Vietnam 1945

A

Philip E. Lilienthal

■   ■   ■

Book

The Philip E. Lilienthal imprint
honors special books
in commemoration of a man whose work
at the University of California Press from 1954 to 1979
was marked by dedication to young authors
and to high standards in the field of Asian Studies.
Friends, family, authors, and foundations have together
endowed the Lilienthal Fund, which enables the Press
to publish under this imprint selected books
in a way that reflects the taste and judgment
of a great and beloved editor.

Ho Chi Minh and Vo Nguyen Giap in Hanoi in early
September 1945. Ho often signed himself "Hoo" when
communicating with Americans, in this case Major
Allison Thomas, head of the OSS Deer Team. Giap's
fedora hat was his trademark in 1945. Courtesy of
Allison K. Thomas.

Vietnam 1945
The Quest for Power

DAVID G. MARR

University of California Press

BERKELEY   LOS ANGELES   LONDON

University of California Press
Berkeley and Los Angeles, California

University of California Press, Ltd.
London, England

© 1995 by
The Regents of the University of California

Library of Congress Cataloging-in-Publication Data

Marr, David G.
    Vietnam 1945 : the quest for power / David G. Marr.
      p.   cm.
    "A Philip E. Lilienthal book."
    Includes bibliographical references and index.
    ISBN 0-520-07833-0 (alk. paper)
    1. Vietnam—Politics and government—1858–1945.
    2. Vietnam—History—August Revolution, 1945. 3. Vietnam
(Democratic Republic)—History. I. Title.
    DS556.8.M36 1995
    959.7′03—dc20   95-15856
                                                         CIP

Printed in the United States of America
9 8 7 6 5 4 3 2

The paper used in this publication meets the minimum requirements of
American National Standard for Information Sciences—Permanence of
Paper for Printed Library Materials, ANSI Z39.48-1984.

For our children
Danny, Aileen, and Andy

Contents

Illustrations

Maps follow page xxviii

Abbreviations

AGAS	Air Ground Aid Section (China).
AOM	Centre des archives d'Outre-Mer (Aix-en-Provence).
c.	*Carton* (box).
CCDVB	Hoang Quang Khanh, Le Hong, and Hoang Ngoc La. *Can Cu Dia Viet Bac (Trong cuoc Cach Mang Thang 8–1945)* [The Viet Bac Base Area (in the August 1945 Revolution)]. Viet Bac: Viet Bac, 1976.
CCP	Chinese Communist Party.
CFLN	Comité français de liberation nationale (Algiers).
CLI	Corps léger d'intervention.
CMCD	Tran Huy Lieu et al. *Tai Lieu Tham Khao Lich Su Cach Mang Can Dai Viet Nam* [Reference Materials on the History of Vietnam's Modern Revolution]. 12 vols. Hanoi: Van Su Dia, 1955–58.
CMTT	Tran Huy Lieu et al., eds. *Cach Mang Thang Tam: Tong Khoi Nghia o Ha Noi va cac Dia Phuong* [The August Revolution: General Insurrection in Hanoi and Various Localities]. 2 vols. Hanoi: Su Hoc, 1960.
CMTT-H	Vietnam. Dang Lao Dong Viet Nam. *Cuoc Van Dong Cach Mang Thang Tam o Ha Noi (cuoi 1939–1946)* [Mobilizing the August Revolution in Hanoi (end of 1939–1946)]. Hanoi: Ban Nghien Cuu Lich Su Dang Thanh Uy Ha-noi, 1970.
CP	Fonds conseiller politique (AOM).
d.	*Dossier* (folder).
DGER	Direction générale des études et recherches.

DGI	Institut Charles-de-Gaulle. *Le Général de Gaulle et l'Indochine, 1940–1946*. Paris: Plon, 1982.
DOS	U.S. Department of State.
DRV	Democratic Republic of Vietnam.
FMM	French Military Mission.
FRUS	U.S. Department of State. *The Foreign Relations of the United States*. Washington, D.C.: Government Printing Office, various years.
GBT	Gordon-Bernard-Tan (intelligence network in Indochina led by Laurence Gordon, Harry Bernard, and Frank Tan).
GF	Gouvernement de fait (AOM file).
HCMTT	Ho Chi Minh. *Ho Chi Minh Toan Tap* [The Complete Works of Ho Chi Minh], vol. 3, *1930–1945*. Hanoi: Su That, 1983.
ICP	Indochinese Communist Party.
IMTFE	International Military Tribunal for the Far East (collection of documents translated and presorted as evidence at Tokyo War Crimes trials).
INF	Indochine nouveau fonds (AOM file).
JSEAS	*Journal of Southeast Asian Studies* (Singapore).
LSQD	Viet Nam, Quan Doi Nhan Dan. Ban Nghien Cuu Lich Su Quan Doi. *Lich Su Quan Doi Nhan Dan Viet Nam* [History of the People's Army of Vietnam], vol. 1. Hanoi: Quan Doi Nhan Dan, 1974.
NCLS	*Nghien Cuu Lich Su* [Historical Research] (Hanoi).
NCO	Noncommissioned officer.
NGS	Kashima Heiwa Kenkyūjohen. *Nihon Gaikōshi* [A History of Diplomacy in Japan], vol. 24. Tokyo, Kashima Kenkyūjo Shuppankai, 1971.
NSKLSD	Vietnam. Dang Lao Dong Viet Nam. Ban Nghien Cuu Lich Su Dang Trung Uong. *Nhung Su Kien Lich Su Dang* [Party Historical Events], vol. 1, *1920–1945*. Hanoi: Su That, 1976.
OSS	Office of Strategic Services.
OWI	Office of War Information.
PJI	U.S. Office of Strategic Services, *Programs of Japan in Indochina*. Honolulu: OSS, Aug. 1945.
PTT	Postes, Télégraphes et Téléphones.
SA	Service d'action.

SEAC	South East Asia Command.
SMS	Bōeichō [Japan Defense Agency]. Bōei Kenshujo Senshitsu [War History Office]. *Shittan Meigō sakusen: Biruma sensen no hōkai to Tai, Futsuin no bōei* [The Sittang and Meigō Operations: The Collapse of the Burma Front and the Defense of Thailand and French Indochina]. Tokyo, Chōun Shinbunsha, 1969.
SOE	British Special Operations Executive.
TVKD	Vietnam. Dang Cong San Viet Nam. Ban Tuyen Huan Trung Uong. *Lich Su Dang Cong San Viet Nam: Trich Van Kien Dang* [History of the Vietnam Communist Party: Extracts from Party Documents], vol. 1, *1927–1945*. Hanoi: Sach Giao Khoa Mac Len-Nin, 1979.
UBND	Uy Ban Nhan Dan [People's Committee].
UBNDCM	Uy Ban Nhan Dan Cach Mang [Revolutionary People's Committee].
USNA	U.S. National Archives (Washington, D.C.).
VKQS	Vietnam. Quan Doi Nhan Dan Viet Nam. *Van Kien Quan Su cua Dang, 1930–1945* [Military Documents of the Party, 1930–1945]. Hanoi: Quan Doi Nhan Dan, 1969.
VNQDD	Hoang Van Dao. *Viet Nam Quoc Dan Dang, 1927–1954* [Vietnam Nationalist Party, 1927–1954]. Saigon: Nguyen Hoa Hiep, 1965.

Main Historical Actors

AYMÉ, GENERAL GEORGES. Commander of French Indochina Army, July 1944–March 1945.

BAO DAI. Emperor of Annam until abdication in August 1945.

CHANG FA-KWEI, GENERAL. Commander of Chinese Fourth War Zone (Kwangsi and western Kwangtung provinces) during World War II.

CHIANG KAI-SHEK, GENERALISSIMO. President of China.

CHU VAN TAN. Nung ethnic minority guerrilla leader, founder of small National Salvation Army north of Hanoi.

CHURCHILL, WINSTON. Prime minister of Great Britain until July 1945.

DE GAULLE, GENERAL CHARLES. Free French leader in London from June 1940, president of Algiers-based Committee of National Liberation 1943–44, president of provisional government in Paris from 1944.

DECOUX, ADMIRAL JEAN. French governor-general of Indochina, 1940–March 1945.

DUCOROY, NAVY CAPTAIN MAURICE. Head of Indochina General Commissariat for Physical Education, Sports, and Youth until March 1945.

DUONG DUC HIEN. Chairman of Hanoi General Student Association, founder of Vietnam Democratic Party in 1944, minister of youth in first DRV cabinet.

HO CHI MINH. Senior member of ICP, founder of Viet Minh in 1941, chairman of National Liberation Committee announced in mid August 1945, president of Democratic Republic of Vietnam inaugurated 2 September 1945.

HOANG QUOC VIET. Deputy to ICP General Secretary Truong Chinh, specializing in clandestine liaison. Dispatched to Cochinchina in late August 1945.

HSIAO WEN, GENERAL. Senior staff aide to General Chang Fa-kwei, responsible for Indochina affairs.

LUNG YÜN, GENERAL. Governor of Yunnan province, adjacent to Indochina.

MATSUSHITA MITSUHIRO. Japanese merchant long resident in Indochina. Wartime intermediary between Japanese officials and Cao Dai religious leaders.

MINODA FUJIO. Japanese governor of Cochinchina, March–August 1945.

MORDANT, GENERAL EUGÈNE. Commander of French Indochina Army until July 1944, then head of de Gaulle's covert resistance organization in the colony until March 1945.

MOUNTBATTEN, ADMIRAL LORD LOUIS. British supreme commander South East Asia, based at Kandy, Ceylon.

NGUYEN HAI THAN. Senior Vietnamese émigré participant in various Chinese-sponsored organizations, notably the Vietnam Revolutionary League.

NGUYEN KHANG. Member of the ICP Northern Region Committee, responsible for Hanoi operations.

NISHIMURA KUMAO. Japanese resident superior for Tonkin, March–August 1945, as well as supreme counsellor to Phan Ke Toai, Tonkin imperial delegate.

PATTI, CAPTAIN ARCHIMEDES L.A. American OSS officer in China responsible for Indochina operations. First Allied representative to arrive in Hanoi, 22 August 1945.

PHAM KHAC HOE. Private secretary to Emperor Bao Dai.

PHAM NGOC THACH. Physician, leading Saigon intellectual in contact with both Japanese and ICP, chairman of Vanguard Youth organization, minister of health in first DRV cabinet.

PHAN ANH. Lawyer, prominent Hanoi intellectual, minister of youth in Imperial Vietnam government, April–August 1945.

PHAN KE TOAI. Imperial delegate (Kham Sai) for Tonkin, May–August 1945.

ROOSEVELT, FRANKLIN D. President of the United States until death on 12 April 1945.

SABATTIER, GENERAL GABRIEL. French commander of Indochina Army contingents in Tonkin. Leads remnant units in retreat to China following 9 March 1945 Japanese coup.

SAINTENY, JEAN. Free French intelligence officer, head of Mission 5 in Kunming. Accompanies Archimedes Patti to Hanoi in August 1945.

TERAUCHI HISAICHI, FIELD MARSHAL COUNT. Commander of Japan's vast Southern Army Area, with headquarters in Singapore and subsequently Saigon.

THOMAS, MAJOR ALLISON K. Head of American OSS team parachuted to Ho Chi Minh's mountain headquarters in July 1945.

TON QUANG PHIET. Writer, principal of private school in Hue, covert ICP member, founder of New Vietnam Association, chairman of Thua Thien province people's committee in August 1945.

TRAN HUY LIEU. Journalist, ICP member, deputy chairman of National Liberation Committee in mid August 1945, minister of propaganda in first DRV cabinet.

TRAN TRONG KIM. Writer, historian, retired colonial education inspector, premier of Imperial Vietnam, April–August 1945.

TRAN VAN GIAU. Prominent ICP activist in Cochinchina, head of Southern Vietnam Uprising Committee in August 1945.

TRUMAN, HARRY S. Vice president of the United States, sworn in as president following Franklin Roosevelt's death in April 1945.

TRUONG CHINH. Secretary-general of the ICP from 1941, with clandestine headquarters in the Red River Delta.

TSUCHIHASHI YŪICHI, GENERAL. Commander of Japanese Thirty-eighth Army in Indochina from December 1944. Governor-general of Indochina, March–August 1945.

TSUKAMOTO TAKESHI, CONSUL GENERAL. Civilian deputy to General Tsuchihashi in latter's capacity as Indochina governor-general, March–August 1945.

VO NGUYEN GIAP. Teacher, ICP member, lieutenant to Ho Chi Minh, founder of small Vietnam Propaganda and Liberation Army in December 1944, commander of Liberation Army from April 1945. Minister of interior in first DRV cabinet.

VU HONG KHANH. Leader of Vietnam Nationalist Party adherents in Kunming and along Yunnan railway.

WEDEMEYER, GENERAL ALBERT. American deputy chief of staff to Lord Mountbatten in Ceylon until November 1944, when appointed chief of staff to Generalissimo Chiang Kai-shek and commander of U.S. Army Forces, China Theater.

YOKOYAMA MASAYUKI, AMBASSADOR. Japanese supreme adviser to Emperor Bao Dai, March–August 1945.

Preface

In 1990, while walking back to my room in Ho Chi Minh City, after a long, sticky day reading files at the National Archives No. 2 building on Le Duan (formerly Norodom) Boulevard, I happened to notice several Vietnamese workers patiently painting two tricolors on each side of the main gate to the spacious compound of the French Consulate. Their artistry aroused not the slightest interest among other passersby. And yet, forty-five years earlier no person of any nationality would have dared even to hold blue, white, and red pots of paint together on the streets of Saigon, Hanoi, or Hue, much less create a French flag in public. The sight of a tricolor provoked more than one mass demonstration in 1945; Vietnamese youths vied with each other and were prepared to die for the privilege of removing the offensive symbol.

A few days later in Ho Chi Minh City, I chanced upon a bric-a-brac shop calculated to fascinate any student of the modern history of Vietnam. Most prominently displayed were some Soviet military watches and tins of Russian caviar. A bit further back I noticed a U.S. Army flak jacket, a U.S. Navy ship's clock, and an assortment of American cigarette lighters, pens, sunglasses, and signet rings. Behind everything else, unlikely to be seen by most visitors to the shop, were a French officer's saber, a 1930s Kodak box camera, and a delicately carved ivory badge of rank once worn by a Vietnamese mandarin. The archaeology of this shop made me appreciate once again how intricate and tortured Vietnam's fate over the past half-century had been, and how difficult it might be to communicate to readers the eagerness, the euphoria of August 1945.

Any Vietnamese over sixty can tell you what she or he was doing in the last weeks of August 1945, much as Americans of more or less the same generation can recall their precise behavior on 7 December 1941, the day of the Japanese attack on Pearl Harbor, or those of a later generation remember where they were and how they responded to the news of President John F. Kennedy's assassination on 22 November 1963. As individuals, we sense instantly the magnitude of such events, connect ourselves to them, and treasure our memories. For millions of Vietnamese in 1945, it was not merely a matter of reacting to media evocations, but of taking part directly. They knew they were making history, not just witnessing it. Many sensed that their lives were changing irrevocably, although no one, not even the most prescient, could imagine where all this would lead. "August 1945 was the most revolutionary moment in my life," one aging Communist Party leader told me wistfully in 1994, leaving implied the further point that such a level of idealism, enthusiasm, and simplicity could not possibly be sustained over decades of subsequent struggle.

The idea for this book goes back to 1961, when I listened to my Vietnamese-language teachers at Monterey describe their experiences in the "August Revolution" (Cach Mang Thang Tam). Six years later I had the opportunity to interview some prominent Vietnamese and Japanese participants; unfortunately, I lacked sufficient knowledge of events in 1945 to ask many of the right questions. At any rate, this specific line of inquiry was shelved for years while I studied earlier decades.

With the opening in the mid 1970s of relevant archival collections in France, and the subsequent willingness of librarians in Vietnam to permit foreign researchers to peruse hundreds of local Communist Party histories and "revolutionary memoirs" (*hoi ky cach mang*), I knew it was feasible to write a detailed study of 1945. The Vietnamese customs police made life easier in 1980 by permitting me to carry out eighty pounds of books and journals purchased on the street, which had not been possible on a visit two years earlier. By 1982, I had established the main cast of characters, initiated an ambitious chronological card file, and begun to speculate about various chains of cause and effect.

However, what really put heart into this project was my first encounter in 1983 with captured documents of the 1945 Vietnamese royal government and early Democratic Republic of Vietnam (DRV), now housed at the archives in Aix-en-Provence. Last examined in 1947 by an anonymous French intelligence officer, still laced with Hanoi dirt and mummified insects (I have often wondered what the after-hours cleaners at the archives thought of my grimy desk), a veritable gold mine of information, these thousands of uncatalogued dossiers have lured me back to Aix repeatedly. Some discoveries came as nuggets directly from the files, others as the result of comparing different firsthand accounts of the same episode, still others by the laborious process of accumulating small, unrelated pieces from diverse provinces. These dossiers are a historian's dream, allowing me in many cases to *show*, not merely tell, the reader what happened. Rather than pre-processing the narrative to pabulum-like consistency, I have tried to convey some of the excitement of archival discovery and bring the reader into the temper of the times. I must apologize in advance to those readers who prefer a more clinical layout and museum-like signposting.

Even as I dug deeper among Vietnamese materials, I realized that it was impossible to fathom developments in 1945 by treating them as an exclusively Vietnamese affair. Important roles were played by foreign actors as well. Fortunately, a range of published memoirs and secondary studies shed light on French, American, and British attitudes and behavior. I have also consulted relevant Western archival materials, albeit not nearly as deeply as my colleague Stein Tønnesson, whose valuable monograph on the same period appeared in 1991.[1] Japanese sources, although far less numerous, do manage to shed some light on the actions of Imperial Army officers and civilian representatives of Japan in Indochina. Chinese sources have been the hardest to locate; my requests for access to relevant archival collections in Taiwan were politely rejected.

Often I have uncovered information that leads in a fascinating direction only to see the trail abruptly disappear. In other cases a group suddenly emerges from the records, yet it is impossible to find out when it was founded or how its leaders established bonds of authority. Occasionally, I have risked reader puzzlement by including such material in the text, so that colleagues can pick up the scent if they wish. I have resisted the temptation to analyze where the sources remain fragmentary. With the recent opening of archival collections in Ho Chi Minh City and Hanoi, it should be possible in the next five or ten years to clear up some uncertainties.

One of my original ambitions was to bring a number of the key personalities in this narrative alive for the reader. Repeatedly frustrated by the sources, I refused to make psychological assumptions or ascribe motivation on the basis of flimsy evidence. Here is where historians and writers of historical fiction part company. Nonetheless, enough was learned about a few individuals to advance characterizations beyond the status of cardboard cutouts. Ho Chi Minh represented the ultimate challenge, not for lack of source materials, but because he assumed so many different roles according to circumstances. Indeed, how one refers to the individual now known to

---

1. Stein Tønnesson, *The Vietnamese Revolution of 1945: Roosevelt, Ho Chi Minh and de Gaulle in a World at War* (London, 1991).

the world as Ho Chi Minh involves historiographical compromise, since he employed more than one hundred aliases between 1911 and his death in 1969. Until 1945 he was best known by the pseudonym Nguyen Ai Quoc, a person many people believed had died in a Hong Kong jail. He first used the name Ho Chi Minh on Chinese identification papers in 1940 or 1942, depending on the source, yet very few people knew that Ho was Nguyen Ai Quoc until late 1945.

Sections of this book are heavily dependent on publications released under Communist Party imprimatur. I have routinely excluded large amounts of hyperbole and cross-checked accounts wherever possible, but almost surely failed to avoid some pitfalls resulting from deliberate Party efforts to manipulate the past. Ironically, certain of the more flamboyant assertions in Hanoi publications may be accurate, yet have been set aside here unintentionally because of the larger pattern of official mystification. Earlier Party publications are generally more useful than later ones, which tend toward either ideological bombast or minor additions to the authorized historical record.

Like any other historian I have tried to work critically with whatever is available, hoping that time will expose additional data and facilitate new interpretations. I have spent quite some time looking for original texts, rather than relying on reprints or translations, but much remains to be done in this realm. Reprints and translations are cited in the footnotes along with originals, since the latter may remain difficult for some researchers to consult.

Whereas my first book, *Vietnamese Anticolonialism, 1885–1925* (1971), attempted to show the political will of a minority of Vietnamese in incredibly trying circumstances, and my second book, *Vietnamese Tradition on Trial, 1920–1945* (1981), aimed to demonstrate that the Vietnamese deserved to be taken seriously as thinking people, the present study is not fueled by any particular didactic mission. This undoubtedly reflects both changed conditions since the end of the Vietnam War in 1975 and my own changing attitudes. Rather than arguing some special relevancy for the 1990s or trying to revive the political passions of bygone decades, I simply wish to show how Vietnam became the vortex of intense international and domestic competitions for power, and why by early September 1945, the contest had already been narrowed down to two rivals: France and the Democratic Republic of Vietnam. It has also been rewarding to select this particular slice of Vietnam's history for intensive scrutiny, bringing out character, motivation, style, color, context, and contradiction. In this I must confess to being influenced by the work of Barbara Tuchman, above all her book *The Guns of August* (New York, 1962), on the outbreak of the Great War in 1914. Indeed, I had originally planned to focus entirely on six months in 1945, but I found it necessary to discuss the years leading up to them as well.

History is not all epic events: "small" people doing seemingly inconsequential things can sometimes influence the course of affairs. Even where there is no demonstrable effect, we need occasionally to remember that lives are being pursued, personal crises faced with a logic and rhythm not necessarily subordinate to the will of states, parties, commanders, or opinion makers. Without by any means endeavoring to write a history of the "underside," I have presented occasional views from below when the sources permit. In 1945, a lot of ordinary people were also seeking empowerment, more control over their own fates, without necessarily phrasing it in such terms.

The only truth in history is that there are no historical truths, only an infinite number of experiences, most of them quickly forgotten, a few remembered and elaborated upon by bards, novelists, philosophers, priests, filmmakers, and, of course, professional historians. Historians are different mainly in the spirit of skepticism with which we address the available traces. In common with detectives and lawyers, we appreciate that every source has an axe to grind. Unlike them, we try to avoid being employed by anyone to prove a specific case. In our trade it is also no sin to admit that the world is very seldom divided between heroes and villains, innocent and guilty.

Although historians constantly preoccupy themselves with linear cause and effect, the more sensitive ones also try to show how at any given point in time a variety of forces are at work at different levels of society, in different places, without any necessary causal links to one another. This is no less the case in war and revolution; indeed, the element of chaos is more pronounced and significant. Historians have the obvious advantage over the people being studied in that they know, or presume to know, which particular causal chains make a difference. Too often, however, we are caught in a teleological trap, considering events entirely from the point of view of what occurred subsequently, forgetting the standpoint of history as "becoming." When this happens, it is but a short step to crude deterministic expostulation, rather than history as a study of the possible.

I have been helped in my research for this book by far more individuals than it is possible to acknowledge here. In the first rank stand a number of sympathetic, tireless archivists and librarians, beginning with François Bordes, Lucette Vachier, Sylvie Clair, and their colleagues at the Centre des

Archives d'Outre-Mer in Aix-en-Provence. Somewhat earlier I was assisted by personnel at the former Ministry of Colonies archives in Paris, and at the Bibliothèque nationale. At the U.S. National Archives, John Taylor made sure that my limited time in Washington was well spent.

On my various trips to Vietnam, Nguyen The Duc and his staff at the National Library of Vietnam always provided me with more books than I could handle; only in 1988 did I discover that Mr. Duc's father was well known to me from his many signatures in the 1945 archives. I was also aided by Nguyen Duy Thong and assistants at the Social Science Information Institute (Hanoi), Mme. Tra Ngoc Anh and staff at the Social Science Library (Ho Chi Minh City), and Mme. Huynh Ngoc Thu at the General Science Library (formerly the National Library of the Republic of Vietnam). Duong Trung Quoc has always facilitated my access to the library of the Historical Research Institute, not to mention giving pointers on where to purchase old books on the street. While many among the administrative staff of the Vietnam Social Sciences Institute have helped me over the years, Nguyen Van Ku in Hanoi and the late Trinh Chi in Ho Chi Minh City deserve my special gratitude.

A long string of colleagues have been kind enough to loan me publications, forward photocopies, and offer valuable source leads, including Stein Tønnesson, Georges Boudarel, Pierre Brocheux, Daniel Hémery, Duong Trung Quoc, Kristen Pelzer White, Nguyen Van Trung, Philippe Devillers, Huynh Sanh Thong, Christopher Goscha, Ralph B. Smith, George McT. Kahin, David Elliott, and the late Huynh Kim Khanh. I would also like to thank Colonel Allison K. Thomas (retired) for sending me materials relating to his experiences in Vietnam in July–September 1945, and for responding readily to my subsequent queries. In Canberra, Li Tana and Ton That Phuong helped me to locate and interpret several key Chinese and Japanese texts.

For seven long years Jennifer Brewster provided invaluable support as research assistant, ferreting out Japanese and Western-language sources, taking copious notes, building the chronological file, commenting on my first drafts, and wielding a sharp copyeditor's pencil. Without her it would have proven impossible to grapple effectively with the sheer quantity and variety of source materials.

David Chandler and Stein Tønnesson deserve high accolades for reading each chapter draft as it appeared and reacting both promptly and constructively. At various points in time, Van Tao, Ngo Van Hoa, Duong Kinh Quoc, Tran Van Giau, Dinh Xuan Lam, Le Mau Han, Vu Huy Phuc, Pierre Brocheux, Ralph B. Smith, Greg Lockhart, Patricia Lane, John Legge,

Anthony Reid, Hank Nelson, Bill Gammage, and Robert Cribb read selected portions of the manuscript. Nola Cooke offered a critique of the whole text at a later stage, and Keith Taylor provided valuable comments after reviewing the manuscript for the University of California Press. None of these scholars should be blamed for my gaffes and omissions; some will surely disagree with my interpretations.

Tan Lay Cheng worked her way through the entire manuscript looking for place names, then located and marked them on copies of maps I had acquired in the military thirty years before. Kay Dancey employed these materials to design the four maps incorporated here. Christopher Goscha, Christiane Rageau, and Norah Forster helped to track down photographs and cartoons for inclusion in the book. Ngo Hoang Oanh prepared the Vietnamese-language glossary, utilizing software devised by Evelyn Winburn.

I confess to remaining a pen-and-paper scribbler, even after most of my departmental colleagues have learned to word process their own manuscripts (and extracted a pledge from me to do likewise following this book). With considerable skill, patience, and good humor, Jude Shanahan typed the penultimate and final book drafts; Julie Gordon and Karen Haines did likewise with earlier chapter drafts. At the University of California Press, Sheila Levine, Betsey Scheiner, and Monica McCormick guided the book through its many requisite stages, and I was privileged to work with a most professional and supportive copyeditor, Peter Dreyer.

Finally, a few words about terminology. To make the text more friendly to nonspecialists, I have generally employed English translations of Vietnamese organizational names, administrative titles, and the like, while providing the original Vietnamese in parentheses on first mention. One exception is Kham Sai (imperial delegate), which comes up so often that readers perhaps will be willing to accept the burden. Another, of course, is Viet Minh, the popular abbreviation of Viet Nam Doc Lap Dong Minh (Vietnam Independence League), but this long ago achieved a certain international currency. I have not attempted to homogenize regional designations, since the way in which these geographical terms were employed tells us something about the times and the people involved. Readers thus need to know from the outset that Tonkin = Bac Ky = Bac Bo = northern Vietnam; Annam = Trung Ky = Trung Bo = central Vietnam; and Cochinchina = Nam Ky = Nam Bo = southern Vietnam.

Although word-processing packages now exist to handle Vietnamese-language diacritics, I prefer not to complicate matters by inserting them in the text. Specialists can consult the glossary that precedes the selected bibliography.

Many of the Vietnamese personalities encountered in this narrative, and even a few of the French, employed a variety of aliases. I have used the names by which individuals are best known historically, be these their given names, pen names, code names, or revolutionary pseudonyms.

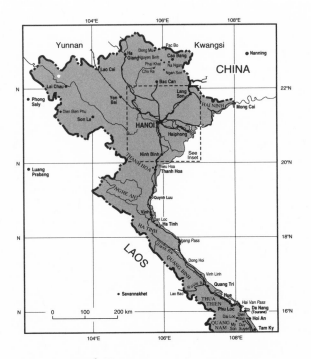

Map 1.   North Vietnam.

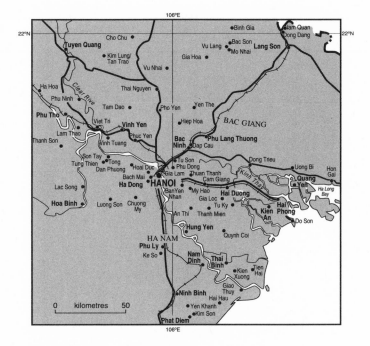

Map 2.   Hanoi and vicinity.

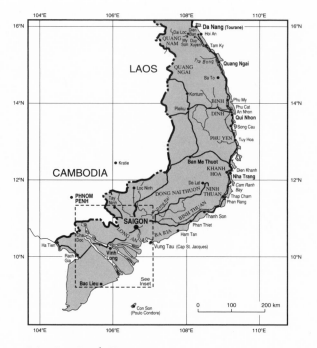

Map 3.   South Vietnam.

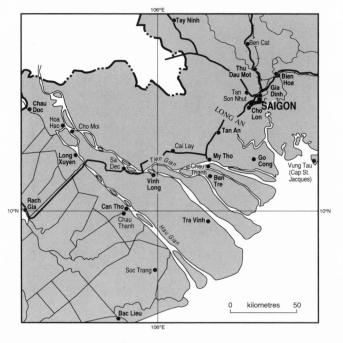

Map 4.   Saigon and vicinity.

Introduction

Nineteen forty-five is the most important year in the modern history of Vietnam. A thousand years of dynastic politics and monarchist ideology came to an end, never to be revived. Eight decades of French rule lay shattered, although its restoration remained an ominous possibility. Five years of Japanese military occupation ceased. Allied leaders in faraway Potsdam determined that Chinese troops would take the Japanese surrender in Indochina north of the 16th parallel, while British forces did likewise south of that line. Even though the United States remained aloof from these occupation tasks, its indirect influence on the course of events was substantial.

On 9 March 1945, Japanese forces had suddenly dumped the French colonial administration in Indochina, after allowing it to function for thirty-nine months following Japan's December 1941 assaults on British, Dutch, and American possessions in Asia. This Japanese *coup de force*, together with a terrible famine then sweeping north and north-central Vietnam, triggered a whole series of changes in the territory. Five months later, again a surprise, Allied radio stations reported Japan's imminent capitulation. During the last two weeks of August 1945, members of the Indochinese Communist Party (Dong Duong Cong San Dang), the Viet Minh, and associated groups seized power from what remained of the Japanese-sponsored royal government. On 2 September, Ho Chi Minh proclaimed the Democratic Republic of Vietnam (Viet Nam Dan Chu Cong Hoa) with himself as president of a provisional government headquartered in Hanoi. The Japanese offered no opposition, and in some places they gave unobtrusive assistance.

Most histories of Vietnam in 1945 stress events in Hanoi, claim a predominant role throughout the country for the Indochinese Communist

Party (ICP), and emphasize revolutionary consciousness over revolutionary spontaneity. This study demonstrates that the reality was much more complicated, and more interesting. The political transformations of 1945 took place in all provincial towns and most rural districts of Vietnam. Particularly in the early stages, from March to June, the ICP was only one force among many provoking change. While most of the upheavals in August were sparked by Viet Minh slogans (created or cleared by experienced ICP members), and while almost everyone came to identify with the Viet Minh flag, soon to become the national standard, many local groups calling themselves Viet Minh had almost no idea of what the organization stood for, much less possessed any connections with the Tong Bo (General Headquarters). The hundreds of "people's committees" and "revolutionary committees" that replaced the assorted royal mandarins and appointed councils soon affirmed their loyalty to the provisional government, yet they were far from being mere appendages of the central authority or fronts for ICP cadres. Many of these committees sought revenge for past injustices or projected radical social revolutionary aspirations, both of which the provisional government tried with only partial success to defer in the interests of mounting an effective defense of national independence.

From another angle this study shows how the political symbols of the various groups active in Vietnam interacted and conflicted, often with surprising results. At this moment of profound uncertainty for everyone, flags, anthems, salutes, slogans, street names, statues, postage stamps, even rubber stamps, possessed inordinate significance. Although at one level these symbols simply represented organizations, at another they took on lives of their own, causing people to act in ways that no leader could predict, much less direct.

Soon after the Japanese coup in March, the provisional government of General Charles de Gaulle in Paris again told the world it would regain Indochina for France. Yet in the following five months, Paris lost touch, failing entirely to appreciate the dramatic changes taking place in Tonkin, Annam, and Cochinchina. With the appointment in mid August of a French high commissioner for Indochina, and the radio announcement that French troops were embarking for the colony, armed confrontation with the Vietnamese became almost inevitable. Nine years later, having suffered military humiliation at Dien Bien Phu, France would abandon its quest in Indochina, even as another foreign power, the United States, was preparing to pick up the gauntlet.

Not enough historiographical attention has been paid to the manner in which war and revolution feed upon each other. While it is impossible to argue that World War II intruded upon Vietnamese society to the degree that World War I undermined czarist Russia, for example, or Japanese aggression disrupted China in the late 1930s, its effects were nonetheless substantial. Wartime economic dislocations ruined the colonial import-export system, upset local class relationships, and raised the specter of famine over half the population. The war was responsible too for the mood of fear, anticipation, and excitement that gripped many Vietnamese from early 1945 on. Violence was becoming commonplace. It seemed a time for quick action rather than patient reflection, for youthful militancy instead of elderly caution. Because the ICP had survived fifteen years of French repression partly by means of quasi-military discipline and secrecy, it was better placed than most political groups to take advantage of these shifts in attitude.

In both war and revolution, opponents are constantly piecing together scraps of information to form pictures, then testing them against preconceived theories or the demands of a particular strategy. What different leaders make of the available evidence depends largely on what they want to believe or fear to believe. Given the high stakes, some underlying optimism is essential. Nonetheless, the group that prepares for the harder alternative, and is willing to act along those lines before the picture is complete, often has the tactical edge. Deferring a decision until one's conceptual or procedural impulses are satisfied can be disastrous in war or revolution. This is unlike "normal" times of peace and social order, when leaders often prefer to delay, to commission another study, in hopes that events will resolve dilemmas for them. As we shall see, the Vietnamese royal government and various noncommunist political groups understood none of these strategic dynamics in 1945, while local ICP activists grasped the essentials, at least intuitively.

The fate of all major revolutions has ultimately been decided on the battlefield, a historical lesson well known to Vietnamese communist leaders, some of whom devoted considerable attention in 1941–44 to building up armed guerrilla units adjacent to the Chinese frontier, only to have them destroyed or dispersed by the French. Following Japanese internment of the French colonial forces in March 1945, however, "Liberation Army" squads and platoons proliferated, and by July the royal government's Civil Guard (Bao An Binh), formerly the colonial Garde indochinoise, refused to patrol the hills and countryside north of Hanoi without Japanese accompaniment. In mid August, when it became obvious that Japanese troops were no longer going to participate, Civil Guard units in this region disbanded or went over to the Viet Minh. From Hanoi southward, most Viet Minh groups possessed few firearms, but because the royal government was too divided to mount a last-minute defense, and most Civil Guard units were unwilling to shoot down demonstrators, the existing system collapsed with very little bloodshed. Power went to those who planted a Viet Minh flag on a government office, held the keys to the Civil Guard armory, or controlled the telegraph key. Thousands of people were imprisoned, leaving the issue of what to do with them for subsequent resolution.

At this point Vietnam had experienced an insurrection of national proportions, but not yet a revolution (although people would soon speak proudly of the "August Revolution"). In most places former colonial employees continued to function, landlords still collected rents, owners of enterprises still told workers what to do, wives deferred to husbands, teenagers obeyed parents. But all such relationships had been thrown into question, and acute awareness that the country was under threat of French reconquest helped to stimulate further alterations. Every citizen's behavior, no matter how innocuous, began to be subjected to the ultimate political litmus test by neighbors: was it patriotic or treasonous? As in all wartime situations, freedom was surrendered to necessity.

The Viet Minh demonstrated its ability prior to the August national insurrection to mobilize resources in one region, north of Hanoi. Now it needed to multiply that capacity tenfold, channeling popular energies away from petty recriminations and toward defense of the Fatherland (To Quoc). Battle would be joined in the south in late September, with the center and north coming in later. Already in the period covered by this book, however, the harsh symbiosis between war and revolution was becoming apparent: 1945 was the first act of an epic, tortuous drama extending over the next thirty years, with influences felt even today throughout Vietnamese society.

Although charting the internal fate of the Vietnamese Revolution was undoubtedly the main reason I embarked on this study, it soon became apparent that other things were happening in and around Vietnam during 1940–45 that deserved scrutiny as well. Vietnam had to be seen in regional and global context, not in isolation. Five foreign powers—France, Japan, China, the United States, and Great Britain—took a direct interest in this territory during World War II. Each government approached the land and its people from a different point of view, with different operational objectives. Moreover, none of these states had a constant, single policy toward Vietnam: always there were several different interests at work, sometimes contradicting each other, sometimes achieving temporary consensus. This was most obvious in the case of Vichy France versus Free France, with important consequences for colonial administration in Indochina. Even among the Free French, there were significant differences. Among the Japanese, Imperial Army officers and civilians dispatched to Indochina from various ministries often disagreed with each other, even worked at cross-purposes. In China, the regional leaders of Kwangsi and Yunnan pursued separate policies vis-à-vis Indochina, and neither agreed with the central government in Chungking, to the point where events in Indochina became an extension of the turbulent politics of southern China. Americans disagreed over whether or not France should retain Indochina as a colonial possession after the war. Great Britain was the most consistent foreign actor regarding Indochina, despite occasional divergencies between Prime Minister Winston Churchill, the Colonial Office, and South East Asia Command (SEAC), located in Ceylon.

During World War II, Indochina became one focus of sustained arguments among the Allies over the future of colonies in general, over China's role as a major power, even over the character of postwar Europe—notably, France's relative strength or weakness. These issues then influenced events in Vietnam, at first only slightly, given Japanese military preponderance, but later with considerable strength, as it became apparent that Allied victory was certain.

A number of historiographical questions have continued to be argued in the years since all these events took place. Perhaps the earliest polemic was between French defenders and denigrators of Admiral Jean Decoux, governor-general of Indochina until March 1945, which eventually broadened into a more fruitful debate over the wisdom of sending British and Free French teams to Indochina to prepare for an Allied invasion. Almost as early, French writers began to accuse the Democratic Republic of Vietnam (DRV) of having had power thrust into its hands by the Japanese, who were said to have delighted in embarrassing the white man even as they grudgingly surrendered to the Allies. DRV writers not only rejected these charges vehemently, but claimed that Viet Minh units had often fought the Japanese heroically, even that Vietnam had conducted a war against Japan. Later, French authors criticized the United States for undermining French sovereignty in Indochina and for providing timely support for Ho Chi Minh. Some Americans accepted these accusations proudly, adding that the United States should have done more to back the Vietnamese; others emphasized the effective collapse of America's anticolonialist pretensions since the first months of 1945. From about 1960 on, historians in Hanoi debated whether the "August Revolution" was primarily political or military in character, and whether actions in the countryside or the cities were more consequential. Eventually, Party arbiters told everyone that all four factors were more or less evenly balanced, an answer that had more to do with Hanoi's 1960s preoccupations with outmaneuvering the Americans than with any reality in 1945. More recently, a few Vietnamese intellectuals have suggested that "revolution" needs to be rescued as a historiographical category, instead of being used to describe everything the Party has done from 1930 to the present.

I have tried to contribute to those debates unobtrusively, without diverting the reader's attention from the 1940–45 period. To be frank, some of the arguments are now of mere antiquarian interest. Rereading my notes from hundreds of Communist Party commemorative articles on the "August Revolution," for example, I found only fifteen or twenty that had stood the test of time, providing useful data and insights. The rest spun political angel hair and repeated historical shibboleths. There is a serious need in Vietnam for fresh research on 1940–45, combining rigorous archival investigation with extensive interviewing before participants die. So far, despite a somewhat less repressive environment for intellectuals since 1986, Vietnam's historians have avoided the challenge.

Curiously, certain significant aspects of the 1940–45 story have never received much attention from historians anywhere. The importance of China has often been ignored or downgraded in both Vietnamese and Western studies. I have tried to redress this deficiency, while often frustrated by the paucity of primary source materials. The Vietnamese royal government that was permitted by the Japanese to function between April and early August 1945 has generally been overlooked or disparaged, when it deserves to be examined seriously. Regional disparities in developments up to early September 1945 warrant frank discussion; Vietnamese writers have tended to paper them over in the interests of producing "national history," while Western writers seem to have lacked the stamina to locate and read the necessary documents. I do not accept the prevailing wisdom that "the Party" was in charge of "the Revolution" from 1930 or 1941 onward. Ironically, communist and anticommunist Vietnamese have agreed with each other on that assertion—the former using it as the linchpin of Party legitimacy to the present day, the latter painting a picture of clever, insidious betrayal of Vietnamese national interests on instructions from Moscow. I shall demonstrate that no one was in control. After 9 March 1945, events took on spontaneous momentum, without any guiding hand. Local Communist Party members and Viet Minh adherents were successful more because of their ability to react quickly to sudden changes than because of any adherence to a master plan.

Each of the first five chapters of this book opens with vital events of 9 March 1945 as seen by a particular set of historical actors, jumps back to the years 1940–44 to provide context for their behavior, then carries the narrative through to the end of July 1945, when matters were coming to a head in Vietnam even without any inkling of imminent Japanese surrender. The purpose of this seemingly labyrinthine structure is to be able to view the same geography and the same period from a number of disparate perspectives. People of diverse backgrounds and intentions contested for hegemony, adjusted their outlooks and behavior, or refused to change. Leaders acted on the basis of insufficient or contradictory information. Often historians are too eager to create a seamless web, to tell a single story, when in fact people saw the world in dissimilar ways, talked past each other, and acted in ignorance of relevant developments elsewhere. Telling multiple stories poses obvious stylistic problems, yet it helps us to remember that history is made up of numerous possibilities, not pseudoscientific necessity.

Chapter 1 focuses on the Franco-Japanese relationship that dominated politics in Indochina from 1940 until the coup of 9 March 1945. We see how military events far beyond Indochina's borders first brought the two parties together, then eventually forced them apart. Ironically, the Japanese need not have attacked the French in March 1945, given American lack of interest in invading Indochina and Governor-General Decoux's sincere desire to return the colony intact to Paris at the end of the war, no matter how intense his dislike of the Free French. Even after they took over, the Japanese permitted many French teachers, technicians, and businessmen to continue working, until mounting Vietnamese antagonism made it too dangerous for them to do so.

Chapter 2 describes the changes that took place among the Vietnamese population even as both the French and the Japanese endeavored to keep everyone quiet and hard-working. Governor-General Decoux, cut off from any metropolitan assistance, promised a bright future for the "Annamites" if they cooperated with him in wartime, a reward remarkably similar, older Vietnamese pointed out wryly, to pledges made by the French during the 1914–18 war, only to be cast aside afterward. Nonetheless, tens of thousands of Vietnamese did take part in the youth and sports organizations that Decoux encouraged as an antidote to Japanese martial arts displays and assertions of Asian racial superiority. Meanwhile, after two decades of looking to the West, Vietnamese intellectuals rediscovered their own history and rural origins. Following the 9 March coup, Vietnamese were able to expand the legal limits of politics by means of public rallies, marches, and lightly censored newspaper articles. The new royal cabinet eventually persuaded the Japanese to relinquish territorial jurisdiction over Co-chinchina and the three cities of Hanoi, Haiphong, and Tourane (Da Nang), but it was unable to do anything about the famine that had begun in northern Vietnam before the Japanese takeover, nor did it know how to deal with underground Viet Minh propaganda or the increasing number of assaults on local officials. It is important to understand how the royal government came under serious challenge some weeks before the Japanese surrender in mid August.

Chapter 3 concentrates on the ICP, undoubtedly the most determined, aggressive Vietnamese organization of the time, as well as the various Viet Minh groups that emerged with increasing frequency from late 1944 on. Although small, dispersed, and beleaguered early in World War II, the ICP still possessed considerable experience and public prestige derived from mounting lively challenges to French colonial exploitation in the 1936–40 period. In 1941–42, Ho Chi Minh set the course of both the ICP and the Viet Minh, at least for the northern part of the country, before he was imprisoned by the Chinese Nationalists. Returning to Vietnam in September 1944, Ho turned the attention of his young lieutenants to building armed propaganda teams, establishing village-level support groups, and spreading the basic Viet Minh credo by word of mouth. With the sudden demise of French administration in March 1945, the ICP saw its opportunity, infiltrating Garde indochinoise units and legal youth organizations, urging people to break into rice warehouses, and stitching together a "liberation zone" in six northern provinces. The Japanese saw little reason to intervene, except in those few places where Viet Minh groups were rash enough to ambush Imperial Army patrols or truck convoys. As the Vietnamese public began to sense Allied victory over the Axis, those of their compatriots who had identified with the antifascist cause years before, when Berlin and Tokyo had looked invincible, took on the aura of prophets. In operational terms, however, the inability of ICP and Viet Minh leaders in the north to reestablish communications with comrades further south led to significant differences of strategy and tactics.

Chapters 4 and 5 examine Allied policies and activities in regard to Indochina up to the end of July 1945. For Chinese and American generals, Indochina represented a troublesome Japanese staging area for possible flank attacks on major Allied air and ground bases in western Kwangsi and Yunnan. For more than four years, both the Allies and the Japanese found it convenient to keep the border region quiet, even to engage in regular cross-frontier commerce. However, American bombers increasingly brought the war to Indochina, curtailing air, sea, and ground transport and reducing its value as logistical hub for Japanese operations to the west and south. Politically, President Franklin Delano Roosevelt made Indochina a test case of Allied intentions respecting postwar international trusteeships over colonial territories. Prime Minister Churchill resisted any Indochina trusteeship proposal, seeing it as the thin end of the wedge in regard to British colonies, and an issue certain to inflame the sensitivities of the French after their wartime humiliations in Europe, but he avoided making an issue of it so long as Roosevelt was alive. Admiral Lord Louis Mountbatten, commander of SEAC, tried with the sparse resources available to him to signal British and Free French concern about the future of Indochina. With the Japanese coup, both China Theater and SEAC lost most of their intelligence sources inside Indochina, which led China Theater quickly to expand links with Ho Chi Minh and the Viet Minh—a sensible military decision that nonetheless went contrary to Washington's increasing readiness to uphold French sovereignty.

The last three chapters are devoted entirely to August and the first days of September 1945. Here it is possible to bring the different narrative threads together, demonstrating how various players interacted with one another during these momentous five weeks. Newly available archival materials of the period allow us to reevaluate scores of published sources, separating substantive wheat from ex post facto ideological chaff. Chapter 6 describes conditions in Vietnam just before word arrived of Japanese capitulation, together with the climactic sequence of events in Hanoi from the 17th to the 19th of August. Chapter 7 takes the reader through the provinces, as well as Hue and Saigon, during the latter half of August. We see that the "general insurrection" carried quickly to every corner of the country, yet its meaning and immediate consequences were far from uniform. As always, Vietnam's unusual geography intruded as silent partner. Chapter 8 swings attention back to Hanoi, especially the rapid formation of a state apparatus and the arrival on the 22d of the first Allied representatives. It concludes with detailed descriptions of the huge 2 September meetings in Hanoi and Saigon to celebrate Vietnamese independence, one gathering proceeding without a hitch, the other degenerating into mob violence that deeply embarrassed Ho Chi Minh's provisional government.

Within a few days of these mass meetings, Chinese troops would arrive in Hanoi, and British and French troops in Saigon. Ho Chi Minh and the provisional government would come under tremendous pressure, all the while encouraging grassroots mobilization against enemies real and imagined. A brief Epilogue describes this historical denouement.

While it might have been preferable to pursue events to December 1946, or even July 1954, this would have meant sacrificing much of the detail of 1945. Specialists will be aware that no book has ever examined a selected episode in the history of Vietnam in depth. There are studies of the outbreak of the Indochina War in December 1946, the 1954 battle of Dien Bien Phu, and the 1968 Tet Offensive, yet no one has succeeded in portraying under one cover the opposite sides of those confrontations. Juggling not just two sides but seven or more has been a major historiographical challenge in this work. Readers will have to decide whether or not the effort was quixotic.

The year 1945 was a critical one throughout the world, shaping much of what has happened since. The month of August was particularly important for Asia. From the windswept plains of Manchuria to the outlying islands of Indonesia, existing institutions disintegrated, and prevailing attitudes were called into question. People understood it to be a turning point of great magnitude, even if few presumed to know where they were going. Vietnam was not alone in experiencing this transformation, just as Vietnamese revolutionaries were hardly unique in determining to take advantage of the unparalleled opportunities offered to them. Nonetheless, each location was different, each set of circumstances unique. Readers familiar with events in China, Korea, Malaya, Singapore, or Indonesia in 1945 should find much here to compare and contrast.

Although much smaller in scope, the Vietnamese Revolution deserves to be placed alongside the French, Russian, and Chinese revolutions for purposes of critical comparison. It is a prime example of radical revolutionary upheaval in a colonial setting, with ample archival and published sources for historical investigation. This book should thus be of interest to all students of revolution, even though it treats only the opening stages of the Vietnamese experience and does not attempt to mount a cross-revolutionary analysis.

There is ample material here too for those who focus explicitly on the relationship between state and society. States often wish to give the appearance of a single coherent entity, quite distinct from society. This is most obvious in a colonial state, where power, being largely derived from outside, is presented as omnipotent, unchallengeable, and external. The reality is different, of course, with society overlapping with the state in many significant ways, producing a more fluid, ambiguous, inconsistent pattern. It is at the beginning of the independence period, when the process of self-definition, relabeling, and reorganization is so vital, so transparent, that we can appreciate how contentious the rationales employed by states to define and present themselves are.[1] During 1945, Vietnam went from colonial state to royal government to democratic republic in six months, offering us a choice opportunity to observe the collapse of state/society boundaries and preliminary attempts to reconstitute them.

In June 1945, eighty-three political prisoners in the Hanoi central jail petitioned the royal government for release, in words that echo through the corridors of time. After itemizing the terrible conditions of their incarceration, and suggesting that government claims to independence could hardly be valid if patriots like themselves remained in jail, they concluded passionately:

> We hope that all the inequities and sufferings in our lives will collapse in the near future, just like French power.[2]

Within months these activists would be in a position to attempt to achieve such lofty ambitions for the entire country.

---

1. For a brief discussion of this issue, see E. Roger Owen, "State and Society in the Middle East," *Items* (New York) 44, no. 1 (Mar. 1990): 1–14.
2. Letter to minister of justice, 25 June 1945, in AOM, INF, GF 13.

1 The French and the Japanese

At 6:00 P.M. on 9 March 1945, the Japanese ambassador to Indochina, Matsumoto Shunichi, walked into the palatial Saigon offices of the French governor-general, Admiral Jean Decoux, to present an ultimatum. Matsumoto had requested the meeting on the pretext of signing annual agreements dealing with rice supplies and French financial support for Japanese troops, the details of which had been worked out laboriously by subordinates, apparently to mutual satisfaction. However, Decoux might have wondered why the ambassador also asked to talk privately following the signing ceremony. During that personal encounter, which began about 6:30 P.M., Decoux recalled that Matsumoto was preoccupied and nervous, "something rare in an Asiatic."[1]

At precisely 7:00 P.M., Ambassador Matsumoto informed the governor-general that Tokyo had conveyed new demands, which required unconditional French acceptance no later than 9:00 P.M. that same evening: all of Indochina's military and police forces were to be put under command and control of the Japanese Army; no unit was to move without prior authorization; railroads, water transport, and radio and telegraph systems were to be placed at Japanese disposition.[2]

It was the moment that Admiral Decoux had dreaded and tried to avoid for the previous fifty-five months. Ever since taking office in July 1940, he had considered himself the custodian of French sovereignty in Indochina, endeavoring even in those tortuous times to retain something of the heroic tradition, at least keeping the colony physically in-

1. Jean Decoux, *A la barre de l'Indochine: Histoire de mon gouvernement général, 1940–1945* (Paris, 1949), 326–28.
2. Ibid., 330.

tact so that it could be presented back to Paris at the end of the world war.

Summer 1940: The Japanese Arrive

Decoux had become governor-general just as Tokyo sought to take maximum advantage of France's disastrous defeat in Europe at the hands of Adolf Hitler. The Japanese government, long bothered about Western supplies reaching beleaguered Chinese armies via Haiphong and the Yunnan railway, first pressed Decoux's immediate predecessor, General Georges Catroux, to close the Tonkin-China frontier and accept a forty-member Japanese inspection team.[3] Faced with reports of imperial troops and naval vessels moving into threatening positions, and failing to obtain American or British pledges of support, Catroux reluctantly agreed. Ironically, he then found himself summarily sacked by the military officers and politicians in France who had just capitulated to Germany, and who were soon to establish themselves at the town of Vichy, a name that became synonymous with collaboration.[4]

Decoux assumed office aware that he could not reverse Catroux's concessions, yet determined to avoid giving the Japanese more. He was im-

3. A considerable amount of confidential debate occurred within the Japanese government and armed forces before this demand was made, and there was no unanimity about what the inspection team was meant to accomplish, much less about longer-term objectives in Indochina and the rest of the Nanyō (Southern Seas) region. See Yoshizawa Minami, "The Nishihara Mission in Hanoi, July 1940," in *Indochina in the 1940s and 1950s,* ed. Shiraishi Takeshi and Furuta Motoo (Ithaca, N.Y., 1992), 9–54; Murakami Sachiko, "Japan's Thrust into French Indochina, 1940–1945" (Ph.D. diss., New York University, 1981), 52–61, 104–6; and Hata Ikuhiko, "The Army's Move into Northern Indochina," in *The Fateful Choice: Japan's Advance into Southeast Asia, 1939–1941,* ed. James W. Morley (New York, 1980), 155–63. Yoshizawa advances the broader argument that myriad points of conflict between and within Japanese organizations had the effect of heightening pressures to expand the war rather than reducing them.

4. Catroux decided not to return to France, instead joining General Charles de Gaulle and the "Free French" in London. Decoux and Catroux traded recriminations in their postwar memoirs. See Decoux, *A la barre,* 56–58, and Georges Catroux, *Deux actes du drame indochinois* (Paris, 1959), 67, 71, 82, 89. It is likely that Catroux was sacked as much for his known sympathy for the alliance with Britain as for his concessions to the Japanese. For a detailed study of these events, see John E. Dreifort, "Japan's Advance into Indochina, 1940: The French Response," *Journal of Southeast Asian Studies* (cited below as *JSEAS*) 13, no. 2 (Sept. 1982): 279–95.

Figure 1.   Admiral Jean Decoux, governor-general of Indochina from July 1940 to 9 March 1945. The photograph heads the admiral's memoirs, *A la barre de l'Indochine*. Courtesy of Librairie Plon.

mediately put to the test. In early August, formal word arrived from France and from the French ambassador in Tokyo that Japan now demanded airfields in Indochina, the stationing of substantial guard units, and transit rights for Japanese combat divisions trying to strangle the Nationalist Chinese.[5] Decoux urged the French government to reject these demands, arguing that, even though Indochina lacked the means to repel a full-scale Japanese military onslaught, it was sufficiently well defended to cause Tokyo to think twice before attacking. Perhaps Indochina could provide Japan with some new economic benefits by way of alternative. French prestige had already been attenuated by the presence of the Japanese inspection group, Decoux asserted. Further military concessions would "alienate us from the Indochinese population and provoke violent reactions against

5. These Japanese requirements had been raised with Governor-General Catroux as early as 3 July, but he had parried by referring the issue to France. Murakami, "Japan's Thrust," 111–12. Hata, "Army's Move," 163–65. Catroux avoids mention of these demands in the opening salvo of his own public defense, a statement made from Moscow, where he was French ambassador, on 1 August 1945 (*New York Times*, 2 Aug. 1945, 7).

France by all the great powers interested in maintaining the status quo in the Far East."[6]

What Decoux could not gauge in the summer of 1940, however, was the ominous shift in elite Japanese thinking toward confrontation with the Western imperial powers. In 1939, Japan had concentrated its pressure northward on the Soviet Union, only to become the victim in August of a sharp Red Army tank attack at Nomonhan on the Manchurian frontier, which nearly annihilated an entire Japanese division. No sooner had Tokyo received news of this loss than word arrived of conclusion in Moscow of the Nazi-Soviet nonaggression pact.[7] After stomaching their fury at both the Nomonhan defeat and being kept in the dark by their de facto German allies, some Japanese strategists began arguing that reducing tensions with the USSR would have the effect of releasing forces for potential action in the direction of Singapore and the oil, rubber, and rice of the Nanyō (Southern Seas) region. Germany's quick victory over France in June 1940 and its preparations to invade Great Britain greatly strengthened the hand of proponents of this "Southern advance" (Nanshin) policy, although many strategists continued to oppose it.[8] The new Japanese ultimatum to the French in Indochina was thus part of an intense, confidential policy struggle in Tokyo over much larger stakes in Asia, the outcome of which remained uncertain until late 1941.

In Vichy, the head of the Colonial General Staff confidently asserted that Indochina could resist Japanese invasion. The United States had already been approached about supplying some planes, the British might release French naval aircraft confiscated in Martinique and Singapore, and there were four thousand Senegalese troops in Djibouti who could be shipped to Indochina. Some foreign policy professionals also argued for a resolute French stand in Indochina as a way of making Washington realize that it had to take a stand against Japanese aggression. If this failed, and France was forced to accommodate the Japanese in Indochina, then at least the Americans would have shared the responsibility. France would not be seen

6. Decoux, *A la barre*, 98, quoting from a message he sent to Vichy on 24 August 1940.

7. Hosoya Chihiro, "The Japanese-Soviet Neutrality Pact," in *The Fateful Choice: Japan's Advance into Southeast Asia, 1939–1941*, ed. James W. Morley (New York, 1980), 17–22.

8. Tsunoda Jun, "The Navy's Role in the Southern Strategy," in *The Fateful Choice: Japan's Advance into Southeast Asia, 1939–1941*, ed. James W. Morley (New York, 1980), 243–77. F. C. Jones, *Japan's New Order in East Asia* (Oxford, 1954), 162–64, 197, 220–25. Yoshizawa, "Nishihara Mission," 43–44.

as having played the Japanese game when the United States eventually and inevitably entered the war against Japan.

Nonetheless, the dominant feelings in Vichy, as represented by Foreign Minister Paul Baudouin, a former general manager of the Bank of Indochina, was that Indochina could not possibly defend itself, and that the United States would refuse to take any decisive measures against Japan so long as England was in peril of German invasion. Thus, the least onerous option was to recognize Japan's special interests in Indochina while retaining French sovereignty and administrative control.[9] If Japanese troops remained in the colony, they would be expected to withdraw once the fight with Chiang Kai-shek ended. A French draft agreement based on this formula proved acceptable to Foreign Minister Matsuoka Yasuko, and on 30 August, the two governments instructed their military representatives in Indochina to work out the details.[10] They would have been better advised to stick to Tokyo-Vichy channels a bit longer.

Still opposed to any stationing of Japanese forces in Indochina, Decoux instructed the commander of the French armed forces there, General Maurice Martin, to play for time in discussions beginning 3 September while he tried to persuade Vichy to toughen its stand. Vichy did ask Berlin to intervene to moderate Japanese demands,[11] with no noticeable effect. Risking the ire of Vichy, Decoux and Martin tried on their own to gain some practical help from London or Washington; they even consulted Chungking on the possibility of joint defense against the Japanese. Foreign Minister Matsuoka knew enough about these communications to complain to the British ambassador that British, American, and Chinese consular representatives in Hanoi were all "encouraging [Decoux] in his policy of procrastination."[12] Decoux never appears to have considered evacuating

9. Paul Baudouin, *The Private Diaries of Paul Baudouin* (London, 1948), 198–99, 223–24. Dreifort, "Japan's Advance," 286–90.

10. Exhibit 620 of the International Military Tribunal for the Far East (henceforth IMTFE) contains a Japanese Foreign Ministry report of these events. See also Hata, "Army's Move," 166–68, 172–75. According to François de Langlade, in Institut Charles-de-Gaulle, *Le Général de Gaulle et l'Indochine, 1940–1946* (Paris, 1982) (cited below as *DGI*), 153, the codes that Decoux, Vichy, and the French ambassador in Tokyo used to communicate with one another were broken by the Japanese, but he does not say when.

11. IMTFE exhibit 625.

12. As quoted in Nicholas Tarling, "The British and the First Japanese Move into Indo-China," *JSEAS* 21, no. 1 (Mar. 1990): 56. Tarling provides an excellent account of British actions and perceptions relating to the Franco-Japanese encounter in June–September 1940, based on documentation at the Public Record Office, London.

French women and children, who numbered about eighteen thousand. Their continued presence in Indochina limited Decoux's options severely, especially given the deservedly brutal reputation of Japanese troops in China.[13]

Meanwhile, the Japanese military representative, General Nishihara Issaku, was saddled with a deputy from the volatile South China Army, members of which were engaged in audacious efforts to force Tokyo to adopt a more aggressive strategy.[14] On 6 September, an infantry battalion from the Twenty-second Army, based in Nanning, violated the Indochina border near the French fort of Dong Dang, giving Decoux sufficient pretext to break off negotiations with Nishihara. On 18 September, however, Nishihara warned General Martin that Japanese troops would enter Indochina from 10:00 P.M. on 22 September whatever the outcome of negotiations.

If this was a bluff, Decoux had no instructions from Vichy to call it. The fact that his naval patron, Admiral François Darlan, occupied a key position in the French government probably helped Decoux decide not to order resistance on his own authority. At the last moment, Vichy did object vehemently to the high Japanese troop levels being specified for positioning in Indochina; Decoux might have used that as sufficient grounds to reject the ultimatum, except that Nishihara reduced the number dramatically on 21 September.[15] By this time Decoux probably also understood that

13. This problem is noted in the memoirs of at least two participants: Eugène Mordant, *Au service de la France en Indochine, 1941–1945* (Saigon, 1950), 27–28, and Claude de Boisanger, *On pouvait éviter la guerre d'Indochine: Souvenirs, 1941–1945* (Paris, 1977), 25. Of course, to have begun such an evacuation would have been seen by Tokyo as evidence of hostile intent, increasing the chances of armed confrontation.

14. For details of the South China Army's political maneuvers in the summer of 1940, often working with members of the Operations Division of the Army General Staff, see Murakami, "Japan's Thrust," 112–14, 121–31, 144–46, 152–62; Yoshizawa, "Nishihara Mission," 29–30, 41–43; and Hata, "Army's Move," 168–72. A rather confusing synopsis of Japanese military actions in 1940 can be found in Sachiko Murakami, "Indochina: Unplanned Incursion," in *Pearl Harbor Reexamined*, ed. Hilary Conroy and Harry Wray (Honolulu, 1990), 141–49. In addition to the South China (Kwantung) Army, the Twenty-second Army, based in Nanning, sometimes had its own political agenda as well.

15. In league with the Operations Division of the Army General Staff, which sent General Tominaga Kyoji to Hanoi to cow Nishihara, the South China Army fervently argued for stationing 25,000 troops in Tonkin. Imperial General Headquarters never believed so many were necessary, and finally succeeded in having the figure reduced to 6,000. Murakami, "Japan's Thrust," 150–54, 166–72, 174–76. Hata, "Army's Move," 175–90.

members of the South China Army were trying to sabotage Nishihara's negotiating efforts and provoke an armed confrontation, in the wake of which Tokyo would agree to full-scale occupation of northern Indochina. Seven hours and thirty minutes before expiry of the deadline, Martin and Nishihara finally signed an agreement authorizing the Japanese to station six thousand troops in Tonkin north of the Red River, to use four Tonkin airfields, to move up to twenty-five thousand men concurrently through Tonkin into Yunnan, and to arrange for a division of the Twenty-second Army to transit Tonkin via Haiphong for operations elsewhere.[16]

Martin and Nishihara had agreed that the first Japanese units would come by sea, and indeed a convoy was poised off Hainan Island for that purpose. However, the Twenty-second Army was equally intent on moving its crack Fifth Infantry Division across the border near Lang Son at precisely 10:00 P.M. Although messages reached all the appropriate command echelons by 9:00 P.M., one hour later, when troops began to advance on the French position at Dong Dang, they quickly became involved in a fierce exchange of fire.[17] During the night, fighting spread to other frontier posts. Despite repeated messages, Japanese armored units pressed on to surround Lang Son, forcing the French garrison to hoist the white flag on 25 September. By now other colonial units were in panic-stricken retreat; hundreds of Indochinese riflemen deserted entirely. Several forts held out desperately.[18] To avoid having their 155 mm heavy artillery pieces captured intact, French commanders ordered the breechblocks to be tossed down a ravine into the river. They were painfully aware of the 1885 historical precedent, when French units fleeing Chinese attack had dumped all their impediments at the same location.[19] Nothing seemed to stand in the way of a triumphal advance on Hanoi by the Japanese Fifth Division.

Meanwhile, eager troop commanders aboard the convoy standing off Haiphong, aware that their comrades had seized the initiative at Dong

16. Hata, "Army's Move," 191–92. Decoux, *A la barre*, 112. Georges Gautier, *9 Mars 1945, Hanoi au soleil de sang: La Fin de l'Indochine française* (Paris, 1978), 43–45.

17. Murakami, "Japan's Thrust," 180–91. Hata, "Army's Move," 192–93. Hata uses Japan time, requiring one to subtract two hours.

18. *Histoire de l'Indochine: Le Destin, 1885–1954*, ed. Philippe Héduy (Paris, 1983), 254–57. Claude Hesse d'Alzon, "L'Armée française d'Indochine pendant la seconde guerre mondiale, 1939–1945," in *L'Indochine française, 1940–1945*, ed. Paul Isoart (Paris, 1982), 86–89. Hata, "Army's Move," 194–98.

19. Later, when fishing out the breechblocks, colonial soldiers also recovered some trunks filled with Mexican dollars from the 1885 debacle. Decoux, *A la barre*, 121–22.

Dang and Lang Son, were furious when the fleet admiral decided to postpone any landing until the border hostilities had been resolved. In a blitz of radio telegrams, each side sought confirmation of its position from superiors in Tokyo. On the evening of 25 September, the Navy General Staff persuaded the Army General Staff to order its units to delay landing until at least 10:00 A.M. the next morning, but a staff intermediary on Hainan deliberately held this message back. The fleet admiral very reluctantly allowed landing craft to be launched in the early morning of the 26th, then withdrew his escort ships toward Hainan in protest at army behavior. The troops beached their boats with no resistance from the French, who allowed their garrison at Do Son to be forcibly disarmed and forty-five hundred imperial troops to take possession of a large camp in Haiphong. At daylight, nine Japanese bombers flew over Haiphong, one dropping a stick of bombs, allegedly by accident, that left thirty-seven civilians dead.[20]

The situation was remarkably similar to that in Manchuria in the early 1930s, when a cabal of militant Japanese field and staff officers had repeatedly forced the hand of their more cautious superiors. Locally initiated violence had combined with deliberate delay, misinterpretation, even ignoring of orders, to help propel Japan into northern China. This parallel could not have been lost on some of the highest-ranking generals of 1940, since they owed their own positions to such prior acts of calculated disobedience. Perhaps for that reason, they were unusually severe in retaliation. They were also particularly embarrassed by the fact that the Shōwa Emperor himself had questioned them skeptically on 13 September about the decision to make the deadline for successful negotiations and the entry of Japanese troops into Indochina exactly coincide, asking, "What will you do if the negotiations are concluded just before the deadline?" He was assured that a peaceful entry would be carried out.[21] Now the emperor had to be called to endorse orders to the South China Army to abide by the 22 September Nishihara-Martin agreement, to halt offensive operations, arrange a cease-fire, release prisoners (who now numbered twenty-five hundred), and return Lang Son and Do Son to French control. Formal apologies were conveyed to Vichy and to Admiral Decoux over the whole affair. The commander of the South China Army was summarily retired, the Oper-

20. Murakami, "Japan's Thrust," 191–99. Hata, "Army's Move," 198–203. Claude Hesse d'Alzon, *La Présence militaire français en Indochine (1940–1945)* (Paris, 1985), 75–77.
21. Hata, "Army's Move," 184.

ations Division purged, the Fifth Infantry Division commander replaced. General Tōjō Hideki, the minister of war, emerged as a tough advocate of centralized control and punishment for those who dared bypass the army chain of command. As a sop to the militants, however, General Nishihara's resignation was accepted, and he never again received an important assignment.[22]

The militants had aimed to create conditions whereby the Japanese government's policy of retaining the French administration was abandoned in favor of outright military occupation or establishment of several dependent native regimes, similar to that of Wang Ching-wei in occupied China. For either of those contingencies, the South China Army had already recruited, trained, and armed Vietnamese auxiliaries, who marched under the banner of the Viet Nam Phuc Quoc Dong Minh Hoi (Vietnam National Restoration League), established by the émigré Prince Cuong De in Shanghai the previous year.[23] Immediately following the Japanese attack on 22 September, this group was greatly expanded, perhaps to as many as two thousand men, drawing recruits from surrendered native colonial soldiers as well as civilians anticipating the demise of French rule. In the wake of Tokyo's firm reaffirmation of the Martin-Nishihara agreement, however, South China Army support for these Vietnamese units evaporated. Some members straggled toward western Kwangsi and were disarmed by the Nationalist Chinese. Others chose to fight the returning French, often together with local followers of the Indochinese Communist Party (see chapter 3); by December, all had been killed, captured, or dispersed.[24] Still others who decided to remain with

22. Murakami, "Japan's Thrust," 199–204. Hata, "Army's Move," 203–8. A rather different Japanese military explanation, emphasizing "misunderstandings" and communications problems, is translated in *War in Asia and the Pacific, 1937–1949*, ed. Donald S. Detwiler and Charles B. Burdick, vol. 6, *The Southern Area* (New York, 1980), 1–3. Within a year of these events, General Tōjō bought two of the offending staff officers back to key positions.

23. David G. Marr, "World War II and the Vietnamese Revolution," in *Southeast Asia under Japanese Occupation*, ed. Alfred W. McCoy (New Haven, 1980), 131, 138.

24. Shiraishi Masaya, "La Présence japonaise en Indochine (1940–1945)," in *L'Indochine française, 1940–1945*, ed. Paul Isoart (Paris, 1982), 219–21. Shiraishi Masaya, "Vietnam under the Japanese Presence and the August Revolution," in *1945 in South-East Asia*, pt. 2 (London: Suntory Toyota International Centre for Economics and Related Disciplines, London School of Economics and Political Science, 1985), 3–4. Vu Ngu Chieu, "Political and Social Change in Viet-Nam between 1940 and 1946" (Ph.D. diss., University of Wisconsin–Madison, 1984), 20–21.

Japanese Army units may have been used later for undercover work inside Indochina.[25]

Thai Irredentism

No sooner had the difficulties between Hanoi and Tokyo been ironed out than Admiral Decoux faced escalating threats from Thailand, where the military regime of Premier Pibul Songgram saw an opportunity to recover Khmer and Lao territories ceded to the French in the late nineteenth and early twentieth centuries. Decoux managed to stall Bangkok for almost two months, meanwhile frantically shifting troops from Tonkin to Cochinchina and Cambodia. However, morale had suffered in the colonial army as a result of the Lang Son debacle. Among Vietnamese infantrymen, there was widespread talk about refusing to fight. In November, the French uncovered a plot whereby Vietnamese troopers and raw conscripts would join with the Indochinese Communist Party in outright rebellion. After suspect units were transferred or confined to barracks, farmers in several Mekong Delta provinces nevertheless mounted demonstrations and seized local authority. In a display of ruthlessness not seen for fifty years in Indochina, white battalions used aircraft, armored cars, artillery, and machine guns to destroy whole villages.[26] The French then passed out thousands of pamphlets in Vietnamese and romanized Khmer arguing that the natives really loved them, and that the claims of the Thai to be "brothers" of the local people were rank delusion.[27]

In a more realistic vein, the governor-general obtained Vichy's agreement to transport four Senegalese infantry battalions from Africa to Saigon, but British warships intercepted and turned back the French vessel involved. Finally, with Thai air sorties and small-scale ground attacks too numerous to endure much longer, Decoux authorized a counteroffensive for 16 January 1941. Advancing Indochina Army units quickly suffered serious reversals, with many Vietnamese soldiers deserting the battlefield entirely. Disaster was averted the next day, however, when French warships scored a clear-cut victory over the Thai fleet near Ko Chang Island.[28]

25. *Histoire de l'Indochine*, ed. Héduy, 256.

26. See chapter 3 for a more detailed account of these Mekong Delta confrontations.

27. See, e.g., Georges Marie Kerneis, *Su That ve viec loi thoi giua Nuoc Phap va Nuoc Xiem* [The Truth about the Troubles between France and Siam] (Hanoi, 1941). Preface dated 20 Dec. 1940.

28. André Gaudel, *L'Indochine française en face du Japon* (Paris, 1947), 94–109. Gautier, *9 Mars 1945*, 46–47. Decoux, *A la barre*, 132–41. Hesse d'Alzon, "L'Armée

At this point, Tokyo instructed Vichy and Bangkok to accept Japanese mediation. Neither side was happy at that prospect, the French correctly surmising that Tokyo would favor their adversary, and the Thai government eager to mobilize the country for a patriotic armed crusade, not negotiations. However, the fate of several Cambodian and Laotian provinces was now linked to overriding strategic issues being hotly debated in faraway capitals. The British, realizing that Tokyo's mediation demand represented a potentially grave new Japanese step southward, as distinct from ongoing attempts in Tonkin to throttle Nationalist China, worked hard in Bangkok to recruit allies. However, when Britain was asked explicitly whether it would come to Thailand's aid if the latter were attacked or threatened by Japan, no answer was forthcoming. London had already tried to interest Washington in alternative Western mediation, but to no avail.

In Tokyo, meanwhile, there was no consensus except on the necessity of blocking the British diplomatic initiative, which was seen to be linked to Dutch refusal in Batavia to sign a new oil export agreement. The Army General Staff pressed for an outright alliance with Bangkok that would enable Japan to position troops and aircraft in Thailand for a possible attack on Singapore, in the spirit of the Tripartite (Axis) pact signed four months earlier. However, Foreign Minister Matsuoka adamantly opposed such a move unless the Soviet Union could first be neutralized in the north. Top echelons of the Japanese Navy were divided, some prepared to risk early confrontation with Britain and even the United States, others working hard to avoid it.[29] Eventually a bureaucratic compromise was pieced together, with Japanese warships being dispatched to the vicinity of Saigon, ground forces strengthened in Tonkin, and preparations made to advance forcibly into southern Indochina if Vichy and Admiral Decoux refused to deliver some territory to Thailand.[30]

On 31 January, faced with this sort of pressure, Decoux boarded a Japanese battleship on the Saigon River to sign a cease-fire with representatives from Bangkok, leaving to Vichy and the French Embassy in

---

française d'Indochine," 93–96, and *La Présence militaire française en Indochine*, 90–96.

29. Murakami, "Japan's Thrust," 228–41. Nagaoka Shinjirō, "The Drive into Southern Indochina and Thailand," in *The Fateful Choice: Japan's Advance into Southeast Asia, 1939–1941*, ed. James W. Morley (New York, 1980), 218–30.

30. Tanemura Sako, *Daihon'ei himitsu nisshi* [Imperial Headquarters Secret War Diaries] (Tokyo, 1952), 38–45.

Tokyo the thankless task of minimizing territorial losses.[31] When talks opened a week later in Tokyo, the Thai negotiator began by demanding "retrocession" of all Laos and Cambodia. The Japanese soon reduced this to the two Laotian provinces acquired by the French in 1904 and the three Cambodian provinces gained in 1907. When the French negotiator procrastinated, Japan once again mobilized ships and troops, threatening to move forcibly if no agreement were reached by 28 February. At one point the ultimatum was delayed because the Imperial Navy became worried about growing American press opposition to Japanese actions. However, on 11 March, France formally accepted the terms of mediation, which were to be enforced by Tokyo and contained a clause precluding either France or Thailand from entering into any understanding with a third party deemed prejudicial to Japan.[32] At this point, tensions receded, and the focus shifted to discussions between French and Japanese specialists about increased economic cooperation. A few months later, however, Indochina was thrust back onto the international stage, with the strategic stakes higher than ever before.

Southern Indochina Takes on Global Significance

Even as portents accumulated of an ominous turn in German-Soviet relations, Foreign Minister Matsuoka refused to be deterred from negotiating a neutrality pact with Moscow, which was duly signed on 13 April 1941. Not until 5 June, when word arrived from the Japanese ambassador of his visit to Hitler's villa at Obersalzberg in order to hear heavy hints about war, did the army and navy begin intense discussions about the implications for Japan. Yet Matsuoka and many other Japanese leaders refused to take Hitler's remarks seriously until the 22d, when word arrived of Germany's invasion of the Soviet Union. Bitter arguments ensued about how to take advantage of this dramatic development. Army proponents of a "Northern advance" (Hokushin) strategy called for an attack on Siberia, yet under questioning, they had to agree that they were poorly prepared to act decisively during the short summer season. Admitting his prior miscalculation, Matsuoka vehemently supported the Siberian invasion option. On the other hand, "Southern advance" advocates in the army pointed out that Germany's attack greatly reduced the need for imperial forces in

31. Decoux, *A la barre*, 141–47. Gaudel, *L'Indochine française en face du Japon*, 110–16.

32. Murakami, "Japan's Thrust," 242–54. Nagaoka, "Drive into Southern Indochina and Thailand," 231–34. Tsunoda, "Navy's Role," 283–84.

the north, hence making possible a decisive move on Singapore. Naval strategists were divided as well, some endorsing the idea of an attack on Singapore, others fearful of American retaliation. On 28 June, a compromise was reached whereby Japan would demand French permission to station troops and operate air and naval bases in southern Indochina, meanwhile undertaking large-scale mobilization at home for subsequent advances in either a southern or northern direction. Confusion over strategic priorities continued until the end of July, when Northern advance proponents reluctantly acknowledged that the German invasion had not forced Stalin to shift enough Far Eastern units westward to make a Japanese attack certain to succeed in 1941. Matsuoka had already been sacked as foreign minister on the 18th.[33]

On 14 July, Bastille Day, the Japanese ambassador at Vichy informed Foreign Minister Darlan of Tokyo's new requirements, emphasizing the need for a quick affirmative response to forestall any British or American interference. Two days later Darlan confidentially alerted the American ambassador, in the desperate hope that a U.S. naval squadron might sail from Manila to Saigon.[34] He also requested Berlin to intercede with Tokyo. Before any replies were received, however, the Japanese ambassador returned with a deadline, which Admiral Darlan felt compelled to accept to avoid senseless bloodshed. Imperial Twenty-fifth Army units began landing in southern Indochina on 28 July. Unlike in September the previous year, Governor-General Decoux did not try to delay or alter Japanese plans.[35]

In Washington, President Roosevelt knew about Japanese intentions to advance into southern Indochina before the French did, thanks to MAGIC, the top-secret system able to decode a significant portion of Japan's clas-

---

33. IMTFE exhibits 588, 1095, 1108, 1306. Jones, *Japan's New Order*, 217–20. Kashima Heiwa Kenkyūjohen, *Nihon gaikōshi* [A History of Diplomacy in Japan], vol. 24 (Tokyo, 1971) (hereafter *NGS*, 24), 198. Nagaoka, "Drive into Southern Indochina and Thailand," 235–36. Murakami, "Japan's Thrust," 286–301. Hosoya, "Japanese-Soviet Neutrality Pact," 82, 89–106. B. V. A. Röling, the Dutch judge at the Tokyo war crimes trials, took a special interest in the relationship between the Tripartite pact, Tokyo's dealings with Moscow, and Japanese moves in Indochina. See *The Tokyo Judgement: The International Military Tribunal for the Far East*, vol. 2 (Amsterdam, 1977), 1078–88.

34. U.S. Department of State, *The Foreign Relations of the United States, 1941* (Washington, D.C.), 5:210, 213–14, 246. In early July, Governor-General Decoux had already alerted Vichy to likely new Japanese demands. Decoux, *A la barre*, 150–51.

35. Gaudel, *L'Indochine française en face du Japon*, 117–21. Decoux, *A la barre*, 151–53. Tanemura, *Daihon'ei Himitsu Nisshi*, 71–72. Murakami, "Japan's Thrust," 322–37. Nagaoka, "Drive into Southern Indochina and Thailand," 236–38.

Figure 2.   A bicycle unit of the Japanese Army enters Saigon in late July 1941, following Tokyo's ultimatum to Vichy. Reproduced from Philippe Héduy, *L'histoire de l'Indochine*, vol. 2. Courtesy of Société de production littéraire / Henri Veyrier.

sified radio traffic.[36] A longtime naval buff and avid map reader, Roosevelt readily appreciated that new Japanese bases in southern Indochina would place Singapore, Sumatra, and Borneo within range of bomber assault for the first time, threaten all movement in the South China Sea, and flank American bases on Luzon. Subsequent Japanese claims that these moves into southern Indochina were not aimed at Dutch, British, and American possessions, but rather a further effort to resolve the "China Incident," were treated with derision.[37]

On 25 July, the Roosevelt administration announced a freeze on Japanese assets in the United States, while simultaneously starting to reinforce ground and air units based in the Philippines. Roosevelt did not intend a complete embargo on Japan. The freeze was meant to be selective, with

36. Jonathan G. Utley, *Going to War with Japan, 1937–1941* (Knoxville, Tenn., 1985), 151.
37. Surprisingly, confidential Tokyo policy papers also sometimes gave the same "China Incident" justification, apparently as a rhetorical compromise to accommodate those in the Japanese Navy and Foreign Ministry who feared Western counteraction. See Murakami, "Japan's Thrust," 309, 311–12.

funds being released depending on the commodity the Japanese wished to buy. Nonetheless, middle-level administrators quickly devised a system that amounted to full-scale economic warfare. In particular, the original guideline, which permitted purchase of gasoline below 80 octane, was modified to allow only a limited amount of diesel fuel, and even this quantity never reached Japan. Meanwhile, Britain, the British Dominions (Canada, Australia, New Zealand, and South Africa), and the Netherlands East Indies administration all prohibited export to Japan of petroleum and other strategic products. Appreciating the gravity of the situation, Prime Minister Konoe Fumimaro sought a face-to-face meeting with President Roosevelt, but this idea was scuttled by Secretary of State Cordell Hull, who had abandoned his cautious position and now wanted a Japanese commitment to withdraw from most of China, not just Indochina.[38]

As discussions dragged on into the autumn of 1941, it became evident that neither side would budge. On 15 October, Konoe's cabinet fell, and he was replaced by the hard-line General Tōjō Hideki as both prime minister and minister of war. In November, Japan offered to remove its troops from southern Indochina in return for the United States rescinding the freeze, helping Japan obtain oil from the Netherlands East Indies, and cutting off aid to China. While an American counterproposal was passed around numerous Washington bureaus for consideration, Secretary of State Hull effectively gave up looking for compromises and accepted the likelihood of war.[39] Meanwhile, most of the Japanese naval officers who had long opposed moves southward concluded that time was on the side of the Americans, who were steadily increasing the size of their fleet, while Japan was depleting its stockpiles of raw materials, especially the oil needed to fuel its warships. From this logical, yet disastrous, assessment emerged the final decision to attack Pearl Harbor.

For the Japanese to be able simultaneously to attack the Philippines, Borneo, Malaya, and Burma, Indochina served as the ideal "pivot point of a folding fan," the apt metaphor of General Tsuchihashi Yūichi, who had been there as an official visitor in late 1939, and who would later mastermind the *coup de force* against the French.[40] Shortly after Pearl Harbor, eighty-eight Japanese bombers and torpedo planes took off from southern Indochina to accomplish what British and American intelligence had regarded as impossible—the sinking of the two British battleships *Prince of*

---

38. Utley, *Going to War*, 151–61.

39. Ibid., 161–75.

40. Tsuchihashi Yūichi, "Furansugun o busō kaijo" [Disarming the French Army], *Shūkan yomiuri* (Tokyo), special ed., 8 Dec. 1956, 156.

Wales and *Repulse*.[41] Cam Ranh Bay proved an ideal staging area for Japanese naval operations throughout the southwestern Pacific and the Indian Ocean. Saigon soon hosted the Japanese Army's Southern Area command, encompassing all South Pacific and Southeast Asian units.[42] The road from Saigon to Bangkok was used extensively by Japanese forces in the early stages of the invasion of Burma.

All of these Japanese movements in and around Indochina in late 1941 were legitimated by a joint defense clause contained in the July agreement with Vichy. However, the Japanese Army wanted to spell things out to the French more clearly. A few hours before the attack on Pearl Harbor, 6,500 miles away, General Chō Isamu sent army units to surround the governor-general's residence in Hanoi and other key locations. At 9:00 A.M. local time on 8 December, after the French had heard about Pearl Harbor from American shortwave broadcasts, he marched into Admiral Decoux's office to present yet another ultimatum. The French authorities in Indochina would now be required to "offer every facility to the operation, maintenance, and establishment of military installations of the Japanese forces," assume primary responsibility for defense in the north against possible Nationalist Chinese attack, and cooperate militarily with the Japanese in a number of other ways.[43] Besides demanding that the French provide food and shelter for Japanese units, as well as native laborers, Chō wanted the right to approve the movements of all French warships and merchant vessels, French exclusion from Cam Ranh Bay, and scheduling priority for the Japanese in rail and road transport, with Japanese liaison officers stationed at key locations such as PTT (Postes, télégraphes et téléphones) bureaus, the censorship office, and coastal defense positions.[44]

For almost twenty-four hours Admiral Decoux attempted to dilute the Japanese demands, without success. Even token military resistance was out of the question, as most French units had been surrounded by surprise and communications cut. If Decoux delayed further or refused to sign, General Chō was ready to place Indochina under complete military control, which meant disarming French troops, terminating French administration, and possibly interning the forty thousand French citizens in the colony. Decoux

41. H. P. Willmott, *Empires in the Balance: Japanese and Allied Pacific Strategies to April 1942* (Annapolis, Md., 1982), 168–69.

42. Field Marshal Terauchi Hisaichi remained commander throughout the war. Southern Area command was shifted to Singapore in December 1942, then back to Saigon in November 1944. IMTFE exhibit 663.

43. Murakami, "Japan's Thrust," 364–67.

44. IMTFE exhibit 656.

reluctantly accepted the Japanese terms, thus escaping the imminent fate of his British, Dutch, and American colonial counterparts in Rangoon, Kuala Lumpur, Singapore, Batavia, and Manila. He consoled himself that French military units would not be called upon to participate in Japanese operations outside Indochina.[45] Although later arguing that the colonial administration had remained neutral as the result of his efforts, Decoux knew only too well the multifold military uses to which Japan put French Indochina during the Pacific War. Wanting to give French nationals in Indochina a specifically non-Japanese focus of attention, Decoux drew from his own reservoir of antirepublican, Pétainist convictions to form a quasi-fascist "Légion des combattants et des volontaires de la Révolution nationale," to purge the administration of Jews and suspected Free French sympathizers, and to demand repeated public affirmations of support for Vichy policies.[46]

Undoubtedly, many Japanese Army officers would have preferred to dump Decoux entirely, humble the Europeans in front of the local people, and operate a straightforward military government. With all the other white imperialists east of India being driven out or imprisoned, why keep the French? However, Prime Minister Tōjō and other top-ranking army men considered this anomaly a small price to pay for avoiding the costs and uncertainties of outright occupation, not to mention a likely rupture with Vichy and strained relations with Berlin.[47] In December 1941, Japanese strategists were anxious to husband troop reserves for much more distant locations like Burma and India, or Papua New Guinea and Australia. From Tokyo's perspective, the French made useful administrative contractors in Indochina, even if they could hardly be expected to collaborate eagerly.[48]

Wartime Economic Activities

Besides military bases and French responsibility for local order, the Japanese expected substantial economic benefits from Indochina. Essentially

45. Decoux, *A la barre*, 157–60, 202–7. Gautier, *9 Mars 1945*, 54–57.

46. P. L. Lamant, "La Révolution nationale dans l'Indochine de l'amiral Decoux," *Revue d'histoire de la deuxième guerre mondiale et des conflits contemporains*, no. 138 (Apr. 1985): 21–41.

47. *Yoshizawa Kenkichi jiden* [The Diary of Yoshizawa Kenkichi], ed. Nakano Keishi (Tokyo, 1964), 169. *NGS*, 24:200–201. Shiraishi Masaya and Furuta Motoo, "Taiheiyō sensō ki no Nihon no tai-Indoshina seisaku: Sono futatsu no tokuisei o megutte" [Japan's Policy toward Indochina during the Pacific War: Concerning Two Peculiarities], *Ajia kenkyū* (Tokyo) 23, no. 3 (1976): 8–9. This latter essay has been translated in *Indochina*, ed. Shiraishi and Furuta, 55–85.

48. The term "administrative contractors" is borrowed from Vu Ngu Chieu, "Political and Social Change in Viet-Nam," 34.

this meant obtaining favored access to Indochina's rice, corn, rubber, jute, coal, zinc, and vegetable oils in exchange for whatever manufactured goods, textiles, processed foods, and medicines Japan could spare after meeting the needs of its armed forces and domestic market.[49] Between June 1940 and December 1941, the French had little reason to complain. Each side needed the other. The European War quickly undercut Indochina's commercial ties with France, and, by mid 1941, with all other Western trading partners. Into this gap stepped Japanese buyers for Indochina's rice and rubber. For the moment, owing to the glut caused by growing restrictions in Japan's traditional Western markets, Tokyo also had products to offer in return. In November 1941, a team of Japanese economic specialists arrived in Indochina to study investment and longer-term development prospects, including possible construction of a Saigon-Rangoon railway.[50]

From early 1942 on, however, this economic marriage of convenience began to work against Indochina. Japan displayed a voracious appetite for food and raw materials, yet proved unable to supply much by way of finished products in exchange.[51] A big yen surplus accumulated in Indochina's accounts in Tokyo. Up until the end of 1942, it was possible to use a portion of the surplus to buy commodities in Thailand, Singapore, or occupied China, but then Japan compelled the Vichy government to convert all accounts to "special" yen, worthless except for the occasional shipment of soap or medicine from Japan, or to cover the living expenses of French diplomatic personnel in Japanese-occupied areas.[52] Although

49. After much wrangling between Vichy and Tokyo, the general terms were codified in the economic and commercial agreements of 6 May 1941. Gaudel, *L'Indochine française en face du Japon*, 199–205. Murakami, "Japan's Thrust," 216–26. See also Shiraishi Masaya, "Dainiji daisenki no Nippon no tai—Indoshina keizai seisaku" [Japanese Economic Policy toward Indochina in World War II], *Tōnan Ajia: Rekishi to bunka* 15 (1986): 28–62. Tabuchi Yukichika, "Dai Tōa kyōeiken to Indoshina: Shokuryō kakutoku no tame no senryaku" [The Greater East Asia Co-Prosperity Sphere and Indochina: A Strategy for Securing Food Supplies], *Tōnan Ajia: Rekishi to bunka*, no. 10 (June 1981):39–68, emphasizes Tokyo's growing concern about grain supplies and provides useful prewar and wartime trade information.

50. Interview with Yokoyama Masayuki, Tokyo, 16 Nov. 1967. Ambassador Yokoyama headed this group of 150 experts to Indochina.

51. Shiraishi, "Vietnam under the Japanese Presence," 8–9, contains relevant Indochina-Japan trade figures expressed in both tonnages and French francs.

52. Gaudel, *L'Indochine française en face du Japon*, 221–24. Nonetheless, Gautier, *9 Mars 1945*, 131, reports that at the end of the war, the Bank of Indochina office in Tokyo held thirty-two tons of gold, subsequently added to the reserves of the Bank of France.

exports to Japan's home islands began to drop off rapidly after mid 1943 as a result of American submarine and air attacks on Japanese merchant shipping, substantial quantities of Indochinese rice, corn, jute, castor oil, and coal continued to be exported to southern China and parts of Southeast Asia. Both French and Japanese authorities permitted modest trade with Nationalist China to continue (see chapter 4). In 1944, as sea communications declined further, Japanese officials in Indochina took the further precautions of stockpiling grain and fuel, commandeering civilian vehicles, and raising their monthly demands on the French for transport tonnage. Some Indochinese rice was shipped to the Philippines in anticipation of an American amphibious invasion there.[53]

Japanese business conglomerates like Mitsui and Mitsubishi endeavored to replace or absorb truncated French trading firms, while colonial administrators in Indochina thought up new ways to protect them.[54] By 1943 a number of Japanese companies were shifting attention toward local production. Some enterprises leased land to cultivate jute, castor beans, hemp, and cotton. Others imported sawmill machinery to tap Indochina's large timber reserves, using the lumber to construct wooden ships, bridges, barracks, and warehouses, as well as cutting railroad ties.[55] Japanese firms also prospected energetically for minerals, opening some modest phosphate, manganese, and chromite mines as a result.[56]

Meanwhile, local French entrepreneurs and technicians were not sitting on their thumbs. Either on their own initiative or with financial inducements from the colonial administration, they developed a surprising number of substitutes for goods previously imported. With the help of Viet-

53. *War in Asia and the Pacific,* ed. Detwiler and Burdick, 6:13. The effects of U.S. sea and air interdiction can be seen in the severe drop in Japanese imports of Indochinese rice, from 973,000 tons in 1942, to 662,000 in 1943, to only 38,000 in 1944. Meanwhile, the French counted 1,023,471 tons of rice being exported from Indochina in 1943 and 499,000 in 1944, some measure of the shift to southern China and Southeast Asia, although an unknown portion of that export total went to the bottom of the ocean.

54. Gaudel, *L'Indochine française en face du Japon,* 212–17.

55. USNA, OSS (Research and Analysis) Washington, report no. 2594, 1 Jan. 45. One of the most active medium-sized companies was Dainan Koosi, whose proprietor, Matsushita Mitsuhiro, had come to Indochina in 1912.

56. Joint Intelligence Collection Agency / China Burma India / South East Asia report, 19 Sept. 44, in USNA, OSS record 96622. American intelligence monitored such Japanese initiatives in Indochina closely. For example, having been bombed repeatedly by the U.S. 14th Air Force, a phosphate mine near Lao Cai was reported in August 1944 to be producing only 5,000 tons per month. Phosphate also piled up in Haiphong for lack of shipping.

namese and Chinese technicians, artisans, and skilled workers, a rolling mill was pieced together, iron reinforcing rods were extracted, and a limited number of grinders, mixers, pistons, and sawblades were manufactured. Before the war, despite the local abundance of latex, tires for both motor vehicles and bicycles had been imported from France. Now it became possible to produce low-quality bicycle tires and to retread automobile and truck tires locally. After imported Egyptian gypsum ran out, a local source was identified to produce cement. Small factories began to make carbonate of soda for soap and potassium chlorate for matches, although never in sufficient quantities to meet demand. Paper, also imported in prewar years, was successfully fabricated at Dap Cau, northeast of Hanoi, until shortages of chemicals and machine parts intervened.[57] Cotton, previously almost driven out of local production by metropolitan French yarn and textiles, quickly regained favor during the war. The Japanese government subsidized six companies to plant cotton experimentally in different parts of the colony.[58] Although cotton acreage jumped from 7,000 hectares in 1939 to 52,000 in 1944, insect pests, too-hasty choice of seeds, and improper soil types kept yields low. Farmers also found themselves being ordered to sell both boll and seed at fixed prices. When Allied bombers damaged the main spinning and weaving mills in Nam Dinh and Haiphong, operations continued in nearby villages. However, cumulative shortages of cotton and yarn eventually forced tens of thousands of textile workers out of employment. Women fashioned crude pullovers and vests out of ramie and kapok. The French tried to ration existing stocks of cloth to Europeans, colonial troops, and native functionaries, while also reluctantly selling some to Japanese quartermasters. Ordinary Vietnamese could only look to the black market, where cloth prices were exorbitant.[59] By 1944, poor adult Vietnamese often owned only one tattered pair of shorts and a shirt, while

57. U.S. Office of Strategic Services, *Programs of Japan in Indochina* (Honolulu, Aug. 1945) (cited below as *PJI*), 14 June 1943, 27 Oct. 1943, 15 July 1944. *Thanh Nghi* (Hanoi), 1 Apr. 1943, 26 May 1945. *Cach Mang Can Dai Viet Nam* (cited below as *CMCD*), 8:121–33. Gaudel, *L'Indochine française en face du Japon,* 227–28. André Angladette, "La Vie quotidienne en Indochine de 1939 à 1946," *Comptes rendus trimestriels des séances de l'Académie des sciences d'Outre-Mer* 39, no. 3 (1979): 482–85.

58. Murakami, "Japan's Thrust," 388.

59. *CMCD,* 8:184. Angladette, "Vie quotidienne," 471–72. René Bauchar [René Charbonneau], *Rafales sur l'Indochine* (Paris, 1946), 114–15. USNA, OSS (Research and Analysis) Washington, report no. 2594, 1 Jan. 1945. In February 1945, just before the Japanese coup, Tonkin Resident Superior Chauvet removed the requirement that cotton cultivators must sell their output to the government. AOM, INF, GF 65.

their children went naked. They would suffer miserably during the unusually cold winter of 1944–45, when the temperature dropped to 6° C. in Tonkin's Red River Delta.[60]

With the fall of Paris in June 1940, Indochina's normal source of fresh coins and banknotes evaporated. Later that year the École pratique d'Hanoi was authorized to fabricate zinc one-centime coins, and in 1941 the San Francisco Mint shipped ten- and twenty-centime copper-nickel coins to Indochina. From 1942 on, the Osaka Mint contracted to produce quarter-centime zinc coins, but during most of 1943 and all of 1944, supplies never left Japan for lack of sea transport. Already in 1942, prewar bronze coins were being hoarded or withdrawn from circulation because of the inflated value of copper. Meanwhile, the Imprimerie d'Extrême-Orient in Hanoi produced notes in denominations from five centimes to 500 piastres, but as chemicals ran short and spare parts had to be improvised for the presses, the quality deteriorated rapidly. In some parts of the colony, the scarcity of small denominations led people to tear notes in half to make change.[61]

As the Pacific War dragged on, and economic strains increased, the colonial authorities ordered ever more money to be printed. Banknotes in circulation increased from 494 million piastres in December 1942 to 740 million in December 1943, and jumped to 1.344 billion a year later. Japanese demands for money to support their operations in Indochina proved especially onerous. Between September 1940 and the end of 1943, the Indochinese treasury turned over a relatively manageable 229 million piastres to the Japanese, but in 1944 the amount leaped to 353 million, helping to fuel the rampant inflation of early 1945.[62]

One predictable French response to wartime shortages was to increase the amount of paperwork necessary to purchase, transport, store, or sell key commodities like rice, salt, cooking oil, cloth, coal, matches, or water filters. In Tonkin, the Service économique local was charged with enforc-

60. Nghiem Xuan Yem, *Thanh Nghi* (Hanoi), 5 May 1945.

61. Howard A. Daniel III, *The Catalog and Guidebook of Southeast Asian Coins and Currency*, vol. 1, *France*, 2d ed. (Postage, Ohio, 1978), 13–14.

62. Shiraishi, "Vietnam under the Japanese Presence," 10, 12. In view of uncertainties about piastre-yen conversion rates in the records available, transfers from the Indochina treasury should be considered rough approximations only. It is interesting to compare wartime printing of banknotes in French Indochina with British India, where the nominal money supply increased from 3.17 billion rupees in 1939 to 21.9 billion in 1945. Sugata Bose, "Starvation amidst Plenty: The Making of Famine in Bengal, Honan and Tonkin, 1942–45," *Modern Asian Studies* (Cambridge) 24, no. 4 (1990): 715.

ing a maze of control regulations, both through the government hierarchy, which extended out to several thousand village headmen, and via a range of private companies authorized to trade in specific goods. In the end, the system appears to have become clogged by huge quantities of telegrams, letters, commodity samples, price lists, internal memos, and formal complaints requiring investigation.[63] The idea that the state must exercise such minute economic controls was assimilated passionately by many Vietnamese, with consequences far beyond the end of the Pacific War.

Because Indochina possessed no oil wells, and the Japanese lacked petrol even for their own garrison troops in Indochina, all motor vehicles, pumps, turbines, and engines in the colony had to be converted to operate on either charcoal gas or alcohol. Coal from the Hon Gai region near Haiphong was shipped south by train or junk until Allied air attacks in 1944 made this too dangerous. In early 1945, the Saigon electric power plant was running on unhusked rice.[64] Also using rice as the main raw material, French-owned distilleries managed to increase alcohol production from 5,000 tons before the war to 15,500 tons in 1942. From early 1943 on, a shortage of sulfuric acid cut industrial alcohol production, but the Japanese converted two distilleries at Cholon to production of butanol for aviation gasoline. From February 1944 on, the distilleries therefore became prime Allied bombing targets. Nonetheless, Allied intelligence reported an increase in production of alcohol in Tonkin in the summer of 1944, just as food shortages began to assume critical proportions.[65] Japanese efforts to induce Vietnamese farmers to shift to cultivating cash crops such as cotton, jute, hemp, ramie, peanuts, and castor oil seed posed few problems in rice-rich Cochinchina, but they proved extremely risky in Tonkin and northern Annam, where grain deficits were already endemic. When villagers tried to evade instructions, the Japanese sometimes sent troops or Kenpeitai (military police) teams to enforce planting con-

63. Today, much of this paperwork for the early 1945 period, at least, can be found scattered throughout the AOM, INF, GF collection.

64. *Shittan Meigō sakusen: Biruma sensen no hōkai to Tai, Futsuin no bōei* [Sittang and Meigō Operations: Collapse of the Burma Front and Defense of Thailand and French Indochina], ed. Bōeichō (Tokyo, 1969) (cited below as *SMS*), 684. Overall coal production dropped from 2.3 million tons in 1941 to 0.5 million in 1944. Vu Ngu Chieu, "Political and Social Change in Viet-Nam," 159.

65. USNA, OSS (Research and Analysis) Washington, report no. 2594, 1 Jan. 1945. Angladette, "Vie quotidienne," 479–82, contains a detailed description of wartime production of both *gazogène* and industrial alcohol. See also Vu Ngu Chieu, "Political and Social Change in Viet-Nam," 160–62.

versions and harvesting.[66] Some French officials warned of the danger of a food crisis, to little avail. By mid 1944, the Viet Minh was distributing leaflets exhorting farmers, "Don't turn over a single kilogram of rice, don't give a single peanut, don't grow another jute plant for the [fascist] bandits!"[67]

Daily Life among the French and Japanese

Amidst all these pressures and uncertainties, some forty thousand Europeans tried to live as normally as possible, retaining their contingents of servants, dressing formally for dinner, gathering to talk at the cafés, taking weekend trips to the beach or to the hill stations of Dalat in the south and Tam Dao in the north. Even the horse races continued. Some families possessed shortwave receivers, around which they would gather to listen to broadcasts from Europe, America, and Australia. From 1942 on, ration tickets were issued to Europeans, which at least ensured them adequate quantities of rice, salt, sugar, cooking oil, soap, matches, "quality" cigarettes, and fuel. Meat and condensed milk were controlled by licensed retailers, who apparently allocated supplies first to Europeans.[68] If the French colonials reflected on their favored status, it was justified on the grounds that "Annamites" were accustomed to privation and simple diets, whereas Europeans would become ill without variety, and had already suffered by not being able to take home leave for the duration of the war. Without their customary twenty thousand tons per year of imported wheat flour, boulangeries tried to make bread from various combinations of corn, rice, and glutinous rice. French families complimented their native cooks for inventing new ways to disguise rice, or for using soy bean derivatives as substitutes for milk, cheese, and curds. Despite numerous experiments, however, no one was able to produce an acceptable local wine. As prewar stocks of wine dwindled relentlessly, the French had to settle for local beer, rum, and fruit liqueurs.[69]

The most worrisome shortage for Europeans was medicine. Insulin became extremely scarce, threatening the lives of diabetics. Prewar quinine stocks had to be limited to Europeans working in the worst malarial zones;

66. *CMCD*, 9:86, estimates that forced crop conversions reduced paddy output in northern Vietnam by 64,000 tons.

67. *CMCD*, 10:110.

68. Bauchar, *Rafales*, 106, 113. Angladette, "Vie quotidienne," 486–87.

69. Angladette, "Vie quotidienne," 469–70. Bauchar, *Rafales*, 106–7, 112, 114. According to Pierre Brocheux, who lived in Saigon at this time, a slightly sparkling white wine was made from local tamarind fruit.

the rest used locally grown quinquina as an imperfect suppressant. The Japanese allowed *émétine* (for dysentery) to be supplied by the International Red Cross, via Nationalist China. Late in the war the Allies parachuted sulfanilamide to clandestine Free French teams in Indochina, and some of this showed up in European hospitals.[70] The Indochina authorities also sponsored an urgent search for pharmaceutical substitutes, eventually claiming four hundred innovations. Vietnamese pharmacists led by Ho Dac An succeeded in producing histidine, cholesterol, benzoic acid, feramine, and other substances locally. Traditional practitioners were also called in to present their wares for scientific scrutiny. Highest priority was assigned to identifying, producing, and distributing remedies for amoebic dysentery and intestinal parasites.[71]

The Japanese in Indochina had a different lifestyle from the French. As members of military units being shifted to and from various parts of Asia, most were not in the colony for more than six months or a year. Generally they lived in spartan camps, relying on the quartermaster corps to secure adequate food, drink, clothing, fuel, and medicines. Undoubtedly Japanese quartermasters and French wholesalers competed for some of the same scarce goods—for example, fresh vegetables from Dalat, cattle from Cambodia (the Yunnan supply being cut off), and cloth from Nam Dinh.[72] When permitted to go outside camp on leave, Japanese soldiers visited temples, wandered the city streets, or frequented bars and houses of prostitution. While a few Japanese, Korean, and Taiwanese shopkeepers and prostitutes had arrived with the early military units, most soldiers' haunts were run by Chinese or Vietnamese. By 1944, a large percentage of Japanese troops in Indochina were either resting from exhausting campaigns in Burma or raw recruits from the homeland.

From 1940, Japanese proficient in French were recruited to work in Indochina as diplomats, interpreters, liaison officers, journalists, intelligence specialists, and commercial representatives. Together with high-ranking military officers and staff personnel, they occupied scores of villas in the European sections of Saigon and Hanoi, much to the irritation of the French. Nonetheless, business between Japanese and French officials was conducted in a civilized manner, each inviting the other to cocktail receptions and formal dinner parties, sharing their dwindling stocks of delicacies.

70. Bauchar, *Rafales*, 117.
71. A. Gibot and R. F. Auriol, "Le Problème des médicaments en Indochine de 1940 à 1945," *Produits pharmaceutiques* (Paris) 2, no. 3 (Mar. 1947): 109–19. Angladette, "Vie quotidienne," 474–75.
72. Bauchar, *Rafales*, 111–12, 115.

Governor-General Decoux hosted General Tsuchihashi at a dinner party on 2 March 1945, and then Ambassador Matsumoto on the 7th.[73] The Japanese did not have a chance to reciprocate before their coup two days later.

A relatively small number of Japanese made friends among the indigenous population. The French authorities tried to insist that all substantive contacts be handled through them, for example, when recruiting workers, purchasing supplies, or negotiating business contracts. The Japanese found this convenient much of the time, but they also did not hesitate to arrange deals with Vietnamese or Chinese contractors directly if the terms were better. They wanted as well to cultivate sufficient sources among the local people to help them keep informed of French activities. Thus, the Nishihara inspection team sent to Tonkin in 1940 already included several intelligence personnel, who quickly befriended the handful of established Japanese families in Hanoi and, through them, made contact with sympathetic Vietnamese. One energetic member of the Nishihara team joined a Vietnamese-language class, took a Vietnamese mistress, and recruited three young Vietnamese and one Chinese to collect information—all before the end of 1940.[74] Although the French Sûreté worked hard to neutralize such Japanese-directed networks, they had to be extremely careful not to kill, arrest, or harass any Japanese citizens in the process. This became all the more difficult as the civilian Japanese population in Indochina climbed from only two hundred in 1940 to an estimated four thousand in 1944.[75]

The War Comes Closer

In 1943, as the Allies forced Japan and Germany onto the defensive, the 1940–41 agreements between Vichy and Tokyo became subject to new

73. Gautier, *9 Mars 1945*, 152.

74. Yoshizawa Minami, "Watashitachi no naka no Ajia no sensō—Nihon to Betonamu no aida" [The War Among Us in Asia—Between Japan and Vietnam], *University Press* (Tokyo), no. 141 (July 1984): 6–9; no. 142 (Aug. 1984): 10–15. Inevitably, a few Japanese were prepared to work against the Imperial Army. For example, Yamamoto Kishi, a former Foreign Ministry officer who had settled in Indochina before the war, took part in an Allied intelligence network centered on Dalat, where his French wife was employed in the telephone exchange. Gilbert David, *Chroniques secrètes d'indochine (1928–1946)* (Paris, 1994), 1:83–85, and 2:616–18.

75. USNA, OSS, "Economic Developments in Indochina, June 1939–June 1944," 46n. Murakami, "Japan's Thrust," 411. AOM, INF, GF 53 contains wartime telephone books for Hanoi, Haiphong, and Hue, with numerous Japanese numbers listed.

strains. Perhaps the most serious challenge came from Japanese General Staff officers who favored granting conditional independence to Southeast Asian peoples, in the expectation they would then participate enthusiastically in collective defense against a Western counterattack. In late May, the Japanese government accepted this policy for Burma and the Philippines, but rejected it for Indochina, Malaya, and Indonesia.[76] Once again the Foreign Ministry's argument that French administration in Indochina undermined Japan's overall policy of Greater East Asian liberation was ignored. Some army officers continued to press for change. During a July 1943 visit to Indochina, retired General Matsui Iwane created a stir when he criticized the French in front of Vietnamese journalists and hinted at independence.[77] Local Japanese personnel responsible for maintaining contacts among Vietnamese nationalists made similar comments.

The French decided to call the Japanese bluff, ordering the arrest or interrogation of a number of Vietnamese *"malfaisants."* Local Japanese officials took no counteraction except to spirit five well-known Vietnamese out of the colony (see chapter 2).[78] Tokyo remained silent. By early September 1943, Admiral Decoux felt confident enough to cable Vichy reconfirming French sovereignty over Indochina and asserting that only certain lower-ranking Japanese "secretly favored the subversive activities of anti-French elements."[79]

Nonetheless, Admiral Decoux could read a world battle map and appreciate how the following year might well bring dramatic changes. As if to punctuate his ruminations, from September 1943 on, American B-24 bombers based in Kwangsi launched repeated attacks on the port of Haiphong and other priority targets in Tonkin.[80] Perhaps at Decoux's behest, a Vichy diplomat stationed in Tokyo, who had spent two months in 1943 touring Indochina, submitted to the Swedish ambassador in Japan a detailed report on conditions in the colony, probably hoping it would

76. Kiyoko Kurusu Nitz, "Japanese Military Policy towards French Indochina during the Second World War: The Road to the Meigō Sakusen (9 March 1945)," *JSEAS* 14, no. 2 (Sept. 1983): 334.

77. Ralph B. Smith, "The Japanese Period in Indochina and the Coup of 9 March 1945," *JSEAS* 9, no. 2 (Sept. 1978): 271.

78. Shiraishi, "La Présence," 224–26.

79. Telegram of 8 Sept. 1943, reprinted in full in *Histoire de l'Indochine*, ed. Héduy, 251.

80. Decoux, *A la barre*, 191–93. USNA, OSS report no. 2594, 1 Jan. 1945. Vu Ngu Chieu, "Political and Social Change in Viet-Nam," 111–12, cites Sûreté reports of two earlier American air raids on Haiphong, in August and November 1942.

reach the Free French in Algiers. Above all, this diplomat cautioned against Allied actions that might provoke Japanese annexation of Indochina.[81] In October, at the urging of Claude de Boisanger, Indochina's chief of diplomatic service, Decoux secretly dispatched a representative to Algiers (via China) to establish contact with the Free French.[82] Of greater concern for the moment, however, was possible Chinese intervention, whether by means of overt military attack, sponsorship of native insurgents, or promotion of disruptive activities by local Chinese businessmen.[83] Because the ultimatum from General Chō on 9 December 1941 had designated the Tonkin frontier as a French defense responsibility, Admiral Decoux not only allocated substantial resources to upgrading fortifications there, but was also able quietly to sustain diplomatic contacts with Chungking. This was no mean feat, as Vichy no longer possessed a representative in Chungking and was inclined to recognize the Wang Ching-wei regime in Nanking, a move successfully opposed by Decoux in relation to Indochina.[84]

With the successful Allied landings in Normandy in June 1944, both Japanese and French officials reassessed their positions. In Tokyo, proposals to dump the French in Indochina were once again considered and rejected. At a time when increasingly scarce resources were being devoted to the massive Ichigō (Joint Operation No. 1) offensive in southern China and to preparations for defense of the Philippines, it seemed unwise to disrupt a key rear area. Besides, Ichigō was designed partly to seize Kwangsi province and thus reopen land communications between China and Southeast Asia (accomplished in October by the capture of Nanning), in which case French forces in Indochina would pose even less of a threat to the Japanese garrison.

The Vichy regime faded from the picture as Allied armies swept toward Paris in early August. A delicate question arose: to whom did the governor-general of Indochina owe allegiance? Eighteen months earlier, Admiral

---

81. Stein Tønnesson, *The Vietnamese Revolution of 1945: Roosevelt, Ho Chi Minh and de Gaulle in a World at War* (London, 1991), 45.

82. Boisanger, *On pouvait éviter la guerre*, 68–69, 77. Gautier, *9 Mars 1945*, 95. *DGI*, 27, 56, 90–91. Apparently unknown to Decoux, his military subordinates in Indochina had already sent a colonel to Algiers in March 1943, who returned in mid August. See chapter 5.

83. Decoux, *A la barre*, 196. *Histoire de l'Indochine*, ed. Héduy, 251. The Japanese also kept close watch on Chinese activities and worked to link Chinese in Indochina with the puppet Wang Ching-wei regime in Nanking. *PJI*, radio intercepts of 25 Dec. 1941, 16 Feb. 1943, and 10 Oct. 1943.

84. Boisanger, *On pouvait éviter la guerre*, 70–72. By contrast, Vichy withdrew its representative in Chungking in 1943 and recognized the Nanking regime.

Decoux had secured Vichy approval to take "exceptional powers" in the event of a sustained breakdown in radio contact. On that tenuous basis he now published an edict giving himself unprecedented authority.[85] An austere workaholic with no confidants or friends, Decoux tended to treat both French and native subordinates like a ship's crew. He seemed to thrive on traveling around the colony and participating in ceremonies designed to manifest French sovereignty.[86] Simultaneously, by means of discreet public references and alterations in political symbolism—for example, changing the official letterhead of French Indochina from the Pétainist "État français" back to "République française"—Decoux signaled that ultimate sovereignty and legitimacy resided in Paris, where the provisional government of General Charles de Gaulle was officially at war with Tokyo and trying to send units to fight the Japanese.

The Free French had already bypassed Governor-General Decoux, secretly selecting General Eugène Mordant as their legitimate representative in Indochina. A clandestine muddle ensued (see chapter 5), with the Japanese well aware of the different French viewpoints. In mid September, however, Tokyo still felt it could afford to play a waiting game. If the governor-general continued to cooperate, it was desirable to maintain the status quo.[87] If he declined, Japanese officers would need to take over some high-level positions, but they would still endeavor to maintain the colonial infrastructure. If either Decoux or the French Army commander initiated violence, Indochina would be resecured by means of full-scale military action.[88]

By December 1944, however, conditions had changed again. Most of the Imperial Navy's remaining capital ships had been lost in the 24–26 October battle of Leyte Gulf. Japanese forces would not be able to prevent American recapture of the Philippines, which had commenced in October. The Ichigō offensive had just about run out of steam; a final unsuccessful attempt to take Kunming involved some Japanese troops from Indochina, moving via

85. Decoux, *A la barre*, 300–302. Gautier, *9 Mars 1945*, 67–68. Philippe Devillers, *Histoire du Vietnam de 1940 à 1952* (Paris, 1952), 118.

86. Boisanger, *On pouvait éviter la guerre*, 30–32. Decoux's wife had been killed in an auto accident in 1944, which caused him to become even more aloof.

87. In November, Japanese officials reported to Tokyo that Decoux had asked de Gaulle to persuade the other Allied leaders not to invade Indochina. Tønnesson, *Vietnamese Revolution*, 190, based on routine American decrypting of Japanese radio messages (MAGIC), copies of which can be found in USNA.

88. These three options were spelled out in a Supreme War Leaders' Council written "Understanding" of 14 Sept. 1944. *Indochina*, ed. Shiraishi and Furuta, 14–16. Nitz, "Japanese Military Policy," 337.

Lang Son and Nanning.[89] In mid December the British Fourteenth Army crossed the Chindwin River in upper Burma, aiming to reach Rangoon in early 1945. There was some Japanese fear that Thailand might become the Italy of Asia, reversing allegiances at this awkward moment.[90] Finally, Japanese intelligence had pieced together a sufficiently detailed picture of Free French covert activities in Indochina to be convinced that Governor-General Decoux was either lying about his willingness to adhere to the 1941 mutual defense agreements or losing control of his subordinates.[91]

General Tsuchihashi Sizes Up the French

In late 1944, both the Japanese ambassador to Indochina and the army garrison commander were recalled. In their places came Ambassador Matsumoto and General Tsuchihashi, whose force was renamed the Thirty-eighth Army and put on a "campaign" footing.[92] General Tsuchihashi, a slight, solidly built man, whose completely shaven head reinforced a habitually severe expression, was a logical choice for this sensitive assignment. Posted to France several times before the war, and an official visitor to Indochina in late 1939, Tsuchihashi had been deeply involved in efforts to isolate Chinese Nationalist forces from outside supplies. He seems to have favored diplomacy backed up by credible force, which put him at odds with General Tominaga Kyōji and others in the Operations Division who preferred ultimatums or preemptive strikes. However, Tsuchihashi also earned respect as commander of large combat contingents in the Philippines and Java in 1941–42, subsequently being put in charge of forces on Timor.[93]

89. *War in Asia and the Pacific*, ed. Detwiler and Burdick, 6:19–20. U.S. military attaché, Kunming, report, 15 Dec. 1944, in USNA, OSS record 110965. Throughout the war, neither side attempted to use the Hanoi-Yunnan railway for attack, apparently because its many bridges and tunnels could easily be collapsed as formidable obstacles.

90. *Indochina*, ed. Shiraishi and Furuta, 66. The Thai elite also worried about a possible Japanese coup in Bangkok. See Thainsook Numnonda, *Thailand and the Japanese Presence, 1941–45* (Singapore, 1977), 52–59.

91. It is possible the Japanese had cracked the Free French code. General Jean Lecomte, in *DGI*, 152, reports postwar conversations with a British officer who claimed to have seen decrypted Gaullist messages in Marshal Terauchi's files. Of course, these could have been captured in the wake of the coup.

92. Shiraishi and Furuta, "Taiheyō sensōki," 19, 21, 35. Nitz, "Japanese Military Policy," 339. Tsuchihashi, "Furansugun o busō kaijo," 156.

93. Hosoya, "Japanese-Soviet Neutrality Pact," 33–34. Hata, "Army's Move," 158, 159, 204, 207, 320–21. Murakami, "Japan's Thrust," 85, 104–6, 108–9. Archimedes L. A. Patti, *Why Viet Nam? Prelude to America's Albatross* (Berkeley and Los Angeles, 1980), 159, 495.

Figure 3. General Tsuchi-
hashi Yūichi, commander
of Japanese forces in Indochina during the critical period from December 1944 to
the end of World War II.
Courtesy of the family of
General Tsuchihashi.

Although some of his military peers probably considered Tsuchihashi a
Francophile, he had little in common with those Japanese diplomats and
writers who sustained the Meiji-period fascination with French culture and
savoir faire. One of Tsuchihashi's first acts was to shift units to positions
where they could better monitor and possibly attack specific French units,
a maneuver quickly noted by General Gabriel Sabattier, the Tonkin troop
commander.[94] In Tokyo, the Army General Staff, which throughout 1944
had favored maintaining the status quo in Indochina, now worried that the
United States would soon possess the capability to mount an amphibious
landing from the Philippines. Perhaps it was better to neutralize the French
first rather than risk an attack from the rear.[95]

When a Japanese official queried Decoux in mid December about whether
he considered de Gaulle's government to be legitimate or not, the governor-

94. Gabriel Sabattier, *Le Destin de l'Indochine: Souvenirs et documents, 1941–
1951* (Paris, 1952), 112–13.
95. Shiraishi, "La Présence," 229–30. Tanemura, *Daihon'ei Himitsu Nisshi,*
205. *War in Asia and the Pacific,* ed. Detwiler and Burdick, 6:17.

general lamely responded that it was only transitional.[96] "Our motherland has been liberated by the Anglo-American armies," Decoux affirmed in a radio address in early February. The Japanese were not amused; immediately after the 9 March coup, a Tokyo news report rated this as "no different from a declaration of war with Japan."[97] On first meeting General Georges Aymé, commander of French ground forces in Indochina, General Tsuchihashi asked bluntly whether he would honor their mutual defense agreement in the event of an American landing or Chinese invasion. According to Tsuchihashi, Aymé looked disturbed and replied that it would depend on discussions.[98] From that point on, Tsuchihashi felt the French were more of an impediment than a help in fulfilling his mission.

This feeling hardened to conviction after American carrier-based aircraft launched devastating attacks on the port of Saigon and Japanese shipping in the South China Sea in early January 1945. Some twenty-four ships, a total of 128,000 tons, were sunk, and thirteen others damaged.[99] Saigon's relative importance to the Japanese Navy had increased in 1944, because it was the mainland Southeast Asian port most distant from Allied bombers stationed in China and India.[100] In one stroke, the U.S. Navy had severely reduced Saigon's maritime utility and begun the process of isolating Indochina for a possible invasion. The Japanese already possessed evidence that French port officials and coastal watch personnel were secretly providing detailed information to the Allies on cargoes, shipping movements, and battle-damage assessments. In late January, the Japanese Army General Staff and subordinates in Indochina exchanged messages about a probable U.S. invasion and hence the need to overthrow the French. On 1 February, final authorization for the takeover was worked out in Tokyo, with the exact date and tactics to be decided.[101]

96. Tønnesson, *Vietnamese Revolution*, 190, based on MAGIC intercepts.

97. Domei news, Tokyo, 10 Mar. 1945, as translated in *Dan Bao* (Saigon), 12 Mar. 1945.

98. As cited in *SMS*, 596.

99. *NGS*, 24:209. Murakami, "Japan's Thrust," 507. Jacques Mordal, *Marine Indochine* (Paris, 1953), 61–64. French intelligence claimed that at least 1,500 Japanese soldiers were killed aboard transports at Cap Saint-Jacques (Vung Tau). DGER report, 13 Mar. 1945, in AOM, INF, c. 123, d. 1108. According to Tønnesson, *Vietnamese Revolution*, 193, the Americans reported forty-four ships sunk. This seems to be either mistaken intelligence or it incorporates further Japanese losses when the carrier task force swept north to Hainan, Hong Kong, and Taiwan.

100. USNA, OSS record L54936.

101. *NGS*, 24:210–14. IMTFE exhibit 661. Tønnesson, *Vietnamese Revolution*, 195, based on MAGIC intercepts in USNA.

In reality, U.S. strategic planners had no intention of mounting an amphibious attack on either Indochina or southern China.[102] Rather, their attention was already focused on Okinawa, 1,500 miles to the northeast and only 450 miles from the Japanese home island of Kyushu. It was useful to keep the Japanese guessing, however, and to that end the U.S. Office of War Information (OWI) seems to have planted stories suggesting an imminent invasion of Indochina or China, which were faithfully printed and then repeated in Allied shortwave broadcasts. An American article was headed "Allied Pincers on Indo-China Hold Key to Far Eastern War."[103] An Australian newspaper asserted that Indochina would become "the main gateway to the re-conquest of East Asia,"[104] while a Chinese journal argued the logistical benefits of capturing Haiphong.[105]

Interestingly enough, in January the Imperial General Headquarters in Tokyo estimated correctly that U.S. forces would bypass Indochina.[106] Japanese naval officers in Saigon also argued in February that an American landing in Indochina was no longer likely. They were supported by Ambassador Matsumoto, who transmitted their assessment to Foreign Minister Shigemitsu Mamoru and pleaded for postponement of the coup. To cap his argument, Matsumoto expressed concern that Japan's attack on "neutral" French Indochina might be used as a pretext by the Soviet Union to break neutrality too and invade Manchuria. This factor had indeed troubled some in Tokyo, since Paris had formally concluded an alliance with Moscow in early December 1944.[107] Also, some civilian officials in Tokyo

---

102. As early as September 1944, military planners in Washington had concluded that such a landing was unnecessary. Christopher Thorne, *Allies of a Kind: The United States, Britain and the War against Japan, 1941–1945* (London, 1978), 428. However, as explained at some length in Tønnesson, *Vietnamese Revolution*, 162–70, President Roosevelt retained the desire to land at some point in the future.

103. *Christian Science Monitor*, 18 Jan. 1945, 11. In early February, United Press speculated publicly over who would command the invasion of China. Some French listeners, at least, were deceived by radio broadcasts of such articles. See Jean Marchand, *L'Indochine en guerre* (Paris, 1954), 27–28.

104. *Sunday Telegraph* (Sydney), 21 Jan. 1945, as quoted by Tønnesson, *Vietnamese Revolution*, 195.

105. *Chung Yang Jih Pao* (Chungking), 12 Feb. 1945, cited in Tønnesson, *Vietnamese Revolution*, 203.

106. S. Woodburn Kirby, *The War against Japan*, vol. 5, *The Surrender of Japan* (London, 1969), 95–96.

107. Tønnesson, *Vietnamese Revolution*, 213. Murakami, "Japan's Thrust," 516–17. At about this time, in Yalta, Stalin was promising Roosevelt and Churchill that Soviet troops would invade Manchuria three months after Germany's unconditional surrender, a pledge he kept.

and Indochina, quietly adjusting to the likelihood of an ignominious Japanese defeat, saw no merit in encouraging yet another Western country, France, to seek postwar retribution.[108]

General Tsuchihashi had other worries besides an American amphibious landing, however. Wherever the next main attack fell, it would probably cut his command off from the homeland except for radio communications and the occasional high-priority airplane flight. If Tokyo decided to order the withdrawal of the remaining Southern Area forces into China, Indochina would become absolutely vital as a way station for seven hundred thousand troops coming from Indonesia, Malaya, Burma, and Thailand.[109] As it happened, Japanese forces in Kwangsi began retreating eastward with such haste in January and February that General Tsuchihashi once again had to consider seriously the prospects of a Nationalist Chinese attack into Tonkin.[110] Militarily speaking, it was time to stockpile more grain and fuel, to commandeer transport, and to recruit local people to strengthen defense positions, yet the French kept throwing up diplomatic objections to each of these initiatives. The joint defense agreements of 1941 were outmoded from Tsuchihashi's point of view. Either the French had to accept drastic new limits on their authority and mobility or they must be forcibly interned.

In January 1945, General Tsuchihashi had no shortage of coup plans to look at, some dating back almost a year. Clearly strategic surprise was impossible, given the need to bring in battle-hardened reinforcements, which arrived in February from southern China and Thailand (and were duly noted by the French). However, tactical surprise became a key ingredient of General Tsuchihashi's operational plan, the objective being to forestall evasive movements by colonial troops, and even to catch many of them unawares in their barracks. Elaborate security measures were em-

---

108. Interview with Nishimura Kumao, Tokyo, 27 Nov. 1967. Amb. Nishimura was consul general in Hanoi until the coup, then resident superior of Tonkin and adviser to the Kham Sai (imperial delegate), Phan Ke Toai, until the Japanese capitulation in August. In 1951 Nishimura became Japan's first postwar ambassador to France.

109. The big weakness in such a plan was transport and communications. One serious bottleneck was Lang Son–Nanning, which had no railway, only a vulnerable, bomb-damaged road. Allied intelligence watched carefully for any signs of upgrading this link. As of August 1945, some 490,000 Japanese troops remained in Indonesia, 116,000 in Malaya, 60,000 in Burma, and 55,000 in Thailand. John J. Sbrega, "The Japanese Surrender: Some Unexpected Consequences in Southeast Asia," *Asian Affairs* (New York) 7, no. 1 (Sept.–Oct. 1979): 46.

110. Tsuchihashi, "Furansugun o busō kaijo," 156.

ployed, including tightened cryptographic procedures, hand delivery of all operational orders, and putting General Tsuchihashi in a lieutenant colonel's uniform as he toured subordinate units.[111] As far as can be ascertained, no Indochinese associates were informed of Japanese plans until the day before the takeover, although rumors abounded.

The French Dilemma

French commanders and staff officers had discussed plans for battle against the Japanese from July 1944 on. However, all their contingencies assumed Allied troop commitments from outside. For example, a September plan approved by General Mordant proposed resolute defense of selected airports, extensive use of parachuted Free French sabotage teams, and close coordination with incoming Allied combat units. General Aymé even requested one month's notice of Allied attack, so that European women and children could be escorted to safety (where and how was not indicated). Such expectations of Allied involvement in the near future were quite unrealistic, a point made to General Mordant in early December by a Free French envoy from South East Asia Command (SEAC) in Kandy, Ceylon. Nonetheless, Mordant persisted with plans to defend fixed positions, especially at Tong, twenty-five miles west of Hanoi, and at Lang Son.[112] At no time, it seems, did the French seriously consider a surprise attack on the Japanese.

The colonial army in Indochina had been designed to ensure order among the natives and to patrol the frontier against incursions by smugglers, brigands, and political dissidents. Despite some frantic reorganization efforts in 1938, events at Lang Son in September 1940 and along the Thai border in January 1941 had demonstrated the army's incapacity to engage in large-scale modern combat operations.[113] Since those debacles, officers and many of the enlisted men had aged four years, while tropical humidity had eaten into military equipment and ammunition.[114] Geographical iso-

111. Ibid., 158.
112. Hesse d'Alzon, "L'Armée française d'Indochine," 111–13. Tønnesson, *Vietnamese Revolution*, 159–60. It appears that Mordant also failed to convey clearly to subordinates the unlikelihood of Allied intervention, so that many of them retained hopelessly unrealistic expectations. See chapter 5.
113. Hesse d'Alzon, "L'Armée française d'Indochine," 76–96.
114. René Charbonneau and José Maigre, *Les Parias de la victoire: Indochine–Chine, 1945* (Paris, 1980), 62–66. A late 1944 Allied intelligence report indicated that Indochina Army recruiters were having difficulty signing up native volunteers,

lation, shortages of matériel, and the Japanese occupation had sapped the morale of the European contingent, who were about one-fifth of the total.[115] One remedy might have been to enroll and train more native officers and noncommissioned officers. Incredibly, by the early 1940s the French had only permitted about twenty Indochinese to become officers, out of a total officer corps of fourteen hundred. In 1943, a plan was finally approved to train 6 Indochinese captains and 108 lieutenants over the next three years.[116] In late 1944, Paris pressed General Mordant to begin recruiting natives into armed resistance organizations, but that idea was deliberately ignored.[117]

Mordant was the quintessential peacetime general, anxious to keep his men busy, concerned about amenities, enforcing an elaborate set of colonial military traditions and ceremonies. He was pleased when the Japanese assigned his forces responsibility for defending the northern Indochina frontier, not because he expected any serious combat but because it gave his men (and accompanying coolies) something to do, in particular construction of a string of forts from Lang Son to Lao Cai.[118] Mordant kept his troops housed at a level such that they would not "lose face" in front of the Japanese. He counted it a victory when he persuaded his Japanese counterpart that neither side was required to salute the other. Above all, Mordant worked to sustain the spirits of his French personnel, cut off from their occupied homeland, humiliated by the Japanese presence in Indochina, feeling abandoned in the debilitating tropics.[119] All of this made sense when it came to preserving colonial institutions, waiting

---

despite the pay and perquisites. U.S. Opintel report, Indochina, 2 Dec. 1944, in Virginia Thompson file, Cornell University Library.

115. In colonial army parlance, "Europeans" included individuals of French parentage, personnel recruited from other colonies (Algeria, Senegal, etc.), and foreign legionnaires. They constituted 12,211 out of a total of 60,605 in the Indochina Army as of the winter of 1944–45. Hesse d'Alson, *La Présence*, 292.

116. Hesse d'Alzon, "L'Armée française d'Indochine," 97–98. According to Hesse d'Alzon, *La Présence*, 292, 294–95, Tonkin units in early 1945 contained thirty-three Indochinese officers, thirteen of them in combat units.

117. Paul Isoart, "Aux origines d'une guerre: L'Indochine française (1940–1945)," in *L'Indochine française*, ed. id., 36–39. Mordant, *Au service de la France*, 94.

118. Mordant was furious to hear in 1946 that Chinese troops had dismantled or blown up his forts, labeling it "odious devastation." Mordant, *Au service de la France*, 59–61. One cannot help here but recall the British colonel played by Alec Guinness in the 1957 movie *The Bridge on the River Kwai*.

119. Mordant, *Au service de la France*, 48–49, 51, 52–54.

for better times. It was not the best frame of mind for a resistance leader, however. De Gaulle could hardly have chosen a man less suitable for this task.

As Japanese reinforcements arrived in Indochina and adjacent areas, the French quandary became acute. Should their armed forces fight or not? The logic of Admiral Decoux's policy inferred that it was preferable to endure almost any Japanese insult or restriction rather than losing the colony entirely. Given rapidly declining Japanese fortunes elsewhere in Asia, it would be foolish to agree to participate in Japanese combat operations, but perhaps it would not come to that, especially if the Americans headed straight for the home islands of Japan.[120] If the Japanese still felt it necessary to reduce the potential threat posed by the Indochina Army, perhaps they would permit some units to retain individual weapons and help maintain local order. If the army had to be disarmed and interned, perhaps the colonial police, militia, and supply and medical services could continue to function.[121] When Allied forces arrived, it might be necessary to face charges of collaboration with the enemy, yet Indochina, the jewel in France's colonial crown, would have been saved.

On the other hand, most ranking French military officers also believed that some line had to be drawn, beyond which point their honor was irredeemably sullied. If the Japanese attacked suddenly or delivered an unacceptable ultimatum, resistance had to be offered. It was a matter of self-respect, of career prospects in the postwar French armed forces, and perhaps in a few cases appreciation of General de Gaulle's intention to demonstrate France's commitment to the overall anti-Japanese alliance (see chapter 5). Even Admiral Decoux accepted that it might be necessary to fight: on 19 February he alerted his regional resident superiors that a state of siege might have to be ordered suddenly, putting all French citizens in Indochina under military control, relying on the French Revolution's famous law of 19 July 1791 and a Napoleonic decree of 24 December 1811.[122]

---

120. According to Gautier, *9 Mars 1945*, 68, Decoux commented as early as November 1942 that American forces would strike for the heart of Japan and not worry about Indochina. Gautier's assistant, Camille Bailly, recalls Decoux making a similar statement when U.S. forces secured Saipan in July 1944. *DGI*, 93.

121. This line of reasoning is suggested by a mid-February instruction from Tonkin Resident Superior Paul Chauvet to civilian subordinates, although he also tells them in the event of a Japanese coup to offer assistance to military units continuing to resist. Reprinted in Sabattier, *Le Destin de l'Indochine*, 124–26.

122. Reprinted in ibid., 119–23.

If the armed forces did mount a defense, what tactics were best? As General Mordant admitted later, to offer resistance to the Japanese was like "squaring a circle."[123] Although orders had been issued to defend a number of fixed positions, it is hard to believe that Mordant, Aymé, and other French generals expected such positions to hold out for more than a few days, or a week at most. In the case of forts and camps inside cities like Hanoi, Haiphong, Saigon, and Hue, they may have intended only a few shots to be exchanged before hoisting the white flag, since anything more risked heavy artillery exchanges, possible Japanese air attacks, and an urban conflagration that would threaten thousands of French civilians. Although Mordant and his staff discussed various plans to withdraw to the hinterlands to mount extended guerrilla operations, it was hard to formulate practical plans without knowing the level of Allied air support. When General Sabattier requested permission to use coolies or pack animals to establish caches in the mountains for future guerrilla action, Mordant refused on the grounds this might alert the Japanese.[124] There was also the seldom-mentioned, but haunting, prospect of leaving families behind in the cities to face possible Japanese or native retaliation.

French staff officers in Hanoi must have led schizophrenic lives in early 1945, in effect being called on to devise plans to fulfill four radically different missions. First, the army was expected to help maintain the colonial status quo, including internal security, anti–Viet Minh operations, and the manning of numerous posts along the Chinese frontier. Second, it had to demonstrate to the Japanese, at least occasionally, a continuing commitment to common defense against Allied invasion. Third, it needed secretly to develop the capacity to attack the Japanese in support of Allied landings. And, finally, it had to be ready to defend itself against a sudden Japanese attack. Some of these missions called for concentration of forces, others for dispersion. With the Japanese monitoring every move, deception was difficult. To be able to shift three battalions away from likely Japanese encirclement, for example, the French devised an operation against Viet Minh–dominated districts in the Cao Bang area, to begin March 10th, and dutifully informed General Tsuchihashi in advance.[125]

---

123. Mordant, *Au service de la France*, 56. Apparently written only twelve to eighteen months after the Japanese coup, Mordant's memoirs are very useful in understanding the mental turmoil of responsible French officers, but they cannot be relied upon in detail.

124. Sabattier, *Le Destin de l'Indochine*, 103. Mordant, *Au service de la France*, 57.

125. Charbonneau and Maigre, *Les Parias*, 72–74.

Even assuming that staff officers could sort out the logical contradictions, and either General Mordant or General Aymé could issue clear advance instructions to their subordinate commanders throughout Indochina, it was unlikely that the army's communications system would stand up under battle strain. Existing telegraph and telephone lines could easily be cut or monitored by the enemy. Except for a few British and American radios parachuted in during 1944, the army had to depend on prewar transmitters and receivers, whose replacement parts were all made locally. Spare condensers were laminated at the colonial mint, using specially created paper. Battery cells were reconstructed from Tonkin zinc, Chinese or Laotian mercury, and *chlorhydrate d'ammoniac* and agar purchased in the marketplace. Only the small 10-watt transmitters could be transported by horse; the rest were either fixed stations or required vehicles.[126]

Coup Preparations

General Tsuchihashi's main problem was not unconnected with the French dilemma of dispersion or concentration. He had been ordered by Tokyo to give Governor-General Decoux precisely two hours to accept or reject the ultimatum to be presented by Ambassador Matsumoto. While this left the door open for a continuing peaceful Japanese-French relationship, and might convince the outside world that Japan was not launching yet another Pearl Harbor–style surprise attack, it also jeopardized Tsuchihashi's plans for action if the ultimatum were rejected.[127] The solution was to link every Japanese unit by radio with the Southern Area Headquarters communication center in Saigon, ready to attack or hold according to coded signal, while simultaneously attempting to isolate Admiral Decoux and his top commanders from contact with subordinate units. Much time was spent worrying whether Decoux would come from Hanoi to Saigon at the right time. Later, plans almost had to be reconsidered when Decoux decided to drive from Saigon to Dalat on March 4th to visit his wife's grave. When Decoux returned on the 6th, Tsuchihashi still worried that he might suddenly decide to go back to Hanoi to supervise French military operations against the Viet Minh.[128]

126. Ibid., 67–69.
127. *SMS*, 607.
128. Tsuchihashi, "Furansugun o busō kaijo," 159. In his account, Tsuchihashi mistakenly has Decoux going to Dalat on the 5th and returning the 7th.

On paper, Japanese forces in early March were still slightly outnumbered by French forces, about 55,000 against 60,000.[129] However, General Tsuchihashi had a higher proportion of combat soldiers at his disposal, perhaps 35,000 versus 30,000. Also, all of his units were Japanese, whereas the Indochina Army was made up of Europeans, Vietnamese, Cambodians, Laotians, Thai, Tho, Nung, and Rhadé. Both sides knew that the main confrontation would occur in Tonkin, where the French had 37,000 men (about half in combat units) and the Japanese had managed to position 24,000, including units of the Twenty-second Division in Kwangsi poised to attack Lang Son. If Indochina Army units in Tonkin succeeded in retreating toward Laos, Tsuchihashi planned to block them with elements of the Fourth Division, which had already reached Luang Prabang from Thailand.[130]

The need for surprise dictated that any Japanese attack begin after nightfall, yet it was highly unusual for an ambassador to ask to see the governor-general in the evening on a routine matter, in this case a ceremonial signing of papers. The latest hour that could be proposed without arousing suspicion was judged to be 6:00 P.M. The governor-general's office accepted.

Meanwhile, administrative affairs proceeded as usual. On 8 March, the Association professionnelle des fonctionnaires d'Indochine en service au Gouvernement Général sent letters of admission to four new members.[131] On the 9th, the *résident* of Ha Dong province forwarded to Hanoi an application from M. Pham Vu Phiet, aged fifty-four, to pursue his calling as a dispenser of traditional medicines.[132] The *résident* of Yen Bai sent in a small Japanese-language newspaper that had been dropped as propaganda by American aircraft.[133] The chief inspector of the Tonkin branch of the

129. Because extensive discrepancies exist in available sources, these are estimates at best. Japanese sources tend to inflate enemy numbers and vice versa. Also, no one discriminates clearly between combat and support units or between mobile and territorial forces. Hesse d'Alzon, "L'Armée française d'Indochine," 119–20, and *La Présence*, 291–93. Charbonneau and Maigre, *Les Parias*, 62. Tsuchihashi, "Furansugun o busō kaijo," 158–59. *War in Asia and the Pacific*, ed. Detwiler and Burdick, 6:20, 22. AOM, INF, c. 123, d. 1108, subdossier 2.

130. Tsuchihashi, "Furansugun o busō kaijo," 159. According to L. H. Ayrolles, *L'Indochine ne répond pas* (Saint-Brieux, 1948), 32, Japanese troops had already occupied Xieng Khouang, closer to Annam and Tonkin, in mid February.

131. AOM, INF, GF 23.

132. AOM, INF, GF 25.

133. Yen Bai to *résident supérieur*, 9 Mar. 1945, in AOM, INF, GF 66. This correspondence took a while, but was dutifully stamped as received on 5 Apr. 1945.

Garde indochinoise received the consignment of office stationery he had requested one week earlier.[134] Functionaries at the Résidence Supérieure in Hanoi leafed through a file from the *procureur général* concerning trooper Nguyen Van Chinh, who had refused to sell a portion of his family's rice crop to the government at the fixed rate.[135] In the afternoon of 9 March, in reaction to political demonstrations five days earlier, Decoux's secretary-general, Georges Gautier, signed an order dissolving the Union of Vietnamese Students of the University of Hanoi.[136] On the Japanese side, General Tsuchihashi scheduled a reception for the late afternoon of the 9th, so that he could be seen relaxing and eating with his guests. At 5:30 P.M., he slipped out and headed for headquarters.[137]

The French had had ample evidence of danger in the days preceding 9 March. A spy within the Japanese security services is said to have conveyed precise coup plans via a clandestine network of Freemasons and Cao Dai believers.[138] On the 5th, word arrived at General Aymé's office of Chinese employees at a gambling den having overheard Japanese soldiers talking of disarming the French in a few days' time.[139] On the evening of the 8th, the Tonkin Sûreté compiled and urgently circulated a report predicting a Japanese attack on one of the next three nights. Japanese nationals had been observed stocking up on scarce commodities and evacuating homes or shops close to the Hanoi Citadel, where fighting was most likely to occur. Ammunition had been distributed to Japanese troop units. Among the Annamites, rumors circulated that independence would be proclaimed on 10 March.[140] Local tailors were dis-

---

134. AOM, INF, GF 22.

135. AOM, INF, GF 25.

136. Gautier, *9 Mars 1945*, 14–15.

137. Tsuchihashi, "Furansugun o busō kaijo," 160. I am assuming that Tsuchihashi's recollection of 7:30 P.M. is Japan time, which corrects to 5:30 in Indochina.

138. David, *Chronique secrète*, 1:254, 411–13, 424–26, 431–33.

139. Sabattier, *Le Destin de l'Indochine*, 114–15.

140. Charbonneau and Maigre, *Les Parias*, 124. Mordant, *Au service de la France*, 136–37. Sabattier, *Le Destin de l'Indochine*, 425–26. Nguyen Huy Tuong diary entry for 9 March, in Le Quang Dao et al., *Mot Chang Duong Van Hoa* [A Segment of the Cultural Road] (Hanoi, 1985), 121. Several publications refer to intelligence from Australian sources that the Japanese planned to seize control specifically on 9 March. According to *Comptes rendus trimestriels des séances de l'Académie des Sciences d'Outre-Mer* (Paris) 36 (1976):410, 414, this information was transmitted by the French military attaché in Australia to Paris, and to one Gaullist clandestine group in the hills of Indochina on 1 March. According to Gautier, *9 Mars 1945*, 158–59, the military attaché cabled Paris on about 5 March, but there is no indication that the message was relayed to General Mordant.

covered sewing batches of armbands for the Kenpeitai to distribute to Annamite auxiliaries.[141]

Despite growing fears among intelligence analysts, Mordant and Aymé refused to order a general alert. Undoubtedly they faced a "Wolf! Wolf!" problem, as similar intelligence reports in previous weeks already had precipitated several false alarms. They also did not wish to take overt actions that would be seen as provocative by the Japanese, and thus trigger a preemptive attack. Mordant further worried that if he and his subordinates fled to the bush and no Japanese attack occurred, they would lose face irremediably.[142] Among top commanders, only General Sabattier considered the most recent intelligence sufficiently grave to place his troops on armed "exercise," at 8:30 P.M. on 8 March. The next morning, Mordant canceled Sabattier's exercise, but a number of outlying units either did not receive this message or chose to ignore it.[143] During the day, telegrams reporting local Japanese troop movements came in to both Hanoi and Saigon headquarters. At 6:00 P.M., a battalion of the Nineteenth Colonial Infantry Regiment, moving from its barracks near Haiphong to its predetermined alert position in the west, came under heavy, if brief, fire from Japanese units at a Red River ferry crossing. Although General Aymé ordered inquiries to be made at Japanese headquarters in Hanoi, he still did not issue a new alert.[144]

The French had ruled Indochina for half a century, coming to regard it as their most important overseas possession after Algeria. Not until the late 1930s had any force, foreign or indigenous, posed a serious threat to French control. In 1940 and 1941, it had been necessary to make substantial concessions to both Japan and Thailand in the hope that fundamental French interests could be sustained. The Japanese tolerated this small remaining outpost of white colonialism in Greater East Asia until the potential risks

---

141. Gautier, *9 Mars 1945*, 142. Mordant suspected these armbands might be no more than a Japanese trick designed to test French reactions. Mordant, *Au service de la France*, 137.

142. Sabattier, *Le Destin de l'Indochine*, 97–98. Mordant, *Au service de la France*, 138.

143. Sabattier, *Le Destin de l'Indochine*, 131–32. Charbonneau and Maigre, *Les Parias*, 124–25. Incredibly, Mordant, *Au service de la France*, 138, suggests that Sabattier's sudden departure from Hanoi may have been considered provocative by the Japanese and hastened their attack.

144. Gautier, *9 Mars 1945*, 143. *SMS*, 626. It seems that Gautier notified Decoux's office in Saigon very quickly of this shooting, but it is not clear whether Decoux himself knew of it before Matsumoto delivered the ultimatum at 7:00 P.M. See *DGI*, 108.

appeared to outweigh the benefits. By the afternoon of 9 March 1945, it must have been apparent to General Tsuchihashi that the Indochina Army was in no position to derail his takeover plans. It only remained to be discovered whether the French would accept the new constraints peacefully or attempt armed resistance.

Boxed In

After being presented with the ultimatum in Saigon at 7:00 P.M., Decoux's first reaction was to call in Claude de Boisanger, who apparently was meant to serve as a witness while the governor-general protested vigorously to Ambassador Matsumoto and sought amelioration of the draconian instructions. De Boisanger also found a pretext to go to the adjacent office, where he told someone to alert the French military commanders. Decoux insisted to Matsumoto that he needed to consult General Aymé and others before replying formally to the ultimatum, but the ambassador replied repeatedly that the governor-general possessed sufficient authority to accept or reject it on his own. Matsumoto did not want to leave without a written response, and even presented Decoux with suitable wording, but eventually, at 8:15 P.M., he agreed to depart the palace, specifying that the reply must come to army headquarters, and that a Japanese troop unit would remain outside to "assure security."[145]

Assuming that Decoux's bureau tried to contact Aymé's headquarters in Hanoi from about 7:30 P.M. on, there is no evidence that any message arrived. Quite possibly the Japanese had cut the relevant telephone and telegraph lines and jammed standard French radio frequencies. General Tsuchihashi apparently knew the content of outgoing telegrams to Hanoi, later expressing surprise that no state of emergency order from Decoux accompanied information about the Japanese ultimatum.[146] Apparently, Decoux still hoped desperately to avoid armed conflict, to gain an extension of the ultimatum deadline in order to parley further. On the other hand,

145. Decoux, *A la barre*, 330–33. Boisanger, *On pouvait éviter la guerre*, 97–101. Because French sources use Indochina time, whereas Japanese sources sometimes use Tokyo time (two hours later), without alerting the reader, the exact sequence of events on the evening of 9 March is still subject to question. I do my best to sort things out in subsequent paragraphs.

146. *SMS*, 659, quoting Tsuchihashi's unpublished memoirs. It is possible Tsuchihashi only learned this after the coup, when the Japanese had direct access to French confidential records.

de Boisanger felt the ultimatum was both completely unacceptable to the French and truly nonnegotiable for the Japanese, hence the prime need to alert military commanders. General Delsuc, troop commander in Cochinchina, and Admiral Bérenger, Indochina naval commander, were summoned to the governor-general's palace immediately after Ambassador Matsumoto's departure, a foolish decision, making it easy for the Japanese to locate and detain them one hour later.[147] At 8:45 P.M., Decoux dispatched his commissioner for Franco-Japanese affairs, Navy Captain Robin, to Matsumoto with a written response, essentially urging continuation of discussions beyond the 9:00 P.M. ultimatum deadline.[148]

In a final tragicomic scene to almost five years of Franco-Japanese diplomacy over Indochina, Captain Robin went to the wrong building. There a Japanese interpreter toting a submachine gun allowed Robin to telephone Ambassador Matsumoto, who sent a vehicle to fetch the errant French messenger. Meanwhile, General Tsuchihashi postponed his radio transmission. At 9:18 P.M., however, a disconcerting message arrived that fighting had already begun in Hanoi. Tsuchihashi's first thought was to court-martial the Japanese officer who had failed to wait for the signal, if it turned out that Decoux had accepted the ultimatum. On quick reflection, however, he realized that fighting could break out all around Indochina with no signal from him, upsetting carefully laid plans and causing greater loss of life.[149] Apparently, Tsuchihashi was still unaware that another subordinate in Haiphong had launched assaults as early as 7:25 P.M., probably in reaction to a local French alert, as well as lack of confidence in radio reception from Saigon. At 8:45 P.M. in Lang Son, a Japanese detachment had attacked the French officers' mess.[150]

At 9:23 P.M., with Captain Robin still not present, General Tsuchihashi decided to assume that Decoux had failed to meet the ultimatum terms and ordered code "7.7.7." to be transmitted repeatedly, signifying French refusal. Two minutes later, Robin was ushered into the adjacent room to present Decoux's letter to Matsumoto, who read it quickly, then called out in a loud voice for Tsuchihashi's benefit, "This is without doubt a rejec-

147. Admiral Bérenger did manage to get a message to his headquarters at 8:50 P.M., thirty-three minutes before Tsuchihashi ordered the attack. Mordal, *Marine Indochine*, 69.

148. Decoux, *A la barre*, 333–34. Claude de Boisanger, "L'Ultimatum japonaise de 1945 aux forces françaises d'Indochine," *Le Monde* (Paris), 11 Mar. 1975, 13.

149. Tsuchihashi, "Furansugun o busō kaijo," 160.

150. *SMS*, 625–26. *Histoire de l'Indochine*, ed. Héduy, 266–67, 271.

tion."[151] Almost immediately thereafter a burst of shooting was heard in another part of town, then silence.[152]

Denouement

French military units reacted to Japanese hostile action in different ways, ranging from immediate capitulation to resolute defense of their positions to attempted escape and evasion. In Cochinchina and Cambodia, almost all troop units offered little resistance and had surrendered to the Japanese by noon of 10 March, possibly on orders from the detained General Delsuc. Several groups did attempt to establish resistance bases in the Mekong Delta or fled in the general direction of Thailand, but within a few weeks only a handful of European stragglers remained, cadging food from villagers, constantly fearing betrayal to the Japanese.[153] In Laos, such small-scale resistance efforts were more successful, as Free French teams could rely on particular Meo (Hmong), Thai, and Lao aristocratic families for assistance in obtaining provisions, porters, and information about Japanese movements.[154]

In Annam, the only colonial unit to put up a determined fight was the garrison at the royal capital of Hue. Most of the Vauban-style Hue Citadel was lost early. A Japanese commando unit disguised as Vietnamese civilians hid inside the massive gates before routine closing time, tied up the gatekeepers at 9:00 P.M., and then fretfully awaited the attack signal, which came twenty-five minutes later.[155] A number of French nationals had gone to a Tarzan movie in downtown Hanoi, only to be rounded up by a Japanese squad shortly after the shooting began.[156] Resolute French resistance centered on the Mang Ca barracks, which surrendered on the afternoon of 10 March after the commander was wounded and ammunition ran short.[157]

151. Tsuchihashi, "Furansugun o busō kaijo," 160. Gaudel, *L'Indochine française en face du Japon*, 149–51, describes events from Robin's perspective.

152. Murakami, "Japan's Thrust," 532–33.

153. *CMCD*, 8:50–51.

154. *Histoire de l'Indochine*, ed. Héduy, 273. Ayrolles, *L'Indochine ne répond pas*, 80–119.

155. Kaneko Noboru, "Annan himitsu butai" [Annam Secret Unit], *Shūkan Yomiuri*, special ed., 8 Dec. 1956, 162.

156. Trinh Xuan An, in Hoang Anh, Le Tu Dong et al., *Binh Tri Thien Thang Tam Bon Lam: Hoi Ky* [August 1945 in Binh Tri Thien Province: Memoirs] (Hue, 1985), 147–48.

157. *War in Asia and the Pacific*, ed. Detwiler and Burdick, 6:26. *CMCD*, 8:51, says 251 out of 1,140 French soldiers at Hue were killed, a very high proportion for twenty hours of combat.

The emperor of Annam, Bao Dai, managed to avoid the entire fray. He left on a hunting excursion on the 9th, was stopped at a Japanese roadblock on his return, and received an armed escort back to the royal palace in the early hours of the 10th.[158] Elsewhere in Annam, several thousand colonial troops fled westward toward the hills, to no avail, as food soon ran short and native soldiers abandoned their French officers and NCOs. Within a few weeks Gaullist intelligence agents advised that further resistance in Annam was impossible, "due to the hostility of the inhabitants and maneuvers of many Japanese agents." A few of the French made it to Laos; the remainder died or were captured.[159]

As expected on both sides, most of the serious action occurred in Tonkin. In Hanoi, Japanese troops, who had trained meticulously to be able to seize a number of different locations simultaneously, were deployed quietly commencing at 7:00 P.M. on 9 March, catching some French officers at their desks or at home. At 7:55 P.M., General Mordant was at his residence, talking with Paul Mus, a Free French undercover agent, when the armed forces headquarters telephoned to report the earlier shooting incident at the ferry crossing. After ordering subordinates to contact the Japanese, with an eye to containing the altercation, Mordant gave Mus the use of his automobile and driver to recross the still silent city. A few minutes later, Mus heard high-pitched cat-meow sounds all around the car—the passing of Japanese bullets. He had been driven into the first Hanoi shooting, near the headquarters building. Colonel Guyot organized the immediate defense and was later killed, while Colonel Cavalin concentrated on burning classified documents.[160] The Japanese commander, realizing that he was ahead of General Tsuchihashi's deadline, hesitated to press the attack. When the "7.7.7." signal did eventually arrive and units moved forward again, the French resisted stubbornly. The armed forces headquarters endured three assaults before surrendering at 5:00 A.M. on the 10th.

Having slipped from his residence to the Citadel during the shooting lull the previous evening, General Mordant spent some time destroying documents and giving advice to General Massimi, the garrison commander, then proceeded to walk to the house of a friend with the apparent intention

158. Shiraishi, "La Présence," 234. The French wife of Consul Yokoyama was in Bao Dai's hunting party, an indication that the Japanese knew the emperor's every move and may have contrived his absence during the coup.

159. AOM, INF, c. 123 d. 1108, subdossier 3. Charbonneau and Maigre, Les Parias, 134–36.

160. Paul Mus, "L'Indochine en 1945," Politique étrangère (Paris) 11 (1946): 355–57. Mus himself managed to slip out of the city and escape to China.

Figure 4.   Indochina Army personnel captured by the Japanese at the Citadel in Hanoi. *Binh Minh* (Hanoi), 25 March 1945. Courtesy of the Bibliothèque nationale.

of escaping Hanoi. In the morning, however, Mordant gave himself up to the Japanese authorities.[161] Meanwhile, General Massimi's men at the Citadel had withstood repeated attacks. The Japanese pressed the captured General Aymé to order General Massimi to capitulate, without success. A captured French trumpeter blew "Cessez le feu!" without effect. On the afternoon of the 10th, the situation having become hopeless, General Massimi blew up the fuel dump and motor vehicle park before surrendering. Although the fighting in Hanoi had lasted less than twenty-four hours, its intensity is revealed by the losses: 87 Europeans and about 100 Vietnamese were killed on the one side, 115 Japanese on the other.[162]

In Haiphong, the Japanese concentrated on the Bouet barracks, headquarters of the First Tonkin Brigade, commanded by Colonel Henry Lapierre. They employed heavy mortar and machine-gun fire to cover platoon-sized infiltrations and assaults on surrounding buildings. By 10:00 A.M. on 10 March, it was impossible for any colonial troopers to move without exposing themselves to murderous fire. As the Japanese began

161. Mordant, *Au service de la France*, 142–45.
162. SMS, 629. *War in Asia and the Pacific*, ed. Detwiler and Burdick, 6:25. Charbonneau and Maigre, *Les Parias*, 131–33. *Binh Minh* (Hanoi), 25 Mar. 1945, contains seven photographs of operations at the Hanoi Citadel.

using cannon to destroy one position after another, Colonel Lapierre ordered his men to cease fire. Escorted by a Japanese lieutenant to meet the attack commander, Colonel Lapierre found himself being instructed repeatedly to sign a paper ordering subordinate units at other locations to surrender. After it became clear that Lapierre would not agree, a search began for his code books so as to fabricate a surrender message, but only ashes were located.[163] Late in the day, the Japanese reconciled themselves to dealing forcefully with remaining First Brigade garrisons.

Once again, as in 1885 and 1940, Lang Son was fated to be the scene of the heaviest French losses. It began with a ruse. The local Japanese commander invited General René Lemonnier, Third Tonkin Brigade commander, to dinner at 6:30 P.M. on the 9th. Lemonnier politely declined, but not wishing to cause diplomatic offense, authorized three senior officers to accompany the civilian *résident* of Lang Son province to the banquet. At 8:00 P.M., the host informed his French guests that they were under arrest. General Lemonnier's headquarters at Lang Son Citadel underwent bombardment and attack from 9:00 P.M. on, and before noon on the 10th, he was forced to surrender. Instructed by the Japanese to order subordinate units to lay down their arms as well, Lemonnier refused and was beheaded. With Japanese units continuing into the 11th to encounter stiff resistance at nearby forts, the same brutal tactics were employed on the four former dinner guests, with identical results.[164] Colonel Robert was even offered a pistol to commit honorable suicide, but refused and was beheaded.[165]

Shortly after midnight on 12 March, the Japanese threw two infantry regiments against Dong Dang, the last French position, which ran out of ammunition and surrendered at 10:00 A.M.. Apparently furious at his own high number of casualties, the Japanese commander ordered the senior French surviving officer to kneel in front of his own colonial troops, who watched stupefied as he was executed. By the next morning, fifty-three other survivors of Dong Dang had been either beheaded or bayoneted to death.[166] The total number of European and Indochinese prisoners killed

163. *Histoire de l'Indochine*, ed. Héduy, 267–70.

164. Ibid., 270–71.

165. Colonel Robert had assisted Free French agents in 1944 and tried to interest the Allies in a coordinated attack on the Japanese while they were understrength in Indochina in late November. *DGI*, 96. U.S. military attaché, Kunming, report, 15 Dec. 1944, in USNA, OSS record 110965.

166. *Histoire de l'Indochine*, ed. Héduy, 262. One Frenchman, trooper Cron, survived a sword wound and feigned death until the Japanese departed.

by the Japanese in the Lang Son area may have exceeded two hundred.[167] General Tsuchihashi arrived at Lang Son about one week after the fighting ended and interrogated officers carefully about these incidents. Consul General Nishimura Kumao, who accompanied Tsuchihashi to Lang Son, heard from a lieutenant-interpreter that the French officers had gone to their executions bravely, singing the "Marseillaise."[168] Meanwhile, tardy bombing attacks by the U.S. Fourteenth Air Force apparently killed several hundred Vietnamese colonial riflemen who had been incarcerated by the Japanese inside the Lang Son Citadel.[169]

For some reason, on the evening of 9 March, the Japanese did not attack General Sabattier's two forces positioned just to the west and northwest of Hanoi, which gave them time to evacuate their camps and begin moving in the general direction of the Yunnan frontier. However, Sabattier quickly lost communications contact with most of his subordinate units; artillery pieces and motor vehicles had to be destroyed at river crossings for lack of adequate ferries or rafts; and the Japanese succeeded in blocking the two most important border exits at Lao Cai and Ha Giang.[170] On 11 March, the Second Tonkin Brigade commander, General Marcel Alessandri, decided to disarm his Indochinese riflemen and leave them behind to their own devices.[171] This may have relieved some of them, but it undoubtedly hurt others deeply, and it was soon being used by Vietnamese nationalists to symbolize the perfidiousness of French colonialism. Paul Mus, who encountered some of these native NCOs and enlisted men as they descended from the hills, could not answer their impassioned questions about why the common struggle against the Japanese enemy had

167. Jean Dubourg, *Les Crimes japonais après le 9 Mars 1945* (Saigon, 1948), 26, asserts that "about 400" French prisoners were killed at Lang Son, but no source is given. This would have represented more than one-third of the total "European" complement at Lang Son, some of whom had already been killed in combat.

168. Interview with Ambassador Nishimura, Tokyo, 27 Nov. 1967. Nishimura also identified a Colonel Yamagata as responsible for the atrocities, and said he was hanged by the returning French authorities after Japanese surrender. No published Japanese source that I have seen mentions these incidents.

169. Charbonneau and Maigre, *Les Parias*, 160.

170. Sabattier, *Le Destin de l'Indochine*, 134–35, 151–87. The French commander at Ha Giang was captured while refereeing a soccer match between Japanese soldiers and Chinese soldiers who had crossed the border for the occasion. He was subsequently executed. From the photographs in *Binh Minh* (Hanoi), 15 Apr. 1945, it appears that the large concrete fortifications at Lao Cai were surrendered to the Japanese without serious resistance.

171. Sabattier, *Le Destin de l'Indochine*, 174. See chapter 5 for additional discussion of the French retreat toward China.

disintegrated so suddenly, leaving them alone, without weapons, vulnerable to retaliation.

General Sabattier received radio orders from General de Gaulle in Paris to maintain a physical presence in northern Indochina at any cost, thus symbolizing the persistence of French sovereignty. However, relentless Japanese pursuit, growing supply shortages, illness, and declining troop morale made this impossible. Veteran colonial officers were particularly upset to discover some highland minority groups teaming up with the Japanese to hunt down isolated French units.[172] Substantial American and Chinese assistance could have enabled Sabattier to defend several mountain redoubts, but, despite entreaties from Prime Minister Churchill, neither President Roosevelt nor Generalissimo Chiang Kai-shek were inclined to divert resources to French forces that only a few weeks earlier had been party to a defense agreement with the Japanese. In April and May, about 5,700 Indochina Army stragglers, including 2,469 Europeans, were permitted by the Chinese to cross the frontier at various locations, disarmed, and treated with ill-disguised contempt.[173] General Tsuchihashi declared mopping-up activities complete as of 15 May, having already released several brigades for operations elsewhere.[174]

French Nationals after the Coup

Throughout Indochina, some 2,100 European officers and enlisted men were killed or disappeared in the Japanese seizure of power on 9 March 1945.[175] Losses among native colonial soldiers were not compiled, but they probably exceeded European deaths. About 15,000 members of the Indochina armed forces were interned by the Japanese, 12,000 of them European.[176] Conditions were harsh, above all for the wounded and sick. Food was scarce, although for a while the Japanese permitted French wives and Vietnamese *congai* (girlfriends) to bring them supplementary fare. Those who tried to escape were generally captured by Vietnamese civilians

---

172. Charbonneau and Maigre, *Les Parias*, 104–5. AOM, INF, c. 123, d. 1108, subdossier 3.

173. Sabattier, *Le Destin de l'Indochine*, 231, contains a detailed breakdown of escapees, including 858 packhorses and 79 saddle horses.

174. Nitz, "Japanese Military Policy," 344. *SMS*, 666.

175. Hesse d'Alzon, "L'Armée française d'Indochine," 130. This figure may include those who died in captivity. I have not been able to ascertain Japanese casualties.

176. AOM, INF, c. 121, d. 1102

or the Civil Guard and turned over to the Japanese.[177] Able-bodied internees had to perform heavy labor, and almost all contracted malaria, dysentery, typhoid, or cholera. Most feared was the "camp of slow death" at Hoa Binh, forty miles southwest of Hanoi, where Japanese and Korean guards pushed internees ruthlessly to clear fields of fire and dig defensive positions.[178] At Viet Tri, northwest of Hanoi, an internment camp was bombed by Allied aircraft. Elsewhere a few internees were taken off for interrogation and torture, sometimes never to return. Nonetheless, all but about 180 military internees managed to survive the six months until the arrival of Allied forces.[179]

French civilians had no idea what to expect after the Japanese coup on 9 March, and neither had Japanese officials formulated clear plans for a postcoup administration (see chapter 2). General Tsuchihashi took over Admiral Decoux's office as governor-general, while Gaimushō (Foreign Office) personnel assumed other top-level colonial positions. Former French incumbents were assigned lightly guarded villas together with their families and servants. Thus, the Gautiers and the Chauvets lived on Boulevard Gambetta in Hanoi, occasionally obtaining old newspapers or bits of information from authorized visitors.[180] The Japanese made an exception of Maurice Ducoroy, the former commissioner-general for youth and sports, turning him over to the Kenpeitai for interrogation and imprisonment.[181]

Unlike top officials, French middle- and lower-echelon civilian personnel were instructed by the Japanese to remain on the job after the coup. We know from archival records that most complied, thus continuing to draw salaries and rations. For example, the chief of Tonkin's Service économique local, M. Lamarque, resumed his functions only days after the coup, among other things responding to a 9 March letter from Denis Frères d'Indochine concerning disposition of 737.2 meters of cloth.[182] In late March, Dr.

177. See, e.g., Bac Ninh to Kham Sai, 6 July 1945, reporting Civil Guard capture of Cavalry Sergeant Stoffel and Second Class Cannoneer Vendomme. AOM, INF, GF 22.

178. *Histoire de l'Indochine*, ed. Héduy, 278–80.

179. Jean J. Bernardini, *Sous la botte nippone* (Paris, 1971), 38–41, 59–111. Lucien Félixine, *L'Indochine livreé aux bourreaux* (Paris, 1959), 38–63. Françoise Martin, *Heures tragiques au Tonkin (9 mars 1945–18 mars 1946)* (Paris, 1948), 89. Gaudel, *L'Indochine française en face du Japon*, 187, 190. Dubourg, *Les Crimes japonais*, 25.

180. Gautier, *9 Mars 1945*, 186–96.

181. Maurice Ducoroy, *Ma Trahison en Indochine* (Paris, 1949), 205–9.

182. Dossier on "Articles mises à la disposition de l'OCR," in AOM, INF, GF 50. By June, Lamarque had been replaced by Nguyen Manh Ha, who two months later would be named to Ho Chi Minh's first cabinet.

Figure 5. Senior French prisoners lined up for Japanese cameras. Included are General Mordant, General Aymé, Assistant Governor-General Gautier, Resident Superior Chauvet, and three unidentified officials. *Binh Minh* (Hanoi), 1 April 1945. Courtesy of the Bibliothèque nationale.

Simon, director of public health in Tonkin, dutifully provided the newly appointed resident superior, Nishimura Kumao, with detailed reports on typhus and cholera outbreaks in particular provinces, together with the information that the Pasteur Institute in Hanoi had a reserve supply of one million doses of cholera vaccine.[183] Other French health administrators, physicians, and hospital supervisors remained equally active, even helping to screen requests from Vietnamese members of the administration for sick leave.[184] French teachers, accountants, engineers, technicians, railroad dispatchers, harbor pilots, and prison wardens continued to work as well.

On the other hand, the Japanese Army showed its distrust by insisting that French nationals surrender all firearms, leave doors unlocked, not

183. AOM, INF, GF 25. On behalf of his detained compatriots, Dr. Simon added a comment that prisons and army detention centers currently represented dangerous breeding grounds for epidemics.

184. AOM, INF, Gouvernement Revolutionnaire/GF 141. A DGER report of 8 May 1945 admits that many public services and commercial operations were still being managed by French civilians, under Japanese supervision. AOM, INF, c. 123, d. 1108, subdossier 3.

move around after dark, and not congregate in groups of more than three. Radios, cameras, binoculars, and typewriters also had to be turned in to the Kenpeitai. Limits were placed on bank withdrawals. Europeans not part of the civil administration were instructed to select representatives to communicate with Japanese officials, especially on matters of food allocation. Often Catholic priests or monks, who seem to have kept the respect of the Japanese, assumed this role. Through such channels, too, dependents of military personnel tried to ascertain the whereabouts of husbands and fathers. As the number of robberies and assaults on French nationals increased in late March and April, these spokesmen also pleaded with the Japanese for more police protection.[185] A rumor swept Vietnamese in Hanoi that French wardens on Con Son Island had killed all political prisoners, sparking much indignation and undoubtedly making the position of French nationals more vulnerable.[186]

By late April, General Tsuchihashi's ad hoc policy of French participation in postcoup administration was in urgent need of clarification. "Transitional rules" were issued distinguishing European government employees already discharged without remuneration from those to be retired with "reasonable compensation" and "indispensable" personnel to be kept on with full pay and allowances.[187] Every bureau was ordered to submit lists of French personnel as of 9 March, indicating who had been removed, who had left without authorization, and who continued to function.[188] Meanwhile, Vietnamese province chiefs were warned not to remove European specialists, especially those responsible for dikes, irrigation, road and rail transport, water supply, and electric power.[189]

However, most Vietnamese members of the administration disliked having their former colonial bosses looking over their shoulders. Some

185. Martin, *Heures tragiques*, 10–15, 59–60, 63–65, 70, 87–88. Smith, "Japanese Period," 287. Claude Paillat, *Dossier secret de l'Indochine* (Paris, 1964), 40. Jacques Le Bourgeois, *Saigon sans la France* (Paris, 1949), 117–18. Some Viet Minh adherents were shocked to hear of Vietnamese entering French homes to pillage and rape. See, e.g., Nguyen Huy Tuong, diary entry, 14 Mar. 1945, in Le Quang Dao et al., *Mot Chang Duong Van Hoa*, 123.

186. Nguyen Huy Tuong, diary entry, 4 Apr. 1945, in Le Quang Dao et al., *Mot Chang Duong Van Hoa*, 125.

187. "Règlement transitoire," 26 Apr. 1945, signed by Tsukamoto Takeshi on behalf of General Tsuchihashi, in AOM, INF, GF 44. Those in the second category, to be retired with compensation, began to receive formal letters from 7 May on.

188. Although these orders went out during the first days of May, replies were slow to come in, so that some consolidated lists could not be prepared until early August, when conditions were quite different. AOM, INF, GF 42.

189. Resident superior to province chiefs, 5 May 1945, in AOM, INF, GF 61.

complained to the Japanese that these French associates did little or no work, that their bad attitudes provoked incidents, and that they posed a potential security threat.[190] Others invoked public opinion. The provincial chief of Yen Bai, for example, after reporting that several French personnel continued to work, added that "the population wishes at all cost to see them disappear from the province."[191] By May, participants in Vietnamese demonstrations permitted by the Japanese had taken to yelling slogans demanding removal of all French personnel from government institutions.[192] French nationals became subject to an increasing amount of physical and verbal abuse from Vietnamese—a new and very disorienting experience. Native policemen appeared to show little sympathy for the French in such circumstances; domestic servants disappeared or even turned against their masters.[193] As rumors circulated among the French of fellow countrymen being massacred in outlying provinces, and as Vietnamese heard stories of Frenchmen poisoning the water supply or sabotaging valuable equipment, the mood became increasingly volatile.[194] To try to bolster flagging French morale, representatives petitioned for permission to organize public sports or cultural performances. Thus, the president of the Hanoi Horseracing Society, G. Guerrier, sent an urgent request to Nishimura to authorize race events on the Sunday afternoons of 13 May and 3 June, with any profits to be donated to welfare.[195]

During June, probably in response to growing tensions, most French civilians in the provinces were withdrawn to the cities to live under various degrees of Japanese guard.[196] Nonetheless, some plantation owners

190. See, e.g., the request from the Ha Nam provincial chief to Nishimura on 3 Apr. 1945 that six French Public Works employees be sacked, in AOM, INF, GF 25.

191. Yen Bai to Kham Sai, 1 June 1945, in AOM, INF, GF 42.

192. Phan Anh, "Con Duong di toi Cach Mang Thang Tam cua Toi" [My Path to the August Revolution], *Nhan Dan* (Hanoi), 21 Aug. 1960, 4. In our interview in Hanoi on 7 March 1988, Phan Anh asserted that his main reason for participating in Japanese-sanctioned activities was to make sure the French were removed from all positions of authority or influence.

193. AOM, INF, c. 121, d. 1102. Martin, *Heures tragiques*, 62, 85–87.

194. Martin, *Heures tragiques*, 99. Nguyen Ky Nam, *Hoi Ky, 1925–1964* [Memoirs, 1925–64] (Saigon, 1964), 2:133–34. *L'Action* (Hanoi), 4 July 1945. Do Thuc Vinh, *Mua Ao Anh* [Season of Mirages] (Saigon, 1962), 52–54, tells of a French company manager destroying machinery and inviting native employees to appropriate movable property rather than see it fall into Japanese or pro-Japanese hands.

195. AOM, INF, GF 25.

196. AOM, INF, Gouvernement Revolutionnaire/GF 141 and GF 5. Pay for all European members of the Tonkin Schools Service terminated from 1 June, which

and managers chose to stay on their properties rather than delegate authority to Vietnamese subordinates, and a few government employees remained scattered around the colony as well. Thus, at the end of June, M. Dauriac, a tax collector in Ninh Binh province, sixty miles south of Hanoi, sent a sharp official protest about Japanese troops destroying property-registration files.[197] French railroad agents and PTT technicians continued to function at certain provincial locations, presumably guarded closely by the Japanese.[198] In July, when Viet Minh groups gained the upper hand at several coal mines north of Haiphong, they chose to keep French supervisors and technicians on the job in the interests of maintaining output.[199]

As of 1 July, 172 French citizens had been removed from the Saigon-Cholon police force; 9 remained, including 3 naturalized Frenchmen, 2 *métis*, and 2 Indians.[200] At the Hanoi Central Prison, European personnel continued to exercise their functions under Japanese observation. An inventory of the prison of 18 July was signed by François Garien, *gardien chef*, with particular attention to 2,564.56 piastres' worth of property lost "since the events of 9 March."[201] Shortly thereafter, in the wake of wide-ranging discussions between General Tsuchihashi and Vietnamese officials, French guards began to receive release notices. Each guard received a polite letter from Resident Superior Nishimura informing him that "following installation of His Excellency the Délégué extraordinaire impérial at the head of the Tonkin administration, I have the honor to inform you that you are requested to cease your functions from 15 August 1945."[202] We do not know if similar notices were sent to several French officials who continued to work under Japanese supervision in the General Government's Financial Control Service.[203] However, at the port of Haiphong, French agents and technicians remained on the job throughout

---

presumably meant they had to rely on in-kind handouts along with their nongovernmental compatriots. AOM, INF, GF 16. A group of Europeans were still at the hill resort of Tam Dao, thirty-three miles northwest of Hanoi, when the Viet Minh attacked a Japanese unit there on 16 July. See chapter 3.

197. AOM, INF, GF 10.

198. AOM, INF, GF 4 and GF 25.

199. Viet Nam, Dang Cong San, Ban Nghien Cuu Lich Su Dang Quang Ninh, *Lich Su Dang Bo Tinh Quang Ninh* [History of the Quang Ninh Province Party Apparatus], vol. 1, *1928–1945* (Hanoi, 1985), 187–88.

200. Tønnesson, *Vietnamese Revolution*, 291.

201. AOM, INF, GF 22.

202. AOM, INF, GF 2.

203. AOM, INF, GF 25.

Figure 6.   A French prisoner of the Kenpeitai taking out the night-soil bucket. Reprinted from Jacques Le Bourgeois, *Ici Radio-Saigon*. Courtesy of Imprimerie française d'Outre-Mer à Saigon.

the ferment of August, finally being ordered to cease work forthwith on 10 September.[204]

Between March and July, the Kenpeitai also jailed about five hundred French civilians,[205] starting with anyone suspected of aiding the Allies, and followed by Sûreté officers who had previously maltreated natives sympathetic to the Japanese. Subsequently, other civilians were arrested for disobeying Japanese edicts. Communications personnel were particularly vulnerable to detention on suspicion of having used their equipment and expertise to facilitate Allied attacks. Jacques Le Bourgeois, director of Radio Saigon, was consigned to the infamous Maison centrale prison for this reason, yet treated reasonably well.[206] Others were less fortunate, being subjected to repeated interrogations, savage torture, and atrocious living

204. AOM, INF, GF 4.

205. A 29 Jan. 1947 report in AOM, INF, c. 121, d. 1102, claims the Kenpeitai jailed 1,500 French nationals. This figure appears to be contradicted by Dubourg, *Les Crimes japonais*, 24, who states that 242 were arrested in Hanoi, the most active location for Kenpeitai roundups according to other evidence, with Saigon a close second.

206. Le Bourgeois, *Saigon sans la France*, 23–44, 93–141.

conditions. Fear surrounded the Shell Oil building in Hanoi, the Chartered Bank in Haiphong, and the Chamber of Commerce building in Saigon, where Kenpeitai operations centered. Prisoners were packed together for months in small bamboo cages, without washing water or medicine. Dysentery was rampant. Struggles sometimes broke out with Vietnamese prisoners in the same cells over food.[207]

Conclusion

The French population in Indochina, military and civilian, emerged from World War II deeply embittered and humiliated. Many were convinced that the Japanese had dumped them in March 1945 out of simple spite—to sabotage the last white outpost in Asia when it was clear their 1941–42 Pacific victories had turned to ashes. The French remembered every example of Japanese maltreatment after 9 March, while forgetting that the Japanese had at least ensured them a minimum food supply during a time when hundreds of thousands of Vietnamese were dying of starvation nearby.

Although some Japanese undoubtedly took pleasure in finally dismantling the anachronistic French colonial structure in Indochina, and some enjoyed maltreating French nationals after the 9 March coup, there is no historical evidence to suggest that such feelings formed the basis of Japanese policy. The French were toppled for straightforward military reasons, probably unnecessarily, given American intentions to strike much closer to the Japanese home islands, yet a sensible precaution considering intelligence data available at the time.

Careful Japanese preparation and the element of tactical surprise reduced the risk of protracted conflict with the French, or even military reversal. On the other hand, bilateral relations were so tense by early March that neither General Tsuchihashi nor Admiral Decoux could follow the precedent of 1940–41 and combine the imminence of violence with a last-minute negotiated solution. For Tsuchihashi this produced a minor leadership embarrassment when local Japanese units moved against the French before receiving the signal to do so. For Decoux it meant complete disaster, the last threads of control slipping away quickly as fighting spread. For almost five years he had set his course by the star of resumed French grandeur in

---

207. *Histoire de l'Indochine*, ed. Héduy, 260–61, 281. Le Bourgeois, *Saigon sans la France*, 45–92. Dubourg, *Les Crimes japonais*, 10–25. Dubourg also indicates that a total of 220 French civilians were killed, disappeared, or died in captivity in Tonkin alone between 9 March and the end of the war.

Indochina, navigating adroitly through Japanese ultimatums, Thai ambitions, Vichy stipulations, increasing Allied pressure, and growing native aspirations.[208] From his place of detention in tiny Loc Ninh, eighty miles north of Saigon, Decoux contemplated his fate and awaited the end of the war.

Shortly after the Japanese coup, Free French intelligence officers in Calcutta were stunned to lose contact with one radio transmitter after another in Indochina. "L'Indochine ne répond plus," they signaled. The silence was broken only by a station in Laos.[209] Control of events had passed out of French hands.

On the night General Tsuchihashi scored his victories in Indochina, 150 American B-29s blanketed Tokyo with incendiary bombs, causing incredible firestorms and 125,000 casualties, the worst losses from a single raid in all of World War II.[210] In the following weeks, Tsuchihashi must have wondered whether a secure Indochina meant anything at all to his compatriots at home.

208. Sbrega, "Japanese Surrender," 53
209. Ayrolles, *L'Indochine ne répond pas*, 49.
210. Hata, "Army's Move," 513. Gautier, *9 Mars 1945*, 234. Masuo Kato, *The Lost War* (New York: Knopf, 1946), 209–16, contains a vivid description of the Tokyo fire-bombing.

2 The Vietnamese Deal with Two Masters

On the evening of 9 March 1945, Pham Khac Hoe, private secretary to the emperor of Annam, Bao Dai, was relaxing at home when the city of Hue was shaken by explosions. As the din continued, he picked out the thud of artillery and stutter of heavy machine guns, much of it from the direction of the French military barracks and administrative bureaus. Next morning, the gunfire having died down, Hoe drove to the royal palace to report for work, but found the gates locked and plastered with Japanese martial law proclamations. As he turned around, Hoe was intercepted by a heavily armed Japanese patrol, whose leader coldly ordered him out of his automobile and took him to the local officer in charge, a bespectacled young captain toting a samurai sword. Seeing Hoe's ivory mandarin badge, the captain saluted him respectfully and explained in French, "The Japanese Imperial Army has simply removed the French colonialists from power, but has not interfered with the royal court." Hoe was then escorted home.[1]

Late the previous night, a Japanese patrol had halted another automobile as it entered Hue from the north. Captain Kaneko Noboru, commander of a covert operations unit, but now wearing an armband with the character *an* (to mean "Security" and perhaps An-Nam) superimposed on a rising sun, identified the occupants in the rear seat as Emperor Bao Dai and Empress Nam Phuong. Through an interpreter, Kaneko informed them that French colonial oppression was over, and that "from tomorrow, the Annamite people and the country of Annam can look forward to glorious prosperity." Allegedly shaking with emotion and weeping profusely, the

1. Pham Khac Hoe, *Tu Trieu Dinh Hue den Chien Khu Viet Bac* [From the Hue Court to the Viet Bac War Zone] (Hanoi, 1983), 9–10.

emperor told Kaneko that he hoped to be able to cooperate with Japan to overcome all difficulties.[2]

Some of Bao Dai's emotion that night may have been linked to uncertainty about his personal future, as it was widely rumored that the Japanese intended to replace him with Prince Cuong De, pretender to the Nguyen throne, long resident in Tokyo. The next afternoon, however, a senior Japanese diplomat, Yokoyama Masayuki, entered the royal palace to tell Bao Dai that Tokyo expected him to head a government dedicated to "maintaining social order."[3] Yokoyama further stated that Japan was prepared to acknowledge an Annamite declaration of independence within the Greater East Asia Co-Prosperity Sphere. Undoubtedly much relieved, Bao Dai instructed Pham Quynh, his minister of the interior (and de facto premier), to draft a proclamation in French and show it to Yokoyama, who found it proper except for a clause expressing gratitude to the Japanese armed forces.[4] That passage deleted, Pham Quynh scheduled a meeting of the full cabinet for the next morning, 11 March, where he read out the text solemnly in the presence of the monarch. The "government of Vietnam"—a new designation—abrogated the 1884 protectorate treaty signed with the French, proclaimed its independence, and affirmed its determination to collaborate with Japan.[5] There being no objections or amendments from the other five cabinet members, Bao Dai instructed his secretary, Pham Khac Hoe, to prepare a formal document for signature. The minister of rites, Ung Uy, adjudged 14 March to be an auspicious day to conduct the ceremony notifying the dynastic ancestors of this dramatic turn of events.

2. Kaneko Noboru, "Annan himitsu butai" [Annam Secret Unit], *Shūkan yomiuri*, special ed., 8 Dec. 1956.

3. Interview with Yokoyama Masayuki, Tokyo, 16 Nov. 1967. Yokoyama had arrived back in Hue toward the evening of 9 March and spent a perilous night in the consulate building, with shells exploding nearby and bullets spattering the walls.

4. This is Yokoyama's recollection. By contrast, Nguyen Ky Nam, *Hoi Ky, 1925–1964* [Memoirs, 1925–64], vol. 2 (Saigon, 1964), 168–69, quotes Pham Quynh as complaining that the original text had been drafted by Yokoyama.

5. French and Vietnamese texts of this proclamation can be found in AOM, INF, GF 25. A slightly different French text is reprinted in Philippe Devillers, *Histoire du Vietnam de 1940 à 1952* (Paris, 1952), 125. See also Bao Dai, *Le Dragon d'Annam* (Paris, 1980), 101–5. Radio Tokyo broadcast a Japanese text that same day, reprinted in U.S. Office of Strategic Services, *Programs of Japan in Indochina* (Honolulu: OSS, Aug. 1945) (cited below as *PJI*), 11 Mar. 1945. Vietnamese newspapers also published the brief 11 March proclamation; see, e.g., *Dan Bao* (Saigon), 12 Mar. 1945. Kenneth Colton, "The Failure of the Independent Political Movement in Vietnam, 1945–1946" (Ph.D. diss., American University, 1969), 57–69, contains an interesting textual analysis of it.

Bao Dai closed the meeting by inviting everyone to his mother's chambers that evening to play mah-jongg and eat wild buffalo meat from his latest hunting excursion.[6] If those present speculated about the fate of their former French masters at the hands of the Japanese, there is no record of it.

Wartime French Treatment of the Vietnamese

Following France's defeat in 1940 and Japan's forcible entry into Indochina, the colonial authorities had implemented a number of policies designed to neutralize any threat from the indigenous population. Acutely aware of Indochina's strategic isolation, with no hope of reinforcements from France, the new governor-general, Jean Decoux, was ruthless when dealing with internal armed opposition. Besides deploying military units to sensitive locations, Decoux reinforced the dreaded Sûreté générale and gave it wider powers.[7] Dossiers were opened on any natives associating with the Japanese, although generally it was not possible to harass, arrest, or torture them in the same manner as other categories of troublemakers. Looking through captured Sûreté files after they took over on 9 March 1945, Japanese officials were impressed at the quality of the information collected. They also concluded that some of the most effective Sûreté agents were *métis* whose French fathers had abandoned them when returning to the métropole, but to whom the colonial government had offered education and subsequent employment.[8]

As we have seen, Governor-General Decoux, a temperamentally aloof career naval officer, took advantage of the lack of contact with the métropole to govern Indochina autocratically, much in the manner of the colonizing French admirals of the 1860s. Whenever his authoritarianism needed to be justified, Decoux simply publicized political edicts emanating by radio from wartime France. The Vichy slogan "Work–Family–Fatherland" was hoisted on banners and splashed on walls, since, in the opinion of the governor-general, it "corresponded marvelously with the deep-seated and traditional aspirations of the [Indochinese] masses, and

6. Pham Khac Hoe, *Tu Trieu Dinh Hue den Chien Khu Viet Bac*, 11–14.

7. Just prior to the 9 March 1945 coup, the Cochinchina branch of the Sûreté had 1,994 personnel on its rosters, 86 percent of them native. AOM, INF, CP 186, Feb. 1946 Sûreté report to the *conseiller politique*. I have yet to locate similar figures for Tonkin and Annam.

8. Interview with Urabe Kiyoji, Tokyo, 15 Nov. 1967. Urabe was consul in Hue, 1943–45.

tallied with Confucian morality."[9] A 1942 Vietnamese school primer described Marshal Pétain in distinctly Confucian terms, at the same time instructing pupils how to line up in formation at precisely 7:50 A.M. each morning to salute the French tricolor.[10] A big portrait of the marshal was attached to the back of St. Mary's Cathedral in downtown Saigon, with the caption, "A single chief: Pétain. A single duty: to obey. A single motto: to serve."[11]

Decoux dissolved all elected bodies in Indochina save the French-dominated municipal councils, a particularly disruptive act in the Vietnamese countryside, where individuals on the tax rolls had become accustomed to approving members of village councils long before the French arrived. By contrast there does not seem to have been much anguish in the cities, where representative institutions were only a few decades old and of Western derivation. Decoux began his reorganization at the top, in 1943 establishing a new Federal Council composed of thirty native and twenty-three French members. According to an official press release, by thus providing natives with numerical superiority, the Indochina government "wished to prove its desire to give the elite of the country the importance that in equity should be theirs."[12] However, the governor-general appointed every council member, made sure that all five committee chairmen were French, specified that the council's role was strictly advisory, and set the agenda of annual meetings.[13] The council met only twice before the Japanese takeover.[14]

In working to secure Indochina from internal unrest, Decoux was not content to rely solely on physical repression and administrative fiat. He showed greater ritual deference to the royal families of Annam, Cambodia, and Laos than previous governors-general had. He publicly upheld the legitimacy of local patriotisms, providing they were not directed against the

9. Jean Decoux, *A la barre de l'Indochine* (Paris, 1949), 360. For further discussion of the cult of Pétainism in Indochina, see Vu Ngu Chieu, "Political and Social Change in Viet-Nam between 1940 and 1946" (Ph.D. diss., University of Wisconsin, 1984), 100–111. AOM, INF, GF 66 contains a copy of a book titled *Paroles du Máréchal* (Hanoi, 1941) on which some clerk has drawn funny faces.

10. Direction de l'instruction publique, *Van Quoc Ngu (Nam Ky)* [National-Script Reader: Cochinchina] (Saigon [?], 1942), 114–16.

11. *Indochine* (Hanoi), no. 71 (8 Jan. 1942): 8. Of course, such Pétainist propaganda was directed equally at the 39,000 Europeans in the colony.

12. *PJI*, Radio Saigon (in French), 23 June 1943.

13. Roger Pinto, *Aspects de l'évolution gouvernementale de l'Indochine française* (Paris, 1946), 58–59.

14. Decoux, *A la barre*, 393.

French; native elites were encouraged to join with him in building an "Indochina Federation" in which the French would be first among equals, not colonial masters.[15] To this end, the salaries of native functionaries were brought closer to those of French functionaries with identical job specifications, and several hundred Vietnamese were promoted to middle-level administrative positions. As inflation gripped the colony, Decoux tried to ensure that the standard of living of native as well as French public employees did not slip too far. The base salary of a provisional district mandarin, for example, was increased by 41 percent in 1943, and 33 percent in 1944.[16] Indochinese employees of the Gouvernement général were allowed to operate a professional association that allocated ration tickets for rice and cloth, offered a modest gift to retiring members, and organized funerals.[17] Nonetheless, Indochinese readers of the government budget prepared for 1945 could not help but note that the average French public servant in the colony would still be paid more than nine times as much as the average native public servant.[18]

With commodity imports from Europe cut off after 1940, Decoux encouraged Chinese and Vietnamese manufacturers, entrepreneurs, and inventors to apply their talents without fear of intruding on traditional French business privileges. Some of these families amassed considerable wealth in only two or three years. To symbolize the enhanced status of native elites, old and new, the colonial government in 1943 published a glossy illustrated volume titled *Souverains et notabilités d'Indochine*.[19]

---

15. Ibid., 388–90. It seems that Decoux was the first top French administrator to use the name "Viet-Nam," which he did in a 1942 degree-conferring ceremony. Paul Isoart, "Aux origines d'une guerre: L'Indochine française (1940–1945)," in *L'Indochine française, 1940–1945*, ed. id. (Paris, 1982), 16.

16. AOM, INF, GF 3. See also AOM, INF, CP 108, which contains a 25 Dec. 1943 annex to an inspection report by A. Renou dealing in large part with the question of salaries for Indochinese employees.

17. AOM, INF, GF 23. At least until the end of 1942, the sports section of the association also received an annual allocation of tennis balls, which were extremely scarce.

18. Nguyen Khac Dam, *Nhung Thu Doan Boc Lot cua Tu Ban Phap o Viet-Nam* [Exploitative Methods of French Capitalists in Vietnam] (Hanoi, 1957), 301–2. To be more precise, 3,691 French employees were allocated 36 million piastres, while 41,745 Indochinese employees were to receive 46 million.

19. Indochina, Gouvernement général, *Souverains et notabilités d'Indochine* (Hanoi, 1943). For a valuable analysis of the 141 of these "sovereigns and notabilities" who resided in Cochinchina, see Ralph B. Smith, "The Vietnamese Elite of French Cochinchina, 1943," *Modern Asian Studies* 6, no. 4 (1972): 459–82.

Almost all the individuals selected for inclusion were royal family members, officials, landlords, professionals, and entrepreneurs. Only 9 of the 342 Vietnamese listed were prominent writers, a reflection of the general alienation of this group from the colonial establishment.

Decoux's most dramatic innovations focused on the youth of the colony. He deliberately ignored French *colons* who warned that too many native children were going beyond village hedges to acquire unrealistic expectations. School enrollments in Tonkin, Annam, and Cochinchina jumped from 450,000 in 1939 to more than 700,000 in 1944.[20] Although this still constituted only about 14 percent of the school-age population, to be able to appropriate the funds, recruit the teachers, and open the buildings necessary to accommodate 250,000 new pupils amid wartime uncertainties was no mean achievement. Most of the expansion took place at elementary-school level, but secondary vocational training also received special attention. For example, two schools were opened in Ben Cat (Cochinchina) to instruct forestry and rubber plantation cadres. Each dawn at the Forestry School, one could see fifty trainees in formation saluting the tricolor and singing marching songs.[21]

Since the war prevented either Indochinese or French *baccalauréat* students from going to France for tertiary education, the University of Hanoi took on greater importance. A new science faculty was opened in 1941.[22] By 1944 there were 1,109 Vietnamese students at the university: 681 from Tonkin, 216 from Annam, and 212 from Cochinchina.[23] In line with Decoux's overall political strategy, the student body was permitted to hold rallies at which "national consciousness" was demonstrated and policy resolutions were adopted, including one calling for creation of a "French Indochina National United Movement."[24] Inside classrooms, the few Vietnamese members of the university faculty sometimes set aside normal lectures in favor of impromptu patriotic talks. At the Cité universitaire, students organized songfests in the evenings that featured the most recent rousing creations of Luu Huu Phuoc, Van Cao, and Hoang Quy. During summer vacations, students went to camps in the nearby

20. "Tableau statistique de l'enseignement en Indochine" (1946 [?]), AOM, INF, c. 1323. Devillers, *Histoire*, 85.

21. *PJI*, Radio Saigon (in French), 11 Nov. 1943 and 11 Oct. 1944.

22. Ibid., 8 Nov. 1944.

23. Total enrollments were 1,528, including at least 300 French students. "Tableau statistique," AOM, INF, c. 1323.

24. *PJI*, Radio Saigon (in French), 20 May 1943.

Figure 7.   Maurice Ducoroy, head of the General Commissariat for Physical Education, Sports, and Youth, addressing a young audience in Saigon. The stand to his left contains French youth cadres, while the one to his right (out of the photograph) contains Vietnamese. Behind Ducoroy is a large statue of Joan of Arc, and behind that is St. Mary's Cathedral. Reproduced from Ducoroy's memoir, *Ma trahison en Indochine.* Courtesy of Éditions internationales.

countryside.[25] Younger residents of Hanoi soon eagerly imitated the university students, especially gathering in the evenings to sing new patriotic songs and play tunes on the harmonica.[26]

Parallel to the enlarged colonial school system, Decoux established a General Commissariat for Physical Education, Sports, and Youth, headed by Maurice Ducoroy, an energetic naval captain. Ducoroy felt that the need to finesse Japanese attempts to woo young Indochinese clearly outweighed the admitted dangers to French rule of allowing large numbers of

25. *Cach Mang Can Dai Viet Nam* (cited below as *CMCD*), 9:175–77.
26. Van Ngoc, "Pho toi ngay ay" [My Street in Those Days], *Doan Ket* (Paris), no. 368 (Mar. 1985): 10. The author, who was only ten in 1944, also loved to sing romantic Tino Rossi and Mistinguett songs.

Figure 8.   Poster for the first Tour d'Indochine cycling race, linking Tonkin, Annam, Cochinchina, Cambodia, and Laos. Reprinted from Maurice Ducoroy, *Ma trahison en Indochine*. Courtesy of Éditions internationales.

young people to congregate regularly. In his mind, Indochina's natives had to identify with either Tokyo or Paris, colonial youths had to pledge either "Mikado, we are here" or "Marshal [Pétain], we are there."[27] The idea that youths might possess or develop passionate local loyalties does not seem to have occurred to Ducoroy. Two training institutions were opened in Phan Thiet (Annam) to accommodate cadres coming from all parts of Indochina; smaller schools on the same pattern were set up in eleven provincial towns.[28] By 1944, Ducoroy could claim 1,109 new sports

27. Maurice Ducoroy, *Ma trahison en Indochine* (Paris, 1949), 91, 105.
28. PJI, Radio Saigon (in French), 1 and 27 June 1943, 23 June 1944.

instructors and 86,075 registered members of sporting societies.[29] Associations of Young Buddhists, Boy Scouts,[30] Girl Guides, Red Ribbon Youth, Christian Workers Youth, and Jeannettes (named for Joan of Arc) were also encouraged to expand their memberships and to participate in public competitions and ceremonies. Ducoroy was especially proud of the cycling races organized annually from 1942 to 1944, with the tour route extending 4,100 kilometers across all five parts of Indochina. He sponsored a big footrace from Phnom Penh to Hanoi, each part of the federation contributing one hundred relay runners. When the Japanese consul general asked if Japanese nationals might compete in these sporting events too, Ducoroy allowed them to sign up for cycling and pelota, but excluded them from swimming and track and field, where they were known to be strong.[31]

Through a Looking Glass Darkly

Behind these wartime colonial initiatives lay certain fixed assumptions about native character. Most important, the French felt they had to demonstrate that ignoble defeat in Europe did not undermine their capacity to suppress opposition in the colonies. According to General Gabriel Sabattier, even the gentlest of followers was capable of the "worst reversals should they establish that we were definitely the weakest." As an old Asia hand, he added, "One can never be too careful in a yellow country."[32] The French mayor of Haiphong complained, "The Annamese, less dominated by us, let themselves take advantage of their natural flaws," becoming once again too casual, lacking in conscientiousness and obedience.[33]

Most French officials continued to regard militant opposition as the work of small, disgruntled groups encouraged by outside powers to thwart

29. Ducoroy, *Ma trahison*, 103.

30. There were about 20,000 Boy Scouts throughout Indochina, of whom one-fifth were adult leaders or teenage explorers. Tran Van Su, "Ket qua buoc dau suu tam Nghien Cuu ve Luc Luong Huong Dao Sinh tham gia cuoc Cach Mang Thang Tam" [Preliminary Research Results Concerning Scout Force Participation in the August Revolution] (MS, Hanoi, Oct. 1989).

31. Ducoroy, *Ma trahison*, 94, 132–33.

32. Gabriel Sabattier, *Le Destin de l'Indochine: Souvenirs et documents, 1941–1951* (Paris, 1952), 159–60, 161. Although Sabattier wrote these words after trudging to China in April 1945, sometimes in disguise and fearful of being denounced to the Japanese, he undoubtedly formed such opinions much earlier.

33. AOM, INF, RST, F 70 (7), as quoted in Vu Ngu Chieu, "Political and Social Change," 233.

France's beneficent efforts to maintain peace and order throughout Indochina. This was certainly the attitude of Paul Arnoux, whom Decoux appointed to the top police position in June 1942. Based on thirty-five years' experience in the colony, Arnoux saw his main job as isolating the tiny groups of malcontents who revolted against constituted authority from the "elites and middle-class Annamites" who hoped for evolution under French protection, as well as from the vast majority of the population who simply sought to "live quietly."[34] Behind this colonial formula, however, lay grudging recognition that professional agitators needed to be pursued constantly and jailed or eliminated, otherwise they might infect the majority with disloyal thoughts.[35] The idea that the majority of Vietnamese, Lao, or Cambodians might want independence from France could not be entertained. At most, natives wanted a better share, hence the need to offer trustworthy elements more opportunities for advancement within the Indochina Federation.

News of French capitulation at Compiègne in June 1940 had indeed shocked the Vietnamese elite. Some collaborator politicians were said to have broken into tears in public.[36] Truong Van Ben, a prominent landlord, rice merchant, and soap manufacturer, declared his willingness to sacrifice everything to "make sure the French tricolor continues to fly over Indochina."[37] Less sympathetic observers mocked previous French confidence. Sarcastic poems pictured the "mother country" waving the white

---

34. As quoted in Isoart, "Aux origines d'une guerre," 15.

35. This viewpoint had been expressed in its most sophisticated form some years earlier by an anonymous Sûreté officer:

> The peasant stooped in his rice-field does not appear until now to have been seriously affected: but it is certain that, from some time or another, by means of a letter from a relative, by way of conversation with a boy or with a petty indigenous functionary, through a fragment of a newspaper discussed among friends, there reaches the villager an attenuated echo of the dreams which caress certain of the town-dwellers; he hears talk of emancipation of Indochina and now and then he pricks up his ears at the announcement of land reform.

AOM, Service de liaison avec les originaires de territoires de la France d'outre-mer, ser. III, 56, "Le Communisme et les colonies" (1927). Translated and quoted in Geoffrey Gunn, "Road through the Mountains: Vietnamese Communist Power in the Lao Struggle for National Independence: 1901–1954" (Ph.D. diss., Monash University, Sept. 1983), 193.

36. Dang Thai Mai, "The Intelligentsia and the August Revolution," *Vietnam Courier* (Hanoi), Nov. 1980, 14.

37. *Luc Tinh Tan Van* (Saigon), 24 June 1940, as quoted in Tam Vu [Tran Van Giau], *Cuoc Khoi Nghia Nam Ky* [The Southern Region Uprising] (Hanoi, 1960), 23.

flag frantically before the victorious Germans, betraying allies, and bluffing some colonies into swearing fidelity to the Vichy puppets. Better for colonial "children" to abandon their "mother," one such poem concluded bluntly.[38] Three months later, even anticolonialist Vietnamese were flabbergasted at the ease with which Japanese troops landed at Do Son, then moved into Haiphong without a single casualty, forcing the French to turn over valuable installations, equipment, and supplies.[39] One year later, it was the turn of Vietnamese believers in the Soviet Union to agonize about German armies sweeping eastward through Byelorussia and Ukraine; in Hanoi, however, two prominent noncommunist intellectuals, Nguyen Van To and Nguyen Van Luyen, made a point of predicting that Moscow would not fall to the Nazis.[40]

Viewing events in 1940–44, older Vietnamese intellectuals inevitably made comparisons with Indochina's fate in World War I. Both conflicts put a premium on native talent, yet simultaneously caused the French to feel less secure, more inclined to suppress opposition. If anything, the larger numbers of educated Vietnamese pushing for concessions, the French trauma over German occupation of the métropole, the greater physical isolation of Indochina, and the distasteful necessity of sharing the colony with the Japanese made these tendencies more pronounced in World War II. Remembering 1914–18, knowledgeable observers could not help but smile wryly at French efforts to mobilize indigenous support, complete with promises of eventual self-rule within the framework of the French empire.[41] Once France was no longer in danger, both opportunities and promises might well vanish. Because of that prior experience, and because Vietnamese intellectuals in 1940 understood more about international affairs, French politics, and the nature of colonial rule than their parents had done, even many of those who benefited directly

---

38. Tran Huy Lieu, "Phong Trao Cach Mang Viet Nam qua Tho Van" [The Vietnamese Revolutionary Movement Seen in Poetry], *Nghien Cuu Lich Su* (Hanoi) 29 (8-1961): 14–15.

39. *CMCD*, 8:21. As noted in chapter 1, the French did offer brief resistance at the Sino-Indochina frontier. Vietnamese were stunned subsequently to see a trainload of casualties arrive in Hanoi.

40. Le Quang Dao et al., *Mot Chang Duong Van Hoa* [A Segment of the Cultural Road] (Hanoi, 1985), 83, 139, 151–52. There were lively debates among political prisoners as to whether Germany or the Soviet Union would win the war. See, e.g., *Lich Su Dang Cong San Viet Nam Tinh Song Be* [History of the Vietnam Communist Party in Song Be Province], ed. Nguyen Ba Tho, vol. 1, *1930–1945* (Ho Chi Minh City [?], 1989), 165.

41. David G. Marr, *Vietnamese Tradition on Trial, 1920–1945* (Berkeley and Los Angeles, 1981), 5–6, 63–64, 152–53.

from French wartime concessions remained skeptical of the postwar implications.

Japanese Approaches to the Vietnamese

Meanwhile, the Japanese also sought to influence the inhabitants of Indochina in their own behalf. Although Tokyo did not wish to undermine French capacities to maintain internal order, it remained committed to "Asia for the Asiatics" and allowed civilian and military personnel to organize projects designed to convince Indochinese of Japanese superiority and the longer-term merits of participation in the Greater East Asia Co-Prosperity Sphere. Japanese-language classes were opened in all major towns.[42] Films were shown to rural as well as urban audiences.[43] The Japanese Embassy published a Vietnamese-language magazine titled *Dong A* [East Asia]. Books on judo, Japanese Buddhism, and the Japanese national character were translated into Vietnamese and cleared for distribution by colonial censors.[44] Professors, religious dignitaries, musicians, painters, and movie stars arrived periodically from Tokyo, making public appearances at cultural centers established in Hanoi, Saigon, and Hue. A few Vietnamese journalists, Buddhist priests, and artists were selected to visit Japan.[45] Japanese personnel opened two small hospitals in Hanoi and Saigon for native patients. Gifts of medicine, food, and money from the home islands to ill or injured Vietnamese received wide publicity.[46]

Although Indochina's radio stations remained under French jurisdiction, the Japanese eventually gained the right to broadcast occasional programs in local languages. One can imagine the ire of French censors when they heard the following exhortation in Vietnamese:

> You must realize that Asians are the most civilized peoples in the world. Asia possesses the wealth of the world which can be utilized to fight our common enemies. Remember what happened to Haiphong, Hanoi and other cities of Tonkin which were bombed by enemy planes. Don't you like to be independent? Do you like your country enslaved by the Anglo-Americans?

42. *PJI*, Radio Tokyo (in Japanese), 5 and 12 Apr. 1943, 2 Mar. and 7 May 1944. Radio Tokyo (in English), 27 July 1943, 8 Apr. 1944. Radio Tokyo (in French), 27 Dec. 1943.

43. *PJI*, Radio Tokyo (in Japanese), 28 Oct. 1943.

44. *PJI*, Radio Tokyo (in English), 19 Oct. 1942. Radio Tokyo (in Japanese), 18 Sept. 1943, 9 Dec. 1944.

45. *PJI*, Radio Tokyo (in Japanese), 26 Oct. 1942, 6 Jan. and 2 Mar. 1944. Radio Tokyo (in English), 13 Dec. 1944.

46. *CMCD*, 9:18–19.

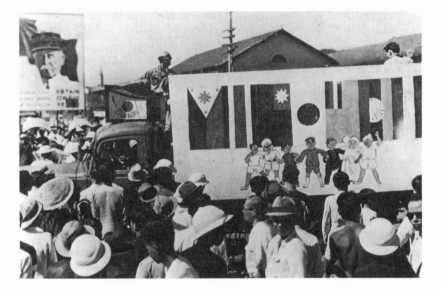

Figure 9.   A Japanese sound truck making the rounds of Saigon, sporting the flags of Greater East Asia Co-Prosperity Sphere members. Note the competing billboard dedicated to Marshal Pétain in the background. Reproduced from J. M. Pedrazzani, *La France en Indochine de Catroux à Sainteny*. Courtesy of Flammarion.

> No. Your mind is better than [that of] an animal, so you must help Japan fight the enemy.[47]

Most of the time the French managed to prevent such outbursts, leading one Japanese broadcaster to complain on the air about the "inconvenient circumstances" in Indochina as compared with occupied areas.[48]

Besides such public efforts, the Japanese pinpointed Vietnamese groups deserving more discreet cultivation. Already in 1939 they possessed a covert network of informants owing allegiance to Prince Cuong De, recruited by Matsushita Mitsuhiro, a merchant long resident in Indochina.[49] However, this network lost much of its effectiveness in late 1940, when widespread rumors of Cuong De's triumphant return to head an independent state were dashed by the Franco-Japanese accord. After the Japanese

---

47. *PJI*, Radio Saigon (in Vietnamese), 6 Dec. 1943.
48. *PJI*, Radio Saigon (in Japanese), 13 Dec. 1943.
49. For Prince Cuong De's earlier activities, see David G. Marr, *Vietnamese Anticolonialism, 1885–1925* (Berkeley and Los Angeles, 1971), 102, 105, 126–27, 141, 154–55, 216–17, 223–24, 236–38.

South China Army abandoned most of its Vietnamese auxiliaries, Cuong De was forced to return to Tokyo, where he met occasional visitors from the homeland and continued to encourage them to prepare for Japanese liberation.[50] Whatever their motives, some Vietnamese in sensitive positions continued to provide useful information to Japanese agent handlers. It was a native member of the colonial army who in late 1944 gave the Japanese incontrovertible evidence of the French secretly taking instructions from the Allied enemy.[51] Just prior to the 9 March takeover, Vietnamese in the colonial PTT may have sabotaged or delayed certain key French telegraphic communications.[52] In the midst of the coup, General Mordant was stunned to discover that one of his own servants was a spy for the Japanese.[53]

Generally speaking, the Japanese found more friends among Vietnamese religious organizations (excluding the Catholics) than among the secular political parties or publishing coteries. This was especially true in Cochinchina, where a variety of mystics and mediums openly predicted the demise of French colonial rule and Japanese support for Vietnamese independence, moral regeneration, and prosperity. Taking advantage of this favorable climate, Matsushita obtained from Prince Cuong De formal recognition as emissary to the eclectic Cao Dai Church, which claimed over a million members. When the French heard that Cao Dai leaders had professed fidelity to Cuong De, they first withdrew Matsushita's residence privileges, then in August 1940 raided the largest Cao Dai temple, in Tay Ninh.[54] A year later the French arrested the Cao Dai "pope," Pham Cong Tac, and five other church dignitaries, packing them aboard the *Dumont d'Urville*, one of the last Vichy ships permitted by the British to sail the Indian Ocean. The prisoners were sequestered in the Comoros Islands off Madagascar for the next five years.[55]

50. Tung Lam, *Cuoc Doi Cach Mang Cuong De* [The Revolutionary Life of Cuong De] (Saigon, 1957), 140.

51. Tsuchihashi, "Furansugun o busō kaijo," 156.

52. Sabattier, *Le Destin de l'Indochine*, 154.

53. Eugène Mordant, *Au Service de la France en Indochine, 1941–1945* (Saigon, 1950), 75.

54. Interview with Matsushita Mitsuhiro, Saigon, 2 June 1967. French treatment of Matsushita produced media indignation in Japan. See, e.g., Hayashi Kyujiro, "Glimpses of the South Sea Region," *Contemporary Japan* 9, no. 10 (Oct. 1940): 1296. Matsushita was allowed to return to Indochina in 1942.

55. Ralph B. Smith, "The Japanese Period in Indochina and the Coup of 9 March 1945," *Journal of Southeast Asian Studies* (cited below as *JSEAS*) 9, no. 2 (Sept. 1978): 273. Vu Ngu Chieu, "Political and Social Change," 131–32, 210–12. Nguyen Ky Nam, *Hoi Ky*, 101–5.

As the Indochina authorities continued to hound other Cao Dai dignitaries, however, the Japanese began to offer shelter. By February 1943, a
mutually beneficial relationship existed: the Japanese endeavored to protect
selected Cao Dai leaders from French wrath in exchange for regular intelligence reports and provision of thousands of Cao Dai laborers for
Japanese military installations.[56] Cao Dai leaders also pressed the Japanese
for military training and weapons, but these requests were politely ignored.
Eventually, in 1944, the three thousand Cao Dai workers at the Japanese
shipyard in Saigon began to receive parade drill and basic tactical instruction from Imperial Navy personnel, but still no firearms. This was sufficient
encouragement for provincial Cao Dai leaders to enroll thirty thousand
more youths for military service whenever the opportunity arose.[57]

The Japanese also established contact with members of the Hoa Hao, a
Buddhist reform movement sweeping the southwestern provinces of Cochinchina. In 1942, the Kenpeitai liberated Huynh Phu So, the charismatic
founder of the Hoa Hao, just as the French were transferring him from
detention in Bac Lieu to distant Laos. From a well-guarded building in
Saigon, the "Mad Monk" proceeded to disseminate prophesies of dam-
nation for nonbelievers and independence for Vietnam, much to the fury
of the French, who had to be content with striking at his disciples in the
countryside.[58]

Japanese contacts with secular Vietnamese intellectuals tended to be the
responsibility of junior diplomats and a variety of free-lance journalists or
"private consultants." One of the most interesting figures was Komatsu
Kiyoshi, a middle-aged writer deeply influenced by association with André
Gide and André Malraux in Paris during the 1920s.[59] He projected firm

56. Jayne Werner, "The Cao Dai: The Politics of a Vietnamese Syncretic
Religious Movement" (Ph.D. diss., Cornell University, 1976), 212–34. Tran Quang
Vinh, "Lich Su Dao Cao Dai trong thoi ky Phuc Quoc" [History of the Cao Dai
Religion in the Period of National Restoration] (MS provided to me by the author,
Saigon, 1967).

57. Werner, "Cao Dai," 234–40. Devillers, *Histoire*, 94–95. A few Cao Dai
leaders skeptical of Japanese intentions, or simply wishing to sustain contacts with
both sides, took part in Allied espionage activities. Gilbert David, *Chroniques
secrètes d'Indochine (1928–1946)*, vol. 1 (Paris, 1994), 108–10, 154–61.

58. A. M. Savani, "Notes sur le Phat Giao Hoa Hao" (mimeograph, Saigon [?],
1951), 1–21. Hue-Tam Ho Tai, *Millenarianism and Peasant Politics in Vietnam*
(Cambridge, Mass., 1983), 115–28.

59. Komatsu advocated French behaviorism in Japanese literary circles after
returning to Tokyo in 1931. He was back in Paris when the Germans arrived in 1940,
promoted Prince Cuong De's cause in Tokyo in 1941–42, and departed for Indochina
with the blessing of the Ministry of Foreign Affairs in early 1943. Sources differ

anticolonialist and antifascist opinions, convincing many Vietnamese listeners of Tokyo's intention to remove the French and foster Vietnamese independence.[60] However, Komatsu was considered a deadly opponent by some ICP activists because of his alleged capacity to turn patriotic intellectuals away from revolutionary commitment.[61] Another indefatigable proselytizer was Komaki Oomi, the recipient of a Paris law degree and an early admirer of Henri Barbusse who was active in Tokyo's Marxist circles during the 1920s but then compelled by dramatically changing political circumstances to put his language skills at the service of a series of diplomats, businessmen, and military commanders. By 1944, Komaki headed the Hanoi office of the Japan Cultural Institute (Nihon Bunka Kaikan), among other things helping to establish a Vietnamese writers' association called the Today Society (Konnichi-sha).[62] It must have been difficult for Vietnamese intellectuals to evaluate Japanese like Komatsu and Komaki, who clearly remained passionately Francophile in literary and philosophical terms, condemned the vast disparity between French ideals and colonial

---

as to whether Komatsu also visited Indochina in 1941. Masaya Shiraishi, "La Présence japonaise en Indochine (1940–1945)," in *L'Indochine française, 1940–1945*, ed. Paul Isoart (Paris, 1982), 222. Kiyoko Kurusu Nitz, "Independence without Nationalists? The Japanese and Vietnamese Nationalism during the Japanese Period, 1940–45," *JSEAS* 15, no. 1 (Mar. 1984): 115, 119; *Gendai sakka jiten* [Contemporary Authors Dictionary], ed. Yoshida Kirō (Tokyo, 1973), 162; *Dai jinmei jiten* [Great Biographical Dictionary], 10 vol. (Tokyo, 1953–55), 299; *Nihon jinmei daijiten: Gendai* [Japan Great Biographical Dictionary: Contemporary Era] (Tokyo, 1979), 328–29.

60. Interview with Ho Huu Tuong, Saigon, 3 Mar. 1967. From June 1944 on, *Trung Bac Chu Nhat* (Hanoi) serialized a novel by Komatsu about an "Annamese" youth educated in France who upon return regains his self-consciousness as an "East Asian." *PJI*, Radio Tokyo (in Japanese), 10 July 1944.

61. Hoc Phi, "Dom Lua ban dau" [Opening Tongues of Flame], in Le Quang Dao et al., *Mot Chang Duong Van Hoa*, 138, 160.

62. Nitz, "Independence," 116, 118–19; *Nihon shakai undō jinmei jiten* [Who's Who of Japanese Social Movements], 251; *Konsaisu jinmei jiten* [Concise Biographical Dictionary], ed. Ueda Masaaki (Tokyo, 1990), 469. Komaki had more prestigious literary credentials than Komatsu and a more radical past to live down. His 1920s journal, *Tane maku hito* [The Sower of Seeds], played an important role in disseminating Communist Third International policies in Japan. In early 1927, he was scheduled to attend the widely publicized Pan-Pacific Anti-Imperialism Conference in Canton, which had to be cancelled owing to Chiang Kai-shek's violent coup against the Chinese Communist Party. Between 1929 and 1939, Komaki worked for the Turkish Embassy in Tokyo. He arrived in Indochina in August 1939, serving as troubleshooter for Japanese entrepreneurs and officials in their dealings with the French. What individuals like Komaki and Komatsu said and did in Indochina, especially in relation to Vietnamese contacts, deserves further research.

practice, yet drew their pay and presumably received instructions from a militarist Japanese dictatorship that maintained an accord with Vichy and Governor-General Decoux.

In 1943, however, it began to look as if Japan might force political changes favorable to its Vietnamese friends. The Vietnam National Restoration League was revived and enlarged; when necessary, leaders got official employment cards or Japanese military uniforms from the Kenpeitai to enable them to move around and convene meetings without fear of arrest by the Sûreté. Most trusted by the Japanese was the Vietnam Patriotic Party (Viet Nam Ai Quoc Dang), an affiliate of the league's. One of its leaders, Vu Dinh Dy, traveled to Tokyo to meet Prince Cuong De and discuss formation of a government in exile.[63] Not surprisingly, rumors spread throughout Indochina of impending Japanese action against the French. As mentioned earlier, Governor-General Decoux decided to call the Japanese bluff, launching police sweeps against Vietnamese known to be associating with the Japanese. Much to the chagrin of Restoration League members and their Japanese contacts, the Japanese authorities refused to retaliate, instead merely offering refuge to some of those who had not been picked up by the Sûreté. Four Vietnamese employees of the Kenpeitai asked bluntly why Japan was so concerned about the interests of a "handful of Frenchmen," as opposed to "twenty-five million Indochinese." In their opinion, Annam deserved to be returned to those Annamites "who possess the heart and the energy necessary to participate in the grand offensive that Japan would not fail to launch unceasingly against the Anglo-Americans."[64] In November 1943, when Domei News Agency featured stories of a Greater East Asia Assembly in Tokyo, opened by Prime Minister Tōjō Hideki and including such Southeast Asian personalities as Prince Wan Watthayakon of Thailand, José Laurel of the Philippines, and Dr. Ba Maw of Burma, league members bitterly noted the absence of any reference to Indochina in general or Vietnam in particular.[65] In the opinion of the Indochina Army com-

63. Vu Ngu Chieu, "Political and Social Change," 53–56, 144, 146–47. Shiraishi Masaya, "Vietnam under the Japanese Presence and the August Revolution," in *1945 in South-East Asia*, Part 2 (London, 1985), 4–5, and "The Background to the Formation of the Tran Trong Kim Cabinet in April 1945: Japanese Plans for Governing Vietnam," in *Indochina in the 1940s and 1950s*, ed. Shiraishi Takashi and Furuta Motoo (Ithaca, N.Y., 1992), 117.

64. Undated *renseignements* (reports) of Nguyen Duy Que, Nguyen Duc Kinh, Hong Phong, and Bui Kien, in AOM, INF, GF 67. Mention of particular events in the text allows one to date this document to the second half of 1943.

65. Nguyen Ky Nam, *Hoi Ky*, 176–80. Once again the league was in a shambles. For contrasts with the situation in Burma, the Netherlands East Indies,

mander, General Eugène Mordant, Japan lost the opportunity to win over the Annamites to its cause.[66]

The continuation of French administration in Indochina almost surely saved tens, perhaps hundreds of thousands of Vietnamese, Cambodians, and Lao from being rounded up by the Japanese and transported to other parts of Southeast Asia as "laborers in the war effort" (*romusha*).[67] From late 1943 on, as many as three hundred thousand Indonesian laborers were shipped to distant locations, with perhaps one-half dying as a result of appalling conditions at the work sites. Sukarno and certain other Indonesian nationalist leaders actively assisted the Japanese in securing laborers[68] —a role Vietnamese nationalists, if placed in a similar position by the Japanese, might have found it equally difficult to avoid.

Privately, Japanese officials continued to disagree among themselves about what kind of regime ought to be established if it became desirable or necessary to present an ultimatum to Governor-General Decoux. Members of the Greater East Asia Ministry argued vehemently that any mobilization of the peoples of Indochina against Allied attack required the granting of some form of independence. This position had strong support in the Foreign Ministry as well, although some of the senior diplomats working in Indochina disagreed, either because they sensed the war was lost, and hence believed it foolhardy to infuriate the Gaullists by abrogating French sovereignty entirely, or simply because postultimatum administration would be less onerous if the French civilian infrastructure continued to function.[69] Although growing fears of an Allied invasion of Indochina eventually shattered the consensus in the imperial armed forces favoring continuation of the Franco-Japanese accord, that did not necessarily translate into support for native self-government. Rather than attempt any

---

and Malaya, see *Japan in Asia, 1942–1945*, ed. William H. Newell (Singapore, 1981).

66. Mordant, *Au Service de la France*, 47–48.

67. This is not to say that Indochinese avoided Japanese transportation entirely. In a personal communication (Jan. 1991), Anthony S. Reid reports the inclusion of the names of Vietnamese workers on a commemorative plaque on a monument erected by the Japanese in 1944 to those who died constructing the Burma railway.

68. Theodore Friend, *The Blue-Eyed Enemy: Japan against the West in Java and Luzon, 1942–1945* (Princeton, 1988), 162–66. Benedict R. O'G. Anderson, *Java in a Time of Revolution: Occupation and Resistance, 1944–1946* (Ithaca, N.Y., 1972), 13.

69. Interview with Nishimura Kumao, Tokyo, 27 Nov. 1967. Interview with Yokoyama Masayuki, Tokyo, 16 Nov. 1967. Shiraishi, "Background," 121–27.

experiments at such a risky moment, most high-ranking officers favored retention of the existing colonial structure where possible, and establishment of military rule where necessary.[70]

Nonetheless, within the Imperial Army there also existed a group favoring abrogation of French sovereignty and the granting of independence to native rulers, who would then be expected to show their gratitude by supporting Japanese military operations. This position was argued most persistently by Lieutenant Colonel Hayashi Hidezumi, a Kenpeitai officer who first arrived in Indochina in early 1944, prepared a detailed plan on postcoup arrangements by December, and apparently even dared to criticize the contrary plans of his new commanding officer, General Tsuchihashi, in the presence of Japanese civilian officials.[71]

During January and February 1945, as telegrams arguing various positions continued to be exchanged between Tokyo and Saigon, the Kenpeitai and several covert units stepped up activities among Vietnamese dissidents, again fueling rumors of imminent independence. It remains unclear to what degree these special operations were known to superior officers—being justified by the need to gather tactical intelligence prior to moving against the French—and to what degree they occurred quite separately, with different motives in mind.[72]

On 1 February 1945, when the Supreme War Leadership Council in Tokyo affirmed the necessity of presenting the Indochina authorities with an ultimatum, it still deferred any decision about administrative arrangements if the French decided to resist and had to be neutralized. As with several prior policy documents, vague mention was made of "Annam, etc."

70. Shiraishi Masaya and Furuta Motoo, "Taiheiyō sensōki Nihon no tai-Indoshina seisaku: Sono futatsu no tokuisei o megutte" [Japan's Policy toward Indochina during the Pacific War: Concerning Two Peculiarities], *Ajia kenkyū* 23, no. 3 (1976): 14–16. Tanemura Sakō, *Daihon'ei kimitsu nisshi* [Imperial Headquarters' Secret War Diaries] (Tokyo, 1952), 192.

71. Shiraishi and Furuta, "Taiheiyō sensōki no Nihon no tai-Indoshina seisaku," 20, 22–23. Shiraishi, "Background," 119–21. Hayashi's plan contained some contradictions, specifying, for example, that Japan would continue to "look after" powers held by the colonial governor-general, which gave Tokyo room for maneuver on the issue of sovereignty.

72. In a 1962 interview with Tsuchihashi, Kiyoko Nitz asked about the "Yasutai" unit in particular. Tsuchihashi replied that if such a unit existed, it had been organized without his knowledge or permission. Nitz, "Independence," 126. It is possible that Tsuchihashi knew of the unit by another name and gave it a mission different from the one that participants, including Hayashi, considered important.

gaining independence at a time yet to be determined.[73] Not least of all, the Imperial Army was concerned that independence might give the civilian ambassador in Indochina and the Ministry of Foreign Affairs more influence than they deserved. In the following weeks, the issue of independence became submerged in a bureaucratic dispute over which Japanese organization should take responsibility for civil affairs in the event of French internment. Eventually, a compromise was struck whereby General Tsuchihashi was assigned Decoux's position of governor-general, while most other top positions held by Frenchmen went to diplomats. The monarchs of Annam, Cambodia, and Luang Prabang would be urged to declare independence "spontaneously," a fiction ironically aimed more at deflecting anticipated Soviet ire at Japan's breach of a neutrality pact than at impressing the peoples of Indochina.[74]

Lieutenant Colonel Hayashi had assumed that Prince Cuong De would replace Bao Dai as emperor of Annam. He also had groomed Ngo Dinh Diem, a stiff-necked Catholic former mandarin, as replacement for Pham Quynh, the Francophile prime minister.[75] Both of these anticipated changes had become common gossip among Vietnamese intellectuals by mid 1944,[76] forcing Diem to request Japanese protection from almost certain arrest by the Sûreté. Diem was driven by auto from Hue to Tourane dressed in army uniform, flown to Saigon, and placed in a Japanese military hospital.[77] In

73. Kashima Heiwa Kenkyūjohen, *Nihon Gaikōshi* [A History of Diplomacy in Japan] (Tokyo, 1971) (cited below as *NGS*), 24:210–14. IMTFE exhibit 661 (document 2664A).

74. Shiraishi, "La Présence," 231–33. Shiraishi, "Background," 128–33. Shiraishi and Furuta, "Taiheiyō Sensōki no Nihon no tai-Indoshina seisaku," 23, 25–26. Tanemura, *Daihon'ei Kimitsu Nisshi*, 216. Smith, "Japanese Period," 278–79, 282–85. As we shall see, following the 9 March coup, Tokyo did not formally recognize Vietnam's independence, but rather the aspiration to be independent.

75. French disapproval of Ngo Dinh Diem was symbolized by his exclusion from the 1943 *Souverains et notabilités* volume, cited above, while four of his five brothers rated inclusion. Japanese diplomats in Hue had developed a close relationship with Diem. Interview with Urabe Kiyoji, Tokyo, 15 Nov. 1967. See also Shiraishi, "La Présence," 224–26. As early as November 1944, Truong Chinh, secretary-general of the Indochinese Communist Party, denounced Diem in print as a lackey of the Japanese. Minh Tranh, "Cach Mang Thang Tam va Khang Chien la mot cuoc Cach Mang Quan Chung duoi su Lanh Dao cua Dang" [The August Revolution and Resistance Were a Mass Revolution under the Party's Leadership], *Van Su Dia* (Hanoi), no. 44 (9-1958): 1, citing *Co Giai Phong*, no. 8 (Nov. 1944).

76. Interview with Hoang Xuan Han, Paris, 3 Nov. 1984.

77. Nitz, "Independence," 117, based on a 1962 interview with Ishida Masao, who was assistant consul in Hue 1943–45. See also Komatsu Kiyoshi, *Betonamu* [Vietnam] (Tokyo, 1955), 238.

January 1945, despite Hayashi's promptings, General Tsuchihashi decided that Bao Dai should remain on the throne in the interests of "social order," and in late February he bluntly rejected a proposal that Cuong De be flown from Tokyo to Saigon.[78] This decision would confuse most Vietnamese and leave the National Restoration League again demoralized at its moment of seeming triumph.

Vietnamese Attitudes toward the Japanese

On the eve of General Tsuchihashi's *coup de force*, the predominant mood among Vietnamese was anticipation of dramatic changes but not particular support for the Japanese versus the French. In 1940–41, the appearance of Japanese troops on city streets and country roads had deeply impressed many people. Above all, they noted the crisp, haughty presence of the officers in their light khaki uniforms, who invariably toted samurai swords. They winced at the barked commands of tough Japanese noncommissioned officers, admired the instant obedience of the enlisted men. By comparison, the French colonial army seemed flabby and ill-disciplined.[79] Partly it was a matter of style: the Japanese military summoned visions of the epic *Tale of Three Kingdoms*, of posturing generals in classical opera, of heroic Vietnamese warriors overcoming the Mongols. A Japanese officer prancing skillfully down the street on a horse evoked admiration, despite the anachronism of the scene.[80] Even the perceived tendency of the Japanese to sense a slight where none was intended, and summarily to execute individuals guilty of relatively minor infringements, fitted the traditional military mold. Bushidō was not new to Vietnam, although the particular Japanese passion for worshipping their emperor did seem peculiar. The Japanese presence even helped to spark renewed interest in classical learning among young Vietnamese who had disparaged it previously.[81]

---

78. Tsuchihashi Yūichi, "Tsuchihashi nikki" [Tsuchihashi Diary] (unpaginated MS located in the Japanese Self-Defense Agency Archives). The handwriting is not Tsuchihashi's, and there is reason to believe certain portions were deleted. Ton That Phuong kindly gave me a copy of this manuscript. See also Shiraishi and Furuta, "Taikeiyō Sensōki no Nihon no tai-Indoshina seisaku," 21–22. Hayashi's redrafted plan, sent to Tokyo in late January, obediently reflected Tsuchihashi's views on retaining Bao Dai.

79. Discussion with Nguyen Phu Phong, Paris, 22 Oct. 1983. As a boy in Da Nang in 1944–45, Phong observed Japanese behavior closely.

80. Do Thuc Vinh, *Mua Ao Anh* [Season of Mirages] (Saigon, 1962), 92.

81. Nghiem Ke To, *Viet-Nam Mau Lua* [Vietnam in Blood and Flames] (Saigon, 1954), 20.

Besides style, the Japanese exuded power. Vietnamese watched in awe as Imperial Army tanks, trucks, and artillery pieces rumbled through Indochina. Sleek Japanese bombers and fighter aircraft made prewar French biplanes and Potez transports look quaint indeed. Japanese ships soon dominated the harbors of Haiphong, Da Nang, Cam Ranh, and Saigon. People crowded in eagerly to view Japanese newsreels that portrayed victories over the white man at Pearl Harbor, Singapore, Corregidor, and Rangoon. They also saw Japanese citizens in the homeland stretching every sinew to support the battlefront: bustling factory assembly lines, hardworking peasants, trains filled with eager young recruits, mass demonstrations of children celebrating the emperor's birthday. In Indochina itself, groups of curious Vietnamese would observe Japanese soldiers cleaning their rifles, practicing bayonet drill, operating field radios. Soldiers sometimes gave sweets to children, cigarettes to adults. When approaching a Vietnamese home, they accepted a cup of tea courteously, respected the family altar, and left without appropriating anything. Stories circulated of Japanese siding with Vietnamese in street arguments with *colons*, even to the point of slapping the Frenchmen.[82] Although such incidents must have been very rare, French officials in the countryside as well as the cities noted uncomfortably how any mention of Japanese victories over Europeans produced expressions of satisfaction among Vietnamese.[83] Being de facto partners of the Japanese, the French could hardly retaliate.

Vietnamese also wondered, however, why the seemingly invincible Japanese had neglected to eliminate the French colonialists as they had the British, Dutch, and Americans elsewhere in Asia. Indeed, the Franco-Japanese accord seemed to make a mockery of Japanese claims to be siding with fellow Asians. Stories circulated of Japanese refusal to protect individuals who supported their cause. Dr. Ton That Tung, the colony's most prominent native surgeon, operated on a wounded Restoration League follower, then was shocked to see colonial troops seize the patient and take him off for execution.[84] Gradually other, more sinister stories began to spread, about Japanese brutality to Vietnamese, detention of individuals by the Kenpeitai, torture, and beheadings. Some Vietnamese wondered if the

---

82. Ibid., 20–21.

83. AOM, INF, Résident Supérieur Tonkin F 70 (7), as quoted in Vu Ngu Chieu, "Political and Social Change," 232.

84. Ton That Tung, *Duong vao Khoa Hoc cua toi* [My Path to Science] (Hanoi, 1978), 41–42.

Japanese might prove to be more oppressive than the French.[85] As word circulated of Japanese defeats in the Pacific, the image of Bushidō invincibility also began to lose its luster. Perhaps Vietnamese ambiguity toward the Japanese is best expressed in a short story by Nguyen Hong in which a group of arrogant imperial soldiers scare and offend people gathered at a public water hydrant, yet one soldier, quite ugly in appearance, goes over to hug a child, whose mother stands petrified until the innocence and humanity of the gesture become clear.[86]

Rediscovery

Not all Vietnamese political and intellectual activity during the 1941–44 period focused on the French and the Japanese. Some individuals preferred to throw themselves into writing popular children's stories and literacy primers, or organizing private classes for workers and peasants. Others continued to publish on the theme of modernization, which had dominated prewar discourse. The Hanoi weekly *Thanh Nghi* (Clear Opinion), for example, projected a lively message of national renaissance—stressing science, technology, industry, education, and public health. Although it proved difficult for anyone to ascertain in detail what was happening beyond Indochina's borders, most intellectuals sensed that the world war would change their lives forever. Already in early 1941, while accepting that French weakness vis-à-vis the Germans and Japanese could not quickly be translated into dramatic political change, some argued that the eventual end of global conflict would bring major new opportunities for Vietnam. In June 1944, just after the Allied landings in Normandy, Vu Dinh Hoe, a regular contributor to *Thanh Nghi*, accepted that only "Heaven" knew exactly when the country's chance would arise, but stressed that it was within human capacity to prepare to seize that moment whenever it came.[87]

85. Doan Quoc Sy, *Ba Sinh Huong Lua* [Three Generations in the Flames] (Saigon, 1962), 36–37. The ICP accused the Japanese of grabbing food in markets, confiscating property without compensation, and forcing peasants to grow industrial crops. *CMCD*, 8:83–84.

86. Nguyen Hong, "Buoi Chieu Xam" [Gray Afternoon], in *Tuyen Tap Nguyen Hong* [Selected Works of Nguyen Hong], vol. 1 (Hanoi, 1983), 363–71. Originally published in *Tien Phong* (Hanoi), no. 1 (Sept. 1945). It is interesting to compare Vietnamese and Thai responses to the Japanese during World War II. For an assessment of Thai attitudes, see E. Bruce Reynolds, "Aftermath of Alliance: The Wartime Legacy in Thai-Japanese Relations," *JSEAS* 21, no. 1 (Mar. 1990): 66–87.

87. Cited in Pierre Brocheux, "Le Revue « Thanh Nghi » : Un Groupe d'intellectuals vietnamiens confrontés aux problèmes de leur nation (1941–1945)," *Revue d'histoire moderne et contemporaine*, 3-1987, 318.

For other thoughtful Vietnamese, 1941–44 was more a time to take stock, to evaluate what had been said and done during the previous two decades, perhaps to look much further back in a reassessment of Vietnam's heritage. Although radicals condemned this tendency as diversionary or defeatist, the majority of intellectuals felt that such a reappraisal was overdue and might well put everyone in a better position to grapple with future challenges. Vietnamese intellectuals who previously had disparaged tradition and mocked the behavior of their country cousins now discovered much to admire on both fronts. They sought out elderly Confucian-educated scholars who could help them read Chinese and *nom* character texts. They revisited native villages, collected folklore and folk poetry, listened to peasants reminisce—and used this information to write short stories, poetry, or descriptive essays. Colonial censors could afford to be lenient, as such writings rarely touched on current affairs and seemed to conform with both the cultural conservatism of Vichy and the benign attitude of the governor-general toward local patriotism. Indeed, the French got into the spirit of things by sponsoring literary competitions on traditional "Annamite" themes, by attending public commemorations of Vietnamese victories over the Chinese, and by approving Boy Scout pilgrimages to ancient historical sites. In 1943, Ernest Hoeffel, governor of Cochinchina, agreed to the proposal of a Vietnamese banker friend to open a summer camp outside Saigon that engaged young people in a variety of literary, musical, athletic, and social activities.[88] That year Hoeffel also offered the keynote speech at an anniversary observance for Nguyen Dinh Chieu (1822–88), southern Vietnam's most famous poet. Hoeffel took the opportunity to urge young people to return to Confucian moral principles and dedicate themselves to a "Franco-Vietnamese renaissance."[89]

88. Mai Van Bo, "Phong Trao Thanh Nien, Sinh Vien va Tri Thuc trong nhung Nam 40" [The Youth, Student, and Intellectual Movement in the 1940s], *Tap Chi Khoa Hoc Xa Hoi* (Ho Chi Minh City), no. 18 (4-1993), 23–24. The banker, Michel Van Vi, also secured approval from Hoeffel to establish the Cochinchina Association for the Dissemination of Quoc Ngu (Vietnamese writing system).

89. Tran Nghia, "Nhin lai Viec Su Dung Noi Dung *Luc Van Tien* duoi thoi Phap Thuoc" [Looking Back on Uses to which *Luc Van Tien* was put in the French Colonial Period], *Tap Chi Van Hoc* (Hanoi) 1-1965, 65. French attempts to appropriate Nguyen Dinh Chieu had begun when he was still alive in the late nineteenth century. A year after Hoeffel's 1943 speech, the authorities sponsored the most impressive edition of *Luc Van Tien* yet to appear, printed on quality paper that was extremely scarce by that time, including abundant footnotes, and featuring a French translation by Duong Quang Ham.

"Vietnamese tradition" became a lively polemical battleground between 1941 and 1944, perhaps the only one admissible to the censors. At one end of the spectrum, very much in tune with Governor Hoeffel, the leader of the near-defunct Constitutionalist Party, Bui Quang Chieu, complained that Vietnamese intellectuals had become too neglectful of their native land, too enamored of radical Western ideas; it was time to accept Confucius again.[90] At the other end of the spectrum, writers ignored Confucius entirely to focus on epic Vietnamese struggles against foreign aggressors, or to describe the timeless efforts of Vietnamese peasants to survive the predations of feudal rulers, landlords, moneylenders, and the elements. As always among Vietnamese intellectuals, the proper attitude to take toward China had to be debated. Covert supporters of the Viet Minh were in a particularly delicate position, as it was organizational policy to endorse the Chinese Nationalist invasion of Indochina. Their solution was to draw a sharp line between bad feudal China and "progressive" China, with special attention to the writings of Sun Yat-sen, Hu Shih, Chen Tu-hsiu, and Lu Hsün.[91] By 1944, some writers were skating close to direct criticism of French colonial policy without being heavily censored. Meanwhile, other intellectuals explored Buddhism, Taoism, Wang Yang-ming, Tagore, and a range of precolonial Vietnamese writers. A key forum was provided by the weekly journal *Tri Tan* [To Know the New], which appeared in Hanoi from 1941 to early 1945.[92]

There was a romantic thrust to intellectual activity in this period, with the popularizing, dramatizing, and idealizing of the Vietnamese past being only the most obvious component. Romanticism had also been fashionable in the 1930s, but mainly as a self-conscious imitation of the nineteenth-century French variety. Now it spread in many directions, with unexpected consequences. Thus, a poet's vague melancholy or despair over unrequited love could move quickly to passionate identification with his exploited fellow countrymen. An essayist moved by a corner of a rural landscape, the spectacle of a village marketplace, or the sights, sounds, and

90. *Tribune indochinoise* (Hanoi), 28 Sept. 1942, as quoted in Megan Cook, *The Constitutionalist Party of Cochinchina, 1930–1942: The Years of Decline* (Melbourne, 1977), 108.

91. Clandestine Viet Minh writers went even further, arguing that Vietnamese culture had its roots in China, that revolutionary currents were more advanced in China than anywhere else in Asia, and that it was a deliberate French plot to promote anti-Chinese sentiments among contemporary Vietnamese. See, e.g., *Cuu Quoc* 11-1944, 3, 7, 15–16, 19–20.

92. Marr, *Vietnamese Tradition*, 279–81.

smells of the countryside could rapidly expand his vision to the entire nation.[93] Students of human character argued vehemently that adversity tempered men and women, made them great, enabled them to overcome fate. Moralists attacked the corruption of the Vietnamese bourgeoisie. Musicians began by concentrating on variations of sad European love songs, but then switched to a martial Western beat, created lyrics harkening back to Vietnamese battle heroes, and were amazed to find teenagers singing their tunes enthusiastically in every town.[94]

By 1944, romanticism increasingly pointed in the direction of collective action. Optimism and group sacrifice were exalted, personal introspection and caution condemned.[95] Intellectuals could either uphold their integrity and join with the progressive, vanguard elements of society or remain pen-and-ink prostitutes for the ruling class.[96] At certain junctures in history, extraordinary measures were required, pushed forward by the dictates of circumstance, not the product of quiet examination.[97] Such ideas clearly animated many of the participants in youth and sport organizations: even as Vietnamese chanted slogans, flexed their muscles, and kept neat and clean ostensibly for the French Indochina Federation or the Greater East Asia Co-Prosperity Sphere, they thought of ancient struggles against the Mongols and wondered when their own patriotic opportunity would arise. In the meantime, citizens could struggle against individual frailty and try to improve their health, strength, and martial prowess— and thus their ability to deal with external reality. Strong individuals made strong countries. Young Vietnamese who previously had looked for role models to Confucian literati, priests, or (more recently) intelligentsia

93. Nguyen Khac Vien, *Glimpses of Vietnamese Literature* (Hanoi, 1977), 117–18.

94. Tu Ngoc, "Nhan xet chung ve nen Am Nhac Viet-Nam tu 1930 den nay va anh huong qua lai giua no va Van Hoc" [General Observations on Vietnamese Music from 1930 to the Present and Its Interaction with Literature], *Tap Chi Van Hoc* (Hanoi), 5-1970, 29–30.

95. Dang Ngoc Tot, Duong Duc Hien, and Nguyen Dinh Thi, *Suc Song cua Dan Viet Nam* [The Strength to Live of the Vietnamese People] (Hanoi, 1944). Reprint of three speeches at the Hanoi University Student Union.

96. Dang Thai Mai, *Van Hoc Khai Luan* [An Introduction to Literature] (Hanoi, 1944), excerpted in *Hop Tuyen Tho Van Viet-Nam* [A Collection of Vietnamese Poetry and Prose], vol. 5, *1930–1945* (Hanoi, 1963), 489.

97. Vu Dinh Hoe et al., *Vai Van De Dong Duong* [Some Indochina Problems] (Hanoi, Feb. 1945), 171. See also Phan Anh, "Con Duong di toi Cach Mang Thang Tam cua Toi" [My Path toward the August Revolution], *Nhan Dan* (Hanoi), 21 Aug. 1960, 4; and Mai Van Bo, "Phong Trao," 24–25.

writers, now expected their paragons to combine physical skills with total emotional commitment.[98]

Apocalypse

With grim irony, the physical and moral fiber of many Vietnamese patriots was about to be challenged by that most primeval of enemies: famine. Unnoticed by all but a few administrators, the specter had been sneaking up for many years. Paddy (unmilled rice) output in Tonkin had fallen by 20 percent during the previous two decades because of gradual reductions in acreage and failure to introduce new methods of cultivation.[99] Meanwhile, Tonkin's population had expanded by at least 36 percent,[100] forcing both a reduction in per capita food intake and increasing dependence on imports of rice from Cochinchina. During 1941–44, an unknown quantity of Tonkin rice land was converted to production of industrial crops, particularly castor oil seed and jute.[101] Drought and insects reduced the spring 1944 rice crop by 19 percent compared to the previous year. Then a series of typhoons damaged the main autumn crop. Many Tonkin farmers had already realized by October that they would not bring in enough to feed their own families, much less pay taxes and sell an obligatory amount of rice to the government at ridiculously low prices. Much the same grim dilemma was emerging in the northern Annam provinces of Thanh Hoa and Nghe An.

98. In *Len Duong Thang Loi* [On the Road to Victory] (Hanoi, 1960), 135–46, Bao Dinh Giang offers a rare insight into attitude changes among rural youth of southern Vietnam.

99. Nguyen The Anh, "La Famine de 1945 au Nord-Vietnam," *Vietnam Forum* (New Haven), no. 5 (Winter–Spring 1985): 84–85. For a provocative comparison of three wartime famines, emphasizing demographic and market pressures, the deleterious role played by the state, and uneven social distribution of the costs, see Sugata Bose, "Starvation amidst Plenty: The Making of Famine in Bengal, Honan and Tonkin, 1942–45," *Modern Asian Studies* (Cambridge) 24, no. 4 (1990): 699–727.

100. Ngo Vinh Long, *Before the Revolution: The Vietnamese Peasants under the French* (Cambridge, Mass., 1973), 123, citing figures from various *Annuaires statistiques de l'Indochine*.

101. Subsequent discussions of the early 1945 famine probably overstate the deleterious effects of these crop transfers, however. Industrial crops occupied 42,546 hectares in Tonkin in 1944, according to the *Annuaire statistique de l'Indochine*, vol. 11, 1943–46, 92–93. Even assuming that all of this land was suitable for grain cultivation, its availability would have added only about 3 percent to total acreage, producing at most another 55,000 tons of paddy or equivalent. On the other hand, official figures may understate the amount of land transferred to industrial crops, especially since the Japanese sometimes bypassed the French to sign contracts and enforce compliance.

Although both French and Japanese officials were aware of the problem, no decision was made to reduce taxes or obligatory sales of rice.[102] Landowners tried to evade quotas by signing property over to their children or relatives, but the government saw through this artifice, ordering local functionaries to collect rice according to old records. Farmers also hoarded rice, causing the authorities to forbid them to store beyond fixed limits. Inspectors roamed the villages looking for caches. Peasants who in truth lacked enough rice to meet obligatory quotas either had to purchase rice at black market rates and sell it to the government at one-tenth the price or risk being sent on forced labor projects far from home.[103] The colonial system still struck fear into the hearts of most subjects, causing them to obey rules even at grave personal cost.

Divided equitably, Tonkin's 1944 official output of 1.68 million tons of paddy would have provided 171 kilograms for each of the 9,851,000 inhabitants, perhaps barely enough for everyone to survive until June 1945, when the next crop could be harvested.[104] However, both the French and the Japanese in Tonkin insisted on stockpiling substantial amounts of rice for their own future use. For example, each day between January and early March, the French sent ten or more boatloads of rice from the Tonkin Delta upriver to military depots at Phu Tho, Yen Bai, Tuyen Quang, and Thai Nguyen.[105] Presumably General Tsuchihashi took similar precautions at

102. Indeed, *CMCD*, 8:175, claims that obligatory sales quotas set by the French increased from 130,205 tons (7.4 percent of output) to 186,180 tons (11.1 percent) in 1944. See also Nguyen The Anh, "La Campagne nord-vietnamienne de la dépression économique de 1930 à la famine de 1945," *Revue française d'histoire d'outre-mer* (Paris) 74, no. 274 (1987): 52.

103. Tran Van Mai, "Ai Gay Nen Toi?" [Who Committed This Crime?], as translated in Ngo Vinh Long, *Before the Revolution*, 224–26. See also *Trung Bac Chu Nhat* (Hanoi), 1 July 1945; and Van Tao, "Qua Trinh Thanh Lap Mat Tran Viet Minh va Thang Loi cua Mat Tran trong Cach Mang Thang Tam" [The Process of Establishing the Viet Minh and Its Victory in the August Revolution], *Van Su Dia* (Hanoi), no. 43 (Aug. 1958): 7–9.

104. In this admittedly hypothetical exercise, everyone would thus get 14.17 kilograms of unmilled rice a month. However, about 5 percent needed to be taken out for seed, and an additional 10 percent might well be lost to rodents and spoilage, leaving 12.04 kilograms per capita. This would reduce to about 9.03 kilograms of rice after milling. In the past, poor families in such straitened circumstances had tended to consume at closer to their "normal" rate of 12–15 kilograms per member for seven or eight months of the year, expecting somehow to buy or borrow rice for the remaining four or five months. In early 1945, unfortunately, such a calculation could well prove fatal.

105. Jean J. Bernardini, *Sous la botte nippone* (Paris, 1971), 51–55. The author was in charge of organizing these shipments. He also describes the harsh conditions under which his Vietnamese coolies labored.

the same time, and after 9 March, he was able to appropriate the French stocks as well. In May, in anticipation of an Allied invasion, Tsuchihashi approved a plan to accumulate a minimum of six months' provisions for the Thirty-eighth Army.[106]

Any attempt at equitable distribution of scarce grain supplies was further neutralized by rapid deterioration of the civilian economy. By late 1944, commodity scarcities, transportation difficulties, the readiness of the authorities to print ever more paper money, and growing uncertainties about the future had produced uncontrollable inflation. Hoarders, speculators, and "fixers" came to dominate the economy, often in league with corrupt officials at various levels. In Tonkin and northern Annam, some big landlords and wholesale grain merchants deliberately held back large quantities of rice in anticipation of windfall profits just before the next harvest in June. Certain Tonkin plantation owners converted their rice to alcohol rather than sell it at the official price.[107] Black market operations largely overshadowed legal transactions, except for that small segment of the population authorized to present ration cards for receipt of rice and cooking oil.[108]

Between 1943 and May 1945, the price of rice on the Tonkin black market climbed at least 1,400 percent, whereas the official price was allowed to go up only 71 percent.[109] People shifted frantically to corn, yams, manioc, or beans, but soon those too became incredibly expensive or disappeared from the market. The cost of food for a working-class Hanoi family jumped 373 percent in the first three months of 1945.[110] Wage increases fell far behind such price rises; indeed, many workers found themselves being laid off

106. *War in Asia and the Pacific, 1937–1949*, ed. Donald S. Detwiler and Charles B. Burdick (New York, 1980), vol. 6, Appendix I. According to Nitz, "Independence," 129, Marshal Terauchi arranged for storage of food sufficient to feed Japanese personnel for three years. This probably refers mainly to silos constructed in western Cochinchina, although plans did exist to shift large quantities to a facility in northern Laos. The main Japanese depot in Tonkin was at Hoa Binh. It is also possible that some Tonkin rice was shipped to Japanese units in Kwangsi in 1944 and early 1945.

107. René Bauchar [René Charbonneau], *Rafales sur l'Indochine* (Paris, 1946), 100–101.

108. AOM, INF, GF 23, contains a 5 Jan. 1945 petition from clerks at René Robin Hospital explaining the current impossibility of sustaining their families and asking for ration tickets. A pen notation indicates that the request was denied or ignored.

109. *CMCD*, 8:184.

110. Fédération indochinoise, *Indices economiques indochinois: Troisième série* (Saigon, 1947), 33. Middle-class Vietnamese families in Hanoi faced a 295 percent increase. By contrast, Saigon working-class and middle-class families encountered 52 percent and 49 percent rises respectively.

because of supply disruptions and equipment failures. Government employees eligible for rice rations found the amount cut from fifteen kilograms per month in early 1943 to twelve kilograms in late 1943, ten in the spring of 1944, and nine by the end of 1944. It became impossible to survive without primitive barter arrangements, including exchange of treasured household items (chinaware, tobacco pipes, furniture, ancestral altars) for small amounts of rice. In early December 1944, wishing to avoid "alienating the population" with further increases in the price of foodstuffs, Governor-General Decoux's newly formed Indochinese Council discussed possible countermeasures.[111]

The only solution to the threat of mass famine emerging unmistakably by October 1944 would have been for the authorities to arrange emergency transport of at least 60,000 tons of rice from Cochinchina, where large surpluses had accumulated.[112] Admittedly the task was formidable. Allied aircraft had cut the long railway line between Saigon and Hanoi into numerous shorter segments, forcing portage by ferry, wagon, and gangs of coolies.[113] American submarines, air patrols, and harbor-mining operations had reduced most coastal shipping to the level of wooden-hulled junks, moving furtively at night from one inlet to another. Trucks plying Colonial Highway Route 1 northward were impeded by destroyed bridges, equipment breakdowns, and the scarcity of motor fuel.[114] As a result of all these difficulties, shipments of southern rice to Tonkin had already dropped to a mere 6,830 tons in 1944, compared to 29,700 in 1943 and 126,670 tons in 1942.[115]

---

111. Stein Tønnesson, *The Vietnamese Revolution of 1945: Roosevelt, Ho Chi Minh and de Gaulle in a World at War* (London, 1991), 292.

112. This is my estimate only. Sixty thousand tons might have kept at least a million people from starving for the five months from January to May 1945, providing of course the rice reached the right locations in time and was distributed to the most needy. News of its impending arrival might also have persuaded hoarders to put a similar quantity on the market.

113. Georges Gautier, *9 mars 1945, Hanoi au soleil de sang: La Fin de l'Indochine française* (Paris, 1978), 12–13. Both before and after the 9 March coup, provincial mandarins routinely forwarded reports of damage and casualties caused by Allied air attacks; periodic summaries can be found in the AOM, INF, GF collection.

114. The French authorities offered private trucking companies in Saigon 200 piastres per ton to carry rice northward, a mere 4 percent of the black market value in Hanoi. Considering the risks involved, and French insistence that payment be made only on delivery, few truckers volunteered. *Thanh Nghi* (Hanoi), 5 May 1945.

115. André Gaudel, *L'Indochine française en face du Japon* (Paris, 1947), 230. These figures would not include military shipments by both the French and the

Nonetheless, French and Japanese officials alike possessed the knowledge and means to reverse this grim trend had they wished. The most reliable system involved transporting supplies by oceangoing junk from Saigon to Tourane (Da Nang), using trains from Tourane to Nam Dinh, and then distributing by river junks and sampans to various parts of the Red River Delta.[116] Vietnamese workers, students, clerks, and intellectuals would have responded enthusiastically to any call to assist in moving the rice north. Neither the French nor the Japanese, however, put a high transport priority on rice to feed starving Vietnamese civilians. Both remained preoccupied with their own military logistics. In January 1945, the Japanese insisted on using two-thirds of all rail capacity for military purposes.[117] We may assume the French allocated most of the remainder to the Indochina Army. In February, the Japanese purchased a large quantity of small junks in Cochinchina, leading the French on 6 March to lower to ten tons the weight above which owners needed official permission to sell their boats. In a radio message of 8 March, General Mordant requested Paris to urge the Americans to stop bombing ports from Vinh northward because of the growing shortage of food. On the 9th, only hours before the Japanese takeover, the governor of Cochinchina sought an increase in rationed fuel allotments for local rice mills to enable them to process additional grain for shipment north.[118]

Following the takeover, Japanese officials ignored the deepening famine for at least two weeks; when they got around to acting, it was merely to reaffirm French policies. Tonkin's resident superior, Nishimura Kumao, restated the draconian 1944 rules for compulsory sale of rice, then proceeded to cajole Vietnamese subordinates as follows: "With a view to ensuring general revictualling, now under great threat, I take the liberty of directing your special attention [to this problem], in order that all producers loyally fulfill their task. I particularly count on your influence and competence to achieve a favorable outcome."[119] Nishimura also authorized the Nam Dinh provincial mandarin to take 320 tons from local warehouses and to release 613 tons of "Saigon rice" to a Japanese delegate

Japanese. By way of comparison, Annam received 60,050 tons of Cochinchina rice in 1944, compared to 104,600 in 1943, and 97,175 in 1942. *CMCD*, 8:174, citing *Bulletin économique de l'Indochine 1944*, 163.

116. Bauchar, *Rafales*, 104.
117. DGER report, 9 Mar. 1945, in AOM, INF, c. 123, d. 1108.
118. Tønnesson, *Vietnamese Revolution*, 294.
119. Nishimura to provinces and bureaux, 29 Mar. 1945, in AOM, INF, GF 61.

for immediate transport to Hanoi.[120] One month later, he queried Ambassador Yokoyama in Hue about an estimated one hundred junks that had been reported making their way up the Annam coast, yet had not arrived on schedule. Probably fearing diversion en route, Nishimura emphasized that "revictualling [of the] population administered [in] Tonkin necessitates utilization to the full of the transported tonnage."[121]

By all accounts, rural areas of Tonkin and northern Annam felt the famine earlier and more severely than cities and towns. Already in December 1944, many poor villagers had been reduced to eating ground-up rice husks, wild tubers, roots of banana trees, bark, and clover. Unusually low temperatures that winter, combined with widespread lack of cloth, put people at further risk. By the time of Tet, the Lunar New Year, in early February, thousands were dying of starvation. Whole families sometimes shut themselves up in their homes, shared the few remaining morsels, then died one by one in silence. More often, they heeded rumors of abundant grain elsewhere, sought out relatives in nearby villages, drifted along the main roads, and looked for help in district centers. After the Japanese takeover, police barricades at city entrances were abandoned, allowing tens of thousands of rural folk to wander the streets, begging pitifully, often clad in nothing but straw matting.[122] As one Vietnamese resident of Hanoi recorded in his diary: "Sounds of crying as at a funeral. Elderly twisted women, naked kids huddled against the wall or lying inside a mat, fathers and children prostrate along the road, corpses hunched up like foetuses, an arm thrust out as if to threaten. Wanted to photograph."[123] Crowds clustered near heavily guarded warehouses, hoping for even a few handfuls of grain. Although the Japanese did release some grain from captured French depots, perhaps partly to discredit the former colonial regime,[124] it seems to have been allocated mostly to urbanites.

On 20 April, Nishimura instructed public and private institutions to reduce their stockpiles by 30–50 percent. Households were ordered to limit holdings of rice to thirty-five kilograms per individual over five years of

120. Nam Dinh to *résident supérieur*, 22 Mar. 1945, in AOM, INF, GF 53; and *résident supérieur* to Nam Dinh, 26 Mar. 1945, in AOM, INF, GF 61.
121. *Résident supérieur* to Yokoyama, 26 Apr. 1945, in AOM, INF, GF 61.
122. Tang Xuan An, "Nan Doi Nam At Dau (1945)" [Famine in the Year of the Chicken (1945)] (MS), 38. Bang Ba Lan, "Doi, Doi . . ." [They Starved, They Starved . . .], *Vietnam Forum* (New Haven), no. 5 (Winter–Spring 1985): 101–7. Translation by Huynh Sanh Thong.
123. Nguyen Huy Tuong, 8 Apr., in Le Quang Dao et al., *Mot Chang Duong Van Hoa*, 125–26.
124. Bauchar, *Rafales*, 209.

age, seventeen kilograms per small child. For those possessing tickets, the public grain ration was reduced from nine to seven kilograms per month.[125] That meant that even ration-card holders had to acquire about three additional kilograms per family member on the black market, at up to seven piastres per kilogram. As many clerks were still making less than one hundred piastres per month, clearly money had to be borrowed or personal effects sold in order to survive.[126] Employees of private firms not eligible for ration tickets were in an even more precarious position.[127]

After installation in April of Tran Trong Kim as premier (see below), the new supply minister was sent to Saigon to try to arrange transport. Attention was given to at least five oceangoing French vessels confiscated by the Japanese in Cochinchina, but the French crews would need to be replaced and Allied mines cleared from the rivers before they could exit.[128] In May, Phan Ke Toai, the newly appointed Kham Sai (imperial delegate) in Tonkin, discovered that 2,000 tons of rice had been cleared by the Japanese Army in Saigon for rail transport north, yet was stuck at various locations en route. Another 1,000 tons was held under Hue government control at Nam Dinh, which Toai requested be released. Searching desperately for more fundamental solutions, Toai proposed that train cars and junks returning empty from Tonkin be used to carry thousands of famine victims to settle in Cochinchina.[129] Meanwhile, cables went back and forth between Hanoi and Hue concerning the whereabouts of particular shipments of rice north, some of which began to spoil along the way, while others were pillaged for lack of reliable guards.[130] Viet Minh adherents in Quang Ngai intercepted several junkloads of rice heading north, secreting

125. AOM, INF, GF 25. In mid March the Japanese had also displayed an edict prescribing the death penalty for speculators, which may have helped to stimulate a drop in rice prices for several weeks. *Tin Moi* (Hanoi), 17 Mar. 1945, as cited in Nguyen The Anh, "La Famine," 92.

126. *CMCD*, 9:80–81, 126.

127. For example, an experienced secretary with five dependents was short 128 piastres per month in January 1945, even though his salary and allowances added up to 303 piastres per month. AOM, INF, GF 23. His situation would degenerate further in coming months.

128. AOM, INF, GF 36.

129. Kham Sai Phan Ke Toai to Minsanté Hue, 14 May 1945; id. to Saigon, 18 May 1945; id. to Minravitaillement Hue, 23 May 1945; all in AOM, INF, GF 58.

130. Messages between 25 June and 20 July, as well as an internal Kham Sai memo dated 2 July 1945, prepared after discussions with Dr. Phan Huy Quat, Tonkin representative of the Ministry of Health, all filed in AOM, INF, GF 58.

the contents or smuggling it to nascent guerrilla units in the hills.[131] Apparently only in late June did junks begin to arrive in the north bearing relief rice from Cochinchina,[132] by which time the immediate crisis had passed.

Meanwhile, a number of Vietnamese social, religious, and philanthropic groups had moved since January 1945 to seek donations of cash or grain and organize cooking of gruel for famine victims. By March, however, participants could see the futility of such scattered efforts, even in the cities. Nguyen Van To, a prominent classical scholar, approached the new Japanese mayor of Hanoi to obtain recognition of a more ambitious General Relief Association (Tong Hoi Cuu Te). It was necessary first to draft bylaws in French and Vietnamese, compile the names and addresses of all founding members, and affix colonial tax stamps to each page of these documents. Although permission to operate was granted on 10 April, Nguyen Van To still felt it necessary two weeks later to petition Nishimura for special organizational status to be able "to come to the effective aid of our compatriots hit by famine, who number in the hundreds of thousands."[133] By May, the General Relief Association had raised a total of 782,403 piastres, which might have enabled it to purchase 1,476 tons of rice from government stocks. In distant Cochinchina, shocked by photographs of famine victims and stories of cannibalism, over twenty groups collected 1,677,886 piastres to help feed their compatriots to the north.[134]

---

131. Dang Bo Huyen Son Tinh, *So Thao Lich Su Dang Bo Huyen Son Tinh* [Preliminary History of the Party Apparatus in Son Tinh District], vol. 1, *1929–1945* (Ho Chi Minh City, 1986), 125.

132. Smith, "Japanese Period," 290–91. Vu Ngu Chieu, "The Other Side of the 1945 Vietnamese Revolution: The Empire of Viet-Nam (March–August 1945)," *Journal of Asian Studies* 45, no. 2 (Feb. 1986): 307. It is possible that several hundred tons of relief grain reached Tonkin earlier, traveling in several stages. Pham Khac Hoe, *Tu Trieu Dinh Hue den Chien Khu Viet Bac*, 39, recalls the supply minister telling him in late July that "almost 2,000 tons of rice" had been transported from the south to the center and north. Although I have not found any total figure in the AOM, INF, GF records, scattered evidence suggests that 2,000 tons might be about right.

133. Tong Hoi Cuu Te to Nishimura, 25 Apr. 1945, in AOM, INF, GF 65. The General Relief Association received its *personnalité civile* (official corporate status) on 3 May. Some donations for famine relief were already going to Japanese officials. In early May, for example, the overseas Chinese of Hanoi gave 110,000 piastres to Mayor Konagaya Yutake. *Hai Phong Nhat Bao* (Haiphong), no. 52 (14 May 1945).

134. Vu Ngu Chieu, "Other Side," 308, citing various issues of *L'Action* (Hanoi). Nguyen Ky Nam, *Hoi Ky*, 65–66, describes how members of the Thanh Nien Tien Phong (Vanguard Youth) risked life and limb sailing rice-filled sampans up the coast. On the other hand, Do Thuc Vinh, *Mua Ao Anh*, 69–75, recounts with obvious

No one knows how many people perished in the famine. In late May, the Kham Sai's Office in Hanoi requested mortality statistics from all Tonkin provinces for the year so far. Eventually, twenty replies came in, reporting 380,969 deaths from starvation and 20,347 from "illness."[135] However, a number of the replies emphasized the inability of officials to go into the countryside to make careful checks. Also, losses in northern Annam were not included in the compilation. In late 1946, a policy paper prepared for internal use by officials of the Democratic Republic of Vietnam estimated that 1,000,000 people had died in northern Vietnam and 300,000 in central Vietnam.[136] By that time it had become standard practice in public for DRV spokesmen to assert that in early 1945 "French colonialists and Japanese fascists" had been responsible for at least 2,000,000 citizens starving to death, a figure subsequently enshrined in government history books.

One million deaths seems a more credible estimate. The implications are still horrific: about 10 percent of the population of the region affected perished in a five-month period.[137] Certain provinces were far more heavily hit: Nam Dinh, Thai Binh, Ninh Binh, Hai Duong, and Kien An accounted for 81 percent of deaths reported in the Kham Sai's compilation. Nam Dinh alone was 32 percent.[138] Although some of the victims undoubtedly had drifted in from elsewhere, the Kham Sai's figures still suggest that these five provinces may have lost between 11 and 20 percent of their populations. Particular districts suffered even worse. Hai Hau district in Nam Dinh province, for example, reported 26,080 deaths, whereas nearby districts reported from 4,000 to 6,000. Kien Xuong district in Thai Binh

---

discomfort how Cochinchinese sometimes competed with one another at benefit auctions to demonstrate their wealth, forgetting the humanitarian purpose.

135. AOM, INF, GF 3. Nine provinces never reported. Six provinces refused to distinguish "starvation" from "illness," considering it unrealistic or impossible in the circumstances. In those cases, the representative of the Kham Sai totting up the figures attributed all deaths to starvation.

136. AOM, INF, GF 12, "Cuu te va y te" dossier. Nonetheless, Hoang Van Duc, who had access to 1945 *résident supérieur* files one year later as part of DRV efforts to ward off further starvation, clearly recalls the figure of two million somewhere amid the documents he consulted. Interview in Hanoi, 19 Feb. 1994.

137. Here I assume the region affected to be the heavily populated Red River Delta and the two Annam provinces of Thanh Hoa and Nghe An, a total of 9,999,200 people in 1943 according to the *Annuaire statistique de l'Indochine*, vol. 11 (Saigon, 1948), 28.

138. It may be that knowledge of Nam Dinh's status as a reception point for grain from Cochinchina caused large numbers of famine victims to gravitate there from other provinces.

reported 14,920, compared to Quynh Coi with 1,532. Particular villages lost half their populations.[139]

Bare statistics can only begin to convey the psychological effects on those who survived the famine. No disaster of this magnitude had afflicted Vietnamese society in living memory. The sounds of lamentation among starving compatriots, the sight of bodies strewn alongside rural roads and hedges, or encountered each morning on city sidewalks, continued to haunt several generations in northern and north-central Vietnam.[140] As one eyewitness recounted in poetry:

> Along all highways famished bodies moaned,
> lying curled up in sun, in dust and filth.
> Amidst those rags the hollow eyes alone
> still harbored sparks of soul soon to go out.
>
> . . . .
>
> And day by day, toward cities, toward Hanoi
> more corpses, yet more corpses dragged themselves,
> bringing the trail of flies, the stench of smells,
> then crumbled down along some street or lane.
> At dawn you'd gingerly push your door ajar
> to check if there was someone dead outside.[141]

Another witness remembered how his landlord father had instructed him to ladle out bowls of thin rice soup to gaunt peasants standing obediently in line, but also how one old man climbed over the fence, entered the kitchen, and grabbed a chicken bone that had just been thrown on the ground for the dog to eat.[142]

People's assumptions about human behavior and morality were shaken profoundly. How could the authorities hold back thousands of tons of grain while so many people perished before their eyes? How could patrons, old friends, and even relatives refuse to share their food surpluses, or merely

---

139. *Thanh Nghi* (Hanoi), 26 May 1945.

140. Neither the French nor the Japanese seem to have left behind detailed eyewitness accounts. Japanese sensitivities may have been dulled by witnessing worse famines in China. However, Nishimura Kumao, resident superior of Tonkin, was clearly upset by what he heard and saw. He was also frank in blaming the Imperial Army for extracting too much grain from Tonkin farmers. Interview in Tokyo, 27 Nov. 1967.

141. Bang Ba Lan, "Doi, Doi . . . ," 103–5.

142. Nguyen Tien Hung and Jerrold L Schecter, *The Palace File* (New York, 1986), 14. Before Nguyen Tien Hung's family walked to daily mass, his father would go alone to the gate of their house to clear away bodies that had collected there overnight.

provide token quantities and discourage any further approaches? How could one's own parents, with bags of grain in reserve, bolt the door against all beggars? If one tried to share, how did one avoid a chaotic stampede and loss of everything? How could parents sell their children for a few tins of grain? On the other hand, how could others reject all food in favor of their children or their elderly parents? Why did some victims refuse to beg, instead simply selecting a spot to lie down and await death, hoping someone there might grant them a decent burial? Why did the Hanoi Hygiene Department accept severed ears as proof in paying teams hired to collect and dump corpses in large pits? Was it true that some thugs carved up bodies and sold human flesh to soup vendors?[143] On 10 May, a Civil Guard patrol in Ha Dong province stopped a woman, Nguyen Thi Lao, and discovered in a box the remains of a three-month-old child, allegedly dismembered for cooking.[144]

In disasters like this, survivors want to assign blame. The colonial authorities quickly became prime culprits in the eyes of most Vietnamese. Many even believed that the French had deliberately created the famine to weaken opposition to their presence.[145] The Japanese received less condemnation by contrast, perhaps because people knew that the French were in administrative control until 9 March, and because Japanese officials made widely publicized (if token) gifts of grain to victims after the takeover. Emperor Bao Dai's new cabinet, announced on 17 April, was perceived widely to lack the means to do more than exhort hoarders, merchants, and creditors to be less selfish, although some observers did credit it with persuading the Japanese to terminate the system of obligatory rice sales by early June.[146] Surprisingly, famine survivors only rarely directed their ire

143. All of these questions, and more, were raised in essays and short stories about the famine that appeared in subsequent years. See, esp., Tang Xuan An, "Nan Doi Nam At Dau," 37–41; Tran Van Mai, as translated in Ngo Vinh Long, *Before the Revolution*, 221–76; Nguyen Hong, "Tieng Noi" [Speech], in *Truyen Ngan Chon Loc, 1945–75* [Selected Short Stories, 1945–75] (Hanoi, 1976), 189–95; and Kim Lan, "The First Comer," in *Vietnamese Literature*, ed. Nguyen Khac Vien and Huu Ngoc (Hanoi, 1983 [?]), 731–37.

144. Ha Dong to Kham Sai, 17 May 1945, in AOM, INF, GF 51. Another cannibalism case, where a group admitted eating three persons, is reported in Kien An to Kham Sai, 7 May 1945, also GF 51.

145. Tran Van Mai, in Ngo Vinh Long, *Before the Revolution*, 221–22, 276.

146. Nonetheless, Kham Sai archival records clearly indicate that such obligatory sales continued, albeit at a reduced rate. See discussion below. The Hue government's frustration over the famine is suggested by the blunt comment of Ho Ta Khanh, the new minister of the economy, to a journalist from the north: "If

at the Allies for disrupting Indochina's economy and strangling transport. Nor was the Viet Minh castigated for supporting those Allied attacks. As we shall see, citizens paid more attention to Viet Minh calls in early 1945 to storm government and landlords' granaries.

Postcoup Perceptions

The Japanese seizure of power in Indochina was announced on Radio Tokyo in the early hours of 10 March; martial law proclamations signed by General Tsuchihashi went up on city walls throughout the colony that same day.[147] A quick succession of orders followed, telling all civilians to remain calm, to go about their normal duties, and to avoid doing anything prejudicial to the interests of the Imperial Army. Government employees—French and non-French alike—were invited to continue working. Although policemen had to turn in their weapons, native police received assurances that this measure was temporary, pending reorganization. The Japanese forces, while fulfilling their defense duties, stood ready to "support any endeavor to satisfy the eager desire for independence." Severe penalties were prescribed for espionage, causing harm to Japanese personnel, destruction of equipment or installations used by the army, spreading anti-Japanese propaganda, and black-marketeering or other behavior "liable to disturb the economic system." The Bank of Indochina was closed for five days, then reopened with a withdrawal limit of 2,000 piastres per month. The bank was not without some reserves: in a Saigon vault, the Japanese discovered gold ingots weighing 1,200 kilograms.[148] On 13 March, General Tsuchihashi announced the names of Japanese appointed to key government positions, most notably the resident superior of Tonkin, Nishimura Kumao, the supreme adviser to the emperor of Annam, Yokoyama Masayuki, and the governor of Cochinchina, Minoda Fujio.[149]

---

people continue to starve and we just talk politics, it is really senseless." Quoted in *Hai Phong Nhat Bao* (Haiphong), no. 52 (14 May 45).

147. *NGS*, 24:124, 217–18. Gautier, *9 mars 1945*, 199, 359–60. Vietnamese-language versions of these proclamations were somewhat different from the French ones. See Nguyen Ky Nam, *Hoi Ky*, 144–47. *Tri Tan* (Hanoi), no. 181 (29 Mar. 1945), contains a Vietnamese description of the fighting in Hanoi on 9–10 March.

148. Hélène Tournaire, *Livre jaune du Viet-Nam* (Paris, 1966), 79.

149. IMTFE exhibit 664 (document 2634). *PJI*, Radio Saigon (in French) 11 Mar. 1945. Françoise Martin, *Heures tragiques au Tonkin (9 mars 1945–18 mars 1946)* (Paris, 1948), 59–63. Smith, "Japanese Period," 285. On 16 March, Nishimura telegraphed all Tonkin echelons: "J'ai l'honneur de vous faire connaître que j'ai été

Figure 10. Vietnamese employees of the colonial Sûreté under review by Japanese Army officers before being reinstated. The placard in Chinese translates as "Tonkin Investigation Bureau." *Binh Minh* (Hanoi), 1 April 1945. Courtesy of the Bibliothèque nationale.

We know much more about what Nishimura did than about what Yokoyama or Minoda did. Immediately on taking office, for example, Nishimura asked all provincial mandarins to tell him what problems they considered most serious. A number of mandarins requested permission to release paddy stored in local government warehouses for famine relief distribution or sale on the open market. The provincial chief of Nam Dinh appealed for 10,026 tons of paddy from elsewhere to halt the starvation that had already claimed at least 4,000 lives. He also asked that people be allowed to plant rice, potatoes, or corn on the 2,000 hectares in his province allocated to producing jute for the Japanese. The Son Tay provincial chief asked whether he was responsible for feeding Japanese troops, while the Vinh Yen chief wanted to know who would deal with the 1,000 European civilians at the Tam Dao hill resort. Almost every mandarin urgently requested that Vietnamese members of the Garde indochinoise be rearmed, to prevent

chargé provisoirement de la direction de l'Administration du Tonkin. Je vous prie de m'apporter votre entière aide pour assurer la marche des services qui devrant fonctionner comme auparavant." AOM, INF, GF 25.

pillaging and to recover firearms that had fallen into the hands of male-factors during the takeover. Only the Thai Nguyen provincial chief referred specifically to "Viet Minh rebels" and pirates, saying that they had formed large bands to "sow disorder."[150]

Despite the flood of rumors in previous months, the takeover when it came left most Vietnamese incredulous.[151] How could the French, who had lorded it over the Vietnamese for more than eighty years, have been quashed in a mere forty-eight hours?[152] Each public humiliation of the French by the Japanese was savored and communicated widely. On faraway Con Son prison island, fifty miles off the coast of Cochinchina, Vietnamese inmates observed with relish as defeated legionnaires were ordered to line up to witness the Japanese haul down the French flag, tear it to shreds, and stamp the pieces into the ground.[153]

For several months the Imperial Army took on new luster. More young men took to imitating the mannerisms of Bushidō warriors, learning judo, and participating in military drills. Japanese commanders found it much easier to recruit laborers. Selected Vietnamese members of the former colonial army were put in Japanese uniforms and organized as *heiho* (aux-iliary) companies.[154] Military academies sprouted in a number of towns

---

150. AOM, INF, GF 6. Nishimura also convened a meeting of province chiefs on 21 March, but the only decision we know about was to send a delegation to Hue, and this was cancelled the next day because of "communication difficulties." AOM, INF, GF 61.

151. Only a handful of Vietnamese took part in the takeover, as members of Japanese-directed teams. Five killed in the Hanoi area were honored in a subsequent public ceremony, according to Paul Isoart, *Le Phénomène national vietnamien* (Paris, 1961), 324. Nguyen Ky Nam, *Hoi Ky*, 126–27, quotes a Cao Dai leader describing how his unit was trucked secretly into Saigon by the Japanese and employed on the evening of 9 March to help block any French attempt to escape from a key garrison. Apparently no blood was shed. If French units in Cochinchina had resisted, it is likely that General Tsuchihashi would have armed other Cao Dai contingents.

152. Nghiem Ke To, *Viet-Nam Mau Lua*, 22. Nguyen Ky Nam, *Hoi Ky*, 123, 153.

153. Nguyen Hai Ham, *Tu Yen Bai den Con Lon* [From Yen Bai to Con Lon] (Saigon, 1969 [?]), 198–200. Nonetheless, the author was dismayed when the Japanese refused to release him and other political prisoners; he had been jailed in 1930 for participation in the Vietnam Nationalist Party's abortive uprising at Yen Bai.

154. Bōeichō [Japan Defense Agency], Bōei Kenshujo Senshitsu [War History Office], *Shittan Meigō sakusen: Biruma sensen no hōkai to Tai, Futsuin no bōei* [The Sittan and Meigō Operations: The Collapse of the Burma Front and the Defense of Thailand and French Indochina] (Tokyo, 1969), 684. I have not been able to ascertain how many *heiho* units were established, or what jobs were assigned to them. Shiraishi, "La Présence," 240, asserts that the Japanese Army also re-cruited natives to *giyutai* (volunteer) units, each of the five Indochina regions

under loose Japanese sponsorship. Vietnamese who had previously been the objects of French harassment as Japanese sympathizers now tried to take center stage. Members of the National League (Quoc Gia Dong Minh) declared that, after so many years languishing under the "white man's tyranny of imperialistic France," it was a joy for people to be able "through the might of Japanese forces to establish in a single day the foundation for the independence of Annam."[155] A Saigon newspaper exalted: "Liberation day for our country of Vietnam has arrived."[156] Broadcasting from Singapore in the name of the Restoration League, Tran Van An expressed his satisfaction at seeing "those French pirates and assassins thrown to the floor forever."[157] Speaking from Tokyo in a more sober vein, Vu Van An emphasized that people at home ought to concentrate on total prosecution of the war, as without victory over the Allies there would be "no real liberation of our Indochinese race."[158]

To mark the new era, public demonstrations were organized in a number of cities. In Hanoi, an estimated five thousand youths participated in a rally and street parade on the Sunday afternoon immediately following the takeover.[159] As many as twenty thousand people gathered in Hanoi on 20 March to celebrate the anniversary of the Trung sisters, who had led a revolt against Chinese rule in the first century A.D.[160] In Hue, a public meeting took place next to the stone ramparts surrounding the royal palace and administrative compound.[161]

The most ambitious early organizing took place in Saigon, where members of the Cao Dai, the Vietnam National Independence Party (Viet Nam

---

providing one thousand men. One of these may be the "Nghia Dong Quan" group pictured in *Tan A* [New Asia] (Saigon), no. 69 (20 July 1945): 8–9.

155. *PJI*, Radio Tokyo (in Japanese and English), 12 Mar. 1945.

156. *Dan Bao* (Saigon), 12 Mar. 1945. Vietnamese readers could not help but notice, however, that this exuberant claim was contradicted at three other places in the same issue by Japanese (Domei) references to "future independence," "preparing the basis for deserving independence," and support for the "aspirations of Indochinese peoples to achieve independence."

157. Devillers, *Histoire*, 125–26, quoting *Non Song* (Saigon), no. 17 (1 Sept. 1947).

158. *PJI*, Radio Tokyo (in Italian), 11 Mar. 1945. The theme of cooperating with Japan to prevent return of the French can be seen most consistently in the Saigon weekly *Tan A*, even as late as 10 August 1945.

159. *PJI*, Radio Tokyo (in English), 12 Mar. 1945. *Dan Bao* (Saigon), 12 Mar. 1945, also reports a meeting in Hanoi of "pro-Japanese organizations" on 10 March that agreed to establish a Greater Vietnam National Union (Tong Hoi Quoc Gia Dai Viet).

160. Martin, *Heures tragiques*, 68.

161. Smith, "Japanese Period," 286.

Figure 11. A pro-Japanese political meeting in Hanoi following the 9 March coup. The building is on Trang Tien Street, adjacent to Hoan Kiem Lake. Courtesy of the Centre militaire d'information et de documentaiton sur l'Outre-Mer.

Quoc Gia Doc Lap Dang), and the Restoration League passed out leaflets inviting citizens to demonstrate their gratitude to the Japanese Army at a mass rally on Sunday, 18 March. In a downtown park, a large yellow panel was erected bearing the word "Viet Nam," before which stood an ancestral altar, a podium, and loudspeakers.[162] From 7:00 A.M. on, about fifty thousand people surged into the park, some marching behind the banners of previously repressed political and religious groups. Nothing of this size had been seen in Indochina since the Popular Front period in the late 1930s. The formal proceedings began at 8:00 A.M. with a moment of silence for those patriots who had sacrificed themselves for the anticolonial cause. The ashes of the anticolonialist literatus Duong Ba Trac, brought back from Singapore, where he had fled to escape French persecution, were placed before the altar. Ho Van Nga, representing the National Independence Party, delivered a speech stressing Vietnamese gratitude to the Japanese. When

162. Nguyen Ky Nam, *Hoi Ky*, 151. By contrast, *PJI*, Radio Saigon (in French), 18 Mar. 1945, reported the word "An Nam" on the panel. I suspect some Japanese were simply following the French practice of ignoring the term "Vietnam" when translating. Neither source makes it clear whether the word was written in Chinese characters or *quoc ngu*.

he got the crowd to cheer "Total Victory for the Japanese Army!" at least one listener thought this most amusing, considering what he had heard on Radio New Delhi.[163] Tran Quang Vinh, speaking for the Cao Dai, seemed truly to believe in the legitimacy and continuing vitality of the Greater East Asia Co-Prosperity doctrine. Another Cao Dai representative led singing of the "Youth March" ("Thanh Nien Hanh Khuc"), using the popular melody of "Luu Huu Phuoc" with altered lyrics. A Japanese student spoke briefly in Vietnamese, much to the delight of the audience. The crowd dispersed in orderly fashion after further mass cheers, including "Independent Vietnam! Unified Vietnam!"[164]

The next day, Vietnamese functionaries and schoolteachers met at locations around Saigon to pass motions requesting replacement of all French supervisory personnel. In several cases they went further, electing their own new bosses. Some of these motions contained identical wording, probably inserted at the suggestion of Independence Party members, offering to "collaborate totally with the Japanese authorities in order to ease their tasks and to lay the foundations of Vietnam's independence."[165]

Before the end of March, however, the Japanese showed public concern that Vietnamese political enthusiasm was getting out of hand. The Imperial Army specifically condemned the dissemination of rumors, incitement of strikes in factories, and acts of violence against French residents. "The defense of Indochina against the enemy outside the country will be completely ineffective if domestic order is not perfectly maintained," the army pointed out.[166] In Cochinchina, where pro-Japanese groups were most visible and hopes for immediate institutional change most pronounced, Governor Minoda found it necessary to threaten dire punishments to any natives who dressed in Japanese uniform, claimed falsely to represent the government, tried to recruit followers or collect money without official authorization, or committed acts of violence. Office personnel, both public and private, were ordered not to abandon their positions or remove any files.[167] In early April, Minoda called all of the Vietnamese replacements

163. Nguyen Ky Nam, *Hoi Ky*, 154.
164. *Tan A*, no. 54 (20 Apr. 1945): 7–8. Nguyen Ky Nam, *Hoi Ky*, 151–63. On 24 March, the nineteenth anniversary of Phan Chu Trinh's death was also commemorated publicly. See Nguyen Ky Nam, *Hoi Ky*, 175–76.
165. National Archives of Vietnam No. 2 (Ho Chi Minh City), Fonds du Goucoch (Divers), dossier 286. Some motions have notations indicating that they were transmitted to the Japanese by the Vietnam National Independence Party.
166. *PJI*, Radio Saigon (in French), 25 Mar. 1945.
167. Ibid., 27 Mar. 1945 and 31 Mar. 1945. Governor Minoda emphasized that no one of Annamese origin had been enrolled in the Japanese Army, which was

for French provincial officials to the Governor's Palace in Saigon, where he lectured them about Imperial Army priorities. Because the Cochinchina government was "merely part of the overall war strategy," everyone would have to wait for a "more propitious moment to carry out needed reforms."[168] Many Saigon intellectuals, overflowing with enthusiasm only a few weeks earlier, now worried that Minoda had simply replaced Governor Pagès, and that Vietnam still was far from being independent.[169]

Japan and Bao Dai

It remained to be seen whether Emperor Bao Dai could do anything more under Japanese tutelage than he had under the French. Bao Dai had been studying in France when his father, Emperor Khai Dinh, died in 1925. Brought home to ascend the throne at the age of thirteen, Bao Dai was then sent back to the métropole and kept under the supervision of a former resident superior for another six years. In 1932, permitted to return to Hue, and given a verbal promise by the governor-general that he would rule as a real king, Bao Dai soon discovered that neither the current resident superior of Annam nor the Vietnamese ministers wished to concede him any authority. Frustrated by vapid court ceremonies, yet warned by older members of the royal family that any aggressiveness on his part would cause the French to depose him as they had two previous emperors, Bao Dai soon turned his undoubted intelligence to gambling and organizing expeditions into the nearby mountains in quest of wild game. Meanwhile, the royal capital became increasingly isolated from political and intellectual developments elsewhere in Indochina and beyond. By the time Japanese troop units moved into Annam in 1941, only two small groups in Hue remained in touch with events, one centered around the aging reformist literatus Huynh Thuc Khang and his *Tieng Dan* (Voice of the People) newspaper, the other propelled by the Ngo Dinh family, well-positioned Catholics from Quang Binh province. Resident Superior E. Grandjean and Interior Minister Pham Quynh monopolized Annam's administrative affairs. The abrupt

---

technically correct, but evaded the fact that *heiho* units wore Japanese uniforms (minus imperial insignia) and sometimes abused their position.

168. *PJI*, Radio Saigon (in French), 9 Apr. 1945. Nguyen Ky Nam, *Hoi Ky*, 164–65, contains a list of twenty-two Vietnamese appointed by Minoda. In an interview in Tokyo, 20 Jan. 1967, Minoda hinted to me that he had not been at all happy with the Japanese Army's political inflexibility. Nonetheless, Minoda had more contact with a wider variety of Vietnamese groups than Nishimura in Hanoi or Yokoyama in Hue.

169. Nguyen Ky Nam, *Hoi Ky*, 165–67.

Figure 12. Emperor Bao Dai in Vietnamese formal garb. Reproduced from Maurice Ducoroy, *Ma trahison en Indochine.* Courtesy of Éditions internationales.

replacement of Grandjean by Yokoyama on 10 March at least gave Bao Dai an opportunity to test whether, like the French, the Japanese would prevent him from issuing written instructions on his own account or not.

Although Consul General Yokoyama urged Bao Dai to proclaim the independence of his kingdom, and Bao Dai complied eagerly, the constitutional situation remained murky. Most important, Tokyo had merely stated that it had no territorial designs on Bao Dai's kingdom and endorsed his *desire* for independence. When Radio Tokyo said, "It is Japan's duty to serve as a godmother in the establishment of an independent nation,"[170] it left obscure how long the "child" would require to grow up. Also, because the Japanese continued to refer to Bao Dai as ruler of "Annam," generally

170. *PJI,* Radio Tokyo (in English), 10 Mar. 1945. On the other hand, the puppet state of Manchukuo was reported as promptly recognizing the independent state of Annam, and an Indonesian spokesman hailed Japan's decision to support Annamese independence. More cautiously, the Nanking Chinese government offered support to the citizens of French Indochina "in the event they make efforts to defend their territory, prevent Allied invasion, and emancipate themselves and East Asia from foreign rule." *PJI,* Radio Tokyo (in English), 11 Mar. 1945; Radio Hsinking (in English), 13 Mar. 1945; and Radio Hong Kong (in English), 13 Mar. 1945. Nguyen Ky Nam, *Hoi Ky,* 149–50, recalls other congratulatory telegrams to Saigon political parties from Thailand, Burma, and Sumatra.

avoiding use of the term "Vietnam,"[171] it remained unclear whether they acknowledged his even nominal authority in Tonkin and Cochinchina. To further complicate matters, although the 11 March proclamation of independence unilaterally abrogated the 1884 treaty recognizing French protection of Annam and Tonkin, it failed to mention the treaties that had ceded Cochinchina and the cities of Hanoi, Haiphong, and Tourane. Finally, there was no indication in either Japanese or Vietnamese royal court statements whether Indochina-wide institutions established by the French would remain indefinitely under Japanese control or be divided and parceled out to the areas concerned.[172] Since these institutions were responsible for defense, security, taxation, commerce, education, and information, the question was important. In short, the independence and territorial integrity of Bao Dai's "Vietnam" remained to be proven. Many thoughtful Vietnamese wondered whether, in exchange for concrete demonstrations of loyalty to the Japanese cause, they were being given a chimera—precisely the tactic employed by the French in 1914–18 and again in 1940–44. As if to confirm this, a proclamation from General Tsuchihashi on 11 April ordered everyone to set aside personal feelings and group loyalties, to "melt into a unified bloc in the pursuit of their tasks, according to the present organizational and hierarchical order." Those who did not would be "severely punished in conformity with military discipline."[173]

Nonetheless, many politically astute Vietnamese still saw the period of Japanese control as an unparalleled opportunity to move toward independence. To this end, a wide variety of functionaries, educators, writers, and professionals approached Japanese commanders, diplomats, and journalists to ascertain what was legally possible. In particular, new censorship guidelines made it possible for writers to expose the evils of French colonialism and heap praise on anticolonial figures like Phan Dinh Phung, De Tham, Phan Boi Chau, Phan Chu Trinh, and Nguyen Thai Hoc.[174] Much attention

171. Some Domei press releases in Vietnamese did, however, employ the name "Viet-Nam." See Nguyen Ky Nam, *Hoi Ky*, 148–49, 169–71.

172. King Norodom Sihanouk proclaimed Cambodia's independence on 13 March, and Sisavangvong declared his kingdom of Luang Prabang independent on 8 April.

173. IMTFE exhibit 664 (document 2634).

174. Nguyen Van An and Trinh Nhu Luan, *Giai Phong va Doc Lap* [Liberation and Independence] (Hanoi, Apr. 1945). The frontispiece contains a wood-block print of Bao Dai. *Tan A*, no. 53 (13 Apr. 1945): 3–5, 12. During April–July 1945, *Tan A* also serialized a revisionist history of the French conquest titled "Phap Quan Xam Viet Su" [History of the French Invasion of Vietnam]. Starting on 21 April 1945, *Tu Tri* (Hanoi) serialized an article by "N.N.M." explaining why French Indochina's foreign trade policy was deeply exploitative, despite endless claims to the contrary.

also focused on selection of a royal cabinet to replace the one headed by Pham Quynh, which resigned on 19 March. As we have seen, most people assumed that the Japanese would pick Ngo Dinh Diem as prime minister. However, General Tsuchihashi never seems to have approved of that idea, perhaps mindful of Diem's unmalleable character, or knowing that Diem would push for the replacement of Bao Dai by Prince Cuong De.[175] None of the Dai Viet Party or Ai Quoc Party intellectuals who had worked closely with the Japanese in previous years received the nod either, probably because they lacked public stature and would have found it difficult to gain the respect of court officials or provincial administrators. Bao Dai's private secretary, Pham Khac Hoe, tried to persuade Huynh Thuc Khang to head a govern-ment, but Khang refused even to meet the king unless he showed his good intentions by remitting taxes for 1945.[176] In any event, Khang doubted the Japanese would allow a new Vietnamese cabinet any leeway.[177] Even some of those individuals ready to cooperate with the Japanese argued that it might be unwise to compromise too many prominent personalities like Khang in this way.[178] On the other hand, some joined as part of a broader

175. Much speculation has surrounded the nonparticipation of Cuong De and Ngo Dinh Diem in government after the Japanese takeover on 9 March. When queried, knowledgeable Japanese become evasive, often referring vaguely to Cuong De being "too old" and infirm, or to Diem being sent a message in Saigon but not responding. Some Vietnamese believe Diem received an offer but declined, it being apparent that the Japanese would not allow him sufficient powers. Given the en-ergetic political maneuvering of the entire Ngo family at this point in time, I don't find that explanation any more convincing than the Japanese ones. Most likely General Tsuchihashi deliberately excluded both Cuong De and Diem when he reject-ed key portions of the coup and postcoup plans developed by Colonel Hayashi in late 1944. In late July 1945, Cuong De was bidden farewell at a banquet in Tokyo's Imperial Hotel, yet then could not secure a seat on any departing aircraft. In Saigon, someone informed Cao Dai leaders of Cuong De's expected arrival; they even con-structed a welcoming arch, which then had to be dismantled quietly in the middle of the night. The most recent discussion of these curious events can be found in Tøn-nesson, *Vietnamese Revolution*, 284–85, which draws intriguingly from a French translation of an English translation of Hayashi's Japanese-language diary located in AOM, Haut Commissaire 57. According to Shiraishi, "Background," 137–39, once Diem understood from talks with Hayashi in late March that military plans had changed, he did write to Bao Dai declining any invitation for "reasons of health."

176. Pham Khac Hoe, *Tu Trieu Dinh Hue den Chien Khu Viet Bac*, 18–23. Huynh Thuc Khang had corresponded earlier with Prince Cuong De in Japan, probably one reason why the French closed down his *Tieng Dan* newspaper in Hue in 1943.

177. Nguyen Quoc Thang, *Huynh Thuc Khang: Con Nguoi va Tho Van (1876–1947)* [Huynh Thuc Khang: His Life and Letters] (Saigon, 1972), 219. As if in rebuttal, a Japanese-supported newspaper in Da Nang criticized those "heroic patriots who have already sacrificed so much for the country," yet now chose to "remain silent and look on." Ibid., 135.

178. Pham Khac Hoe, *Tu Trieu Dinh Hue*, 23, attributes this opinion partic-ularly to Tran Dinh Nam, who became minister of the interior.

effort to persuade the Japanese to sack the remaining French personnel, while simultaneously finessing the rabidly pro-Japanese elements who were seeking positions.[179] No one had any inkling that Japan would be compelled to surrender in a mere five months' time.[180]

By the end of March, attention centered on Tran Trong Kim, a retired school inspector and respected writer who had been forced to seek Japanese protection from the Sûreté in 1943. A Japanese Army lieutenant was sent to collect Kim in Bangkok, and on 7 April he received an audience with Bao Dai.[181] Kim first urged the king to cable Diem again, but, when days went by without any reply, he agreed to accept responsibility for forming a cabinet. On 17 April, he offered Bao Dai a list of eleven nominees, including four lawyers, four physicians, two teachers, and one engineer. Bao Dai assented. Yokoyama, who was also present, asked to see the list and complimented Kim on his selections.[182] Apparently by mutual agreement, no defense portfolio was established.[183]

179. These justifications were given subsequently by Phan Anh, a member of the Thanh Nghi publishing group, who became youth minister. Interview with Phan Anh, Hanoi, 7 Mar. 1988. See also Tønnesson, *Vietnamese Revolution*, 287, and Phan Anh, "Con Duong," 4.

180. Among intellectuals called to Hue in late March for consultations about forming a new cabinet, the estimate was that Japan could hold out for another year, perhaps a bit more. Hoang Xuan Han, "Tuong Nho Phan Anh" [Remembering Phan Anh], *Doan Ket* (Paris), Feb. 1991, 9.

181. Shiraishi, "La Présence," 235–36. Pham Khac Hoe, *Tu Trieu Dinh Hue*, 25, strongly suggests that Tran Trong Kim's name was put forward by the Japanese, not by any Vietnamese source. If so, neither Hoe nor anyone else seems to have expressed reservations. Hoang Xuan Han, a graduate of the prestigious Ecole polytechnique in Paris, played a key role in the deliberations over a new cabinet in late March and early April. He also happened to be a relative of Pham Khac Hoe's.

182. Apparently only two individuals, Kim himself and Hoang Xuan Han, coincided with six names presented to Kim by the Japanese when he passed through Saigon en route to Hue. On the other hand, six individuals coincided with a list of fourteen names prepared on 19 March by Pham Khac Hoe in consultation with two ministers of the outgoing cabinet (Bui Bang Doan and Ung Uy) and two left-wing intellectuals (Ton Quang Phiet and Ta Quang Buu). These were Tran Dinh Nam, Ho Ta Khanh, Luu Van Lang (who eventually declined the invitation), Hoang Xuan Han, Vu Van Hien, and Phan Anh. The remaining members of the new cabinet were Tran Van Chuong, Trinh Dinh Thao, Vu Ngoc Anh, and Nguyen Huu Thi. Tran Trong Kim, *Mot Con Gio Bui* [A Puff of Dust] (Saigon, 1969), 42–43, 51–53. Pham Khac Hoe, *Tu Trieu Dinh Hue*, 22–23, 26–27. It seems obvious that, while not choosing to dictate any particular cabinet, the Japanese narrowed the range of potential candidates and, by Yokoyama's act of requesting the list, made it clear that they retained a final say in such matters. In the opinion of Shiraishi, "Vietnam," 16, only one cabinet member, Tran Van Chuong, could be considered "pro-Japanese."

183. Tran Trong Kim, *Mot Con Gio Bui*, 57–58, argues that this made it more difficult for Japan to pull Vietnam into war against the Allies. Phan Anh, in our

Figure 13.   Ministers of the new royal government at the inaugural ceremony in Hue, 8 May 1945. From left to right: Hoang Xuan Han, Ho Ta Khanh, Trinh Dinh Thao, Tran Trong Kim (hidden behind microphone), Vu Ngoc Anh, Tran Van Chuong, Tran Dinh Nam, Vu Van Hien, Phan Anh, and Nguyen Huu Thi. *Trung Bac Chu Nhat* (Hanoi), 20 May 1945. Courtesy of the Bibliothèque nationale.

Tran Trong Kim seems to have been picked to head the royal cabinet largely because of his widely known conservative views. His morality textbooks had been used extensively in colonial schools, his *Viet-Nam Su Luoc* [Outline History of Vietnam] had offered a new generation access to the traditional chronicles, and his *Nho Giao* [Confucianism] had precipitated an important intellectual polemic in the 1930s.[184] Like almost everyone else in the new cabinet, he had had only limited administrative experience. No mandarins were included in the cabinet, perhaps because in the public's eye they had become tainted by corruption and long collaboration with the French. In the larger sense, however, since no Vietnamese

7 Mar. 1988 interview in Hanoi, made the same point. However, according to Hayashi's diary, discussed in Tønnesson, *Vietnamese Revolution*, 288, Japanese Army headquarters had already specified that it would not accept designation of a minister of war.

184. Marr, *Vietnamese Tradition*, 106–9, 114–15, 175, 273, 275–77, 279. See Vu Ngu Chieu, "Other Side," 300–301, for additional biographical details on Kim.

had been permitted to exercise policy-making authority since the 1880s, the cabinet's weakness was generic, not specific.

Tran Trong Kim Cabinet Policy

Because of transportation difficulties, the full cabinet was unable to convene until 4 May. Its first policy statement, read by Tran Trong Kim to a small assemblage of dignitaries four days later, emphasized that Vietnam "could not think of conducting war with anyone," although it was necessary to "cooperate sincerely with Japan in building Greater East Asia." The government promised to honor past patriotic heroes, release political prisoners, provide relief to famine victims, standardize the tax system, and encourage young people to "protect the independence that is being constructed."[185] Quickest off the mark was Phan Anh, the youth minister, who appears to have spent little time subsequently in his office, instead traveling from one town to the next, exhorting anyone who would listen to form paramilitary groups, practice marching, heighten one another's patriotic awareness, and serve as exemplars for the citizenry at large. Although he was quite short, Phan Anh's deep voice, forceful demeanor, and use of his fist to emphasize points must have made a considerable impression on urban audiences.[186] The youth minister's close associate, Ta Quang Buu, made the rounds of existing organizations, particularly Ducoroy's network and the Boy Scouts, urging them to serve as disciplined foci for the much larger youth movement.[187] Back in Hue, plans went ahead for a Frontline Youth (Tien Tuyen Thanh Nien) school, designed to produce reserve officers for a future Vietnamese army. Candidates had to be male, at least 1.63 meters tall, unmarried, and possess a first-class *baccalauréat*, which gave the endeavor a distinctly elitist hue.[188] Once enrolled, students especially enjoyed train-

185. The text of this statement is reprinted in Nguyen Ky Nam, *Hoi Ky*, 206–8. Nguyen Duy Phuong, *Lich Su Doc Lap va Noi Cac Dau Tien Viet-Nam* [Vietnam's Independent History and First Cabinet] (Hanoi, 1945), contains articles from the *Viet Dong* newspaper supporting the Hue government.

186. Interview with Phan Anh, Hanoi, 7 Mar. 1988. Although he was in his late seventies when we met, Phan Anh had lost none of his rhetorical skills, even reaching over to tap my knee to reinforce arguments.

187. Tran Van Su, "Ket qua buoc dau suu tam Nghien Cuu ve Luc Luong Huong Dao Sinh," 7–10, 12–15, contains information on some scout leaders and scout troops that accepted this challenge and continued to be significant after the 2 September 1945 establishment of the DRV.

188. Undated (probably early June 1945) Youth Ministry planning paper on Tien Tuyen Thanh Nien, in AOM, INF, GF 41. Among the public at large, the Frontline Youth was often called the "Phan Anh Youth," and it appears as such

Figure 14. Phan Anh, minister of youth in the royal government, addressing a June 1945 audience estimated at twenty thousand in front of the Hanoi Opera House. Courtesy of the Centre militaire d'information et de documentation sur l'Outre-Mer.

ing with real firearms, even if they had to surrender them to a locked armory at the end of each session.[189]

Except for Phan Anh, cabinet members seem to have spent a lot of time discussing constitutional problems and matters of national political symbolism. The former would require extended discussions with Yokoyama and other Japanese officials, but the latter could be resolved unilaterally. Thus, the name of the country was reaffirmed to be "Viet Nam"; all internal government documents had to be labeled *Viet Nam De Quoc* (Empire of Vietnam).[190] The national flag was the red character $\equiv$ (*ly*)

in some memoirs. Most later studies invert the title of the organization (Thanh Nien Tien Tuyen) to conform with Vietnamese rather than Chinese syntax.

189. Thach Ha, *Mat Troi Chieu* [Afternoon Sun] (Saigon, 1963), 16–23. Although this book is fictional in nature, internal evidence suggests that its author witnessed events in Hue in 1945.

190. Kham Sai circular to all provinces dated 7 May 1945, in AOM, INF, GF 34. Facing an acute paper shortage, clerks used rubber stamps bearing the words "Viet Nam De Quoc" to overprint the *résident supérieur*'s stationery. In the case of French file folders, they often turned them upside down before stamping them, a perhaps unconscious statement of revolutionary enthusiasm.

from the ancient *Book of Changes*, signifying south, fire, and civilization, on a regal yellow field. The national anthem was the solemn "Dang Dan" ("Ascending the Altar").[191] When presenting themselves ceremonially to the monarch, the cabinet resolved to wear the traditional Vietnamese tunic and turban, yet also retain their Western suits and shoes. Pham Khac Hoe assured them it was not necessary to kowtow; all they need do was simply clasp their hands together and bow respectfully.[192]

On 23 May, to further symbolize the end of colonial subjugation, and pursuant to the Confucian practice of "rectification of names," the Ministry of the Interior ordered provincial chiefs to get rid of all French toponyms.[193] While undoubtedly a popular initiative, as it meant eliminating from street signs and parks the names of precisely those Frenchmen who had masterminded the invasion and pacification of Vietnam in the late nineteenth century—for example, Francis Garnier, Henri Rivière, François-Jules Harmand, Jules Ferry, Joseph Gallieni, and J. J. C. Joffre—the selection of suitable Vietnamese substitutes proved a complicated and potentially divisive matter. Local committees were established, maps drawn up, and biographies compiled on those individuals not likely to be known by higher officials, who carefully reserved the right to reject proposals. Most provinces tended to favor ancient military leaders like the Trung sisters, Ngo Quyen, Ly Thuong Kiet, Tran Hung Dao, and Le Loi, as well as notable opponents of French colonial rule, such as Phan Dinh Phung, Phan Boi Chau, Phan Chu Trinh, and Nguyen Thai Hoc. To demonstrate their affinity with the "empire" centered in Hue, some provinces also made a point of naming streets after Nguyen dynasty rulers, beginning with Gia Long. Delicate problems arose, however, when localities proposed to eliminate not only French toponyms but also certain Vietnamese ones, particularly the names of individuals who had collaborated with the colonizers. Prominent among these were Emperor Dong

---

191. Royal edict 6 June 1945, in AOM, INF, GF 25. Tran Trong Kim, *Mot Con Gio Bui*, 60–61. The Nguyen dynasty's simple yellow flag was rejected on the grounds that yellow faded too quickly in the sun, and because that color possessed certain "mistaken international implications," perhaps a reference to ships flying yellow pennants when under quarantine.

192. Pham Khac Hoe, *Tu Trieu Dinh Hue*, 27–31, describes with some amusement how he initiated the new cabinet to court ritual and royal family politics.

193. The first initiative of this kind, however, seems to have come from a Japanese military commander in Nam Dinh, who on 12 April induced the provincial chief to convene the municipal commission of the city of Nam Dinh to discuss replacing French street names with those of "grands hommes et héros annamites." AOM, INF, GF 24.

Khanh and Emperor Khai Dinh, father of Bao Dai. On 22 June, Hanoi administrators sent messages to all northern provinces complaining that name changes were poorly thought out, and especially suggesting they keep all toponyms that were not French.[194] Incredibly, even in the middle of the August upheavals, the Northern Kham Sai's Office and local officials continued to send toponym documentation back and forth. In Saigon, on 24 August, only hours before ICP-led seizure of key installations around the city, a noncommunist newspaper urged readers to assist a name-changing committee established by officials loyal to the royal government in Hue.[195] One of the earliest messages of the new regime in Hanoi, sent on 25 August, sternly queried those provinces that had failed in previous months to submit name lists and maps.[196] Needless to say, further name changes would be made in subsequent months and years.

Of greater long-term significance was the Tran Trong Kim cabinet's firm commitment to using the Vietnamese language rather than French for official communication. Looking at government dossiers many years after events, the abrupt change in language remains startling. The log book of incoming correspondence for the Second Bureau of the Northern Kham Sai's Office, for example, switched from French to Vietnamese on Tuesday, 22 May.[197] Archival dossiers reveal that these Kham Sai clerks had no difficulty composing outgoing messages in Vietnamese. All but a handful of province and district officials made the transition with equal flair.[198] Hanoi clerks delighted in ordering workers to paint over French signs inside each building and replace them with Vietnamese renditions.[199] Meanwhile, in Saigon, Vietnamese lawyers requested and received Japanese permission to conduct criminal court proceedings in their native language. French

194. AOM, INF, GF 8 and GF 24. In Saigon, by contrast, French street signs remained intact under Governor Minoda. *Tan A* (Saigon), no. 69 (20 July 1945): 16, complains about this, while praising shop owners for blanking out French shop names.

195. *Hung Viet* (Saigon), no. 21 (24 Aug. 1945). Ironically, the editorial address of this paper was still "99B Verdun Street."

196. AOM, INF, GF 2.

197. AOM, INF, GF 10. Chinese characters had been employed for official communications until the early twentieth century. After the 1920s, no one seriously considered returning to Chinese, although characters continued to be brushed on ceremonial awards until 1945, and some people signed their names in characters.

198. A stubborn exception was the Bac Ninh province chief, Than Trong Hau, who in late July still sent his correspondence in French. The pen notations by a Kham Sai official on his letters were in Vietnamese, however. AOM, INF, GF 20.

199. Nha Kinh Te to Tuc-me-cuc,5 July 1945, in AOM, INF, GF 41.

lawyers were reduced to asking furtively for summary translations, much to the amusement of their Vietnamese colleagues.[200] One wonders how everyone coped. Probably the relatively smooth shift reflected the avid involvement of many functionaries in nonofficial Vietnamese publishing during the previous two decades.[201] As Vietnamese spread through the administrative system, the minister of national education, Hoang Xuan Han, urged everyone to master an orthographic convention that dropped the diacritics entirely in favor of extra letters at the end of words. This was not a new idea,[202] having been employed for some years on colonial telegraph machines, but Han now proposed that it be expanded to office typewriters (which contained only French diacritics), and perhaps eventually to printed publications and handwriting.[203] By July and August, some correspondence was being typed in this manner, an innovation retained by the Democratic Republic of Vietnam.

French could not be eliminated entirely. Most important, Japanese officials corresponded with government bureaus in French and expected significant Vietnamese-language reports and messages to be translated into French for their benefit. Thus, on 2 June, the Northern Kham Sai's Office instructed members of the Local Economic Service to append French translations to Vietnamese messages in order to facilitate examination by the Japanese financial controller.[204] Nonetheless, no bureau bothered to translate the vast majority of its documents, some quite sensitive, and it was not unusual for French renditions to be deliberately different from the Vietnamese original. Presumably the Japanese knew they were getting less than adequate compliance, yet chose not to make an issue of it. Meanwhile, for reasons of scientific accuracy, government health officials and physicians

200. Nguyen Ky Nam, *Hoi Ky*, 141–44.

201. Marr, *Vietnamese Tradition*, 44–52, 161–82. Within the colonial structure, Vietnamese writing had also managed to infiltrate certain less sensitive realms. Thus, the internal notes for 1943–44 of the Association professionnelle des fonctionnaires indochinois en service au Gouvernement général were often written in Vietnamese, not French. AOM, INF, GF 23. In Annam from the 1930s on, some district and provincial reports previously prepared in Chinese were allowed to be submitted in Vietnamese, not French. My thanks to Nola Cooke for this information.

202. See, e.g., Le Mai, *Quac Am Tan Che* [A New System of National Language] (Saigon, 1927 [?]).

203. AOM, INF, GF 34. Hoang Xuan Han also prepared ambitious plans for upgrading Vietnamese-language instruction at all school levels, none of which could be implemented before August. Vu Ngu Chieu, "Political and Social Change," 366.

204. AOM, INF, GF 34.

continued to employ French as the primary means of correspondence, although sometimes formal letters were translated into Vietnamese before posting.[205] Government letters to Chinese- and French-owned companies were written in French.[206]

Although indiscriminately labeled Japanese puppets by the Viet Minh, postcoup Vietnamese administrators proved in reality to be cut from diverse bolts of cloth. Some continued to know only slavishness. When Governor Minoda was traveling in the Mekong Delta, he encountered a Sadec dignitary who suffered an embarrassing verbal lapse, greeting Minoda with "Vive la France!" instead of "Vive la Grande Asie orientale!" After being corrected, he apologized profusely and followed Minoda all the way to his automobile, promising never to make the same mistake again.[207] Officials of two villages in Bac Giang province, far to the north, were quicker to learn the new rhetoric, thanking the Japanese Army for overthrowing the French and "liberating the Vietnamese to be independent." What they really wanted, however, was annulment of a 1940 French zoning decision placing them inside the limits of the town of Phu Lang Thuong.[208] Cung Dinh Van, provincial mandarin of nearby Thai Nguyen, wishing to support the "continuing fight to reestablish this country's independence," requested permission of the local Imperial Army commander to establish a Buddhist altar to pray for the souls of Japanese soldiers killed in Indochina, to send cakes, fruit, and flowers to casualties hospitalized in Hanoi, and to put Japanese flags at the head of a planned Vietnamese youth procession.[209] Some officials used personal contacts with local Japanese commanders to try to influence higher-echelon decisions in their favor. In at least two cases, this tactic backfired, however, with the Kham Sai sticking to his decision to transfer individual mandarins and being backed up by his Japanese "advisers."[210]

Another case simultaneously demonstrated the royal government's desire not to offend the Japanese and its wish to assert administrative jurisdiction. During the takeover, when the incumbent chief of Bac Ninh province had fled office, the Japanese Army installed one of its Vietnamese

205. AOM, INF, GF 25.

206. AOM, INF, GF 37. French continued to be used even with those companies where owners had delegated authority to a Vietnamese associate after the 9 March coup.

207. Nguyen Ky Nam, *Hoi Ky*, 181.

208. AOM, INF, GF 25.

209. Tuan Phu Tinh Truong Thai Nguyen to Quan Tong Tu Lenh Quan Doi Dai Nhat Ban o Thai Nguyen, 5 Apr. 1945, in AOM, INF, GF 67.

210. AOM, INF, GF 34.

associates, Nguyen Van Sy, who remained as deputy after the errant chief returned. On 14 July, the Kham Sai asked Tran Trong Kim to confirm Sy's appointment, adding that it would help to dispel possible Japanese irritation at three other favorites being removed in Bac Giang and Mong Cai provinces, demonstrating that the government did not have a policy of sacking all Imperial Army selections. "The appointment of Nguyen Van Sy is merely a temporary expedient in the period of incipient independence," he concluded. Nonetheless, by the end of the month Sy's resignation had been accepted by the prime minister, with a formal letter of thanks for his services.[211]

Particular incidents sometimes soured relations between Vietnamese functionaries and the Japanese. Thus, Japanese Army units passing through Ninh Binh decided to billet themselves in government offices, ruining the provincial archives in the process and pestering clerks at their desks.[212] In Hoa Binh, Japanese officers ordered a district mandarin to mobilize hundreds of villagers to cut and deliver bamboo poles to put up a one-hundred-meter-long horse stable—then proceeded to pack up and move elsewhere without paying for anything.[213] The troops departed minus at least seven horses, allegedly killed and eaten by tigers, but quite possibly consumed by hungry villagers.[214] Troops in Lang Son made off with property belonging to the Customs Service, apparently including the safe where contraband money, opium, and firearms were meant to be stored.[215] At the psychiatric hospital in Bac Giang, the local Japanese commander decided to confiscate all poisons "as a precautionary measure," provoking a protest from the Tonkin Medical Bureau.[216] In Hanoi, a Japanese guard at the Indochina Meteorology Service accosted, slapped, and threatened to behead a Vietnamese employee of the Office of Agriculture, who had come to obtain weather data. Obviously the soldier had been stationed there to

211. AOM, INF, GF 20.

212. AOM, INF, GF 10 and GF 27.

213. Unidentified *tri phu* (prefectural mandarin) to Tinh Truong Hoa Binh, 20 July 1945, in AOM, INF, GF 51. Earlier, the Hoa Binh mandarin had queried Hanoi about overall compensation prospects, given the large number of Japanese troops in his province.

214. Thu Y Hoa Binh to provincial mandarin, 31 July 1945, in AOM, INF, GF 51. The speculation about the villagers is mine.

215. AOM, INF, GF 25. It is unclear from the report whether the contraband was taken as well.

216. Than Kinh Benh Vien to Bac Giang, 27 June 1945; Y Te Bac Ky to Kham Sai, 9 July 1945; Shibaraki to Kham Sai, 25 July 1945; all in AOM, INF, GF 66. Another Japanese unit confiscated poisons in Ha Nam province on 26 June, which suggests a coordinated response to some perceived threat.

prevent weather information being secretly transmitted to Allied air units, while the employee was seeking information relevant to crop selection and planting. This episode stimulated a formal protest from the Office of Agriculture to the Kham Sai, suggesting that the government's honor was at stake.[217]

Intractable Problems

Although the Tran Trong Kim cabinet discussed the famine still ravaging northern and north-central Vietnam, it was unable to accomplish much before the June harvest alleviated the immediate crisis, causing black market rice prices to drop 65 percent in a few weeks. Nonetheless, the government had reason to fear yet another famine in September or October, since the June harvest was said to be down 150,000 tons from that of 1944, and transportation of surpluses from Saigon remained inadequate.[218] The Japanese made matters worse by ordering huge quantities of piastre notes to be printed. Between March and early August 1945, some 770 million piastres were put at the disposal of the imperial armed forces, more than Governor-General Decoux had supplied during the previous 53 months.[219] Powerless to prevent such Japanese excesses, the royal government devised new regulations to encourage movement of grain, punish hoarding, and ensure minimum rations for the neediest. Plans were drawn up to repair the Red River dike system, damaged during the 1944 typhoons.[220] To relieve pressure on impoverished citizens, an imperial edict of 23 May allowed repayment of private loans to be deferred until further notice.[221] A reduction in the head tax was ordered for households in the lowest income bracket.[222]

---

217. AOM, INF, Gouvernement Revolutionnaire/GF 141, Phong Vien Chuc dossier.

218. AOM, INF, GF 34. It should be noted, however, that the capacity of local officials to measure crop yields declined substantially during the summer of 1945.

219. Shiraishi, "Vietnam," 10. It is quite possible that the Tran Trong Kim cabinet was not told the magnitude of currency printing.

220. Thirteen pages of instructions were issued to twelve provinces on 25 June 1945. AOM, INF, GF 25. See also the May (?) 1945 hydraulic engineering diagrams in AOM, INF, GF 4.

221. AOM, INF, GF 8. No additional interest was meant to be levied during the hiatus. The deferral did not apply to debts owed to the government.

222. Vu Ngu Chieu, "Other Side," 308. On the other hand, Tonkin Resident Superior Nishimura ordered that the head tax be kept at 1944 levels. Nishimura to Chef du Bureau local des contributions directes, RST, 4 May 1945, in AOM, INF, GF 66.

Of most immediate concern to farmers, however, were obligatory rice sales and the collection of paddy for land taxes. As early as 23 April, the Vinh Yen provincial mandarin took the incident of a local collector of paddy being shot and killed to warn Nishimura of future opposition to government impositions. In the villages, the mandarin added, such violent events produced "a certain satisfaction among most of the smallholders, worn out by poverty and unceasing previous deductions of paddy, which make them very susceptible to extremist conspiracies."[223] Although the government obtained Japanese agreement to discontinue colonial regulations on obligatory sales, Vietnamese officials in Hanoi still ordered farmers possessing three *mu* (1.08 hectares) or more rice land to sell a percentage of their crops to the state at less than half the black market price.[224] According to one internal government calculation, the Japanese themselves intended to collect 35,000 tons of June harvest paddy in Tonkin by one means or another, and actually obtained about 11,500 tons.[225]

Meanwhile, the government's refusal to remit or reduce the land tax led to serious trouble in the countryside. By early July, provincial mandarins were reporting substantial shortfalls in tax collections, in some cases owing to Viet Minh–organized resistance. Than Trong Hau, head of Bac Ninh province, just north of Hanoi, revealed that only one of the ten district mandarins had met his tax collection quota, for which he deserved immediate promotion. Four others needed to be cashiered in Hau's opinion for failing to report any collections whatsoever.[226] The Hung Yen province chief condemned the An Thi district mandarin, Le Van Hien, as "extremely soft-hearted" for not collecting any taxes, and suggested he be replaced forthwith. Less than two weeks later, Hanoi ordered Hien reassigned.[227] When the Ha Nam provincial chief reported collection of 1,088,759.11 piastres in land taxes, slightly more than half the intended amount, he was anxious to blame the shortfall on poor climatic conditions and transport problems rather than the admitted local "propaganda against paying," which he stressed had not led to violence.[228] Nonetheless, as officials in

223. Vinh Yen to resident superior, 23 Apr. 1945, in AOM, INF, GF 51.

224. Viet Nam Hoang De Du #14, 13 May 1945, in AOM, INF, GF 41. See also AOM, INF, GF 37. In their own defense, the Vietnamese authorities pointed out that they had raised the fixed purchase price from 25 to 120–40 piastres per quintal, at a time when the black market price was 280–320 piastres.

225. AOM, INF, GF 34.

226. AOM, INF, GF 25. Bac Ninh to Kham Sai, 9 July 1945.

227. AOM, INF, GF 25. Hung Yen to Kham Sai, 5 July 1945, and Kham Sai to Hung Yen, 16 July 1945.

228. Ha Nam to Kham Sai, 15 Aug. 1945, in AOM, INF, GF 61.

Hanoi tried to estimate overall revenues, they were forced to admit that northern Vietnam's entire budget might be gravely threatened by a "widespread and rapidly rising anti-tax movement."[229]

As part of his general concern to set a tone of sincerity, dedication, and incorruptibility in government, Tran Trong Kim insisted that information be collected on corrupt mandarins, and that measures be taken to remove and punish them. On 22 May, Vietnamese officials in Hanoi reported the removal of five province chiefs on grounds of incompetence, and the detention of six district heads on corruption charges, to Resident Superior Nishimura.[230] Not to be outdone, the Ministry of the Interior in Hue warned all government echelons of plans to sack corrupt or oppressive officials.[231] The minister of justice, Trinh Dinh Thao, abolished rules that excluded members of the royal family from arrest and court prosecution. As a deliberate warning, Thao then briefly detained one particular prince who had achieved notoriety for his gambling protection racket.[232] These early actions unleashed a flood of accusations from below aimed at scores of individual functionaries. The Hung Yen provincial chief, for example, conveyed public complaints concerning four district heads and one senior interpreter, adding that he had long tried to get them to change their ways, without success. Similar letters came from the provincial chiefs of Hai Duong and Hoa Binh.[233] After a particular canton head in Son Tay was denounced for peculation, the provincial chief recommended that he be dismissed and stripped of all honors.[234] Local youth organizations dared to petition the authorities in Hue and Hanoi directly. In Hung Yen, a youth group accused one official of opium addiction and extortion. On being queried by Hanoi, the official's immediate superior admitted that he probably did smoke opium, but suggested that "the extortion evidence is not strong."[235] A young Ninh Binh activist condemned the town's police chief for black-marketeering and packing his office with relations. The head of Hai Duong's youth organization, Vu Ngoc Cu, forwarded a four-page

229. AOM, INF, GF 5. Tai Chinh Phong budget simulation, July (?) 1945.

230. AOM, INF, GF 34. Not until a week later did Phan Ke Toai bother to inform the Ministry of the Interior in Hue. May–June 1945 dossiers on allegedly corrupt mandarins can be found in Indochine GF 14.

231. AOM, INF, GF 4.

232. Trinh Dinh Thao, "Ngay hom truoc Cach Mang Thang Tam 1945 [The Days Preceding the August Revolution], *To Quoc* (Hanoi), 9-1984, 8–9.

233. AOM, INF, GF 14.

234. AOM, INF, GF 10.

235. AOM, INF, GF 9. This box contains a number of other June–July 1945 dossiers dealing with sackings, suspensions, and forced transfers.

indictment of the province's examining magistrate, Tran Duc Tao, for allegedly raping, molesting, and otherwise maltreating numerous women in the area.[236]

By late June, the staff of the Bureau of Personnel in Hanoi must have realized that the government's cleanup campaign posed a serious dilemma. Swamped with reports from every province, they created dossiers assiduously for each case, hoping to ascertain which accusations were accurate, which the product of local vendettas or rumor-mongering. Aside from the obvious problems of time and resources, each investigation at the local level produced further rumors, suspicion, and acrimony. Although some additional officials were dismissed in July and early August,[237] most of the dossiers seem to have been filed away, perhaps for perusal in quieter times. To have done otherwise would have jeopardized the entire administrative system from within precisely when it faced unprecedented challenges from without. The government's difficulties were compounded by an unusually high number of requests from mandarins to be relieved of their positions, to retire early, or to take long-service leave. Although the reasons given were invariably personal—for example, illness, infirmity, being an only son, or honoring a recently deceased parent—we may assume that many mandarins felt profoundly uncomfortable in the new, unpredictable political circumstances. In any event, most of these requests were denied or deferred. Routine summer vacations were canceled, or limited in some cases to a mere three days.[238] Some officials left their posts without permission, provoking dire warnings from their Japanese and Vietnamese superiors alike.[239]

The Administrative Tangle

One of the more momentous decisions taken after the Japanese takeover involved establishment of an administrative apparatus in Tonkin (Bac Ky) largely autonomous from the ministries in Hue. In the first instance, this probably reflected the wishes of General Tsuchihashi to conduct business with as few bureaucratic complications as possible: he assigned Tsukamoto Takeshi responsibility for Indochina-wide institutions, mostly headquar-

236. AOM, INF, GF 34.
237. AOM, INF, GF 34, contains a letter of 2 Aug. 1945 from the minister of the interior, Tran Dinh Nam, to the Kham Sai in Hanoi, authorizing him to relieve one provincial chief and six district heads on charges of graft and embezzlement. A 7 February 1946 list of mandarins dismissed between November 1944 and December 1945 can be found in Indochine GF 3.
238. AOM, INF, GF 3, GF 7, and GF 34.
239. AOM, INF, GF 4, GF 25, and GF 34.

tered in Hanoi, and, as we have seen, designated Nishimura Kumao as resident superior of Tonkin. On 27 April, undoubtedly after consultations with the Japanese, the royal government announced that a Kham Sai would assume the functions of the resident superior, minus responsibility for the cities of Hanoi and Haiphong, but would continue to "ask the opinion of the Japanese adviser in north Vietnam."[240] On 2 May, Phan Ke Toai, then provincial chief of Thai Binh, was appointed Kham Sai. Nonetheless, Nishimura continued to sign himself "resident superior" as often as "supreme counselor." What might have been a hopelessly confusing situation was probably saved by Nishimura's increasing willingness to let the Kham Sai's Office take on responsibilities not affecting Japanese security, simply retaining the right of oversight.[241] The so-called "local services" in Tonkin, subordinate to the governor-general's "general services," and responsible for finances, customs, public works, and education, among others, came increasingly under the Kham Sai's authority as well.

However, such Kham Sai powers, derived from long-standing French colonial regulations making the Tonkin resident superior almost entirely autonomous of the royal government in Hue, could not be squared with Japanese professions of support for Hue's authority in the north as well as the center. In mid June, Tran Van Chuong, the minister of foreign affairs, brought this anachronism to the attention of the Japanese, stimulating a written clarification by Yokoyama. Henceforth the Kham Sai, although holding powers formerly invested in the resident superior, would be "directly responsible to the imperial government in Hue instead of the governor-general of Indochina." Local services would also subordinate themselves to Hue rather than to the governor-general.[242] Yokoyama's letter

240. AOM, INF, GF 25. In Vietnamese, the full title of this new position was Bac Ky Kham Sai Dai Than (northern imperial delegate high official), usually abbreviated to Kham Sai. The French translation was Délégué extraordinaire imperial au Tonkin.

241. Nishimura said Phan Ke Toai was the only Vietnamese political figure he came to know well, characterizing him as a "good patriot" of strong character. Although originally nominated by the Japanese Army, Toai became disenchanted when "real power" remained in foreign military hands. Toai showed disapproval by staying away from his office, an act that Nishimura quietly admired. Interview in Tokyo, 27 Nov. 1967. Whether Toai was seen at his desk or not, the archival records show that his large staff was quite active and maintained contact with most provincial bureaus.

242. AOM, INF, GF 25. Letter dated 21 June 1945 addressed to "SE TV Chuong, VP du Gouvernement imperial du Viet Nam, ministre de aff. étranger à Hue." It is perhaps significant that this letter did not come from Governor-General Tsuchihashi, or even his deputy Tsukamoto.

Figure 15. Phan Ke Toai, imperial delegate for
northern Vietnam. *Trung Bac Chu Nhat* (Hanoi),
13 May 1945. Courtesy of the Bibliothèque nationale.

provoked a detailed rebuttal from the Kham Sai's head of financial services,
essentially arguing that as long as the Gouvernement général and its
various services existed side by side with the imperial government and its
ministries, the "principles" set forth in Yokoyama's letter could not be
applied.[243] Implicitly accepting this reasoning, Hue tried to persuade General Tsuchihashi to transfer general service bureaus to its jurisdiction,
obtaining some success on paper, but not in practice, before the royal
cabinet resigned in early August.[244] The Japanese could always reply that

243. AOM, INF, GF 25. "Note au sujet des principes énoncés dans la lettre no.
691—Cab du 21 Juin 1945 de S.E. le conseiller suprême à Hue," (?) July 1945. The
same dossier contains a proposal for abolition of the Financial Control Service
subordinate to the governor-general, because it operated on the French colonial
principle of "divide and rule."
244. The paucity of personnel to staff the Hue ministries was another motivation for gaining control of the general services. For example, the entire Ministry
of Foreign Affairs had barely ten staff members, the Ministry of National Education
only two. Shiraishi, "La Présence," 237. Apparently to resolve structural confusion,
the government established a small Judicial and Financial Administrative Reform
Council (Hoi Dong Cai Cach Cai Tri Tu Phap va Tai Chinh), composed of the
minister of finance, Vu Van Hien, the Kham Sai, Phan Ke Toai, and two eminent

it took time to divide Indochina-wide institutions among the three kingdoms.[245] In Hanoi, meanwhile, Phan Ke Toai and his subordinates marched to their own drum, a fact of enormous consequence when the time came to respond to the Japanese surrender and Viet Minh moves to seize power.[246]

Concerning the reversion of Cochinchina, Hanoi, Haiphong, and Da Nang (Tourane) to Vietnamese imperial jurisdiction, the issue was more clear-cut: either the Japanese accepted that these places were part of Vietnam or they did not. On 11 June, passing through Hue, General Tsuchihashi discussed the matter with Emperor Bao Dai.[247] In a remarkably blunt imperial statement, issued the same day, Bao Dai revealed that he had intended to announce the independence of all Vietnam in March, but "owing to circumstances, I [*Tram*] found it necessary to follow operational instructions." He thanked Japanese officials for "temporarily supervising" certain territories, claimed they were ready to "return the right of administration of all the land of Vietnam to the Vietnamese Government," and instructed his ministers to make the necessary preparations.[248] This pronouncement, which represented both an apology by the monarch to his subjects in traditional Confucian style and a deliberate nudge to the Japanese, provided the political focus for an elaborate ceremony in Hue to commemorate the one hundred forty-third anniversary of the Nguyen dynasty's accession to power.[249] On 13 July, Tran Trong Kim traveled to

academics, Nguyen Van Huyen and Nguyen Huu Tao. Minutes of its first meeting, on 18 July, are contained in AOM, INF, GF 5.

245. AOM, INF, GF 55 is entirely composed of General Government personnel lists as of 15 June 1945, presumably with an eye to subsequent reallocation. The lists for each bureau are still divided between "Cadres européens" and "Cadres indochinois," even though all the names are now indigenous, not French.

246. As late as 30 July, Tran Trong Kim felt it necessary to obtain from the Japanese authorities an agreement placing the Kham Sai under the Vietnamese imperial government. AOM, INF, GF 47. We can surmise that Kim had failed to gain satisfaction from Phan Ke Toai directly, and that each individual continued to use his Japanese connections against the other. As we shall see in chapter 6, Kim sought Toai's removal in early August.

247. Shiraishi, "La Présence," 239–40. On the same day, probably not by coincidence, a large Vietnam unification rally was held in Hanoi, the featured speaker being Phan Anh, minister of youth. Martin, *Heures tragiques*, 95. In our interview in Hanoi on 7 March 1988, Phan Anh gave the Tran Trong Kim cabinet considerable historical credit for pushing the Japanese repeatedly on unification issues. By contrast, the Communist Party continues to condemn the 1945 royal government as "pro-Japanese," "reactionary," and "traitorous."

248. Tuyen Chieu, 11 June 1945, in AOM, INF, GF 66.

249. Smith, "Japanese Period," 293.

Hanoi to discuss reversion with Tsuchihashi, probably prepared to resign if no progress was made. Tsuchihashi, it seems, had already decided to transfer the cities: within a week, Konagaya Yūtake was replaced as mayor of Hanoi by Tran Van Lai, a close associate of the Japanese.[250] Haiphong and Da Nang soon witnessed similar transfers.[251]

Tsuchihashi was less forthcoming on Cochinchina, presumably reflecting his reluctance to overturn long-established administrative patterns rather than any particular Japanese designs on the region. To complicate matters, new irredentist claims on several Cochinchina border provinces were being advanced from Phnom Penh. In early July, perhaps after hearing from Vietnamese compatriots stationed in Cambodia, the central branch of the Vietnam Public Servants Association protested vehemently to the Hue government about "Cambodia requesting to divide territory," then attempted to alert its brother organization in Hanoi.[252] According to Tran Trong Kim, Tsuchihashi argued that the Cambodian assertions needed to be resolved before Cochinchina could be returned. Kim flatly rejected these Cambodian claims, and after a full day of talks, he and Tsuchihashi agreed that transfer should take place in Saigon on 8 August, with both of them present.[253] Tsuchihashi made the appointment, but Kim remained embroiled in a cabinet crisis in Hue, as we shall see.[254]

Meanwhile, in Cochinchina itself, Governor Minoda had largely ignored developments to the north, including the efforts of the Hue government to assert jurisdiction over the colony. He appointed a number of Vietnamese to fill administrative positions vacated by the French, brought Tran Van An back from Singapore to spearhead formation of a quasi-legislative Council of Cochinchina, and encouraged his assistant Iida to

250. Shiraishi, "La Présence," 239. Photographs of the transfer ceremony are featured on the cover of *Trung BacChu Nhat* (Hanoi), no. 255 (29 July 1945).

251. Vu Trong Khanh became mayor of Haiphong, and Nguyen Khoa Phong mayor of Da Nang. Ministry of the Interior appointments for all three individuals were signed 19 July. AOM, INF, GF 4.

252. AOM, INF, GF 58. On 10 July 1945, an unidentified official in the Hue government tried to cancel this cable to Hanoi at the PTT. If the cable had already gone, he instructed the PTT to retrieve it and tell the northern branch of the Vietnam Public Servants Association, "Don't do anything hasty."

253. Tran Trong Kim, *Mot Con Gio Bui*, 78–81. In a 1962 interview with Kiyoko Nitz, Tsuchihashi indicated that he was willing quite early to transfer both the cities and Cochinchina, but repeatedly found Bao Dai hesitant to accept them. Nitz, "Japanese Military Policy," 347. In his unpublished diary, cited above, Tsuchihashi also blames the Hue court for "ignoring" the question of Cochinchina's reversion. I find these statements by Tsuchihashi less than convincing.

254. See chapter 6.

convert Maurice Ducoroy's youth and sports organizing into a regionwide paramilitary Vanguard Youth (Thanh Nien Tien Phong) organization.[255] Minoda does not seem to have excluded any existing group from coming forward and participating in his institutions, providing it did not contest Japanese hegemony. By July 1945, therefore, a remarkable variety of Constitutionalist landlords, colonial functionaries, Cao Dai adepts, monarchists, Trotskyists, and covert ICP members were jostling for leadership positions.[256] A former member of the Nguyen An Ninh "Secret Society" and wartime Kenpeitai associate, Nguyen Hoa Hiep, for example, was selected to head the Saigon Sûreté.[257]

The Vanguard Youth first came to the attention of the public in the wake of an American B-29 raid on Saigon on 12 June, which killed twenty-two Europeans and at least two hundred Vietnamese.[258] Hundreds of young men in dark shorts and white shirts marched to the ruins with picks and shovels, digging out survivors, assisting in the identification of victims, and transporting bodies to the mortuary. The operation was led by Pham Ngoc Thach, who would play a pivotal role in the events of August–September in Cochinchina. The son of a royal princess, Thach had obtained a medical degree in prewar Paris, married a Frenchwoman, and returned home to specialize in the treatment of lung disorders, especially tuberculosis. Through his private practice, he came to know a number of Japanese officials, including Minoda, whose French wife made sure they met socially

255. In late March, Iida formed a Vietnam Youth and Sports Union Committee (Uy Ban Viet Nam Thanh Nien The Thao Tong Hoi), which was dominated by Cao Dai representatives and cadres from Ducoroy's group. On 15 April, Iida addressed a youth assembly, urging Vietnamese to step up activities if they wanted to achieve full independence. By May, the Vanguard Youth, originally only one component of the committee, had come to dominate youth organizing in Saigon. Nguyen Ky Nam, *Hoi Ky*, 54–59. I have not been able to ascertain Iida's given name.

256. The Hoa Hao do not appear to have played much of a role in these organizations, although they were busy mobilizing in their own strongholds in the western Mekong Delta. See Hue-Tam Ho Tai, *Millenarianism*, 132–35. Huynh Phu So did consult a variety of secular intellectuals, most notably the prominent Trotskyist Ta Thu Thau. See Phuong Lan, *Nha Cach Mang Ta Thu Thau (1906–1945)* [The Revolutionary Ta Thu Thau] (Saigon, 1973), 350–61. Catholic clergymen also seem to have kept a low profile.

257. *Lich Su Dang Cong San Viet Nam Tinh Song Be*, ed. Nguyen Ba Tho, 173, 175, 196. AOM, INF, CP 158, "Activities rebelles au Nam Bo," d.10. Huynh Van Phuong, a 1930s Trotskyist activist, was appointed chief of the Sûreté for all Cochinchina, probably a less sensitive post.

258. Michel Desiré, *La Campagne d'Indochine, 1945–1954: Bibliographie*, vol. 1 (Vincennes, 1971), 11. Four months earlier, on 7 February, a similar B-29 raid had killed an estimated one hundred fifty Vietnamese and thirty Europeans.

as well. As former secretary of the Cochinchina Scout Association, Thach had some experience in motivating young people. Most surprisingly, given his background, Thach had recently accepted secret membership in the ICP.[259]

The following weeks saw membership of the Vanguard Youth movement expanding into the tens of thousands, with branches in a number of provincial towns. Although building on Ducoroy's efforts, and borrowing extensively from Boy Scout manuals, the Vanguard Youth was permitted by the Japanese to be much more political in orientation, displaying its own flag (yellow with a red star), hanging banners across the street calling for "National Liberation" (Giai Phong Dan Toc), and publicly exhorting members to "reorganize society, improve the lives of our countrymen." At a solemn oath-taking ceremony on 1 July, attended by Iida, members swore readiness to sacrifice themselves for the Fatherland (To Quoc). Two days later in Hue, Emperor Bao Dai received a 38-person Vanguard Youth delegation and officially acknowledged Pham Ngoc Thach as the royal government's youth representative in the south.[260] A "Vanguard Youth Honor Court" was established to punish any member who committed a crime.[261] In some areas, Vanguard Youth units issued identification cards to replace the hated colonial head-tax certificate, as well as trying to enforce their own system of travel permits.[262] To some degree, the Vanguard Youth succeeded because it helped fill an administrative vacuum left by the French, not only carrying out disaster relief, but repairing public bomb shelters, standing guard duty, and attempting to ship rice north.

259. Interviews with Tran Van Giau, Ho Chi Minh City, 25 Mar. 1980 and 12 Feb. 1990. At our interview in Ho Chi Minh City on 19 March 1988, Duong Quang Dong (Nam Dong) remembered Thach being sworn into the ICP in May 1945. Minoda, in an interview with me in Tokyo on 20 January 1967, recalled Thach as a "sincere and honest friend," although he had "certain suspicions about his political loyalties." Kiyoko Kurusu Nitz, "Independence without Nationalists? The Japanese and Vietnam Nationalism during the Japanese Period, 1940–45," *JSEAS* 15, no. 1 (Mar. 1984): 119, mentions Thach as a friend of Komatsu Kiyoshi's as well. Further biographical information on Pham Ngoc Thach is contained in AOM, INF, c. 360, d. 2848.

260. Nguyen Ky Nam, *Hoi Ky*, 60–71. Besides Thach, other members of the Vanguard Youth leadership committee in Saigon included Nguyen Van Thu, Tran Buu Kiem, Huynh Van Tieng, Mai Van Bo, Luu Huu Phuoc, and Le Van Huan. Mai Van Bo, "Phong Trao," 27–28, recalls the first oath-taking ceremony as taking place on 15 July, with up to 50,000 youths participating.

261. *Tan A* (Saigon), no. 70 (27 July 1945): 5. The Vanguard Youth also had its own uniform (black or blue shorts, white shirt, straw hat), salute, and "official song."

262. Interview with Tran Bach Dang, Ho Chi Minh City, 17 Mar. 1988.

Texts prepared for Vanguard Youth propaganda efforts and training sessions reveal a mélange of ideas, with no attempt yet to project a firm organizational line.[263] Thus, while the Vanguard Youth stood for representative, constitutional democracy, one document also opined that dictatorship might be necessary "for a limited period," and that the franchise ought not be extended to those who had "followed the imperialists for their own profit, forgetting the interests of the country." The Vanguard Youth was prepared to enroll anyone possessing a "good attitude," refusing explicitly to discriminate by social class. A training brief on the Indochinese economy warned that no nation could sustain political independence while "remaining economically dependent on some foreign power." Fortunately, Indochina contained the necessary raw materials, labor force, and market to underpin future industrial development. Vanguard Youth adherents were urged by the writer of this brief to reject pessimism stemming from awareness of Vietnam's high mortality rates, a "popular tendency toward discouragement," or the current lack of a national army. Instead, members should appreciate that "the period of using armed force [a circumlocution for the Pacific War] has determined that the fate of this region will soon be decided." Those ethnic groups who were not "meek," who acted with discipline, could seize a favorable position. In this new, hopeful historical period, there would no longer be "the shame of carrying the yoke of foreign rule."

A few southern intellectuals sensed that it was vital to find out what was happening in distant Hanoi, the traditional focal point of Vietnamese political and cultural activity,[264] and a much better place to try to learn about events in China and the world at large. Most determined was Ta Thu Thau, a Trotskyist leader of the 1930s jailed repeatedly by the French. Shifted from Con Son prison island to forced residence in Long Xuyen in 1944, he had been able to return to Saigon soon after the Japanese took over. After consulting with other Vietnamese activists across the political spec-

263. Three undated (but probably June or July 1945) documents in Vietnam National Archives No. 2 (Ho Chi Minh City), Fonds du Goucoch (Divers), d. 612.

264. Although Hue had been the royal capital since 1802, Hanoi had enjoyed that status for the preceding eight centuries. From the late nineteenth century on, the French concentrated commercial and some administrative functions in Saigon; it was there that the new Vietnamese intelligentsia blossomed in the 1920s. Following the victory of the French Popular Front in 1936, however, colonial censorship restrictions on Hanoi publications were eliminated and a veritable explosion took place in writing, printing, and dissemination of Vietnamese-language materials, accompanied by a lively literacy campaign. Marr, *Vietnamese Tradition*, 45–49, 178–80.

trum, Thau began the difficult journey northward, almost surely sped on his way by those Japanese who saw him as the potential leader of a popular anti-French national united front.[265] In Hue, he sought out Ho Ta Khanh, minister of the economy and a fellow southerner, who voiced growing disenchantment with the royal government.[266] In Hanoi, Thau linked up with fellow Trotskyists in the Han Thuyen publishing group, met some miners, stevedores, and textile workers, purchased a shortwave receiver, and explored opportunities to travel on to Kunming. Throughout his trip, he made no secret of his opposition to the ICP-led Viet Minh. The Allied call for Japan's unconditional surrender in the Potsdam Declaration, the terms of which were broadcast over New Delhi radio in late July (see chapter 4), convinced Thau that time was running short, but his frantic attempts to mobilize an anti-imperialist alternative to the Viet Minh in the north bore little fruit.[267] As we shall see, his return trip south immediately following Japanese capitulation would end brutally in Quang Ngai, with Thau being executed by a local Viet Minh group.

Within weeks of the takeover, as mentioned above, censorship rules had been altered significantly. It remained impossible, of course, to criticize the Japanese overtly or praise the Allies, yet the printing of brief Domei news bulletins—for example, about the invasion of Okinawa, the surrender of Germany, and the intensified bombing of Tokyo—led many Vietnamese readers to conclude that Japan's fate was sealed. One author intimated that Japan was facing disaster because it had unjustly attempted to achieve its geographical objectives by brute force, cutting across the "road of human progress." Vietnam could learn from this mistake and achieve complete independence, he added, by "fighting within the ranks of the international movement to eliminate colonial systems."[268]

Writers were free to condemn colonial practices in vivid detail, to publicize Vietnamese patriots who had died fighting the French, and to discuss in general outline a future Vietnam free of foreign occupation or

265. Ho Huu Tuong, another prominent Fourth International activist of the 1930s, indicated to me that Komatsu Kiyoshi discussed such a front with Ta Thu Thau, and traveled with Thau to Hanoi. If Tokyo surrendered to the Allies, Komatsu hoped that some Japanese like himself could take Vietnamese citizenship and participate in resistance to French recolonization. Interview with Ho Huu Tuong, Saigon, 3 Mar. 1967.

266. Interview with Ho Ta Khanh, Paris, 1 Nov. 1984. According to Nguyen Ky Nam, *Hoi Ky*, 39, Thau also met Trinh Dinh Thao, minister of justice, the other southerner in the cabinet.

267. Phuong Lan, *Nha Cach Mang Ta Thu Thau*, 362–415.

268. Que Lam, "Ngoai Giao" [Foreign Relations], *Tu Tri* (Hanoi), 22 June 1945.

exploitation. Two ideas permeated the press: to love one's country and to serve the nation. Writers preached unity, dynamism, and abnegation.[269] While such principles had characterized earlier Pétainist propaganda as well, the imagery in the spring and summer of 1945 was far more vibrant, the message more compelling. The territorial integrity of Vietnam was constantly reaffirmed in the press, even though the Japanese remained noncommittal. In a public "Letter to the South," for example, the Hanoi-based General Association of Vietnamese Students offered a range of historical, economic, and cultural reasons why Vietnam was a single "bloc," which could become a modern nation if people heeded the call to unite; the letter was prefaced by a cartoon showing individuals linking hands from Saigon to Hanoi, captioned, "There are no central, southern, and northern regions, only the country [*nuoc*] of Vietnam."[270] The press proved reluctant to criticize the royal government, partly because of continuing censorship, but mainly because writers did not wish to violate the spirit of unity in the face of major national problems. Besides, a number of royal government appointees had long been colleagues in a variety of publishing endeavors.[271]

Nonetheless, in northern Vietnam especially, many who had cheered the Japanese in March and hailed the new Tran Trong Kim cabinet in April were deeply disappointed by June or July. The economy remained a shambles. Fear of another terrible famine was never far from anyone's mind. Grandiose imperial edicts proliferating from Hue failed to translate into practice at any level. A Ministry of Interior prohibition on gambling promulgated on 28 May took a month to be mimeographed by the Kham Sai's Office for distribution to northern mandarins and then seems to have produced only confusion and acrimony. Youthful militants complained that the gambling ban failed to cover small-scale card games and mah-jongg. The Hoa Binh provincial chief argued sarcastically that because people were so preoccupied with material privations and Japanese confiscations and corvée demands, they had no time to think about gambling. The chief of Lang Son province, after pointing out that a substantial portion of his provincial budget derived from taxes on public gaming establishments, curtly requested to be excused from making monthly reports on implementation of the ban. In early July, police in Hai Duong raided a mah-jongg

---

269. Brocheux, "La Revue *Thanh Nghi*," 325–28.
270. *Tu Tri* (Hanoi), 4 May 1945.
271. For example, four out of the ten members of the Tran Trong Kim cabinet had participated actively in the weekly *Thanh Nghi*: Hoang Xuan Han, Phan Anh, Vu Van Hien, and Vu Ngoc Anh.

parlor and arrested the provincial treasurer and education mandarin among others. Although the incident was reported in a Hanoi newspaper and the offenders scheduled for trial, superiors in the Kham Sai's Office apparently decided to let the two officials off with a reprimand and transfer.[272] In the midst of such disputes about government probity, the head of the Economic Service in Hanoi, Nguyen Manh Ha, quietly complained to the Kham Sai that his Rice Office currently possessed only two employees, yet was supposed to be responsible for supplying grain to the Japanese and the city population, purchasing rice in Saigon, supervising commercial rice trans-actions, and punishing violators of relevant edicts.[273]

Partly to meet such needs, the Japanese established in Hanoi an École des fonctionnaires indochinois. After processing applications and conduct-ing medical examinations in May, courses for forty advanced and ninety-seven elementary students commenced in early June, designed to last for three months. All enrollees swore to assume responsibilities as "warriors building a new Indochina," which included disciplining both body and spirit, uniting to protect the Fatherland, and "zealously advancing first to serve and to lift high the level of people's livelihood [*dan sinh*]." The regimen was quasi-military, with a daily schedule extending from 0700 to 2400 hours that embraced physical exercise and marching drill as well as seven hours of classroom instruction. Each week also saw an excursion to some central or provincial government office. Within a week, nineteen students had dropped out, most citing physical inadequacies; their places were taken by Vietnamese former members of the colonial army. From surviving school records, we know that Japanese personnel kept a close watch over twice-daily roll calls, classroom attendance, and individual grades. The school was still functioning in late August.[274]

Action from Below

Between March and May, most politically inclined groups in north Viet-nam meekly accepted the restrictions imposed by the authorities.[275] Thus,

---

272. AOM, INF, GF 22 and GF 25. Anti-gambling initiatives enjoyed popu-larity across the political spectrum. See, e.g., *Tan A* (Saigon), no. 69 (20 July 1945): 5–7.

273. Nha Kinh Te to Kham Sai, 22 June 1945, in AOM, INF, GF 41.

274. "Ecole des fonctionnaires indochinois," in AOM, INF, GF 43.

275. Besides the Japanese military proclamations mentioned above, restrictive colonial laws remained in force until further notice. A royal edict of 8 May gave citizens the right to form organizations, providing (a) they entertained no illegal purposes; (b) the founders had no criminal records; and (c) thirty days' prior notice

when the Vietnam Patriotic Youth Association (Hoi Viet Nam Thanh Nien Ai Quoc) submitted its bylaws and request to operate to Resident Superior Nishimura in mid April, it stressed its noninvolvement in politics and readiness to support any government "providing it is legal [*hop phap*]."[276] Five individuals in Lac Son district, Hoa Binh province, were more forthcoming when they applied to establish a branch of the Greater Viet National Alliance (Dai Viet Quoc Gia Lien Minh), presenting themselves as protectors of the country's independence. Perhaps for this reason, the district head disparaged them as "merchants of little education and no political talents" who would upset the Muong ethnic group, a majority in his district.[277] A new Vietnam Women's Association (Hoi Phu Nu Viet Nam) sought approval from the Ministry of the Interior in Hue, politely proposing the queen mother and the queen as honorary chairwomen.[278] Carefully phrased petitions and draft bylaws came in from a host of other groups, from the highly visible Hanoi University Student Union to small societies in distant provinces espousing uncontroversial cultural, moral, or religious ideals. The civil servants of Bac Ninh province requested organizational recognition, as did Vietnamese workers at the French-owned Gros Company and an association of Haiphong entrepreneurs.[279]

By June, however, many organizations simply sought clearance from local authorities, or proceeded to ignore administrative red tape entirely. Accepting this fact, a royal edict of 9 July transferred official responsibility for organizational supervision to provincial and district mandarins, even though the youth minister, Phan Anh, complained that some of these

---

was given. False statements could incur fines of from 15 to 1,000 piastres. Individuals who failed to disband on government order might receive six days to one year in prison and fines of between 15 and 10,000 piastres. AOM, INF, GF 25. In Tonkin, Resident Superior Nishimura issued his own instructions on 3 May and maintained dossiers on about forty organizations. AOM, INF, GF 39. See also the 19 June 1945 Kham Sai list of voluntary and charity groups, in AOM, INF, GF 65.

276. AOM, INF, GF 3. The writer of this application, Vo Van Cam, claimed that the "Japanese military staff" had already agreed. Nishimura approved the organization on 5 May, specifying that every member had to carry a pass with photo and tax stamps. Not until 15 June did the Kham Sai's Office receive notice of these actions.

277. AOM, INF, GF 3. The provincial chief forwarded the dossier to Nishimura, recommending rejection of the application and requesting a list of organizations approved by the resident superior.

278. Approval was granted 23 May, and the first meeting was convened at the Hoi Khai Tri Tien Duc hall in Hanoi on 11 June. Respectable bourgeois ladies took most of the seventeen elected offices. AOM, INF, GF 3.

279. AOM, INF, Gouvernement Revolutionnaire/GF 141, GF 3, and GF 8.

officials deliberately obstructed young people wishing to participate in relief efforts, literacy classes, or the Civil Guard.[280] The Kham Sai's Office seems to have encouraged provincial chiefs to bring proliferating local youth groups under one officially sponsored provincial youth committee. The result was bureaucratic chaos, however, with some provincial chiefs continuing to forward group applications and bylaws to Hanoi, others complaining sharply about political agitators from Hanoi forming branches in their areas, and still others compelled to approve organizations on the "recommendation" of local Japanese military commanders.

Indochina in early 1945 contained an inordinate number of prisoners, both "common" and "political," many of whom saw the Japanese coup as an opportunity to gain their freedom by one means or another.[281] Quickest off the mark were 200 political prisoners at the Ba Ra penal camp in Thu Dau Mot province, north of Saigon, who chose to liberate themselves on 10 March after French wardens fled and before a Japanese Army unit arrived.[282] In late March, the authorities suddenly released 150 prisoners from the Quang Tri provincial jail.[283] For others the road to freedom was more tortuous. On 2 April, for example, Le Quang Tao headed a group of common criminal inmates at the Hanoi Central Prison who unsuccessfully petitioned Commandant Oshima of the Kenpeitai for release. On 6 May, Tao and 23 colleagues tried again, this time addressing Phan Ke Toai, the newly appointed Kham Sai. All the signers admitted their crimes, ranging from accessory to murder (sentence of twenty years) to black-marketeering (three years), but blamed their actions partly on the French colonial system, expressed repentance, and promised to serve the Fatherland.[284] This petition had yet to be acted upon when, ten days later, 44 prisoners in the Hanoi Central Prison dug a hole and crawled to freedom, although half

280. AOM, INF, GF 3. Bo Thanh Nien to Kham Sai, 12 June 1945, in AOM, INF, GF 41.

281. The Japanese appear to have supervised prisons until August, relying on Vietnamese mandarins and French wardens to maintain operations. In early April, General Tsuchihashi ordered all province chiefs to submit monthly status reports on prisons and to seek his approval for any increase in the number of inmates, whether political prisoners or common criminals. AOM, INF, GF 61.

282. *Lich Su Dang Cong San Viet Nam Tinh Song Be*, ed. Nguyen Ba Tho, 178–79. Probably fewer than half of the Ba Ra camp departees were ICP members, and only twenty of these ended up participating in subsequent Party operations. For another example of early "self-release," see the discussion of Ba To penal camp in Quang Ngai in chapter 3.

283. Hoang Anh, Le Tu Dong, et al., *Binh Tri Thien Thang Tam Bon Lam: Hoi Ky* [August 1945 in Binh Tri Thien: Memoirs] (Hue, 1985), 160.

284. Petitions in AOM, INF, GF 45.

were recaptured within a few days.[285] To the east of Hanoi, in Hai Duong, about one-quarter of the inmates in the provincial jail tried to escape at dinnertime on 12 May; 2 were killed, 40 recaptured quickly, and 27 remained at large the next day. Well to the south, in Quang Tri province, 16 escapees from the mountain penal colony of Lao Bao managed to evade recapture.[286]

Many political prisoners expected to be released immediately following the 9 March coup; when this did not happen, both inmates and their families outside began to bombard the authorities with petitions, often expressing polite exasperation or bewilderment at "anti-French patriots" being kept behind bars.[287] A royal edict of 20 April did order the release of colonial-period political prisoners, but implementation was in the hands of local administrators, who wished to examine each dossier separately and had the backing of their Japanese supervisors. Even the pro-Japanese magazine *Tan A* (New Asia) felt the 178 politicals released in Saigon in June were "very few" in light of the total number incarcerated by the French.[288] A petition from 83 politicals in the Hanoi Central Prison on 24 June asked that they be allowed to follow 181 others already freed.[289] Newspapers began openly to criticize the authorities for selectively keeping some anticolonialists in jail. *Tan A* persisted in its belief that the Japanese would not "discriminate by political coloration," yet unwittingly contradicted itself by asserting that "Japan will never forget any element that has helped to greater or lesser degree in the current war."[290] Viet Minh adherents submitted pe-

---

285. Hinh Vu So to Kham Sai, 16 and 19 May 1945, in AOM, INF, GF 47. Warden Peuziat had the unenviable task of reporting this breakout to the Kenpeitai.

286. Hai Duong to Kham Sai, 13 May 1945, and Bo Tu Phap to Kham Sai, 17 May 1945, in AOM, INF, GF 57.

287. On 19 June 1945, for example, the Kham Sai's Office sent Nishimura thirteen petitions from families of political prisoners, together with a list of thirty-seven inmates at three locations. The first eighteen were Vietnam Nationalist Party members serving life sentences. Seven others were members of the Vietnam Restoration League. Eleven had been jailed for "political maneuvers aimed at the independence of Vietnam," and one was incarcerated for "communist political maneuvers." AOM, INF, GF 62.

288. *Tan A* (Saigon), no. 66 (30 June 1945): 9. The editors urged families to be patient, as processing was continuing. They also pointed out that the French had put some politicals in the common criminal category, further complicating the screening procedure.

289. Not until 31 July did the minister of justice, Trinh Dinh Thao, forward this petition to Yokoyama with a suggestion that they all be released. On 8 August, the correspondence was forwarded to the Kham Sai in Hanoi, but with no indication of a decision. AOM, INF, GF 13.

290. *Tan A* (Saigon), no. 66 (30 June 1945): 9.

titions too. In early April, for example, Nguyen Huu Than and 11 others jailed in Ha Dong before the Japanese coup requested release on the grounds that their only crime had been to oppose the French and seek Vietnamese independence. "Now Vietnam is independent, hence our aspirations have been satisfied," they added. Such willingness to please did not impress the head of the Tonkin Sûreté, who in fact went beyond this particular petition to recommend that all "communist political prisoners" be kept under detention beyond the expiration of their normal sentences. The Kham Sai's Office accepted the Sûreté's advice, at least in respect to the Ha Dong prisoners.[291] As we shall see, other ICP and Viet Minh prisoners were released or managed to escape between March and July.

Freed political prisoners of any party affiliation posed a delicate problem for administrators, since many returned to their home districts eager to settle old scores or form organizations to influence local affairs. Some former prisoners chose to join government organizations, but that was not necessarily of comfort to the authorities. Provincial and district mandarins—themselves part of the system that had incarcerated these men and women, now hailed by the public as suffering patriots—hardly dared contradict them on policy issues, much less punish them for violating existing laws.

Not only former political prisoners sensed that the local status quo could be altered dramatically. Ordinary farmers began to forward petitions requesting the removal of corrupt, rapacious, or violent village chiefs. Some petitions focused on excessive tax collections or corvée demands. By far the largest number, however, detailed how particular plots of land had been taken unfairly during the colonial period; this was the beginning of a property upheaval from below that no government could control. Thus, residents of Cao Due village in Hai Duong province complained bitterly at being forced previously to sell 35 hectares to René Gilles, leaving only 158 hectares in the hands of local farmers.[292] Villagers in Giao Thuy district, Nam Dinh province, petitioned for return of 27 hectares from a canton head, Nguyen Truc Hien.[293] In Bac Giang province, My Do villagers

---

291. Petition, 10 Apr. 1945; Tong Doc Ha Dong to Kham Sai, 3 May 1945; Mat Tham Bac Ky to Kham Sai, 28 May 1945; and Kham Sai to Tinh Truong Ha Dong, 12 June 1945, all in AOM, INF, GF 57. Meanwhile, Nguyen Huu Than had been released on 19 April, after serving three years.

292. AOM, INF, GF 4. The Gia Loc district head forwarded his assessment of this case to Hanoi on 10 August, and deliberations continued into 1946 under DRV auspices.

293. AOM, INF, GF 1.

requested return of land originally appropriated by the colonial railway service, but now being tilled by "someone else."[294] Residents of Yen Phu village, Ha Nam province, asserted that their ancestors had been compelled to sell 15.3 hectares to the Catholic Church in the twenty-eighth year of the reign of Tu Duc (1875); now they wanted the land back. Apparently the provincial chief showed sympathy for their cause, although no action was taken before the royal government collapsed in August, when villagers proceeded to occupy the property. Like many other land disputes, this one would continue well into the DRV period.[295] For the moment, no one dared challenge more recent Japanese expropriations of land for military purposes at ridiculously low rates.[296]

Kham Sai records reveal a steady growth in incidents of armed robbery and pillaging after April 1945. The number of individual petitions complaining about losses to "bandits" (*bon cuop*) increased markedly compared to previous months. Officials could be held up too. In mid June, five men pretending to be Kenpeitai officers drove up to the Bac Ninh Mines and Industry Bureau in a V-8 deluxe automobile, seized 20,000 piastres plus a quantity of documents, then forced the bureau chief to accompany them out of town.[297] However, it was the bigger attacks that soon preoccupied the authorities. Most worrisome at first were the assaults on coal-mining towns in Quang Yen, just north of Haiphong, culminating in the storming of the Clothilde Louise mine and Port Redon loading facility at Uong Bi one June night, which resulted in the deaths of a number of Vietnamese guards and civilians, as well as two Frenchmen. When the remaining French nationals tried to flee carrying the two bodies, they were intercepted on the road and another killed, along with a Japanese woman accompanying them. Several days later, a combined Japanese-French group returned to Uong Bi by boat to find extensive destruction of equipment and loss of property; as

294. AOM, INF, GF 25.

295. AOM, INF, GF 1. One of the most serious disputes involved 1,066 hectares in Ninh Binh province. In May 1945, the Catholic Church, which claimed credit for developing this land, found itself under challenge by adjacent non-Catholic villagers.

296. AOM, INF, GF 16. For example, the village of Phu Lo Doai, Kim Anh district, Phuc Yen province, received a mere 135.88 piastres indemnification (the equivalent of less than 50 kilograms of rice) for Japanese use of 14.508 hectares. See also the village files in AOM, INF, GF 39 and GF 71. Some of this land had been acquired to establish a Japanese airbase at Noi Bai, now Hanoi International Airport.

297. Groupement d'achats to Japanese General Staff HQ Hanoi, 17 June 1945, in AOM, INF, GF 58. Before allowing the official to escape, the five men identified themselves as Viet Minh.

the boat departed, it was attacked and sunk by Allied aircraft.[298] Shortly thereafter, the "pirate" (*giac*) problem expanded to adjacent Bac Giang province, where armed bands swept into villages, demanded money, and, when that was not produced, seized water buffalo, clothing, and other movable property. Most disturbingly, the An Chau Civil Guard post was surrounded by a 400-strong band led by "General" Luc Van Loi; the twenty-seven guardsmen resisted for six hours, by which time their paltry allocation of fifteen cartridges per rifle had almost been expended. Some guardsmen used their last bullet to commit suicide; others were executed after surrender; nine managed to escape alive.[299]

By July, reports of banditry involving ten to one hundred gang members were coming in from other provinces as well. The Lang Son provincial chief requested assistance from local Japanese units to deal with a large group of "pirates" of Nung and Chinese ethnic origin, although the situation here was complicated by the arrival of increasing numbers of Chinese Army troops, some of whom crossed and recrossed the frontier at will. In Cao Bang, the Japanese apparently forced several local officials and Vietnamese guardsmen to cross the border with them in pursuit of offenders, where they were killed or captured by the Chinese.[300] Closer to Hanoi, the Bac Ninh province mandarin informed the Kham Sai of a shoot-out with about twenty "brigands" and requested reinforcements. In Ha Dong, guardsmen were called to the scene of several homes being pillaged, but failed to pursue the perpetrators because they were so well armed.[301]

Although previous district and provincial reports had often lumped Viet Minh actions together with "bandits" and "brigands," by early June the Viet Minh was seen as a separate, increasingly serious threat. Local efforts to deal with Viet Minh challenges soon took on a frenetic character. Not surprisingly, functionaries adjacent to the Sino-Vietnamese frontier were hardest pressed. Thus, the chief of Cao Bang province reported that the "Viet Minh Party" had made communication with his subordinates impossible, except when Japanese units were on the move and willing to carry messages. In such uncertain conditions, he added, "local authorities are afraid the

298. R. Huas to Consul Nojiri, 23 May 1945, and "Bao cao ve mo than Uong Bi cua nguoi Phap," 6 June 1946, in AOM, INF, GF 47.

299. Bao An Bac Giang to Kham Sai, 20 June 1945, and La Van Lo to Bac Giang, 13 July 1945, in AOM, INF, GF 58.

300. Trung Khanh district mandarin to Cao Bang province chief, 23 July 1945, in AOM, INF, GF 66. AOM, INF, GF 45.

301. Bac Ninh to Kham Sai, 19 July 1945, and Ha Dong to Kham Sai, 11 July 1945, in AOM, INF, GF 58.

revolution will jeopardize their lives."[302] The Lang Son province chief requested and obtained an order from the Kham Sai cashiering the Binh Gia district head for abandoning a joint operation with Japanese troops designed to suppress the Viet Minh.[303] A group of government employees and citizens of Ha Giang province forwarded an eight-page letter to the Kham Sai explaining the degenerating situation in their area because of increased Viet Minh activity, despite "our reliance on the Japanese Army to exterminate them." They particularly urged replacement of the incumbent provincial chief, who allegedly did nothing but "push papers around in his office."[304] In Bac Can, seventy-five miles north of Hanoi, the provincial chief was anything but a paper-pusher. In early June, aiming to induce Viet Minh adherents to relinquish firearms, he posted an announcement that began: "Today our Vietnam is independent. Everyone must obey the orders of the Vietnamese government. . . . Whoever does not obey, whoever flees or resists when Japanese or Vietnamese soldiers enter their village, will be considered rebels. If they are shot and killed, no one should feel resentment."[305] Privately, he requested Hanoi urgently to place five hundred additional civil guardsmen at his disposal, because moving through villages the Viet Minh had "pressured" parents and friends of existing guardsmen, precipitating desertions. Several of his subordinate officials had been captured or disappeared, and others were now "weak and incapable of work." He nominated two new assistant district heads on the basis of their close collaboration with the Japanese Army and their courage in the face of enemy reprisals. "Those who accept the post of mandarin now expose themselves to risks that are not compensated for by the perquisites attached to their functions," he added.[306]

Certain provinces closer to Hanoi also began to report serious problems with the Viet Minh in June. In Thai Nguyen, forty miles north of Hanoi, where the provincial chief, Cung Dinh Van, had already alerted Nishimura ten weeks earlier to "Viet Minh rebels and pirates forming large bands in the interior to sow disorder,"[307] a Viet Minh unit now managed to seize

302. AOM, INF, GF 3.

303. AOM, INF, GF 2. In four Lang Son districts, officials evacuated their bureaus, at least temporarily, enabling the Viet Minh to destroy records, which made it impossible to respond to the Kham Sai's queries about famine deaths. AOM, INF, GF 3.

304. AOM, INF, CR 141.

305. Bac Can thong cao, 7 June 1945, in AOM, INF, GF 51.

306. AOM, INF, GF 20. Bac Can to Bac Bo, 30 June 1945, in AOM, INF, GF 58. Bac Can to Kham Sai, 6 July 1945, in AOM, INF, GF 44.

307. AOM, INF, GF 6.

the Dinh Hoa district seat and abduct the district head, leading the Japanese to intervene in force. However, Cung Dinh Van, who had earned a reputation for ruthlessness against the Viet Minh, was summarily shifted to the Kham Sai's Office in the city.[308] The provincial chief of Hung Yen, thirty miles southeast of Hanoi, reported that security was compromised in four of his districts; rice warehouses had been pillaged, and Viet Minh propaganda was making it very difficult to collect additional paddy.[309] On 21 June, Viet Minh adherents managed to destroy a blockhouse in the Van Lam district seat (Hung Yen) and seize thirty-one firearms. A Japanese detachment rushing to the scene encountered a crowd of about one hundred persons marching behind the Viet Minh's red flag with yellow star. Opening fire, the Japanese killed one demonstrator, arrested four others, and recovered a few weapons.[310] Meanwhile in Bac Ninh province, just across the river from Hanoi, the head of Phu My village was killed by the Viet Minh, apparently while collecting taxes. To facilitate continued collection of taxes "despite the Viet Minh menace," the provincial chief, Than Trong Hau, recommended that this village head be promoted posthumously and his family awarded 5,000 piastres.[311] In early July, Hau warned Hanoi that unless a deltawide counterpropaganda campaign were launched urgently, government rice purchases, tax collections, and dike maintenance would all be jeopardized; "AID US AND COUNSEL US," his message concluded in capital letters.[312]

Events were, however, quickly going beyond any mere propaganda contest; armed confrontation was in the offing. The royal government had at most fifty civil guardsmen to each provincial seat, and twenty to a district, all equipped with antiquated firearms and unreliable ammunition.[313] More-

---

308. AOM, INF, GF 34. As we shall see, Cung Dinh Van was one of the few mandarins hauled before a "people's court" and executed following the August Revolution.

309. AOM, INF, GF 25. By early July, Hung Yen described "extremist Viet Minh propaganda" as a major obstacle to paddy purchases and tax collection throughout the province. Meanwhile, on the other side of Hanoi, the Phu Tho province chief insisted that the Viet Minh had disrupted purchases and collections in only two of his districts. AOM, INF, GF 61.

310. AOM, INF, GF 25. Report of Civil Guard Second Lieutenant Nguyen Thuy Hung, who accompanied the Japanese unit. Also in Hung Yen, a deputy canton chief was reported killed on 27 June by three persons claiming to be Viet Minh.

311. AOM, INF, GF 25. Nishimura annotated this recommendation: "Il faut faire, à mon avis, quelque chose; et cela vite." Phan Ke Toai approved the promotion, but no mention was made of money.

312. AOM, INF, GF 25.

313. Tran Trong Kim, *Mot Con Gio Bui*, 57–58.

over, it could not simply rely on the Japanese Army. At the late July meeting between General Tsuchihashi and Premier Tran Trong Kim, mentioned earlier, agreement was reached to release additional Vietnamese members of the French Army from detention to encadre a substantially expanded Civil Guard force. Kim selected Captain Vu Van Thu to draft urgent reorganization, recruitment, and training programs, which, however, would take from five to twelve months to reach fruition. In the meantime, the Japanese made available two thousand firearms, plus ammunition, for immediate use in the north.[314] Several other members of the cabinet in Hanoi with Premier Kim doubted whether two thousand guns would be sufficient, given the stories they were hearing from friends among the intelligentsia about Allied delivery of arms to anti-Japanese forces in the nearby hills.[315]

In late June, deciding that Viet Minh activities in Hanoi and several provincial towns had reached disturbing proportions, the Kenpeitai launched a series of preemptive sweeps, imprisoning at least three hundred suspects, mostly youths, students, and government clerks, and subjecting some to brutal interrogations. This Japanese operation, known in the files as "the Viet Minh affair," created a furor as far away as Hue, with Premier Tran Trong Kim calling in Yokoyama and adding it to his list of reasons for traveling north. Petitions poured into the Kham Sai's Office in Hanoi from the families of those jailed. Rumors circulated that the Japanese had detained thousands of people rather than hundreds. In mid July, the Kenpeitai unilaterally arrested a further twenty-two Viet Minh suspects in Thai Binh, including a district education officer and the head of the provincial youth bureau, Nguyen Cong Hoan, who was better known as a novelist and short-story writer. The provincial chief protested that he had not been forewarned, and warned that such arrests "throw the population into disarray, above all the good officials whose threatened liberty is not effectively protected." By the end of the month, the Japanese had released about 150 individuals; the others would have to await the events of mid August.[316]

---

314. Ibid., 82–84. Decisions (*dinh*) issued by Tran Trong Kim, 26 July 1945, in AOM, INF, GF 66. In the north, as of 16 August, the former Garde indochinois, provincial guards (*linh co*), and police were all to reform as the Bao An Binh (Civil Guard). No mention was made of arrangements for the center and south.

315. Hoang Xuan Han, "Tuong Nho Phan Anh," 9.

316. Nishimura to Yokoyama (draft message), 26 June 1945; Thai Binh to Kham Sai, 18 and 20 July 1945: in AOM, INF, GF 66. Tran Trong Kim, *Mot Con Gio Bui*, 77, 82–83.

Despite such altercations, the focus in Hanoi was still more on talking than on fighting. In early July, the Hue government had foreshadowed a National Consultative Conference (Hoi Nghi Tu Van Quoc Gia) and established three committees to draft a constitution and propose reforms to the administrative and educational systems.[317] Prominent intellectuals published tracts and articles pressing the government to take action on a wide variety of economic, political, and cultural fronts.[318] Potentially the most influential group, consisting of about thirty-five writers and professionals dedicated to eliminating all vestiges of colonial rule, called itself the New Vietnam Association (Tan Viet Nam Hoi).[319] However, it was not until 30 July that the government selected the individuals it wished to participate in the northern branch of the National Consultative Council.[320] The first meeting was scheduled for 17 August in Hanoi.

Conclusion

Governor-General Decoux's carrot-and-stick approach succeeded in finessing native discontent at a very difficult time for France in Indochina. If not for the Japanese coup, Decoux almost surely could have kept the colonial system intact, quelled any disturbances at the end of the war, and delivered Indochina back to the French government of the day. This is not to say that time stood still between 1940 and February 1945. The Japanese managed to influence Vietnamese attitudes and behavior more than the French dared to admit, helping to stir a sense of pride in precolonial traditions, an interest in the martial arts, and a recognition that Europeans were not invulnerable.

317. Vu Ngu Chieu, "Other Side," 466, contains membership lists for the three committees. Although as it turned out none of these committees had an opportunity to convene, individual members did stimulate considerable discussion. AOM, INF, GF 5, contains May–June 1945 correspondence between the Kham Sai's Office and provincial chiefs designed to identify prominent personalities to participate in these and other institutions. Several provincial chiefs outside the Red River Delta stressed the paucity of suitably educated or experienced individuals.

318. See, e.g., Le Quang Loc, *Mot Chuong Trinh Kien Thiet* [A Program for Development] (Hanoi, June 1945), which proposes nationalization of agriculture and a platform of "constitutional socialism."

319. *Thanh Nghi* (Hanoi), no. 107 (5 May 1945), contains a list of members. The general secretary was Vu Dinh Hoe, who had just published an influential essay titled *Nhung Phuong Phap Giao Duc o cac nuoc va Van De Cai Cach Giao Duc* [Educational Methods in Various Countries and the Question of Educational Reform] (Hanoi, May 1945). It is unclear whether this New Vietnam Association was connected with a group of the same name active simultaneously in Annam.

320. AOM, INF, GF 5. Presumably central branch and southern branch meetings also were planned, but Hanoi files make no mention of them.

Simultaneously, Indochina's relative isolation from the battlefield gave Vietnamese intellectuals four years to reassess reality according to their own lights rather than the priorities set by foreigners. All this counted for something when the outside world, in the form of the relentlessly advancing Allied forces and awareness that Japan could not avoid defeat, began to crowd Indochina once again.

The Japanese takeover revived Vietnamese respect for the Imperial Army and led a variety of groups to try to exploit new opportunities. However, they soon discovered that General Tsuchihashi and most of his subordinates were disinclined to alter the colonial system in Indochina dramatically, even preferring to continue employing French personnel wherever possible. This was unacceptable to almost all Vietnamese groups, helping to spark an upsurge of unauthorized political activity, threats to the safety of the French civilian population, and increasing pressure on the Kenpeitai, native police, and Civil Guard units. By May 1945, Tsuchihashi was ready to give more authority to Emperor Bao Dai and the Tran Trong Kim cabinet. However, they were mostly unprepared for the challenge, assuming that government meant reading reports, working one's way through agendas, signing documents, issuing decrees. There was a disposition, too, among members of the royal administration at all levels not to prepare for the harder alternative, not to act on what they suspected to be true.

The terrible famine of early 1945 cut across all other events and calculations, at least for the ten million inhabitants of Tonkin and northern Annam. In those regions, society was disrupted at a level deeper than anyone, Vietnamese, French, or Japanese, realized at the time. Outraged at the wielders of power who had permitted such horrors to occur, the survivors were open to Viet Minh explanations and exhortations, yet also haunted by the moral dilemmas that had been forced upon them. Above all, they wished to avoid yet another encounter with starvation later in the year, if necessary by taking matters into their own hands.

If the Japanese and the Vietnamese royal government had been given several years to begin to devise alternatives to the colonial system, as happened in Indonesia, for example, Vietnam's fate might have been very different. It is not hard to imagine someone like Phan Anh taking on the role of a Sukarno and learning through experience what national leaders were expected to do. Like Sukarno, he might have helped the Japanese round up and transport countrymen to their graves at distant work sites. As it was, Phan Anh and the rest of his colleagues had only four months, at a time when Japan's star was waning, although no one could know how rapidly. While a few Vietnamese appointees felt it necessary to stick with the Japanese as the only safeguard against French return, most were sophisticated enough to start looking for alternatives, not least of all the Viet Minh, who had the advantage of being both anticolonial and pro-Allied. Meanwhile, quite separate from such higher-level calculations, ordinary villagers were busy discovering the parameters of life without French tax inspectors, post commanders, and plantation owners.

3 The Indochinese Communist Party and the Viet Minh

On 8 March 1945, hearing that Governor-General Decoux had been called to Saigon for consultations with the Japanese, and observing Imperial Army units preparing for possible combat, underground Communist Party activists in Hanoi sent an alert to the headquarters of the Party Central Committee, located in a clandestine "safe zone" (*an toan khu*) less than twenty kilometers north of the city.[1] Truong Chinh, the highly intelligent, if pedantic, secretary-general of the Party, decided to convene a meeting of the available members of the Central Committee to discuss how to react to violent termination of the fifty-three-month-old Franco-Japanese relationship, which he had been predicting in Party periodicals for almost a year. As members began to gather the next evening at a pagoda in Dong Ky village, Bac Ninh province, the first Japanese sapper explosions and artillery salvos against French positions in Hanoi could be heard in the distance.[2] Soon Vietnamese colonial *tirailleurs* were reported fleeing along nearby Route 1, and several participants in the Party meeting rushed out

---

1. We are entirely dependent on Communist Party sources for the events described here and much that follows. As indicated in the preface, I have ignored unconfirmed assertions apparently designed to convince readers of the infallibility or omnipresence of the Party.

2. Other ICP leaders at this meeting included Nguyen Luong Bang, Le Duc Tho, Le Thanh Nghi, and Nguyen Van Tran. Ban Nghien Cuu Lich Su Dang Trung Uong, *Nhung Su Kien Lich Su Dang* [Party Historical Events] (hereafter *NSKLSD*), vol. 1, 1920–1945 (Hanoi, 1976), 601–2. Because participants were observed entering the pagoda, the meeting shifted that same night to the nearby village of Dinh Bang, only sixteen kilometers from Hanoi. *Cach Mang Thang Tam* [The August Revolution] (hereafter *CMTT*), vol. 1, ed. Tran Huy Lieu (Hanoi, 1960), 200.

to encourage local supporters to collect stray firearms discarded along the road.[3]

Eschewing any other hasty actions, Truong Chinh and his colleagues spent almost three days deliberating the overall situation and formulating a Party response. The remarkable 1,750-word set of instructions, drafted by Truong Chinh and issued on 12 March in the name of the Standing Bureau of the Central Committee, conveyed succinctly the unparalleled opportunities offered the Party and its Viet Minh front groups. Drawing on the scattered battle information available up to that moment, the instructions assumed correctly that French colonial forces would not be able to recover from the initial shocks delivered by the Imperial Army. On the other hand, the victorious Japanese would find it difficult to govern Indochina in their own right, particularly given the perceived threat of Allied invasion. As a result of this turn of events, it was appropriate for the Party to stop condemning the French—Vietnam's overlords for six decades—and instead attempt to link up with them in attacking the Japanese. If French commanders decided to reject these overtures, it would still be possible to win over some of the rank-and-file members of the colonial army.

Mindful of earlier disastrous attempts by Party branches to seize power before conditions were ripe, the Standing Bureau instructed subordinate echelons to concentrate first on organizing anti-Japanese meetings, demonstrations, strikes, and armed marches. People should be persuaded not to work for the Japanese, not to pay taxes, not to be deceived by claims of independence under Japanese aegis. Where possible, famished citizens should storm government granaries. In some localities it would be feasible to convene military training courses, build guerrilla units, and establish revolutionary councils to assume administrative responsibilities. If the Japanese retaliated, activists would need to fade in among the villagers for protection, then try to make life sufficiently difficult for enemy troops to cause them to withdraw from the area. However, the Standing Bureau instructions cautioned readers that Japanese forces were still united and resolute. Moreover, many Vietnamese citizens would need to go through a period of disillusionment with the results of the Japanese takeover before they would support the Viet Minh, and many nascent Viet Minh groups would need strengthening before a general uprising was possible.

3. Le Thanh Nghi, "May net hoi ky ve Tien Khoi Nghia o Chien Khu 2" [Some Recollections of the Early Insurrection Period in War Zone 2], *Nhan Dan* (Hanoi), 31 Aug. 1960.

Aware that it was only a matter of time before Allied forces in the Philippines, southern China, or Burma invaded Indochina, the Standing Bureau tried to prepare Party followers for such contingencies. Mindful of disasters that had befallen overeager Italian, Polish, and French insurgents in 1943–44, they cautioned especially against rising up at the moment of Allied assault; instead, communists should wait until Allied and Japanese units were locked in combat, then proceed to attack Japanese rear-area camps, warehouses, transport, and communication lines. Simultaneously, Vietnamese guerrilla leaders would make contact with Allied commanders to coordinate attack strategies. However, at no time would the Party allow its plans for a general insurrection to be contingent on Allied operations, as that would mean "relying on others, tying one's hands when conditions were changing to advantage." It was possible that revolution might break out in the Japanese homeland, or that Japan might be occupied like France in 1940, causing the imperial forces overseas to lose hope. In those cases, "even if the Allies have not yet invaded [Indochina], our general insurrection could still break out and be victorious."[4]

Copies of the Standing Bureau instructions of 12 March quickly reached Party branches in Hanoi and adjacent provinces. Within a month, most other Party members in Tonkin and northern Annam had either read the instructions or been briefed on their contents.[5] Southward beyond Nghe An province, however, Party communications remained erratic or nonexistent. Although key branches in Ha Tinh, Hue, and Phu Yen had managed to get hold of copies of the instructions and discuss their implementation by late May, most Party cells in between had to depend on the occasional Viet Minh leaflet or on simple word-of-mouth interpretations.[6] Further south, in Cochinchina, no copies of the Standing Bureau instructions

4. "Nhat Phap Ban Nhau va Hanh Dong cua Chung Ta," in Dang Lao Dong Viet Nam, *Chat Xieng: Nhung Tai Lieu Lich Su tu Chinh Bien Thang Ba den Cach Mang Thang Tam 1945* [Breaking Our Chains: Historical Documents from the Political Changes of March to the August Revolution], 3d ed. (Hanoi, 1960), 9–19. Text also contained in Quan Doi Nhan Dan Viet Nam, *Van Kien Quan Su cua Dang, 1930–1945* [Military Documents of the Party, 1930–45] (Hanoi, 1969) (hereafter VKQS), 264–73. An English translation can be found in *Breaking Our Chains: Documents of the Vietnamese Revolution of August 1945* (Hanoi, 1960), 7–17.

5. CMTT, 1:21, 281, 337, 383–84. Pham Cuc, "Khoi Nghia gianh chinh quyen Thang Tam 1945 o Thanh Hoa" [The August 1945 Insurrection to Seize Power in Thanh Hoa], *Tap Chi Lich Su Dang* (Hanoi), 4-1991, 30.

6. CMTT, vol. 2, ed. To Lich Su Cach Mang Thang Tam (Hanoi, 1960), 23, 30, 50, 70, 149.

appear to have reached the Party Regional Committee(s) or anyone else until August.

Setbacks in 1939–1940

Truong Chinh and his colleagues had reason to be confident of the Party's ability to win power, although substantial hurdles remained, and no one imagined that the moment of truth would come in only five months' time. Formed in 1930, the Indochinese Communist Party (ICP) had weathered early internal doctrinal disputes, condemnations from both left (Trotskyists) and right (Constitutionalists, nationalists, royalists), and repeated police suppressions.[7] During the Popular Front period (1936–38), the ICP had been able to emerge from the shadows, organize large public meetings and peaceful demonstrations, publish extensively, and recruit new members from rural as well as urban backgrounds—effectively reaching beyond its initial small base among the intelligentsia and proletariat. Its policy of pressing the Popular Front government in Paris for fundamental reforms to the Indochina colonial system garnered considerable public support, even though the French failed to concede much in practice.[8]

In September 1939, following the Nazi-Soviet pact and France's declaration of war on Germany, the authorities in Indochina moved to arrest as many ICP, Trotskyist, and other left-wing Vietnamese activists as they could find. ICP leaders, while mindful of growing physical danger since the fall of the Popular Front government in Paris in April 1938, nonetheless failed to turn many members away from the attractions of open speechmaking or publishing and back toward the type of covert politics that had characterized Party efforts prior to 1935. Very tardily, in late September 1939, the ICP Central Committee sent out instructions to all branches to go underground, to comprehend the grave circumstances under which all members and sympathizers now had to function, yet not to lose faith in the Party's ultimate victory.[9] Over the next fourteen months, thousands

7. Huynh Kim Khanh, *Vietnamese Communism, 1925–1945* (Ithaca, N.Y., 1982), 57–231. William J. Duiker, *The Communist Road to Power in Vietnam* (Boulder, Colo., 1981), 14–55.

8. Tran Huy Lieu, *Mat Tran Dan Chu Dong Duong* [The Indochina Democratic Front] (Hanoi, 1960). Daniel Hémery, *Révolutionnaires vietnamiens et pouvoir colonial en Indochine: Communistes, Trotskystes, Nationalistes à Saigon de 1932 à 1937* (Paris, 1975), 281–424. David G. Marr, *Vietnamese Tradition on Trial, 1920–1945* (Berkeley and Los Angeles, 1981), 315–21, 347–62, 373–99.

9. Vien Lich Su Dang, *Tong Khoi Nghia Thang Tam 1945* [The August 1945 General Uprising] (Hanoi, 1985), 17–18. *NSKLSD*, 1:477–81.

of ICP members were thrown into prison, others fled to southern China, and still others ceased operations in hopes of avoiding police attention.[10] In a number of localities, the Sûreté relied on spies within the Party or confessions obtained through torture to track down and arrest entire provincial and district-level committees.[11] The Annam (Trung Ky) Regional Committee lost and reconstituted its membership three times before running out of suitable volunteers.[12] The Haiphong Committee, also responsible for the coal-mining region immediately to the northeast, was smashed in December 1939.[13]

Even as ICP members tried desperately to avoid arrest, they had to digest the policy implications of the Soviet Union's nonaggression pact with Germany in August 1939. Suddenly Adolph Hitler, archenemy of socialism, freedom, and the working class, became the associate of their hero Joseph Stalin. At a special session of the Supreme Soviet in late October 1939, Foreign Minister Molotov asserted that it was no longer Germany but Britain and France who must be looked upon as the aggressors. The Communist International, having prior to the pact urged all member parties to mount the barricades against fascism, now denounced former Popular Front allies as reactionaries, ceased its criticism of Hitler, and pictured the war as a struggle between rival imperialists to decide who would dominate the world.[14] This volte-face, according to a later official Vietnamese communist history, "could not help but cause some surprise and misunderstanding among a number of Party members and revolutionary cadres."[15]

To counter such confusion, the ICP Central Committee, meeting twenty kilometers northwest of Saigon in November 1939, circulated a resolute defense of Moscow's position. It argued that since the September 1938 Munich encounter with Hitler, London and Paris had been "maneuvering

10. *CMTT*, 1:81–82, 128, 330, 406, 428–29. *CMTT*, 2:39–42, 65–66, 103, 146, 206, 215.

11. *CMTT*, 1:420. *CMTT*, 2:5, 20–21, 65. One example of the devastating effect of a Party cadre confessing is provided in Luong Van Dai, "Chap Moi" [Tying the Knot], in *Thai Binh Khoi Nghia* (Thai Binh, 1965), 95–105. In this case, at least two hundred ICP members were captured as a result, with four dying in Sûreté hands, others becoming ill and dying later in jail.

12. *CMTT*, 2:41, 65.

13. *CMCD*, 10:9.

14. Julius Braunthal, *History of the International, 1914–1943*, vol. 2 (London, 1967), 496–515.

15. Vien Lich Su Dang, *Tong Khoi Nghia Thang Tam 1945*, 17. Tran Huy Lieu, *Mat Tran*, 60, states that both the Moscow show trials and Stalin's pact with Hitler undermined ICP credibility, at least temporarily.

vilely" to embroil the Soviet Union in a war with Germany. As a result of the nonaggression pact, however, "not only 180 million Soviet citizens, but billions of other workers and peasants around the world could avoid being drawn into a second terrible war of plunder provoked by the British, French, and German imperialists."[16]

Another passage in this resolution suggested, however, that everyone would probably become embroiled in this global war, whether they liked it or not. It predicted that the "American and Italian imperialists would push and deceive their citizens into the killing," that Japan would expand its war in the Far East, and that hence:

> Many millions of corpses will pile up like a mountain of blood and bones. Innumerable homes, countless amounts of property will be reduced to ashes. Pitiful sights of children crying for fathers, older brothers for younger brothers, wives for husbands, persons missing, houses destroyed, famine and misery will exceed comprehension. The world will be a giant extermination furnace. Humanity will have to endure several generations of doleful existence.[17]

In all likelihood this apocalypse would extend to Indochina, since the Japanese had already occupied Hainan and the Spratly Islands offshore, and French concessions had only further "whetted the insatiable appetite of the bald-headed Nipponese."[18] Imperialists—whether white or yellow—had to be fought by the peoples of Indochina if they hoped to avoid extinction. Fortunately, global war would weaken the imperialists and strengthen the international revolutionary movement. Furthermore, "ruthless exploitation by French imperialists in Indochina to support the war effort will cause the Indochinese to become progressively revolutionary."[19] The struggle needed to be carefully modulated to avoid spontaneous outbursts that the enemy could quickly repress. On the other hand, it was erroneous to retreat in the face of terror or to believe that "urging the masses to struggle in wartime amounted to leading them to slaughter." Such capitulationist

---

16. Ban Tuyen Huan Trung Uong, Dang Cong San Viet Nam, *Lich Su Dang Cong San Viet Nam: Trich Van Kien Dang* [History of the Vietnam Communist Party: Extracts from Party Documents] (hereafter *TVKD*), vol. 1, *1927–1945* (Hanoi, 1979), 228. A direct comparison was also made between this "second imperialist world war" and the 1914–18 conflict, although without mentioning the precedent of the draconian Brest-Litovsk treaty imposed by Germany on the Bolsheviks in March 1918. Ibid., 224–25.

17. Ibid., 227.

18. Ibid., 231–32. "Bald-headed" presumably alludes to the close-cropped heads of imperial soldiers.

19. Ibid., 251–52.

attitudes would "impede the struggle movement, alienate the masses from the Party, exterminate the revolution."[20]

These Central Committee exhortations led some ICP members to reject any thought of passive self-protection or defensive regroupment in favor of violent counteraction. France's capitulation to Germany in June 1940, and especially the Indochina Army's humiliating defeat at the hands of the Japanese in September (see chapter 1), gave further impetus to arguments within the ICP favoring overt challenges to the imperialists, even plans to launch an uprising (khoi nghia).[21] However, the two most notable episodes originated to some degree outside Party ranks, being taken up in hasty, ill-coordinated form by local or regional leaders without approval from the ICP Central Committee.

In late September, as colonial troops fled the debacle around Lang Son, hill people of Tay, Nung, and Yao ethnic origin disarmed some of the stragglers, persuaded others to desert, and collected hundreds of rifles thrown down alongside roads and paths. Emboldened by rumors of complete collapse of the Indochina administration, they sacked several police stations and terrorized local families who had served the French. Simultaneously, a small group of ICP members escaped from Lang Son jail in the confusion of the Japanese attack, met with a village-level Party cell, and together decided to mount an uprising. On the night of 27 September, about six hundred people armed with captured French rifles, old hunting flintlocks, machetes, and quarterstaves marched on the Bac Son district seat, forty kilometers west of Lang Son. The district mandarin fled, together with his platoon of guards, leaving the crowd free to liberate the nearby Mo Nhai military post, make a bonfire out of official documents and seals, and cheerfully declare an end to imperialist oppression. Then everyone dispersed. Three days later, a French-led Garde indochinoise unit retook the district center without opposition and reestablished contact with local colonial appointees.[22]

The original decision to march on Bac Son had been reached without consulting Chu Van Tan, the Party secretary for the area. He hurried to

20. Ibid., 268.
21. Trung Chinh, "Hoi Nghi Trung Uong Lan Thu 6 va hai cuoc Khoi Nghia dau tien do dang ta lanh dao" [The Central Committee's Sixth Plenum and the First Two Uprisings Led by Our Party], NCLS 146 (5-1972): 5–8.
22. Tong Bo Viet Minh, Bac Son Khoi Nghia [The Bac Son Uprising], 4th printing (Hanoi, 1946). Hoang Quang Khanh, Le Hong, and Hoang Ngoc La, Can Cu Dia Viet Bac (Trong cuoc Cach Mang Thang 8-1945) [The Viet Bac Guerrilla Base (in the August 1945 Revolution)] (Viet Bac, 1976) (hereafter CCDVB), 17–19.

the delta to report to the Tonkin (Bac Ky) Regional Committee, which quickly dispatched one of its members, Tran Dang Ninh, to Bac Son to take charge. On 16 October, Ninh and Tan formed a twenty-man guerrilla unit, set up an uprising headquarters, and publicly reaffirmed the dissolution of imperialist rule. Homes of local "reactionaries" were stormed and their property (rice, clothing, money) given to those said to have suffered most at the hands of the colonialists. Alleged secret agents of the French were executed. On 28 October, more than a thousand people gathered at the village of Vu Lang to listen to revolutionary speeches and prepare for recapture of the Mo Nhai military post. However, a local French plantation owner, hearing of the meeting in advance, guided soldiers from Mo Nhai via a mountain shortcut to attack the crowd by surprise, causing the participants to flee in all directions. The colonial authorities followed up this success with public executions, burning of houses and crops, and confiscation of cattle and grain.[23] The Japanese had no objections to these operations, despite earlier promotion of anticolonial sentiments in the area; it was convenient to have the French take responsibility for "law and order" following the 22 September accord.

Far to the south, a much more substantial challenge to French rule occurred. Beginning in March 1940, the ICP's Cochinchina (Nam Ky) Regional Committee circulated a pamphlet on general preparations for a revolt.[24] Subsequent clandestine meetings focused on three constituencies: trade union members in the Saigon-Cholon area; poor peasants, tenants, and agricultural laborers in the Mekong Delta; and Vietnamese conscripts in French military units. The soldiers were deemed crucial, since they had access to firearms and were known to be increasingly disturbed at the prospect of either being sent to fight in the European war or ordered to defend French Indochina against the Japanese or the Thais. When Governor-General Decoux issued instructions to mobilize more native troops and civilian labor brigades to meet the growing threat from Bangkok,

---

23. Chu Van Tan, *Ky Niem Cuu Quoc Quan* [Recollections of the Army for National Salvation] (Hanoi, 1977), 8–10. This entire memoir has been translated by Mai Elliott as *Reminiscences on the Army for National Salvation*, Cornell Southeast Asia Data Paper 97 (Ithaca, N.Y., 1974). CMCD, 10:10–17. NSKLSD, 1:489–91, 493–94. Ban Nghien Cuu Lich Su Quan Doi, *Lich Su Quan Doi Nhan Dan Viet Nam* [History of the People's Army of Vietnam] (Hanoi, 1974) (hereafter *LSQD*), 52–57. After the ICP gained power in 1945, the "Bac Son Uprising" was placed on a historiographical pedestal, which my scrutiny of the available evidence fails to support.

24. Tam Vu [Tran Van Giau], *Cuoc Khoi Nghia Nam Ky* [The Southern Region Uprising] (Hanoi, 1960), 34.

Vietnamese soldiers garrisoned in Saigon approached ICP members to cooperate in a general uprising before their units were dispatched to the Cambodian front.[25]

Although the Cochinchina Regional Committee, headed by Ta Uyen, clearly favored mounting an uprising, Party rules dictated that it obtain authorization from the Central Committee. This was no easy matter, the Standing Bureau of the Central Committee having been reconstituted in the north for the first time since the founding of the ICP. In October, Phan Dang Luu, one of the more fervent proponents of the uprising, and also a member of the Central Committee, made the long trip north, hoping to gain approval and return safely to Saigon before the plot was uncovered by the police or participating troops were shifted to Cambodia. However, the Central Committee, gathered secretly in a village near Hanoi for its Seventh Plenum (6–9 November 1940), rejected the Regional Committee's proposal as premature. Phan Dang Luu had difficulty getting back to the south, and then was captured as he approached Party headquarters in Saigon on 22 November.[26]

Having heard nothing from the Central Committee by early November, and pressed by members of the Regiment de Tirailleurs annamites and 5^e Regiment d'Artillerie coloniale to make a commitment, the Cochinchina Regional Committee decided on its own initiative to schedule

---

25. *CMCD*, 10:17–19. Nguyen Ngoc Ty et al., "Revolutionary Upsurge, 1930–1945," in *Vietnamese Studies* 45 (Hanoi, 1976 [?]), 79–82. According to the latter source, a clandestine French Communist Party cell, led by a naval lieutenant, supplied local ICP contacts with information, a radio set, twenty-seven pistols, and other weapons.

26. Trung Chinh, "Hoi Nghi Trung Uong Lan Thu 6," 8–9. Pierre Brocheux, "'L'Occasion favorable,' 1940–1945," in *L'Indochine Française, 1940–1945*, ed. Paul Isoart (Paris, 1982), 136–37. *NSKLSD*, 1:494–96. Available sources fail to tell us why or how the ICP's Standing Bureau ended up in Tonkin. It probably reflected the ICP's increasing attention to events in China. We know that the general secretary, Nguyen Van Cu, spent some time in the north prior to his arrest in June 1940. With so many other leaders in jail, Truong Chinh's group near Hanoi may simply have promoted itself and sought regional recognition later. Stein Tønnesson, *The Vietnamese Revolution of 1945: Roosevelt, Ho Chi Minh and de Gaulle in a World at War* (London, 1991), 115–16, suggests that the Standing Bureau remained in the south in late 1940, with Phan Dang Luu going north, not to participate in an alleged seventh plenum of the Central Committee, but to instruct the Tonkin Regional Committee to participate in a general insurrection. Tønnesson's hypothesis would help to account for the very poor communications between the southern and northern wings of the Party during the next four years. However, he has no solid evidence to place against the scores of Communist Party histories and autobiographies that assert a legitimate seventh plenum near Hanoi in early November 1940. It is an intriguing question for some future student of the ICP.

the uprising for the night of 22 November. Several days before the 22d, however, colonial intelligence services learned enough to convince French commanders to transfer suspect units out of Saigon or confine them to barracks and lock away all weapons. On the 22d, the secretary of the ICP's Saigon-Cholon Committee was captured and quickly confessed what he knew of the uprising plan, leading the governor of Cochinchina to place guards at key installations, close schools, order a curfew, and send squads into working-class neighborhoods to round up suspects. The ICP's urban network was smashed in a few hours. Although some workers went to assigned locations that night prepared to act, nothing happened. In nearby Gia Dinh, a crowd gathered in front of the local theater wearing special scarves as a code sign, expecting to receive firearms from soldiers with which to attack the main Saigon prison, where a number of ICP leaders were incarcerated. When no one arrived, they dispersed.[27]

With both soldiers and workers neutralized, everything depended on the peasants. In a few provinces, ICP cells received last-minute orders to abort the uprising. In at least eight locations, however, ICP members led large crowds of villagers to march on provincial or district centers, armed mostly with machetes and bamboo spears. In other places, hearing news of demonstrations and land seizures, villagers moved on their own without any Party members being present.[28] Police posts and administrative bureaus were attacked, telegraph offices burned, bridges damaged, roads torn up, local collaborators killed or detained, and revolutionary committees formed. Residents of My Tho province experienced revolutionary rule for almost four weeks. All debts and taxes were abolished, property of particularly hated landlords distributed to poor participants, and tribunals set up to try alleged French agents and other "enemies of the people." At least three colonial employees were executed. People gathered in a festive atmosphere to burn tax certificates and loan contracts. The red flag with yellow star was

---

27. Trung Chinh, "Hoi Nghi Trung Uong Lan Thu 6," 9. *CMCD*, 10:19–21. Tam Vu [Tran Van Giau], *Cuoc Khoi Nghia Nam Ky*, 37–49, 53–54. Vu Ngu Chieu, "Political and Social Change in Viet-Nam between 1940 and 1946" (Ph.D. diss., University of Wisconsin–Madison, 1984), 24–26.

28. Bao Dinh Giang, in Chanh Thi et al., *Len Duong Thang Loi*, 138–43. In one province, Long Xuyen, ICP leaders received the uprising order six days late, when word of failures elsewhere was already at hand, yet they nonetheless decided to mobilize people to attack three targets. The only success was the burning of the Cho Moi telegraph office, after which the participants retreated to the countryside, where many were subsequently killed or captured. Ban Nghien Cuu Lich Su Dang, *Lich Su Dang Bo Tinh An Giang (1927–1945)* [History of the An Giang (1927–1945)] (An Giang, 1986), 149–56.

flown for the first time. Local landlords and merchants found it prudent to donate money, gold, jewelry, cattle, cloth, and even land and several rice mills to the revolution.[29]

Elsewhere, however, the French counterattacked more quickly, employing European troop units and Cambodian tirailleurs rather than Vietnamese.[30] In several cases, aircraft, armored cars, and artillery were used to destroy whole villages. Police and local colonial officials then moved in to arrest suspects, in some cases shooting them on the spot.[31] For want of sufficient handcuffs or chains, detainees had their hands and feet pierced with telegraph wire. When all existing prison facilities were full, the French packed detainees onto ships moored in the Saigon River. No one knows how many people died in this "white terror," but the number almost surely exceeded two thousand. Up to eight thousand were detained, some later dying in jail or being executed.[32] On the other side, three Frenchmen and thirty militiamen or local Vietnamese notables were killed.[33]

Partly to divert the attention of the colonial authorities, partly to reduce the negative political implications of defeat, ICP committees at a distance from both the Bac Son and Cochinchina uprisings organized support meetings, collected money, and distributed leaflets praising the heroism of the insurgents.[34] In Hanoi, women traders, students, and elderly folk contributed sweaters, quilted jackets, and cloth to send to combatants in the chilly hills of Bac Son.[35] The poet Truong Son evoked the suffering of villagers in the face of French repression:

> Blood spilled in resistance zones,
> People strung together, piling up in prisons.

29. *Nam Ky Khoi Nghia* [The Southern Region Uprising], ed. Luu Phuong Thanh (Ho Chi Minh City, 1990). *CMTT*, 2:329, 385. *LSQD*, 57–69. Ban Nghien Cuu Lich Su Dang, *Tien Giang trong cuoc Khoi Nghia Nam Ky* [Tien Giang in the Southern Region Uprising] (Ho Chi Minh City, 1985), 46–89. Tam Vu [Tran Van Giau], *Cuoc Khoi Nghia Nam Ky*, 50–53.

30. Brocheux, "'L'Occasion favorable,'" 142.

31. René Bauchar [René Charbonneau], *Rafales sur l'Indochine* (Paris, 1946), 71.

32. *CMCD*, 10:21–30. Tran Huy Lieu, *Lich Su Tam Muoi Nam Chong Phap* [History of Eighty Years Resisting the French], vol. 3 (Hanoi, 1961), 61–63.

33. Brocheux, "'L'Occasion favorable,'" 138. AOM, INF, CP 158, d. 12. Vu Ngu Chieu, "Political and Social Change," 26–27. One French source speaks of "a hundred insurgents killed," either a deliberate downgrading of the overall bloodshed or a figure restricted to known opponents with police files. AOM, INF, 7F27.

34. *CMTT*, 1:350–51. *CMTT*, 2:43.

35. *CMTT*, 1:8. *CMCD*, 10:26–29, reprints an urgent message from the Standing Bureau of the ICP Central Committee, issued about 3 Dec. 1940, chastising Party members in Tonkin and Annam for not mobilizing more public support for the Cochinchina uprising.

Hatred fills our stomach,
Revenge torments us endlessly.
Who knows how much broken flesh and blood
On the Liberation road,
Building the long wall.[36]

Another poet, after recalling past violent Vietnamese encounters with Mongol, Ming, and Ch'ing invaders, stressed how recent events had demonstrated that Frenchmen bled and died just like anyone else.[37]

Despite such bravado, ICP losses during 1940 had been very high. Those leaders captured and subsequently executed by the French included the Party's general secretary, Nguyen Van Cu; a former general secretary, Ha Huy Tap; the Comintern's representative to the ICP, Le Hong Phong; and the ranking female ICP member, Nguyen Thi Minh Khai. Many provincial and district-level committees were in a shambles, particularly in Cochinchina; it would take three or four years to regain momentum.[38]

French faith in the loyalty of Vietnamese colonial soldiers had already been shaken by the events of late 1940, when in January 1941, Nguyen Van Cung, a Vietnamese sergeant in the Garde indochinoise entrusted with command of a small post in Nghe An province, decided with possible prompting from supporters of Prince Cuong De to kill the local French customs inspector and his wife, cut the telegraph wires, and lead some of his comrades against a larger military post down the road. Sergeant Cung told subordinates that Cuong De was waiting offshore with eight boats, but beyond that he apparently lacked any operational plan and simply hoped that his violent initiative would generate action up and down the Annam coast. While he was trying to persuade several other Vietnamese NCOs to join the uprising and help him kill the French garrison commander, two shots rang out from somewhere, the commander telephoned higher echelons for assistance, and the plot quickly collapsed. Sergeant Cung and ten others were executed by a firing squad composed of French and Rhadé minority soldiers.[39]

---

36. Quoted in Tran Huy Lieu, "Phong Trao Cach Mang Viet Nam qua Tho Van" [The Vietnamese Revolutionary Movement in Letters], *NCLS* 29 (8-1961), 16.

37. Trung Chinh, quoted in Tran Huy Lieu, "Phong Trao," 16–17.

38. Huynh Kim Khanh, *Vietnamese Communism*, 250. CMCD, 10:9–10.

39. *CMCD*, 10:30–34. AOM, INF, CP 158, d. 12. Brocheux, "'L'Occasion favorable,'" 143. Vu Ngu Chieu, "Political and Social Change," 28. Although Sergeant Cung's mutiny had no links with events in Bac Son or Cochinchina, and indeed may have been inspired by rumors of Cuong De returning with Japanese assistance, it was soon labeled the "Do Luong Uprising" by ICP writers and

Meanwhile, some survivors of the Bac Son uprising managed in early 1941 to regroup themselves into the first platoon of the ICP-controlled "National Salvation Army" (Cuu Quoc Quan).[40] However, for the next forty months, it proved impossible for this "army" to operate at more than squad level. Garde indochinoise units, district gendarmes (*linh dong*), and Sûreté agents searched the area regularly. On several occasions they were reinforced by French infantry and native tirailleurs, forcing adherents of the Army of National Salvation to scatter and subsist perilously in the deepest forests or across the border in Kwangsi, returning only after colonial search-and-destroy operations had terminated. At best, Cuu Quoc Quan members were able to protect Party leaders on the move, conduct a few classes, and collect food from villagers.[41] Although some Bac Son activists continued to plot another local uprising, the focus of the ICP more generally had shifted in favor of patiently reconstructing the Party's covert network, establishing Viet Minh nuclei in villages, arranging basic training sessions for as many individuals as possible, and disseminating the broad anti-imperialist credo by every means conceivable.

Ho Chi Minh Returns

Undoubtedly the person most responsible for this momentous shift in ICP strategy was Ho Chi Minh. Finding some excuse to depart Moscow for Yenan in 1938, Ho had the opportunity to observe the united front policy of the Chinese Communist Party (CCP) in action. Permitted to travel to Kwangsi in a delegation led by CCP General Yeh Chien-ying, Ho had considerable difficulty making contact with ICP representatives. Between June and September 1939, he used his language skills to monitor foreign broadcasts for the staff of a combined Kuomintang-CCP training school in Hunan province. During the winter of 1939–40, Ho spent some time in Chungking, residing at the same place as Chou En-lai, who undoubtedly knew his true identity from earlier days shared in Paris.[42] Moving to Kunming in February 1940, and relying on the CCP to put him in contact

---

incorporated into revolutionary history. Another desperate attempt at armed resistance to the French in 1941, involving more than one hundred ICP members and sympathizers in the hills of Thanh Hoa province, appears to have been ignored for many years.

40. *NSKLSD*, 1:506–7. *LSQD*, 77–91.

41. Chu Van Tan, *Ky Niem*, 12–211. *CCDVB*, 41–49, 64–72. Duong Thi An, *Nguon Vui Duy Nhat* [The Sole Source of Joy] (Hanoi, 1974), 22–63.

42. Huang Cheng, *Hu Chih-ming yü Chung Kuo* [Ho Chi Minh and China] (Beijing, 1987), 53–61.

with several covert ICP cells, Ho spent the next nine months or so re-connoitering, gaining the trust of a number of small groups of Vietnamese anticolonialists on the Chinese side of the border, and trying to ascertain which Chinese Nationalist commanders were prepared to sponsor clandestine cross-border operations against the French and Japanese.[43]

One of Ho Chi Minh's most valuable contacts was Ho Hoc Lam (also known as Ho Ngoc Lam), a Vietnamese follower of Phan Boi Chau in Japan and China in earlier years, more recently an officer in the Chinese Army, and now eager to lend his name to serious efforts to liberate Vietnam. Lam introduced Ho to a number of potentially sympathetic Chinese and Vietnamese friends, and let Ho use the name of the émigré nationalist organization he had founded in Nanking in 1936—the Vietnam Independence League (Viet Nam Doc Lap Dong Minh Hoi).[44]

Ho Chi Minh's main rival at this time for leadership of anti-imperialist operations along the Sino-Vietnamese frontier was Truong Boi Cong, a member of the Vietnam Nationalist Party (Viet Nam Quoc Dan Dang) faction sustained in Nanking during the early 1930s.[45] Like Ho Hoc Lam, Cong had graduated from a Chinese military academy and made his way up the ranks of the officer corps. As a senior staff officer in Nanning, Cong came to the attention of General Chang Fa-kwei, commander of the Fourth War Zone,[46] who selected him to coordinate recruitment and training of Vietnamese irregulars and intelligence agents. With the June 1940 capit-

43. Hoang Quang Binh, "In Yunnan," in *Uncle Ho* (Hanoi, 1980), 205–20. Vu Anh, "From Kunming to Pac Bo," in ibid., 221–25. William J. Duiker, *Communist Road*, 64–66.

44. Hoang Van Hoan, *Giot Nuoc Trong Bien Ca* [A Drop of Water in the Sea] (Beijing, 1986), 131–34. King C. Chen, *Vietnam and China, 1938–1954* (Princeton, 1969), 43–48. See chapter 4 for additional information on Ho Hoc Lam. By 1943, if not earlier, the last word in this organizational title, "Hoi," had been dropped, probably to avoid confusion with another anticolonial group, the Vietnam Revolutionary League (Viet Nam Cach Menh Dong Minh Hoi). Many later Western authors fail to notice this change, causing considerable semantic confusion in the literature.

45. The Vietnam Nationalist Party was formed in 1927 by young northern intellectuals, clerks, and village functionaries attracted to the writings of Sun Yat-sen and impressed by recent Kuomintang victories in China. Dedicated to Vietnamese independence, it naturally came under increasing pressure from the Sûreté. In February 1930, fearing elimination, the Nationalist Party joined with a few Vietnamese noncommissioned officers in the Indochina Army to attempt a violent coup. The French executed or imprisoned a number of participants, while others managed to flee to China. Attempts to rebuild the Nationalist Party in exile had only limited success.

46. Archimedes L. A. Patti, *Why Viet Nam? Prelude to America's Albatross* (Berkeley and Los Angeles, 1980), 480.

ulation of France to Germany and the September 1940 agreement of Governor-General Decoux to cooperate with Japan, General Chang had reason to be concerned about his southern defenses. Truong Boi Cong not only had the existing Vietnamese émigré community in Kwangsi and Yunnan from which to recruit, but also about five hundred Vietnamese former members of the Japanese-sponsored Restoration Army (Phuc Quoc Quan) who had fled to territory held by the Chinese Nationalists in October, as well as several hundred ethnic minority survivors of the Bac Son uprising and several hundred intellectuals fleeing the Sûreté.

Realizing that these new arrivals represented an important pool of potential followers, Ho Chi Minh dispatched three trusted ICP members, Vo Nguyen Giap, Pham Van Dong, and Hoang Van Hoan, to join Truong Boi Cong's team. Soon they were able to identify an initial batch of forty-three young men prepared to return to the frontier for action. Later, on Ho's instructions, Hoang Van Hoan drafted a letter in Chinese for the forty-three men to sign and send to General Chang, criticizing Cong's leadership. Checking the text, Ho deliberately inserted some grammatical errors to convince General Chang's staff that the letter was genuinely non-Chinese in origin.[47]

All of Ho Chi Minh's activities in southern China required the utmost dexterity. Because of his Comintern background—anathema to most Kuomintang personnel and not a few Vietnamese nationalists—Ho had to be careful not to reveal his true identity to more than a tiny circle of ICP confidants. He thus employed a variety of disguises, aliases, and travel documents when moving around southern China. In Kwangsi in late 1940, for example, Ho disguised himself as a French-speaking Chinese press correspondent, with Pham Van Dong serving as interpreter. Only once did Ho slip inadvertently into Vietnamese, when a comrade's coat began to smolder from dropped cigarette ashes.[48] On the other hand, to secure the respect of young Vietnamese patriots or gain the ear of Chinese officers, Ho Chi Minh had to be something more than he appeared on the surface, conveying the aura of an experienced, totally dedicated revolutionary.

47. Hoang Van Hoan, *Giot Nuoc*, 139–41. A few months later, Hoan also recruited about forty former members of the Restoration Army, eight of whom went for additional military training at Nanning and Liuchou, the others returning to Vietnam. Ibid., 145–48. Hoan's memoir serves as a useful counterpoise to memoirs published in Hanoi, since it was written after he fled Vietnam for Beijing.

48. Vu Anh, "From Kunming to Pac Bo," 227–28. Hoang Van Hoan, *Giot Nuoc*, 138.

Having built a network of contacts on the Chinese side of the border, Ho Chi Minh's next objective was to establish a secret and reasonably secure base inside Vietnam. He excluded the region adjacent to Yunnan, because that province's warlord, Lung Yün, already possessed a working relationship with the avowedly anticommunist Vietnam Nationalist Party group led by Vu Hong Khanh, and because the ICP counted very few followers in the Tonkin border provinces of Ha Giang and Lao Cai.[49] In December 1940, Ho dispatched Vu Anh to reconnoiter possible sites adjacent to Kwangsi, the choice soon falling on a complex of limestone caves known as Pac Bo, just across the border in Cao Bang province. The area was difficult for colonial patrols to approach from the south, easy to abandon if necessary in favor of the Chinese side of the frontier, yet not too close to Chinese troop concentrations. It also was thinly populated by Nung villagers, who for almost a decade had provided covert assistance to ICP cadres. Before crossing into Vietnam in early February 1941—after thirty years abroad—Ho made a point of receiving three key members of the ICP Central Committee: Truong Chinh, Hoang Van Thu, and Hoang Quoc Viet.[50] Presumably at this meeting the three younger men acknowledged Ho's overall leadership, based on his long-standing Comintern affiliation and his key role in establishing the Party in 1930, while Ho affirmed his confidence in the current membership of the Standing Bureau, most notably Truong Chinh, the acting general secretary. Ho appears deliberately to have remained outside the ICP apparatus, in this way modeling himself on Lenin rather than on Stalin or Mao Tse-tung. To have assumed formal control of the ICP would have limited his room for maneuver, particularly when creating a new united front and, eventually, a government. Beyond that, Ho liked to take on different personas, depending on the audience, not be bound by institutional conventions. As one Western scholar has observed perceptively, Ho Chi Minh "was always in the process of reinventing himself."[51]

Ho Chi Minh's third priority was to set a new strategic direction for the ICP. His venue was the Eighth Plenum of the ICP Central Committee, which met at Pac Bo on 10–19 May 1941.[52] The resolution passed at this

49. Hoang Van Hoan, *Giot Nuoc*, 130–31.

50. Vu Anh, "From Kunming to Pac Bo," 228–29. On the other hand, *NSKLSD*, 1:499, mentions only Hoang Van Thu.

51. Patricia M. Pelley, review of *Ho Chi Minh: De l'Indochine au Vietnam*, by Daniel Hémery (Paris, 1990), *JSEAS* 23, no. 1 (Mar. 1992): 217.

52. Other participants included Truong Chinh, Hoang Van Thu, Phung Chi Kien, Hoang Quoc Viet, Vu Anh, "Comrade San" from the Annam Regional

plenum drew heavily on Ho's knowledge of international relations and his recent experiences in China among Red Army units. On the other hand, Truong Chinh probably drafted the passages on the resolution dealing with political and social conditions inside Indochina, and Ho soon demonstrated that he had no wish to interfere in the month-to-month operations of the Standing Bureau located close to Hanoi.[53]

Although he had been a Comintern agent for almost two decades, Ho Chi Minh chose in May 1941 to ignore the current Comintern line entirely. At a time when Stalin was still trying to maintain his nonaggression pact with Hitler and expecting all communist parties faithfully to support this position, Ho assumed that Germany would soon attack the Soviet Union and force Stalin urgently to seek an alliance with Great Britain, China, and the United States. Beyond that, the Eighth Plenum resolution predicted that Japan's continuing aggression in China, its September 1940 move into Indochina, and its transparent preparations to attack British, Dutch, and American colonies further south would soon embroil humanity in truly global conflict. For colonized peoples everywhere, this would result in more suffering, yet also an unparalleled opportunity to participate in struggles leading to liberation. For the peoples of Indochina specifically, these changes meant the necessity of tying in closely with China's fight against Japan.[54]

Six weeks later, after Hitler had begun his invasion of the Soviet Union, the Comintern proceeded to tout exactly the position taken by Ho Chi Minh at faraway Pac Bo. Six months later, after Japan had attacked Pearl Harbor and begun its clean sweep of Western colonies in Southeast Asia,

---

Committee, and "Comrade Thao" from the Cochinchina Regional Committee. Vu Anh, "From Kunming to Pac Bo," 232. Chu Van Tan, *Ky Niem*, 16. NSKLSD, 1:508. Hoang Van Hoan participated in several sessions, but spent more time moving back and forth across the frontier, guarding against disruption from the Chinese side. Interview with Hoang Van Hoan, Beijing, 13 Sept. 1980. Hoang Van Hoan, *Giot Nuoc*, 159. There is some evidence to suggest that the Eighth Plenum actually took place on Chinese soil, not at Pac Bo, but after 1945 it became an article of faith to assert otherwise.

53. The Eighth Plenum resolution is reprinted in *TVKD*, 1:303–45, as well as in *VKQS*, 168–208.

54. *TVKD*, 1:303–10. Ho Chi Minh was not entirely prescient. For example, the Eighth Plenum resolution predicted an imminent, massive Chinese counteroffensive against the Japanese. It also argued that workers in Germany and Japan posed ever more serious problems for fascist rulers, when in fact most remained docile or supportive of them. And it seems to have assumed that the Soviet Red Army would soon join the attack against the Japanese, which did not happen for another fifty months.

China assumed central importance in President Franklin Roosevelt's plans for Allied counteraction. Meanwhile, the Atlantic Charter, already affirmed by Roosevelt and Prime Minister Winston Churchill in August 1941, promised that the Allies would "respect the right of all peoples to choose the form of government under which they will live."[55] Tongue in cheek, Ho Chi Minh might have claimed to be the first antifascist "Ally," a stance he had taken before others could bring themselves to do so, and long before the others knew of the ICP's existence.

In the most abbreviated fashion, suitable for widespread oral transmission, readers of the Eighth Plenum resolution were instructed to "oppose the French, resist the Japanese, join with the Chinese [*Hoa*], [achieve] independence."[56] Plenum participants were acutely aware that affirming the necessity of a close Sino-Vietnamese relationship went against the country's historical grain, which included a millennium of Chinese over-lordship and four subsequent invasions from the north. They acknowledged that the Decoux government was appealing to Vietnamese patriotism partly in order to blunt native support for any Chinese intervention. Nonetheless, the logic of the ICP position demanded cooperation with "the Chinese Army in entering Vietnam" (*Hoa Quan Nhap Viet*) to attack Japanese and French forces.[57]

The organizational vehicle for accomplishing ICP objectives was to be the Viet Nam Doc Lap Dong Minh (Hoi) [Vietnam Independence League], or Viet Minh in common parlance.[58] In contrast to the ICP's 1930–31 anti-imperialist front, class struggle was rejected in May 1941 as a means of bringing different social elements together to achieve a single objective. Instead, the Viet Minh front would try to position workers and peasants side by side with those landlords, capitalists, mandarins, soldiers, intellectuals, clerks, and shopkeepers increasingly antagonized by outrageous Franco-Japanese behavior and prepared to struggle for Vietnam's national liberation. Unlike the ICP's 1937–39 democratic front, the Viet Minh would scorn "reformism" or incremental bargaining with the authorities, dedicating itself instead to violent overthrow of the colonial system and establishment of a republic. Finally, unlike the 1939–41 anti-

---

55. U.S. Department of State, *The Foreign Relations of the United States: Diplomatic Papers*, vol. 1 (Washington, D.C., 1958), 367–68.

56. *TVKD*, 1:331.

57. Ibid., 335–36.

58. The Eighth Plenum also anticipated assisting the Lao and Khmer to form similar organizations, after which an "Indochina Independence League" could be established. Ibid., 331.

imperialist front, the Viet Minh would identify itself entirely with one side in the global confrontation, those who soon styled themselves the Allies.[59]

Up until 1941, front groups had tended either to be passive auxiliaries of the Party or loose affiliates that owed far more to traditions of mutual aid and blood brotherhood than to Leninist organizational principles. Auxiliaries expanded only to the degree the Party maintained a high profile, whereas affiliates often reacted spontaneously to local issues and fell apart under enemy pressure. The Viet Minh concept was designed to overcome such weaknesses, offering a more flexible, sophisticated prescription for ICP initiative and control, while keeping the Party's profile as low as possible. On the one hand, ICP members would occupy key Viet Minh leadership positions, coordinating their actions internally even as they worked together with representatives of other groups. On the other hand, ICP members would assume active roles within "national salvation organizations" (*doan the cuu quoc*) affiliated with the Viet Minh. The united front would thus take shape both "from above" and "from below" (although these terms were not employed). To further reduce the chances of any front leaders operating independently of ICP intentions, the Viet Minh was to be structured horizontally but not vertically, presumably leaving the Party solely responsible for communication between upper and lower echelons. However, this rule appeared to be contradicted by other passages in the Eighth Plenum resolution that encouraged enrollment of existing political and religious organizations if they accepted the Viet Minh program and bylaws. This particular ambiguity would lead to suspicion and recriminations in later years.

Ideologically, the Eighth Plenum resolution was most important for its indefinite deferral of specific working-class and poor peasant demands in favor of a "national liberation revolution" (*cach mang giai phong dan toc*). Henceforth Party members would devote themselves totally to preparations for a widespread armed uprising, which would be ordered when objective conditions warranted, "such as the Chinese Army decisively defeating the Japanese Army, revolution breaking out in France or Japan, the democratic side winning decisively in the Pacific, the Soviet Union being victorious, revolutions occurring in other French and Japanese col-

59. The Eighth Plenum resolution referred to the "Democratic Front" or "Democratic side" fighting the "fascist gang" or "aggressors." Ibid., 323, 336, 339.

onies, and especially in the event of Chinese or Anglo-American armed forces pouring into Indochina."[60] To operate on the basis of such eventualities in the dark days of 1941 required a combination of informed imagination and faith that only Ho Chi Minh could provide. Following a successful armed uprising, a Vietnamese revolutionary government would be established in the spirit of "new democracy," which the plenum resolution defined as belonging, not to any particular class, but to all the people, "minus puppets of the Franco-Japanese, traitors, and [other] enemy elements."[61]

Realizing that workers and poor peasants might well feel that their interests were being ignored, the Eighth Plenum resolution urged both constituencies to look at the wider political canvas, to be patient, yet to call on the Party whenever capitalists or landlords acted viciously. In such cases, a struggle could be mounted, not on class grounds, but because the behavior of such capitalists or landlords undermined the national united front against Franco-Japanese exploitation.[62] Any attempts to expropriate property had to be limited to national enemies: the French, the Japanese, and a small minority of Vietnamese traitors. In particular, this meant that poor peasants would have to defer to a later phase of the revolution any broad struggle for land. "At the present stage everyone knows that unless the French and Japanese are driven out, not only is it the fate of our people to be draft animals forever, but we shall never be able to solve the agrarian question either," the resolution noted.[63] Indeed, to try to overthrow landlords now would quickly push them into the enemy camp, thus harming the primary struggle for national liberation.[64]

The Eighth Plenum resolution did not mark a complete departure from previous ICP policies. The Party reaffirmed its adherence to dialectical materialism, considering national liberation as simply one step along the road to socialism. The proletariat remained the vanguard revolutionary force, even though Indochina's working class was minuscule and most ICP members did not come from proletarian families. By leading the people to

60. Ibid., 339.
61. Ibid., 322. The "new democracy" (*tan dan chu*) idea was borrowed without attribution from Mao Tse-tung.
62. Ibid., 337.
63. Ibid., 328.
64. Another passage in the resolution, more often quoted, argues that for the Party not to demand independence and freedom first for all the people would mean that no sector or class could achieve its interests for ten thousand years. Ibid., 321.

national liberation, the ICP would position itself strategically to initiate further revolutionary changes, thus achieving socialism more quickly.[65] This readiness to concentrate on the "national issue" (*van de dan toc*) had become evident following the 1937 outbreak of the Sino-Japanese war, as Vietnamese Marxist-Leninists marveled at the willingness of millions of ordinary Chinese to fight in defense of their homeland.[66] The Sixth Plenum resolution, formulated in November 1939, had called explicitly for preparations to mount a national liberation revolution in Indochina, citing as precedent the heroic achievements of 450 million Chinese fighting the Japanese.[67] One year later, the Seventh Plenum resolution spoke of forming "anti-imperialist national salvation associations" (*phan de cuu quoc hoi*), and of linking efforts in Indochina with the anti-Japanese front in China.[68]

Nonetheless, neither in 1939 nor in 1940 had the ICP Central Committee been willing explicitly to downgrade class struggle or defer the agrarian issue indefinitely. The 1941 ideological changes were undoubtedly the work of Ho Chi Minh, and they were to be as important to the Party's future as his sophisticated analysis of global politics or his understanding of how to build a united front both "from above" and "from below." We do not know if any Central Committee members argued with Ho about class struggle or the land question, but subsequent events suggest that some province-level cadres, if not higher-ranking ICP leaders as well, chose to ignore these instructions when it suited them. In Cochinchina, Party members remained unaware of the new line.

Early Viet Minh Operations

Following the Eighth Plenum, Ho Chi Minh turned his attention for the next fourteen months to organizing training courses and setting the overall tone of Viet Minh propaganda.[69] He focused first on the districts imme-

65. Ibid., 329–30.

66. Marr, *Vietnamese Tradition*, 278, 397–98. Previously the ICP had denounced such motivations as parochial chauvinism. For a more detailed discussion of the influence of events in China on ICP thinking in 1938–39, see Greg Lockhart, *Nation in Arms: The Origins of the People's Army of Vietnam* (Sydney, 1989), 66–72.

67. *TVKD*, 1:231, 267.

68. Ibid., 297–98, 301–2. Otherwise, however, the Seventh Plenum resolution seemed to back away from detailed discussion of national liberation or a Vietnamese front organization designed to achieve that objective.

69. Phan Ngoc Lien, "Tim Hieu ve Cong Tac Van Dong, Giao Duc Quan Chung cua Ho Chu Tich trong thoi gian Nguoi o Pac-Bo" [Investigating President Ho's

diately surrounding Pac Bo. Men and women came in groups of twenty or thirty, studying for no more than two weeks, the duration determined as much by the amount of food they could carry as by pedagogical rationales.[70] Instructors offered a capsule view of the world at war, explained the perfidious nature of Franco-Japanese cooperation in Indochina, and provided a concise statement of Viet Minh objectives. Equal time was devoted to more concrete matters: how cadres should investigate local conditions, proselytize, organize the first national salvation associations, arrange training sessions, and conduct initial struggle operations. Because many of the local people of Cao Bang spoke little Vietnamese or Chinese, it was often necessary to rely on several interpreters.

None of the men and women who took these classes had any idea that the thin, middle-aged man wearing a faded Nung jacket and supervising instruction was the mysterious revolutionary Nguyen Ai Quoc, although they did note the special respect given to him by other teachers. Whenever Ho Chi Minh taught classes, the emphasis was on simplicity and practicality. He devised poetry to be memorized by illiterate cadres, stressed that personal habits of hard work, economy, cleanliness, and punctuality were just as important as a correct political outlook or military skills, and sometimes employed a Socratic style of questioning to induce students to think for themselves.[71] Occasionally, Ho would use role-model techniques—for example, acting the part of a farmer and encouraging students to try to recruit him into the Viet Minh.[72] Ho's teaching assistants traveled to more distant villages to conduct courses of four or five days' duration.[73]

Ho Chi Minh insisted that Viet Minh propaganda be succinct, employ popular Vietnamese or highland minority imagery, stimulate patriotic emotions, and make no mention of socialism or the Communist Party. His 6 June 1941 "Letter from Abroad," under the name of Nguyen Ai Quoc, offered a prototype. It was only about six hundred words long, stylistically vivid, and more akin to the fervently nationalistic writings of Phan Boi

---

Mass Mobilization and Education Efforts while at Pac Bo], *NCLS* 149 (3/4-1973): 13–21, 30.

70. The first such course had actually taken place in late January 1941, across the frontier in Kwangsi. *NSKLSD*, 1:501. *CCDVB*, 33–34.

71. It should be noted, however, that when some of these Socratic exchanges were copied down and reprinted, they became catechisms, to be memorized as received truth.

72. *NSKLSD*, 1:502–3. *CCDVB*, 52.

73. Vo Nguyen Giap, *Tu Nhan Dan ma ra* [From the People] (Hanoi, 1964), 63.

Chau and other classically educated writers of the early twentieth century than to the publications of the new intelligentsia during the 1920s and 1930s. The opening passages give one the flavor:

> Elder citizens!
> Sages and heroes!
> Scholars, farmers, workers, merchants, and soldiers!
> France has been lost to the Germans. French strength here is dissipated, yet still they raise our taxes to loot us, still they mount white terror against the people. In foreign dealings they hold their breath fearfully, giving some land to Siam, kneeling down in surrender to Japan. Meanwhile, our people have to wear two yokes, continuing to serve as buffalo and horses for the French, but now also being slaves of the Japanese.
> In such painful, tormenting conditions shall we simply fold our arms and wait to die?
> No, absolutely not! More than twenty million descendants of Lac and Hong are determined not to be perpetual slaves without a country![74]

In 1941 and 1942, Ho Chi Minh also authored at least twenty poems, ranging from a 4-line exhortation to unite to achieve independence, to a 208-line "History of Our Country."[75] Using his battered portable typewriter, Ho wrote "Cach danh du kich" ("Guerrilla Fighting Methods"), a 43-page essay drawing heavily on Chinese Red Army precedents.[76] He translated a history of the Communist Party of the Soviet Union into Vietnamese for internal ICP circulation.[77] He also established a two-page,

---

74. Ho Chi Minh, *Ho Chi Minh Toan Tap* [The Complete Works of Ho Chi Minh] (hereafter *HCMTT*), vol. 3, *1930–1945* (Hanoi, 1983), 147–49. Also included in *VKQS*, 215–17, and *Tong Tap Van Hoc Viet Nam* [General Collection of Vietnamese Literature], ed. Nguyen Khanh Toan, vol. 36 (Hanoi, 1980), 544–46. Translated in Ho Chi Minh, *Selected Writings* (Hanoi, 1977), 44–46. "Letter from Abroad" circulated widely during the next four years in both Chinese and Vietnamese (*quoc-ngu*) versions. The Chinese version and a slightly different Vietnamese version can be found in *CMCD*, 10:55–63. *NSKLSD*, 1:517, asserts that Hoang Van Hoan translated Ho Chi Minh's Vietnamese original into Chinese. However, Hoan makes no such claim in his 1986 memoirs, and it seems unlikely from what we know of Ho's language abilities. In fact, there is some reason to believe that Ho originally wrote the letter in Chinese.

75. *HCMTT*, 3:150–59, 210–37.

76. "Cach danh du kich," reprinted in *LSQD*, 93–94. *HCMTT*, 3:165–209. Besides conveying new battle concepts, it was necessary for Ho and others to convert traditional Chinese military terminology into colloquial Vietnamese. For some examples, see Ngo The Son, "Lop Huan Luyen Quan Su Dau Tien" [The First Military Training Class], in *Thai Binh Khoi Nghia*, 28–45.

77. Vo Nguyen Giap, *Tu Nhan Dan ma ra*, 51.

thrice-monthly newspaper, *Viet Nam Doc Lap* (Independent Vietnam), which continued to appear with only minor interruptions until September 1945. Ho insisted that no article be included unless it had been read first and comprehended by one of his literate, but poorly educated, comrades in camp.[78] Until his departure for China in August 1942, Ho not only participated in writing and editing this periodical, but occasionally contributed line drawings and helped with the printing as well.[79]

During the time the Cao Bang base was being established, training classes conducted, and the Viet Minh message disseminated elsewhere in Tonkin, the ICP was careful not to neglect its "rear area" in southern China. One month before the Eighth Plenum, Pham Van Dong, Vo Nguyen Giap, and Hoang Van Hoan had taken part in formation at Chinghsi of the "Vietnam National Liberation League" (Viet Nam Dan Toc Giai Phong Dong Minh), under the patronage of Li Chi-shen, a left-leaning Kuomintang leader. The more senior members of the Liberation League were avowed noncommunists or anticommunists, anxious like the ICP to recruit followers from among the young Vietnamese crossing the frontier, to receive specialized military training, and, they hoped, to obtain military equipment. About all that Liberation League leaders could agree on was the need for a single, officially acknowledged point of contact with the Chinese authorities. In June 1941, Dong, Giap, and Hoan obtained permission from Li Chi-shen to bring an additional eighty youths from Cao Bang for military instruction.[80] By the end of 1941, several other members of the Liberation League were sufficiently worried about such Viet Minh successes to denounce Giap and Dong as covert ICP cadres to General Chang

78. Le Quang Ba, "Souvenirs de clandestinité," *Etudes vietnamiennes* (Hanoi), no. 15 (1967): 53–54.

79. *NSKLSD*, 1:523–27. After Ho's departure, Pham Van Dong took responsibility for *Viet Nam Doc Lap* until May 1945. About four hundred copies of each issue were printed, using a rudimentary stone and gelatin technique. Another system involved grinding a stone surface very smooth, using acid to inscribe letters in mirror image, then spreading an ink and sugar-juice solution over the stone for each paper sheet printed. Luong Quang Chat, "Hai Nam Bao Ve Bao Dang" [Two Years Protecting the Party's Newspaper], in *Thai Binh Khoi Nghia*, 69–81. Tønnesson, *Vietnamese Revolution*, 125–38, 145–47, provides a detailed content analysis of *Viet Nam Doc Lap*.

80. *CCDVB*, 55–56. This group included several individuals who would become ranking People's Army commanders: Hoang Van Thai, Nam Long, Dam Quang Trung, and Thanh Phong. Vo Nguyen Giap, *Tu Nhan Dan ma ra*, 39. Ten youths were assigned to study military communications at Liuchou; they later became the core of ICP and army radio, telegraph, and telephone operations. "Lich Su Nganh Thong Tin Buu Dien Viet Nam (Du Thao)" [A History of Vietnam's Postal Communications Branch (Draft)] (Hanoi, 1989), 1:62.

Figure 16.   One of Ho Chi Minh's cartoons for use in the serial *Viet Nam Doc Lap* (Independent Vietnam) in 1942. A French capitalist and a Japanese militarist burden the Vietnamese people with taxes and rising food costs. Courtesy of the Revolutionary Museum, Hanoi.

Fa-kwei's headquarters.[81] Sensing a sudden change in the Chinese attitude, Giap and Dong sought and received Ho Chi Minh's permission to recross the frontier.[82] At about this same time, Truong Boi Cong, one of the most prominent members of the Liberation League, was jailed by the Chinese

---

81. Chen, *Vietnam and China*, 49–51.
82. Vo Nguyen Giap, *Tu Nhan Dan ma ra*, 45–47.

authorities in response to formal protests by French diplomats in Chung-king at his alleged sale of certificates promising official rank to wealthy Chinese residents in Tonkin.[83] The Liberation League became an empty shell after these incidents.

During 1942, Chinese staff officers in the Fourth War Area preferred to identify Nguyen Hai Than, a sixty-four-year-old expatriate, as the ranking Vietnamese intermediary.[84] Hoang Van Hoan continued under-cover recruitment for the Viet Minh, relying on his close link with Ho Hoc Lam to avoid arrest. At one point, Lam and Hoan were summoned to Fourth War Area headquarters to listen to plans to establish a "Viet Nam Anti-Aggression League" (Viet Nam Phan Xam Luoc Dong Minh) in antici-pation of major Chinese operations inside Indochina. When Hoan realized that the Fourth War Area staff intended to rely mainly on overseas Chinese (*Hoa Kieu*) leaders rather than Vietnamese, he and other Viet Minh representatives persuaded Nguyen Hai Than to criticize the planning pro-cedures at a large meeting chaired by General Chang Fa-kwei himself, which led to expanded Vietnamese involvement. However, some Viet-namese participants soon began to denounce Viet Minh participants as communists, forcing Hoan and others to withdraw across the frontier to Pac Bo.[85]

Hoping to improve ties with both the Kuomintang and the CCP, Ho Chi Minh recrossed the frontier to Kwangsi in August 1942, only to be arrested by the local authorities as a possible spy for the French or the Japanese. Although they clearly did not guess his real identity, any foreigner car-

83. Hoang Van Hoan, *Giot Nuoc*, 158–59. Purchasers of these certificates could present them to incoming Chinese or Vietnamese units as proofs of prior support. Although this was the stated reason for Cong's arrest, Hoan suggests the Chinese really wished to express their displeasure at his ineffectiveness and as a warning to others. A Chinese source quoted by Chen, *Vietnam and China*, 51, says Cong was arrested for working with ICP members against the Kuomintang. However, this more serious charge does not conform to the fact that Cong was released after a short time.

84. Nguyen Hai Than (1878–1955) left Vietnam in 1905 to join Phan Boi Chau, with whom he was associated until 1924. According to Chen, *Vietnam and China*, 50, Than "served in the Chinese army for more than 30 years." However, this was probably a sinecure.

85. Hoang Van Hoan, *Giot Nuoc*, 171–94. How to relate to the overseas Chinese in Vietnam remained a delicate problem for the ICP / Viet Minh. Little time seems to have been devoted to winning them over. For one exception, see the fictional letter in *Cuu Quoc* (11-1944), 10–11, addressed to "Anh Phoong," which empha-sizes Japanese and French maltreatment of Chinese in the colony and argues that only when those two enemies are "killed completely" can the "lives of both of our peoples [*dan toc*] be saved."

rying forged travel papers in wartime China was liable to face indefinite incarceration or execution. For nine months, Ho was shuttled from one jail to another, living among petty gamblers, diseased prostitutes, opium addicts, and the family members of army deserters. To keep his sanity, Ho composed poetry in classical Chinese.[86] In early 1943, various friends learned of Ho's predicament and began quietly to lobby for his release. In Chungking, Chou En-lai persuaded General Feng Yü-hsiang and Vice President Li Tsung-jen to approach Generalissimo Chiang Kai-shek on the matter. In Kwangsi, two Vietnamese students at a special Fourth War Area training program gained the ear of the school's commandant and pleaded for Ho's release, even to the extent of revealing his identity as Nguyen Ai Quoc. The commandant then approached General Hsiao Wen, a staff aide to General Chang specializing in Indochina affairs. In May, Ho was transferred to the Liuchou military prison, identified as a "political prisoner" of some status, given better food, allowed to sit in his cell unshackled, and even provided with books and periodicals to read. In September, Chang agreed to Hsiao's suggestion that Ho be permitted to participate in a reorganized version of the Vietnam Revolutionary League (see chapter 4). When formal permission for his release came from Chungking, Ho was taken to a ceremonial luncheon with Fourth War Area staff members. Not until August 1944, however, was Ho permitted to recross the frontier.[87] He would not be jailed again.

Ho Chi Minh's capture was a serious blow to his ICP comrades, especially for the eight months or so during which they believed he had died in prison. In Cao Bang, a solemn memorial service was planned, then deferred while ICP members in Kwangsi tried to confirm the report and ascertain where Ho had been buried.[88] As it happened, Ho Chi Minh's two-year absence served as a practical test of the ICP's institutional maturity. Few serious misunderstandings or policy disputes appear to have occurred, although communication between ICP units remained difficult,

86. Some of these poems were compiled and published subsequently under the title *Nguc Trung Nhat Ky* [Prison Diary]. *Tong Tap Van Hoc Viet Nam*, ed. Nguyen Khanh Toan, 603–785, contains both Chinese originals and Vietnamese translations. English translations by Huynh Sanh Thong can be found in *Reflections from Captivity*, ed. David G. Marr (Athens, Ohio, 1978), 59–98.

87. Huang Cheng, *Hu Chih-ming yü Chung Kuo*, 95–96. Tran Dan Tien, *Nhung Mau Chuyen ve Doi Hoat Dong cua Ho Chu Tich* [Stories about Chairman Ho's Life of Action] (Hanoi, 1975), 95–99. This latter work, originally written in 1948, is now considered by many scholars to have been authored by Ho Chi Minh himself. See also Chen, *Vietnam and China*, 55–60, 64–66, 82.

88. Vo Nguyen Giap, *Tu Nhan Dan ma ra*, 96.

sometimes impossible for a year or more at a time. Different units moved at different rhythms, reflecting local conditions, but at least in Tonkin and northern Annam, most ICP members attempted to implement the Eighth Plenum strategy of organizing, prosyletizing, and training under the Viet Minh's banner.

Highest priority was given to developing a network of village-level Viet Minh groups in the three mountain provinces of Cao Bang, Bac Can, and Lang Son. It was demanding work, calling for physical stamina, cultural sensitivity, patience, and a readiness to pick up the institutional pieces after each setback and rebuild. Malaria or dengue fever periodically attacked each activist, with local herbs the only available remedy.[89] Most important, ICP leaders of ethnic Vietnamese (Kinh) origin had to learn how to gain the trust and participation of the various non-Vietnamese peoples (Tay, Nung, Yao, Meo), who together constituted a clear majority in the area.[90] Competence in several local languages was essential. Customs needed to be understood and at least outwardly respected, even to the point of taking part in blood oaths and other traditional rituals.[91] Vietnamese intellectuals discovered that their passion for literacy could sometimes be counterproductive, as when a Viet Minh cadre encountered total rejection in a Yao village after insisting on writing down the names of prospective front members. Subsequent investigation revealed that his behavior had been equated with that of the hated colonial tax collector. No progress was possible until Vo Nguyen Giap devised a ritual whereby the names of both villagers and outside cadres were inscribed on a single piece of votive paper, then ceremoniously burned as an offering to the spirits.[92] Despite such ingenious Kinh efforts to bridge the ethnic gap, many minority people remained suspicious. When the Viet Minh lacked local contacts, the next

89. Ibid., 47, 54, 79–80, 82–83, 118, 217.

90. John T. McAlister, Jr., *Viet Nam: The Origins of Revolution* (New York, 1969), 123–29. Nguyen Van Rang, "Nam Thang o Giai Phong Quan Khang Nhat" [Five Months with the Anti-Japanese Liberation Army], in *Rung Yen The* [The Yen The Forest] (Hanoi, 1962), 69–70.

91. Thus, Vo Nguyen Giap, *Tu Nhan Dan ma ra*, 72, describes participation in a fidelity ritual of the Man Tien, a Yao subgroup, which involved dousing burning incense sticks in water to symbolize what would happen to someone who betrayed his comrades. According to Huang Cheng, *Hu Chih-ming yü Chung Kuo*, 78, Ho Chi Minh and several comrades had also become sworn brothers of a group of peasants on the Chinese side of the frontier by means of a ceremony in which a chicken was slaughtered, its blood mixed with wine, and the concoction shared among the celebrants. Ho was ranked "second brother" among forty-eight participants.

92. Vo Nguyen Giap, *Tu Nhan Dan ma ra*, 93, 95.

best tactic was to rely on a cadre from one minority group to recruit members of another.[93]

Viet Minh cadres repeatedly asserted that since all ethnic groups in Indochina were suffering equally under the Franco-Japanese yoke, they needed to unite to drive out the common enemy. Cadres also promised ethnic self-determination in a future independent Vietnam, although non-Kinh readers of clandestine ICP and Viet Minh texts of the time must have noted curious ambiguities. Thus, the Eighth Plenum resolution had endorsed self-determination, yet it also referred to most ethnic minorities as being at a "low level of existence, dumb and naive, hence readily deceived"; and it assumed that all nationalities wished to "live in line with progress, advancing on the road to genuine civilization." The Vietnamese had a responsibility to "lead and assist" the Khmer, the Lao, and the ethnic minorities of Indochina in struggling for freedom and independence. As the "most numerous and strongest nationality in Indochina," the Vietnamese would certainly establish a "new democracy" government; what the others might do was left deliberately vague. In the meantime, Party committees in the south and center were given responsibility by the Eighth Plenum for building up ICP networks in Cambodia and Laos respectively.[94] During 1942–44, Party publications gave more attention to the idea of Indochina than did Viet Minh publications, as might be expected. Nonetheless, even Viet Minh newspapers sometimes spoke of all nationalities in Indochina being "brothers of a common family," who would "volunteer to unite" in a single independent state.[95]

Whatever the doctrinal nuances, it is likely that more minority people were won over to the revolutionary cause by the fact of rapid promotion of kin in Viet Minh ranks than by political rhetoric. Hoang Van Thu, who was of Tay origin, had risen to head the ICP's Tonkin Regional Committee even before 1941. At the time of his capture in Hanoi in September 1943, he was second only to Truong Chinh in the Standing Bureau.[96] Between

---

93. Duong Thi An, *Nguon Vui Duy Nhat*, 64–69, describes how her background as a Nung enabled her to build a network among the Man (Yao) in the Lang Son–Thai Nguyen border districts.

94. *TVKD*, 1:318–23, 344. These references to the Khmer and Lao were deleted from reprintings of the Eighth Plenum resolution in the 1960s and early 1970s.

95. Tønnesson, *Vietnamese Revolution*, 124–25, with citations from *Co Giai Phong* 3 (15 Feb. 1944) and 6 (28 July 1944) and *Viet Nam Doc Lap* 170 (1 Aug. 1943) and 174 (11 Sept. 1943).

96. Aside from formal rankings, it is evident from later provincial Party histories and memoirs that Hoang Van Thu played a crucial role in reconstituting the Tonkin network between 1940 and 1943. Thu was executed by firing squad on 24

Figure 17. Hoang Van Thu, member of the ICP Standing Bureau, captured by the French and executed in 1944. Courtesy of the Vietnam News Agency.

1941 and 1944, Chu Van Tan, a Nung, led development of the Bac Son–Vu Nhai guerrilla base area, which straddled the Lang Son–Thai Nguyen border.[97] Other minority activists came quickly to chair district-level Viet Minh committees. At the village level, Ho Chi Minh had insisted that ethnic Vietnamese not take any leadership roles,[98] and this rule seems to have been observed in practice. Because many minority families had kin across the frontier in Kwangsi, Viet Minh cadres depended on them for introductions in both directions. Lacking external funding, cadres had to depend on minority sympathizers for food, usually corn or manioc, from which a simple soup was prepared. In villages where Viet Minh members were numerous enough, a small monthly grain tax could be

May 1944. *CMTT,* 1:5, 13–14, 105. *NSKLSD,* 1:582–83. *CMCD,* 10:75. Another prominent Tay in the ICP was Luong Van Chi, a member of the Tonkin Regional Committee when wounded and captured in August 1941. He died in prison, allegedly as a result of torture. *CCDVB,* 42. A third Tay, Le Quang Ba, took part in formation of the earliest armed Viet Minh groups in Cao Bang province, eventually (1951) becoming commander of the crack 316th Division and chairman of the DRV Nationalities Commission (1960).

97. Chu Van Tan, *Ky Niem,* 34–230.
98. Hoang Van Hoan, *Giot Nuoc,* 215.

gathered, the amount varying according to the success of the crop and time of year.[99]

Precisely because food was so scarce, Viet Minh cadres discouraged young men and women from leaving their villages to join full-time units hiding in the upland forests. Instead, such recruits received on-the-spot training and began to establish local Viet Minh affiliates (Peasant Salvation Association, Women's Salvation Association, etc.), to seek out weapons to form a "self-defense" (*tu ve*) squad,[100] and to isolate people in the village suspected of retaining ties with the colonial system. The objective was to create a "perfect village" or "complete village" (*xa hoan toan*) in which the vast majority supported the Viet Minh in a variety of practical ways, while the uninvolved minority dared not serve the French for fear of retaliation. Perceived opponents might have leaflets affixed to their houses, warning of elimination if they did not mend their ways soon.[101] If such efforts proved successful in adjacent villages, the next objective was to create a "complete canton," and so on. Although colonial appointees remained in position at village and canton levels, continuing to collect taxes and enforce corvée, a shadow Viet Minh government was being established as well.[102]

Since the full-time Viet Minh units in the upland forests had only a few score modern firearms and perhaps a couple of hundred old muskets and hunting rifles, no attempt was made to attack colonial posts or ambush military patrols. Instead, most such weapons were used to train much larger numbers of adherents in the internal functioning and maintenance of firearms, as well as to practice sighting and shooting (using black powder or out-of-date, unreliable cartridges). Elite squads were issued highly prized pistols to guard important meetings, escort ICP Central Committee members on missions, or seek out and execute alleged spies and traitors. Ordinary Viet Minh squads were lucky to be issued two or three rifles,

99. Le Hien Mai, in Le Thiet Hung et al., *Rung Yen The*, 117.

100. *Vietnam: The Definitive Documentation of Human Decisions*, ed. Gareth Porter (Stanfordville, N.Y., 1979), 11–13, contains excerpts from a February 1944 pamphlet by Vo Nguyen Giap on organizing self-defense units.

101. See, e.g., an undated (but probably 1942–43) leaflet of the "Group to Uphold Goodness and Eliminate Evil" (Doan Ho Luong Giet Ac), in the Revolutionary Museum, Hanoi. Aimed at "enemy agents," the leaflet's threatening text is reinforced by drawings of a sword and a pistol.

102. Vo Nguyen Giap, *Tu Nhan Dan ma ra*, 51–54, 58–63, 67–71, 91–93, 98–99, 104–5. Ban Nghien Cuu Lich Su Dang Khu Tu Tri Viet Bac, *Khu Thien Thuat trong cuoc van dong Cach Mang Thang 8 o Viet Bac* [The Thien Thuat Zone in Activating the August Revolution in Viet Bac] (Viet Bac, 1972), 22–48.

using them for defense if ambushed, but especially to impress villagers and local officials. Thus, Tran Do found that waving his firearm in the air persuaded more than one village chief to allow a public meeting to be convened and not to dare report Viet Minh activities to the district authorities.[103] On at least one occasion, Ho Chi Minh seems to have become exasperated at the petty competition among his followers for custody of scarce weapons. To convince them that guile was much better protection than a pistol with two or three questionable cartridges, Ho assumed the disguise of an old blind man, hand resting on a young comrade's shoulder for guidance, then walked right in front of a colonial military post without any challenge from the sentries. After that, cadres thought twice before requesting a firearm when traveling, although some still carried wooden pistols to try to trick opponents and villagers into believing they were armed.[104]

Local colonial officials did not remain passive in the face of Viet Minh efforts. Most commonly, a district mandarin would dispatch a patrol to a village known to contain Viet Minh adherents, forcing the most active to flee to the forest. Relatives were then arrested, with promises of release if their younger, more impetuous kin could be persuaded to surrender. Kinship ties, which had been an asset when first establishing a Viet Minh presence, now became a potential liability. Even when local activists refused to give themselves up, contact might well be lost with the village, and the problem of finding food magnified. In such "hot" circumstances, it was sometimes necessary for Viet Minh cadres to withdraw from the area for several months, allow matters to "cool," then make contact again. Those Viet Minh participants in the village who had best withstood enemy pressures were praised and promoted to more responsible positions.[105]

By the end of 1943, Viet Minh activities in the border provinces had become sufficiently bothersome to cause the French commander of the Second Military Region to order a series of special operations. Patrols increased markedly in size and frequency, new military posts were estab-

---

103. Tran Do, "Cong Tac Doi," in Chanh Thi et al., *Len Duong Thang Loi* [On the Road to Victory] (Hanoi, 1960), 83–99.

104. Be Van Khai, "His Adoptive Nephew," in *Uncle Ho* (Hanoi, 1980), 225–56. For at least two years, Vo Nguyen Giap evidently carried only a dud grenade strapped to his waist, while his partner, Le Thiet Hung, who had been trained professionally in China, possessed a pistol and several unreliable cartridges. Good ammunition was more highly prized than firearms. Vo Nguyen Giap, *Tu Nhan Dan ma ra*, 91, 123.

105. Vo Nguyen Giap, *Tu Nhan Dan ma ra*, 75–85, 101–3, 106–12. CMCD, 10:69–73.

lished, police checkpoints proliferated to be able to check identification papers and restrict the movement of food, salt, and medicine. Rewards of as much as 20,000 piastres were offered for the heads of ranking Viet Minh leaders. In certain areas, colonial units burned down whole villages and herded the inhabitants into makeshift "regroupment" camps. Over a three-month period by official French count, such search-and-destroy efforts netted fifty ICP members, one hundred tons of hidden paddy, two collections of revolutionary publications, and considerable intelligence data on the "anti-French rebels."[106]

Completely outgunned, very few Viet Minh groups attempted armed resistance, instead fleeing villages and, if necessary, withdrawing deeper into the forest or across the frontier. The number of activists who had "gone into secrecy" (*di bi mat*) rapidly increased beyond the capacity of the network to feed them. In some locations, Viet Minh leaders instructed villagers to destroy their houses and crops and flee into the forest ahead of enemy sweeps, a tactic that could provoke considerable bitterness, especially when cadres lacked sufficient food to support such refugees for very long.[107] In May 1944, when regular French military units withdrew to the lowlands with the advent of the summer monsoon, leaving an expanded grid of Garde indochinoise posts and Sûreté informers, Viet Minh fortunes in the mountains looked far from promising. Many supporters were demoralized, and the essential network of safe houses, local informants, guides, and tax collectors was a shambles. The two main guerrilla bases of Cao Bang and Bac Son–Vu Nhai had lost touch with each other, and neither had contact with the ICP Standing Bureau operating undercover near Hanoi.[108]

Beyond the Mountains

Meanwhile, in the populous Red River Delta to the south, ICP members faced rather different conditions from their comrades 50–150 kilometers

---

106. DGER report on 2^e Territoire militaire, 1 June 1945, in AOM, INF, c. 122, d. 1106. See also *CCDVB*, 43; Hoang Van Hoan, *Giot Nuoc*, 217; and Vo Nguyen Giap, *Tu Nhan Dan ma ra*, 111.

107. Ha Thi Que, in Le Thiet Hung et al., *Rung Yen The*, 91–95. This Viet Minh tactic of "bare gardens and empty houses" (*vuon khong nha trong*) remained controversial for many years, with some cadres avoiding it, others insisting it was necessary to prevent people and property from falling into the hands of the enemy.

108. *CMTT*, 1:90–92, 120. Vo Nguyen Giap, *Tu Nhan Dan ma ra*, 117–25. *LSQD*, 101–4.

away in the mountains. The Standing Bureau of the Party managed to operate from the same "safe zone" close to Hanoi for almost four years, but at the cost of elaborate secrecy precautions and much time spent worrying about basic food needs. Commerce provided both a cover and a means of livelihood, while small restaurants served as clandestine meeting places.[109] ICP liaison agents sometimes purchased opium in the mountains and sold it to delta addicts, even though the Party vehemently denounced opium smoking as a colonial plot to weaken the Vietnamese people.[110] The Standing Bureau's mastermind was General Secretary Truong Chinh, backed up by Hoang Van Thu until the latter's capture, and by Hoang Quoc Viet. Disguised as a petty merchant, village clerk, or, most effectively, a rural schoolteacher (black silk tunic and turban, white pants, glasses, umbrella), Truong Chinh moved constantly from one village to another, occasionally entering a provincial town or even Hanoi itself. Once, when confronted on a dike by a police checkpoint, Truong Chinh avoided certain arrest by acting as if he was the overseer of some peasants planting jute nearby, cursing them loudly for not working harder to fulfill the production quotas set by the Japanese, then managing to slip away in the opposite direction.[111]

Having obtained copies of the basic Viet Minh program by early 1942, most Party branches began to organize "national salvation associations" in selected villages, only to find that most existing local officials appointed by the French remained hostile. ICP activists were arrested and imprisoned by the score, forcing the Tonkin Regional Committee to spend most of its time finding suitable replacements and helping them to establish contact with local cells or non-Party sympathizers.[112] The Regional Committee relied heavily on a cluster of ICP cells in Hoai Duc district (Ha Dong), just west of Hanoi; one particular village, Van Phuc, only six kilometers from the

109. Nguyen Duc Thang, "Khu An Toan cua Dang Cong San Dong Duong tren Dat Ha Noi" [The ICP's Safe Zone on Hanoi Land], *Van Hoa Nghe Thuat* (Hanoi), 9-1981, 43–46.

110. Nguyen Tu Thuy, "Don cac Anh ve" [Greeting Older Brothers on Return], in *Hoi Ky Cach Mang Ha Tay* [Ha Tay Revolutionary Memoirs], vol. 1 (Ha Tay, 1970), 50.

111. Tran Do, in Le Quang Dao et al., *Mot Chang Duong Van Hoa* [A Segment of the Cultural Road] (Hanoi, 1985), 99–100. For a moment Truong Chinh considered going down to the nearby rice field to pretend to be defecating, but he realized that this ruse had not saved several comrades from capture on earlier occasions. Thanh Tin [Bui Tin], *Hoa Xuyen Tuyet* [Snowdrop Flower] (Irvine, Calif., 1991), 129–30, makes the point that Truong Chinh enjoyed far more rapport with ordinary people in these clandestine days than after he became a high official.

112. *CMTT*, 1:164, 332, 406, 408, 430.

Governor-General's Palace, provided cover for a variety of organizing, training, and printing efforts.[113]

Because rules of secrecy required horizontal compartmentalization, it was not unusual for several different Viet Minh groups to emerge in the same district or province, each perhaps suspicious of the other's credentials. Thus, for more than a year in Ha Dong province, Van Tien Dung was suspected of being an "A.B." (Anti-Bolshevik), or agent provocateur, until an ICP Standing Bureau member, the peripatetic Hoang Quoc Viet, showed up in March 1943 and vouched for him.[114] Not until late 1943 did the Party's efforts in the Red River Delta begin to regain momentum, bolstered by the return of some cadres from jail, by news of Allied victories in both Europe and the Pacific, by the failure of either the Decoux administration or the Japanese to offer the Vietnamese rural elite a viable nationalist alternative, and by growing economic dislocation.[115] Even then, several delta provinces remained nearly devoid of Viet Minh activity until after the Japanese coup in March 1945.[116]

In the mountainous region west of the delta, a few ethnic Vietnamese managed to establish a Viet Minh group in the town of Hoa Binh at the end of 1943, but found little support among the surrounding Yao people until early 1945.[117] In Son La province, a small Thai People's National Salvation Association was founded in 1943, broke apart under colonial repression, then managed to regroup in 1944, distributing five or six issues of a bilingual Vietnamese and Thai newspaper.[118] However, very few tribal

113. Dang Cong San Viet Nam, *So Thao Lich Su Cach Mang Huyen Hoai Duc (1926–1945)* [Preliminary History of the Revolution in Hoai Duc District (1926–45)] (Hanoi, 1982), 60–72.

114. Van Tien Dung, in Chanh Thi et al., *Len Duong Thang Loi* [On the Road to Victory] (Hanoi, 1960), 69–82.

115. *CMTT*, 1:145, 183–85, 295. Phan Thi Khoi, "Nhung Nam Thang Khong Quen" [Unforgettable Months and Years], in *Hoi Ky Cach Mang Ha Tay*, 1:27–47. A report by four Vietnamese employees of the Kenpeitai in Tonkin in late 1943 argues that recent Russian victories had invigorated the ICP and implies that Japanese refusal to emancipate the local population from the French gives some credence to communist rhetoric. Undated *renseignements* in AOM, INF, GF 67.

116. *CMTT*, 1:163, 238, 315, 367. Delta provinces slow to see Viet Minh activity included Hai Duong, Ha Nam, Thai Binh, and Yen Bai (only partially in the delta). *CMCD*, 12:127–28, tantalizingly reprints a leaflet of 1 May 1945, which almost surely originated somewhere in the Red River Delta, employing rhetoric characteristic of 1939–40, signed "Indochinese Communist Party," and making no mention whatsoever of the Viet Minh.

117. *CMTT*, 1:399–400.

118. Ibid., 447–48. Cam Trong, *Nguoi Thai o Tay Bac Viet Nam* [The Thai People in Northwest Vietnam] (Hanoi, 1978), 503–11. Important ICP and Viet

leaders in this region were inclined to shift their loyalty away from the French until well after the Japanese took control.

In the three urban centers of Tonkin—Hanoi, Haiphong, and Nam Dinh—most people appear to have paid little attention to the Viet Minh until early 1944, when it became obvious that the Axis powers were everywhere on the defensive and probably destined to lose the war. Viet Minh calls to seize independence whenever Allied forces invaded Indochina or Japan capitulated no longer seemed so fanciful.[119] Urban intellectuals in particular sought information about the Viet Minh's program and clandestine operations. Because the French chose to try individuals accused of Viet Minh participation before secret military tribunals, routine court reports in the daily newspapers proved unenlightening. Precisely for that reason, the prominent lawyer Phan Anh was fascinated to listen privately to the stories of an ICP activist who had just escaped from prison.[120]

Anticipating this sort of interest among the intelligentsia, Truong Chinh had drafted brief "Theses on Vietnamese Culture" for internal ICP circulation in 1943. Henceforth all cultural output had to be judged by the degree to which it stimulated patriotism, mass consciousness, and scientific objectivity.[121] Simultaneously, a National Salvation Cultural Association (Hoi Van Hoa Cuu Quoc) was established to recruit urban intellectuals to the Viet Minh cause and find ways of insinuating anti-French, anti-Japanese propaganda into legal newspapers and journals. With almost all prominent ICP writers in jail or out of touch in the south, however, Truong Chinh had to rely on unknown students or minor journalists to make covert contact with noncommunist luminaries, most of whom seemed to appre-

---

Minh efforts also were under way in Son La and Nghia Lo (Yen Bai) prisons, but with little impact on the population outside the walls.

119. In February 1943, the ICP Standing Bureau chided even Party members who continued to think they were operating in peacetime rather than grasping the urgent conditions of war and revolution. *TVKD,* 1:373.

120. Phan Anh, "Con duong di toi Cach Mang Thang Tam cua toi" [My Path to the August Revolution], *Nhan Dan,* 21 Aug. 1960. The ICP member was introduced by "H.X.H.," almost certainly Hoang Xuan Han, who like Phan Anh became a minister in the Tran Trong Kim cabinet.

121. "De Cuong ve Van Hoa Viet-Nam" [Theses on Vietnamese Culture], in Dang Lao Dong Viet Nam, *Ve Su Lanh Dao cua Dang tren Mat Tran Tu Tuong va Van Hoa, 1930–1945* [Concerning the Party's Leadership on the Ideological and Cultural Front, 1930–45] (Hanoi, 1960), 187–93. The "Theses" show evidence of ICP familiarity with the results of the CCP's May 1942 Yenan Conference on the Problems of Art and Literature.

ciate exchanging ideas but avoided any organizational involvement. Rigorous colonial censorship prevented Viet Minh formulas from surfacing in the public media, leaving intellectuals to rely on word of mouth and occasional copies of clandestine papers like *Cuu Quoc* (National Salvation) and *Co Giai Phong* (Liberation Flag).[122]

Party leaders were even more anxious to reestablish effective links with urban factory workers, artisans, and coolies. For an organization that prided itself on its vanguard proletarian status, this proved surprisingly difficult. The ICP's Hanoi network had been hit hard by six Sûreté roundups between April 1940 and April 1943.[123] In Haiphong, only the Party cell at the large cement works escaped destruction. Among the Nam Dinh textile factories, no ICP cells could be restored until mid 1943.[124] More fundamentally, the tenuous economic conditions characterizing wartime Indochina seemed to drive a wedge between those men and women permitted by employers to continue working and those who were retrenched and forced to work as day laborers or return to their home villages to survive.[125] When employees did dare to strike, it was to try to obtain a bit more money or rations to offset inflation and product scarcities, with no mention of prewar political demands, much less any call for national independence.[126] On the other hand, Viet Minh calls for workers to join together with supervisors and even managers in "Worker National Salvation Associations" offended those who continued to believe that only militant class struggle could achieve better living conditions.[127] Finally, despite Viet Minh condemnations of the fascist war effort, some unemployed laborers were quick to sign up when the Japanese offered them jobs constructing airfields, repairing equipment, or sawing timber.[128]

To the south of Tonkin, along the extended coast of Annam, although ICP members in many localities had been able to resume activity within a year or two of the 1939–40 colonial crackdown, knowledge of Eighth Plenum decisions and the new Viet Minh strategy remained spotty. Activists

---

122. Le Quang Dao et al., *Mot Chang Duong Van Hoa*, 37–79, 135–60.

123. *CMTT*, 1:5, 9. Ban Nghien Cuu Lich Su Dang Thanh Uy Ha-Noi, *Cuoc Van Dong Cach Mang Thang Tam o Hanoi* [Activating the August Revolution in Hanoi] (Hanoi, 1970) (cited below as *CMTT-H*), 58.

124. *CMTT*, 1:265–66, 420–21.

125. *CMCD*, 9:148–64.

126. *CMCD*, 9:165–69. *CMCD*, 10:116–23.

127. Workers who took this position were sometimes labeled "Trotskyists" by Viet Minh organizers, although no evidence exists of groups in Tonkin who called themselves by this name.

128. *CMTT-H*, 33–34.

in Quang Nam possessed details by August 1941; those in Quang Tri learned in early 1942; those in Thanh Hoa in September 1942.[129] However, ICP cells in the provinces of Nghe An, Quang Binh, Thua Thien, Quang Ngai, Binh Dinh, and Khanh Hoa remained ill informed until 1943 or even 1944.[130] Also, it was not uncommon for one or two ICP cells in a particular province of Annam to obtain instructions yet fail to pass them on to others, or to meet with disbelief and suspicion from members who assumed that the Sixth Plenum resolution of November 1939 remained in force. Such problems were supposed to be overcome by the Party's Regional Committee for Annam, but it had been smashed in mid 1941, reconstituted, then broken again in mid 1942.[131] In some cases, central Vietnamese activists first learned of Eighth Plenum instructions inside prison, from northern comrades arrested after May 1941. Upon release or escape from jail, they gravitated to their home districts and often managed to persuade others to start organizing Viet Minh affiliates.[132] However, because rumors continued to circulate that political prisoners had been suborned by the Sûreté prior to release or being allowed to escape, some ICP members preferred to work alone, not trusting anyone else.[133] Provinces in the central highlands remained almost devoid of Viet Minh organizing until early 1945,[134] and for reasons unknown the coastal province of Ha Tinh, sandwiched between Nghe An and Quang Binh, lacked any Viet Minh groups until June 1945.[135]

Further south, in Cochinchina, after the Nam Ky uprising in November 1940 and subsequent colonial repression, those ICP members not in jail spent most of their time trying to avoid capture and locate a few comrades, from among whom it might be possible to establish local cells. Many peasant followers of the ICP had gravitated toward the Hoa Hao religious movement, which in addition to its millenarian vision of imminent salvation seemed to offer more chance of public organizing under Japanese protection.[136] By 1942, some local ICP members had managed to reestablish

129. *CMTT*, 1:380. *CMTT*, 2:46–47, 88, 91.

130. *CMTT*, 2:14, 34, 68, 104, 106, 137, 157.

131. Truong Sinh, in Bui Cong Trung et al., *Nguoi Truoc Nga, Nguoi Sau Tien* [The First Rank Falls, the Second Advances] (Hanoi, 1960), 59–74.

132. *CMTT*, 2:137, 139, 157.

133. This problem is admitted in many provincial-level memoirs. The mood of suspicion seems to have been especially debilitating in Nghe An province. See *Co Giai Phong*, no. 8 (26 Aug. 1943), quoted in Dang Lao Dong Viet Nam, *Ve Su Lanh Dao*, 145–46.

134. *CMTT*, 2:186, 207, 216.

135. Ibid., 30.

136. Hue-Tam Ho Tai, *Millenarianism and Peasant Politics in Vietnam* (Cambridge, Mass., 1983), 122–31.

clandestine contact with labor union branches, "mutual assistance associations" (*hoi tuong te*), and sporting groups established during the 1936–38 Popular Front period. In a few cases, they rehabilitated anti-imperialist front groups set up in 1940 in accordance with Sixth Plenum instructions. However, in Cochinchina it proved very difficult to revive coherent ICP efforts beyond the district level.[137] The Sûreté had infiltrated the Party to the extent that it could follow internal debates in detail, sow confusion, and pounce on selected members at times of its own choosing.[138]

In 1943, young employees of the colonial Agricultural Bureau smuggled copies of Viet Minh publications from Hanoi to the Mekong Delta town of Can Tho, where they shared them with local militants.[139] That may have been the impetus for an ICP group led by Bui Van Thu to start a new journal under the title *Giai Phong* (Liberation) and to rename existing front groups in Viet Minh parlance as "national salvation associations." In mid 1944, someone else from the north sought out Bui Van Thu and his comrades, this time bringing an ICP Central Committee resolution as well as more copies of Viet Minh newspapers. Perhaps at the urging of this northern contact, preparations began for an insurrection, to take place in November under the aegis of the "Cochinchina Section" of the Viet Minh.[140] Although ICP cells in Can Tho, Long Xuyen, Rach Gia, and perhaps Saigon accepted this dangerous challenge,[141] Bui Van Thu encountered resolute opposition from Tran Van Giau, claiming to speak for the Cochinchina Regional Committee of the Party, who instead argued for building links with the Free French in anticipation of Japanese defeat at the hands of the Allies.[142]

137. To Tranh, "Cuoc dau tranh nham cung co va giu vung chinh quyen cach mang o Nam Bo" [The Struggle to Consolidate and Uphold the Revolutionary Government in Southern Vietnam], *NCLS* 229 (4-1986): 15. Nam Moc, in Le Quang Dao et al., *Mot Chang Duong Van Hoa*, 85–86.

138. "Rapports mensuels de la Sûreté interieure en Cochinchine, décembre 1942 à octobre 1944," in AOM, CP 161. My appreciation to Stein Tønnesson for making his notes on these reports available to me.

139. *CMTT*, 2:349.

140. "Rapports mensuels de la Sûreté," esp. those for 20 Dec. 1942–19 Jan. 1943, 16 June–15 July 1943, 16 June–15 July 1944, 16 July–15 Aug. 1944, and 16 Aug.–15 Sept. 1944. See also Tønnesson, *Vietnamese Revolution*, 139–41. Bui Van Thu headed the ICP's "Interprovincial Committee of the West [Delta]," also known as the "Hau Giang Interprovincial Committee." He may be the same person as Nguyen Van Tay, mentioned in later sources as heading the Giai Phong ICP group in the south.

141. *CMTT*, 2:336–37, 385.

142. "Rapports mensuels de la Sûreté," 16 Aug. 1944–15 Sept. 1944. In my interview with Tran Van Giau, 12 Feb. 1990, he also made a point of criticizing the

Whatever the reasons, the proposed Viet Minh insurrection did not go ahead.

Tran Van Giau—a graduate of Moscow's Oriental Workers' Institute ("Stalin School"), a Popular Front activist in Saigon in the late 1930s, and an escapee from the Ta Lai colonial penal camp in 1941—had indeed reestablished a Cochinchina Regional Committee in late 1943, but this initiative was angrily rejected by the ICP group headquartered in Can Tho, which then proceeded to form its own regional committee. As each committee dispatched representatives around the Mekong Delta to argue its case and recruit adherents, it was not long before most provinces contained two small groups competing for revolutionary legitimacy.[143] During 1944, several meetings were convened between rival regional leaders, without result.[144] Such chaos was both unacceptable from the point of view of Leninist organizing principles and dangerous in the opportunities it offered enemy security services. Normally the ICP Standing Bureau would have stepped in early to impose unity or anoint one regional committee, but this did not happen.

It is important to appreciate that between December 1940 and perhaps as late as June 1945, no direct organizational contact existed between the ICP Standing Bureau, located far to the north, and any regional-level committee in Cochinchina.[145] Several factors contributed to this serious breakdown of communication: continuing dissension among ICP members in Cochinchina; effective wartime control by the Sûreté of movement between regions; and the apparent inability of the ICP to restore its influence among those railway or maritime workers who moved routinely up and down the long coast of Vietnam.

ICP leadership in the north in 1944 for not giving sufficient attention to joining with "progressive French" in anticipation of a Franco-Japanese confrontation.

143. *Lich Su Dang Cong San Viet Nam Tinh Song Be* [History of the Vietnam Communist Party in Song Be Province], ed. Nguyen Ba Tho, vol. 1, *1930–1945* (Ho Chi Minh City [?], 1989), 157–58, 172.

144. Interviews with Tran Van Giau and Duong Quang Dong (Nam Dong), Ho Chi Minh City, 19 Mar. 1988. Interview with Tran Bach Dang, Ho Chi Minh City, 17 Mar. 1988. The one person who might have been accepted as a compromise regional chairman by both groups was Ha Huy Giap, partly because of the prestige of his older brother, Ha Huy Tap, who had been executed by the French in 1941.

145. Clearly copies of clandestine papers and occasional policy pronouncements did manage to make their way in both directions, but there is no evidence of specific orders being transmitted successfully by the Standing Bureau or of detailed reports being received from the south.

More fundamentally, it may be that some ICP leaders in the south, still disgruntled at the 1940 transfer of Standing Bureau / Central Committee operations to Tonkin after many years in Cochinchina, preferred not to receive instructions from General Secretary Truong Chinh and his associates. In an interview much later, Tran Van Giau intimated that he would not have followed Central Committee orders based on the 1941 Eighth Plenum resolution even if he had received them. Giau particularly insisted that workers and peasants ought to be able to develop their own class-based organizations, rather than subordinate themselves to front control. Also, any united front should involve a variety of groups in free association, not function merely as a tool of the covert ICP.[146] As Giau summarized his revolutionary outlook on another occasion, fully appreciating the irony of what he said: "I'm a Westerner!"[147] While some members of the alternative Cochinchina Regional Committee in Can Tho undoubtedly accepted the Eighth Plenum resolution, they do not appear to have succeeded in communicating the new concepts, except to the limited extent of local groups changing their names from "anti-imperialist" to "national salvation." Deep down, almost all ICP members in the south aimed to replicate the 1917 Bolshevik Revolution, not appreciating the degree to which the Viet Minh strategy as developed in the north drew on more recent CCP precedents.

In such circumstances, it ought not surprise us that many ICP members and sympathizers in Cochinchina remained unaware, perplexed, or skeptical about what was happening in the next district or province, much less in faraway Tonkin. Even those who used the Viet Minh name do not seem to have understood the underlying change in revolutionary strategy. Most local ICP groups continued to advocate general land redistribution, class struggle, and a proletarian identity distinct from any national united front.[148] ICP members in only one Cochinchina province, Rach Gia, attempted seriously to establish a jungle base to train followers in guerrilla combat.[149] Meanwhile, intellectuals outside the ICP, hearing of a new

---

146. Interview with Tran Van Giau, Ho Chi Minh City, 12 Feb. 1990. While it should be obvious that Giau made these comments in the context of the Vietnamese debates about "openness" in 1990, that does not mean he was fabricating 1941–45 attitudes. The same general points were made to me in our 25 Mar. 1980 interview, minus details about internal Party discussions.

147. In Vietnamese, "Toi la Tay ma!" The French enemy was called the "Westerner" in common parlance. Interview with Tran Van Giau, Ho Chi Minh City, 19 Mar. 1988.

148. *CMTT*, 2:222, 231–32, 245, 250, 275, 283, 403.

149. Ibid., 398–99. At his 1980 interview, Tran Van Giau also mentioned sending three comrades to the forest north of Bien Hoa in late 1944 to establish a guerrilla base. It does not appear to have flourished.

organization calling itself the Viet Minh, tried without success to locate a Cochinchina representative.[150]

During 1941–44, at least three thousand ICP members remained in jail, yet far from inactive. Those with prior prison experience took the lead in organizing protective networks among inmates, initiated clandestine training courses, devised techniques for communicating with comrades outside, and plotted escapes. Those in jail for the first time discovered that social class and formal education counted for little, whereas ingenuity, dependability, and the capacity to withstand physical and psychological adversity counted for a great deal. Individuals who had never before traveled beyond their home provinces gained a new sense of national identity by being shipped from one prison to another, meeting inmates from diverse locations and backgrounds, forging friendships that would last a lifetime. Thanks to the routine arrival of new prisoners, ICP members inside jail had a better chance of learning about the Eighth Plenum resolution and other key Party decisions than many activists at liberty, yet out of touch with higher echelons.

Hundreds of political prisoners were either released by the colonial authorities or managed to escape. Those who chose to return home and resume operations had the advantages of enhanced prestige, extraprovincial links, and knowledge of Party directives. In late 1942, for example, several escaped inmates made it back to Bien Hoa, where they established contact with a group of deportees from other provinces, as well as some Party members hiding out on local rubber plantations.[151] In early 1943, after escaping from jail, To Huu convened the Thanh Hoa provincial committee to begin organization of Viet Minh units. Released from Son La Prison in 1943, Tran Quang Binh returned to action in Yen Bai. Escapees from Hanoi Central Prison (Hoa Lo) and Son La gravitated back to Thai Binh in mid 1944, reestablished contact with old comrades, and soon had a provisional province committee functioning.[152] Nonetheless, it was not unusual for such escapees to be recaptured within a few months, perhaps because of informers within local ICP cells, or in some cases because local members suspected them of being Sûreté plants.[153]

In June 1944, despite all its efforts to proselytize, train, and organize people, the Viet Minh remained only a minor irritant to the French

150. Nguyen Ky Nam, *Hoi Ky, 1925–1964* [Memoirs, 1925–64], vol. 2 (Saigon, 1964), 29.

151. *CMTT*, 2:307.

152. *CMTT*, 1:164, 380, 431.

153. *CMTT*, 2:22, 68, 104.

authorities and of no consequence whatsoever to the Japanese Army. Whatever their faith in inevitable victory, some ICP leaders must have wondered if they were any closer to power than at the Eighth Plenum three years prior. Hundreds had been killed, thousands compelled to live in constant fear and privation. Nonetheless, what had happened to this small group of Vietnamese militants between 1941 and 1944 would prove of major consequence to the country for the next three or four decades.

The Tempo Increases

From mid 1944 on, the pace of clandestine political activity picked up markedly in Vietnam and along the Chinese border. Official Japanese press releases (Domei News Service) contained sufficient information about Axis reversals to enable educated Vietnamese to plot the course of events on a world map. Allied landings in Normandy and the Soviet Army's penetration of Germany's eastern frontier made it obvious that Hitler's days were numbered.[154] American victories in the central Pacific and Allied counterattacks in Burma suggested that Japan would either have to sue for peace or eventually face total defeat, although the Japanese counteroffensive in China during the second half of 1944 put a question mark over Nationalist Chinese abilities to contribute to either outcome. Such developments offered new opportunities for the ICP and the Viet Minh.

One option available to ICP and Viet Minh leaders was to try to link up with French Gaullists also committed to eliminating the Axis presence in Indochina. Already in February 1943, the ICP Standing Bureau had pointed to the existence of significant anti-Japanese sentiment among the French in Indochina, hence the desirability of entering into a "democratic front" relationship. It also predicted that any Allied invasion of Indochina would cause some French colonial forces suddenly to turn against the Axis, as had happened in North Africa in late 1942.[155] A year later, the Standing Bureau's periodical *Co Giai Phong* (Liberation Flag) printed a call for active cooperation between Free French, Chinese, and "Indochinese revolutionary" forces to defeat the "Vichy traitors" and the Japanese.[156] However, in July 1944, aware of Free French pronouncements

154. Immediately on hearing of the Normandy landings, the Viet Minh issued an appeal urging readers to prepare to rise up, throw out the Japanese and French, and win back "food, clothing, independence and freedom." *CMCD*, 10:110.

155. *TVKD*, 1:366–67, 370–72.

156. *Co Giai Phong* 3 (15 Feb. 1944), reprinted in *CMCD*, 8:33–36, and in Truong Chinh, *Cach Mang*, 271–73.

that seemed to exclude any idea of autonomy or self-government for postwar Indochina, the ICP accused the Gaullists of rank hypocrisy in preaching liberation of France from the Nazis but continued French subjugation of other nationalities.[157] "We want total liberty," a Viet Minh pamphlet warned, adding that "the Allied powers do not have the right to put a yoke on other peoples."[158]

Despite such misgivings, the ICP Standing Bureau retained contact with local Gaullists via a clandestine French Communist Party group still surviving in Hanoi.[159] Simultaneously, the respected teacher and writer Dang Thai Mai served as secret liaison between the ICP and Gaullist sympathizers within the local branch of the French Socialist Party.[160] After the liberation of Paris in August 1944, the ICP tried without success to ascertain whether General de Gaulle intended to abrogate the authority of the French collaborator administration in Indochina or work with it to ensure colonial continuity following Japanese defeat. At a more modest level, Truong Chinh met secretly in November with two Gaullist lieutenant colonels, requesting that they use their positions to try to stop Japanese rice confiscations, to obtain release of Vietnamese political prisoners, and to provide firearms to the Viet Minh. Apparently the Gaullists did manage to engineer release of one hundred fifty political prisoners in Hanoi, but they flatly rejected the request for weapons, and proved incapable of preventing continued rice confiscations.[161]

Another option, publicly advocated by the Viet Minh since 1941, was to work closely with the Chinese Nationalists to attack both Japanese and French forces in Indochina. The longer the war ground on, however, the less capacity Chinese generals in either Kwangsi or Yunnan had to launch an invasion. In the latter half of 1944, Japan's massive Ichigō counterof-

157. Co Giai Phong 6 (28 July 1944), reprinted in Truong Chinh, Cach Mang, 287–89.

158. Quoted in Paul Isoart, Le Phénomène national vietnamien: De l'indépendance unitaire à l'indépendance fractionée (Paris, 1961), 321–22. See also quotations from Viet Minh tracts in Philippe Devillers, Histoire du Vietnam de 1940 à 1952 (Paris, 1952), 110–11.

159. Jacques Doyon, Les Soldats blancs de Ho Chi Minh (Paris, 1973), 47–49. The French communists also put the ICP in touch with antifascist Germans, Austrians, and Spaniards in Foreign Legion units.

160. Le Quang Dao et al., Mot Chang Duong Van Hoa, 144.

161. CMCD, 10:83–84. Thomas Hodgkin, Vietnam: The Revolutionary Path (London, 1981), 318. The intermediary for the Truong Chinh meeting with Gaullist officers was Erwin Borchers, an anti-Nazi Alsatian German enrolled in the French Foreign Legion. It seems very unlikely that General de Gaulle would have approved of such contacts with the ICP or Viet Minh.

fensive in southern China threw the entire frontier region into confusion. General Chang Fa-kwei, who as Fourth War Area commander had earlier sponsored establishment of the coalition Vietnam Revolutionary League (Viet Nam Cach Menh Dong Minh Hoi) to cooperate in cross-border operations, now faced far more pressing problems of evacuation and defense in northern Kwangsi. Ho Chi Minh, who had been released from jail to take part in the Revolutionary League, was permitted in August to depart for Indochina carrying a military map, some medicine, and 76,000 Chinese dollars (U.S. $150).[162] He was not alone: French intelligence reported that more than two hundred Vietnamese anticolonial activists either deserted Chinese military units or were released from prison in the wake of the Japanese offensive, most crossing into Indochina with weapons in hand.[163]

Eager to recruit more Vietnamese émigrés to its cause, the Viet Minh in late October issued an open letter to overseas organizations, arguing that the political divisiveness that had long prevented Vietnam from casting off the foreign yoke could now be overcome by the Revolutionary League in southern China cooperating with the Viet Minh inside the country.[164] Internationally, the open letter highlighted Hitler's collapsing fortunes, remarked upon heightened tension between the Japanese and the French in Indochina, and argued that the Imperial Army's counteroffensive in China represented a last desperate attempt to avoid total defeat. With the prospect of revolution "knocking on our door at any moment," it was essential for patriotic groups to come together to agree on a program for building a strong, progressive Vietnam after enemy armies had been cleansed from the country. Only given such unity, the letter concluded, could Vietnam achieve "happiness, independence and freedom." Other materials issued at the same time as this letter disingenuously denied assertions that the Viet Minh was communist-dominated, quoted Chiang Kai-shek, Chang Fa-kwei, and Nguyen Hai Than approvingly, and reendorsed the proposal that Chinese troops invade Indochina.[165]

162. Chen, *Vietnam and China*, 64–85. Ho's request for 1,000 firearms and 4,000 grenades was denied. Chinese setbacks in late 1944 did not silence Viet Minh calls for Sino-Vietnamese cooperation, as we shall see in chapter 4.

163. DGER report, 1 June 1945, in AOM, INF, c. 122, d. 1106. Not all of these individuals would have joined the Viet Minh, however.

164. "Thu cua Tong-Bo Viet-Minh gui cho cac doan the cach mang Viet-Nam o Hai ngoai" [Viet Minh General Headquarters Letter to Overseas Vietnamese Revolutionary Groups], reprinted in *Cuu Quoc*, 11-1944, 12–14. Specifically excluded from this cooperation was the Nationalist Party leader Vu Hong Khanh, labeled an "opportunist" and "fake revolutionary."

165. *Cuu Quoc*, 11-1944, 4–6, 9, 14, 16–18, 21.

In July 1944, the ICP's Interprovincial Committee for Cao Bang, Bac Can, and Lang Son convened a meeting of local cadres to plan future operations. Participants were buoyed by their recent success in restoring the Viet Minh network, badly damaged earlier in the year, and by the prospect of the Vichy government's imminent demise in France, which would inevitably demoralize the Decoux administration in Indochina. The meeting became quite animated, with a majority apparently favoring urgent preparations for an armed uprising. As one Nung speaker picturesquely summarized it, "For a long while the child has been without milk. Now its mother will let [it] suckle. This time we're determined to wipe out the enemy."[166] However, Vu Anh argued that such talk was dangerously premature. As the ranking Party member present, his opinion could not be ignored, leading to compromise approval of two months of preparations for "guerrilla war," rather than an "uprising," and leaving the precise date of the first offensive action to be decided later.[167]

After the cadres dispersed to their respective districts, many continued to talk eagerly about an armed uprising. They organized special leadership training sessions, urged villagers to donate grain for placement in secret caches, and devised plans to withdraw civilians from areas adjacent to colonial posts and roads. Armed units tried to accumulate sufficient ammunition and supplies for a possible six months' conflict.[168] Persons who contributed money to help the Viet Minh obtain weapons were promised that the Fatherland would inscribe their names for posterity. On the other hand, those who voluntarily helped the enemy or used the "troubled times to get rich" would have their names "blanked out."[169] A mood of excitement suffused participants, leading Vo Nguyen Giap to ruminate on how "Revolution really was the New Year's festival [*Tet*] of the oppressed."[170] On the other hand, Vu Anh was so concerned that at one point he ordered Giap to cease efforts to establish a regular Liberation Army unit.[171]

With battle plans completed and the Interprovincial Committee close to issuing the implementation order, Ho Chi Minh returned, listened to reports by the worried Vu Anh and eager Vo Nguyen Giap, then instructed them immediately to put off any uprising. Conditions were not ripe else-

166. Vo Nguyen Giap, *Tu Nhan Dan ma ra*, 131–32.
167. Hoang Van Hoan, *Giot Nuoc*, 226–27.
168. *CCDVB*, 72–74. Vo Nguyen Giap, *Tu Nhan Dan ma ra*, 132–35.
169. Viet Minh appeal, 10 Aug. 1944, reprinted in *CMCD*, 10:112–13.
170. Vo Nguyen Giap, *Tu Nhan Dan ma ra*, 134.
171. Hoang Van Hoan, *Giot Nuoc*, 227. Contact had been lost for many months with the ICP's Standing Bureau in the Red River Delta, so it was impossible to refer the issues to higher authority.

where in the country, he emphasized. Contact was lacking even with Chu Van Tan's group in the nearby Bac Son–Vu Nhai base area. Following an uprising, the French would be able to isolate the three provinces of Cao Bang, Bac Can, and Lang Son and would launch a repression more merciless than that of early 1944. In the face of this harsh critique, Vo Nguyen Giap now revealed his own concern that any evacuation of civilians into the forest would soon encounter serious problems of sustenance.[172] The Interprovincial Committee's operational plan was aborted, a negative decision possessing considerable positive consequences, as French retaliation undoubtedly would have been severe, perhaps crippling Viet Minh operations in this area well into 1945.

Ho Chi Minh had already conceived a plan to turn the energies of some of his most militant followers in less dangerous directions. To the crestfallen Giap, he gave responsibility for organizing a nascent regular army, which would constitute a third level of military force, complementing the existing village-level and district-level guerrilla units. By early December, the first platoon of the Vietnam Propaganda and Liberation Army (Viet Nam Tuyen Truyen Giai Phong Quan) had been formed.[173] On 24 December, one of its squads donned colonial uniforms, gained entry in the late afternoon to the militia post of Phai Khat, twenty-six kilometers west of the town of Cao Bang, and captured it without a shot.[174] According to a later account by Vo Nguyen Giap, following a fifteen-kilometer forced march, the same tactic was employed to capture the tirailleur post at Na Ngan the next morning; five enemy soldiers who offered resistance were killed, at the cost of one slightly wounded Propaganda and Liberation Army member. The thirty-seven captured soldiers from the two posts were offered the choice of either joining a Viet Minh unit or returning to their home villages. Most took the latter option and were given back their haversacks, blankets, and personal effects, then issued with travel papers and a small sum of money.[175]

172. Vo Nguyen Giap, *Tu Nhan Dan ma ra*, 136–39. NSKLSD, 1:584–85.
173. VKQS, 262–63. LSQD, 114–19. Vo Nguyen Giap presided over a solemn oath-taking ceremony on 22 December, which later came to be designated as the birthday of the People's Army of Vietnam. His speech is translated in *Vietnam: The Definitive Documentation*, ed. Porter, 14–17. The concept of "armed propaganda" underlying Giap's efforts is discussed in Lockhart, *Nation in Arms*, 92–102.
174. Vo Nguyen Giap, *Tu Nhan Dan ma ra*, 139–65. After Phai Khat had been captured, the absent French officer in charge returned on horseback from nearby Nguyen Binh and was shot dead.
175. Vo Nguyen Giap, *Tu Nhan Dan ma ra*, 166–70. CCDVB, 74–81. LSQD, 119–20. According to colonial accounts, by contrast, a French corporal was captured and fifteen troopers had their throats cut. Sûreté report, 10 Jan. 1945, in AOM, CP 161.

The army unit eagerly reequipped itself with the forty rifles, two pistols, and 3,000 cartridges captured,[176] distributing its old hunting rifles and muskets to local Viet Minh self-defense units that had cooperated in the attacks by collecting intelligence, screening movement, and stripping the posts of everything usable.

News of these two victories spread quickly, enhancing Viet Minh prestige considerably throughout the region. Letters of congratulations and gifts of clothing, blankets, mosquito nets, and food flowed into the Interprovincial Committee headquarters. To avoid French counteraction, the Propaganda and Liberation Army platoon took refuge in a particularly inaccessible valley, where it also received more than a hundred new recruits, giving it sufficient men to form a company composed of six platoons.[177]

In mid January 1945, a more ambitious assault was mounted on Dong Mu, seven kilometers from the Chinese frontier. Assuming that the same daytime ruse could not work again, Propaganda and Liberation Army members this time crawled toward the Dong Mu post in darkness, only to be challenged at the foot of the main blockhouse. In the ensuing firefight, both sides suffered casualties. After three hours, the Viet Minh attackers were ordered to withdraw, taking with them three prisoners and five captured firearms.[178] Although a subsequent French report declared this particular enemy assault defeated, it admitted that all Viet Minh attacks since Christmas had been carried out with "perfect technique and executed with calm cold-bloodedness and method."[179] In February, several ambushes and assaults on smaller posts netted almost fifty rifles.[180] Not far to the south, in Bac Son district, the French managed to expose part of the Viet Minh network, disrupt organizing efforts, and capture two leaders. The district mandarin, having put a bounty on Hoang Van Han, another Viet Minh leader, was able proudly to display his head on a pole in mid February.[181]

176. DGER report, 1 June 1945, in AOM, INF, c. 122, d. 1106.

177. Vo Nguyen Giap, *Tu Nhan Dan ma ra*, 171–72. The company commander was Hoang Sam, and the political commissar Xich Thang. Hoang Van Thai, who had had four years' military training in China, was given responsibility for intelligence and planning. Giap remained in overall charge.

178. Ibid., 173–78. According to the prisoners, the post had been on 50 percent alert for fear of an attack from an entirely different source—"bandits" positioned just across the frontier.

179. Sûreté report, 10 Jan. 1945, in AOM, CP 161.

180. Vo Nguyen Giap, *Tu Nhan Dan ma ra*, 189–90.

181. Ban Nghien Cuu Lich Su Dang Tinh Uy Lang Son, *Lich Su Dau Tranh Cach Mang Huyen Bac Son (1935–1945)* [A History of Bac Son District's Revolutionary Struggle (1935–45)] (Lang Son, 1974), 55.

The French realized that the Viet Minh could not be allowed to continue its activities unhindered. In January, Paul Arnoux, general intendant of the Indochina Sûreté, ordered that a list be compiled of all incidents since 1940 provoked by this "terroristic, criminal, antisocial and anti-French" organization, for covert dispatch to General de Gaulle's government.[182] Presumably Arnoux hoped that such evidence would persuade Allied intelligence services to ostracize the Viet Minh. Meanwhile, the colonial authorities began to construct three concentration camps preparatory to launching search-and-destroy operations in the hills north of Hanoi. With Franco-Japanese relations becoming ever more tense, however, Indochina Army commanders understandably focused their attention almost entirely on the Imperial Army. To shift a number of colonial battalions from established camps into the mountains would immediately have aroused Japanese suspicions of a preemptive maneuver directed against them. In early March, as mentioned earlier, the French nonetheless notified General Tsuchihashi's headquarters of their intention to move against the Viet Minh in force, starting with the transfer of one battalion of tirailleurs from Lang Son to Cao Bang on 12 March.[183] These plans evaporated on the night of 9 March.

Meanwhile, in Hanoi during the second half of 1944 and early 1945, popular interest in the Viet Minh had increased greatly compared with previous months and years. On 30 June, the Vietnam Democratic Party (Dang Dan Chu Viet Nam) was formed by a group of young patriotic intellectuals led by Duong Duc Hien, and sought covert contact with the Viet Minh.[184] Several Hanoi University students were assigned to listen routinely to Allied shortwave radio broadcasts, taking notes to convey to writers and organizers.[185] In December 1944, the main National Salvation Cultural Association group of five was uncovered by the Sûreté in Hanoi and members jailed for a few weeks, then released or ordered to reside in

---

182. Tønnesson, *Vietnamese Revolution*, 118–19, based on documentation in AOM, Service de Protection du Corps Expeditionnaire, c. A-8. Of ninety-five incidents listed, eighty had occurred in 1944.

183. DGER report, 1 June 1945, in AOM, INF, c. 122, d. 1106. Because such troop movements also met General Sabattier's desire to get some units out of camp before a likely Japanese attack (see chapter 1), it is difficult to know how seriously the French regarded anti–Viet Minh operations at this time.

184. Other founders of the Democratic Party included Hoang Minh Chinh, Vu Dinh Hoe, and Do Duc Dung. Early support came mainly from the Thanh Nghi writers' group, university students, and clerks in the colonial bureaucracy. Interview with Hoang Van Duc, Hanoi, 19 Feb. 1994.

185. Interview with Tran Lam, 5 Mar. 1988. Tran Lam's long hours hunched over a receiver with earphones led in early September 1945 to his appointment to establish the DRV's "Voice of Vietnam," which he was still directing forty-three years later.

their home villages.[186] By early 1945, nonetheless, up to thirty essayists, short-story writers, poets, dramatists, and folklorists in and around Hanoi were eager to promote the Viet Minh line, without necessarily being part of any apparatus. The undisputed doyen of this coterie was Dang Thai Mai, a classically trained essayist and teacher of literature.[187]

The involvement of these creative minds had an immediate and salutary effect on the quality of Viet Minh propaganda—for example, circulating poems that celebrated the heroic feats of guerrillas in the Cao-Bac-Lang "battle zone" (*chien khu*), employing imagery drawn from traditional operas about China's Warring States period or the *Tale of the Three Kingdoms*.[188] Van Cao composed the patriotic march "Advancing Army" ("Tien quan ca"), had it printed in the Democratic Party's clandestine journal, and was amazed one month later to hear it being played in downtown Hanoi. In early 1945, "Advancing Army" became the informal anthem of young city folk in Tonkin.[189] Other Viet Minh activists preferred surprise and simplicity. Flags, banners, and leaflets began to pop up at the most evocative times and places—for example, when more than one thousand students visited the Huong Tich pagoda outside Hanoi on Christmas Day 1944,[190] and at the Voi Phuc temple during a Tet 1945 ceremony to commemorate victory over invading Ch'ing dynasty troops in 1789.[191] Although most Hanoi residents still knew very little about the Viet Minh, their curiosity had been whetted.

Actions Following the Japanese Takeover

While ICP analysts had long predicted the violent breakdown of Franco-Japanese cooperation,[192] they do not appear to have been particularly well

---

186. The individuals arrested were Vu Quoc Uy, Nhu Phong, Nguyen Dinh Thi, To Hoai, and a fifth person whom all memoirs choose not to identify. Le Quang Dao et al., *Mot Chang Duong Van Hoa*, 44, 59, 67, 118–19.

187. Ibid., 43, 52, 56–57, 115, 119–20. *CMTT-H*, 73–76. Other significant writers and artists in this pro–Viet Minh circle included Nguyen Hong, Nam Cao, Van Cao, and Nguyen Huy Tuong. Interestingly enough, no historians, scientists, physicians, or lawyers seem to have been involved.

188. Tran Huy Lieu, *NCLS* 29 (8-1961): 18–19.

189. Van Cao, "Ky Niem ve Bai Hat 'Tien Quan Ca'" [Anniversary of the "Advancing Army" Anthem], *Van Hoa Nghe Thuat* (Hanoi) 171–72 (Aug. 1985): 9, 19. Le Quang Dao et al., *Mot Chang Duong Van Hoa*, 109–13.

190. *CMTT*, 1:18.

191. *CMTT-H*, 77–78. *CMTT*, 1:20.

192. See, e.g., the insightful analysis of deteriorating Franco-Japanese relations written by Truong Chinh and published in *Co Giai Phong*, 28 Sept. 1944, available in translation in the *Vietnam Courier*, 8-1985, 10–11.

informed about the growing tensions in early 1945, as seen, for example, in Ho Chi Minh's decision to travel again to China in February to improve contacts with Allied forces. Once the 9 March coup had taken place, however, ICP leaders were not slow to enunciate a new line and take advantage of fluid conditions. On 15 March, a short, vivid Viet Minh proclamation appeared, describing how the Japanese had become the primary enemy, explaining why they were certain to suffer defeat, and calling on people to demonstrate, strike, destroy communications, and attack small Japanese posts or patrols. It concluded:

> If you want sufficient food and clothing,
> If you wish to protect your home and country,
> To avoid conscription or corvée,
> To escape falling bombs and stray shells,
> To live proudly in the world,
> Then stand up, rich and poor, women and men, old and young, a million
>   individuals as one.
> Kill the enemy, eliminate traitors.
> Create a strong, free, and independent Vietnam.[193]

No such rhetoric was necessary to energize existing ICP-led units, although Japanese forces were generally avoided. Thus, upon hearing that the Japanese had attacked the colonial post at Nguyen Binh (Cao Bang) and taken French personnel away as prisoners, Vo Nguyen Giap decided without waiting for any higher authorization to march his main Propaganda and Liberation Army company southward to link up with Chu Van Tan's National Salvation Army unit in the Bac Son–Vu Nhai area and reestablish contact with the ICP Standing Bureau near Hanoi. In contrast to all previous troop movements, which had been conducted in secrecy at night, Giap this time ordered the company to march in open terrain during daylight, Viet Minh flags carried proudly. As Giap recalled:

> After so many years of clandestine operations, surviving deep in the forests, slipping past villages in the dark, repressing any cough, placing each foot gingerly one after the other, now suddenly we were able to come out of the trees, walk easily along roads amidst the fields, and be received warmly by our countrymen.[194]

By the end of March, this unit was already adjacent to the town of Cho Chu (Thai Nguyen), 110 kilometers south of Cao Bang town and more than halfway to Hanoi.

193. Quoted in *CMCD*, 11:26–27. Allegedly 150,000 copies of this proclamation were printed and circulated in northern Vietnam.
194. Vo Nguyen Giap, *Tu Nhan Dan ma ra*, 191.

The first practical test of ICP policy came when armed Viet Minh groups of various types encountered French colonial units fleeing the Japanese. It will be recalled that the Standing Bureau's instructions of 12 March urged ICP members to set aside deeply rooted animosities toward the French colonials and try to work with them against the now-dominant Japanese. Similar instructions were issued by the Cao-Bac-Lang Interprovincial Committee.[195] In Cao Bang, a ranking French officer, Commandant Reul, had already initiated contact with Viet Minh agents before the Japanese coup. In late March, a Viet Minh representative promised to provide military intelligence on the enemy, as well as local guides, and food for about six hundred colonial soldiers (including fifty Europeans), in exchange for Reul obtaining approval from his superiors to furnish firearms, ammunition, and instructors to the Viet Minh. The agreement seems to have held for at least ten days, particularly in regard to Viet Minh provision of food. However, the question of firearms remained unresolved, and on 12 April, the Viet Minh liaison officer abruptly departed Reul's camp. At this point, Reul also learned of Viet Minh attacks on colonial units elsewhere, as well as Viet Minh removal of an arms cache to a secret location. Three days later, a ranking Viet Minh leader arrived, violently criticized French colonial policies, and gave only vague replies to Reul's queries about recent attacks, detentions, and disappearances. Native soldiers continued to desert colonial units. On 20 April, Reul broke off contact, eventually withdrawing what remained of his unit across the frontier to China.[196]

About thirty kilometers south, the French officer in charge of Ngan Son post agreed to march his unit out before the Japanese arrived and join forces with Vo Nguyen Giap's main Propaganda and Liberation Army company. However, by the time both units arrived in Cho Ra (Bac Can), most of the native colonial soldiers had decided they wanted to turn their weapons over to Giap's company and return home, leaving the French officer and his wife to make their way to the Chinese frontier.[197] At Cho Ra, Giap also met Inspector Pierre de Pontich, who was in charge of Garde indochinoise forces in the region. They agreed to cooperate in harassing the Japanese, with Giap

---

195. Ibid., 200.

196. DGER report, 1 June 1945, in AOM, INF, c. 122, d. 1106. René Charbonneau and José Maigre, *Les Parias de la victoire: Indochine–Chine, 1945* (Paris, 1980), 103–4, 172–73. Gabriel Sabattier, *Le Destin de l'Indochine: Souvenirs et documents, 1941–1951* (Paris, 1952), 235–37. On the Vietnamese side, *CMTT*, 1:96–97, argues that several of Reul's French subordinates sabotaged the agreement and had to be attacked. In the end, "several thousand" colonial weapons came into Viet Minh hands in this area.

197. Vo Nguyen Giap, *Tu Nhan Dan ma ra*, 192–93.

receiving 165 Remington rifles and 40 old muskets in exchange for local Viet Minh supporters providing Garde units with food and guides. Through de Pontich, Giap also endeavored to meet the colonel commanding colonial units retreating up the Clear River Valley to the west, in hopes of negotiating a military alliance. On 1 April, however, a Viet Minh squad suddenly opened fire on one Garde group, wounding de Pontich. Soon most Garde members had drifted away, leaving de Pontich and four other French nationals effective prisoners of the Viet Minh until late March 1946, when they were taken to Hanoi and released.[198] Four French military men, headed by Lieutenant Tudy Bernier, were willing to serve as instructors of Viet Minh recruits; they would march triumphantly into Hanoi together in late August.[199]

At a number of other locations, Viet Minh cadres met retreating French officers or NCOs, decided they were too arrogant to work with, and thenceforth concentrated on winning over rank-and-file members of colonial units. Still elsewhere, armed Viet Minh groups made no effort at all to parley, simply ambushing colonial units to demonstrate their superiority and collecting firearms.[200] Following one skirmish at Deo Khe, on the border between Thai Nguyen and Tuyen Quang provinces, Viet Minh guerrillas reaped a surprise bonus when Allied aircraft parachuted in weapons and ammunition intended for the retreating colonial forces.[201] In the end, the idea of tactical cooperation between Viet Minh and French colonial units proved hopelessly impractical, and it appears not to have been taken seriously by more than a small minority on either side. However, those French personnel who experienced what they perceived to be Viet Minh duplicity or outright hostility subsequently conveyed their outrage to

198. Charbonneau and Maigre, Les Parias, 343. Vo Nguyen Giap, Tu Nhan Dan ma ra, 193–94. J. J. Fonde, "Giap et le maquis de Cho ra (mars 1945–mars 1946)," Revue historique des armées (Paris) 2 (1976): 113–26. Fonde adds that Inspector de Pontich returned to Bac Can in October 1947 together with attacking French paratroopers, "hoping to savor the sublime joy of revenge" by capturing Ho Chi Minh and Vo Nguyen Giap.

199. Fonde, "Giap et le maquis," 118, 125–26.

200. Le Thiet Hung, "Lay Sung" [Getting Guns], in Le Thiet Hung et al., Rung Yen The, 46. It is clear that Le Thiet Hung, who had worked closely with Vo Nguyen Giap in previous years, had little or no sympathy for attempts to work with the French. See also CMTT, 1:133–35; Ban Nghien Cuu Lich Su Dang Khu Tu Tri Viet Bac, Khu Thien Thuat, 55–56; and Le Thanh Nghi, "May net hoi ky," Nhan Dan, 31 Aug. 1960. A DGER report of 28 Apr. 1945 mentions a post at Tampril (?) where Garde indochinoise members allegedly killed all Europeans. AOM, INF, c. 123, d. 1108, subdossier 3.

201. CMTT, 1:71.

higher echelons, coloring the attitudes of Gaullist officials who would soon have to decide what position to take vis-à-vis this new force in the Indochinese political equation (see chapter 5).

In April, four cadres approached Vo Nguyen Giap to ask when they would receive guns. Giap, having finally replaced his own dud grenade with a Colt .45 pistol, told them to go out and bring back more firearms to build the army. "Our armory is thanks to the enemy, not any weapon's factory around here," he added.[202] Besides firearms obtained directly from colonial units, local Viet Minh groups probably secured even larger numbers by persuading isolated stragglers to exchange weapons for food and villagers to turn over rifles and ammunition abandoned along roads and pathways, or dumped into the water, to them.[203] Party cells in Hoai Duc district, adjacent to Hanoi, received several hundred firearms from various sources, forwarding some to the mountains, putting aside others for the eventual urban uprising, and distributing still others for use in training sessions.[204] The biggest haul occurred in Bac Giang province, where local Viet Minh adherents uncovered a French cache of five hundred firearms.[205] Another major catch took place in Bien Hoa province, far to the south, after the French warship *Tourane* ran aground on the Dong Nai river and was abandoned, the crew trying to flee northward to Ban Me Thuot. Local ICP members and forestry workers managed to round up enough compatriots to strip the vessel of all portable weapons, ammunition, and equipment before the Japanese arrived. Eventually, most of the booty was carried to hiding places in Thu Dau Mot province.[206]

In line with Bolshevik experience in 1917 Russia, ICP leaders always assumed that it would be necessary to win over or neutralize a majority of the enemy's military forces in order for any revolution to succeed in Indochina. Although prior attempts at "mobilizing the military" (*binh van*) hardly inspired confidence, conditions were far more favorable now. French troops were conveniently out of the picture, Japanese troops needed to concentrate on a possible Allied invasion, and native Indochinese troops remained in suspended animation without their French officers and NCOs.

202. Nguyen Van Rang, "Nam Thang o Giai Phong Quan Khang Nhat," 67.

203. *CMTT*, 1:354, 410. *CMTT*, 2:224–25, 302, 331, 368. Le Thiet Hung, "Lay Sung," 44–45. Truong Do Thanh, "Mua Sung" [Buying Guns], in *Hoi Ky Cach Mang Ha Tay*, 2:3–18.

204. Dang Cong San Viet Nam, *So Thao Lich Su Cach Mang Huyen Hoai Duc*, 73–74.

205. Le Thanh Nghi, "May net hoi ky," *Nhan Dan*, 31 Aug. 1960.

206. *CMTT*, 2:299.

Small Garde indochinoise units at the district level proved particularly vulnerable to Viet Minh efforts, although the Japanese tried to make sure they were paid regularly and received rations adequate for family needs. Within weeks of the 9 March coup, leaflets purporting to come from the Viet Minh appeared in the vicinity of many such posts, urging military personnel to cooperate in fighting the Japanese. Letters were sent to individual soldiers, and local Viet Minh members approached wives and relatives to persuade soldiers to defect. In some cases, small armed Viet Minh groups detained soldiers for "education sessions," then let them return to their posts.[207]

As might be expected, such tactics proved most successful in the provinces to the north of Hanoi, where rumors of Viet Minh strength had some basis in fact. For example, soldiers at the Hiep Hoa district post in Bac Giang opened the gate on the night of 8 April to enable a Viet Minh group to seize fifteen firearms, execute one "reactionary" civilian functionary, and escort the district mandarin to a forest hideout. One week later, at nearby Yen The, after simply receiving a written threat of attack, both the Civil Guard unit and the district mandarin surrendered, turning over fourteen rifles, some ammunition, and one typewriter.[208] Units of Chu Van Tan's National Salvation Army, which had been depleted and dispersed by colonial sweeps in late 1944, moved quickly after the Japanese coup to seize several posts in Thai Nguyen province, then marched further westward into Tuyen Quang.[209] Perhaps their most satisfying accomplishment, however, was to join with a unit of Vo Nguyen Giap's Propaganda and Liberation Army to take the Mo Nhai and Binh Gia posts in Bac Son, site of the late September 1940 abortive uprising, without firing a single shot.[210] Elsewhere, the district mandarin of Thanh Mien (Hai Duong) tried to hide eleven rifles plus ammunition under a pile of mud camouflaged to look like animal dung, but Viet Minh adherents

---

207. *CMTT*, 1:202. Such leaflets and letters also were addressed to civilian officials. For two good examples, see *CMCD*, 12:134–37.

208. *CMTT*, 1:205. After the Japanese escorted a replacement mandarin to Yen The, the post was "liberated" once again on 16 July.

209. Chu Van Tan, *Ky Niem*, 239. *CMTT*, 1:72–73. These National Salvation Army units also linked up with a Viet Minh force of several hundred in Yen Bai province. Ngo Minh Loan, "Doi Du Kich Au Co" [The Au Co Guerrilla Unit], in Le Thiet Hung et al., *Rung Yen The*, 28–29.

210. Ban Nghien Cuu Lich Su Dang Tinh Uy Lang Son, *Lich Su Dau Tranh Cach Mang Huyen Bac Son*, 56–59. *CMTT*, 1:106. Booty in Bac Son included paddy from the government warehouse, seventy-five rifles, a stockpile of salt, and some very scarce cloth and clothing.

forced the wife of the sergeant in charge of the local post to reveal the cache's whereabouts.[211] In most cases, after being alerted to a Viet Minh takeover at district level and conferring with the ranking Japanese officer, the provincial mandarin would dispatch a mixed, platoon-sized unit to the area, only to discover empty buildings and little reliable information as to where the attackers had gone.

In the Red River Delta, so far as can be determined, only one Civil Guard post was seized in the three months following the Japanese coup. That was at Ban-yen-nhan, in Hung Yen province, where a large crowd of Viet Minh adherents surrounded the post and frightened the soldiers into turning over their twenty-nine firearms and 5,000 cartridges without a fight. Thirty minutes after the crowd dispersed, Japanese troops arrived to take control.[212]

Reacting to Famine

Between March and May, most people in the delta were far more concerned with avoiding starvation than with attacking military posts. They reacted with alacrity to Viet Minh calls to oppose further tax collections, to demand distribution of existing grain stocks, or, failing that, to try to liberate grain from government or landlords' warehouses by force.[213] Because Viet Minh activists in the delta provinces generally still lacked firearms, they often encouraged villagers to petition local officials, to remonstrate with tax agents, perhaps to march in strength on district centers or marketplaces. Viet Minh leaflets and slogans painted on the sides of buildings threatened village officials with "severe punishments" if they assisted higher authorities in collection of grain taxes. Local officials who heeded such threats were sometimes arrested or cashiered by the government. In Binh Giang district (Hai Duong), about three hundred people from three villages marched to a field one kilometer from the mandarin's headquarters, waving the Viet Minh flag, and yelling for abolition of taxes and immediate famine relief. After one hour of speechmaking and waiting to see if the mandarin would retaliate, the participants dispersed in orderly fashion.[214] One canton chief in Yen Bai province agreed to release forty tons of stored grain to feed

211. *CMTT*, 1:249–50.

212. *CMTT*, 1:303–4. The attacks on five posts in northern Hai Duong and Tuyen Quang provinces, on the edge of the delta, are discussed later in this chapter.

213. AOM, INF, GF 62, contains a translation into French (for Japanese perusal) of a Viet Minh leaflet accusing the Japanese of trying to kill off the population through famine. *CMCD*, 11:97–98, reprints a typical Viet Minh leaflet condemning Japanese rice confiscations and suggesting a range of ways to avoid them.

214. *CMTT*, 1:216, 239, 248, 299, 338.

Viet Minh units, but before transport arrangements could be worked out, another official apparently alerted a group of relatives and friends to take away the grain for their own use.[215]

Elsewhere, less sympathetic officials found themselves surrounded by angry compatriots wielding bamboo spears, machetes, or knives, escorted to the village communal house (*dinh*), and compelled to apologize publicly for abusing their powers and denigrating the Viet Minh. If the village possessed a small stock of "charity grain," officials might be persuaded to release it. Grain already collected and about to be turned over to private syndicated tax collectors (the hated *lien doan*) sometimes had to be returned.[216] In Tu Son district (Bac Ninh), when the district mandarin arrived at Phu Ninh village to collect taxes escorted by a Japanese squad, the alert drum sounded and hundreds of villagers surrounded the party. After a standoff lasting all day, the Japanese fired a volley that killed two people, then withdrew.[217] In Ninh Binh province, a bitter fight broke out between the villagers of Lu Phong and a small Civil Guard unit escorting the district mandarin. Two soldiers were killed, while the mandarin escaped after a severe beating and destruction of his car.[218] The district mandarin of An Thi (Hung Yen) reported that most village officials were now more afraid of being killed than of disobeying repeated orders from superiors to collect taxes.[219] Just south of the delta, in Thanh Hoa province, where famine was also rampant, the authorities dispatched fifty soldiers to Thieu Hoa district to enforce tax collections, but apparently met with little success. In at least four villages, crowds instead compelled local officials to let them "borrow" grain to eat.[220]

With all the above initiatives failing to check starvation, people sometimes broke into grain warehouses owned by the government or big landlords. Most commonly a small group of young men armed only with spears and machetes would overpower two or three guards in the middle of the night, break the locks, then urge a much larger group to grab sacks of paddy

215. *CMTT*, 1:167. In Bac Ma (Hai Duong) in early June, Buddhist monks approached wealthy families to donate grain for some two hundred Viet Minh adherents training nearby. Tran Cung, "Khoi Nghia o De Tu Chien Khu" [Uprising in the Fourth War Zone], *NCLS* 126 (9-1969): 50.

216. *CMTT*, 1:201, 299, 338, 340.

217. *CMTT*, 1:319. It is unclear from the source whether the mandarin obtained his taxes or not.

218. *CMTT*, 1:367. Villagers also captured the two firearms and bicycles belonging to the soldiers.

219. AOM, INF, GF 34.

220. *CMTT*, 1:385.

and disperse as quickly as possible. In other cases, large crowds were mobilized first to cow guards and provide a screen against outside interruption as the warehouse was emptied.[221] Occasionally, it was possible to take advantage of Allied air attacks, when warehouse guards ran for shelter, to seize a quantity of paddy and flee.[222] Subsequent published accounts point to break-ins in at least seventy-five locations around the Red River Delta following the Japanese coup.[223] Hung Yen may have seen the most such activity: a contemporary Viet Minh source asserts that forty thousand people in that province received a total of six hundred tons of liberated paddy between 2 May and 8 June.[224] While Viet Minh editors probably inflated such figures for propaganda value, an urgent confidential message from the provincial chief to Hanoi on 12 June, reporting Viet Minh "pillaging of administrative paddy" in four northern districts and requesting troop reinforcements, confirms that Hung Yen was far from quiet during at least the latter stages of the famine.[225] The largest granary seized was also in Hung Yen, containing one hundred tons.[226] If we collate other accounts, about fifteen "liberated" granaries held ten to eighty tons each, but most only two to ten tons, and some raids yielded a mere 500 kilograms.[227] In Kien An province, storage rooms on a plantation owned by Hoang Trong Phu, a prominent mandarin and entrepreneur, yielded three thousand *phuong* of paddy (90,000 liters) to the benefit of three thousand villagers.[228] Members of a Viet Minh self-defense group in Chuong My district (Ha Dong) four times "ambushed" lines of bullock carts filled with rice, either ordering drivers to turn around or encouraging villagers in the

221. Le Tuong and Vu Kim Bien, *Lich Su Vinh Phu* [History of Vinh Phu] (Vinh Phu, 1980), 166.

222. To Huu, "Nho lai thoi ky Cach Mang ve vang" [Remembering the Glorious Period of Revolution], *Tap Chi Lich Su Dang* (Hanoi), 4-1991, 16.

223. This figure is derived primarily from *CMTT*, vol. 1, with some crosschecking of memoirs and provincial Party histories. *CMCD*, 11:103–29, mentions thirty granary break-ins. Although DRV publications generally claim ICP or Viet Minh leadership of these assaults on granaries, it seems likely that some were led by local toughs who cited Viet Minh propaganda for justification, or in later years found it politically expedient to assert Viet Minh inspiration.

224. *Cuu Quoc*, 5 July 1945, cited in *CMTT*, 1:300.

225. Hung Yen to Kham Sai, 12 June 1945, in AOM, INF, GF 62.

226. *CMTT*, 1:301. See also Gérard Chaliand, *The Peasants of North Vietnam* (Harmondsworth, England, 1969), 73–74, 141–43. Le Thanh Nghi, *Nhan Dan*, 31 Aug. 1960, asserts that almost 6,000 tons of grain were liberated from a plantation warehouse in Vinh Yen province, but an account of the same incident in *CMTT*, 1:188–89, makes no such claim. It sounds inflated.

227. *CMTT*, 1:24–26, 150, 201, 253, 299–301, 338, 367, 432–44.

228. Ibid., 282.

immediate vicinity to appropriate the contents.[229] In Hai Duong, having mobilized twenty armed followers and three hundred villagers to cow guards at three warehouses into surrender, a Viet Minh activist named Nguyen Cong Hoa brought in a number of small boats to shift the paddy to more secure locations for distribution.[230]

Perhaps the most audacious attack occurred in Thai Binh province, where a Viet Minh group with several rifles forced two sampans transporting fifty tons of rice on the Luoc River to beach and surrender their cargoes to hundreds of villagers, who spent six hours frantically carrying sacks to other locations until the arrival of a Japanese patrol.[231] Almost equally daring was the decision of a Viet Minh group in several villages immediately adjacent to Hanoi to target grain belonging to the Japanese Army but stored in a local communal building. By employing self-defense unit members to control egress from the neighborhood, sufficient time was gained to fly Viet Minh flags, address a large crowd about French and Japanese responsibility for the famine, and supervise distribution and transport of the grain before disappearing during the wee hours of the morning.[232] Some of the most avid recruits to nascent Viet Minh self-defense teams were unemployed young men who sensed that being part of such a group would at least ensure them a daily ration of rice. Thus, lacking funds to continue studying in Hanoi, unable to find a job, aware of the futility of returning to his home village, where family members had already died of starvation, Tran Trung Thanh eagerly accepted a friend's invitation to join a small Viet Minh group in the city.[233]

Propaganda Inroads

By May 1945, most inhabitants of Tonkin would have heard of the exploits of the Viet Minh, without necessarily coming into contact with someone who claimed to be a member. Propaganda techniques acquired and refined by ICP members over the previous fifteen years were largely responsible. At the most formal level, Viet Minh periodicals like *Viet Nam Doc Lap* and

229. Duong Van Bat, "Vai Mau Chuyen Dau Tranh" [A Few Struggle Stories], in *Hoi Ky Cach Mang Ha Tay*, 2:19–47.

230. *CMTT*, 1:249. In this assault, four firearms and a quantity of ammunition also were collected.

231. Ibid., 433–34. Dao Ngoc Quynh, "Gao Viet Minh" [Viet Minh Rice], in *Thai Binh Khoi Nghia*, 106–15.

232. *CMTT*, 1:25.

233. Tran Trung Thanh, "Nho Mai Ha-Noi" [Always Remembering Hanoi], in *Ha-Noi Chien Dau* (Hanoi, 1964), 10.

Cuu Quoc expanded rapidly in news coverage and circulation. The publishing staff of *Cuu Quoc*, headed by Xuan Thuy and Tran Huy Lieu, operated clandestinely from a house in Van Phuc village only one kilometer from the Japanese post at Dan Phuong district seat, just west of Hanoi. To avoid arrest, everyone was confined to a single blacked-out room, except for the luxury of one walk each night to the edge of the village to defecate. The lithograph machine was positioned elsewhere for security reasons, and the newspapers went to yet a third location to be parceled out to couriers.[234] In at least five provinces, ICP members with access to printing equipment put out their own periodicals, republishing information from scarce copies of central papers and adding local news.[235] In early 1945, however, paper of any kind had become extremely scarce, forcing Viet Minh adherents to improvise—for example, using the backs of sheets from primary school copybooks to print leaflets or daubing slogans on walls with lime paint. In late March, inhabitants of Hanoi were surprised to see "Down with the Japanese Fascists!" inscribed in large letters on the wall of the historic Temple of Literature.[236]

Appreciating that Vietnam remained largely a nonliterate society, the Viet Minh followers employed a variety of visual and verbal communication techniques. Perhaps most imaginative were the laborers at the Yen Phu waterworks who constructed banana-leaf rafts to hold Viet Minh flags, then floated them downriver past Hanoi.[237] More characteristically, several youths would enter a busy marketplace, call for quiet, pull out a Viet Minh flag, address the surprised audience, then melt away before the police arrived. If one of the youths possessed a firearm, he might punctuate his concluding exhortations with a shot or two in the air.[238] On 22 April, at the Tuong Truc marketplace in Ha Dong, three or four young men passed out Viet Minh leaflets and were in the midst of anti-Japanese speechmaking

234. Pham Van Hao, "Lam Bao Bi Mat" [Publishing Papers Secretly], in *Len Duong Thang Loi* (Hanoi, 1960), 128–30. In 1944, *Cuu Quoc* publishing operations had been smashed by colonial roundups, necessitating complete reconstitution. *CMTT*, 1:351. In a short recollection of this period, published posthumously, Tran Huy Lieu describes drolly how the entire staff grappled with scabies, and how he in particular encountered inconveniences with diarrhea. *Hoi Ky Tran Huy Lieu* [Memoirs of Tran Huy Lieu], ed. Pham Nhu Thom (Hanoi, 1991), 340–43.

235. *CMTT*, 1:409. *CMTT*, 2:117, 325. *CMCD*, 11:130–31, lists the names and locations of seventeen Viet Minh papers, plus the ICP's *Co Giai Phong* and the Democratic Party's *Doc Lap*.

236. *CMTT*, 1:22.

237. Ibid., 26.

238. Ibid., 410. Tran Do, "Nhung Mau Truyen . . . Sung" [Stories about . . . Guns], in Chanh Thi et al., *Len Duong Thang Loi* (Hanoi, 1960), 96.

when interrupted by the local authorities. According to a government report of the incident, the perpetrators menaced the authorities with pistols and then escaped on bicycles.[239] At the Olympia Theater in Hanoi, the audience was stunned when the electricity went off, a Democratic Party youth harangued it in the dark for precisely three minutes before vanishing, and the lights went on to reveal a Viet Minh flag and paper slogans pinned to the stage curtain.[240] Occasionally, a local Viet Minh group would wait for a legal organization to gather a crowd, then take over from the sidelines, yelling anti-Japanese slogans, unfurling flags, and barging onto the rostrum.[241] Viet Minh songs, poems, and slogans also circulated spontaneously. The Vietnamese predilection for wordplay and double entendre reached new heights, especially when mocking high officials.[242] It was not unusual for Vietnamese government officials to overhear their children singing an antigovernment ditty, or for policemen to note women traders on an electric tram reciting lines from a Viet Minh call for independence.

As it became evident that neither the Japanese nor the Vietnamese government authorities were enforcing the previous draconian colonial restrictions on public assembly, Viet Minh activists became progressively bolder, drawing on late 1930s Popular Front experience to organize meetings and demonstrations. In early May, a crowd gathered at the foot of a hill in Hiep Hoa district (Bac Giang), only four kilometers from a Japanese garrison, to listen to speeches and chant Viet Minh slogans. In late June, twelve hundred villagers from two districts in Hung Yen province converged on Lung town, only to be blocked by a Japanese patrol equipped with a machine gun. A brief encounter left one demonstrator dead and one wounded. By July, many Viet Minh demonstrations included an armed self-defense contingent, and the organizers aimed at more than popular evocations of enthusiasm. Thus, in Kien An, a crowd of about five hundred surrounded a school where the Dai Viet Party had begun to train youth leaders, forcing all participants to disperse. In Thanh Hoa, more than one thousand people, headed by a big banner and a self-defense group, marched

239. Ha Dong to resident superior, 25 Apr. 1945, in AOM, INF, GF 51. The report also mentions cryptically that a member of the Dai Viet Quoc Gia Lien Minh, said to be investigating Viet Minh activities, was present at the incident.
240. Tran Lam, "Doi Tuyen Truyen Xung Phong Dang Dan Chu nhung ngay tien Khoi Nghia" [The Democratic Party's Propaganda Assault Unit in the Opening Days of the Insurrection], *Doc Lap* (Hanoi), 28 Sept. 1988, 1.
241. *CMCD,* 11:129.
242. *Viet Nam Doc Lap,* 10 May 1945, contains a characteristic play on Vietnamese words: "When the Japanese are beaten, as is inevitable, Bao Dai will also be defeated and overthrown [*Bao Dai cung bai dao*]."

twenty kilometers through four cantons, stopping in each village to convene a meeting and issue warnings to "Vietnamese traitors." After turning over his seal and official records, one canton chief asked to join the Viet Minh.[243]

In Hai Duong, the ICP Provincial Committee instructed subordinates to organize a mass march on the Tu Ky district seat. Equipped with one pistol, one rifle, two bird guns, and about one hundred spears and machetes, a self-defense unit surged into the district compound without opposition, followed by almost one thousand villagers. After confiscating eleven rifles, plus ammunition, belonging to local guards, the demonstration leaders put the district mandarin on public trial. At the end of the proceedings, some in the crowd called for the mandarin's execution, others for his release. Standing on a table to take a vote, Comrade Do Huy Liem ascertained that a majority opposed execution.[244]

As the reputation of the Viet Minh spread, it became more common to find supporters and sympathizers within existing government institutions or legal organizations founded after the Japanese coup. The prominent surgeon Ton That Tung was moved by talking to a dying Viet Minh typesetter, delivered to Phu Doan hospital in Hanoi by the Kenpeitai following brutal torture.[245] Middle- and lower-level members of the administration sometimes quietly sought out Viet Minh participants to offer their services.[246] For example, several Hanoi PTT employees began to convey the substance of royal government message traffic to ICP contacts, as well as helping to camouflage the activities of Nguyen Thi Bich Thuan, a Women's National Salvation Association member recently planted in the PTT.[247] Higher-level officials were in a more difficult position, as the Japanese might hold them personally responsible for any breaches of public order. Some mandarins clearly knew the identities of Viet Minh activists in their provinces or districts, yet chose to turn a blind eye. Others dispatched intermediaries to find out more about the Viet Minh and perhaps offer covert assistance, but then generally backed away when Viet Minh cadres asked for firearms. However, the district mandarin of Ninh Giang

243. *CMTT*, 1:207, 282, 303, 386.

244. Ibid., 243–44. Although the source does not say what happened subsequently, it seems likely the mandarin was detained.

245. Ton That Tung, *Duong vao Khoa Hoc cua toi* [My Path to Science] (Hanoi, 1978), 32.

246. *CMTT*, 1:153. *CMTT*, 2:81. "Etude Service de Documentation Extérieure et de Contre-Espionnage," 25 June 1946, AOM, INF, c. 138–39, d. 1247.

247. "Lich Su Nganh Thong Tin Buu Dien," 1:66.

(Hai Duong) agreed to an elaborate ruse whereby eleven of his guards were "ambushed" by a Viet Minh group and relieved of their rifles and ammunition.[248] In Gia Dinh province, a Viet Minh group was able several times to borrow and return two pistols from local officials. Most remarkably, the provincial mandarin of Quang Binh donated thirty firearms to the Viet Minh via a third party.[249] Depending on the official and the circumstances, such responses might reflect quiet admiration for stated Viet Minh goals, grudging acknowledgment of the ability of the Viet Minh to stir up the local population, or naked fear of retaliation.

Working Autonomously or from Within?

New organizations established with Japanese patronage or benign approval posed both a threat to Viet Minh hegemony and an opportunity for infiltration, legal cover, and recruitment. In Tonkin, many Viet Minh leaders apparently felt they could afford to bypass or ignore these groups, since their own national salvation associations were expanding rapidly. Only in provinces where a particularly energetic mandarin was proving successful in attracting young men and women to legal groups did the Viet Minh feel the need to become involved too. Thus, in Phu Tho province the Viet Minh encouraged sympathizers to join an officially inspired youth group led by Chan Ton, considered a "traitor" (*Viet gian*), to try to redirect group activities from within.[250] In Hai Duong province, three district mandarins managed to form viable youth groups. In one case, however, the mandarin unwittingly appointed two ICP members as leaders, while in a second case, Party members turned several local branches into covert national salvation units, complete with military training by a cadre brought in from the Viet Minh's liberated zone.[251]

In Annam at the time of the Japanese coup, most provinces possessed only a handful of Viet Minh–affiliated national salvation associations. Rather than compete directly with the royal government's new Front Line Youth (Tien Tuyen Thanh Nien) program, headed by Phan Anh, it seemed sensible to many ICP members to join up, then try to turn the attention of participants away from the Japanese and toward the victorious Allies and news of Viet Minh achievements in Tonkin. In the town of Dalat, for

248. *CMTT*, 1:246–47, 249–50, 252, 423.
249. *CMTT*, 2:36, 322.
250. *CMTT*, 1:153–54. A similar effort took place in Ha Nam province. Ibid., 410.
251. Ibid., 241, 245.

example, Party members joined a postcoup amalgamation of one hundred former Ducoroy Youth and thirty-two Scouts. Together they enrolled another one thousand eager participants by early August, including some laborers.[252] In Quang Binh, an activist dispatched from Viet Minh headquarters in Tonkin managed to infiltrate a number of his comrades into the royalist youth group, after which they recruited the "best" elements to a clandestine Viet Minh unit, which proceeded to paint slogans and print leaflets denouncing the Japanese. However, Party activists were less successful when trying to penetrate another youth group identifying itself with the Catholic mandarin Ngo Dinh Khoi and his energetic younger brother Ngo Dinh Diem, both originating from Quang Binh.[253] In Ha Tinh province, members of the royalist youth group, excited after reading copies of Viet Minh propaganda, yet unable to make contact with Viet Minh representatives, took it upon themselves to organize covert national salvation units.[254] In Nghe An, by contrast, Viet Minh representatives faced a new organization, the Vietnam Independence Corps (Viet Nam Doc Lap Doan), which had already attracted a substantial rural following without offending the Japanese, and indeed criticized the Viet Minh for its refusal to take advantage of the opportunities offered.[255]

In fact, a significant number of ICP members in Annam saw nothing wrong in trying to "use" the Japanese in various ways prior to the end of the war, thus putting themselves in a stronger position to resist any postwar return of the French.[256] Not having invested four years in trying to build a Viet Minh network like their comrades in Tonkin, they saw more tactical benefits to be gained by taking some of the leadership positions in organizations permitted by the Japanese to operate openly. As well as in royalist youth groups, ICP members played key roles in the New Vietnam Association (Tan Viet Nam Hoi), a republican, anti-authoritarian organi-

252. *CMTT*, 2:209–10. A similar pattern was followed in Phu Yen and Khanh Hoa provinces. Ibid., 149, 158.

253. Ibid., 35. As mentioned in chapter 2, the Ngo Dinh family remained politically active during 1941–44. Already it possessed a reputation for militant anticommunism.

254. Ibid., 30.

255. Ibid., 9–10. Party members in Nghe An seem to have been divided about the whole Viet Minh strategy. As of May 1945, they still had no links with the Standing Bureau in Tonkin. Ban Nghien Cuu Lich Su Dang Tinh Uy Nghe An, *So Thao Lich Su Tinh Dang Bo Nghe An* [Preliminary History of the Nghe An Party Provincial Branch] (Nghe An, 1967), 76–85.

256. In at least one province, Quang Tri, some ICP members wanted to work to position a Party member or sympathizer as provincial mandarin. This was criticized at a provincial-level Party meeting in May 1945. *CMTT*, 2:50.

zation that had been begun in Hue by Ton Quang Phiet, the principal of the prestigious Thuan Hoa private school, and was soon active in at least four other locations along the central coast.[257] New Vietnam quickly gained adherents among politically alert intellectuals, functionaries, merchants, and landed rural families. By June, it was attracting some peasants and workers as well, which caused members of the ICP to become quite concerned, as they were committed to establishing Viet Minh units among these same constituencies.

The royal capital of Hue presented particular problems for anyone wishing to organize people in the name of the Viet Minh. Immediate or prospective opponents included the forty-five hundred Japanese soldiers stationed in the city, five hundred French military personnel under loose detention, the Vietnamese Civil Guard, the Imperial Guard, and the Front Line Youth. Moreover, Hue retained a unique cultural ambience that no movement seeking to overturn the status quo could afford to ignore. This was typified by the hundreds of families belonging to various branches of the royal family, which often lived in far from prosperous circumstances and voiced every shade of political opinion imaginable. Perhaps it was inevitable in these conditions that three or four different organizations claiming to represent the "true" Viet Minh would emerge in Hue and vicinity soon after the Japanese coup, then proceed to denounce one another as "false," or even as enemy provocateurs. Matters came to a head first between the handful of Party members who continued to operate in rural districts adjacent to Hue and communist returnees from prison, who, finding themselves under suspicion until vouched for by the faraway Standing Bureau, proceeded on their own initiative to proselytize for the Viet Minh cause. These two groups met together secretly in late May, compared what little documentation each possessed from higher echelons, vigorously debated strategy, and finally managed to elect a common five-man Viet Minh standing committee for Thua Thien–Hue.[258]

It soon became evident, however, that yet another group calling itself Viet Minh, also containing some ICP members, and able to affirm connections with activists in Hanoi, was recruiting followers in Hue city from

257. Ibid., 76, 94, 129, 139.
258. Hoang Anh, Le Tu Dong, et al., *Binh Tri Thien Thang Tam Bon Lam: Hoi Ky* [August 1945 in Binh Tri Thien: Memoirs] (Hue, 1985), 7–15, 60–63. Ban Nghien Cuu Lich Su Dang Tinh Thua Thien, *So Thao Lich Su Cach Mang Thang Tam Thua Thien–Hue* [A Preliminary History of the August Revolution in Thua Thien–Hue] (Hanoi, 1970), 38–47.

among students and government employees, as well as starting to generate support in nearby rural districts. The differences here were more fundamental, involving the degree of ICP control, rural versus urban emphasis, clandestine versus open operations, and, above all, the issue of whether to cooperate or not with other organizations. In early July, a unification meeting was convened at which leadership positions were parceled out diplomatically to both Viet Minh groups, yet separate operations persisted into August. Meanwhile, with more and more rumors of Viet Minh success reaching Hue from the north, the New Vietnam Association began to look increasingly redundant, provoking Ton Quang Phiet and other leaders to declare the organization dissolved, a decision cabled to all provincial branches. Many former members of New Vietnam shifted allegiance quickly to the Viet Minh.[259]

Essentially the same issues faced ICP members in Cochinchina, where Governor Minoda Fujio had deputed Iida to develop the paramilitary Vanguard Youth organization (see chapter 2). Tran Van Giau, chairman of one of the two reconstituted Cochinchina regional committees, instructed ICP members to join the Vanguard Youth at every level, using it as a legal cover to restore clandestine contacts, and as a means of linking up with other anticolonialist groups. At the top level in Saigon, Giau and his lieutenant Ha Huy Giap exercised influence via Dr. Pham Ngoc Thach, president of the Vanguard Youth. According to Tran Van Giau, Thach had developed leftist sympathies as a student in France; on his return, he treated ICP patients at no charge. When the idea of accepting Thach into the ICP was raised, many considered it ludicrous, given his French citizenship, French wife, Japanese acquaintances, blood ties to Emperor Bao Dai, and ownership of large tracts of land in the countryside. Nonetheless, Giau and Giap went ahead secretly to enroll Thach. As Giau commented much later, "I felt it was often the well-off who were the firmest believers (my family was certainly not poor), whereas workers who reached the point of material sufficiency often abandoned the struggle."[260]

259. Hoang Anh, Le Tu Dong, et al., *Binh Tri Thien*, 16–17, 63–65, 108–12, 142–50. Ban Nghien Cuu Lich Su Dang Tinh Thua Thien, *So Thao Lich Su Cach Mang*, 50–54. *CMTT*, 2:77. Because Ton Quang Phiet also was close to the Viet Minh group based among Hue students and government employees, dissolution of New Vietnam hardly lessened his political influence.

260. Interview with Tran Van Giau, Ho Chi Minh City, 12 Feb. 1990. Giau's initiative was not a well-kept secret. For example, Ho Huu Tuong, a prominent Trotskyist intellectual and close personal friend of Pham Ngoc Thach's, knew that Thach was a member of the ICP. Interview with Ho Huu Tuong, Saigon, 3 Mar. 1967.

In Cholon, adjacent to Saigon, all province and district Vanguard Youth leaders were ICP members or Party sympathizers.[261] In Gia Dinh province, just north of Saigon, a clandestine ICP member also headed the Vanguard Youth.[262] Sixty-five kilometers southeast of Saigon, in Ba Ria province, ICP members helped organize Vanguard Youth training classes and quasi-governmental guard rosters. The Japanese apparently knew of this "communist influence," yet took no action beyond trying occasionally to sponsor alternative leadership or initiate competing branches. Thus, in Thu Dau Mot province, the Japanese encouraged a breakaway Vanguard Youth group, which debated the original ICP-infiltrated group vigorously, occasionally to the point of physical altercations. In Tra Vinh province, Vanguard Youth leaders, including several ICP members, convened meetings to rouse patriotic sentiment, collected money for victims of Allied bombings, and began a movement against "superstition" at the village level. In Ben Tre province, local ICP members invited Dr. Thach from Saigon to help them take the initiative away from local functionaries and members of the landed elite selected by the Japanese to lead the Vanguard Youth.[263] In all cases, however, ICP members remained a tiny minority in Vanguard Youth units.[264] Left-leaning friends of ICP activists in the Vanguard Youth often found them disconcertingly vague or contradictory about basic political objectives.[265] In Cochinchina, this was not usually an attempt to hide intentions, but instead reflected honest confusion among Party members about strategy.

Although ICP participants in the Vanguard Youth took advantage of their legal status to conduct clandestine Party business—reestablishing links with local cells, recruiting the most reliable Vanguard Youth members to secret "assault squads" (*doi xung phong*), or founding Viet Minh national salvation units—other Party members in Cochinchina vehe-

261. *CMTT*, 2:232–33.

262. Ibid., 316. This appears to have been the case in Can Tho province as well. Ibid., 351. In Can Tho, the left-leaning lawyer Pham Van Bach, appointed judge by the Japanese, sought out an ICP acquaintance to reach a suitable understanding. Bach became chairman of the southern Revolutionary People's Committee in early September. See his memoir in *Nhan Dan* (Hanoi), 22 Aug. 1982.

263. *CMTT*, 2:240, 257–58, 276. *Lich Su Dang Cong San Viet Nam Tinh Song Be*, ed. Nguyen Ba Tho, 187–195.

264. Tran Van Giau, in our 12 Feb. 1990 interview, mentioned that a hypothetical group of a hundred Vanguard Youth might have contained between one and five ICP members. Undoubtedly some Vanguard Youth units had no ICP participation at all.

265. Do Thuc Vinh, *Mua Ao Anh* [Season of Mirages] (Saigon, 1962), 93–99.

mently rejected any participation in an organization sponsored by the Japanese. According to these critics, such collaboration diluted the anti-fascist credentials of the ICP, confused the masses, and inhibited rather than facilitated formation of dynamic Viet Minh units. This position was voiced most coherently in the Can Tho journal *Giai Phong,* in direct opposition to *Tien Phong* (Vanguard), organ of the Cochinchina Regional Committee, led by Tran Van Giau. At this juncture, it seems that *Giai Phong* advocates controlled provincial Party committees in My Tho and Soc Trang, while in six or seven other provinces rival provincial committees condemned one another and asserted their own legitimacy.[266] To distinguish themselves from the Vanguard Youth, even if it meant abandoning clandestinity entirely, ICP members in Long An province commissioned two silversmiths to make badges featuring the hammer and sickle superimposed on a Viet Minh flag.[267] In Long Xuyen, the *Tien Phong*–affiliated committee put a member on the Vanguard Youth executive board, partly to screen Party operations at the village level, while the *Giai Phong*–affiliated committee complained that "youth national salvation" and "women's national salvation" units failed to grow because young people were being drawn into the Vanguard Youth. Meanwhile, "peasant national salvation" units were restricted by the growing influence of Hoa Hao millenarians.[268]

By June, the ICP Standing Bureau in Tonkin had acquainted itself sufficiently with the various lines being taken by Party members in both Annam and Cochinchina to issue stern corrective notices. A letter to the provisional Annam Regional Committee criticized "a few comrades" for believing they could use the Tran Trong Kim regime to political advantage, or even reform it from within.[269] Secretary-General Truong Chinh, cas-

---

266. *CMTT,* 2:285, 322, 330–31, 351. Interview with Tran Van Giau, 25 Mar. 1980. Alain Ruscio, "Tran Van Giau et la révolution d'août 1945 au Nam Bo (sud du Viet Nam)," *Approches Asie* (Nice), no. 10 (1989–90): 182–96. To Thanh, "Cuoc dau tranh nham cung co va giu vung chinh quyen cach mang o nam bo: Thoi ky 1945–46" [The Struggle to Consolidate and Defend the Revolutionary Regime in the South: 1945–46 Period], *NCLS,* no. 229 (4-1986): 15–16. Quite possibly *Giai Phong* advocates had their own regional committee, although this is not stated explicitly in the sources. The unsettling effect of these ICP quarrels on noncommunist friends is captured in Do Thuc Vinh, *Mua Ao Anh,* 113. The available sources are at present insufficient for a proper analysis of this factionalism in the Cochinchina ICP.

267. H.S., "Chiec Phu Hieu Dang Vien" [The Party Member's Badge], *Long An* 336 (30 Aug. 1982): 4–5.

268. *CMTT,* 2:387.

269. Vien Lich Su Dang, *Tong Khoi Nghia,* 80–81.

tigated the *Tien Phong* group in Cochinchina for trying to "exploit the Japanese to gain government."[270] In both regions, he said, the effect was to cloud popular perceptions of the "Japanese bandits and their gang of Vietnamese puppet lackeys," as well as to divert attention away from the Party's prime objective—seizure of state power in an armed uprising.[271] The members in question both overrated the strength of the Japanese and seriously underrated the Party's ability to mobilize the masses via Viet Minh front organizations.[272] Undoubtedly, Truong Chinh was concerned as well that Viet Minh involvement in any Japanese-inspired organizations might come to the attention of Allied intelligence, thus jeopardizing the entire rationale for Viet Minh participation in the final victory and postwar political settlement in Indochina. Almost as an afterthought, Truong Chinh also reproved the *Giai Phong* group for continuing to attack the French after the Standing Bureau had instructed that the entire struggle be directed against the Japanese.[273] More than anything, Truong Chinh hoped to persuade all ICP members to subordinate personal prejudices and policy preferences to the Party line at what he saw to be a crucial historical juncture. "We shall be committing a great crime if we remain divided at this decisive hour," he warned.[274]

Truong Chinh's criticisms were carried south to the Cochinchina Regional Committee in late June, together with an invitation to send delegates to an ICP all-country conference being planned for August.[275] The two men selected to travel north to the conference could be spared because they had only recently resumed activity in the crucial area around Saigon: Ha Huy

270. *Co Giai Phong*, 17 July 1945.

271. *CMTT (1945)*, 120.

272. In a 1946 retrospective, Truong Chinh softened his criticism of the *Tien Phong* group, suggesting that objective conditions in Cochinchina had kept Viet Minh organizations relatively weak, and that poor communications had prevented members from keeping pace with the general Party line. Truong Chinh, *The August Revolution* (Hanoi, 1962), 36. Originally published in *Su That* [Truth], Sept. 1946.

273. In Soc Trang province, Party members had deviated one step further, mounting demonstrations aimed at forcible detention of all Vietnamese of French nationality. *CMTT*, 2:285.

274. *Co Giai Phong*, 17 July 1945.

275. According to Tran Van Giau, in "April or May," the Regional Committee had dispatched Ly Chien Thang north, where he managed to meet "gentlemen of the [ICP] Center" (*may ong Trung Uong*), then return in late June. Interview in Ho Chi Minh City, 12 Feb. 1990. Thang was probably slowed down, not only by transport disruptions, but also by the difficulty of seeking out and gaining access to members of the clandestine Standing Bureau after being out of touch for four years.

Giap was just back from a stint in Ban Me Thuot prison, and Ung Van Khiem had presented himself in June after several years hiding on a distant plantation. Whatever messages these representatives carried north, the Cochinchina Regional Committee appears in practice to have ignored Truong Chinh's warnings against working with Japanese-sponsored organizations. The committee also ruled out formation of guerrilla bases. As Tran Van Giau argued forty-five years later:

> After the 9 March coup it would have been foolish to implement plans for guerrilla bases, like a tortoise lumbering around too late. Our objective was to involve as many people as possible in the direct seizure of power and formation of government, not steal about in small units and assume an elitist posture. The key in the south was the Vanguard Youth.[276]

What the Regional Committee would have done if the Japanese had moved to disband the Vanguard Youth, or replaced the existing leadership, does not seem to have been debated.

In the months immediately following the Japanese coup, more than one thousand ICP members were released from prison or slipped away in the administrative confusion.[277] Although some undoubtedly hoped for a respite before resuming operations, the majority sought contact with Party leaders on the outside and found themselves quickly engaged. Thus, Song Hao and two comrades had barely left the Cho Chu jail before they encountered advancing Propaganda and Liberation Army units and were pressed into service.[278] It was not quite so easy for Nguyen Van Rang, who was seized by a Viet Minh group on suspicion of being an enemy spy, trussed up like a pig going to market, almost executed, then lucky enough to see an old comrade who could vouch for him. He was instructed to read several pamphlets, given a pistol plus two grenades, and that same night took part in the destruction of a Japanese truck.[279] In Ban Me Thuot,

---

276. Interview with Tran Van Giau, Ho Chi Minh City, 12 Feb. 1990.

277. The jail in Cao Bang town may have been a tragic exception. Some Vietnamese sources allege that French warders killed several score inmates there before fleeing across the frontier. At Nghia Lo (Son La), an armed demonstration by political prisoners on 17 March went awry, with guards killing a number of inmates, only a few managing to climb the fence and escape. After French personnel withdrew toward China, the remaining inmates took control of the facility and organized departures. Tran Huy Lieu, *Nghia Lo Khoi Nghia* [The Nghia Lo Uprising] (Hanoi, 1946). Vuong Thua Vu, *Truong Thanh trong Chien Dau* [Growing Up in Fighting] (Hanoi, 1979), 39–55.

278. *CMCD*, 10:174–75.

279. Nguyen Van Rang, *Toi Len Chien Khu* [I Climb to the Battle Zone] (Hanoi, 1961), 41–48. In another memoir, Rang describes former inmates of Son La prison

inmates managed to smuggle a letter to townspeople urging them to press the authorities for release of a long list of political prisoners. The provincial chief subsequently offered political prisoners amnesty if they would agree to participate in a government independence celebration; some saw this as collaboration and chose to remain behind bars, but at least three hundred took the opportunity to gain release and head for the coast. Soon veterans of Ban Me Thuot jail were playing key roles in at least seven Annam provinces.[280] On return to their home provinces, residual suspicions or amour propre sometimes prevented former political prisoners and members of the existing ICP network from working together.[281] In most cases, however, joint meetings were convened, problems discussed, and leadership committees expanded—the result being a more vigorous, focused Party operation.[282] In still other cases, returning home to find no one active, political prisoners resumed Party efforts on their own.[283]

Hot Spots

A different situation arose in two particular locations: Quang Ngai province in southern Annam and the hilly border area between Hai Duong and Bac Giang provinces in Tonkin, which came to be called the "Fourth War Zone" (De Tu Chien Khu). Immediately after hearing of the Japanese coup, political prisoners at the Ba To detention camp in the hills of Quang Ngai had managed to disarm their guards, form a guerrilla platoon, and dispatch cadres to the coastal plains to begin organizing local Viet Minh units. Within four months, Quang Ngai possessed two well-armed guerrilla companies, at least two thousand eager self-defense group participants, and an extensive supply and communications network among villagers in both ethnic minority and Kinh regions of the province. The ICP provincial committee and

---

coming together in the forest to swap anecdotes. Finally someone called out, "Men of Son La! We've got orders to move out. Let's put a full stop on the sentence for now. When Japan has surrendered and the revolution has succeeded, we'll have time to reminisce in detail." Nguyen Van Rang, "Nam Thang o Giai Phong Quan Khang Nhat," in Le Thiet Hung et al., *Rung Yen The*, 64.

280. Tinh Uy Dak Lak, *Lich Su Nha Day Buon Ma Thuot (1930–1945)* [History of Ban Me Thuot Prison (1930–45)] (Hanoi, 1991), 116–21. *CMTT*, 2:50, 111, 139, 148, 157, 175. Tønnesson, *Vietnamese Revolution*, 351–52, based on a 1989 interview with General Le Tu Dong, a former Ban Me Thuot inmate. Meanwhile, released prisoners at Kontum were assisted by residents of Gia Lai to secure motor transport to Qui Nhon. *CMTT*, 2:188.

281. *CMTT*, 2:148, 157, 376.

282. *CMTT*, 1:250, 408. *CMTT*, 2:2, 49–50, 69, 74, 95, 111, 232, 337, 386.

283. *CMTT*, 2:139, 175, 196, 210, 292, 330.

Figure 18.   Color guard of former political prisoners at Ba To detention camp (Quang Ngai), just before their platoon-sized unit infiltrated the coastal plain in late March 1945. The banner behind them says, "Sacrifice for the Fatherland." Courtesy of the Vietnam News Agency.

Viet Minh committee were practically synonymous. Key leaders were all natives of Quang Ngai, hardened by the bitter struggles of 1930–31 and many years in jail. Although prepared to obey specific instructions from higher ICP echelons, they felt quite confident of being able to engineer their own armed uprising the minute any of the preconditions specified in the Standing Bureau instructions of 12 March were present. Meanwhile, they encouraged popular moves against perceived reactionaries and traitors, including hated landlords, village officials, adherents of the Cao Dai religion, members of the local "New Vietnam" branch, and participants in the government-inspired youth organization.[284] In mid July, Quang Ngai provided the venue for ICP activists from seven provinces of Annam to come together, swap information, listen to a report from To Huu, representing the Standing Bureau in the north, and elect two of their number to attend

284. Pham Kiet, *Tu Nui Rung Ba To* [From the Ba To Forested Mountains] (Hanoi, 1977). *CMCD*, 12:66–72. *CMTT*, 2:103–19. Dang Bo Huyen Son Tinh, *So Thao Lich Su Dang Bo Huyen Son Tinh* [Preliminary History of the Party Apparatus in Son Tinh District], vol. 1, *1929–1945* (Ho Chi Minh City, 1986), 115–28.

the national conferences scheduled for Tan Trao in August (see chapter 6).[285] Word of Quang Ngai's aggressive, uncompromising approach to revolution spread through central Vietnam, exciting some people, worrying others.

The Fourth War Zone emerged as the result of a tactical alliance between ICP-inspired units and several Sino-Vietnamese bands with loose connections to Chinese Nationalist forces across the frontier. At the heart of the ICP initiative was Nguyen Binh, an audacious 39-year-old former seaman, former Vietnam Nationalist Party member, and veteran of Con Son prison,[286] who saw the strategic importance of the region just north of Haiphong and determined to fashion an armed force by any means possible. On 8 June, his small group cooperated with a band flying a banner inscribed "China-Vietnam Guerrilla Army" (Trung Viet Du Kich Quan), led by Luong Dai Ban, to launch simultaneous assaults on four Civil Guard posts strung along colonial Route 18, meeting almost no resistance, and netting close to one hundred firearms.[287] When two Japanese infantry companies moved in two days later, both guerrilla groups withdrew north into the hills. One week later they lost fourteen killed and twenty captured when the Japanese attacked by surprise, then withdrew to the plains. The guerrillas responded by destroying a number of bridges along Route 18 and stripping the nearby Kinh Thay River of ferryboats, making Japanese movement difficult.[288]

In early July, independent of the Sino-Vietnamese bands, Nguyen Binh's unit managed with inside help to seize the Civil Guard post at Uong Bi, just north of the Quang Yen province seat, in the process killing four Japanese and collecting ten automatic weapons, almost two hundred rifles, other military equipment, and a quantity of grain. On 20 July, Quang Yen town itself was seized, with no resistance from the three hundred Civil Guard members there. With Nguyen Binh opting to keep moving rather than hold Quang Yen, Vietnamese government officials in the nearby city of Haiphong and Hai Duong province were panic-stricken, yet the Japanese chose not to counterattack in force. By the end of the month, Nguyen

---

285. Dang Bo Huyen Son Tinh, *So Thao Lich Su*, 128–29. *CMTT*, 1:117–18. Nguyen Chi Thanh and Tran Qui Hai were the two delegates.

286. AOM, Gouvernement générale 7F29, "Index des noms cites dans la note sur les partis nationalistes vietnamiens du 24 Jan. 1949." Phung Duc Thang, "Nguyen Binh," *Tap Chi Lich Su Dang* (Hanoi), 6-1991, 35, 43. Nguyen Binh's key lieutenants were Tran Cung and Hai Thanh.

287. These attacks are described in detail in Tran Cung, "Khoi Nghia," *NCLS* 126 (9-1969): 44–57.

288. *CMTT*, 1:214–28.

Binh's force exceeded five hundred well-armed coal miners, plantation workers, middle school students, former members of the Garde indochinoise, former Japanese Navy auxiliaries, and recruits from the Sino-Vietnamese bands. Efforts were made to keep the important coal mines operating, even if it meant retaining the French supervisors and technicians.

Nguyen Binh does not seem to have established contact with the ICP Standing Bureau only forty kilometers or so to the west. Almost no attention had been given to developing Viet Minh national salvation groups or to political proselytizing in general, although small self-defense groups had emerged in six districts in the Fourth War Zone.[289] Moreover, the Sino-Vietnamese units, referred to as "bandits" (*tho phi*) by ICP members, remained autonomous and capable of wreaking havoc. Increasingly, they looked northward, across the frontier, where Chinese Nationalist troops had marched to the coast without Japanese opposition. In late July, a unit of the Chinese-supported Vietnam Revolutionary League seized the border town of Mong Cai, then withdrew as Japanese forces approached. The Revolutionary League unit forcibly disarmed a small Viet Minh group and killed several of its members, the beginnings of a competition for power that soon would extend across all of northern Vietnam.[290]

Consciousness over Spontaneity

As an avowedly Leninist party, the ICP was determined to *make* a revolution, not have it occur spontaneously. To do this required agreement of purpose, operational unity, and increased strategic momentum prior to the moment of general insurrection. The Standing Bureau instructions of 12 March had set the agenda. The next step was to bring the commanders of the two main military contingents in the mountains together with Central Committee members working in the Red River Delta to assign responsibilities and hammer out a unified plan of action. This was accomplished at a Party meeting in Bac Giang province, chaired by General Secretary Truong Chinh, on 15–20 April.[291] Vo Nguyen Giap was made senior member of

289. Ibid., 228–30. Ban Nghien Cuu Lich Su Dang, *Lich Su Dang Bo Tinh Quang Ninh* [History of the Quang Ninh Province Party Apparatus], vol. 1, *1928–1945* (Hanoi, 1985), 169–93.

290. Ban Nghien Cuu Lich Su Dang Quang Ninh, *So Thao Lich Su Cach Mang Thang Tam tinh Quang Ninh* [Preliminary History of the August Revolution in Quang Ninh Province] (Quang Ninh, 1970), 25–38.

291. Other participants included Vo Nguyen Giap, Chu Van Tan, Tran Dang Ninh, Le Thanh Nghi, and Van Tien Dung. Ho Chi Minh was in Chungking (see chapter 4). Hoang Quoc Viet was ill after returning from a mission to China. Pham

the Viet Minh's new Northern Region Revolutionary Military Committee (Uy Ban Quan Su Cach Mang Bac Ky), in effect confirming the trust Ho Chi Minh had placed in him six months prior. To emphasize growing military priorities, the term "propaganda" was dropped from the army's official designation, making it the Vietnam Liberation Army (Viet Nam Giai Phong Quan). Chu Van Tan's "National Salvation Army" was dissolved and units placed under Giap's authority.[292] At this same meeting, almost by accident, Giap learned for the first time of the death in prison three years earlier of his wife, Nguyen Thi Quang Thai. According to Giap's memoirs, this personal shock gave an edge to his determination "to wipe out enemy forces, to sacrifice everything in service to the Party, the people, the country."[293]

The nineteen-page resolution formulated at the end of this Bac Giang meeting focused more on strategic issues than on organizational arrangements.[294] At an international level, the resolution noted recent important developments at Yalta, at Hot Springs, Virginia, and at San Francisco, where delegates from forty-six countries were gathering to found the United Nations (see chapter 4). The global antifascist struggle was almost over: "Although Japan's annihilation is not as near as Germany's, it is no longer that far away." Allied forces were advancing in the central Pacific, China, and Burma. Allegedly, the Soviet Union had torn up its neutrality agreement with Japan and the Red Army was "taking part directly in determining the destiny of oppressed peoples in Asia."[295] A "new democracy" (*tan dan chu*) movement was sweeping the world, the resolution claimed, with communist parties participating in a number of European governments, talks in China between the Kuomintang and Chinese Communist Party showing some progress, and India drawn into the fight against Japan despite unfortunate divisions between Muslims and Hindus. Al-

---

Van Dong and Vu Anh probably remained in charge of Cao-Bac-Lang administration.

292. *NSKLSD*, 1:612. Chu Van Tan, *Ky Niem*, 243–44.

293. Vo Nguyen Giap, *Tu Nhan Dan ma ra*, 207. According to Giap, his wife had died as a result of sustained torture designed to force her to reveal the whereabouts of Hoang Van Thu, which she never did. Published French sources acknowledge her death in prison, but make no mention of torture.

294. "Nghi Quyet cua Hoi Nghi Quan Su Cach Mang Bac Ky" (20 Apr. 1945), in Dang Lao Dong Viet Nam, *Chat Xieng*, 23–42. *VKQS*, 274–91. *CMCD*, 11:37–54. An English translation, probably from Russian, is available in *Documents of the August 1945 Revolution in Vietnam*, trans. C. Kiriloff (Canberra, 1963), 14–30. See also *Vietnam: The Definitive Documentation*, ed. Porter, 29–39.

295. This statement was, of course, premature, undoubtedly reflecting ICP frustration at almost five years of Soviet neutrality toward Japan.

though the resolution of 20 April conceded the possibility that Allied forces might now move directly against the Japanese home islands, bypassing imperial forces elsewhere, it reaffirmed the ICP conviction that sooner or later Allied units would enter Indochina. Besides the obvious military significance of Indochina, the Hot Springs meetings had exposed competition between the French and English on the one hand and the Chinese and Americans on the other that would have the effect of "pushing two different Allied forces to jump into Indochina to reap rewards." Given the paucity of information available to participants at the Bac Giang meeting, this prediction was quite remarkable, not because it presumed an eventual Allied pincer attack, which might have been inferred from campaign reports in the media, but because it sensed the intense intra-Allied competition for control of Indochina, which only became explicit three months later in the wake of the decision taken at Potsdam.

At the domestic level, the resolution of 20 April argued that because the Japanese were relying on the "old feudal apparatus detested by the Vietnamese citizenry," and even restoring some French colonial personnel, a number of people who had initially believed enemy promises of independence were now becoming despondent and leaning toward the Viet Minh front. It was thus essential to step up anti-Japanese propaganda, to mobilize ever-larger numbers of citizens to resist, to eliminate traitors, and to win over more enemy soldiers. Existing guerrilla bases needed to be expanded and new ones created. Attacks had to be small and certain of success. In areas where guerrilla assaults were not yet feasible, meetings, demonstrations, and armed shows of force could still achieve much. The resolution of 20 April also divided all Vietnam into seven battle zones, named after past leaders of heroic struggles against foreign invaders; foreshadowed establishment of a central training school; called on local Viet Minh groups to forward 50 percent of their financial gains to the Central Revolutionary Military Committee; and emphasized the urgent need to establish communications with groups in Annam and Cochinchina. Although the revolutionary movement had grown spectacularly since the Japanese coup, there remained major deficiencies needing correction, including "bandit" and "isolationist" tendencies among some Viet Minh units, substantial disparities in operational capability from one location to another, overconfidence as the result of a few small victories, and lack of vigilance against political saboteurs.

In late April, Ho Chi Minh returned from China to Pac Bo with a greater sense of urgency, particularly in regard to talk of a Chinese invasion of Indochina and the Viet Minh's need to demonstrate to the Allies that it commanded a large following. He instructed Vo Nguyen Giap to select a quasi-capital for a liberated zone (*khu giai phong*) composed of the six mountain provinces where a large number of Viet Minh village and district groups already existed parallel to the increasingly shaky administrative system based in Hanoi.[296] Giap's subordinate Song Hao persuaded him of the defensive merits of Kim Lung, subsequently renamed Tan Trao (literally "New Tide"), a cluster of mountain hamlets inhabited by Tay people astride the Tuyen Quang–Thai Nguyen border, eighty-five kilometers northwest of Hanoi. Within weeks Ho was being escorted from Pac Bo to Tan Trao, still wearing his Nung jacket and being referred to simply as the *Ong Ke*, "Elderly Gentleman" in the Nung language. At Tan Trao, Ho was received with all the military pageantry possible in the spartan circumstances.[297] Tan Trao possessed a radio transmitter capable of communicating with an Allied station in Kunming, and soon the specialists trained at Liuchou had strung combat telephone lines in the immediate region as well.[298]

Throughout his trek from China to Pac Bo and thence to Tan Trao, Ho Chi Minh was accompanied by Frank Tan, a Chinese American educated at Boston Latin School, who represented two or three different Allied intelligence organizations (see chapter 4). Shortly after arriving at Tan Trao, Ho presented Tan with a typed account of the odyssey, replete with details about the rugged topography, the dangers of night marching, the intricate system of local guides and porters along the route, the wild animals encountered, food provided by sympathetic villagers, ruins of former French outposts, and biographical sketches of three Viet Minh activists accompanying them. Amid this lively narrative, Ho sprinkled information about earlier suffering at the hands of the French, current Viet Minh administration in the mountains, literacy classes, women's support groups, and the participation of hundreds of thousands of people in the VML (Viet Minh League), which was "MORE THAN COMMUNIST," allegedly incorporating nationalists, socialists, democrats, big landlords, rich industrialists, high mandarins, and native soldiers in the colonial army. Clearly Ho wished to

296. These provinces were Cao Bang, Bac Can, Lang Son, Ha Giang, Tuyen Quang, and Thai Nguyen. Bits of Bac Giang, Phu Tho, Yen Bai, and Vinh Yen were also included. About one million people lived in this zone. *CCDVB*, 118–19.

297. Vo Nguyen Giap, *Tu Nhan Dan ma ra*, 208–10. Chu Van Tan, *Ky Niem*, 244–45. "Nguoi ve" [He Returns], *Doan Ket* (Paris), no. 370 (May 1985): 31. In practice, the names Kim Lung and Tan Trao appear to have been used interchangeably.

298. "Lich Su Nganh Thong Tin Buu Dien," 1:65. The Tan Trao transmitter was probably linked to the Kunming bureau of the U.S. "Air Ground Aid Section" (AGAS). See chapter 4.

codify and supplement Tan's own impressions of the arduous walk from the border, in the hope that the radio reports Tan sent back to Kunming would create a favorable impression and result in increased Allied support to the Viet Minh.[299]

On 4 June, Ho Chi Minh presided over a Viet Minh conference at Tan Trao that approved a three-month crash program to extend and formalize the village- and district-level "revolutionary people's committees" (*uy ban nhan dan cach mang*) in the liberated zone, to create provincial committees, and to manage this whole network by means of a Provisional Command Committee (Uy Ban Chi Huy Lam Thoi) divided along quasi-ministerial lines, including political affairs, general staff, economics and finance, communications, and cultural and social affairs.[300] Toward the end of this three-month period, Ho intended to convene an all-country Party conference and a National People's Congress (Quoc Dan Dai Hoi).[301] If battle were joined between Chinese and Japanese troops at the end of the rainy season in October, as seemed likely, the Viet Minh could wreak havoc on Japanese supply lines. Clearly, Ho saw the liberated zone as a Vietnamese Yenan, which it was to be hoped might be defended with quantities of weapons received from the Americans, but would in any case serve as a practical training ground and launching pad for the eventual nationwide insurrection. As if to symbolize the transition to state status, a rudimentary postal service was established and crude postage stamps issued bearing a five-pointed star, the slogan "Support the Viet Minh, Oppose the Japanese," the inscription "Vietnam Independence League," and monetary values in both Vietnamese and Chinese.[302]

299. "How We Travel," six-page undated typescript in the possession of Frank Tan, who generously agreed to make a copy available to me in May 1994. What makes this document particularly interesting is the way in which it is crafted entirely as if Tan himself was the author, not Ho Chi Minh (who is referred to in the narrative as "our old friend H"). Ho always enjoyed role-playing; this is not the only example of Ho writing about himself and his movement as if he were someone else.

300. Dang Lao Dong Viet Nam, *Chat Xieng*, 51–55. *VKQS*, 292–96. *CMCD*, 11:61–69. *NSKLSD*, 1:624–25. *Documents of the August 1945 Revolution*, trans. Kiriloff, 37–41, contains a translation of the resolution of 4 June. See also *Breaking Our Chains*, 52–57.

301. *NSKLSD*, 1:614. As early as October 1944, Ho had circulated a letter to Viet Minh groups indicating the need for such a national meeting as soon as possible. *CMCD*, 12:25–26, reprints the text.

302. Theo Klewitz, "North Vietnam," *Society of Indo-China Philatelists Journal*, no. 78 (Aug. 1986): 57–59, discusses and illustrates two extremely rare covers and stamps postmarked from and to Cao Bang province in May and June 1945. Thanks to Stan Blanko for sending me a copy of this article.

As word of this liberated zone circulated beyond the mountains, Viet Minh exploits quickly assumed mythic proportions. Urban intellectuals in particular conjured up images of Viet Minh leaders as swaggering generals in a classical opera, or Garibaldi-like saviors from foreign oppression. As one participant recalled:

> Some imagined the "battle zone" (*chien khu*) as high passes and rugged forests, a green-shirted self-defense member shouldering a musket, a young buffalo boy singing the "Advancing Army" song while tapping out the rhythm on the animal's side. Others dreamed of green hills, blue streams, dazzling white plum blossoms, and pretty, unaffected young women.[303]

In one sense, musket and plum blossom were two sides of the same romantic coin. From the poetic evidence available, however, violence already overwhelmed beauty, as in the following quatrain:

> In your hand a long sword,
> Enemy troops slashed to flesh and bone,
> Their blood steeping the forest verdure,
> Your grand victory banner redder than ever.[304]

Inspired by such rhetoric, hundreds of young men and women in Hanoi, Haiphong, and the Red River Delta started walking into the hills, hoping to join a Viet Minh armed unit. Most were encouraged politely to return home to organize their own self-defense groups; a few were killed as suspected Japanese spies. Those prudent enough to obtain letters of introduction in advance from local Viet Minh leaders might be escorted under armed guard to Tan Trao, where they received revolutionary pseudonyms and eagerly learned how to count off in platoon formation, march in file, maintain route silence, cross open areas with minimum risk, and disperse at sign of danger.[305]

By July 1945, most armed Viet Minh units in the liberated zone possessed experienced instructors and an assortment of printed or typed curricular materials. Classes ranged from basic squad tactics and instructions for small unit leaders to more sophisticated analyses of guerrilla warfare

---

303. Tran Huy Lieu, "Phong Trao," *NCLS* 29 (8-1961): 18.
304. Ibid., 19.
305. Nguyen Van Rang, "Nam Thang o Giai Phong Quan Khang Nhat," in Le Thiet Hung et al., *Rung Yen The,* 74–75. Tran Huy Lieu, "Di Du Quoc Dan Dai Hoi o Tan Trao" [Attending the National People's Congress at Tan Trao], *NCLS* 17 (8-1960): 35–38. Similar short classes were organized at other locations where at least one authentic firearm existed and someone was available who knew basic military drills and tactics. See, e.g., Tran Trung Thanh, "Nho Mai Ha-Noi," 12.

and the responsibilities of political commissars in the army.[306] In early July at Tan Trao, the "Anti-Japanese Military-Political Academy" (Truong Quan Chinh Khang Nhat) was established to train platoon leaders and political commissars, with Hoang Van Thai in charge.[307] Among one hundred members in the first class were nine women, who had to endure snide remarks from men as they practiced creeping and crawling in their traditional tunics.[308] It was to this school that Major Allison Thomas and his "Deer Team" came in mid July (see chapter 4).

Meanwhile, outside the liberated zone, Viet Minh directives focused on attracting new participants to grassroots national salvation associations, then moving to establish "national liberation committees" (*uy ban dan toc giai phong*) from the village or urban work site upward. Brief printed bylaws were distributed for separate associations of peasants, workers, self-defense unit members, women, Catholics, public servants, (royal) soldiers, and even teenage boys.[309] Members were obligated to obey orders from higher echelons, maintain secrecy, eschew divisiveness, assist fellow participants, pay their dues, and try to make the association grow. They had the right to propose, to discuss, to criticize policies or leaders at any level, to vote, and to be elected. Following the principle of democratic centralism, however, once a particular decision was made, the minority had to follow the majority, and lower echelons had to carry out policy in the manner specified from above.[310] Newly formed self-defense teams would be expected to enforce decisions if necessary.

Leaders of different national salvation associations at a particular level were instructed to form a Viet Minh "group" (*doan*), which would coor-

---

306. At least eight of these manuals were reprinted a few months later in Hanoi and copies placed in the government's Dépôt legal, as a result eventually making their way to the Bibliothèque nationale in Paris, where they are available for consultation. See, e.g., *Chuong Trinh Huan Luyen Can Bo Quan Su: Tieu Doi Truong* [Program for Training Military Cadres: Squad Leaders]; *Chien Thuat Co Ban* [Fundamental Tactics]; *Du Kich Chien Thuat* [Guerrilla Tactics]; and *Chinh Tri Vien trong Quan Doi* [The Political Commissar in the Army]. Most are translations from Chinese Red Army manuals, with passages occasionally added to reflect conditions in Vietnam. Lockhart, *Nation in Arms*, 121–25, outlines the content of three manuals.

307. CCDVB, 128. CMTT, 1:154. LSQD, 141–42.

308. Duong Thi An, *Nguon Vui Duy Nhat*, 105.

309. Bylaws reprinted in CMCD, 10:183–98. Such printed bylaws were often recopied by hand at one location and then passed on. By July, copies had reached numerous locations in northern Annam as well as Tonkin.

310. Viet Nam Doc Lap Dong Minh, *Cong Giao Cuu Quoc Hoi: Dieu Le* [Catholic National Salvation Association: Bylaws] (Hanoi, 1945).

dinate activities, receive secret instructions from above, and decide when to found a quasi-official liberation committee composed of representatives of each association plus some unaffiliated notables or elders. To ensure unity, Viet Minh representatives would caucus in advance of any committee meeting. When the time came for general insurrection, these committees were expected to dissolve in favor of elected revolutionary people's committees in villages and revolutionary workers' committees at work sites.[311]

Revolutionary Violence

It should not be assumed that Viet Minh general propaganda was identical to Viet Minh internal instructions, or that internal instructions were interpreted uniformly by groups in different localities. For example, even though Viet Minh propaganda often called with much rhetorical flourish for armed attacks on the Japanese fascists, no military commander or political commissar was expected to risk green troops and newly acquired weapons in attacks on Japanese posts or road convoys, which were invariably well protected. They generally avoided ambushing platoon- or squad-sized Japanese patrols as well. Viet Minh leaders had to consider, too, that killing Japanese soldiers might provoke bloody retaliation against unarmed local villagers.[312]

On the other hand, any Viet Minh unit that somehow managed to kill Japanese became the object of popular awe, its exploits magnified with every telling. In Bac Son district (Lang Son), units of the National Salvation Army chose to clash twice with Japanese patrols only one week after the coup, claiming six enemy dead and keeping their own casualties secret.[313] In Yen Bai province, a unit that had managed to acquire a precious machine gun used it to ambush a Japanese river patrol, killing several and then withdrawing successfully when pursued. The prestige of this unit was enhanced by Japanese comments to villagers that only strong American

311. "Chi Thi ve viec To Chuc cac Uy Ban Dan Toc Giai Phong" [Instructions on Organizing National Liberation Committees], issued 16 Apr. 1945 by the Tong Bo Viet Minh. Reprinted in Dang Lao Dong Viet Nam, *Chat Xieng*, 45–50. English in *Documents of the August 1945 Revolution*, trans. C. Kiriloff, 31–36. See also *CMCD*, 11:55–60.

312. Hoang Van Hoan, *Giot Nuoc*, 230–31. For an example of propaganda claims about fighting and defeating Japanese forces, see Truong Chinh's article in *Co Giai Phong*, 28 June 1945, translated in *Vietnam: The Definitive Documentation*, ed. Porter, 533–54.

313. *CMCD*, 10:159–61.

guns could have penetrated the helmets of the dead soldiers, not weak French guns.[314] In Hai Duong province, a local self-defense unit managed to capture five Japanese soldiers guarding a railroad bridge without a shot, subsequently parading them through a series of villages, preceded by Viet Minh flags and triumphant renditions of the "Advancing Army" anthem. In Thanh Hoa province, however, the killing of a single Imperial Army soldier provoked a month of terror for the nearest village, with Japanese machine gunners spraying houses at random and youths being grabbed for interrogation and torture. In Ninh Binh, after the ICP province secretary killed a Japanese soldier in an unplanned altercation, a Japanese unit eventually tracked him down and shot him as he attempted to escape by swimming a river.[315]

Although the Japanese probably lost fewer than fifty men in such engagements between March and May, they realized that matters might soon get worse, particularly if the Allies chose to equip the Viet Minh with automatic weapons, mortars, and bazookas. In mid May, the Imperial Army launched preemptive sweeps in the mountains north of Hanoi, with minimal results.[316] When a unit of about one hundred Japanese moved into Bac Son district, Viet Minh leaders ordered villagers to burn their homes and evacuate. A week later, the Japanese withdrew again.[317] Local Viet Minh groups made Japanese movement by road very slow by felling trees, digging trenches, and triggering rock slides. In June, the Japanese withdrew units from a number of smaller, more exposed posts, an action quickly noted by Viet Minh intelligence.[318]

On 16 July, the Liberation Army conducted its most ambitious attack yet, against a combined Japanese–Civil Guard position at Tam Dao, fifty-one kilometers northwest of Hanoi. Tam Dao was symbolically significant as the main colonial summer resort in Tonkin, where several hundred

---

314. Ngo Minh Loan, "Doi Du Kich Au Co," in Le Thiet Hung et al., *Rung Yen The*, 25–27. *CMTT*, 1:166. A similar river ambush occurred in Yen The (Bac Giang). *CMTT*, 1:208.

315. *CMTT*, 1:254, 368, 386.

316. *Shittan Meigō sakusen: Biruma sensen no hōkai to Tai, Futsuin no bōei* [Sittang and Meigō Operations: Collapse of the Burma Front and Defense of Thailand and French Indochina], ed. Bōeichō (Tokyo, 1969) (henceforth cited as *SMS*), 684, dates these sweeps to mid June. *LSQD*, 143–45, is probably more accurate in saying mid May, but its claim of at least seventy Japanese killed in action is hardly credible.

317. Ban Nghien Cuu Lich Su Dung Tinh Uy Lang Son, *Lich Su Dau Tranh Cach Mang Huyen Bac Son*, 60–61.

318. Ban Nghien Cuu Lich Su Dang Khu Tu Tri Viet Bac, *Khu Thien Thuat*, 57–58.

French civilians continued to reside. Most of the Civil Guard platoon defected before the shooting began, but the nine Japanese present rejected calls to surrender. After a two-hour firefight, seven were dead, and a major and one soldier had been taken prisoner.[319] The Japanese retaliated severely, but indiscriminately, to this attack.[320] Among the French who had fled into the forest during the fighting, twenty accepted Viet Minh offers of protection and were escorted to a Viet Minh camp, from whence an American air-ground team arranged to fly the women and children to China, while the able-bodied men began the long trek to the frontier.[321]

In practice, most Viet Minh groups probably spent as much time selecting Vietnamese "traitors" and "reactionaries" for elimination as trying to kill Japanese. Although such acts were sanctioned in Viet Minh propaganda and internal instructions, no rules appear to have been distributed for determining which enemies of the Revolution were capable of redemption and which not. Over its fifteen-year existence, the ICP had developed procedures for deciding who should be targeted and how to minimize damage when the enemy retaliated, but following the 9 March coup, local ICP leaders were more eager to seize the political initiative than to wait for higher-echelon consideration of execution requests. Enemy capability to take effective countermeasures was also markedly reduced. A number of Viet Minh "honor teams" (*doi danh du*) materialized, dedicated to eliminating traitors. Leaflets signed by these teams lacked the subtlety of other Viet Minh propaganda. For example, a broadside titled "Merit is Welcome, [but] Crimes Must Result in Execution!" listed government employees falling into the two categories by name and warned everyone to make their political choices quickly or face dire consequences.[322]

319. *CCDVB*, 123. Le Tuong and Vu Kim Bien, *Lich Su Vinh Phu*, 168. *LSQD*, 150, somehow manages to ignore earlier accounts and inflate Japanese deaths to eighteen.

320. Françoise Martin, *Heures tragiques au Tonkin (9 Mars 1945–18 Mars 1946)* (Paris, 1948), 107–11.

321. Patti, *Why Viet Nam?* 128. Tran Dan Tien, *Nhung Mau Chuyen*, 98–99. Although both of these sources state that the twenty French nationals had been incarcerated by the Japanese at Tam Dao, it seems more plausible that the Japanese had simply ordered them to remain at the hill resort after the March coup. In Maurice Bernard and Yvonne Bernard, *Lettre aux amis d'Hanoi* (n.p., n.d., copy kindly provided to me by Allison K. Thomas), printed several months after the events, two of the evacuees stress the discipline of Viet Minh soldiers, the support given by people in the villages through which they passed, and a surprising lack of hatred toward the French.

322. Leaflet probably circulated in late May 1945, reprinted in *CMCD*, 12: 1480150, as well as *NCLS*, no. 255 (2-1991): 48–49.

Rough revolutionary justice made itself felt first in the northern mountain provinces, where many Viet Minh participants, who had themselves only recently been the objects of several "white terror" campaigns, now saw the opportunity for "red terror" (khung bo do).[323] In Lang Son, a village official who earlier had delivered the severed head of a local Viet Minh leader to the French in exchange for a sack of salt was tracked down and dispatched.[324] In Tuyen Quang, a National Salvation Army unit tried and executed a district official together with a native employee of the Japanese. A district mandarin was killed after attempting to escape detention.[325] In Yen The (Bac Giang), another National Salvation Army unit convened a people's court to try a canton chief, who was then executed and his property confiscated, except for an amount deemed sufficient for survival of his wife and children.[326] On entering the town of Cho Ra (Bac Can) in early April, a Propaganda and Liberation Army unit summarily executed the district mandarin, Dong Phuc Quan.[327]

In the Red River Delta, Viet Minh groups were more inclined to threaten or cajole government officials than to eliminate them.[328] However, the ICP did target a number of lower-level opponents. Native Sûreté agents who had terrorized ICP members in the past and continued to work for the Japanese were considered fair game. At least five individuals believed to fit this description were killed in Hanoi in June and July by an "honor team" headed by Cao Ngoc Lien, a local high school student. Most stunning to the public was the street killing of Nga Thien Huong, said to be a female master spy for the Kenpeitai.[329] The Party committee of Hai Duong decided

323. Prior to March 1945, "red terror" was not entirely unknown in the northern mountains, particularly directed at suspected Sûreté agents and leaders of "bandit" gangs. In one 1943 (?) episode, presumably unusual, the village of Ha Vi (Cao Bang) was surrounded and twenty-seven "informers" (cho san) were beheaded. CMTT, 1:92.

324. Hoang Van Hoan, Giot Nuoc, 230.

325. CMTT, 1:134.

326. Ha Thi Que, "Rung Yen The," in Le Thiet Hung et al., Rung Yen The, 98–123.

327. CMTT, 1:124.

328. Naturally there were exceptions. The district mandarin of Tu Son (Bac Ninh) was killed for being an "effective collaborator with the Japanese." CMTT, 1:318. The district mandarin of Thanh Thuy (Phu Tho) was killed in July or early August. Ibid.,151. In Luc Yen (Yen Bai), the district mandarin was captured after fleeing the town, given the opportunity to repent, but then somehow demonstrated by "traitorous actions" his refusal. A court ordered him to be punished "severely" (nghiem tri), in this context almost surely execution. Ibid., 178.

329. Quan Khu Thu Do, Thu Do Ha Noi: Lich Su Khang Chien chong Thuc Dan Phap (1945–1954) [The Capital of Hanoi: History of Resistance to French Colo-

to eliminate Tong Van Kim, who had recently captured two committee members and relentlessly pursued others. It assigned the job to the Ninh Giang district committee, which proceeded to investigate Kim's movements and select a suitable executioner. Kim was shot in late June as he bicycled across a bridge, the killer then coolly doffing a straw hat and palm-leaf raincoat disguise before boarding a bus out of the area.[330]

In Thai Binh, an ICP member named Binh Son, working undercover in the Civil Guard, discovered that one of the sergeants was Truyen, an old Sûreté enemy involved in several torture incidents and deaths. Truyen was utilizing a local firm purchasing cotton, jute, and ramie for the Japanese as a screen to import armed agents to counter growing Viet Minh activities. Binh Son obtained permission from Party superiors to eliminate Truyen, but botched the first attempt. He then gathered over one hundred Viet Minh followers to surround and assault Truyen's house at night, capturing Truyen as well as two assistants. After loudly declaring his Viet Minh credentials, Binh Son shot all three. The next morning, when Truyen's superior arrived suddenly on the scene by car he was shot as well.[331]

Established enemy agents were only the most obvious candidates for elimination. Individuals who "posed as Viet Minh" to collect money were sometimes executed, even though no system yet existed to check the legitimacy of local groups. Anyone actively assisting the Japanese might be killed, although most such people were supposed to be capable of redemption, or at least of switching to a passive stance. Often warnings were delivered; if heeded, plans for elimination would be dropped. However, warnings were not felt necessary in the case of Nguyen Dinh Phach, a village chief in Hung Yen who received five bullets on 19 March, or of Hai An, a Buddhist priest killed as an alleged collaborator in the Fourth War Zone in June. When local activists came to believe that a long-hated notable in Gia Loc district (Hai Duong) had uncovered the ICP identities of three

---

nialism (1945–1954)] (Hanoi, 1986), 48, 52–53. *CMTT*, 1:29–30. Perusal of provincial- and district-level Party histories suggests that an additional twenty or twenty-five alleged Sûreté agents may have been killed in the Red River Delta region between May and July.

330. *CMTT*, 1:245–46.

331. Binh Son, "Tieng Sung Tru Gian" [Shots That Eliminate Traitors], in *Thai Binh Khoi Nghia* (Thai Binh, 1965), 116–27. According to Binh Son, the Thai Binh province mandarin, Nguyen Huu Tri, was moved by these incidents to support the Viet Minh with cash donations. *CMTT*, 1:434–35, has a somewhat different account of the same incidents.

government Frontline Youth leaders, he was shot down at the district cattle market in late July.[332]

Because the overriding political purpose of such killings was to cow opponents and perhaps to garner support from ordinary citizens angry at the way they had been treated by authority, some ICP and Viet Minh leaders did not spend much time evaluating specific proposals for execution or canvassing less drastic options. If the person killed was subsequently declared to be guilty of crimes, and that declaration was believed by enough people, then the action was justified. In Haiphong, Nguyen Binh carried this reasoning a step further, arguing in late March for a series of killings of informers to "speed up the advance of the movement." Although Binh's proposal was turned down, because he lacked written authorization from the Standing Bureau and some members feared Japanese retaliation, it seems that a few Haiphong ICP cells went ahead anyway. In April they killed one "collaborator" on a city street and shot a "reactionary" while he waited for the ferry to Kien An. They also pursued Nguyen The Nghiep, who had betrayed the Party in 1930 and now supported the Japanese, but only managed to catch up with him after the August Revolution. Further tangling the organizational threads, a National Salvation Youth unit in Hanoi trailed a Vietnamese employee of the Kenpeitai to a Haiphong opium den in July and eliminated him.[333]

Persons who identified themselves with the Dai Viet Quoc Gia Lien Minh (Greater Vietnam National Alliance) were considered by the ICP and Viet Minh not only as Japanese lackeys but also as potential rivals for political power. In Bac Giang, Viet Minh adherents killed a Dai Viet leader on sight as he approached their village. In Hung Yen, three Dai Viet members were shot on the assumption that they had come to spy for the Japanese. However, other Viet Minh units were more eager to take over Dai Viet meetings and break up youth training camps than to kill followers. For example, when the Dai Viet organized a patriotic commemoration in Ha Dong in June, attracting about seven hundred people, a small Viet Minh assault team seized the rostrum, denounced Japanese collaborators, and substituted their flag for the Dai Viet's banner (three red stars on a yellow field). Dai Viet camps were invaded in at least four Tonkin provinces.[334]

332. *CMTT*, 1:178, 225, 241–42, 244–45, 256, 305. Hoang Van Hoan, *Giot Nuoc Trong Bien Ca*, 231.

333. *CMTT*, 1:269–70, 273.

334. Ibid., 190, 201, 202, 228–29, 282, 302, 305, 339.

Balance Sheet

In its efforts to control the direction and pace of revolutionary events, the ICP faced two important problems: continuing lack of operational unity and a paucity of Party members to exercise leadership within front groups. As indicated previously, the Cochinchina apparatus remained divided and out of touch with the Standing Bureau. The Annam apparatus was only marginally better off, with participants at the mid July meeting in Quang Ngai still awaiting approval from the Standing Bureau to reestablish a full-fledged regional committee, and several provinces possessing different Viet Minh organizations disputing one another's legitimacy. Even in Tonkin, difficulties abounded. In mid July, Truong Chinh published a severe internal critique, pointing out that whereas some places had advanced to setting up local government, others were depressingly silent, without any signs of struggle, even of a spontaneous character. Some places were "extremist" to the point of establishing courts to try village chiefs simply because they had collected taxes for the Japanese or puppet regime, while others failed to use the political turmoil caused by the Japanese takeover even to organize mass demonstrations. According to Truong Chinh, some cadres led the masses in broad struggle but neglected to recruit and train specialized units, while others limited themselves to training and arming small units but cautiously avoided open struggle. In some localities, people thought that bullets in the heads of a few traitors would solve all problems; in others, they allowed traitors ample room to counterattack and destroy what had already been achieved.[335]

In early August 1945, the ICP counted about 5,000 members,[336] of whom perhaps one-third were still in jail or so recently released that they had not been able to resume activities.[337] Even in Tonkin, some heavily populated delta districts had only a single four- or five-person Party cell.[338] The key province of Bac Ninh contained only 95 ICP members, working amid 3,000 Viet Minh adherents.[339] In Annam, Quang Nam had 180 organized ICP members, plus a number of former political prisoners who

---

335. *Co Giai Phong* 15 (17 July 1945), reprinted in *CMCD*, 11:146–48.

336. Ho Chi Minh, "Our Party has struggled . . . ," in *A Heroic People: Memoirs from the Revolution* (Hanoi, 1965), 12.

337. The largest group of political prisoners, more than one thousand, remained on Con Son (Poulo Condore) island until liberated in September. See chapter 7.

338. *CMTT*, 1:252, 253.

339. Ibid., 331. This Party count probably excludes Standing Bureau or Regional Committee cadres based in Bac Ninh.

still had not resumed activity.[340] Meanwhile, Viet Minh groups were popping up in hundreds of villages and district towns, often with no ICP involvement whatsoever. In the mountain liberated zone, it seems plausible that 100,000 people, or 10 percent of the population, were active in national salvation units by the end of July. Perhaps 1,000 were organized in "main force" (*chu luc*) army units.[341] In the rest of Tonkin, at least 50,000 had probably joined groups styling themselves Viet Minh, with Annam and Cochinchina perhaps enrolling another 20,000 and 10,000 respectively.[342]

The formation of local liberation committees moved much more slowly, probably because few notables or village elders outside the liberated zone were prepared to lend their names overtly to the revolutionary cause in June or July. Many provinces apparently had no liberation committees at all, while others possessed only three or four amid 80–120 villages. In some cases, the liberation committee pushed aside the existing village council entirely; in others, it recruited several council sympathizers; in still others, it remained undercover until the August insurrection.[343] In Annam, rather than start with village-level committees in accordance with Viet Minh instructions, there seems to have been a tendency to establish committees at province or district levels first.[344]

Looked at from a local perspective, groups that called themselves Viet Minh, that shared the vision of an independent postwar Vietnam, and that increasingly threatened the existing power structure had emerged in most districts in the country by July. Fed by rumor, leaflets, and the heady excitement of speeches and demonstrations, participants in these groups felt that revolutionary change was imminent. Because contact between lower and higher echelons remained minimal, local leaders enjoyed considerable leeway when translating Viet Minh policies into action. In many ways the "Viet Minh" in late July was more an amorphous movement, possessing its own momentum and trajectory, than a functioning political organization. ICP members effectively promoted or discouraged particular

---

340. *CMTT*, 2:96.

341. Lockhart, *Nation in Arms*, 104–5, estimates five thousand in main force units by August, but I think that is extremely unlikely.

342. These figures are notional only, based on scattered provincial and district claims. Thus, *CMTT*, 1:353, indicates that Son Tay province had almost 1,000 national salvation members in June and about 2,000 by early August. In Annam, Quang Ngai claimed 110,000 Viet Minh adherents by late July (*CMTT*, 2:118), but 12–15,000 seems more likely. Tuy Hoa asserted 3,000 (*CMTT*, 2:150), also an exaggeration.

343. *CMTT*, 1:170, 204, 282, 340, 356, 386, 435.

344. *CMTT*, 2:29, 74.

types of action at the district or village level, but they could not control events on a day-to-day basis. On the other hand, no alternative leadership had any chance of emerging within the Viet Minh to rival the ICP. Members of Viet Minh district or provincial committees who did not belong to the Party quickly came to understand that ICP activists might view their forming a group to advance their own interests or policies as treason.

Viewed from a countrywide perspective in late July, the Viet Minh clearly held the political initiative in Tonkin and was making rapid progress in Annam, but remained little understood in Cochinchina. The Tran Trong Kim cabinet had begun to fragment, while in Hanoi the imperial delegate, Phan Ke Toai, increasingly ignored messages from Hue. Dai Viet Party branches continued to train young auxiliaries, but at a pace suggesting that they expected the Japanese to remain in control for another year or two. General Tsuchihashi had no desire to mount a substantial campaign against the Viet Minh, although given increasing Allied support to Liberation Army units and growing unrest in the towns, he might have been forced to do so if the Pacific War had not come to an abrupt end.

Sometime in July, General Tsuchihashi dined with Phan Ke Toai and the mayor of Hanoi, Tran Van Lai. His purpose was to encourage one or both of them to make direct, conciliatory contact with ranking Viet Minh leaders. At the end of the month, Tsuchihashi secured Premier Tran Trong Kim's agreement to this initiative.[345] Possibly Tsuchihashi knew that Toai's son, Phan Ke Bao, was a member of the Viet Minh–affiliated Democratic Party.[346] These preliminary feelers by Tsuchihashi would strongly influence events in Hanoi in August.

---

345. *SMS*, 684. Nitz, "Independence," 124. Apparently a young Japanese intelligence agent, Harada Toshiaki, twice carried messages from the Japanese Army to Viet Minh cadres in Thai Nguyen before being killed in a village on a third mission. Nitz, "Independence," 127.

346. Hoang Van Dao, *Viet Nam Quoc Dan Dang, 1927–1954* [The Vietnam Nationalist Party, 1927–54] (Saigon, 1965), 219. Another potential intermediary was the minister of youth's younger brother, Phan My, who was active in the Viet Minh in Hanoi. The Kenpeitai had already searched Phan Anh's home and his wife's large pharmacy in Hanoi for evidence of Viet Minh connections. Interview with Phan Anh, Hanoi, 7 Mar. 1988.

4 The Allies: China and the United States

Within hours of the Japanese takeover on 9 March 1945, Allied commanders in China, Ceylon, and India had in hand fragmentary radio messages from French colonial units under attack, as well as reports from their own clandestine teams positioned inside Indochina. About midnight, Americans in southern China intercepted a transmission from the French garrison at Lang Son, reporting a heavy Japanese assault and requesting Allied air strikes on designated targets. General Claire Chennault, commander of the U.S. Fourteenth Air Force, immediately requested permission from China Theater headquarters to bomb the Japanese. "Give them hell," came the reply.[1] When planes arrived over Lang Son, however, the opposing forces were too close to each other to risk bombing.[2] In Chungking on the morning of 10 March, Chennault asked Generalissimo Chiang Kai-shek whether China would help the French in Indochina if they put up a stiff resistance. "Assistance may be rendered," Chiang answered cryptically, adding that if French units fled across the frontier, they might be permitted to remain at a location designated by the Chinese.[3]

Within a few days of the coup, it was apparent to Allied intelligence units monitoring Indochina radio traffic that although general resistance had collapsed, several substantial colonial combat units had managed to

1. Ronald H. Spector, *United States Army in Vietnam. Advice and Support: The Early Years, 1941–1960* (Washington, D.C., 1983), 31.

2. René Charbonneau and José Maigre, *Les Parias de la victoire: Indochine–Chine, 1945* (Paris, 1980), 160. As mentioned in chapter 1, after the French surrender an American bombing attack killed several hundred Vietnamese colonial riflemen detained inside the Lang Son citadel by the Japanese.

3. Archimedes L. A. Patti, *Why Viet Nam? Prelude to America's Albatross* (Berkeley and Los Angeles, 1980), 64.

evade capture by the Japanese and were retreating in the general direction of Kwangsi and Yunnan. When members of the American Office of Strategic Services (OSS) in China proposed to drop arms, equipment, and guerrilla training teams to one French commander who had been providing information to them previously via a clandestine radio post, China Theater decided to request policy guidance from Washington. A confusing series of consultations and messages followed, reflecting differences of opinion about Indochina extending back several years. While this continued, Chennault was reluctant to drop equipment or supplies other than medicines, but he did quietly authorize a total of thirty-four bombing, strafing, and reconnaissance missions over Indochina between 12 and 28 March.[4]

Meanwhile, senior officers at South East Asia Command (SEAC), headquartered in Kandy, Ceylon, quickly approved drops of arms and ammunition to several retreating French units.[5] With fifteen out of twenty-three British-controlled clandestine radio stations still functioning inside Indochina, it seemed conceivable that extended guerrilla operations could be mounted against the Japanese. By the end of March, however, almost all such radio posts failed to respond. SEAC's 1,210 European and native agents were all either dead, captured, or fleeing to China or northern Laos. With priority assigned to the Allied offensive in Burma, fewer special-duty aircraft were available than before to drop new teams into Indochina and keep them supplied.[6]

Word of the Japanese coup reached Paris via a Free French unit in Calcutta working closely with the British. Press reports of events in Indochina were completely overshadowed by news of American units successfully crossing the Rhine and General G. K. Zhukov's Soviet forces arriving at the Oder, poised to penetrate Germany.[7] Nonetheless, on 12 March, the minister of colonies, Paul Giacobbi, spoke of the "sometimes touching loyalty" of the peoples of Indochina to France, and predicted that "soon our flag will again float over a free Hanoi, Hue and Saigon just as over Strasbourg and Metz" (recently liberated from the

4. Spector, *United States Army in Vietnam*, 32–34.

5. Peter M. Dunn, *The First Vietnam War* (London, 1985), 95–96. Charbonneau and Maigre, *Les Parias*, 214. Admiral Lord Mountbatten, chief of SEAC, was in Chungking at the time of the Japanese coup.

6. Charles Cruickshank, *SOE in the Far East* (Oxford, 1983), 134–35.

7. Philippe Devillers, *Paris-Saigon-Hanoi: Les Archives de la guerre, 1944–1947* (Paris, 1988), 53.

Germans).[8] That same day, French Ambassador Henri Bonnet presented a note to the U.S. State Department requesting immediate help in Indochina.[9] On the 13th, General Charles de Gaulle, head of the French provisional government, berated U.S. Ambassador Jefferson Caffery for lack of American air assistance in Indochina, punctuating his concern by asking if Washington were pushing France into the Russian orbit.[10] Beyond such calculated outbursts, however, de Gaulle could do little to save the remnant colonial troop units in Indochina.

Prime Minister Winston Churchill was so preoccupied with other matters that he asked his subordinates for a one-page memo explaining why there were French troops in Indochina thirty-nine months after the outbreak of the Pacific War.[11] On 17 March, he cabled President Franklin Roosevelt urging that Indochina be placed under the de facto jurisdiction of Admiral Lord Louis Mountbatten, the British supreme commander in South East Asia, but did not try to force the issue of direct military support to the retreating French.[12] Two days later, Roosevelt's military aide, Admiral William Leahy, authorized General Chennault to assist the French in Indochina, providing such aid did not interfere with other China Theater operations already planned.[13] Although the British chiefs of staff encouraged Churchill to ask Roosevelt for more affirmative action, the prime minister demurred, explaining that he had heard the president was very hard pressed, "and I like to keep him as much as possible for the biggest things."[14] Following further interventions from Paris, however, Churchill cabled Roosevelt on 11 April urging that every assistance be given to the French, and telling the president that he had instructed Admiral Mount-

8. Bruce D. Marshall, *The French Colonial Myth and Constitution-making in the Fourth Republic* (New Haven, 1973), 192.

9. Georges Gautier, *9 mars 1945, Hanoi au soleil de sang: La Fin de l'Indochine française* (Paris, 1978), 161–63. General Saint-Didier approached the American and British Combined Chiefs of Staff with a similar plea. Dunn, *First Vietnam War*, 94.

10. U.S.Department of State, *The Foreign Relations of the United States, 1945*, vol. 6 (Washington, D.C., 1969), 300. *Foreign Relations of the United States* is cited below as *FRUS*.

11. Dunn, *First Vietnam War*, 94.

12. Walter La Feber, "Roosevelt, Churchill, and Indochina: 1942–45," *American Historical Review* (Washington, D.C.) 80, no. 5 (Dec. 1975): 1294.

13. Christopher Thorne, "Indochina and Anglo-American Relations, 1942–1945," *Pacific Historical Review* (Berkeley) 45 (1976): 90.

14. John J. Sbrega, "'First catch your hare': Anglo-American Perspectives on Indochina during the Second World War," *Journal of Southeast Asian Studies* 14, no. 1 (Mar. 1983): 72.

batten to conduct "minimum pre-occupational activities" in Indochina, with SEAC merely informing China Theater headquarters in Chungking of its initiatives.[15] The next day Roosevelt was dead.

CHINA

Among the Allies fighting the Axis powers, China had most reason to pay attention to developments in Indochina prior to March 1945. After withdrawal of the national capital to Chungking in 1938, Chinese forces resisting the Japanese became increasingly reliant on supplies coming from Western countries via Indochina, Burma, and India. Japan eliminated the Indochina logistics link in 1940, then occupied Burma in early 1942, leaving only the difficult American airlift operation from India to Kunming, plus the occasional truck convoy from the Soviet Union to Sinkiang. Henceforth the possibility of a Japanese offensive up the Red River toward Kunming had to be taken seriously, although it was appreciated that the more dangerous threat to Nationalist China's survival continued to be Imperial Army units to the east of Chungking.

While the willingness of the French colonial authorities to cooperate with Japan from 1940 on was a source of considerable irritation in China, the authorities in Chungking deliberately chose not to declare war on Vichy or the Indochina administration of Governor-General Jean Decoux. In response, Decoux avoided contact with the Japanese-sponsored Wang Ching-wei regime in Nanking, attempted to limit Japanese depredations among th overseas Chinese in the colony, and tried to persuade Chungking that maintaining French authority in Indochina was a form of resistance to Tokyo.[16] The bearer of this Gallic logic was Claude de Boisanger, Decoux's chief of diplomatic service, who communicated via the Vichy representative in Chungking until the latter's departure in July 1943, then went to the trouble of crossing the frontier himself in October to assure the Chinese government of Hanoi's desire for amicable relations and to seek practical assistance in sending an emissary via China to the Free French government in Algiers.[17] Perhaps as a result of these entreaties, Chiang Kai-shek did

---

15. La Feber, "Roosevelt, Churchill, and Indochina," 1294. Thorne, "Indochina," 87.

16. Charbonneau and Maigre, *Les Parias*, 44. Even the Viet Minh acknowledged grudgingly that Chungking needed to maintain contact with Decoux because of the "overseas Chinese problem." See *Cuu Quoc*, 11-1944, 17.

17. Claude de Boisanger, *On pouvait éviter la guerre d'Indochine: Souvenirs, 1941–1945* (Paris, 1977), 70–75. About the same time, General Eugène Mordant, commander of the colonial armed forces in Indochina, sent his own representative

not declare war on Vichy when he moved to upgrade relations with Algiers in late 1943.[18]

Such diplomatic contortions reflected an underlying fact in the China-Indochina border region: for most of the war it was convenient for all the main actors, Chinese, Japanese, and French, to avoid provoking hostilities. On several occasions, Chinese generals considered, but eventually rejected, plans to launch an offensive into Indochina.[19] A massive, hazardous operation of that kind could only be justified in coordination with American amphibious landings on Hainan or the Indochina coast, which remained out of the question until the Philippines had been retaken. Similarly, Japanese strategists never found Kunming a sufficiently compelling target to risk an offensive through the rugged terrain of southern Yunnan, where each mile gained would bring new logistical problems. In 1944, the Imperial Army did employ the Hanoi-Nanning road to support troops attacking western Kwangsi, but the rest of the frontier remained unaffected. Meanwhile, the French understood that any open Sino-Japanese confrontation in or adjacent to Indochina would jeopardize their survival. In the spirit of the Franco-Japanese accord, they constructed defensive fortifications along the frontier, using native labor for a total of forty million man-hours.[20]

To keep abreast of major Japanese troop movements and other developments, Chinese intelligence relied on clandestine radio reports from overseas Chinese agents in the service of General Tai Li, chief of security for Chiang Kai-shek, supplemented by U.S. Army Air Force photo reconnaissance missions over northern Indochina.[21] Aggressive long-range patrolling on the ground was ruled out for fear of sparking Japanese counteraction. In any event, it proved unnecessary, as hundreds of cross-border traders helped to keep all sides reasonably well informed.

Commerce across the Sino-Indochinese frontier was limited only by the diplomatic need to declare it "contraband" and the American propensity

---

to Kwangsi, who met with one of the subordinates of General Chang Fa-kwei, the Fourth War Area commander. King C. Chen, *Vietnam and China, 1938–1954* (Princeton, 1969), 73.

18. Philippe Devillers, *Histoire du Vietnam de 1940 à 1952* (Paris, 1952), 117.

19. Chen, *Vietnam and China*, 71–73.

20. Gabriel Sabattier, *Le Destin de l'Indochine: Souvenirs et documents, 1941–1951* (Paris, 1952), 76–78. General Sabattier is quite critical of this construction program, ordered by General Mordant.

21. Tai Li initiated his Indochina network in 1939, beginning with Hanoi. Soon it extended to Saigon, Haiphong, Mong Cai, Lang Son, and Hue. Liang Hsiung, "Tai Li Chuan" [A Biography of Tai Li] (Taipei [?], 1981), 212.

to bomb bridges and rail facilities in the area. Owing to the necessity to transship by packtrain between railheads, bulk commodities like coal, rice, tin ore, and raw cotton, which had dominated prewar traffic, gave way to items of much higher value per unit weight. Thus, China exported tin ingots, mercury, wolfram, and antimony, while Indochina exported salt, opium, cigarettes, and cloth. Salt purchased on the Tonkin coast for .20 piastres per kilogram sometimes sold for fifty times that much across the border in Yunnan,[22] thus earning the sobriquet "white gold."[23] An Indian Army officer reconnoitering the frontier region in 1943 found abundant evidence of such trading—for example, observing eighty mules coming from Indochina loaded with locomotive parts to help keep the French-owned Yunnan railway functioning south of Kunming. At the Lao Cai frontier post, a regular ferry service operated, with Japanese soldiers issuing passes to merchants moving back and forth.[24] A major cross-border trading organization in Nanning was run by one of Kwangsi province's military leaders.[25]

Although we know little in detail about Chinese cross-border transactions, the British secret services left a revealing record of their affiliated operations, headquartered in Kunming. The original idea in October 1942 was to purchase rubber from Indochina using agents recruited in China. Soon the plan expanded to moving scarce strategic materials like quinine, agar, catechu, benzoin, and silk from other Japanese-occupied areas via Indochina or Thailand to Kunming, thence on to Great Britain. When all of these schemes foundered for lack of reliable local connections, the British concentrated on using diamonds from South Africa, sulfa drugs, Swiss watches, and cigarette paper to play the black market in southern China. By mid 1944, the main British institution, code-named "Remorse," had become part of a large syndicate of mainly Chinese banks, transport companies, and representatives of provincial administrations, with 6.7 percent of all profits going to General Tai Li's organization as insurance against customs obstruction or hijacking camouflaged as guerrilla raids. "Remorse" served as black market banker for thirty-three Western customers,

22. USNA, OSS collection, U.S. consul, Kunming, to U.S. Embassy, Chungking, 22 Mar. 1943; also OSS, New Delhi, memo D-30, 14 May 1945. An estimated three tons of salt went into China at Lao Cai each day.
23. René Bauchar [René Charbonneau], *Rafales sur l'Indochine* (Paris, 1946), 113.
24. USNA, OSS collection, American Embassy, Chungking, report 1095, 21 Apr. 1943.
25. USNA, OSS collection, OSS report A-43919, 5 Oct. 1944.

including military organizations, diplomatic missions, the Red Cross, the Friends' Ambulance Unit, ICI Ltd., Reuters, and seven other commercial firms. Indochina was only a very minor part of this network. Nevertheless, in April 1945, "Remorse" helped to finance the French colonial units escaping Japanese pursuit, then provided them with food, clothing, medicines, blankets, and shelter in Yunnan and Kwangsi until the Americans eventually agreed to take responsibility for them.[26]

South China in the early 1940s was the scene of a complex struggle for power among Chinese Nationalist leaders, with the war against the Japanese serving as backdrop. Chiang Kai-shek used the Sino-American relationship and his new status as leader of one of the big four Allied powers to undermine the position of long-standing domestic rivals and provincial warlords. This was particularly obvious in Yunnan, where General Lung Yün, who had seized control of the province in 1927, saw his prewar autonomy eroded by the Chungking government's persistent demands for men, money, and matériel. The Central Military Committee established a "Southwest Transport Management Bureau," headed by Tai Li, to finesse local interests. Even Lung Yün's control of cross-border traffic in opium was jeopardized in May 1942, when Tai Li's agents won a pitched battle with Lung Yün's son over three truckloads of raw opium.[27] Lung Yün reacted to such central challenges by siphoning off large quantities of American Lend-Lease supplies coming across the Himalayan "Hump" to Kunming.[28] He also turned a blind eye to the anti-Chiang activities of thousands of Chinese intellectuals who had fled to Kunming in the wake of Japanese occupation of all the eastern cities. However, Lung Yün could not prevent Chiang from stationing ever more central government troops in Yunnan, until by March 1943 they outnumbered local troops by a ratio of four to one.[29]

Somewhat different problems beset General Chang Fa-kwei, commander of the Fourth War Area in Kwangsi and western Kwangtung. As head of the famed Ironsides Army in the Kuomintang's victorious Northern Expedition of 1927, Chang retained many admirers throughout China. However, the fact that he had taken a leading role in several subsequent attempts to depose Chiang Kai-shek made the Generalissimo anxious to

26. Cruickshank, *SOE*, 210–20.
27. Liang, "Tai Li Chuan," 247.
28. Barbara W. Tuchman, *Stilwell and the American Experience in China, 1911–45* (New York, 1971), 316, 362, 364. Patti, *Why Viet Nam?* 487.
29. Lloyd E. Eastman, *Seeds of Destruction: Nationalist China in War and Revolution, 1937–1949* (Stanford, 1984), 13–28.

circumscribe Chang's powers. After the outbreak of war with Japan in July 1937, Chang did receive responsibility for the defense of Shanghai, where for more than three months, his troops demonstrated a relentless will to fight that deeply impressed their countrymen and world public opinion alike.[30] In 1939, Chang was given command of the Fourth War Area, but precisely because of his reputation as one of China's foremost military tacticians, Chiang Kai-shek withheld crucial resources and insisted that key subordinates report directly to Chungking. Kwangsi province benefited from wartime manufacturing and commercial activity until the Japanese Ichigō offensive in mid 1944, which caused the deaths of more than a hundred thousand people, together with the burning of uncounted houses, slaughter of draft animals, destruction of factories, and total disruption of communications.[31]

Sino-Vietnamese Contacts

While most members of the South China elite considered Indochina primarily in the context of their own pressing concerns, they were not unaware of the territory's separate history and unique problems. For all Chinese Nationalists, it was a source of embarrassment that the Ch'ing dynasty had not been able to help the kingdom of Vietnam escape French colonization in the nineteenth century. Many knew of statements by early-twentieth-century luminaries like Liang Ch'i-ch'ao, Sun Yat-sen, and Hu Han-min fervently supporting the efforts of Vietnamese patriots. They might even have heard of Phan Boi Chau, a tireless Vietnamese organizer against the French until his capture in Shanghai in 1925.[32] In the mid 1920s, Kuomintang leaders in Canton encountered a new generation of Vietnamese anticolonial activists, who had come to that city for its vibrant politics, the opportunity to secure military training at the Whampoa Academy, and, they hoped, foreign assistance in liberating their country. Following the violent collapse of the united front between the Kuomintang and the Chinese Communist Party in 1927, Chinese interest in the "colonial question" waned, and Vietnamese activists were forced to scatter. Some Chinese commanders recruited educated Vietnamese to their military units, perhaps partly out of guilt for not helping in a more

30. *Biographical Dictionary of Republican China*, ed. Howard L. Boorman (New York, 1968), 1:56–59. Tuchman, *Stilwell*, 169–70.

31. Diana Lary, *The Kwangsi Clique in Chinese Politics, 1925–1937* (London, 1974), 206.

32. David G. Marr, *Vietnamese Anticolonialism, 1885–1925* (Berkeley and Los Angeles, 1971), 109–15, 125–28, 148, 215–21, 225–26, 238–39, 257–58.

Figure 19. General Ho Ying-ch'in (left), chief of staff of the Chinese armed forces, and General Chang Fa-kwei, commander of the Fourth War Area, which included Kwangsi and western Kwangtung. Courtesy of the U.S. Department of Defense.

affirmative manner, but also because such foreign adherents had no local family connections to complicate loyalties.

During the 1930s and early 1940s, hundreds of anticolonialist Vietnamese continued to navigate the confusing, volatile politics of China. Since most were wanted by the Sûreté in Indochina, they always ran the risk of some Chinese official turning them over to a French consulate in exchange for favors.[33] As political and personal differences developed among Vietnamese émigrés, it was also not unusual for one group to denounce another to the Chinese police or security services. Being jailed as an alleged com-

33. This happened to noncommunist activists as well as communists. See, e.g., Hoang Nam Hung, *Nam Muoi Nam Cach Mang Hai Ngoai* [Fifty Years of Overseas Revolutionary Activity] (Saigon, 1960), 148–49, and Hoang Van Dao, *Viet Nam Quoc Dan Dang: Lich Su Dau Tranh Can Dai, 1927–1954* [The Vietnam Nationalist Party: A Modern Struggle History, 1927–54] (Saigon, 1964), 173–74.

munist or Japanese or French agent became almost routine. In such circumstances, it was essential to be able to get word to a powerful or prestigious Chinese patron prepared to vouch for one's innocence and engineer release.

Several émigrés played key roles as intermediaries between Chinese officialdom and less well placed Vietnamese activists. Most important until at least 1940 was Ho Hoc Lam, a longtime follower of Phan Boi Chau's, a graduate of the Paoting Military Academy near Peking, and, since 1927, a member of the Chinese Army General Staff, with the rank of major. Ho Hoc Lam was respected by Vietnamese communists and noncommunists alike, a rare achievement in the 1930s. He repeatedly attempted to bring together anticolonialists of all different persuasions, coming closest to success in 1935–36, when émigré leaders traveled from Canton, Kunming, and Thailand to the Chinese capital of Nanking to establish the Vietnam Independence League (Viet Nam Doc Lap Dong Minh Hoi). Following this meeting, a delegation was received by Chinese government officials, who authorized the league to function and gave it permission to publish a Chinese-language journal.[34] Disputes among adherents prevented the league from operating as intended, however, and the journal folded after three or four issues.[35] Undaunted, Ho Hoc Lam continued to secure jobs for émigrés, to vouch personally to the Chinese police for jailed Vietnamese, and to offer his home as free accommodation and a meeting place. After outbreak of the Sino-Japanese War in 1937, Ho Hoc Lam and his wife evacuated to Wuhan, then Kweichow, and finally Kwangsi, where he secured employment at Chang Fa-kwei's Fourth Army Area headquarters.[36] It was

34. One source indicates that General Lu Han, a relative and follower of Lung Yün, assisted the Vietnam Independence League to obtain recognition as well from the Central Committee of the Kuomintang Party. U.S. Department of State, "Political Alignments of Vietnamese Nationalists," Office of Intelligence Research report no. 3708, 1 Oct. 1949, 26.

35. Hoang Van Dao, Viet Nam Quoc Dan Dang, 182–83. Hoang Van Hoan, Giot Nuoc trong Bien Ca: Hoi Ky Cach Mang [A Drop in the Ocean: Revolutionary Memoir] (Beijing [?], 1986), 102–8. Calvin E. Mehlert, "Miscellaneous Comments on the Vietnamese Nationalist Movement 1925–1946" (unpublished paper, Berkeley, 1969), 26. Chiang Yung-ching, Hu Chi Ming tsai Chung Kuo [Ho Chi Minh in China] (Taipei, 1972), 120.

36. Hoang Van Hoan, Giot Nuoc, 88, 92–94, 109–13. Hoang Van Hoan came from the same village in Nghe An as Ho Hoc Lam, who also happened to be the uncle of Ho Tung Mau, one of Ho Chi Minh's earliest recruits. According to Chiang Yung-ching, Hu Chi Ming tsai Chung Kuo, 108, Ho Hoc Lam's daughter, Ho Diec Lan, was a member of the ICP. Such personal ties help to explain why Ho Hoc Lam, never sympathetic to Marxism-Leninism, often helped ICP adherents as well as nationalists.

here that Ho Hoc Lam was tracked down by Ho Chi Minh, who soon benefited from the former's extensive contacts.

Another well-connected Vietnamese was Vu Hong Khanh, leader of the
Vietnam Nationalist Party (Viet Nam Quoc Dan Dang) group in Yunnan.[37]
Fleeing the French colonial crackdown of 1930, Vu Hong Khanh was able
to enroll at a Yunnan military academy, and after being commissioned in
the Chinese Twentieth Army Corps, he rose rapidly to the rank of brigadier
general. In 1941 he was appointed superintendent of a school that specialized in training Vietnamese, Thai, and Burmese youths for future
cross-border operations. During his tenure, more than one hundred Vietnamese went through this program.[38] The Vietnam Nationalist Party in
Yunnan also benefited from being able to recruit from among the three to
four thousand Vietnamese workers, shopkeepers, and house servants scattered along the French-owned railroad, although from 1940 on, it met
increasingly stiff competition from the Indochinese Communist Party.[39]

Even though Vu Hong Khanh's organization was listed as a branch of
the Kuomintang, this did not protect him from being arrested three times
by Lung Yün's police. On each occasion, comrades had to contact central
Kuomintang officials to be able to secure his release. Sometimes rank-
and-file members of the Vietnam Nationalist Party were not so fortunate,
being turned over to the French authorities for deportation, or, in at least
one case, facing a Chinese firing squad. At issue were constant French
assertions that the Nationalist Party engaged in murder, banditry, extortion, and the manufacture of explosives. Some of the charges were true,
some arose from the acts of gangs not associated with the Nationalist Party,
and some were fabricated out of whole cloth by the French. Whatever the
facts, Vietnam Nationalist Party members were convinced that Lung Yün
responded more to the lure of French money than to police evidence.[40] After
1940, French capacity to interfere in Yunnan affairs declined dramatically,
but Chungking's growing penetration of Lung Yün's domain ensured that
he would continue to harass Vu Hong Khanh. In response, the Vietnam
Nationalist Party may have sought the patronage of Tai Li's powerful
security network, solving its immediate problem, yet creating others.

37. Vu Hong Khanh came from the same village in Vinh Yen province as
Nguyen Thai Hoc, the most famous of the Vietnam Nationalist Party leaders
guillotined by the French in 1930.
38. Mehlert, "Miscellaneous Comments," 24. As a State Department officer in
Saigon in 1968, Mehlert was able to interview both Vu Hong Khanh and his close
associate Nghiem Ke To.
39. Chen, *Vietnam and China*, 37–40.
40. Hoang Van Dao, *Viet Nam Quoc Dan Dang*, 165–66, 170–71, 175–76, 183.

Conditions were different in Kwangsi, where General Chang Fa-kwei seems to have prided himself on sponsoring meetings of Vietnamese anticolonialists from all over. Mention has already been made in chapter 3 of the 1941 Chinghsi encounter that produced the short-lived Vietnam National Liberation League. By early 1942, the Fourth War Area had enrolled 702 young Vietnamese in five different training programs.[41] A number of older activists had already converged on Liuchou, including Ho Hoc Lam, Nguyen Hai Than (previously sponsored by the Kwangtung provincial authorities), and Truong Boi Cong. In June, a ten-man delegation of the Vietnam Nationalist Party arrived from Kunming. No ICP members were present for these extended discussions, unlike at the 1941 Chinghsi meeting.[42] At stake were formal Chinese recognition, a subsidy of 100,000 Chinese dollars per month (about U.S. $1,200 on the open market), and, it was hoped, weapons for graduates of the training programs and coordinated operations of some kind along the entire Sino-Indochinese frontier. At one point, Vu Hong Khanh sent a colleague to Chungking to encourage the central Kuomintang to take control of the proceedings, which made him unpopular with the Fourth War Area staff for the remainder of the war.[43] When it became clear that the Chinese wanted Truong Boi Cong to chair the new organization, Nguyen Hai Than departed Liuchou in a huff.[44] One participant who protested persistently that China was merely using Vietnamese revolutionaries for its own purposes found himself arrested, labeled pro-Japanese, and subjected to a stern lecture by Chang Fa-kwei.[45]

Whatever the problems, General Chang was determined to have an organization, which duly emerged on 1 October 1942 as the Vietnam Revolutionary League (Viet Nam Cach Menh Dong Minh Hoi), complete with constitution, working program, and officeholders.[46] The head of the

41. Chen, *Vietnam and China*, 51. Chiang Yung-ching, *Hu Chi Ming tsai Chung Kuo*, 152–53. The enrollees included thirty-six women.

42. It is quite possible that Ho Chi Minh was hoping to participate in these deliberations when he was arrested on the Chinese side of the frontier in August 1942.

43. Mehlert, "Miscellaneous Comments," 30–31, states that Nghiem Ke To had received prior encouragement from General Ho Ying-ch'in, chief of the General Staff in Chungking, to draw up a plan to unify all noncommunist Vietnamese revolutionaries.

44. Hoang Van Dao, *Viet Nam Quoc Dan Dang*, 193. Nonetheless, Nguyen Hai Than was still designated a member of the standing committee.

45. Chen, *Vietnam and China*, 61–62. Chiang Yung-ching, *Hu Chi Ming tsai Chung Kuo*, 155–56, suggests that this participant, Hoang Luong, was incited by the ICP.

46. By 1945 at least, the Revolutionary League also boasted a flag, which was red with white and blue stripes in the upper left corner. AOM, INF, GF 67.

Fourth War Area's political department, Lieutenant General Liang Hua-sheng, was appointed "director."[47] Truong Boi Cong took responsibility for establishing the league's main office in Liuchow, while other executive committee members dispersed to Kunming, Chinghsi, and Tunghsing, on the Gulf of Tonkin just across the border from Mong Cai. Within six months, however, Truong Boi Cong had been stripped of his functions, Nguyen Hai Than was accused of embezzling league funds, and Vu Hong Khanh faced growing ICP challenges to his position among Vietnamese émigrés in Kunming.[48] In late 1943, fed up with all the backbiting and signs of incompetence, General Chang decided to return to the 1941 Chinghsi formula and invite ICP participation. Formally, this might be permissible, in the spirit of the second Kuomintang-CCP united front and Sino-Soviet cooperation against fascism, but Chang well understood how his opponents in Chungking would try to use evidence of cooperation with Vietnamese communists against him.

In making his decision, Chang Fa-kwei was undoubtedly swayed by favorable reports received from his aide, General Hsiao Wen, following the latter's extensive discussions with the imprisoned Ho Chi Minh. Chang particularly noted Ho's energy, knowledge of world affairs, and foreign-language abilities. He must have been impressed, too, by the fact that General Feng Yü-hsiang, Vice President Li Tsung-jen, and Sun Yat-sen's son, Sun K'o, had all interceded earlier to recommend Ho's release. For some reason, American consular officials had also taken an interest in Ho's case.[49] This was no minor factional politician. From Chungking sources, Chang knew that Ho was a member of the former Comintern, but not until September 1944 did he receive a report confirming that Ho was the famous Nguyen Ai Quoc.[50] Meanwhile, during the winter of 1943–44, Chinese intelligence agencies tested Ho's capacity to obtain reliable information

47. In May 1943, General Liang was replaced by General Hou Chih-ming, who was apparently more loyal to the central Kuomintang authorities than to Chang Fa-kwei. By January 1944, however, General Chang had managed to lever General Hou aside in favor of General Hsiao Wen. Chen, *Vietnam and China*, 67.

48. Hoang Van Dao, *Viet Nam Quoc Dan Dang*, 193–94. Chen, *Vietnam and China*, 63–64.

49. Chen, *Vietnam and China*, 56–60. Chiang Yung-Ching, *Hu Chi Ming tsai Chung Kuo*, 174–50. Huang Cheng, *Hu Chih-ming yü Chung Kuo* [Ho Chi Minh and China] (Beijing, 1987), 95.

50. Chen, *Vietnam and China*, 83. Given the high-level attention devoted to Ho Chi Minh, I think a range of noncommunist Chinese leaders must have known or guessed Ho's identity as Nguyen Ai Quoc, but chose for various reasons not to expose him.

from Viet Minh sources inside Indochina,[51] while the government radio station put him to work broadcasting propaganda aimed at the colony.[52]

In March 1944, a reunification conference of the Revolutionary League was convened in Liuchou, with most of the old faces, plus Ho Chi Minh, Le Tung Son, and Pham Van Dong representing the ICP under various cover designations. The bickering did not lessen, yet quite possibly General Chang and General Hsiao Wen anticipated that outcome, simply using the meeting as a device to legitimize subsequent bilateral dealings with the ICP and Viet Minh. This is suggested by the tacit support that Hsiao Wen provided the ICP in its moves to wrest control of the Kunming branch of the Revolutionary League away from the Nationalist Party, as well as the careful attention given to Ho Chi Minh's detailed Vietnam operational plan, even though he remained technically a mere alternate in the new eleven-member executive committee of the league.[53]

While anticommunist members of the Revolutionary League were increasingly concerned at Ho Chi Minh's growing influence in Liuchou, they were even more vocal in urging General Chang not to allow him to recross the frontier to Vietnam. With the Japanese Ichigō offensive moving relentlessly toward Liuchou in August, however, General Chang decided to authorize Ho's departure for home, giving him a travel permit, certificate of appointment in the Revolutionary League, a personal letter of introduction, military map, propaganda materials, medicine, and 76,000 Chinese dollars. He also assigned eighteen Vietnamese who had trained for three years to Ho Chi Minh's operations. It was agreed that Ho could send followers to short-term training classes in Tunghsing. If either the French or the Japanese retaliated against the Viet Minh, General Chang authorized Ho's guerrilla units to seek sanctuary in Kwangsi.[54] Arriving in Lung Chou county, close to the Indochina frontier, Ho persuaded the head of a local

51. Patti, Why Viet Nam? 55.

52. USNA, DOS special files RG59, box 7, d. 2, report of 7 Nov. 1944.

53. Chen, Vietnam and China, 68–70, 74–76. Chiang Yung-ching, Hu Chi Ming tsai Chung Kuo, 164–69. Both authors consider Hsiao Wen a "pro-communist." Chen intimates that Hsiao Wen helped Ho Chi Minh in order to foster communist aims in Indochina. However, no Vietnamese communist source accepts this interpretation. Indeed, most regard Hsiao Wen as a dangerous manipulator dedicated to fostering Chinese control of Indochina. On the available evidence, I see him as an opportunist eager to become postwar proconsul in Hanoi, not necessarily in the service of Chinese central government interests. Nonetheless, it is likely that some lower-ranking members of the Fourth War Area staff assisted the ICP as communist sympathizers or undercover members of the CCP.

54. Chen, Vietnam and China, 77–82. General Chang ignored Ho Chi Minh's request for one thousand firearms and ammunition.

CCP-affiliated peasant association to secure civilian clothing to replace the Chinese Army uniforms he and his eighteen associates were wearing.[55] All crossed into Cao Bang at the end of August.

In November 1944, the Viet Minh published a resolute defense of its links with the Chiang Kai-shek government and reiterated its desire for Chinese forces to enter Vietnam to fight the Japanese and French.[56] After admitting that the "Viet Minh–Chungking alliance" had yet to achieve much, that some Chinese officers undoubtedly intended to reap personal benefits from any advance into Vietnam, and that China maintained relations with the enemy French, the editors and authors of this publication addressed each difficulty in turn. Citing various official Chinese statements denying any territorial ambitions in Vietnam, they then argued more bluntly that it was futile for leaders in Chungking to "entertain imperial dreams when one had yet to escape from the imperialist yoke oneself." The Japanese offensive currently under way in China had only been possible, according to these Viet Minh analysts, because Kuomintang and Chinese Communist forces continued to attack each other. In addition to resolving such serious internal disputes, China had to support uprisings elsewhere in Asia, especially Korea and Vietnam, if it hoped to defeat the Japanese. Picking up rhetorical steam, one Viet Minh writer lauded China as the "revolutionary furnace of the Far East" and seemed to endorse the Chinese view of themselves as "eldest brothers" in the Asian anti-imperialist struggle. Another writer emphasized that today's "democratizing China" was fundamentally different from the China that had committed so many crimes in Vietnam in the feudal era. Nonetheless, the need for the Viet Minh to organize in advance of Allied troop arrivals, in order to avoid complete dependence, was emphasized repeatedly—with Yugoslavia being cited as the model.

Indochina and Wartime Chinese Politics

From 1943 on, it was possible for the Chinese to contemplate eventual Axis defeat and the outlines of postwar Asia. While government officials understandably thought first about returning to the coastal provinces, resolving the Kuomintang-CCP cleavage somehow, and beginning to reconstruct the economy, they did not ignore foreign policy questions, including

55. Huang Cheng, 105.

56. *Cuu Quoc*, 11-1944, a 26-page special issue on "The Overseas Question." Although apparently printed on a commercial-quality press somewhere in the Red River Delta, this edition of *Cuu Quoc* seems to have relied partly on documentation received from Ho Chi Minh's headquarters near the Chinese frontier.

future relations with the territories adjacent to China. Already in 1942, Sun K'o, in his capacity as president of the Legislative Yuan, had urged the Allies to declare a "Pacific Charter" to complement the 1941 Atlantic Charter promulgated by President Roosevelt and Prime Minister Churchill, in which postwar independence would be promised for India, Vietnam, Korea, and the Philippines.[57] During 1943, it became clear that most Chinese political and intellectual leaders believed that the French ought to be stripped of sovereignty over Indochina, yet no consensus existed about what or who should take their place. One influential Kunming newspaper, after explicitly ruling out either continued French rule or a "return" to China, argued in favor of an independent Vietnamese republic "cooperating intimately with other republics, notably China."[58] By contrast, a book published in Kunming that same year urged the Indochinese to "wake up from the past errors of their ancestors whose selfishness and greed led them away from their mother country—China."[59] Others preferred to ignore the independence versus annexation issue in favor of spelling out the concrete benefits that ought to be sought—for example, free port status for Haiphong, a more efficient rail service between the coast and Kunming, and fewer restrictions on Chinese trade inside Indochina.[60] At the Cairo Conference in November 1943, when President Roosevelt appeared ready to offer Indochina to Chiang Kai-shek on a platter, the Generalissimo showed no interest in incorporating the territory into China, instead suggesting a joint effort with the United States leading to independence, which was probably the answer Roosevelt wanted to hear in any case.[61]

As the Japanese offensive rolled southward and westward in mid 1944, postwar Chinese plans had to be shelved in the interests of immediate

57. *Chung Yang Jih Bao* (Chungking), 23 Mar. 1942, translated in *FRUS: China, 1942* (Washington, D.C., 1957), 730. No such charter eventuated.

58. *Yunnan Je Bao*, 16 Dec. 1943, as cited in AOM, INF, c. 209, d. 1576. According to the *New York Times*, 7 Jan. 1943, *Ta Kung Bao* (Chungking) ridiculed suggestions that China might accept Indochina in exchange for ceding Manchuria to the USSR.

59. Cited in USNA, OSS collection, U.S. Embassy, Chungking, report no. 2945, 9 Sept. 1944. Unfortunately the book's title is not mentioned.

60. USNA, DOS special file RG59, lot file 54-D-190, box 10, d. 7, U.S. consul general, Kunming, 16 June 1944.

61. William Roger Louis, *Imperialism at Bay, 1941–1945: The United States and the Decolonization of the British Empire* (Oxford, 1977), 279–85. Lloyd C. Gardner, *Approaching Vietnam: From World War II through Dienbienphu* (New York, 1988), 39. Two months earlier, Foreign Minister T. V. Soong already had indicated publicly that unlike Formosa [Taiwan], Indochina was not part of China irredenta. *New York Times*, 15 Sept. 1943.

survival. When Chiang Kai-shek refused to commit many of his better divisions as reinforcements, or even to release Lend-Lease equipment and ammunition to frontline provincial units, Lung Yün and Chang Fa-kwei angrily withdrew some of their units to the hills, prepared to see the Japanese chew up central government forces in the valleys. Instead, central units fled further westward, discrediting Chiang's leadership, yet not quite provoking a cabal of southern Chinese military leaders and prominent civilians to implement their plot to force his replacement. In December 1944, Japanese attacks on both Yunnan and Szechwan seemed imminent, but the Imperial Army had outrun its supply lines, and the possibility of an American landing on the South China coast in early 1945 had to be guarded against.[62]

In this climate of confusion, a number of Chinese units bypassed by the Japanese organized themselves into guerrilla zones and lived off the local populace. The most ambitious such effort was led by Marshal Li Chi-shen, a member of the former Kwangsi warlord clique, who formed an autonomous region in the east-central part of the province, near the border with Kwangtung, designed to serve as magnet for opponents of Chiang Kai-shek.[63] Another focal point for initiatives of this kind was the Sino-Indochina border region west and southwest of Nanning. It was in this context that General Chang Fa-kwei released Ho Chi Minh in August 1944 and encouraged him to build a Vietnamese guerrilla zone linked to Chinese groups across the frontier. Ho's communist background was of little concern to Chang in this period of open alienation from Chungking; indeed, it had a positive aspect, helping to ensure that whatever Vietnamese units took shape would not double-cross Chang and ally themselves with Chiang Kai-shek.

Simultaneously, however, Chungking pursued its own efforts to develop guerrilla bases behind Japanese lines, often relying on local Kuomintang branches or members of Tai Li's security network. In mid 1944, the Vietnam Nationalist Party received radio transmitters from Chungking with instructions to set up three posts inside Vietnam. These would be coordinated by Nghiem Ke To from an operational headquarters at Tunghsing. If successful, this would have enabled the Nationalist Party to break out of its increasing isolation in Yunnan and improve its capacity to recruit followers in Tonkin. Precisely for these reasons, General Hsiao Wen in August ordered the arrest of Nghiem Ke To in Tunghsing, ignored repeated

---

62. Eastman, *Seeds of Destruction*, 28–34. Tuchman, *Stilwell*, 1–2, 457–58, 508–9.
63. Eastman, *Seeds of Destruction*, 29–30. Tuchman, *Stilwell*, 475.

orders from central Kuomintang officials to release him, and finally expelled him to Chungking in December. This arbitrary treatment of To, understandable only in the context of the bitter domestic Chinese rivalries of late 1944, had the effect of seriously demoralizing the Nationalist Party precisely at a time when new opportunities were opening up for all Vietnamese anticolonialists.[64]

By late 1944, the central Chinese government gave increasing weight to Free French maneuvers relating to Indochina. As early as May 1941, Chiang Kai-shek had permitted a small Free French office to be established in Chungking, but only as a "political movement" in contact with the Kuomintang Central Committee, not the Foreign Ministry, which continued to deal with Vichy until mid 1943.[65] Subsequently, the Chinese authorities allowed several Free French representatives to travel to Indochina via Kunming and to depart the same way. In 1943, General Tai Li reached agreement with a Free French representative, Naval Commander Robert Meynier, to expand the transport of strategic goods between China and Indochina, to promote dissidence within the Vichy-affiliated French forces in the colony, and to organize local Indochinese groups in support of Allied military operations.[66] When it became clear that the French Military Mission (FMM) in Chungking was hostile to Meynier because of his affiliation with General Henri Giraud rather than General de Gaulle, Tai Li made life very difficult for the Gaullists. An FMM post at Hok'ou, across the frontier from Lao Cai, found itself besieged by Chinese troops, and the occupants had to be rescued by Americans from a nearby meteorological station.[67] In early 1944, Tai Li ordered the FMM in Chungking to close down its radio links with Indochina.[68] However, once it was understood that General de Gaulle had won the power struggle in Algiers,

64. Hoang Van Dao, *Viet Nam Quoc Dan Dang*, 197–98. By contrast, Chen, *Vietnam and China*, 76–77, ascribes Nghiem Ke To's arrest to charges in Kunming that the Vietnam Nationalist Party had negotiated a working agreement with the British secret services. Although this may have been Hsiao Wen's pretext, Hoang Van Dao is correct to focus on the Tunghsing initiative and its direct links with Chungking.

65. Institut Charles-de-Gaulle, *Le Général de Gaulle et l'Indochine, 1940–1946* (Paris, 1982) (cited below as *DGI*), 39–40.

66. "Tai Li Chuan," 213. It is unclear whether this was the same agreement sponsored by U.S. Navy Captain Milton Miles (discussed below) or a separate Tai Li scheme.

67. Charbonneau and Maigre, *Les Parias*, 38. The killing of a French intelligence officer at Mong Cai in July 1943 may also have been the work of Tai Li's agents. *DGI*, 55.

68. Patti, *Why Viet Nam?* 36.

and especially following Allied recognition of de Gaulle's provisional government in Paris in October, Chungking adopted a correct, if still cool, attitude toward FMM and French embassy personnel.

The Chungking government understood that General de Gaulle was no more eager than Admiral Decoux to see Chinese forces enter Indochina, and knew that he had urged Washington and London not to support any such endeavor. It may have suspected de Gaulle of preferring the Franco-Japanese status quo to any wartime shattering of the French position in the colony. At the end of 1944, however, still facing Japanese threats to its own survival, the Chinese government spared little thought for such matters.

Following the Japanese takeover on 9 March, Chinese intelligence looked first for any signs that the Imperial Army planned to use Indochina as a springboard for flank attacks into Yunnan. On 13 March, the French ambassador in Chungking indicated to Foreign Minister T. V. Soong his government's readiness to discuss future Sino-Indochinese economic relations, a shift in attitude meaning little in the short term, yet deemed worthy of a positive response two days later.[69] Meanwhile, the Japanese limited themselves to chasing remnant French colonial troop units toward the border, generally not pursuing them into China. In several places where French officers tried to create small resistance bases close to the frontier, thus attracting Japanese attack, the Chinese authorities instructed the FMM to order them to desist and withdraw.[70] Local Chinese officials were barely tolerant of the exhausted and demoralized colonials; in many cases, they disarmed them and put them under guard.

In late May, Chiang Kai-shek, as commander in chief of China Theater, formally asserted his authority over Indochinese army units that had escaped to China, as well as any troops continuing to fight the Japanese in Indochina. This was more of diplomatic than of military significance, since neither Chiang nor his American chief of staff, General Albert Wedemeyer, intended to reequip the colonial units for combat, and both knew that all French resistance had ceased inside Indochina itself.[71] By this time, Chungking was preoccupied with efforts to retake huge chunks of South China as the Japanese withdrew. Nanning was liberated on 26 May and Liuchou on 10 June, and by 20 July, a Chinese detachment had crossed

69. AOM, INF, c. 209, d. 1572.

70. Charbonneau and Maigre, *Les Parias*, 190, 200, 336.

71. Patti, *Why Viet Nam?* 106. Sabattier, *Le Destin de l'Indochine*, 225–27, 455–62.

into Indochina to occupy Mong Cai.[72] General Wedemeyer's headquarters put forth ambitious proposals for Chinese armies from both Yunnan and Kwangsi to march on Hanoi, but General Ho Ying-ch'in, chief of the General Staff, preferred a defensive posture, combined with reconnaissance patrols into Tonkin.[73] In mid July, when the French ambassador stressed to the Chinese Foreign Ministry the need for French troops to accompany any Chinese units entering Indochina, he apparently received no satisfaction, leading Paris to place the issue on the agenda for General de Gaulle's meeting with President Truman in August.[74] At almost the same moment in faraway Potsdam, however, American and British generals were agreeing that China Theater had responsibility as far south as the sixteenth parallel in Indochina, with no mention of French participation.

Meanwhile, relations between General Hsiao Wen and the Viet Minh soured as the latter took advantage of chaotic conditions inside Vietnam to extend its authority across hundreds of upland villages and hamlets. Between May and July, Hsiao Wen wrote letters to Ho Chi Minh and sent messages via third parties excoriating the Viet Minh for being communist, for not cooperating with the advancing Chinese troops, and for linking up with the Americans. Members of the Vietnam Revolutionary League attached to Chinese units sent letters to specific Viet Minh groups ordering them to obey instructions or be destroyed.[75] Except for the border region northeast of Haiphong, however, Chinese troops remained clear of Indochina until several weeks after the Japanese capitulation, leaving the field open for the Viet Minh for five months. If anticommunist members of the Revolutionary League like Truong Boi Cong and Vu Hong Khanh realized the opportunity that was being lost, they did not take the risk of separating from their Chinese sponsors and moving followers into Vietnam.[76] One

72. *FRUS: The Conference of Berlin*, vol. 2 (Washington, D.C., 1960), map facing p. 346. AOM, INF, c. 136, d. 1236.

73. Stein Tønnesson, *The Vietnamese Revolution of 1945: Roosevelt, Ho Chi Minh and de Gaulle in a World at War* (London, 1991), 307–9.

74. AOM, INF, c. 209, d. 1572, messages of 17 and 19 July 1945.

75. Major Allison K. Thomas, "The Vietminh Party or League" (report to OSS, 16 Sept. 1945), reprinted in U.S. Congress, Senate Committee on Foreign Relations, *Causes, Origins and Lessons of the Vietnam War* (Washington, D.C., 1973), 268–70.

76. According to Hoang Van Dao, *Viet Nam Quoc Dan Dang*, 189–98, from late 1944 on, Vietnam Nationalist Party leaders in Kunming had conceded operational responsibility inside Indochina to the Dai Viet Quoc Dan Dang (Greater Vietnam Nationalist Party), which took a pro-Japanese position. If this is true, a move into Vietnam in the period April–July 1945 would have compromised them in the eyes of the Allies and compromised the Dai Viet in the eyes of the Japanese.

exception was "Sergeant To," formerly of the French Army, who in the name of the Revolutionary League led forty armed men across the frontier to Gia Hoa, deep in Lang Son province.[77]

Chinese attitudes toward Vietnamese anticolonialists had often combined sincere admiration for their patriotic zeal, ethnocentric assumptions about the need for these "younger brothers" to accept guidance, and pragmatic intentions to use them as auxiliaries in the event of operations inside Tonkin. Astute Vietnamese émigrés learned how to play upon these attitudes to obtain assistance. However, only the Indochinese Communist Party devoted equal or more attention to building an autonomous network inside Vietnam and chose the right moment to hazard Chinese ire by taking independent action.

One should not overstate the significance to China of such wartime maneuvering along the Indochina frontier. From the point of view of leaders in Chungking, developments to the east and northeast were infinitely more important. It is doubtful whether Chiang Kai-shek felt the need to think about Indochina more than once or twice a month. For leaders in Yunnan and Kwangsi, the picture was rather different, however. They needed to keep reasonably well informed about Japanese activities to the south, to reap some benefit from cross-border trade, and perhaps to formulate more ambitious plans for peacetime. Lacking sufficient resources to threaten the Japanese, they contented themselves with recruiting a few hundred Vietnamese émigrés here and training a few dozen there, usually with an eye to rapid expansion when circumstances permitted. Although the war ended before this Sino-Vietnamese relationship could be put to any combat test, the experience of both groups between 1941 and July 1945 would help to shape the course of events in Vietnam during the immediate postwar period.

THE UNITED STATES

During World War II, Indochina occupied the attention of Washington policy makers out of all proportion to its military significance. Only in 1941, when the United States tried unsuccessfully to pressure Japan into withdrawing its forces from southern Indochina because of the threat to the

---

Nguyen Tuong Tam, the key link between the Nationalist Party and the Dai Viet, was in Kunming in June or July, perhaps trying to resolve this dilemma. AOM, INF, c. 360, d. 2848, "La Delégation vietnamienne en France," 15 June 1946.

77. Ban Nghien Cuu Lich Su Dang Tinh Uy Lang Son, *Lich Su Dau Tranh Cach Mang Huyen Bac Son (1935–1945)* [A History of Bac Son District's Revolutionary Struggle (1935–45)] (Lang Son, 1974), 61.

Philippines and Singapore, did the military stakes deserve such attention. After that the issues were political, involving efforts to restore French national pride, the future of colonialism throughout Asia, and the enhanced status that President Roosevelt attempted to bestow on Nationalist China. A host of position papers, memos, records of conversations, and cables about Indochina were exchanged between Washington offices, and beyond the U.S. capital to London, Kandy, Chungking, and Algiers. In much of this discourse, Indochina was a metaphor for broader issues, not a place to be understood and dealt with in any practical sense. Ironically, when the time did come for decisive action, the lack of a military justification for entering Indochina in force helped American officials to opt for the political path of least resistance—reaffirmation of French sovereignty.

President Roosevelt often remarked that the French did not deserve to retain Indochina after the war. He had the conviction, never explained in any detail, that France had treated its natives in Indochina much worse than the British had done in India or Malaya, or of course the Americans in the Philippines. It also rankled Roosevelt that the French colonials had not only buckled under to Japanese coercion in 1940–41, but then continued to work with the invader for what he considered the most narrow and selfish of motives. Beyond such personal opinions, however, Roosevelt employed Indochina as the thin end of the wedge when advancing his overarching concept of postwar international trusteeships in former Western colonies. Understanding this, the British felt compelled to defend the French position in Indochina. Roosevelt earmarked Indochina as a Chinese trusteeship, or a Sino-American one, as part of his grand design of promoting China as a member of the Big Four powers. The British often suspected that Roosevelt was simply inflating Chiang Kai-shek as a screen for American postwar domination of Asia, while Stalin seemed quietly skeptical of the exercise.

President Roosevelt never forced the Indochina issue with Prime Minister Churchill. The personal friendship between these two men, so important to the success of the alliance, received a number of severe tests in regard to European war policy, but Roosevelt appreciated that the future status of Indochina was hardly worth jeopardizing his relationship with Churchill. In turn, Churchill avoided raising Indochina with Roosevelt, even when subordinates gave him convincing reasons why particular differences needed to be resolved. Both men reached past the other to try to influence officials in the opposite camp; both occasionally took unilateral decisions involving Indochina. In this game Roosevelt was at a disadvantage, as many in the U.S. State Department and military establishment doubted the wisdom of his efforts. Moreover, the American wartime bureaucracy grew so rapidly, and Roosevelt's leadership style remained so personal, that policy on secondary questions often eluded his direction for many months at a time.

In April 1942, as part of American efforts to weaken the German grip on France and North Africa, the undersecretary of state, Sumner Welles, publicly promised return of France's authority over all her prewar possessions.[78] The next month, however, Roosevelt contradicted this pledge in specific regard to Indochina when communicating privately with the Pacific War Council in Washington; British members of the council dutifully reported the president's remarks to London.[79] In October, amid intricate maneuvers to neutralize Vichy forces in North Africa prior to Allied landings, the president's personal representative assured General Henri Giraud in writing that the Allies aimed to reestablish French sovereignty "in all the territories, continental and colonial, over which the French flag flew in 1939."[80] Roosevelt subsequently rebuked his representative and disavowed the undertaking to key American officials, yet did not bother to correct the record with the French or the British.[81]

Pursuant to the Atlantic Charter of 1941, in which the United States and Great Britain had proclaimed "the right of all peoples to choose the form of government under which they will live," Roosevelt and his secretary of state, Cordell Hull, maintained that this formula applied to all oppressed or colonized peoples, whereas Churchill related it mainly to the occupied countries of Europe and insisted that any self-government for British possessions would be achieved within the Commonwealth.[82] At times U.S. officials declared publicly that the age of imperialism had ended, that victory in the war would bring liberation to all peoples.[83] The American press embellished on this theme, much to the concern of Churchill and the British Foreign Office. Not without reason, the British sensed behind this exuberant rhetoric a new liberal imperial ideology, whereby America's

78. *FRUS, 1942*, vol. 2 (Washington, D.C., 1962), 561.

79. Thorne, "Indochina," 78.

80. As quoted in Sbrega, "'First catch your hare,'" 65–66. See also the discussion in Edward R. Drachman, *United States Policy toward Vietnam, 1940–1945* (Cranbury, N.J., 1970), 36–40.

81. *Viet-Nam Crisis: A Documentary History*, ed. Allen W. Cameron, vol. 1, *1940–1956* (Ithaca, N.Y., 1971), 8–9.

82. Cordell Hull, *The Memoirs of Cordell Hull* (New York, 1948), 2:1476.

83. See, e.g., the Sumner Welles statement in Department of State *Bulletin*, 20 May 1942, 488. Drachman, *United States Policy toward Vietnam*, 40–43, provides further evidence of American anticolonial rhetoric.

superior economy would draw lesser nations into her free-trade orbit and make them dependent on her for protection and prosperity.

The lack of a clear-cut policy on Indochina left different components of U.S. officialdom ample room to argue and improvise. A 1942 OSS survey confidently declared that "the Annamites have proven themselves capable of self-government."[84] Later the same year, a State Department advisory committee on postwar foreign policy opined that as a result of their surrender to Japanese demands, the French had no claim to regain Indochina.[85] In 1943, however, Sumner Welles told the British ambassador that Indochina ought to be returned to France subject to some form of international inspection, since outright independence might well lead to social and political disintegration. In February 1944, the European and Far Eastern offices of the State Department clashed over Indochina, the former favoring continuation of French administration with some degree of international accountability, the latter an international trusteeship to prepare the natives for self-government or independence.[86] Six months later, William Langdon, U.S. consul general in Kunming, argued that "the Annamites are not yet materially or politically prepared for independence"; if put in that position prematurely, they might soon be smothered by the Chinese. For "practical reasons," Langdon therefore concluded, the French ought to exercise "temporary dominion."[87] Meanwhile, some senior military staff officers in Washington had come to favor modest French participation in the Pacific War, including Indochina operations.[88]

Roosevelt's Indochina Trusteeship

President Roosevelt had a strong emotional commitment to the concept of international trusteeships, whereby for a period of twenty or perhaps thirty years some more advanced, relatively disinterested party would exercise control over the inhabitants of a former colonial territory, accountable to

---

84. USNA, OSS Research and Analysis study no. 719 (Mar. 1942).
85. Thorne, "Indochina," 79.
86. Ibid., 82, 93.
87. USNA, DOS Papers, file 851G, U.S. consul general, Kunming, to DOS, 3 Aug. 1944.
88. Sbrega, "'First catch your hare,'" 69. Some in the OSS also favored the use of French troops for any future amphibious landing in Indochina. USNA, OSS Research and Analysis report no. 2439 (9 Aug. 1944). As Stein Tønnesson has pointed out to me in a personal communication, the U.S. Joint Chiefs of Staff were not interested in employing French troops in China Theater or in General MacArthur's Southwest Pacific command. Admiral Leahy favored British use of French forces within SEAC but opposed raising the issue formally with Roosevelt.

the still-to-be-established United Nations organization, patiently tutoring people in the direction of independence.[89] Roosevelt appreciated that pre-war colonial systems could not be sustained and sensed an upsurge of nationalist feelings in Asia that would not dissipate.[90] On the other hand, it did not occur to Roosevelt or most other American policy makers that this inchoate nationalism might soon be translated into direct political power, that colonized peoples might try to seize the initiative themselves, vigorously contesting the decisions of outsiders, whether in Washington, London, or Paris. With his own patrician background, Roosevelt simply assumed that poor, uneducated natives would see the merits of receiving guidance from those more fortunate or experienced, much as an orphaned minor accepted the decisions of a court-appointed trustee. He considered the Philippines an appropriate model, blissfully ignoring early American terror campaigns and subsequent promotion of a small Filipino oligarchy to safeguard U.S. interests.[91] Despite these limitations, the idea of trusteeship frightened those in Europe who believed the war was being fought to recover empires as well as to smash German and Japanese aggressors, or who wanted to implement changes in their own way without meddling from others.

Roosevelt first broached the Indochina trusteeship question with the British foreign secretary, Anthony Eden, in March 1943, receiving a negative response five months later.[92] In November he raised the matter in Cairo with Chiang Kai-shek, and then at Teheran with Stalin, mentioning twenty to thirty years as a suitable trusteeship period. Both agreed.[93] However, Roosevelt apparently did not take the next logical step and try to badger Churchill into assenting. At a time when tensions were growing between Washington and London about the amphibious landings in France in 1944, Roosevelt undoubtedly appreciated that Indochina, indeed the

---

89. Roosevelt and other trusteeship advocates had in mind an improved version of the League of Nations system of mandated territories. Louis, *Imperialism at Bay*, 3–26, 88–117. For a sensitive evocation of Roosevelt's attitude toward colonial people and his unique political style, see Gardner, *Approaching Vietnam*, 23–32, 40, 52.

90. Henry Wallace, vice president until January 1945, often proclaimed these opinions even more vociferously, reflecting his midwestern populist heritage more than any grasp of contemporary events in Asia.

91. William Brothers Dunn, "American Policy and Vietnamese Nationalism: 1950–1954" (Ph.D. diss., University of Chicago, 1960), 14–19.

92. La Feber, "Roosevelt, Churchill, and Indochina," 1279.

93. *Viet-Nam Crisis*, ed. Cameron, 10–11. Louis, *Imperialism at Bay*, 283–85. Herbert Feis, *Churchill, Roosevelt, Stalin: The War They Waged and the Peace They Sought* (Princeton, 1957), 246–53.

entire trusteeship issue, was not worth provoking the prime minister directly. Instead, with the puckish unpredictability for which he was famous, Roosevelt called the Chinese and Turkish ambassadors, the Egyptian minister, and the Soviet and Persian first secretaries to the White House to inform them that he had been working to prevent Indochina from being restored to France, and that he wanted a United Nations trusteeship backed up by "world policemen" to operate there until the inhabitants were capable of governing themselves.[94]

At this unusual encounter, Roosevelt did not name candidates for trustee or policeman in Indochina, but from his earlier conversation with Chiang Kai-shek and other evidence, it is likely he had China and probably the United States in mind.[95] China had captured Roosevelt's imagination, and support for Chinese resistance to Japanese aggression was extremely popular in America. More than that, Roosevelt believed that the wartime Sino-American partnership could carry over to peacetime joint management of Asian affairs.[96] One place where China could demonstrate its international respectability was Indochina, although exactly how a corrupt Kuomintang oligarchy would implement the lofty ideals of impartial United Nations guardianship was not addressed.[97]

The British Foreign Office, aghast at Roosevelt's late 1943 gambits involving Indochina, urged Churchill to confront the president. Like Roosevelt, however, Churchill wished to limit such personal disputations to vital issues regarding Europe. Aware that many American officials disagreed with the president on Indochina, he instructed Eden to mount a quiet countereffort via the State Department.[98] Queried by Secretary of State Hull about these British Foreign Office arguments, Roosevelt responded that the case for an Indochina trusteeship was perfectly clear: France had "milked

94. La Feber, "Roosevelt, Churchill, and Indochina," 1284–85.

95. At various times, Roosevelt also mentioned Britain, France, the Soviet Union, and even the Philippines as participating in the Indochina trusteeship. I suspect these were offhanded tactical ploys, meant to soften opposition to the essential Sino-American responsibility.

96. Tuchman, *Stilwell*, 249–50, 291, 360.

97. Another place Roosevelt had in mind for Chinese trusteeship was Korea, then a Japanese colony. He may have considered Burma and Thailand as well, but appreciated that Great Britain would oppose both ideas relentlessly. In Roosevelt's view, Thailand's independence had been compromised by its alliance with Japan.

98. La Feber, "Roosevelt, Churchill, and Indochina," 1286. *Vietnam: The Definitive Documentation of Human Decisions*, ed. Gareth Porter (Stanfordville, N.Y., 1979), 1:10–11. U.S. Department of Defense, *United States–Vietnam Relations, 1945–1967*, vol. 1 (Washington, D.C., 1971), A12–A15.

it for one hundred years"; the people of Indochina were entitled to "something better."

During 1944 it became apparent that military success in China was not essential to the defeat of Japan. As early as November 1943, the U.S. War Department's Strategy Section had argued that any land operations in China would come too late to assist in the attack of Japan proper.[99] By mid 1944, the American plan to use China as a platform from which to bomb Japan into submission was being finessed by much more rapid progress in the central Pacific. The subsequent collapse of Chinese armies and loss of U.S. long-range bomber bases in the face of Operation Ichigō simply confirmed the strategic tilt toward the Mariana Islands and the Philippines, although some American planners still worried that the Imperial Army might be able to fight on the Chinese mainland for several years following defeat in the home islands.[100] Increasingly, it was thought in Washington that no amphibious landing on the coast of China would be necessary.[101] In mid October, the battle for the Philippines was joined and the main Japanese fleet lured to its destruction in Leyte Gulf. Manila was secured in early February 1945. With Okinawa already selected as the next main target, both Taiwan and Indochina were dropped by the Joint Chiefs of Staff as candidates for invasion, although this was not made clear to America's allies. U.S. media releases designed to deceive the Japanese may well have confused many Chinese, British, and French analysts.

Despite the dramatic downgrading of China as a military theater, President Roosevelt still had ample political reasons to continue to promote the Sino-American alliance. By late 1944, however, his faith must have been shaken. He had failed in his efforts to persuade or coerce Chiang Kai-shek to accept General Joseph Stilwell as commander of all forces in China, to shake up the entire Kuomintang structure, and to stop violent skirmishing with communist units. Nonetheless, Roosevelt backed away from proposals to terminate American Lend-Lease support to Chiang, and did nothing to enlighten the American public about the growing differences between Washington and Chungking. Propaganda about brave, battling Nationalist China had become part of political reality in the United States, although a few journalists were beginning to ask nagging questions in print.[102]

99. Christopher Thorne, *Allies of a Kind: The United States, Britain and the War against Japan, 1941–1945* (London, 1978), 324. For another six months the Joint Chiefs of Staff continued to emphasize China's potential, however.

100. Tuchman, *Stilwell*, 466–67, 515.

101. Thorne, *Allies*, 428.

102. Tuchman, *Stilwell*, 491–509.

Official policy had cut a deep groove for itself, which Roosevelt was too tired and ill to redirect, while his aides were anxious to save him for more important matters, particularly the upcoming meeting with Churchill and Stalin at Yalta.

With the liberation of Paris in August 1944 and formal recognition of de Gaulle's provisional government in October, France's demands to take part in the fight against Japan and have its sovereignty over Indochina reaffirmed gained ground in Washington. The European office of the State Department took the lead, arguing the need for France to regain its dignity and its overseas possessions if it were to play a constructive role in peacetime.[103] On the other hand, an OSS Washington report argued that, "The use of French forces in ousting the Japanese from Indochina . . . might reduce US chances for directly influencing Indochinese policy or for encouraging greater development and independence in the area."[104] For more than a year, Roosevelt had flatly rejected French and British proposals to incorporate a French military contingent into Lord Mountbatten's command.[105] In October Churchill finally decided himself to approve a small French mission to SEAC, adding, "There is no need for me to telegraph the President."[106] Hearing about this soon after, Roosevelt may have been inclined to accept State Department and OSS reports that Britain, France, and the Netherlands were now in active collusion to retrieve their Asian colonies.[107] Again he chose not to confront Churchill on the issue, instead simply restating to a number of American officials his refusal to recognize French involvement.[108] The U.S. Office of War Information (OWI) was instructed to report nothing about the new French presence at Mountbatten's headquarters.

During these same months, the American commitment to the whole idea of international trusteeships was being gutted. When the Dumbarton Oaks conference on postwar world organization convened in August 1944, the

103. Thorne, "Indochina," 91. La Feber, "Roosevelt, Churchill, and Indochina," 1288–89.

104. USNA, OSS Research and Analysis Washington, report no. 2439 (9 Aug. 1944).

105. Sbrega, "'First catch your hare,'" 69–70. Thorne, "Indochina," 90. Patti, *Why Viet Nam?* 20–21.

106. La Feber, "Roosevelt, Churchill, and Indochina," 1291.

107. *Viet-Nam Crisis*, ed. Cameron, 15–17. Thorne, "Indochina," 75. Thorne, *Allies*, 604. Thorne maintains that no such collusion existed in fact.

108. Hull, *Memoirs*, 2:1597–98. Thorne, "Indochina," 79–80. La Feber, "Roosevelt, Churchill, and Indochina," 1291–95. *Viet-Nam Crisis*, ed. Cameron, 14–15, 17–19. Patti, *Why Viet Nam?* 20, 22.

U.S. proposal on colonies made no mention of ultimate independence for Europe's colonies. The State Department was increasingly fearful that the Soviet Union would take advantage of postwar turmoil in Asia, while the Joint Chiefs of Staff wanted to secure a string of military bases in Japan's former mandated Pacific territories for the United States.[109] When the trusteeship issue was raised at Yalta in February 1945, Churchill exploded, saying that he would never consent to "forty or fifty nations thrusting interfering fingers into the life's existence of the British Empire." After a brief adjournment, Alger Hiss, aide to Roosevelt, offered language that left it to each colonial power to decide whether to place territory under trusteeship or not.[110] With that quick amendment, Roosevelt's ambition to reshape Asia by means of trusteeships was dead.

Nonetheless, Roosevelt still refused to apply the Yalta language about voluntary trusteeship to Indochina. Stein Tønnesson has uncovered evidence that Roosevelt intended to dislodge the Japanese from Indochina by force of arms, thence being able to invoke the alternative trusteeship category of "territories detached from the enemy." In October 1944, the president requested U.S. military planners to investigate whether Indochina might be used as a substitute for the Burma supply route to China. Although the Joint Planning Staff obediently drafted a plan to mount amphibious invasions of first Hainan Island and then Tonkin in March 1945, it also offered numerous reasons why such an allocation of resources would be wasteful in the extreme, forcing six months' delay in the attack on Okinawa, hence probably postponing the invasion of Japan's home islands by a similar period. In January, a more modest version of the plan was circulated to American theater commanders, involving capture of Hainan alone before the summer monsoon season, but it too was shelved. Meanwhile, carrier air attacks on Indochina and Hainan in January had the effect of convincing some Japanese analysts that landings were imminent. Indeed, it is possible that Roosevelt viewed these air assaults, together with various covert deception efforts under way, as a device to trigger Japanese elimination of the French in Indochina. In any event, had Roosevelt lived, he would have continued to look for a way, perhaps in the autumn of 1945, to commit Chinese or American troops to Indochina.[111]

109. Louis, *Imperialism at Bay*, 351–80. La Feber, "Roosevelt, Churchill, and Indochina," 1289.

110. Louis, *Imperialism at Bay*, 459. Language defining three categories of future trusteeship had been put forward at Dumbarton Oaks but not discussed.

111. Tønnesson, *Vietnamese Revolution*, 187–99, 213–14, 260, 273–74, 300–301.

With his typical preference for keeping options open, however, President Roosevelt did not rule out some future understanding with Paris over Indochina. In mid March, he told a State Department official that he would agree to France assuming for herself the obligations of a trustee providing that independence was affirmed as the ultimate goal.[112] General de Gaulle soon made it clear he had no intention of accepting the trusteeship principle or promising independence. Just before Roosevelt's death on 12 April, a draft policy paper emanating from the Far Eastern Division of the State Department suggested that it was impolitic to try to impose conditions on the French that were not being demanded of the British or the Dutch. Beyond that, "a disgruntled, psychologically sick and sovereign-conscious France will not augur well for post-war collaboration in Europe and in the world as a whole."[113] Meanwhile, growing fears of postwar Soviet hegemony in Asia had altered the equation inside the OSS, leading General William Donovan to forward a report to the president arguing that the United States "should realize also its interest in the maintenance of the British, French and Dutch colonial empires."[114] Within two weeks of Roosevelt's death, the European office of the State Department had persuaded the new president, Harry Truman, to accept de Gaulle's terms, with a vague rider about colonial reforms. At the San Francisco Conference in May, when Foreign Minister Georges Bidault poured out French resentment toward American policy, Secretary of State Edward Stettinius and his assistant, James Dunn, went out of their way to placate him, claiming rather disingenuously that "no official policy statement of this Government . . . has ever questioned even by implication French sovereignty over Indo-China." Inside the State Department, Dunn pushed successfully for a moratorium on Indochina discussions with Paris, arguing that France was a "badly beaten and humiliated country" with a special sensitivity about that Asian colony.[115]

112. *FRUS, 1945*, vol. 1 (Washington, D.C., 1967), 124. *Vietnam*, ed. Porter, 22–23. *Viet-Nam Crisis*, ed. Cameron, 32–33.

113. *Vietnam*, ed. Porter, 23–27.

114. OSS memorandum, 2 Apr. 1945, quoted in Richard Aldrich, "Imperial Rivalry: British and American Intelligence in Asia, 1942–46," *Intelligence and National Security* (London) 3, no. 1 (Jan. 1988): 45–46.

115. George C. Herring, "The Truman Administration and the Restoration of French Sovereignty in Indochina," *Diplomatic History* (Wilmington, Del.) 1, no. 2 (Spring 1977): 100–105. *Vietnam*, ed. Porter, 40–46, contains a revealing exchange on 20–21 April between the European and Far Eastern divisions of the State Department.

Theater-Level Concerns

For the first two years of the Pacific War, U.S. theater commanders and staff officers in China and India had no reason to pay much heed to Indochina. Stopping the Japanese from penetrating India, building up Chinese capacity to fight, and establishing a long-range bomber force occupied most of their attention. It was of course useful to know which food and raw materials the Japanese secured from Indochina, how the port and transportation system functioned, and where enemy bases were positioned—for which purposes routine photoreconnaissance flights were scheduled and men assigned to cull reports received from various clandestine sources. As the war progressed, both American and British intelligence services scoured the world for individuals with local expertise. Not surprisingly, these often turned out to be businessmen and colonial officials who had been active in the region before 1941. Such recruitments heightened the degree of intra-Allied rivalry, as such men could not help but concern themselves with the shape of postwar Asia in general or Indochina in particular.[116]

In May 1943, Navy Captain Milton Miles, the senior American intelligence officer in China, stopped in Algiers to discuss Indochina with the Free French. He obtained General Giraud's cooperation in establishing an espionage network, to be headed by Robert Meynier, the young French naval commander mentioned previously, whose wife came from a prominent Vietnamese mandarin family.[117] By the end of the year, Meynier had pieced together a string of informants inside Indochinese government bureaus, who proffered information on bombing targets, Japanese troop movements, field fortifications, and local political developments. Meanwhile, Captain Miles also sponsored special training in the United States for a group of eighteen American and two French military personnel, who would be parachuted into the central highlands of Annam to create a large force of tribal guerrillas. By mid 1944, however, Meynier had been short-circuited and stigmatized by French officers loyal to General de Gaulle, while the highland team was disbanded before ever leaving the United States.[118]

Fortunately another espionage network was proving its value by this time. Known as "GBT," after the last names of its three leaders, Laurence

116. Aldrich, "Imperial Rivalry," 9–10.
117. R. Harris Smith, *OSS: The Secret History of America's First Central Intelligence Agency* (Berkeley and Los Angeles, 1972), 322–23. Several French and British agents are said to have died aiding Mme Meynier, daughter of Hoang Trong Phu, to escape from a German prison camp to participate in these operations.
118. Spector, *United States Army in Vietnam*, 24–27.

Gordon, Harry Bernard, and Frank Tan, this group remained outside either Vichy or Free French control, yet somehow managed to achieve remarkable access to the Indochinese administrative and business establishment.[119] Formed originally to try to protect certain Western commercial interests in wartime, GBT subsequently accepted British secret service sponsorship and linked up with one or more Chinese intelligence agencies. Cross-border black-marketeering helped to finance espionage efforts. GBT's grid of informants, couriers, and clandestine radio posts was coordinated from a headquarters just across the border in Kwangsi. Japanese signal intercept teams knew of these radio communications, but were unable to catch the local perpetrators.[120] As Allied air operations over Indochina expanded in 1944, GBT received stronger radio transmitters and additional money from the U.S. Fourteenth Air Force. The OSS also contributed resources, then made a bid to take over GBT entirely. Amid this flurry of attention, GBT moved well beyond the collection of military intelligence to evaluation of political attitudes and the encouragement of an armed anti-Japanese underground.[121] By the end of 1944, GBT was working with an astonishing range of Chinese, British, French, and U.S. intelligence services, while simultaneously developing contacts among Vietnamese groups on both sides of the frontier.[122]

American aircraft stationed in southern China first bombed targets in Indochina in August 1942, then stepped up the pace from September 1943 on. Haiphong harbor was targeted repeatedly, until by late 1944, Japanese ships appeared to be avoiding it entirely. Other attack priorities included coastal shipping, the rail system, and selected production sites. Phosphate mines near Lao Cai and tin mines in Cao Bang were hit from late 1943 on.[123] Distilleries in Nam Dinh and Thanh Hoa were heavily damaged in Feb-

---

119. Laurence Gordon, a Canadian citizen, had been director of operations for the Texaco oil company in Haiphong before the war. Harry Bernard was a British tobacco merchant. Frank Tan was a young Sino-American entrepreneur. Another key participant was a French priest who was apparently able to tap the wealth of the Catholic mission in Indochina.

120. Undated (but probably late 1943) *renseignements* in AOM, INF, GF 67.

121. Spector, *United States Army in Vietnam*, 27. Patti, *Why Viet Nam?* 43–45. Tønnesson, *Vietnamese Revolution*, 197.

122. Charbonneau and Maigre, *Les Parias*, 35–36. A recent publication connects GBT with the Freemasons, which if true, might help to account for the surprisingly multi-ethnic composition of this clandestine network. Gilbert David, *Chroniques secrètes d'Indochine (1928–1946)*, vol. 1 (Paris, 1994), 75–262.

123. USNA, OSS reports 103144 (15 Oct. 1944), 2594 (1 Jan. 1945), and 12033 (14 May 1945). U.S. Opintel reports, Indochina: 26 Nov. 1944 (fuel supplies); 15 Dec. 1944 (railroads); 22 Dec. 1944 (phosphate); 20 Jan. 1945 (industries).

ruary–March 1944, reducing the availability of butanol for Japanese aircraft and alcohol for motor vehicles. Heavy bombing of the Nam Dinh
textile mill in April–May forced workers to disperse to nearby villages,
where some were reported still to be weaving on hand looms.[124] In May,
the Fourteenth Air Force also began to send B-24 Liberators on night
missions as far south as Saigon, aiming at the docks and rail yards, but
sometimes hitting residential areas instead.[125] An attack on 16 May killed
213 Vietnamese civilians and injured 843.[126] On 7 February 1945, B-29
Superfortresses from Calcutta, flying in low cloud cover and dropping
bombs by radar, mistakenly hit a Saigon hospital and a French military
barracks.[127] Thirty Europeans and about 150 Vietnamese were killed, many
hundreds more injured; as one French report commented bitterly, "There
was not a single Japanese victim."[128]

Until the Japanese coup, Gaullist agents inside Indochina sent quantities
of target information via the British Force 136 network[129] to French military missions in India and China, which in turn routed portions to American intelligence.[130] Not surprisingly, French missions were less keen to
provide data on French-owned factories, mines, power stations, or warehouses than on Japanese targets. Radio reports detailing Japanese ship
movements along the Indochina coast proved especially valuable, climaxing

124. USNA, OSS reports 2594 (1 Jan. 1945).

125. USNA, Joint Intelligence Collection Agency (New Delhi) report of 16 Feb.
1945 (OSS document 118215) contains a detailed target map of Saigon, based
mostly on information obtained in April–June 1944.

126. Jacques Le Bourgeois, *Ici Radio Saigon, 1939–1945* (Paris, 1985),
230–33.

127. Peter M. Dunn, "An Interpretation of Documentation and Oral Primary Source Materials for the Period September 1945 until May 1946 in the
Region of Cochinchina and Southern Annam" (Ph.D. diss., [University of
London] School of Oriental and African Studies, 1980), ch. 2, 21–22; and ch. 5,
34–35.

128. Michel Desiré, *La Campagne d'Indochine (1945–1954): Bibliographie,* vol.
1 (Vincennes, 1971), 10. AOM, INF, c. 123, d. 1108, reports of 24 Feb. and 1 Mar.
1945.

129. Force 136 was the code name used from March 1944 on for the branch of
the British Special Operations Executive (SOE) functioning east of Suez. Before that
it was designated "India Mission." Until October 1943, it was supposed to take
orders on operational matters from India Command, and for the remainder of the
war from South East Asia Command. However, Force 136 and SOE headquarters
in London sometimes kept military commanders ignorant of activities laden with
political implications. Charles Cruikshank, *SOE in the Far East* (Oxford, 1983), 21,
83–84, 88. Aldrich, "Imperial Rivalry," 32.

130. USNA, Joint Intelligence Collection Agency (New Delhi) report of 12 June
1945 (OSS document 114748). Charbonneau and Maigre, *Les Parias,* 41–42.

in attacks by U.S. carrier aircraft in January 1945 that sank twenty-four vessels and damaged thirteen others. Much shipping information came from an unnamed French official with access to local agents from Saigon to as far north as Qui Nhon.[131] A French civilian ship pilot on the Saigon River of leftist political inclination funneled such information to Allied contacts until at least March and continued to work for the Japanese until August without detection.[132] Others were not so lucky, being arrested and brutally interrogated by the Kenpeitai.

By July 1945, American aircraft roamed Indochina at will, bombing and strafing trains, small postal and passenger boats, government buildings, and storage facilities of any description. For example, an attack on the steam launch *Nam Hai* in Nam Dinh province on 4 July left two killed, five missing, and twenty-seven hospitalized, with two dying en route. Several days later, a dredge was sunk in Haiphong harbor and a floating dock badly damaged.[133] Ships formerly anchored at Saigon or Cap Saint-Jacques (Vung Tau) were now hidden upriver in the Mekong Delta to try to escape destruction.[134] Vietnamese-language leaflets dropped by Allied aircraft warned people to stay clear of all rail lines, bridges, and boats or ferries. Nor should anyone assist the Japanese to repair bombed facilities: "Our airplanes will come again, and if you are near the target you will probably be killed by association."[135]

With both China Theater and South East Asia Command interested in Indochina, it was inevitable that a jurisdictional dispute would arise at some point. In October 1943, Chiang Kai-shek and Mountbatten had reached an informal "gentlemen's agreement" whereby both theaters could conduct operations in Indochina (and Thailand) until further notice, providing each kept the other informed and everyone acknowledged Chiang's formal

131. USNA, OSS report L54936 (19 Mar. 1945), contains eight pages of information on ship movements from this official.

132. Interview with Ho Huu Tuong, Saigon, 3 Mar. 1967. Tuong recalled the pilot as "M. Canac," perhaps slang for someone from the South Pacific (*Kanak*).

133. AOM, INF, GF 4. The Haiphong report, from R. Cassoux, port director, one of the French officials permitted by the Japanese to continue working, was received by Vietnamese functionaries in Hanoi.

134. AOM, INF, GF 36, report from members of the former Colonial Economic Bureau to the Provisional Revolutionary Government of Vietnam, 29 Aug. 1945.

135. AOM, INF, GF 66 contains two leaflets dropped over Hung Yen province on 20 July 1945, one in Vietnamese, the other in Japanese. Not all messages were threatening. Thus, a set of U.S. Air Force leaflets in Vietnamese and French, apparently dropped in September 1944, featured photographs of liberated Paris and long quotations from the excited reports of American war correspondents. My appreciation to Allison Thomas for making available copies of these leaflets.

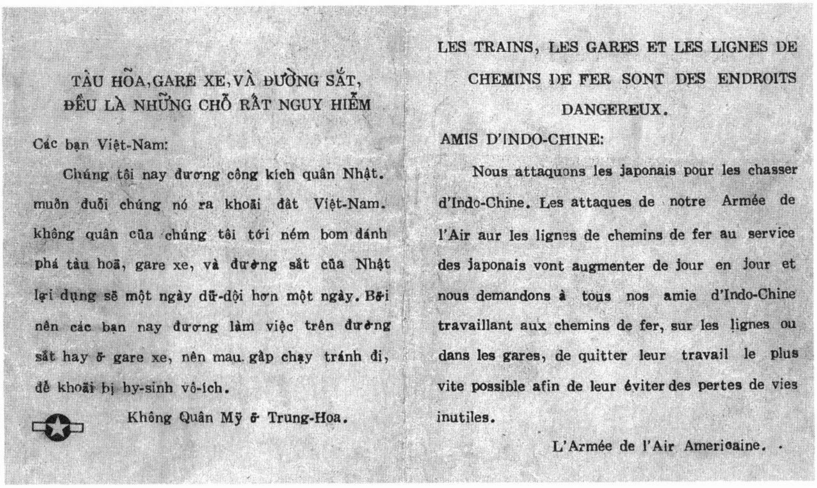

TÀU HỎA, GARE XE, VÀ ĐƯỜNG SẮT, ĐỀU LÀ NHỮNG CHỖ RẤT NGUY HIỂM

Các bạn Việt-Nam:

Chúng tôi nay đương công kích quân Nhật. muốn đuổi chúng nó ra khỏi đất Việt-Nam. không quân của chúng tôi tới ném bom đánh phá tàu hỏa, gare xe, và đường sắt của Nhật lợi dụng sẽ một ngày dữ-dội hơn một ngày. Bởi nên các bạn nay đương làm việc trên đường sắt hay ở gare xe, nên mau gặp chạy tránh đi, để khỏi bị hy-sinh vô-ích.

Không Quân Mỹ & Trung-Hoa.

LES TRAINS, LES GARES ET LES LIGNES DE CHEMINS DE FER SONT DES ENDROITS DANGEREUX.

AMIS D'INDO-CHINE:

Nous attaquons les japonais pour les chasser d'Indo-Chine. Les attaques de notre Armée de l'Air sur les lignes de chemins de fer au service des Japonais vont augmenter de jour en jour et nous demandons à tous nos amis d'Indo-Chine travaillant aux chemins de fer, sur les lignes ou dans les gares, de quitter leur travail le plus vite possible afin de leur éviter des pertes de vies inutiles.

L'Armée de l'Air Americaine.

Figure 20. U.S. Army Air Force leaflet in Vietnamese and French, designed to persuade people to avoid working on railroads for the Japanese. The Vietnamese text is less than perfect, but is notable for addressing "Vietnamese friends" (Các bạn Việt-Nam), not "Annamites" or "Indochinese." Courtesy of Allison K. Thomas.

prerogatives.[136] No one seems to have bothered much about exchanging information until, in July 1944, a senior American OSS officer at SEAC discovered that the British Force 136 had secretly staged a Free French official through Kunming carrying a handwritten letter from General de Gaulle to General Eugène Mordant, the Indochina Army commander. The episode was deemed sufficiently serious by Mountbatten's American deputy, General Wedemeyer, to warrant a top-level staff conference and reports to both London and Washington.[137] The British argued disingenuously that their help to Gaullist agents parachuting into Indochina had "no ulterior political objective whatever."[138] When no solution was forthcoming from higher echelons, China Theater and SEAC continued along separate trajectories, with personal relations between American and British staff officers suffering as a result. Distrust was exacerbated by American and British competition for leadership of anti-Japanese operations inside

136. Thorne, "Indochina," 77–78. Sbrega, "'First catch your hare,'" 73–74. Dunn, First Vietnam War, 79–80. Already in August 1943, SOE and OSS heads had separately reached a similar agreement for all of Southeast Asia, but with no mention of Chiang Kai-shek. Aldrich, "Imperial Rivalry," 17.

137. Patti, Why Viet Nam? 30–31. Aldrich, "Imperial Rivalry," 29–31.

138. La Feber, "Roosevelt, Churchill, and Indochina," 1291.

Thailand, with the OSS and Force 136 building entirely separate networks and each suspecting the other of postwar designs to control that country.[139]

By October 1944, Mountbatten was eager to move from the occasional parachuting of Force 136 and Free French agents into Indochina toward "pre-operational" activities involving more than one thousand saboteurs and leaders of prospective guerrilla bands. At this point, as mentioned previously, Prime Minister Churchill did authorize attachment of a small French military group to SEAC, but a much larger Corps léger d'intervention (CLI), about 1,200 men, had to remain in training camps in North Africa pending a decision on shipping, over which the Americans held veto power. Although the U.S. Joint Chiefs of Staff now accepted the future usefulness of French troops in Indochina, they delayed authorization of transport pending President Roosevelt's agreement.[140] Meanwhile, Mountbatten proceeded to expand slowly the number of Force 136 missions, apparently relying on French personnel recruited in the métropole.[141] American military planners saw utility in the Free French developing a clandestine working relationship with the Decoux administration in Indochina, even though this heightened the danger of a Japanese riposte.[142] In early January 1945, pressed repeatedly from various angles, Roosevelt acknowledged to the British ambassador that if members of his government thought it important to use French nationals for sabotage work, they should go ahead and ask no questions. Nonetheless, through the Joint Chiefs of Staff, Roosevelt continued to block movement of the CLI from North Africa to SEAC.[143] At Yalta, Roosevelt told Stalin that de Gaulle had promised troops whenever he, Roosevelt, found the ships. So far, the president added, perhaps with a twinkle in his eye, there were no ships.[144]

General Wedemeyer, who had replaced General Stilwell as China Theater chief of staff in November 1944, decided to reopen the boundary

---

139. Smith, *OSS*, 288–91, 303–8. Aldrich, "Imperial Rivalry," 20, 24–26. Aldrich advances the more general thesis that SOE and OSS operations in Asia were less important for what they accomplished in terms of political advantage than for the damage they inflicted on Anglo-American relations.

140. Sbrega, "'First catch your hare,'" 70. Gautier, *9 mars 1945*, 122–24. La Feber, "Roosevelt, Churchill, and Indochina," 1295. Drachman, *United States Policy toward Vietnam*, 61–63.

141. Patti, *Why Viet Nam?* 20.

142. U.S. Opintel report, Indochina, 22 Oct. 1944.

143. Thorne, "Indochina," 90. La Feber, "Roosevelt, Churchill, and Indochina," 1291. Dunn, *First Vietnam War*, 88–89, 93.

144. *FRUS: The Conference of Berlin*, vol. 1 (Washington, D.C., 1960), 917. *Viet-Nam Crisis*, ed. Cameron, 21–22.

question, arguing that Indochina was in his sphere of operations.[145] Face-to-face discussions with Mountbatten failed to resolve the dispute, again leaving each theater to go its own way. The danger of this approach was brought home to all concerned when two, perhaps three, Royal Air Force B-24s were reported to have inadvertently been shot down at night over northern Tonkin by Fourteenth Air Force P-61 Black Widow fighters equipped with radar.[146] In mid March 1945, Churchill wrote to Roosevelt seeking agreement to Mountbatten's demarcation interpretation; Roosevelt replied five days later with Wedemeyer's position. By May, the argument had become so personal between Wedemeyer and Mountbatten that General George Marshall, U.S. Army chief of staff, complained that it would be a pity if "good relations should be jeopardized over a dispute arising over matters of such low importance as clandestine operations in Indo-China." Finally, in late July, the U.S. and British Combined Chiefs of Staff gave each theater half of Indochina.[147]

General Marshall's comment reflected the fact that in Washington, both China Theater and SEAC were regarded as military backwaters by early 1945. Attention was riveted on the final push against Hitler and the central Pacific offensive. In Chungking and Kandy, nonetheless, there remained dragons to slay. At one level, the theater demarcation issue seemed a petty squabble between prima donna commanders, egged on by their respective staffs. At another level, both argued their need to make life difficult for the Japanese in Indochina, Mountbatten pointing out that Imperial Army units in Burma and Thailand were supplied from Saigon, Wedemeyer concerned about a flank attack as Chinese divisions marched eastward. Despite the de facto downgrading of both theaters, American production of weapons and equipment had now reached the point where agonizing logistical choices no longer needed to be made; each theater could sustain its own raison d'être

---

145. Peter Dennis, *Troubled Days of Peace: Mountbatten and South East Asia Command, 1945–46* (Manchester, 1987), 28. At the end of 1944, Wedemeyer's staff developed a counteroffensive plan (BETA), which soon came to include a diversionary attack on Tonkin, tentatively scheduled for May 1945.

146. Dunn, *First Vietnam War*, 87–88. Dunn's assertion is challenged in Anthony Short, *The Origins of the Vietnam War* (London, 1989), 58–59, based on recent correspondence with former pilots and British military historians, but no new documentary evidence. At very least, the original report (by the British military representative in Chunking) of the alleged shoot-down would have heightened inter-theater tensions.

147. Dunn, *First Vietnam War*, 95–96, 98, 103, 105–10, 117–18. *FRUS: The Conference of Berlin*, 1:921–22; 2:83–85, 1319, 1465–66. U.S. Department of Defense, *United States–Vietnam Relations*, 1:A15–A22.

and institutional momentum. SEAC thus received enough supplies to mount an offensive toward Rangoon (occupied in early May) and to make preparations for a landing on the Malayan coast in September. China Theater obtained sufficient resources for Chinese troops to regain all the territory lost the previous year and then gaze on the South China Sea by July. The U.S. Joint Chiefs made plans to secure and open the port at Fort Bayard, on the Liuchou peninsula, to be able to reduce dramatically the supply distances for Chinese forces, which currently ran from the United States to Calcutta and over the Hump to Kunming.[148]

Neither personality factors nor military considerations can explain the inordinate amount of time that Wedemeyer and Mountbatten spent arguing over Indochina, however. Both commanders must have appreciated the political stakes involved, with Mountbatten under instructions to facilitate the French return to Indochina, and Wedemeyer determined to make this as difficult as possible. Until Roosevelt's death in April, Wedemeyer had reason to be confident of his position; indeed, the president may privately have confided his intention to invade Indochina later in the year to him. After Truman took over, Washington failed to explain clearly to either Ambassador Patrick Hurley or General Wedemeyer in Chungking that American policy had tilted decisively toward the French. In May, hearing rumors, Ambassador Hurley addressed a personal message to President Truman asking bluntly whether American Lend-Lease supplies were now to be used by Lord Mountbatten to reestablish French imperialism in Indochina. The White House instructed the State Department to reply that there had been no "basic change" in policy, although it did seem unlikely that the French would accept establishment of a trusteeship in Indochina.[149] Hurley was not told of Secretary of State Stettinius's recent assurances to Foreign Minister Bidault, nor of the moratorium on further discussions with Paris about Indochina.

Probably the most revealing instructions received in Chungking were from General Marshall, who informed Wedemeyer in early June that the State Department's position eliminated "the political necessity of curtailing Lord Mountbatten's operations in Indochina," leaving such operations to be judged "strictly on their military merits and in relation to the stand of the Generalissimo."[150] For another two months at least, the "military merits" were not deemed sufficiently compelling to begin to transport

148. *FRUS: The Conference of Berlin*, 2:351.

149. *Viet-Nam Crisis*, ed. Cameron, 33–39. Patti, *Why Viet Nam?* 118–120. *Vietnam*, ed. Porter, 49–50. Herring, "Truman Administration," 106–7.

150. Ronald Spector, "Allied Intelligence and Indochina, 1943–1945," *Pacific Historical Review* (Berkeley) 51 (1982): 48.

French combat units from Europe to the Far East.[151] Meanwhile, General Wedemeyer, on behalf of Chiang Kai-shek, continued until the Potsdam decision of late July to insist that Indochina was entirely within China Theater. In these circumstances, it is not surprising that many American personnel in China Theater with operational duties involving Indochina continued to assume that the French ought not be assisted to regain their colony.

Border Operations

With the Japanese coup in early March, both Gaullist and GBT intelligence nets were smashed. Fearing possible follow-up Japanese attacks into southern Yunnan or western Kwangsi, China Theater headquarters pressured all Allied intelligence agencies to ascertain quickly what was happening inside Indochina. Although efforts commenced to reestablish links with former sources of information, it soon became apparent that conditions had changed so dramatically as to require other approaches. On 20 March, China Theater authorized the OSS to use "any and all resistance groups," a clear departure from President Roosevelt's October 1944 instructions to the OSS to "do nothing" in regard to Indochina resistance groups, whether French or native in leadership.[152] The OSS sent officers into Indochina to make contact with retreating French units, but found them suffering from fatigue and low morale, discarding equipment along the route without bothering to destroy it. Simultaneously, the OSS unit in Kunming worked out an informal understanding with Ho Chi Minh, representing the "League for the Independence of Indochina," whereby his organization—in the spirit of anti-Japanese cooperation—would provide order-of-battle information.[153] Despite this modest beginning, in less than four months an OSS team was deep inside Tonkin training and equipping one hundred league adherents for substantial sabotage missions.

Ho Chi Minh had attracted American interest since late 1942, when the American Embassy in Chungking reported his arrest in Kwangsi. For the next two years, the embassy and the consulate general in Kunming main-

151. The CLI, now renamed the Fifth Colonial Infantry Regiment, which even the British considered an unfortunate choice of terminology, had managed finally to depart Algiers for Ceylon on 13 May, arriving fifteen days later. Dunn, "Interpretation," ch. 2, 25. Dennis, *Troubled Days*, 30. In July, President Truman approved movement of further French forces "in principle," but without a date being set for release of the necessary ships. Thorne, *Allies*, 633.
152. Patti, *Why Viet Nam?* 21, 55, 57, 59, 65.
153. Ibid., 75, 80, 87, 100, 102.

tained a watching brief on "Annamite" politics in general. In mid 1943, the embassy tried without much success to fathom relations between various Chinese government organizations and Vietnam émigrés.[154] As William Langdon, consul general in Kunming, admitted to his Washington superiors in June 1944, all intelligence obtained by him was "second-hand and colored by the divergent interest in Indochina of each source," whether French, British, U.S. military (bombing targets), Chinese, or Annamite. Nonetheless, Langdon found reason to argue that the Chinese Kuomintang had bullied Annamite émigrés into forming the "Revolutionary Alliance," and he approvingly quoted a "local Annamite gentleman" who considered return to French rule the least unacceptable option.[155] Disinformation abounded, as when the American consul in Kweilin sent a detailed report from a Chinese source on the "Democratic Party of Indochina," led by Hsieh Yueh, a lawyer of Cantonese and Annamite parentage, who claimed an armed militia of two hundred thousand men in thirteen locations straddling the frontier.[156] Most American diplomatic observers assumed the inhabitants of Indochina to be incapable of governing themselves, which left a choice between French administration and United Nations trusteeship. In the shorter term, those Indochinese groups hostile to the Japanese were regarded as too divided internally to be of much practical use to the Allies.[157]

By the summer of 1944, Chang Fa-kwei's staff had granted Ho Chi Minh sufficient freedom of movement to spend time at the local bureau of the U.S. Office of War Information, where he avidly read press accounts of the war and chatted with available Americans. This sparked a serious OWI effort to secure a visa for him to travel to San Francisco, where he would broadcast the news in Vietnamese. At the State Department, the European office opposed this initiative, while the Far Eastern office favored it. Responding to criticism, OWI said that "Ho's activities will be thoroughly controlled and in essence merely mechanical."[158] The visa was not granted, probably for fear of offending the French.[159] Meanwhile, apparently un-

154. Ibid., 48. Someone in the State Department was sufficiently interested to send a cable under Secretary Hull's name requesting clarification.

155. USNA, DOS special files, Record Group 59, box 10, d. 7, Langdon to Landon, 16 June 1944. According to Langdon, his source was "regarded as anti-French by the French and a traitor by Annamite nationalists."

156. Ibid., Arthur Ringwalt to Ambassador Gauss, 5 Aug. 1944.

157. U.S. Opintel report, Indochina, 22 Oct. 1944.

158. USNA, DOS special files, Record Group 59, box 7, d. 2, messages from 7 Nov. 1944.

159. Patti, *Why Viet Nam?* 50–51. There was the technical complication of what passport Ho Chi Minh would have his visa stamped in, Chinese or French, neither

known to his American contacts, Ho had left for the Indochina border in late August.

After Ho Chi Minh's departure, a group of Viet Minh activists in Kunming continued to cultivate available OWI and OSS officers, even to the point of securing their assistance in drafting a letter to the American ambassador pleading for an opportunity to fight alongside the Allies and seeking U.S. assistance in their struggle for independence.[160] Nonetheless, William Powell, the OWI air liaison in Kunming, and one of the friendly consultants to the group, judged in his own official report that the Indochinese were not ready for "complete independence," probably requiring "quite a bit of tutelage before they can completely run their country themselves in a responsible a manner as a modern post-war government must be run." Without saying so directly, Powell apparently favored American tutelage, since the French would merely "return to their former policy of 'deceptive liberalism' . . . and stifle any attempts of the Indo-Chinese for self-government," while the Chinese had "definite territorial designs upon at least a portion of Indo-China (Tonkin), and entertain dreams of at least exercising the dominate [*sic*] foreign influence throughout the entire country." Powell also quoted at length from a June 1944 analysis by an unnamed Annamite, quite possibly Ho Chi Minh, who predicted that the Japanese would move to take over Indochina completely, that the French would resist only weakly, and that a puppet Annamite government would be established, perhaps headed by Bao Dai. After the war, this local source continued, the Annamites possessed sufficient personnel for government, but they would need Western support and protection—preferably from the United States, or, if this were not feasible, "some kind of commonwealth" with France.[161]

In early September 1944, Consul General Langdon agreed to meet a delegation from the "League for the Independence of Indochina," the usual

---

of whom were likely to agree. One cannot help but wonder how Vietnam's history might have been altered if Ho Chi Minh had gone to San Francisco on an American laissez-passer.

160. Ibid., 53. USNA, OSS record 110208, American Embassy, Chungking, to secretary of state, 9 Sept. 1944, contains a description of this letter without any mention of American help in drafting it. Perhaps the most sympathetic American was OSS Major Austin Glass, former director of the Haiphong office of the Standard Oil Company of New York. A thirty-year resident of Indochina, Glass was fluent in Vietnamese and had a Vietnamese wife. He was transferred to Washington in late 1944, where he briefed Patti extensively before the latter's posting to Kunming in early April 1945.

161. USNA, OSS record 110308, American Embassy, Chungking, to secretary of state, 9 Sept. 1944.

English designation for the Viet Minh. Langdon certainly was not encouraging. Although acknowledging general U.S. interest in the "political
welfare and advancement of oppressed peoples in the Orient," he told them
bluntly that the Annamite people were "citizens of France," and that it
would not make any sense if "America with one hand at great expenditures
of life and treasure rescued and delivered France from German slavery and
with the other hand undermined her Empire." When the delegation's head,
Pham Viet Tu, tried to back away from the French issue and concentrate
on the need for arms to fight the Japanese, Langdon interrupted to say that
that was a military matter, which the league must take up with the Allied
military authorities.[162] Henceforth the league did indeed concentrate on the
U.S. military and the OSS, but without much success. A December OSS
report from Kunming endorsed the opinion of recently interviewed French
sources that the league lacked any popular support; rather, it was "largely
a facade, composed of a relatively small number of Indo-Chinese intellectuals and other dissatisfied elements in the colony."[163] In February 1945,
Ho Chi Minh recrossed the border and made his way again to Kunming,
seeking to meet General Chennault, partly on the basis of recent Viet Minh
rescue and safe delivery of a downed American pilot. His request was
politely rejected.[164]

Immediately following the Japanese coup, however, Fourteenth Air
Force targeting specialists, the OSS, and the Air Ground Aid Section
(AGAS), responsible for rescuing downed pilots, shared an urgent need to
obtain reliable information from any source, whatever their postwar political aspirations. Charles Fenn, an OSS officer assigned to work with the
GBT group, heard from AGAS about "an old Annamite" who had not only
helped a downed pilot to escape but was connected with a "large political
group." This man could occasionally be found at the OWI bureau, where
he "read everything from *Time* magazine to the *Encyclopaedia Ameri-
cana*."[165] On 19 March, in characteristically colorful language, Ho Chi
Minh affirmed to his American acquaintances that "the French imperialist
wolf [is] finally devoured by the Japanese fascist hyena," then switched

162. Patti, *Why Viet Nam?* 53–54. We know about "Pham Viet Tu" from
Western sources only. He probably needs to be linked to another name in Vietnamese sources.
163. USNA, OSS record 110965, Research and Analysis, Kunming report 0016,
15 Dec. 1944.
164. Charles Fenn, *Ho Chi Minh: A Biographical Introduction* (New York,
1973), 73–75.
165. Ibid., 75–76.

metaphors to argue that Indochina represented the neck of the enemy snake extending all the way from Tokyo to New Guinea, which therefore needed to be attacked by the Allies to prevent any strategic withdrawal.[166] After three meetings with Ho, a check of the files on the league, and consultations with GBT members, Fenn requested and received permission from AGAS Chungking to establish a radio network centered on league headquarters inside Tonkin. On 29 March, Fenn and Harry Bernard escorted Ho to meet General Chennault, who was pleased that Ho knew in detail about the Flying Tigers and readily assented to Ho's request for an autographed photo. A few days later, just before being flown to Chinghsi with a Chinese radio operator, Ho asked Fenn for six new Colt .45 automatic pistols in their original wrappings, which Fenn obtained from OSS stores. Subsequently, Ho displayed the photograph as proof of Allied endorsement and distributed the pistols to selected subordinates as symbols of authority.[167] Fenn confidently placed "Ho Tchih Ming" (nickname Old Man Ho, code name Lucius) on a list of fifty-three agents working for him.[168]

In mid April, the head of the OSS Secret Intelligence (SI) branch in China, Colonel Paul Helliwell, authorized his newly arrived deputy for Indochina, Captain Archimedes Patti, to investigate establishment of an Independence League–based intelligence network that would go well beyond AGAS pilot rescue preoccupations. Patti managed to catch up with Ho Chi Minh near Chinghsi before the latter started the difficult walk back to Pac Bo, and, after a long evening discussion arranged by a Chinese communist intermediary, emerged deeply impressed by Ho's eloquence, sincerity, and refusal to exaggerate his group's capabilities. Unlike the leaders of underground groups with whom Patti had dealt in Europe, Ho did not ask for money in return for information or pretend to lack firearms as a device to obtain large OSS stocks for postwar domestic action.[169]

166. Based on Tønnesson, *Vietnamese Revolution*, 238, 337, who managed to locate this 19 Mar. 1945 document in the USNA.

167. Fenn, *Ho Chi Minh*, 76–79, 81. Ho Chi Minh also arranged through AGAS for his comrades in Kunming to secure and send a set of large Allied flags, to be displayed in camp on appropriate occasions. *Viet Nam Social Sciences* (Hanoi) (1/2-1986): 217.

168. List kindly provided by Charles Fenn in September 1993. Employing a questionnaire containing thirty-five items, Fenn also endeavored to obtain detailed information from Ho Chi Minh and others on Japanese, French, and Vietnamese activities and attitudes. Item no. 15, for example, asks for "Details of Jap or collaborationist participation in gambling, drinking, whoring, other vice."

169. Patti, *Why Viet Nam?* 61–63, 67–71, 82–88. According to French sources, the Viet Minh did subsequently receive at least a million Chinese dollars (U.S. $500) a month from the OSS. AOM, INF, c. 134, d. 1229, "Agissements americains contre

By the end of April, Frank Tan was at Pac Bo, representing AGAS, yet apparently sending regular intelligence reports to OSS Kunming as well. Several Viet Minh members were accepted by GBT or AGAS for radio training.[170] In May, Tan and his radio operator, Mac Shin, joined Ho Chi Minh on the difficult trek from Pac Bo to Tan Trao (Kim Lung), accompanied by a forty-four-man armed escort and about twenty-five porter loads of Sten guns, Thompson submachine guns, carbines, ammunition, medicines, and communications gear acquired from different Allied intelligence organizations. Ho Chi Minh took Tan under his wing like an adopted son, and Tan reciprocated with trust and affection.[171] Laurence Gordon, returning to Kunming after months in Washington trying to ward off OSS control of GBT operations, insisted that Tan be withdrawn, but this did not happen until after the Japanese surrender in August. Meanwhile, by late May AGAS had parachuted in one of its own men, Lieutenant Dan Phelan, who sent back glowing reports of the Viet Minh. A further parachute drop of radio sets, medicines, and weapons caused a sensation among Vietnamese at Tan Trao. Viet Minh work teams carved a small airstrip out of the jungle to accommodate L-5 observer craft.[172]

On 13 May, the head of OSS China, Colonel Richard Heppner, convened a meeting in Kunming to discuss future guerrilla and sabotage missions in conjunction with Chinese units advancing toward the South China Sea. It was agreed to approach General Gabriel Sabattier in Chungking with a proposal to incorporate some French troops into American-directed operations. Simultaneously, Captain Patti was permitted to expand contacts with the Vietnamese communists, providing he operated quietly and "stayed out of politics." Although the U.S. "Dixie Mission" to Mao Tse-tung's headquarters in Yenan offered an obvious precedent, Heppner was acutely aware of the complications that had arisen on that front with Ambassador Hurley and the State Department. Somehow Patti was also expected to screen his

---

le rétablissement de la souveraineté français en Indochine," n.d., but probably early October 1945.

170. *Viet Nam Social Sciences* (Hanoi) (1/2-1986): 216–17. By this time the Vietnamese at Pac Bo must have been aware that AGAS hardly limited itself to pilot rescue but served as cover for OSS operations as well.

171. Ho Chi Minh, "How We Travel," six-page undated typescript in the possession of Frank Tan. Phone interview with Frank Tan, 29 June 1994. Later, Ho gave Tan a solid gold bracelet for his mother and some tiger bone elixir to alleviate her problems connected with old age.

172. Fenn, *Ho Chi Minh*, 80–82. See also Robert Shaplen, *The Lost Revolution: Vietnam, 1945–1965* (London, 1966), 18–29.

relations with Ho Chi Minh from the French and from General Tai Li's espionage network.[173] On 18 May, perhaps frustrated at being finessed by the OSS, Consul General Langdon bluntly queried the State Department: "Could I . . . be informed as to what our policy toward Indochina now is? Whether the late President froze it into mañana status or whether the living are doing something about it?"[174]

It is worth asking why the OSS did not link up as well with Vietnam Nationalist Party and Revolutionary League adherents. Although the sources are not especially helpful, it seems the OSS in South China considered these groups mere auxiliaries of Chinese units, with few connections inside Indochina. Then, too, previous negative experiences with Tai Li's organization, and the assumption that such Vietnamese groups would be deeply infiltrated, may have given OSS officers practical reasons to shy away. Tai Li's earlier obstruction of U.S. efforts in Thailand, causing considerable delay and loss of life, probably lingered in their minds.[175] Finally, the State Department may not have shared with the OSS its information on the Nationalist Party and the Revolutionary League, particularly material available from consular officials in southern China.

Moving to recruit French participants, the OSS discovered that no clear chain of command existed between colonial army remnants in South China and the government in Paris. More seriously, General Wedemeyer's insistence that all operations involving Indochina come under China Theater jurisdiction proved unacceptable to the new representative in China of the clandestine Direction général des études et recherches (DGER), Major Jean Sainteny, who had the backing of General de Gaulle.[176] Then, too, when Captain Patti interviewed French evacuees for possible intelligence missions, he found them out of touch with reality, anxious to restore prewar controls, contemptuous of Annamite political capabilities, and suspicious of American intentions.[177] Other OSS officers found working with the French less onerous. In early June, a joint coast-watch and naval mission in the vicinity of the Hainan Straits enjoyed initial success. In late July, OSS Captain Lucien Conein led a Franco-Vietnamese unit to destroy Japanese installations in the Lang Son area, bringing back two prisoners and a

173. Patti, *Why Viet Nam?* 96–101.
174. As quoted in Gardner, *Approaching Vietnam*, 60.
175. Smith, *OSS*, 298–305.
176. Sabattier, *Le Destin de l'Indochine*, 227–30, 257–67. Sabattier identifies Sainteny as chief of the DGER in China. Other sources identify him as chief of Mission 5 (M.5) in Kunming. These were identical positions.
177. Patti, *Why Viet Nam?* 88–95.

quantity of documents.[178] However, a more ambitious operation along the South China Sea coast was delayed by OSS reservations about the degree of American control.[179]

In late May, Major Allison Thomas led a small OSS "Special Operations" team to camps at Poseh and Chinghsi to prepare for sabotage missions against the Hanoi–Lang Son road and railroad. Initially, Thomas was given two Chinese border patrol companies from General Chang Fa-kwei, then presented with one hundred French and Annamite colonial troops as well. In early June, the Chinese units were reassigned, while training of the French and Annamites was delayed by a dispute over pay and rations. Meanwhile, Thomas was receiving unsettling intelligence reports that he might well be shot at by the natives or denied food if accompanied by French troops. From Kunming, Patti offered him the option of setting aside the French entirely in favor of Ho Chi Minh's adherents. Deciding to learn more at firsthand, Thomas parachuted into Ho's new headquarters near Kim Lung (Tan Trao) village, twenty-seven kilometers east of Tuyen Quang town, on 16 July, actually dropping straight into the main banyan tree of the village, with the rest of his team landing further down the valley. Besides two OSS enlisted men, Thomas brought Lieutenant Montfort, a French officer in American uniform, as well as a *métis* sergeant named Logos and an Annamite sergeant named Phac.[180]

Thomas was greeted at the drop zone by Lieutenant Phelan, Frank Tan, and a contingent of well-armed Vietnamese. Once the six-person OSS "Deer Team" had consolidated under the banyan tree, it formally proceeded to meet the main Viet Minh unit, which was drawn up in formation nearby, then trekked several kilometers to a camouflaged campsite. On arrival, the team was escorted through an archway proclaiming "Welcome to Our American Friends," greeted by an ill Ho Chi Minh, assigned newly constructed bamboo shelters, and given a supper of freshly slaughtered beef, rice, bamboo shoots, and captured beer. Next morning, after identifying Montfort as an officer who had previously served at Cao Bang, Ho told Thomas bluntly that no French personnel were welcome.[181] The *métis*

178. Ibid., 104–7, 113. Conein later joined the CIA, serving as liaison with the Republic of Vietnam generals who overthrew and killed Ngo Dinh Diem in 1963.

179. Ibid., 112–15.

180. Major Allison K. Thomas, "Report on Deer Mission," 17 Sept. 1945, reproduced in U.S. Congress, Senate Committee on Foreign Relations, *Causes, Origins and Lessons*, 251–56. Personal correspondence with Allison Thomas, 26 Apr., 5 June, and 12 Aug. 1991. Patti, *Why Viet Nam?* 124–27.

181. According to a French source, Phelan warned Montfort not to speak French, but some Viet Minh members recognized him anyway. *DGI*, 71–72.

and Vietnamese NCOs might stay, although Ho preferred otherwise. Deeply impressed by what he had seen and heard, Thomas immediately prepared a recommendation to his superiors to parachute more OSS men and equipment to begin training the Viet Minh, to "Forget the Communist Bogy," and to "eliminate all French and Annamese" at the Poseh border camp.[182] Montfort and his two NCOs joined the group of twenty French refugees from Tam Dao for the long trek to China. Additional OSS members parachuted in on 29 July, including a male nurse, who quickly diagnosed Ho Chi Minh as suffering from a serious combination of malaria, dysentery, and other tropical complications, for which he injected him with quinine and sulfa drugs.[183]

The OSS arrival at Ho Chi Minh's headquarters, and OSS members being escorted around the nearby countryside, considerably enhanced the prestige of the Viet Minh. Members of the Tay ethnic group in the area considered that Ho Chi Minh had "worked a miracle" when he told them to go to a particular clearing and wait for men to "fall from the sky."[184] Vietnamese leaders arriving from the lowlands were fascinated by the silk parachutes hung around the camp, the mannerisms of the strange Americans, the GI candy they offered to guests.[185] Whatever the American disclaimers of political involvement, the United States was seen by all Vietnamese coming and going as actively training, equipping, and morally supporting both anticolonial and anti-Japanese causes. For the first two weeks, Major Thomas spent most of his time on reconnaissance treks in four different directions, accompanied by Viet Minh interpreters and guides. At each hamlet he was greeted with fruit, eggs, speeches, and songs, although the people were obviously impoverished and their clothing in "terrible condition." Back at headquarters on 1 August, the entire Deer Team attended a ceremonial opening of the communal assembly hall, complete with Viet Minh

182. "Deer Report #1," 17 July 1945, in U.S. Congress, Senate Committee on Foreign Relations, *Causes, Origins and Lessons*, 244–46. The OSS had not briefed Thomas about either the Viet Minh or Ho Chi Minh, whom he initially refers to as "Mr Hoe" and then in September as "Mr C. M. Hoo."

183. Smith, *OSS*, 332, and photo on p. 323, which bears a caption claiming that the American medic "saved Ho's life." By contrast, most Hanoi publications ignore this medical assistance, sometimes ascribing Ho's recovery to traditional herbal remedies. Much later, Major Thomas commented, "He [Ho Chi Minh] was very sick, but I'm not sure he would have died without us." Quoted in William Broyles, Jr., *Brothers in Arms: A Journey from War to Peace* (New York, 1986), 104.

184. Broyles, *Brothers*, 108.

185. Tran Huy Lieu, "Di du Quoc Dan Dai Hoi o Tan Trao" [Attending the National People's Assembly at Tan Trao], *Nghien Cuu Lich Su* (Hanoi), no. 17 (8-1960): 40.

Figure 21. The OSS Deer Team with Ho Chi Minh and other Viet Minh associates. Standing from left: Phan Dinh Huy (Hong Viet), René Defourneaux, Ho, Allison Thomas, Vo Nguyen Giap, Henry Prunier, Dam Quang Trung, Nguyen Quy, and Paul Hoagland. Kneeling from left: Lawrence Vogt, Allan Squires, and Thai Bach (Thai Ba Chi). This photo was taken at a reunion in Hanoi in September 1945, just prior to the OSS team's return to China. Courtesy of Allison K. Thomas.

songs, skits, speeches on independence and women's rights, and drinks of hot water flavored with anise.[186] With his sure propaganda touch, Ho Chi Minh officially dubbed the contingent about to begin training with Deer Team the "Vietnamese-American Force" (Bo Doi Viet My).[187]

Whenever there was a spare moment, Ho Chi Minh chatted with the Americans, endeavoring to understand more clearly what was happening outside Indochina, to assess the prospects of U.S.–Vietnamese cooperation extending beyond defeat of the Japanese, and of course to influence their radio reports favorably. Lieutenant Phelan, who in May had been reluctant to undertake this particular mission, because he had heard Ho was a communist, was soon sending rapturous accounts of his reception and

186. Personal diary of Major Allison Thomas, who kindly made a subsequent typed copy available to me.

187. Ngoc An, "Bo Doi Viet-My," *Tap Chi Lich Su Quan Su* (Hanoi), no. 10 (Oct. 1986): 19. Dam Quang Trung was made commander of this unit, and Major Thomas is identified as chief of staff.

asserting that the Viet Minh were "not anti-French merely patriots de-ser[ving] full trust and support."[188] Henry Prunier, who had studied at the army Vietnamese-language school (then located on the Berkeley campus of the University in California), was struck by how often Ho wanted to talk about the United States—its history, political ideals, and official support for "free, popular governments all over the world."[189] René Defourneaux, a French-American from New York, later recalled Ho arguing in slightly fractured English:

> Your statesmen make eloquent speeches about helping those with self-determination. We are self-determined. Why not help us? Am I any different from [Indian nationalist Jawaharlal] Nehru, [Philippine leader Manuel] Quezon, even your George Washington? Was not Washington considered a revolutionary? I, too, want to set my people free.[190]

Major Thomas was becoming uncertain about Ho's noncommunist status, but on broaching the question gingerly with him was told, "We are all united now, we will discuss politics later."[191]

None of the Americans talking with Ho Chi Minh appear to have wondered why he called his organization the "League for the Independence of *Indochina*" in English, while calling it the "*Viet Nam* Doc Lap Dong Minh" in Vietnamese. Perhaps they assumed that Ho was simply taking account of foreign unfamiliarity with the name "Vietnam." (They knew he refused to use the terms "Annam" or "Annamite" because of the colonialist implications.) In all likelihood, however, Ho's choice of "Indochina" represented more than a passing nod to established foreign parlance. He probably wished to convey the impression that he represented

188. Fenn, *Ho Chi Minh*, 81.

189. Smith, *OSS*, 334. In a 1968 interview with his hometown newspaper, Prunier further described Ho Chi Minh as a quiet, intense person who knew how to "draw answers out of you" and who "listened to everything you had to say." Because Prunier hailed from Massachusetts, Ho also told him of his brief youthful stint in Boston, working as a waiter. Raymond P. Girard, "City Man Helped to Train Guerrillas of Ho Chi Minh," *Evening Gazette* (Worcester, Mass.), 14 and 15 May 1968.

190. René Defourneaux, "Secret Encounter with Ho Chi Minh," *Look* magazine (New York), 9 Aug. 1966, 32–33.

191. Letter from Allison K. Thomas, 10 Sept. 1986. At a farewell dinner in Hanoi in September 1945 hosted by Ho Chi Minh, Thomas asked the new chairman of the provisional government bluntly if he was a communist. Ho responded: "Yes, I am. But we can still be friends, can't we?" Quoted in *Vietnam: Anatomy of a Conflict*, ed. Wesley Fishel (Itasca, Ill., 1968), 7; confirmed by personal correspondence with Thomas, 5 Sept. 1990.

the interests or at least the aspirations of the Cambodian and Lao peoples as well as the Vietnamese. That was still the intention of the Indochinese Communist Party, although of course this point did not come up in conversations with the Americans. At Tan Trao in late July, no one knew what was happening in Cambodia or Laos, but efforts were under way to remedy this deficiency, relying in the first instance on contacts among the significant Vietnamese minorities in both places. A month later, Ho Chi Minh would set aside any thoughts of establishing an Indochinese state in favor of a "Democratic Republic of Vietnam" limited to the territories of Tonkin, Annam, and Cochinchina. Nonetheless, he and his lieutenants would continue to influence events in Cambodia and Laos via clandestine Viet Minh and ICP channels.

Reports received from OSS teams inside Indochina helped to fuel the debate in Kunming and Chungking over how to relate to both the French and the Annamites. Thus, one OSS memo relayed without comment a French agent's assessment that "the Annamites have developed no ambition for independence," appreciated that they were not ready for self-government, and understood that "the normal evolution of events" would bring self-government to them "in the distant future."[192] This provoked a sharp rebuttal from "an American observer" with eighteen years' experience in Indochina:

> It is notoriously true of French "colonials" that they love to delude themselves into thinking merely because the native peoples have failed to drive them out in the several sporadic and uncoordinated attempts at insurrection, for which they lacked arms, training and leadership, that the people had come to love them and were thoroughly content with their humiliated and subjugated condition under foreign masters in their own land. Such [a] conceited attitude . . . would be ludicrous, were it not so tragic.[193]

This source further doubted that France ever intended to relax strict control over Indochina, or to permit the natives to attain independence, despite General de Gaulle's promise of "statehood."

Those in the OSS who condemned French attitudes and behavior knew they had few supporters in the American Embassy in Chungking, which was supposed to provide guidance on current diplomatic policy. Ambassador Hurley was an outspoken anticolonialist, but his personal eccentricities and

192. USNA, OSS record 130333, 14 May 1945, Research and Analysis/India-Burma Theater memo D-30.
193. USNA, OSS record XL12971, Research and Analysis/SEAC memo K-134, 26 July 1945. The source may have been Austin Glass.

lack of relevant expertise made him a questionable source of guidance. Even those sympathetic or neutral toward the French preferred to obtain policy clarifications via the military chain of command, or directly from OSS headquarters in Washington. By early 1945, the OSS, headed by General "Wild Bill" Donovan, the "Henry Ford of the Secret Services," possessed an international momentum that was not easy to deflect.[194] Given the special wartime relationship of the OSS with President Roosevelt, one can imagine that many members wished to continue promoting his international policies unless told by the new president or General Donovan to desist. Some may even have known of Roosevelt's intention to invade Indochina, treating it as a dying wish. Although Roosevelt's trusteeship dreams had suffered grievously at Yalta, this was not known to the OSS in China. In mid June, Colonel Heppner was shown the ambiguous State Department reply to Ambassador Hurley, mentioned above.[195] Reading between the lines, it could be assumed that Washington now accepted France's future responsibility for Indochina, yet did not wish U.S. military decisions to be made on that basis. The OSS could thus work with any group, the Viet Minh included, that contributed something to the local war effort. Not until well after Japanese capitulation did directives arrive from Washington that sharply altered the ground rules.

American Public Opinion

Despite the amount of confidential attention given to Indochina by American officialdom, civilian and military, very little information spilled into the public domain. Occasionally, the OWI distributed press releases on Allied bombing operations or mentioned Indochina as a candidate for trusteeship. In the current self-satisfied spirit of anticolonialism and the Atlantic Charter, American journalists usually sideswiped the French record in Indochina and assumed the United States would make sure the natives received a better deal after the war.[196] Nonetheless, Indochina's minor news status was reflected in the New York Times choosing to devote only one article to it in 1942, seven in 1943, and four in 1944.[197]

194. The "Henry Ford" characterization is from Claude Paillat, *Dossier secret de l'Indochine* (Paris, 1964), 41.
195. Patti, *Why Viet Nam?* 120. Heppner subsequently divulged pertinent passages of this message to Patti and certain other subordinates.
196. See, e.g., Selwyn James, "French Want to Fight Japs for Indo-China," *PM*, 1 Oct. 1944.
197. By contrast, there were twenty-five articles between January and July 1945. *New York Times Index* (1941–45), 564, 594, 613–614, 705. I have excluded

From August 1944 on, the de Gaulle government operated a press mission in New York, which, as part of its overall objective of promoting the image of a "new France," publicized plans for postwar colonial reform, while simultaneously trying to rebut prevailing American impressions about prewar French exploitation. Thus, a pamphlet titled "France Forever—the Fighting French Committee in the U.S.," written by the mission head, Jean de la Roche, summarized the "grand accomplishments" of France in Indochina, asserted that the majority of both French and Indochinese peoples there were pro-Allied, and made vague promises of future liberal reforms.[198] In October 1944, probably encouraged by de la Roche, the influential American journal *Foreign Affairs* published an article by Gaston Rueff, a French businessman resident in the United States, which criticized Washington sharply for not helping Governor-General Catroux to resist Japanese pressure in 1940, quoted Acting Secretary of State Welles's 1942 recognition of French sovereignty, and promised rather rashly that the French community and French officials in Indochina would assist Allied forces to overthrow Japanese rule. According to Rueff, previous French rule had brought "peace and a certain degree of culture, health and prosperity" to Indochina. Nonetheless, France was aware that mistakes had been made, and that economic policy in particular would need to be changed "drastically." With an obvious eye to his American readers, Rueff proposed detaching Indochina from the French customs system, instituting an "Open Door policy for foreign capital," and establishing some sort of international or regional body to monitor efforts to prepare all native people in the southwestern Pacific for eventual self-government.[199]

In January 1945, the French carried their campaign to the Ninth Conference of the Institute of Pacific Relations, in Hot Springs, Virginia. Jean de la Roche offered three papers, stressing the French government's intention to develop the postwar Indochina economy separate from metropolitan pressures, its commitment to improving living conditions and reducing income disparities, and its plan to strengthen the five regional administrations (Tonkin, Annam, Cochinchina, Cambodia, and Laos),

---

articles on the "Far Eastern Front," in which Indochina generally is treated only in passing.

198. AOM, INF, c. 120, d. 1089. Roche was a colonial administrator with extensive African experience, apparently seconded to Agence Presse France.

199. Gaston Rueff, "The Future of French Indo-China," *Foreign Affairs* 23, no. 1 (Oct. 1944): 140–46. As we shall see, Rueff's article was criticized by the French Ministry of Colonies.

while retaining the governor-general as the embodiment of French sovereignty. However, Roche concluded one of his papers with a quotation from Pham Quynh, at that time still Bao Dai's first minister in Hue, on the desire of the inhabitants of Indochina to be "incorporated forever in the French Community."[200] Gaston Rueff presented a paper that encouraged American investors to look at industrial and mining opportunities in Indochina, suggested a free port to accommodate traffic to and from China, and favored giving more power to the Indochinese authorities at the expense of the métropole, except on matters of "national defense, collective security and relations with foreign countries."[201] Pierre Gourou, a methodical scholar of the prewar rural economy in Indochina, outlined some ways in which the living conditions of peasants in the overcrowded Red River Delta might be improved, while cautioning that no "false hopes" ought to be raised.[202]

Apparently only one American, Virginia Thompson, presented a paper on Indochina at the Hot Springs conference. It chided the French for ruthless labor exploitation before the war, but avoided comment on current issues entirely.[203] Nonetheless, colonial issues sparked considerable controversy during the floor discussions. U.S. delegates emphasized that their country was not fighting the Japanese in order to reconstitute Western colonial empires. "We shall not permit ourselves to be hustled out of evolution into revolution," countered a British delegate, backed up by the Dutch and the French.[204]

Following the Japanese coup in early March, the American media reacted cautiously to General de Gaulle's calls to provide military assistance to the French in Indochina. A *New York Times* editorial acknowledged French

---

200. Jean de la Roche: "French Indo-China's Prospective Economic Regime," French Paper no. 2; "A Program of Social and Cultural Activity in Indo-China," French Paper no. 3; and "Indo-China and French Colonial Policy," French Paper no. 5. An abbreviated version of no. 5 was published in *Pacific Affairs* (Honolulu) 18, no. 1 (Mar. 1945): 62–75. My thanks to Dr. Kristen Pelzer White for making a set of the Institute of Pacific Relations papers available.

201. Gaston Rueff, "Post-War Social and Economic Problems of French Indo-China," Secretariat Paper no. 6. A revised version of this paper appeared in *Pacific Affairs* 18, no. 2 (June 1945): 137–55, and ibid., no. 3 (Sept. 1945): 229–45.

202. Pierre Gourou, "The Standard of Living in the Delta of the Tonkin (French Indo-China)," French Paper no. 4.

203. Virginia Thompson, "Notes on Labor Problems in Indo-China," Secretariat Paper no. 11.

204. Quoted in Thorne, *Allies*, 541. Useful background on this Institute of Pacific Relations conference is provided in Christopher Thorne, *Border Crossings: Studies in International History* (Oxford, 1988), 175–92.

armed resistance, but questioned the degree of native support, and concluded:

> Whether on the basis of international trusteeship or not, the status of the Asiatic nations will not be the same as it was. One of the fruits of the victory over Japan that the people of the West will demand is an extension of self-government, as rapidly as circumstances permit, to the people of the East.[205]

The prestigious Foreign Policy Association printed an analysis by its Far Eastern specialist, Lawrence Rosinger, condemning Governor-General Decoux's crassly opportunistic attempts "to be on the winning side in the war—whichever side that might be." Surprisingly, Rosinger ignored aid to Gaullist elements entirely, instead focusing on the readiness of the "League for the Independence of Indo-China" to cooperate with Allied forces. Whether de Gaulle's promises of a new political status for Indochina would satisfy the league and other nationalists remained to be seen. However, Rosinger saw difficult times ahead: "It is apparent that in Asia, as in Europe, liberation from the enemy will be accompanied by a host of problems, originating in the pre-war decades, but stimulated by experiences under the heel of the Axis conqueror."[206] A subsequent Rosinger article urged France to "make a virtue of the weakness arising from defeat by cooperating with the Indo-Chinese in moving toward full autonomy with the eventual right to complete independence."[207] On the other hand, Eleanor Lattimore argued that de Gaulle's concept of a French Union represented a "revolutionary departure from the traditional French policy of 'assimilating' colonies, or associating them with France in a highly centralized empire." She predicted that the Indochinese would "probably have had enough experience of Japanese 'independence' by the time the war is over to trade it without reluctance for French 'dominion status.'"[208]

The American public had little or no basis on which to evaluate such viewpoints. Nor were they expected to. The war had fostered a pervasive climate of secrecy, trust in presidential leadership, and respect for military commanders, such that open debate on strategic or foreign policy issues was considered unpatriotic. Far more vital issues than Indochina failed to receive a public airing in 1945. It was left to a handful of curious journalists

205. *New York Times*, 17 Mar. 1945, 12.

206. "Resistance Movement Fights Japanese Rule in Indo-China," *Foreign Policy Bulletin* (New York) 24, no. 22 (16 Mar. 1945): 1–2.

207. *New York Times*, 21 May 1945, 3.

208. Eleanor Lattimore, "Indo-China: French Union or Japanese 'Independence,'" *Far Eastern Survey* (New York), 23 May 1945, 132–34.

and academics outside the government to wonder if French troops would be committed to Indochina, which military theater had operational responsibility, and whether or not the principle of self-government was being jettisoned by the Truman administration. In late June, the White House invited General de Gaulle to visit Washington later in the summer, perhaps the most important, yet barely noticed, sign of conciliation toward France and acceptance of French government plans for Indochina.[209]

Policy Paradoxes

Indochina may have been a strategic backwater for most of World War II, yet, as we have seen, it received considerable attention from Chinese and American policy makers and commanders. For Chinese leaders, Indochina was in many ways an extension of the complex maneuvering for power in Kwangsi and Yunnan, as well as a source of income for those able to tap the cross-border trade. The presence of Japanese forces in Indochina was used to secure more supplies and equipment from the Americans, while nonetheless eschewing any action that might precipitate an attack by the Imperial Army. For political, military, and commercial reasons it was helpful to sponsor a variety of Vietnamese émigré organizations and to improve contacts inside Tonkin, although preferably not to a level where such people were in a position to take independent action. By July 1945, Chinese regional commanders were probably prepared to challenge Japanese control of northern Indochina, but they were restrained by the central authorities in Chungking.

President Roosevelt's idea of establishing a trusteeship for Indochina was linked to his vision of a postwar Asia without colonies, his particular distaste for French behavior, and his eagerness to promote China as member of the Big Four. However, none of these considerations were important enough to interfere with prosecution of the war against Germany and Japan. Specifically, Roosevelt did not let differences over Indochina jeopardize his crucial working relationship with Prime Minister Churchill, and neither did he contravene U.S. Joint Planning Staff opinion that amphibious landings on Hainan Island and the coast of Tonkin would prove extremely wasteful of resources, delaying the invasions of Okinawa and

209. Herring, "Truman Administration," 107–8. General de Gaulle had visited Washington in July 1944, making a favorable public impression, but relations with Roosevelt remained strained, especially in the wake of de Gaulle's exclusion from Yalta.

Kyushu by six months. By early 1945, Roosevelt must have sensed that his aspirations for Chiang Kai-shek's China were unrealistic, yet he was not quite prepared to throw in the towel. Thus, he appears to have favored a much less expensive occupation of Indochina by Chinese troops whenever conditions permitted, which helps to explain General Wedemeyer's adamant refusal to concede the territory to Lord Mountbatten's theater.

Meanwhile, U.S. air attacks on targets of opportunity in Indochina continued relentlessly, and the OSS expanded its cross-border operations. Added urgency was provided by the Japanese takeover and the Chinese troop advance southeastward across Kwangsi. Ironically, Indochina was assuming greater theater importance just at the time when President Truman was abandoning Roosevelt's remaining reservations about France's return to its colony. Truman would have preferred the policy change to be unobtrusive, but Ambassador Hurley's acerbic message in May forced his hand. Nonetheless, theater planning went ahead for Chinese entry to Indochina, and this was given the overall Allied imprimatur at Potsdam in late July, at least to the sixteenth parallel. The stage was thus set for both OSS and Chinese involvement in the events of August–September.

5   The Allies: Great Britain and Free France

Although engaged in common struggle against the Axis powers, the Allies found it much more difficult to work together in Asia than in Europe. China understandably treated the Pacific War as central. The United States accepted the primacy of the European War, yet insisted that the Japanese advance not only be halted but rolled back decisively. Great Britain worried that America would allocate too many resources to the Pacific before Germany was vanquished. The Free French were interested in participating in the Pacific War only to the degree that it helped to restore France's status as a global power. Finally, the Soviet Union avoided declaring war on Japan until total victory was a foregone conclusion.

Indochina served to highlight another point of contention among the Allies: the future of colonialism in Asia. As we have seen, China had no problem envisaging postwar independence or temporary trusteeship for Western colonial possessions and Korea. Until late 1944, the United States favored international trusteeships, but Washington then backed away from confrontation with the western European powers as the moment of truth approached. Great Britain, Free France, and the Dutch government in exile resolutely opposed American trusteeship proposals, yet lacked the means to reconquer their colonies alone. The Soviet Union, with no particular strategic interests to protect, limited itself to verbal support for Asian movements.

GREAT BRITAIN

With the fall of France in June 1940, Great Britain had urgent reason to take an interest in the French colonial empire. Above all, London hoped to deny French colonial resources to the Axis powers, redirecting them where possible to the British and American war machines. In order to facilitate new military base arrangements and mobilization of local manpower, Britain also tried to encourage colonial identification with the Free French cause.

Japan's quick assertion of military hegemony in mid 1940 precluded Britain from gaining control of Indochina's resources, although London did succeed in strangling the colony's trade with metropolitan France, and for eighteen months the British managed to purchase significant quantities of Indochinese rice and coal. Both the Japanese presence and Governor-General Decoux's loyalty to Vichy made efforts to promote the Free French banner impossible. During 1941, in fact, the British had a "gentlemen's agreement" with Decoux whereby they banned Free French propaganda to Indochina in exchange for Vichy propaganda not being directed at French territories in the South Pacific.[1] Britain also agreed not to foster Free French efforts in Indochina so long as French warships stationed there refrained from hostile action.[2] Behind these British actions lay a deeper concern not to antagonize the Japanese into attacking Singapore.

The shock of Japan's triumphant sweep of Southeast Asia in early 1942 fell most heavily on the British, since their navy had dominated the region for 150 years. Nonetheless, it did not precipitate any serious reappraisal of established relationships between colonial rulers and ruled. In London it was generally assumed that the natives would not make common cause with the Japanese invaders, instead looking to the Europeans for deliverance. To the degree the white man had suffered a loss of face, it was important he come back with a maximum demonstration of force. Once European authority was restored, discussions could proceed with local elites over delegation of powers, perhaps even self-government within a commonwealth system.

For three years, however, Great Britain was in no position to influence events in Asia east of India. Indeed, rather than try, Prime Minister Churchill anxiously worked to restrain President Roosevelt's inclination to increase military resource allocations to the Pacific and China at the expense of Europe. Partly as a result, 1943–44 counterattacks in the South Pacific were a largely American and Australian affair. In Southeast Asia, the Allies could not come up with enough troops, munitions, aircraft, and

---

1. Peter M. Dunn, *The First Vietnam War* (London, 1985), 57.
2. Charles Cruickshank, *SOE in the Far East* (Oxford, 1983), 74. John J. Sbrega, "'First catch your hare': Anglo-American Perspectives on Indochina during the Second World War," *Journal of Southeast Asian Studies* (cited below as *JSEAS*) 14, no. 1 (Mar. 1983): 64.

road-building equipment to overwhelm even the exposed Japanese position in Burma. To complicate matters, American planners in India looked northeast to China, while British planners aimed southeast to Rangoon and beyond.[3] Formation of the South East Asia Command in late 1943 was meant to reconcile such conflicting objectives, yet this did not stop the British from complaining that the United States was wasting military resources on propping up the Chiang Kai-shek regime, or prevent the Americans from carping that SEAC stood for "Save England's Asiatic Colonies."[4] In Kunming, the chief political adviser to General Stilwell asserted, "The raising of the Union Jack over Singapore is more important to the British than any victory parade through Tokyo."[5] The American mission in Delhi was warned by Washington to keep U.S. psychological warfare activities completely apart from the British, as they could be assumed "to be fighting primarily for the retention, if not expansion, of their Empire."[6]

Simultaneously, the British had some grounds to suspect that the United States intended to shove European interests aside in Asia, either working directly or via the Chinese. As Churchill once remarked, China would be merely "a faggot-vote on the side of the United States in any attempt to liquidate the British Overseas Empire."[7] Sir Alexander Cadogan, permanent undersecretary at the Foreign Office, wrote Churchill that, in view of American attitudes, there was "much to be said for the colonial powers sticking together in the Far East."[8] One of Cadogan's colleagues worried that "we do not know where the US would stop if they were encouraged to imagine that the concept of 'parent states' in the Pacific might be

3. Christopher Thorne, *Allies of a Kind: The United States, Britain and the War against Japan, 1941–1945* (London, 1978), 226.

4. Walter La Feber, "Roosevelt, Churchill and Indochina: 1942–45," *American Historical Review* (Washington, D.C.), no. 80 (Dec. 1975): 1282. Barbara W. Tuchman, *Stilwell and the American Experience in China, 1911–45* (New York, 1970), 369–70.

5. December 1943 memorandum prepared by John Paton Davies, quoted in Richard Aldrich, "Imperial Rivalry: British and American Intelligence in Asia, 1942–46," *Intelligence and National Security* (London) 3, no. 1 (Jan. 1988): 8.

6. Thorne, *Allies*, 292. On similar grounds, the State Department rejected Lord Mountbatten's request for U.S. civil-military affairs officers to be attached to SEAC. Peter Dennis, *Troubled Days of Peace: Mountbatten and South East Asia Command, 1945–46* (Manchester, 1987), 20.

7. La Feber, "Roosevelt, Churchill and Indochina," 1281.

8. Christopher Thorne, "Indochina and Anglo-American Relations, 1942–1945," *Pacific Historical Review* 45 (1976): 84. Another Foreign Office paper argued that "the Colonial Powers had better stick together or hang together." Cruickshank, *SOE*, 123.

discarded."[9] Esler Dening, Lord Mountbatten's top political adviser, argued that one of Britain's major tasks was to convince the Americans that it was "not in their interests to undermine the stability of the British Empire in Asia and the Pacific or to upset the equilibrium in Siam, Indo-China or the Netherlands East Indies." In the next breath, however, he complained of the tendency of "American imperialism . . . to try to elbow us out," as well as of a "smearing campaign which not only attributes to us the meanest motives but tries to belittle everything we do."[10]

Indochina became the front line in a mostly confidential Anglo-American wrangle over the fate of colonial Asia, with the British making up in policy consistency what they lacked in capacity to enforce opinions. President Roosevelt might have the full weight of U.S. war resources behind him, but his views on Indochina lacked bureaucratic consensus. By contrast, the London bureaucracy, deeply concerned about Roosevelt's apparent intention to challenge Britain's imperial mission, closed ranks behind the Foreign Office to formulate countermeasures. Prime Minister Churchill shared these anxieties, yet was determined not to allow the colonial issue to poison cross-Atlantic relations. More than once he cautioned officials against allowing intemperate remarks to reach the Americans. Many a waspish rebuttal to Roosevelt made the office rounds without being communicated to Washington. In response to Roosevelt's criticisms of the French for neglecting native education and welfare in Indochina, for example, one Foreign Office memo writer doubted if southern sharecroppers in the United States were any better off, then asked rhetorically whether such outwardly altruistic reasoning, if allowed to pass for Indochina, might next be used by the Americans to gain control of oil in Borneo or rubber in Malaya.[11]

The British shared French suspicions that China entertained territorial ambitions in mainland Southeast Asia, whatever its professions to the contrary. Thus, one Foreign Office document argued that any international trusteeship in Indochina would open the door to Chinese and, in time, Japanese intrigues; any outright Chinese control would be both "objec-

9. Quoted in D. Cameron Watt, *Succeeding John Bull: America in Britain's Place, 1900–1975* (Cambridge, 1984), 205.

10. Daniel B. Valentine, "The British Facilitation of the French Re-Entry into Vietnam" (Ph.D. diss., University of California, Los Angeles, 1974), 177.

11. William Roger Louis, *Imperialism at Bay, 1941–1945: The United States and the Decolonization of the British Empire* (Oxford, 1977), 38–39. Sbrega, "'First catch your hare,'" 73. Watt, *Succeeding John Bull*, 195, 200–202, 206.

tionable to the natives and probably menacing to ourselves."[12] Prior to the war, British and French colonial administrations had worked to neutralize Kuomintang and Chinese Communist Party influence among the overseas Chinese. In the postwar period, the Foreign Office predicted, both administrations would again need to prevent trouble from expatriate Chinese communities.[13]

Not only Asian imperial issues but also plans for a firm Anglo-French alliance in postwar Europe convinced London officials that they had no choice but to fight for French sovereignty in Indochina. At the end of the war, France would be in an "extremely touchy, indeed almost pathological condition," one Foreign Office paper predicted.[14] British failure to support France on the Indochina issue would be "passionately resented" and produce "incalculable results" on two continents, not just one.[15] Fears even were expressed of a Franco-Czechoslovak-Soviet bloc counterposed to the British Commonwealth and the United States.[16] Even short of such a scenario, it was still undesirable to weaken France by "depriving her of so important a part of her Empire."[17] Apparently only one British official suggested that France might be so debilitated at the end of the war as to make impractical the resumption of all her former commitments, and that it would be better for the French to concentrate on recovery in Europe and the Mediterranean.[18]

While Prime Minister Churchill accepted France's imperial ambitions, including return to Indochina, he was in no particular hurry to dispatch French troops to Asia. Aside from his European preoccupations and Roosevelt's manifest opposition, Churchill took account of his difficult relationship with General de Gaulle, and above all his painful experience in regard to the mandated territories of Syria and Lebanon, where Anglo-Australian and Free French forces had operated at cross-purposes following capitulation of Vichy-affiliated units in July 1941. Whereas Churchill urged the French to defuse native discontent by negotiating seriously with nationalist elements, General de Gaulle preferred to select a notorious Francophile to establish an interim government. Under British pressure,

12. Louis, *Imperialism at Bay*, 278.
13. Thorne, "Indochina," 84.
14. Valentine, "British Facilitation," 81.
15. Ibid., 118. See also Sbrega, "'First catch your hare,'" 71–72.
16. Watt, *Succeeding John Bull*, 203–4.
17. Louis, *Imperialism at Bay*, 278.
18. This was Sir Maurice Peterson, an assistant undersecretary of state, as cited in Thorne, "Indochina," 83–84.

the Free French in 1943 restored the suspended constitutions of Syria and Lebanon, but they then jailed the Lebanese president and most government ministers for proposing to terminate the French mandate. A general strike, protest demonstrations, and further Anglo-American coercion induced de Gaulle to back down, yet tensions flared again in early 1945. After French units mounted a three-day artillery and air bombardment of Damascus, British troops intervened and confined French troops to barracks under threat of military action.[19] De Gaulle's rancor was compounded by the knowledge that his own ministers opposed his Syrian policy, and the French public remained indifferent.[20] French officials responsible for Indochina planning realized that Syria damaged their credibility in regard to promised reforms and made it easier for the United States to reject French military participation in the Far East.[21] In a note to the minister of colonies, Henri Laurentie worried that events in Syria, as well as recent killings of nationalists in Algeria, would greatly increase distrust of France among the Indochinese.[22] He was not mistaken. When the Japanese Domei News Agency gleefully reported Middle East events as evidence of growing schisms among the Allies, Vietnamese writers added their concern that Syria demonstrated France's probable determination to return to Indochina to try to stifle independence in the same manner.[23]

The first Free French request to establish a military mission at SEAC was turned down by the British in October 1943, on the grounds that no prospect yet existed of French operations in the Far East.[24] Six months later the British Chiefs of Staff changed their minds, and, in October 1944, as we have seen, Churchill approved attachment of a French military mission to Mountbatten's headquarters without consulting Roosevelt.[25] Subse-

19. Geoffrey Warner, *Iraq and Syria, 1941* (London, 1974), 122–58. Tabitha Petran, *Syria* (London, 1972), 77–79. French forces eventually withdrew from Syria in April 1946 and Lebanon in December 1946.

20. Don Cook, *Charles de Gaulle: A Biography* (New York, 1983), 282–84. In the last weeks of the European War, de Gaulle also ordered French divisions to occupy several locations in Germany and northern Italy that had been allocated to others by General Dwight Eisenhower. Churchill was incensed, saying, "Between us and France, there can be no bridge via de Gaulle, ever." It was Truman's threatened termination of aid, however, that forced de Gaulle to withdraw.

21. AOM, INF, c. 123, d. 1108, subdossier 3, DGER reports of 29 May and 16 June 1945.

22. Institut Charles-de-Gaulle, *Le Général de Gaulle et l'Indochine, 1940–1946* (Paris, 1982) (cited below as *DGI*), 70–71.

23. *Tan A* [New Asia] (Saigon), no. 53 (13 Apr. 1945); and no. 73 (17 Aug. 1945).

24. Thorne, *Allies*, 349.

25. La Feber, "Roosevelt, Churchill and Indochina," 1286, 1291.

Figure 22. Vietnamese cartoon mocking French setbacks in the Middle East. There is a play on words, with the civilian asking the sailor why he has so many bandages [*bang*], and the sailor replying, "I've just come back from Lebanon [Li-Bang]." *Tu Tri* (Hanoi), 22 June 1945. Courtesy of the Bibliothèque nationale.

quent French offers to provide two infantry divisions were accepted in principle but were not taken seriously until July 1945, and even then the French troops were only scheduled for transport east in early 1946.[26] As for the 1,200-man Corps léger d'intervention (CLI), which Lord Mountbatten certainly wanted available despite American objections, the preferred plan was to subordinate smaller components to British-directed operations rather than giving the French their head.[27] In early February 1945, the Foreign Office, anxious to avoid an open split with the Americans, managed to block a Special Operations Executive (SOE) attempt to ship the CLI to Ceylon.[28]

Force 136 and Indochina

With the CLI stuck in North Africa, the British recruited French personnel from diverse locations into existing British organizations, most notably Force 136, specializing in subversive and sabotage missions.[29] Until rather late in the war, such British clandestine operations tended to suffer from

26. Dennis, *Troubled Days*, 32–33. Georges Gautier, *9 Mars 1945, Hanoi au soleil de sang: La Fin de l'Indochine française* (Paris, 1978), 100.
27. Cruickshank, *SOE*, 124.
28. Watt, *Succeeding John Bull*, 211.
29. As indicated earlier, Force 136 was the code name for SOE functioning east of Suez.

shoestring budgets, tangled lines of authority, and old school amateurism. Serious attention was given, for example, to a scheme to move supplies of natural rubber from Indochina, using agents recruited in China. When this proved impractical, plans developed for acquiring Thai tungsten and Sumatran quinine in exchange for South African diamonds. The end results were deep involvement in the Chinese black market and some useful entrepreneurial covers for British agents, but very little intelligence or sabotage payoff.[30] "As the war progressed, SOE in particular began to resemble empire trade in khaki," according to one recent study.[31]

One of the biggest practical problems for all Western clandestine organizations in Asia was recruitment of suitable native agents. Force 136 made the mistake of accepting hundreds of Chinese trainees from General Tai Li's security organization, including a group destined for Indochina, code-named the "Eagles." Very few proved reliable.[32] In 1943, the British gained access to Vietnamese whom the French had previously deported and jailed in Madagascar. Following extensive interviewing, at least four were selected for training in India. Hoang Dinh Rong was an experienced member of the Indochinese Communist Party, having attended its 1935 congress in Macao, worked undercover in the hills of Tonkin, and survived several long spates of colonial detention. Duong Cong Hoat belonged to an ethnic minority group resident in the Tonkin hills. Le Gian and Hoang Huu Nam were young intellectuals who had been swept up in the anticolonial struggles of the 1930s. In September 1944, the British dropped all four by parachute near the provincial town of Cao Bang, with a mission to liberate Free French prisoners from Japanese detention. They soon managed to link up with nearby Viet Minh units, putting their expertise and equipment to uses that would hardly have been approved by the British.[33]

30. Cruickshank, *SOE*, 212–81.

31. Aldrich, "Imperial Rivalry," 10.

32. Cruickshank, *SOE*, 12–15. U.S. organizations in China made the same error with Tai Li. See R. Harris Smith, *OSS: The Secret History of America's First Central Intelligence Agency* (Berkeley and Los Angeles, 1971), 245–66.

33. Le Gian, "The Story of an Exile," *Vietnam Courier*, Aug. 1980, 17–20. Cruickshank, *SOE*, 14, states that no Annamites from Madagascar were taken in by India Mission / Force 136, although nine were considered. Presumably these four were recruited by another of the total of eleven British clandestine units operating out of India. Hoang Dinh Rong subsequently commanded the Viet Minh brigade sent south to fight the French in late 1945, and was killed in action in 1947. Le Gian became head of the DRV's central security agency. Hoang Huu Nam played a key role in Franco-Vietnamese negotiations in 1946; he drowned while crossing a mountain river in 1947. Some other Vietnamese recruits to Force 136 may have come from among members of the French Army taken off ships intercepted by the

Force 136 relied heavily on François de Langlade, a French planter in Malaya who had visited Indochina in 1941 on behalf of the British, and who subsequently demonstrated he held the confidence of General de Gaulle. In mid 1943, de Langlade was accepted as head of the British Indo-China Country Section in Calcutta. Several months later, a small group of French officers and Vietnamese enlisted men arrived for guerrilla training. Whatever British intentions, the head of this group, Lieutenant Colonel Jean de Crèvecoeur, continued to report to the CLI commander in Algiers and to promote growth of a separate clandestine French Service d'action (SA) network in the Far East.[34] At some point this SA operation came under control of General de Gaulle's intelligence service, the Direction générale d'études et recherches (DGER), presumably with the knowledge, but not necessarily the explicit approval, of London. Exactly how command decisions were made and enforced remains unclear. Meanwhile, Lord Mountbatten, not wishing to keep American officers in SEAC entirely in the dark, and aware that air missions to Indochina were better staged via Kunming, fretted over the operational implications of President Roosevelt's opposition to any French return to Indochina.[35]

In February 1944, Force 136 submitted to SEAC a comprehensive proposal to parachute agents and supplies into Tonkin to begin building a clandestine organization.[36] The first attempt on 9 May ended when the airplane's automatic pilot failed after takeoff. A second try the next day was defeated by thick clouds over the drop zone.[37] Flights like these were extremely perilous and demanding, involving 18–20 hours in the air devoid

---

British following the fall of Paris in June 1940. Two Vietnamese were parachuted to Cochinchina as well, but their activities are unknown. Interview with Tran Bach Dang, Ho Chi Minh City, 17 Mar. 1988.

34. Cruickshank, *SOE*, 74, 122–23. *DGI*, 56. It seems the government of India was not kept informed of French upgrading of operations in Calcutta. See F. V. S. Donnison, *British Military Administration in the Far East, 1943–46* (London, 1956), 404–5.

35. La Feber, "Roosevelt, Churchill and Indochina," 1285. Thorne, "Indochina," 84. Aldrich, "Imperial Rivalry," 32, asserts that Mountbatten was "largely unaware of the extent of SOE's political activities," especially in regard to Indochina. However, I think Mountbatten must have understood the political implications of extensive French participation in clandestine operations, even if he remained uninformed about specific Force 136 missions.

36. Archimedes L. A. Patti, *Why Viet Nam? Prelude to America's Albatross* (Berkeley and Los Angeles, 1980), 30–31. The original French draft of this proposal had specified French personnel, but this passage was deleted to avoid American objections.

37. Cruickshank, *SOE*, 126.

of sophisticated navigational aids, trying to reach pinpoint targets at night in very uncertain weather conditions. In one such transport mission, involving three Dakota aircraft caught in a severe storm, one plane disappeared completely, another had to jettison all its supplies to gain enough altitude to return to base, while the third lost an Australian NCO swept out the door before making a forced landing in open country.[38] Of forty-six sorties to Indochina approved by the end of November, only eighteen succeeded. One Royal Air Force B-24 Liberator squadron lost fourteen aircraft on special-duty missions of this kind throughout the theater.[39]

On the night of 4–5 July 1944, a British airplane staging through Kunming managed to parachute three French agents to a prearranged spot near Lang Son: Major de Langlade, Major Philippe Milon, a colonial army officer dispatched previously from Indochina to contact the Free French, and Sergeant Marmont, their radio operator. From there the party made its way safely to Hanoi and discussions with Indochina Army commanders. Subsequent American objections apparently negated the plan to pick up de Langlade and Milon at an isolated airstrip, forcing them to walk out of Indochina via Lao Cai. A British Force 136 officer negotiated their release from Chinese detention, using a combination of ruse and gifts of a Sten gun, 200 rounds of ammunition, and copies of the *Tatler* and *Illustrated London News*.[40]

By the end of December, thirteen clandestine radio posts had been established in Indochina, each linked individually with Calcutta. In the January 1945 full-moon period, twenty-seven agents were dropped successfully, although on one night only two out of eleven Liberators accomplished their missions, and three planes failed to return to base. By the end of February, the resistance had been provided with sixty more men, 3,400 Sten guns, over a million rounds of ammunition, 6,000 grenades, 800 pistols, 94 Bren guns with a quarter of a million shells, and large quantities of explosives. A Force 136 officer conducted training courses at three locations for Indochina Army personnel.[41] Another three hundred French

---

38. L. H. Ayrolles, *L'Indochine ne répond plus* (Saint-Brieux, 1948), 7–11.
39. Dunn, *First Vietnam War*, 85, 86.
40. Cruickshank, *SOE*, 126–29.
41. Ibid., 130–31. Dunn, *First Vietnam War*, 87. René Charbonneau and José Maigre, *Les Parias de la Victoire: Indochine-Chine, 1945* (Paris, 1980), 53–54. Ayrolles, *L'Indochine ne répond plus*, 19–25, contains a vivid description of a mission on 22–23 December in which one Liberator parachuted commandos over the Plain of Jars in Laos, while two others were forced to turn back. It required seven attempts before the full team and equipment were in position.

officers and NCOs were awaiting dispatch to Indochina, having undergone intensive training at various Force 136 camps in India.[42]

In commando efforts of this kind, a delicate line often exists between building up capabilities for effective action and moving with such enthusiasm that the enemy retaliates before all the pieces are in place. Force 136 planners seem to have assumed that more men and matériel could be dropped into Indochina, and elaborate preparations to attack undertaken, without triggering Japanese preemptive measures. This made sense in isolation, given the local balance of forces, but it failed to take sufficient account of Japanese worries about American amphibious landings. Moreover, the British and French decision to link the Force 136 network closely to the existing colonial administration, obviating the need to build a resistance organization from the ground up as in most other occupied countries, left the commandos extremely vulnerable if the Japanese decided to overthrow the administration in advance of possible enemy landings. Ironically, the lack of any Allied plans for a major offensive in or near Indochina, and most particularly SEAC's inability to approach the colony in force before early 1946, meant that Force 136 teams had no D-day around which they could orient intelligence and sabotage operations, unlike previous SOE experiences in Europe. They were teams without a clear-cut military mission, inserted partly as markers in the SEAC territorial dispute with China Theater, partly to demonstrate an Allied commitment to French sovereignty in Indochina.

Following the Japanese takeover on 9 March, the Force 136 network of 1,210 commandos fell apart quickly. Minus the French colonial apparatus, it proved difficult to secure the necessary food, guides, and porters from native villages. Accustomed to functioning with radio sets, batteries, acid for the batteries, blankets and groundsheets, Sten guns and ammunition, spades, medicine, and other paraphernalia,[43] Force 136 units had trouble evading Japanese patrols. Drops of rations and mail from India occasionally relieved the hunger and isolation. However, during this same period, Force 136 was increasingly committed to supporting the Fourteenth Army offensive in Burma. Owing to operational losses and maintenance backlogs, special-duty Liberator squadrons were seventeen planes short. Missions to Indochina fell to seventeen in April and fourteen in May, compared to an average of forty-four a month in January–March.[44] Aircrews forced down

42. Cruickshank, *SOE*, 19.
43. Ibid., 29.
44. Ibid., 135.

in Indochina were less likely to receive local assistance than before. Thus, two B-24 crew members captured by Cao Dai adherents in the Mekong Delta were promptly turned over to the Japanese, whose offers of a reward were politely refused.[45] By late April the Annam elements of Force 136, previously the largest in Indochina, were reduced to 150 Europeans and 80 natives.[46] They, like survivors from Tonkin and Cochinchina, hoped to escape to Laos and reorganize. Meanwhile, drawing on profits from large-scale black market operations in China, the British were able to resupply exhausted French colonial units retreating into Yunnan and Kwangsi. The British were not amused, therefore, to discover the French entering the black market as unacknowledged competitors. Later, when the French Military Mission asked for a large consignment of Chinese dollars at black market rates, the British provided only a fraction of the quantity requested, at an exchange rate more than twice the amount quoted to other Allied clients.[47]

Force 136 parachute drops continued in June and July, with the focus shifting to northern Laos, where some of the upland ethnic groups had proven willing to cooperate.[48] A standard drop included woolen caps and sweaters, shoes, battledress, socks, mosquito nets, blankets, tent cloths, waterproofs, sacks, 100 kilograms of salt, medicines, toilet articles, tobacco, cigarettes, cigars, pipes, chocolate, three bottles of whisky, three of brandy, fifty kilograms of silver, and 10,000 piastres. Since much of this bounty could not be carried far from the drop site, it was offered to local notables in order of precedence.[49] Some attempts were made to insert new Force 136 commandos, employing three-man "Jedburgh teams" with previous experience in occupied Europe.[50] None of these teams reestablished a foothold in Tonkin, however, leaving the initiative there almost entirely in the hands of the American OSS.

With the head of the French Military Mission at Kandy, General Roger Blaizot, desperate for affirmations of SEAC action in Indochina, Lord Mountbatten in late April indicated that following the recapture of Singapore, it might be possible to mount a pincer attack on Indochina, one

45. *Tan A* (Saigon), no. 53 (13 Apr. 1945). News items in this issue extend to late June, so the date is quite misleading.

46. AOM, INF, c. 123, d. 1108, subdossier 3, DGER report, 25 Apr. 1945.

47. Cruickshank, *SOE*, 218–20. Charbonneau and Maigre, *Les Parias*, 307–8.

48. Ayrolles, *L'Indochine ne répond plus*, 35–36, 43–49.

49. Ibid., 120–23.

50. Philippe Héduy, *Histoire de l'Indochine: Le Destin, 1885–1954* (Paris, 1983), 273. For a partial list of French Force 136 / SA officers killed in Indochina, see Jean-Pierre Pisardy, *Paras d'Indochine, 1944–1954* (Paris, 1982), 215.

force moving through Thailand, the other landing on the Cambodian coast.[51] At the end of May, Mountbatten set 9 September for landings in the Port Swettenham / Port Dickson region of the Malayan peninsula, with Singapore to be occupied by the end of the year.[52] Two weeks later, Mountbatten offered Blaizot two British divisions after recapture of Singapore. However, when Blaizot met with de Gaulle in early July, the offer was refused, apparently a reflection of continuing Anglo-French tensions over Syria.[53]

On 24 July, Mountbatten arrived at Potsdam to learn that SEAC's area of responsibility had been extended to include Borneo, Java, the Celebes, and part of Indochina. Shortly afterward, Churchill told him in utmost confidence about American plans to use the atomic bomb against Japan, and advised him to be prepared for possible Japanese surrender soon after the middle of August. Without being able to provide any reason, Mountbatten cabled his SEAC staff instructions to begin planning on a much shorter time frame than previously understood. Staff members reacted by putting forth numerous reasons why the agreed timetable could not or should not be advanced.[54] Meanwhile, defeat of the Conservatives in the July elections in Great Britain gave further cause for policy uncertainty. It soon would become evident, however, that the new Labour prime minister, Clement Atlee, and his foreign minister, Ernest Bevin, were more inclined to placate General de Gaulle than Churchill had been.[55]

THE FREE FRENCH

Indochina was an essential part of the French concept of empire. Although it could not be a factor in Free French plans to liberate the métropole, given its geographical remoteness and Japan's strategic preponderance, Indochina symbolized France's continuing commitment to Asia and the Pacific. In the broader sense, French power and prestige throughout the world could not be reaffirmed without reversing France's humiliation at the hands of the Japanese as well as the Germans. Charles de Gaulle, while not himself a product of the colonial military tradition, still felt that France required

51. AOM, INF, c. 123, d. 1108, subdossier 3, DGER report 27 Apr. 1945.

52. S. Woodburn Kirby, *The War against Japan*, vol. 5, *The Surrender of Japan* (London, 1969), 5, 8, 65.

53. *DGI*, 66, 67, 71.

54. Dennis, *Troubled Days*, 10–12.

55. Cook, *Charles De Gaulle*, 192.

"vast enterprises" to be able to counterbalance "the ferments of dispersal which are inherent in her people."[56]

As German armies swept toward Paris in early June 1940, Indochina was far from the minds of French leaders trying to decide how to respond to disaster. Nonetheless, General de Gaulle's decision to flee to Great Britain and organize armed resistance to Hitler was premised partly on the conviction that France's overseas possessions could provide the wherewithal to return triumphantly to Paris and reconstruct the politics of the métropole. As de Gaulle insisted in his emotional 18 June radio appeal from London: "Believe what I tell you, for I know of what I speak, and I say that nothing is lost for France. For France is not alone. She is not alone. She is not alone. . . . She has a vast Empire behind her."[57] In Indochina, those who heard this appeal, or obtained second-hand accounts of it, realized that nothing could be done without first considering Japanese reactions. Governor-General A. J. Catroux, who received a personal message from de Gaulle inviting him to join the Free French cause, jousted for a few weeks with both the Japanese and his métropole-appointed replacement, Admiral Jean Decoux, then conceded defeat and departed for London.[58]

In September 1940, de Gaulle received a confidential letter from Colonial Inspector Cazaux, a senior official in Indochina, explaining the current powerlessness to act in support of the Free French. De Gaulle's reply was conciliatory, admitting his own inability to assist in Indochina, asking to be kept informed, and expressing hope that the spirit of resistance would grow in the colony.[59] Ironically, it was Governor-General Decoux who demonstrated the limits of French resistance a few months later, when he accepted battle with encroaching Thai forces and moved by sea to threaten Bangkok, only to be compelled by the Japanese to cede two portions of Indochina to Thailand (see chapter 1).

De Gaulle and Decoux shared a fervent desire to preserve French sovereignty over Indochina, but a gap that was much more than geographical separated them, reflecting the different ways in which proud military officers reacted to the humiliations of 1940. Having declared his fidelity to Marshal Philippe Pétain, Decoux expected all his subordinates to do likewise. Those in Indochina who expressed admiration for the Free French or dislike of the Vichy regime found themselves disciplined, harassed by right-wing

56. Ibid., frontispiece, 315. De Gaulle refers here to domestic tendencies to fragment, not any particular French inclination toward overseas settlement.

57. David Shoenbrun, *As France Goes* (New York, 1957), 214–15.

58. *DGI*, 47, 77, 87. Georges Catroux, *Deux actes du drame indochinois* (Paris, 1959), 68–69.

59. *DGI*, 47, 48.

extremists, sometimes imprisoned. Thus, Inspector Cazaux was stripped of his position, ordered back to the métropole, and court-martialed.[60] A few military men managed to depart the colony illegally. André Jubelin, a naval aviation officer, secretly converted a Pelican training plane for long-distance flight, recruited two compatriots, and flew to Malaya in November 1940. Three months later, de Gaulle put Jubelin in temporary command of a battleship; fifty-five months hence he would captain the first French warship to drop anchor in the Saigon River following the Japanese surrender.[61]

During 1941 a group of Free French sympathizers in Saigon established contact with the British SOE. In October, the SOE arranged for Professor Meyer May, formerly of the Hanoi Medical School, to sail from Singapore equipped with a radio set, explosives, and a spy plan. Learning of the plot, the Japanese prepared to ambush Professor May and his associates at a beach near Cap Saint-Jacques. The group in Saigon, sensing a leak, succeeded in canceling the rendezvous in time.[62] For the next two years, at least, no Free French organization challenged either the Japanese or the Pétainists in Indochina.

For General de Gaulle, the idea of the entire French empire rallying behind him to help liberate the métropole was sufficient reason to make the occasional public statement in 1940–41 calling for Indochina's participation. Privately, however, he told the British he did not wish action to be taken that would result in Japanese overthrow of the Decoux administration. Such willingness to put French colonial interests ahead of slowly growing Western efforts to stop the Japanese strategic push southward caused resentment in the United States, as the Free French representative in Washington, René Pleven, duly informed de Gaulle in August 1941.[63] From de Gaulle's point of view, however, Washington had no right to preach, as it had ignored Catroux's pleas for material assistance the previous year and still showed little readiness to challenge the Japanese militarily.[64]

---

60. Paul Isoart, "Aux origines d'une guerre," in *L'Indochine française, 1940–1945*, ed. Paul Isoart (Paris, 1982), 6–7, 20–21.

61. André Jubelin, *The Flying Sailor* (London, 1953), 32–34, 43–44, 51–53, 270–71. First published as *Marin de métier, pilote de fortune* (Paris, 1951). After escape from Indochina, Jubelin carefully arranged to ship the Pelican from Singapore back to Saigon.

62. Cruickshank, *SOE*, 74–75. During 1941, François de Langlade was able to travel legally from Singapore to Indochina on a British passport, collecting information for both British and Free French use. *DGI*, 94–95.

63. *DGI*, 23–24, 48–49, 50.

64. The Free French collected information on this issue so as to be able later to rebut American charges. See, e.g., the 8 Feb. 1944 position paper in AOM, INF, c. 120, d. 1087.

Immediately following the 7 December 1941 Japanese attack on Pearl Harbor, the Comité français de libération nationale (CFLN) joined Washington and London in declaring war on Japan. General de Gaulle appealed specifically to the peoples of Indochina to resist Japanese aggression.[65] However, de Gaulle refrained from publicly condemning Decoux or the rest of the Indochina administration for continuing to cooperate with Tokyo. Some attempts were made to establish covert intelligence links via Chungking, but those in Indochina who were prepared to supply information to the Allies generally found it necessary to rely on British, American, or Chinese spy networks, not the Free French. One of the more colorful examples was Mario Bocquet, a World War I veteran and prominent planter in Cochinchina, who formed his own civilian network to collect information on the Japanese and funnel it to British and American agencies.[66] A former officer in the colonial army, code-named Gabaon, allegedly relied on his Freemasonry contacts throughout East Asia and his Vietnamese wife's exalted rank in the Cao Dai religious hierarchy to build and sustain a large network connected by radio to the commander of the Fourteenth Air Force, General Chennault, in Kunming.[67]

In March 1943, uncomfortable at such dependence on foreigners, a group within the Indochina Army secretly dispatched Captain Philippe Milon to Algiers, where he met General Catroux and was introduced to staff officers loyal to General de Gaulle. Milon was instructed to work with the French Military Mission in Chungking, newly directed by Colonel Zinovi Pechkoff,[68] a colorful one-armed Russian émigré and Foreign Legion officer, and to urge comrades in Indochina to sustain the modus vivendi with the Japanese until ordered otherwise. Rather than receiving Free French code books for future radio exchanges, Milon had to arrange for Indochina Army code books to be smuggled out to Pechkoff. By September, the nascent Free French group in Hanoi could communicate with Algiers via Chungking.[69]

65. DGI, 27, 51.

66. Philippe Devillers, Histoire du Vietnam de 1940 à 1952 (Paris, 1952), 115, 153. DGI, 87. Patti, Why Viet Nam? 310, 564 n. 6. On release from Japanese detention in late August 1945, Bocquet vehemently opposed the fledgling Vietnamese government.

67. Gilbert David, Chroniques secrètes d'Indochine (1928–1946), vol. 1 (Paris, 1994), 87–176.

68. In late 1943, Colonel Pechkoff became chargé d'affaires in Chungking, while Colonel Emblanc replaced him as head of the French Military Mission.

69. Charbonneau and Maigre, Les Parias, 37. DGI, 50, 53, 54–55, 88–92. Devillers, Histoire, 117. The key person in the Free French group inside Indochina seems to have been Captain Marcel Levain, head of the China Section of the Bureau

For some months plans to use this radio link were hindered by confusion surrounding the struggle for power within the CFLN between General de Gaulle and General Giraud. As mentioned previously, Giraud had selected Commander Meynier to work with the Americans in developing a clandestine Indochina network. Pechkoff's team in Chungking and Kunming refused to cooperate with Meynier and lobbied for his recall. General Eugène Mordant, commander of the colonial army in Indochina, was inclined to funnel information via the Meynier network even after being informed by Captain Milon of contact with the French Military Mission.[70] To further complicate matters, in October 1943 Governor-General Decoux dispatched his own emissary to Algiers, a civilian banker named François, who received a hearing from Léon Pignon (later high commissioner of Indochina) in the Colonial Commissariat. Perhaps because everyone was preoccupied by the de Gaulle–Giraud dispute, or because Decoux was considered too fervent a Pétainist, this opportunity was allowed to lapse.[71] By early 1944, de Gaulle had vanquished Giraud in Algiers, yet a multiplicity of intelligence agencies continued to exist and occasionally to operate at cross-purposes.

General de Gaulle Acts

From early 1944 on, de Gaulle moved to assert his authority over the colonial establishment in Indochina, starting with the armed forces. "The moment has come for Indochina to be subordinated to the Committee of National Liberation," he wrote General Mordant on 29 February, saying he should prepare to resist an eventual Japanese attack. De Gaulle also assured Mordant that he was working to influence Allied policies affecting Indochina, mentioning adverse propaganda, bombing, and especially warding off proposals to launch Chinese forces into the colony. Without mentioning President Roosevelt by name, de Gaulle explained that certain "tendentious opinions" about the temporary weakness of France in the Far East made it imperative that the French play a key role in the liberation of Indochina from Japanese occupation. For that purpose, a Corps léger d'intervention was being formed, which by the first half of 1945 would total about fifty thousand men.[72]

---

de statistiques militaires (i.e., secret military intelligence), who was from the same Saint-Cyr class as Captain Milon, an artillery officer.

70. *DGI*, 55, 56, 58.

71. Claude de Boisanger, *On pouvait éviter la guerre d'Indochine: Souvenirs, 1941–1945* (Paris, 1977), 68–70, 76–77, 130–31. Gautier, *9 Mars 1945*, 95. *DGI*, 135.

72. Gautier, *9 Mars 1945*, 96–97, 101–6. Charles de Gaulle, *Mémoires de guerre: L'Unité (1942–1944)* (Paris, 1956), 680–83.

This important statement of Free French policy did not reach Mordant until April, and it was not until early July, as we have seen, that François de Langlade was able to parachute in to provide an authoritative Gaullist gloss.[73] De Langlade was under instructions to meet Decoux, but General Mordant told him that this was impossible, given the difficulty of traveling to the governor-general's summer residence in Dalat during the rainy season. It seems more likely that Mordant either feared Decoux's negative reaction, or wished to retain sole responsibility for building the resistance in Indochina.[74] Major Milon, who accompanied de Langlade carrying instructions from General Blaizot, found General Mordant quite pessimistic about the prospects of success, given the "tired" nature of the Indochina Army and its long lack of contact with the métropole. "If you do nothing, the Japanese will take all of you in garrison," Milon recalled saying in response.[75]

Not happy with his Mordant encounter, de Langlade also provided Colonel Robert at the Lang Son fortress with a letter authorizing him to communicate with the Free French without Mordant's knowledge.[76] Meanwhile, Mordant devised a scheme whereby his statutory retirement later in July could be used to screen his Free French activities. Mordant's proposed replacement, General Georges Aymé, was prepared to accept him as de facto superior. Decoux opposed Aymé's appointment, claiming in a message to the Vichy premier, Pierre Laval, that Aymé had displayed disloyalty by failing to include in his routine orders of the day a phrase affirming the fidelity of his troops to Marshal Pétain.[77] Aymé took over as armed forces commander all the same, and in late August the CFLN secretly confirmed Mordant as resistance head in Indochina.[78] The outlines of civil-military confusion, conflict, and potential disaster were drawn.[79]

73. According to *DGI*, 59, General de Gaulle's letter of 29 Feb. was received in segments by radio during April.

74. *DGI*, 28, 95–97, 99–100, 102. De Boisanger, *On pouvait éviter la guerre*, 86, 136–38.

75. *DGI*, 100–101. Mordant also took exception to being placed under the orders of his junior, Blaizot, commenting sardonically that Blaizot had been given his brigade by Vichy, his division by Giraud, and his corps by de Gaulle.

76. *DGI*, 101–2.

77. Isoart, "Aux origines d'une guerre," 30. Nine months earlier, Decoux had informed Vichy that Aymé was against any resolute resistance to a "Sino-American" invasion.

78. *DGI*, 60. Mordant's formal title was *délégué général du Comité d'action pour la libération de l'Indochine*.

79. Some idea of the tangled lines of French authority and communication can be obtained from studying the chart titled "Organisation politique et militaire

Not until late October did General Aymé inform Governor-General Decoux of Mordant's status. According to Decoux, rumors of Mordant's activities had been circulating for months among French citizens and the "annamites évolués" alike. Now, confronted directly, Decoux decided to radio Paris asking either to be reconfirmed in his powers or relieved as governor-general.[80] Paris rejected both options, instructing Decoux to serve as a screen from the Japanese. Decoux acquiesced, but the poisoned atmosphere between him and the military chiefs made construction of any policy to deal with growing pressures from both the Japanese and the Allies all the more difficult.[81]

Aside from personal resentment at having been bypassed by the CFLN and lied to by subordinates for more than a year, Decoux remained opposed to any plans for either Allied invasion of Indochina or trying to turn the colonial apparatus into a device to sabotage the Japanese. He particularly objected to Gaullist assumptions that Indochina was "occupied" and hence needed to be "liberated." On 31 August 1944, Decoux had joined with the still-recognized Vichy ambassador in Tokyo and the chargé d'affaires in Peking to advise the new authorities in Paris to maintain the neutrality of France and Indochina in the Pacific, in return for which "we hope to see out the end of the fighting without loss." Any Allied attack on Indochina would provoke disastrous consequences:

> The protected populations of Indochina, whose loyalty and gratitude toward France rests primarily on the maintenance of peace, will neither understand nor tolerate a different policy. Any change of policy, however temporary, runs the risk of creating very serious obstacles to the reestablishment of French sovereignty, especially in Tonkin, should there be Chinese interference.[82]

(hiver 1944–1945)," in Claude Hesse d'Alzon, *La Présence militaire française en Indochine (1940–1945)* (Paris, 1985), 297.

80. Jean Decoux, *A la barre de l'Indochine: Histoire de mon gouvernement général, 1940–1945* (Paris, 1952), 306–8. Gautier, *9 Mars 1945*, 89–91, 121. Devillers, *Histoire*, 118–19.

81. Decoux, *A la barre*, 308–10, 316–20. De Boisanger, *On pouvait éviter la guerre*, 83–86, describes being called in late October 1944 from Dalat to Hanoi by Mordant, who introduced him to de Langlade; presumably de Boisanger tried thence to serve as intermediary with Decoux. Gabriel Sabattier, *Le Destin de l'Indochine: Souvenirs et documents, 1941–1951* (Paris, 1952), 99–100, 146–50, contains a detailed comparison of Decoux and Mordant, based on the author's four-year experience dealing with both men.

82. Decoux, *A la barre*, 302–3. Gautier, *9 Mars 1945*, 351–53. Héduy, *Histoire*, 252. Stein Tønnesson has located a somewhat different version of this "message à trois" in the Swedish archives, which does not mention anything about neutrality.

Perhaps fearing that these words had not reached top levels, or had not been considered seriously, Decoux sent another message to a naval colleague in Paris on 9 October, urging examination of the relevant Vichy dossiers and acknowledgment that French sovereignty had been sustained since 1940. "Any harsh change of this policy would have very serious consequences for French Indochina, and I signify my explicit and categorical reservations," he concluded.[83] Decoux seems deliberately to have ignored the fact that the CFLN had declared war on Japan in December 1941, so that any policy of neutrality would have required the Free French to exclude themselves from operations in Asia and the Pacific. Only days after the liberation of Paris, however, the Free French publicly voided Decoux's authority to collaborate with Japan and asserted that the fate of Indochina would be settled by armed confrontation between the French Republic and the Japanese government.[84]

For General de Gaulle the overriding objective was to reassert France's status as a global power, which in the wartime context demanded a French contribution to the Allied victory over Japan, preferably in Indochina. Already in July 1943, de Gaulle had designated Indochina's liberation to be the highest-priority operation outside the métropole.[85] The next month General Blaizot was selected to begin piecing together a Far Eastern expeditionary force in North Africa, and in September de Gaulle and Giraud jointly proposed "a substantial participation by French troops in the liberation of Indochina" to Churchill, Stalin, and Roosevelt.[86] In December, acutely mindful of President Roosevelt's disparaging attitude, de Gaulle

Stein Tønnesson, *The Vietnamese Revolution of 1945: Roosevelt, Ho Chi Minh and de Gaulle in a World at War* (London, 1991), 47–48. Decoux had also summarized his position in a 10 August radio report to Vichy, apparently anticipating that it would soon be read by the approaching Free French.

83. Decoux, *A la barre*, 500. The messages of both 31 August and 9 October relied on Vichy codes, which, as suggested in chapter 1, may well have been cracked by the Japanese. In September and November, Decoux apparently sent two additional personal emissaries to Paris. See *DGI*, 27, 136, and USNA, OSS record no. 110965 (15 Dec. 1944), 6, 9. Curiously, in their memoirs, neither Decoux nor de Boisanger mentions these representatives. An unnamed French diplomat in Tokyo also sent a message via Swedish channels, going so far as to argue that "the situation in Indochina represents a justification of the French and Western presence in the Far East." See Tønnesson, *Vietnamese Revolution*, 46.

84. Radio France (Algiers), announcement of 30 Aug., quoted in the *New York Times*, 31 Aug. 1944, 16.

85. Philippe Devillers, *Paris-Saigon-Hanoi: Les Archives de la guerre, 1944–1947* (Paris, 1988), 21–22.

86. Devillers, *Histoire*, 115. Dennis, *Troubled Days*, 29. *DGI*, 13, 56.

publicly chided the "great democracies" for not providing aid to French Indochina in 1940, thus forcing it, "after a heroic but vain resistance, to submit to the demands of the enemy."[87] On another occasion de Gaulle opined that French troops in Indochina would at his bidding rise up and massacre the Japanese, a claim regarded as "nonsense" by the British.[88] For de Gaulle, the legend of heroic resistance, both in the métropole and overseas, provided a cloak of honor with which French citizens might cover the bitter truths of submission to foreigners.

In the summer of 1944, de Gaulle established an interministerial Comité d'action en Indochine, chaired by the commissioner of colonies, René Pleven.[89] Its essential objectives were to arrange participation in the liberation of the colony, and to prepare political, economic, and administrative reforms "likely to assure actual acknowledgment of our position in Indochina."[90] The question of what to do about American objections to Free French participation in the Pacific War had become more pressing as the liberation of Paris approached and U.S. forces made ready to invade the Philippines. Reports of American secret service contacts with Annamite revolutionaries added another note of urgency.[91] From Chungking, Pechkoff proposed offering special postwar commercial privileges to the United States in Indochina, but this idea was rejected by the government, at least until the Americans first agreed to recognize France's "indisputable political rights."[92] Others argued that the Americans would respond favorably to some French declaration of liberal intentions regarding the peoples of Indochina. Nonetheless, Free French attitudes were probably best symbolized by René Pleven's suggestion that two torpedo boats just

87. *Viet-Nam Crisis: A Documentary History*, ed. Allan W. Cameron, vol. 1, *1940–1956* (Ithaca, N.Y., 1971), 11.

88. Thorne, *Allies*, 349.

89. *DGI*, 62. Other institutions represented included Defense (General Alphonse Juin), Foreign Affairs (Jean Chauvel), and DGER (Jacques Soustelle). General Blaizot and Henri Laurentie also participated. Commissariats became ministries after the shift from Algiers to Paris. In December 1944, Paul Giacobbi replaced Pleven as minister of colonies. In February 1945, the organizational title was changed from Comité d'action to Comité interministériel de l'Indochine (COMININDO), with the président du conseil (Charles de Gaulle) taking over as chairman.

90. AOM, INF, c. 120, d. 1087, message, Algiers (Massigli) to Chungking (Pechkoff), 1 Aug. 1944.

91. AOM, INF, c. 120, d. 1087, Pechkoff to Algiers, 19 June 1944.

92. AOM, INF, c. 120, d. 1087, Pechkoff to Massigli, 3 Apr. 1944; Massigli to Free France Chungking, 1 Aug. 1944; and Colonies Alger to Free France Chungking, [?] Aug. 1944. After discussions with William Langdon, Pechkoff seems to have concluded that economic favors would improve American attitudes.

received from U.S. forces in Europe be renamed *L'Indochinois* and *L'An-namite*.[93]

In late 1944, still unable to get more than a forward planning team to Kandy because of Roosevelt's opposition, the French Foreign Ministry approached the American ambassador with a proposal to contribute troops to any move that General Douglas MacArthur might make from the Philippines toward Indochina.[94] In late January 1945, blocked on this front as well, Paris instructed General Mordant to ensure that the colonial armed forces in Indochina maintained neutrality in the event of American action, a message that managed thoroughly to confuse and perplex the recipients.[95] From the archival record, which the historian Stein Tønnesson has examined meticulously, it seems that many Free French officials were as much the victims of American disinformation about an impending invasion of Indochina as the Japanese. As late as 1 March, French intelligence analysts argued that Allied control of Indochina was indispensable prior to the final push on the Japanese home islands, as it enabled the Southwest Pacific, Central Pacific, and China commands to link up with one another.[96]

Like Vichy diplomats before them, Free French representatives in Chungking were especially concerned to monitor and if possible divert any Chinese plans to attack into Indochina. Assuming that only the United States could prevent such a move, the CFLN representative in Washington was employed in October 1943 to present a memorandum arguing that the Annamites, because of their hereditary animosity toward China, would turn completely against the Allies in the event of a Chinese invasion.[97] Perhaps realizing that the Americans might consider such words self-serving, a subsequent message from Chungking to Algiers suggested the need to assuage their "ignorant anticolonialism" by somehow communicating the "liberal intentions" of France regarding the Indochinese populations.[98] Nonetheless, in mid 1944, Ambassador Pechkoff was still pre-

93. AOM, INF, c. 120, d. 1087, DGER intelligence report, 17 Nov. 1944.

94. Gautier, *9 Mars 1945*, 171. Aside from diplomatic obstacles, the initial selection of a number of black African units for the CLI was criticized by both British and American military sources. Jean Marchand, *L'Indochine en guerre* (Paris, 1954), 98.

95. Sabattier, *Le Destin de l'Indochine*, 102–3. Decoux, *A la barre*, 323–24, sardonically expresses his "great surprise" at this Paris directive.

96. Tønnesson, *Vietnamese Revolution*, 199–204, 215. Curiously, the French ignored SEAC in this assessment.

97. *DGI*, 131.

98. AOM, INF, c. 120, d. 1087, Coiffard to Diplofrance, 5 Nov. 1943.

pared to justify the French position primarily in terms of long-term defense against China. In Indochina, unlike the situation in the Philippines or Indonesia, Pechkoff asserted:

> Our establishment in the colony has as its basic objective the protection of the population from the seductive power of the East, historically displayed, to a greater or lesser degree, through the proximity of China. The Annamites are well aware that, left to themselves, they would not be in a position to defend themselves against the patient infiltration of the Chinese mass. The presence of a foreign power in Indochina is thus the essential prerequisite of peaceful development.[99]

Throughout this period, French officials monitored the Chinese press closely as a possible barometer of intentions regarding Indochina. In early 1945, newspapers in Chungking and Kunming seemed less hostile, although they still denounced French imperialism and France's quick surrender to the Japanese in 1940, as well as continuing to allude to China's strategic and economic interests in Indochina.[100]

The Moment of Truth Approaches

Since the liberation of Paris in late August 1944, many French citizens in Indochina had made no effort to hide their patriotic enthusiasm. A few went further, showing public contempt for the Japanese.[101] Meanwhile, Allied radio broadcasts made open reference to resistance preparations inside Indochina, leading General Mordant to request "extreme prudence" for fear of precipitating a Japanese ultimatum.[102] As Force 136 / Service d'action teams dropped into Indochina and established contact, their presence became the subject of excited conversation within the French community. Allied weapons and equipment, even Allied cigarettes and razor blades, made their way into colonial military bases and civilian villas.[103] Even

99. Ibid., Pechkoff to Algiers, 19 June 1944.

100. AOM, INF, c. 209, d. 1576, Pechkoff to Ministry of Foreign Affairs, 2 Feb. 1945.

101. Kiyoko K. Nitz, "Japanese Military Policy towards French Indochina during the Second World War: The Road to the *Meigō Sakusen* (9 March 1945)," *JSEAS* 14, no. 2 (Sept. 1983): 336, 337.

102. Sabattier, *Le Destin de l'Indochine*, 101. As early as December 1943, the outgoing governor of New Caledonia was quoted publicly on the beginnings of a Free French movement in Indochina linked with missions in India and China. *New York Times*, 18 Dec. 1943, 4.

103. Charbonneau and Maigre, *Les Parias*, 53–54. Héduy, *Histoire*, 259. Jacques Mordal, *Marine Indochine* (Paris, 1953), 66–67. Tsuchihashi Yūichi, "Furansu-gun o busō kaijo" [Disarming the French Army], special ed. of *Shūkan Yomiuri*, 8 Dec.

Decoux seems to have become imprudent: in the traditional governor-general's New Year's message, he rejoiced at the liberation of France and hoped for reunification of the empire in 1945.[104] More remarkably, the 28 February issue of *Indochine*, a pictorial magazine edited in Hanoi by the Gouvernement général, repeated General de Gaulle's comments on Indochina at the Lunar New Year's festivities in Paris.[105] During this time, the Japanese patiently compiled information on particular Allied air drops, French pickups, French failure to fire on enemy planes, and French refusal to turn over captured American airmen.[106]

The Anglo-French and American establishments were now engaged in a secret service steeplechase to Saigon and Hanoi. With no idea when the CLI might get as far as Ceylon or India, much less Indochina, the authorities in Paris put ever more hope and operational responsibility on the Service d'action (SA), modeled after the resistance network developed in France prior to the June 1944 Normandy landings.[107] A covert hierarchy was to be constructed parallel to the existing military and civilian chains of command in Indochina. General Mordant was the point of contact between these hierarchies, while Lieutenant Colonel Cavalin, chief of the Bureau de statistiques militaires, maintained regular radio contact with the DGER in Calcutta. To ensure secrecy and external control, local SA radio teams were to communicate with each other only through Calcutta, never directly. Only French men and women would be recruited to the SA. Names of suitable Annamite sympathizers were to be submitted to higher echelons for consideration, since "one of the distant objectives of the Resistance is to associate the entire Annamite population, especially in the villages, with guerrilla operations against the Japanese."[108]

1956. According to Yokoyama Masayuki, consul general in Hue at the time, Japanese intelligence knew of at least thirty persons who had parachuted into Indochina, carrying radios, maps, and thousands of paper piastres, in the three months prior to the 9 March coup. Interview with Yokoyama in Tokyo, 16 Nov. 1967.

104. Gautier, *9 Mars 1945*, 133–34, 354–55. Paris subsequently rebuked Decoux for this broadcast, reminding him that his role was to "act as cover for the Resistance and to inspire confidence in the Japanese."

105. AOM, INF, c. 123, d. 1108, subdossier 3, DGER report, 23 June 1945.

106. *PJI*, 9 Mar. 1945 (Tokyo, in English).

107. If units from the CLI could be inserted, the SA was expected to operate like General Orde Wingate's "Chindits" in Burma, attacking Japanese lines of communication. *DGI*, 58, 101.

108. "Instruction du 10 septembre," issued by General Mordant and reprinted in Sabattier, *Le Destin de l'Indochine*, 387–90. See also Mordant's modifications of 10 Dec. 1944, reproduced in ibid., 390–92.

In practice, much time seems to have been devoted in Hanoi to evaluating the political trustworthiness of existing French officers and administrators. General Gabriel Sabattier, commander of army units in Tonkin, was disgusted one day to see General Mordant poring over a list of naval officers and using a blue pencil to tick reliable men, a red pencil to mark suspects.[109] Although Mordant was supposed to control all clandestine SA teams, Colonel Cavalin often used his radio connection with Calcutta to function semi-autonomously, while Calcutta routinely bypassed both Mordant and Cavalin with direct orders to dispersed teams.[110] Following a second mission to Indochina in November–December 1944, de Langlade reported pessimistically about breaches of security, the inability of middle-aged colonial personnel to withstand future guerrilla operations, and the lack of experienced cadres from outside who might replace them.[111]

In late January 1945, General de Gaulle and General Alphonse Juin, Armed Forces chief of staff, sent General Mordant a detailed "plan of defense" for Indochina, trying to anticipate from a distance various Japanese actions and appropriate French counteractions. It must have made sobering reading, since it predicted no substantial Allied intervention for at least six months, yet ordered the entire colonial establishment, military and civilian, forcibly to resist any Japanese attempt to take over the colony. De Gaulle and Juin envisaged troop withdrawals to several mountain redoubts, yet said almost nothing about how these units would be fed or resupplied with ammunition.[112] When General Sabattier subsequently requested permission from General Mordant to use coolies or pack animals to establish caches in the mountains for future guerrilla action, Mordant refused on the grounds that this might alert the Japanese.[113]

Unlike in France, clandestine SA units in Indochina were not permitted to refine their skills in practice—for example, by blowing up bridges and power lines or ambushing Japanese trucks. Yet they might be called upon subsequently to expose themselves to full-scale repression some months prior to any arrival of Allied forces. Confined to passive training, resistance attitudes in fact barely penetrated an army and administration still oper-

109. Ibid., 89, 106.
110. Gautier, *9 Mars 1945*, 116–19.
111. Devillers, *Paris-Saigon-Hanoi*, 48–49.
112. "Directive au sujet du plan de défense de l'Indochine," 26 Jan. 1945, reprinted in Sabattier, *Le Destin de l'Indochine*, 410–17. For more details on Free French military planning on Indochina, dating back to May 1943, see Tønnesson, *Vietnamese Revolution*, 158–60.
113. Sabattier, *Le Destin de l'Indochine*, 103.

ating according to long-established routines, amid a native population more or less indifferent to French political choices.[114] Above all, while the resistance in Europe had been conducted among people of the same skin color, in Indochina it would somehow be carried out by a tiny minority of whites in a sea of "yellow" Asians.[115]

A new ingredient was added at the end of January 1945, when Captain Paul Mus, code-named Caille, dropped into Indochina charged with beginning to organize resistance among selected native elements, the so-called *autochtones évolués*. Mus enjoyed many acquaintances among the Vietnamese elite, having grown up in the colony, where his father was a ranking education official, and then spent some years there as a bright young archaeologist and historian.[116] Since early 1944, General de Gaulle had urged his subordinates to consider how to associate the Indochinese peoples with the French resistance, yet concrete proposals radioed to the colony or Kunming met with skepticism or outright hostility.[117] When Mus explained his mission in person to Decoux in February, the governor-general made clear his opposition. Fearing that his five-year effort to maintain order and discipline was about to dissolve into "anarchy and a confusion of powers," Decoux once again queried Paris critically, trying to obtain acknowledgment of his authority over at least the civilian echelons of the Indochina administration.[118] General Mordant proved more receptive to Mus's ideas, but his commander of Tonkin troop units, General Sabattier, disagreed with any development of a clandestine Annamite apparatus.[119]

In late February, another Free French representative who parachuted into Indochina encountered widespread opposition to any incorporation of indigenous elements into resistance units.[120] Many French men and women in the colony felt it was a serious mistake to educate the natives, much less allow them to participate in preparations to overthrow the Japanese.[121] Even members of the French Socialist Party in Hanoi were

114. Jean Marchand, "Les Origines du drame indochinois," *Revue de défense nationale*, Oct. 1952, 318.

115. René Bauchar [René Charbonneau], *Rafales sur l'Indochine* (Paris, 1946), 152. *DGI*, 123.

116. John T. McAlister, Jr., and Paul Mus, *The Vietnamese and Their Revolution* (New York, 1970), 7–15.

117. Isoart, "Aux origines d'une guerre," 36–37.

118. Decoux, *A la barre*, 320–23.

119. Sabattier, *Le Destin de l'Indochine*, 106.

120. Isoart, "Aux origines d'une guerre," 39.

121. Françoise Martin, *Heures tragiques au Tonkin (9 mars 1945–18 mars 1946)* (Paris, 1948), 27–28.

against making major concessions to the natives. When a group of Vietnamese intellectuals approached them with a proposal to recognize Vietnam's independence following the war and negotiate cooperative agreements as between diplomatic equals, the Vietnamese were reproached for being greedy and ill informed.[122]

General Sabattier believed that the attitude of the native peoples would make it impossible to sustain guerrilla zones of any kind for very long.[123] Nonetheless, in late February, he issued a detailed operations order designed to prepare troop units for a fighting retreat to selected upland positions, where they might hope to be resupplied from China. The objective, according to Sabattier's order, was to "prolong resistance so that the French flag remains flying over the greatest possible area . . . right up to the moment of intervention by the liberating forces." Units that found themselves encircled and unable to break out were to "defend themselves to the utmost of their abilities."[124] Although not stated in the operations order, Sabattier apparently intended that his key combat groups would avoid being confined to particular upland zones, instead withdrawing closer to the Yunnan frontier and anticipated assistance. Relations between Paris and Chungking had shown signs of improvement, and French representatives had already approached the Chinese about permission for some units to cross into Yunnan.[125] We do not know how the Chinese reacted, but the U.S. State Department proceeded to bend President Roosevelt's earlier ban on aid to resistance groups in Indochina by authorizing at least medical supplies.[126] Still, the issue remained very sensitive, causing the head of OSS China to instruct his subordinates on 4 March to refer all proposals for supplies to Indochina or dealings with the French to him.[127]

In the Wake of the Japanese Takeover

When the Japanese struck on 9 March 1945, the Free French resistance network established during the previous six months collapsed like a house

---

122. Phan Anh, "Con duong di toi Cach Mang Thang Tam cua Toi" [My Road toward the August Revolution], *Nhan Dan* (Hanoi), 21 Aug. 1960, 4.

123. Isoart, "Aux origines d'une guerre," 38.

124. "Ordre général d'opérations no. 4," 28 Feb. 1945, reprinted in Sabattier, *Le Destin de l'Indochine*, 393–410.

125. Sabattier, *Le Destin de l'Indochine*, 95. Gautier, *9 Mars 1945*, 126–27.

126. Patti, *Why Viet Nam?* 64. Macy W. Marvel, "Drift and Intrigue: United States Relations with the Viet Minh, 1945," *Millennium* (London) 4, no. 1 (1975): 12.

127. Patti, *Why Viet Nam?* 63.

of cards. Most civilian groups had no idea where to go or what to do, reflecting Governor-General Decoux's quietly successful effort to shield his administrative hierarchy from General Mordant's meddling, as well as the preference of most Indochina Army officers to treat resistance as a strictly military operation. Yet it is indicative of the military's own lack of preparedness that only three out of thirteen general officers escaped Japanese incarceration or execution.[128] As noted previously, many military units surrendered without a fight, while others defended themselves for a while in fortified positions with no hope of breaking out. Large quantities of French weapons, ammunition, motor vehicles, and other supplies and equipment were seized intact by the Japanese.

Those troop units that did manage to evade the Japanese dragnet found themselves out of radio contact with one another, forced to abandon everything that could not be carried by mule or human, and increasingly preoccupied by the search for food.[129] Some isolated mountain posts employed passenger pigeons to communicate—until hungry soldiers ate them.[130] A Force 136 / SA radio post and cache of parachuted supplies had been established earlier thirty-five kilometers northwest of Vinh (Nghe An), the plan being for units in the city to retreat there, reequip, and commence guerrilla operations. Japanese forces got there first, however, killing or capturing almost all of the 303 defenders, 76 of whom were European.[131] Further south, in Quang Nam province, four French SA officers dropped before the coup were forcibly detained by the local Viet Minh adherents, not to be released until fifteen months later.[132]

Such altercations between fleeing French personnel and local inhabitants were rare, however. If the colonial unit was large, villagers often ran into the forest at first sight.[133] Smaller units might encounter people

128. These were General Sabattier, General Marcel Alessandri, commander of the Tonkin Second Brigade, and General Turguin, commander of the Annam-Laos Brigade, who lost contact with his troops, and, on escape to China, was ordered back to Paris. Sabattier, *Le Destin de l'Indochine*, 195. Those captured were Admiral Decoux, General Mordant, General Aymé, General Delsuc, General Noël, Admiral Bérenger, General Massimi, General Chamagne, and General Froissart-Broissiat. General Lemonnier was beheaded at Lang Son.

129. Sabattier, *Le Destin de l'Indochine*, 92–93, 152–87. Charbonneau and Maigre, *Les Parias*, 179–234. Hesse d'Alzon, *La Présence*, 219–50.

130. Charbonneau and Maigre, *Les Parias*, 69.

131. Ibid., 134–35.

132. AOM, INF, CP 186, "Bulletin quotidien du Sûreté," no. 126 (19 June 1946).

133. Sabattier, *Le Destin de l'Indochine*, 161–63. In Laos the situation was different, partly owing to several months of preparatory Force 136 / SA work

armed with spears and machetes, intent on protecting food stores and livestock, but not impeding passage. Paul Mus and a compatriot, escaping Hanoi in the direction of Son La, found Vietnamese quite willing to facilitate their departure, offering food, shelter, local guides, and advice for evading the Japanese.[134] But this was not done out of "loyalty." As Mus reflected later:

> Even in the most remote villages, the peasants knew that the positions of power in Indochina were now reversed. Their prescience and self-confidence made them seem like a company of actors suddenly adapting to new roles in a new play even though their previous production closed only the night before.[135]

Georges Condominas, later to become a famous anthropologist, was hidden from Japanese patrols by a Vietnamese monk, only to be captured when he slipped back to a French plantation to obtain food and money. Japanese threats to shoot him and other French prisoners if they did not reveal their weapons caches were forestalled by local Vietnamese affirmations that no firearms existed, which happened to be the truth.[136]

General Sabattier was unable to reestablish contact with Calcutta and Paris until reaching a Force 136 radio post at Lai Chau on 23 March, at which point he assured General de Gaulle of his loyalty and resolve to defend Indochina to the end against the Japanese aggressors.[137] This being precisely the sort of statement that de Gaulle wanted, Sabattier's message was released to the media and gained wide currency. However, the regular air drops of supplies, which Sabattier, Alessandri, and other troop commanders now needed so desperately, failed to materialize. Occasionally, a few British aircraft would appear and parachute arms and ammunition to a particular French column.[138] From 18 March on, U.S. aircraft were

---

among the upland peoples, most notably those Meo (Hmong) clans owing fidelity to Touby Lyfong. Ayrolles, *L'Indochine ne répond plus*, 19–25, 35–36, 43–49, 54–60. Héduy, *Histoire*, 273. Charbonneau and Maigre, *Les Parias*, 242–58.

134. Paul Mus, "L'Indochine en 1945," *Politique étrangère* (Paris) 11 (1946): 358–60, 365–66, 372–74. According to Mus's first confidential report of 28 March 1945, discussed in Tønnesson, *Vietnamese Revolution*, 244, the Vietnamese were disappointed that the shooting didn't signify American arrival.

135. McAlister and Mus, *Vietnamese and Their Revolution*, 16.

136. Discussion with Professor Condominas in Hanoi, 8 Mar. 1990.

137. Sabattier, *Le Destin de l'Indochine*, 171.

138. Charbonneau and Maigre, *Les Parias*, 214, 238, mention particular drops on 12 March and 27 April, the latter mostly composed of material too heavy to carry from the site. On 4 May, according to ibid., 336, the British dropped a substantial quantity at Fong Senh, on the Chinese side of the frontier. Ayrolles, *L'Indochine*

authorized by Washington to assist the French, yet General Wedemeyer seems to have interpreted this not to include drops of arms and ammunition.[139] Fourteenth Air Force planes did bomb and strafe Japanese units pursuing the French; on 30 March, OSS Lieutenant Robert Ettinger flew into the airstrip at Dien Bien Phu to improve coordination of such attack missions.[140] Between 31 March and 13 April, American aircraft flew ninety-six attack sorties at direct French request.[141]

In Paris, General de Gaulle and some of his aides were convinced that Roosevelt continued deliberately to withhold assistance. Press leaks accused the United States of failing to support legitimate French resistance efforts, of excluding its European allies from the Pacific War, and of entertaining its own designs on Indochina.[142] Trying to defuse French anger, the U.S. State Department urged the War Department to order at least a token drop of supplies. Blankets and medicines were provided, but General Wedemeyer, citing extreme shortages in China Theater, continued to reject appeals for arms and ammunition, much less a puzzling French request for gasoline.[143] After hearing by radio of President Roosevelt's death on 12 April, General Sabattier ordered a solemn memorial ceremony at his Phong Saly headquarters in Laos, which was attended by two American officers.[144] Meanwhile, Sabattier was being blitzed with orders from de Gaulle to remain inside Indochina for as long as possible and not to trust the advice of Americans or others on this

---

ne répond plus, 119–23, describes drops by two Liberators at Sakok, in Laos, on 25 April. Sabattier, *Le Destin de l'Indochine,* 212, and *DGI,* 65, are therefore apparently incorrect in stating that the Royal Air Force parachuted its last arms to resistants on 19 April.

139. Charbonneau and Maigre, *Les Parias,* 146, do, however, mention "American Liberators" dropping equipment that helped in confrontations with the Japanese on 21–22 March.

140. Smith, *OSS,* 328. Sabattier, *Le Destin de l'Indochine,* 200–201. Ronald Spector, "Allied Intelligence and Indochina, 1943–1945," *Pacific Historical Review* (Berkeley) 51 (1982): 34–35.

141. USNA, DOS, Record Group 59, 54-D-190, box 9.

142. *New York Times,* 13 Mar. 1945, 11; 15 Mar. 1945, 15; 22 Mar. 1945, 5; and 31 Mar. 1945, 13.

143. Spector, "Allied Intelligence," 35–36. Tønnesson, *Vietnamese Revolution,* 258–60. Charbonneau and Maigre, *Les Parias,* 299, say that the commander of the Sixty-ninth Transport Group, General Kennedy, allowed his pilots to drop some supplies. Sabattier, *Le Destin de l'Indochine,* 200–201, 204–6, confirms this, and describes the efforts of Kennedy's liaison officer, Major Lloyd Gibbons, to obtain more, until he was apparently ordered to desist.

144. Sabattier, *Le Destin de l'Indochine,* 201–2.

crucial issue. No money arrived from Paris to pay the troops or purchase food, however, and Sabattier's store of piastres and opium was almost gone.[145] In mid April, he desperately requested authority to negotiate assistance from the Chinese military in exchange for promises of a future "open port" in Tonkin, but this was denied.[146] Receiving a personal letter from Wedemeyer on 21 April offering only medicines, Sabattier realized his position was hopeless. At the end of the month, his bedraggled column crossed into China.[147]

Although General de Gaulle had hoped that the Japanese would not overturn the colonial administration in Indochina, once this happened he resolved to take maximum political advantage. No longer did he need to endure American barbs about Franco-Japanese collaboration. For French citizens everywhere, the last physical remnant of Vichy was gone. In a radio broadcast on 14 March, de Gaulle claimed to have created the conditions whereby a great battle was being fought against the Japanese. "Not for a single hour did France lose the hope and the will to recover Free Indochina," he declared. French unity was indivisible, "whether it be at Brazzaville, Algiers, Hanoi, or even at Nantes, Lyon, or Paris."[148] The next day, de Gaulle affirmed that "by the trials of all and the blood of the soldiers at this moment a solemn pact is sealed between France and the peoples of the Indochinese Union."[149] Members of the French Consultative Assembly provided the chorus, with Gaston Monneville, for example, asserting that France had to choose whether "to remain a second-rank nation or instead, thanks to the contribution of her overseas territories, to become once again a great power."[150] Addressing the assembly himself, de Gaulle told it not to pay any particular attention to interpretations of events in Indochina offered by foreign journalists, then stirred the patriotism of his audience by reading a telegram from a beleaguered French garrison.[151]

145. Ibid., 192–96, 202, 204. Charbonneau and Maigre, *Les Parias*, 179–200. In Cao Bang province, Colonel Reul took with him both stockpiled opium and the silver piastres meant to pay the producers. Charbonneau and Maigre, *Les Parias*, 309–12.

146. AOM, INF, c. 123, d. 1108, subdossier 3, DGER report, 17 Apr. 1945.

147. Sabattier, *Le Destin de l'Indochine*, 206–7, 213–17.

148. D. Bruce Marshall, *The French Colonial Myth and Constitution-making in the Fourth Republic* (New Haven, 1973), 133, 135, 192–93.

149. *New York Times*, 15 Mar. 1945, 15, as cited in Ellen Hammer, *The Struggle for Indochina* (Stanford, 1966), 43.

150. Marshall, *French Colonial Myth*, 195.

151. Ibid., 193.

With Indochina capturing worldwide attention, General de Gaulle decided to issue a broad policy declaration on 24 March, which continued to be cited by government officials for several years thereafter, despite dramatic changes in context. The image was projected of brave French and native peoples fighting for a lofty common goal—an "Indochina Federation" within a "French Union." Mention was made of equal access to all government positions, democratic liberties, trade unions, economic autonomy, and industrialization. Such undoubted reforms were hedged, however, by metropolitan hegemony over foreign affairs and defense, the right of the French Constituent Assembly to determine conditions of participation in the French Union, and the right of a governor-general to arbitrate between different parts of the Indochina Federation. Most important for the Vietnamese, this 24 March declaration foreshadowed that in view of differences of "civilization, race and traditions," Tonkin, Annam, and Cochinchina would be treated as three separate "countries."[152] No provision was made for voluntary adherence to, much less withdrawal from, either the Indochina Federation or the French Union.

The "Brazzaville Spirit"

The declaration of 24 March was not a hasty reaction to the Japanese coup or Bao Dai's proclamation of independence, although the timing of its release was hardly fortuitous.[153] As early as October 1940, General de Gaulle had stressed that the French empire belonged to the national patrimony. In June 1942, at the Albert Hall in London, de Gaulle outlined Free French responsibilities in relation to the colonies and protectorates.[154] A CFLN declaration on 8 December 1943 promised Indochina a new political status within the French community in recognition of the "loyal attitude of the Indochinese peoples in the struggle against Japan and Siam." It also anticipated a deliberate loosening of metropolitan controls over Indochina's

---

152. Text in France, *Journal officiel de la République française: Ordonnances et décrets*, 25 Mar. 1945, 1606–7. English translations can be found in *Viet-Nam Crisis*, ed. Cameron, 33–35, and *New Cycle in Asia*, ed. Harold Isaacs (New York, 1947), 159–61. The declaration of 24 March is discussed in Marshall, *French Colonial Myth*, 134–37; Devillers, *Histoire*, 144–45; Hammer, *Struggle*, 43–45; Joseph Buttinger, *Vietnam: A Dragon Embattled* (New York, 1967), 302–3, 609–10; John T. McAlister, *Viet Nam: The Origins of Revolution* (New York, 1969), 274–75; Bernard B. Fall, *The Two Viet-Nams* (New York, 1967), 66–67; and André Teulieres, *La Guerre du Vietnam, 1945–1975* (Paris-Limoges, 1979), 26–27.

153. According to Léon Pignon, as cited in Tønnesson, *Vietnamese Revolution*, 316–17, the text had been revised at least seven times in the preceding few months.

154. *DGI*, 24.

fiscal and tariff systems, as well as closer "intellectual and economic relations" with China.[155]

In late January 1944, representatives of Free France met in Brazzaville for ten days to deliberate postwar colonial policies. There had not been a serious French debate about the "colonial question" since 1930, when Socialist and Radical members of the National Assembly argued in favor of "provisional tutelage" and commitment to eventual independence, but were outvoted by a conservative coalition favoring "restoration," the recapturing of lost initiative, and modernization of colonial institutions. When the left gained power in 1936, the Socialist minister of colonies, Marius Moutet, ignored his previous advocacy of "dominion" or "self-government" status for some colonies, including Indochina, instead focusing on gradual improvements to the existing system.[156] The Brazzaville Conference reasserted France's mission to "elevate" native peoples and to promote mutually beneficial economic growth. Participants, mostly colonial administrators, acknowledged past errors and discussed a range of reforms, but they excluded self-government "even in the most distant future," and rejected any notion that France should account to the international community for the conduct of colonial affairs. Whatever changes were made, France would accomplish them within the family, much as the United States might decide to modify the status of Puerto Rico or the Virgin Islands.[157]

One year later, at the Institute of Pacific Relations Conference in Hot Springs, French participants tried to spell out to an international audience some of the implications of Brazzaville for Indochina.[158] Paul Émile Haggiar, the senior French delegate, revealed that Indochina had been selected as the first venue for an experiment in colonial politics.[159] According to Jean

155. *Viet-Nam Crisis*, ed. Cameron, 11–12. *DGI*, 13, 25–26, 56–57. Jean d'Arcy, "Confrontation des thèses françaises et vietnamiennes," *Politique étrangère* (Paris) 12 (1947): 330. Tønnesson, *Vietnamese Revolution*, 314–15, indicates that Henri Laurentie and Léon Pignon authored this Dec. 1943 declaration.

156. Daniel Hémery, "Aux origines des guerres d'indépendance vietnamiennes: Pouvoir colonial et phénomène communiste en Indochine avant la seconde guerre mondiale," *Mouvement social* (Paris), no. 101 (Oct.–Dec. 1977): 3–35.

157. Louis, *Imperialism at Bay*, 43–46. Donald Lancaster, *The Emancipation of French Indochina* (London, 1961), 122–23.

158. French archival records demonstrate that Paris took the Hot Springs Conference very seriously. See, e.g., the correspondence contained in AOM, INF, c. 120, d. 1089. At one point the French feared that a Vietnamese delegate, "Tao Kim Hai," might make his way to Hot Springs and be allowed by the IPR secretariat to participate.

159. *Christian Science Monitor* (Boston), 18 Jan. 1945, 11. Internal government preparations for this experiment are discussed in Andrew Hardy, "La politique

de la Roche, France would rely on a spirit of cooperation rather than subordination in future relations with Indochina; maintenance of a "single supreme authority" would be tempered by "wide local franchises, which will be allowed to develop freely."[160] After admitting that the rural population of Indochina was "reduced to living miserably in a permanent state of undernourishment on a land which cannot feed them," he advanced a variety of ambitious economic and social programs—without, however, indicating where all the necessary money would come from. De la Roche also voiced concern about the effects of a "jump of six centuries" in the customs and habits of people deeply attached to their traditions, a problem he claimed was aggravated by "the inertia and fatalism common to Oriental peoples."[161] As mentioned earlier, Gaston Rueff proposed the industrialization of Indochina, an end to the French monopoly on financial initiative, and encouragement of American and other foreign investment.[162] Perhaps because he was not a French government employee, Rueff dared to speak, too, of Indochina attaining independence rapidly, albeit within the larger French community. Nevertheless, he expected Europeans to remain in Indochina indefinitely—for example, working among the mountain peoples, where "experience has proven that indigenous peoples prefer new methods to be applied to them by a white man than by a man of their own color but of a different race."[163]

The efforts of de la Roche and Rueff in the United States had already provoked confidential criticism in Paris. Opponents wondered whether it was possible to apply the allegedly liberal "Brazzaville spirit" to Indochina, and whether Rueff in particular was jeopardizing French economic interests in the colony by talking about an open door for foreign investment. The French Embassy in Washington had attempted to stop pub-

économique française en Indochine, 1944–1948" (Maîtrise d'histoire, University of Paris, 1991).

160. Jean de la Roche, "Indo-China in the New French Colonial Framework," *Pacific Affairs* (Honolulu) 18, no. 1 (Mar. 1945): 65.

161. Jean de la Roche, "A Program of Social and Cultural Activity in Indo-China" (paper delivered at the Ninth Conference of the IPR, Jan. 1945), 5, 11.

162. Gaston Rueff, "Postwar Problems of French Indo-China: Economic Aspects," *Pacific Affairs* (Honolulu) 18, no. 2 (June 1945): 137–55.

163. Gaston Rueff, "Postwar Problems of French Indo-China: Social and Political Aspects," *Pacific Affairs* (Honolulu) 18, no. 3 (Sept. 1945): 232, 243. In his article "The Future of French Indo-China," *Foreign Affairs* 23, no. 1 (Oct. 1944): 140–46, Rueff had spoken more cautiously of moving steadily in the direction of "social and economic independence," and eventually achieving the ultimate goal, "self-government."

lication of Rueff's October 1944 *Foreign Affairs* article, "The Future of French Indo-China." Meanwhile, de la Roche complained about lack of support from Paris for his New York press office and forwarded clippings from American periodicals to demonstrate the magnitude of the problem he faced in overcoming "anti-French" attitudes on Indochina. His pleas did persuade the Ministry of Colonies to get permission from the Ministry of Finance to dispatch additional press personnel to New York.[164]

From late 1944 on, the French government also labored hard to persuade its own citizenry of the need to commit resources to the liberation of Indochina. The Ministry of War appears to have been most energetic on this topic. Numerous issues of the ministry's glossy periodical, *L'Armeé française au combat*, were devoted to florid rhetoric on the subject, reminiscent of the 1870s. For example, the cover of a January 1945 special issue titled "Indochine: Terre française" depicted a Sherman tank with the Cross of Lorraine painted on its front crashing through bamboo scrub in front of the massive Jayavarman VII faces at Angkor. Inside, the minister of war, André Diethelm, pledged to deliver Saigon and Hanoi from Japanese oppression, while the minister of colonies, Paul Giacobbi, spoke poetically of the *Arabian Nights* magic of the temples and rice fields of Indochina. Other articles recalled the heroic nineteenth-century exploits in Indochina of French missionaries, explorers, and military officers, as well as the grand public works projects of the early twentieth century. In an especially impassioned essay, Commandant Gabriel Bonnet argued that this particular colony was the "jewel in the crown" of France's empire, declaring, "If we abandon Indochina we abandon ourselves." For him, France without its empire was no more than a "withdrawn coin on the chessboard of the old continent." France possessed a colonial vocation, which needed to be conveyed to its youth. For Bonnet, the empire without Indochina was a mistress "no longer able to dispense the bloom of her breath, the honey of her lips, the warmth of her embraces." Inside the back cover of this issue was printed a call to reserve officers, NCOs, and young men to enroll in the Far East Expeditionary Corps.

Soon after the 9 March coup, an anonymous author in this periodical, now retitled *L'Armeé française*, insisted that the Japanese action had changed nothing, since Japan had in fact exercised military control for a long time prior, and since France was still determined to humble the aggressor. General de Gaulle had long ago inscribed Indochina, one of the

164. AOM, INF, c. 120, d. 1089.

"fairest flowers in our empire," in his liberation program.[165] Four months later, a more subdued article admitted that the Expeditionary Corps had yet to be committed for lack of transport, but claimed that French resistance groups continued to immobilize important Japanese forces and asserted that France had "made known" its expectation to take part in any attack if Japan rejected the Potsdam ultimatum to surrender.[166]

In contrast to such outpourings from the Ministry of War, the French left was practically silent on Indochina, reflecting its continuing preoccupation with events in Europe and especially postliberation political maneuvering in the métropole. Having accepted de Gaulle's offer of two cabinet posts, the French Communist Party found him receptive to domestic programs for raising the workers' standard of living, implementing price controls, and nationalizing key economic sectors. In January 1945, Maurice Thorez, recently returned from exile in the Soviet Union, actively discouraged the plans of some former resistance leaders to go up against de Gaulle.[167] The Communist Party strongly supported French military participation in the final defeat of "Japanese fascism," above all in Indochina, where France could guarantee the people "a leap toward independence protected from the ventures of external interests, the foreseeable activities of which would be detrimental as much to France as to Indochina."[168] This latter reference pointed obliquely, yet unmistakably, at the predatory designs of American capitalism, which the French right also wished to exclude from Indochina. Similarly, the French Communist Party and the Gaullists shared a fear that any victory by Vietnamese nationalists would simply be prelude to Indochina being taken over by another great power, probably the United States.[169]

165. *L'Armeé française* (Paris), Apr. 1945, 44. Copies of this serial can be found in the Bibliothèque nationale, Paris.

166. André Pierre, "Les Derniers Evénements dans le Pacifique," *L'Armeé française* (Paris), Aug. 1945, 47–49.

167. Cook, *Charles De Gaulle*, 254, 263. Cook indicates that de Gaulle and Stalin had struck a deal on the return of Thorez, both apparently preferring him to Jacques Duclos, the underground Communist Party leader inside France during the resistance.

168. *L'Humanité* (Paris), 25 Oct. 1944, as quoted in Alain Ruscio, *Les Communistes français et la guerre d'Indochine, 1944–1954* (Paris, 1985), 81. According to Ruscio, 77, the French Communist Party considered the Brazzaville statements on colonialism of February 1944 a "positive tendency," and endorsed the intent of the declaration of 24 March 1945 to bring the French and Indochinese peoples closer together. See also *DGI*, 191–92.

169. Martin Shipway, "France's Colonial Crisis, 1944–47: The Liberal Laurentie" (seminar presented at the Modern History Faculty, Oxford, 10 June 1988).

Although no figures are available, it seems that a significant minority of the French Expeditionary Corps that eventually reached Saigon in late 1945 were young men of leftist, anti-imperialist persuasion.[170] We know that the military experienced difficulty locating recruits, to the point where one general proposed enrolling youths imprisoned for political, black market, and vagrancy offenses.[171] Up until the troops arrived, the assumption remained that all native opposition to French return was being masterminded by the Japanese. Even some government ministers in Paris had little inkling of the changes taking place in Indochina. In late July, the aviation minister, Charles Tillon, a Communist Party member, quietly charged Captain Rouen with a mission to fly to the Far East and make contact with Annamite political organizations in China and Tonkin, including the Indochinese communists. When this became known to the Gaullists, Rouen was apparently stopped in India and subsequently diverted to the Mekong Delta, where he was wounded and hospitalized in late 1945.[172]

The Gaullists were not unmindful of the need to influence native Indochinese opinion as well as American and French domestic attitudes. At his Lunar New Year (Tet) speech on 13 February 1945, mentioned earlier, General de Gaulle stressed the bonds of sympathy between Frenchmen and Annamites, and promised that France would make the development of Indochina "one of the principal goals of her activity in her reborn power and rediscovered grandeur."[173] Such statements were relayed to a shortwave radio unit in Madagascar, which began each of its broadcasts with the announcement, "This is Tananarive, the Free Empire speaking to Indochina." Each transmission in some way stressed that France had never abandoned Indochina and was currently trying to contribute to its liberation. After the 9 March takeover, a new team arrived in Tananarive, broadcasting in French, Vietnamese, Cambodian, and Tho (appropriate Lao speakers could not be found). French officials in Indochina were urged not to collaborate with the Japanese, and the natives were encouraged to resist even if weapons were lacking. On 9 April, one month after the coup,

170. G. Madjarian, *La Question coloniale et la politique du Parti communiste français, 1944–1947* (Paris, 1977), 127, as cited in Ruscio, *Les Communistes*, 82.

171. AOM, INF, c. 123, d. 1108, subdossier 3, DGER report, 18 May 1945.

172. AOM, INF, CP 222, de Raymond to Colonies, 6 Aug. 1945; Giacobbi to de Raymond, 17 Aug. 1945. AOM, INF, CP 225, intelligence report, 31 Dec. 1946. See also AOM, INF, c. 123, d. 1108, subdossier 6, DGER note, 8 Aug. 1945.

173. Marshall, *French Colonial Myth*, 191–92. *DGI*, 63–64.

Vietnamese listeners received a wildly unrealistic description of continued fighting against the Japanese.[174]

Tananarive was under pressure from Paris to paint an even more optimistic picture. The Ministry of Colonies complained about one March broadcast that had mentioned disaffection among "certain classes of indigenous people who are turning toward the United States." The Ministry of Information, which was in charge of the station, instructed the staff to refute vigorously American radio commentary that French resistance in Indochina was futile.[175] Radio Tananarive repeatedly stressed that Allied forces were being shifted from Europe to the Far East, so that Indochina's liberation could not be far away. On 8 May, when eagerly announcing the capitulation of Germany, a broadcaster asked rhetorically: "How could you not want us to share around our good fortune when, on the crosses on the [European] battlefields, alongside the names of Dupont or Durand, one finds those of Nguyen van or Le van—impossible names that are so difficult to pronounce?" Another commentary that same day urged listeners to "accept without reservation the independence that our Republic offers you in the ranks of the French Union." Having uttered the delicate word *indépendance*, this broadcast nonetheless went on to argue that the destinies of France and Indochina were indissoluble, and concluded: "Long live de Gaulle, our liberator! Long live the Allies! Long live the French Republic. Long live Indochina!"[176]

It was not yet in the power of listeners in Indochina to communicate their reactions to such Free French rhetoric. In France, however, Vietnamese took advantage of relatively open conditions following the liberation of Paris to voice strong reservations. A conference at Avignon in December 1944, after passing motions condemning French colonial practices in Indochina, established a "Délégation générale des Indochinois en France" to communicate with French labor unions, political parties, and journalists. Although the Ministry of Colonies preferred to deal only with a more conservative group, known as the *juristes*, because so many participants held law degrees, the ministry's top Indochina expert, Léon Pignon, did agree to receive leaders of the Délégation. Meanwhile, the 15,000

---

174. Etienne Boulé, *Ici Tananarive: L'Empire libre parle à 'Indochine* (Tananarive, 1945). Besides Boulé, another reporter at this radio station was Jean-Michel Hertrich, who witnessed events in Saigon from September on and published the critical *Doc-Lap! (L'Indépendance ou la mort!): Choses vues en Indochine* (Paris, 1946).

175. AOM, INF, c. 137, d. 1242

176. Boulé, *Ici Tananarive*, 38–40.

Vietnamese workers residing in guarded camps in southern France, known as "MOI" (Main d'oeuvre indigène), were able to elect their own administrators, to join French unions, and to publicize a range of economic and political grievances.[177] This ferment quickly reached Vietnamese members of French military units in Europe, causing the Ministry of War to hesitate over including them in contingents earmarked to go to Indochina.[178] Vietnamese members of the French Communist Party supported incorporation of Indochinese into the Expeditionary Corps,[179] while Vietnamese Trotskyists and many nationalists opposed it.[180]

In early April 1945, the increasingly vocal Délégation published a point-by-point criticism of the French government's declaration of 24 March, stressing its failure to accord Vietnam a diplomatic personality or to guarantee political freedoms and universal suffrage.[181] In June, two moderate Vietnamese intellectuals published a more detailed critique, focusing particularly on apparent French unwillingness to acknowledge the national unity of Tonkin, Annam, and Cochinchina.[182] The government chose to ignore these warning signals on the political front, while substantially alleviating the material difficulties of Vietnamese workers in the métropole. In late July, Pignon invoked his own understanding of Vietnamese public opinion to refute the Délégation and other nationalists: "Even if the intellectual youth . . . is now apparently dedicated to the idea of Viet Nam, nothing proves that the masses have ceased being indifferent or even hostile to the unification of the three Ky [regions]."[183] From September on, the Délégation would vigorously support the fledgling Democratic Republic of Vietnam, an embarrassment that the French

177. Virginia Thompson, "The Vietnamese Community in France," *Pacific Affairs* 25, no. 1 (Mar. 1952): 49–51. Anh Van, "Les Travailleurs vietnamiennes en France: 1939–1950," *Chroniques vietnamiennes* (Paris), no. 4 (1987 [?]): 10–17. N. N., "Ngoai Hang Van dam luon huong ve To Quoc Cach Mang" [Overseas Tens of Thousands Look toward the Revolutionary Fatherland], in Nguyen Duy Trinh, Chu Van Tan, et al., *Nhung Ngay Thang Tam* (Hanoi, 1961), 247–53. DGI, 109–10.*Cach Mang Thang Tam* [The August Revolution], vol. 2, ed. To Lich Su Cach Mang Thang Tam (Hanoi, 1960), 445–46.

178. AOM, INF, c. 2705, "Notes sur l'amicale Annamite (1945)." Tønnesson, *Vietnamese Revolution*, 323.

179. Ruscio, *Les Communistes*, 81–82.

180. Le Huu Khoa, "Communauté des stratégies collectives dans l'enjeu de l'indépendance du Vietnam," *Approaches Asie* (Nice), no. 10 (1989): 104–32.

181. Thompson, "Vietnamese Community," 51–52. Paul Isoart, *Le Phénomène national vietnamien* (Paris, 1961), 331. DGI, 65.

182. Nguyen Quoc Dinh and Nguyen Dac Khe, *Le Statut futur de l'Indochine* (Paris, 1945).

183. As quoted in Tønnesson, *Vietnamese Revolution*, 317.

government chose to endure in the name of domestic freedom of expression.

Free French Efforts in Southern China

Besides intellectuals and workers in France, the only other Vietnamese with whom the Free French could talk following the Japanese coup were located in South China. About 3,200 native members of the Indochina Army had withdrawn across the frontier, together with the 2,469 Europeans, but they were unlikely to express themselves forthrightly on political questions. Not surprisingly, the Free French regarded all Vietnamese anticolonial groups with deep suspicion, if not hostility.[184] The Vietnam Nationalist Party and Vietnam Revolutionary League were considered particularly dangerous because of their close ties with the Chinese, who might invade Indochina at any moment. The French Embassy in Chungking protested often about Chinese support to these organizations, receiving only evasive replies.[185] In April, Ambassador Pechkoff complained specifically about recent "Annamite revolutionary demonstrations" in Kunming, but was merely told that such activities were prohibited in the capital, Chungking.[186] Earlier, Pechkoff had secured permission from Paris to evacuate 3,000 troublesome Indochinese from Yunnan to French Pondicherry in India or Madagascar. Only in early May was this plan discarded.[187] In July, Léon Pignon assessed the Vietnam Nationalist Party as still hostile, yet possibly vulnerable to "defections."[188] At the end of July, Jean Sainteny met in Kunming with Nguyen Tuong Tam, probably one of the Nationalist Party leaders Pignon had in mind.[189]

It had always been less difficult to arrange meetings with Vietnamese communists. In April 1944, the Free French consul in Kunming had discussed future political aspirations with two representatives of the League

184. An earlier background analysis is contained in AOM, INF, c. 1576, "Les Partis revolutionnaires annamites en Chine," 2 Mar. 1944.

185. AOM, INF, c. 134, d. 1229, "Agissements chinois," 3 Oct. 1945.

186. AOM, INF, c. 209, d. 1576, Pechkoff to Minister of Foreign Affairs, 28 Apr. 1945.

187. Tønnesson, *Vietnamese Revolution*, 216. How Pechkoff would have accomplished this forcible evacuation under the noses of the Chinese, and with whose trucks and ships, is not explained.

188. AOM, INF, c. 123, d. 1108, subdossier 3, DGER report, 20 July 1945.

189. Jean Sainteny, *Histoire d'une paix manquée: Indochine, 1945–1947* (Paris, 1953), 54–56. Sainteny's encounter was arranged via a Vietnamese lieutenant in the colonial army. Nguyen Tuong Tam (Nhat Linh), Vietnam's most prominent novelist, editor, and publisher of the 1930s, helped to found the Dai Viet Party in 1939 and then sought links with noncommunist émigrés in southern China.

for the Independence of Indochina (Viet Minh).[190] Reading the report in Algiers, René Pleven requested more details on the league, which were provided in July. Pleven subsequently instructed François de Langlade to make contact with the league, but this does not appear to have happened. Another meeting between league representatives and the French consul in Kunming in January 1945 led nowhere.[191] Then, in mid May 1945, Sainteny suddenly radioed from Kunming that it would be perilous, if not impossible, to attempt to penetrate northern Tonkin without Viet Minh assistance, while Pignon expressed his intention to meet the Viet Minh leadership. At this same time, Paris received from Kunming a dossier compiled by the Sûreté in Indochina just prior to the Japanese coup, which established conclusively that Ho Chi Minh was none other than Nguyen Ai Quoc, founder of the Indochinese Communist Party and believed dead for thirteen years.[192] On 12 June, the minister of colonies, Paul Giacobbi, authorized Sainteny to enter into relations with the ICP, possibly to include delegation of powers in specific regions, as well as provision of weapons and money, providing the ICP promised "to bind itself only to the members of the French resistance, to the exclusion of any other French authority and any outside authority." For some reason this message was not relayed from Calcutta to Kunming until 3 July, by which time the increasingly frustrated Sainteny was already preparing to fly to Paris to try to obtain backing at the highest level.[193]

By July 1945, the French already knew that the Viet Minh considered the declaration of 24 March a poor basis for discussion, especially in regard to allegedly exorbitant powers accorded to the governor-general and the perpetuation of three separate Annamite states.[194] Toward the end of the month, the French Military Mission in Kunming received via OSS Major Thomas in Kim Lung (Tan Trao) a five-point proposal from Ho Chi Minh

190. Devillers, *Paris-Saigon-Hanoi*, 39–43. One of the representatives was Pham Viet Tu, who, as we have seen in chapter 4, met with the American consul general five months later.

191. Tønnesson, *Vietnamese Revolution*, 135–37.

192. Devillers, *Paris-Saigon-Hanoi*, 59–61. Tønnesson, *Vietnamese Revolution*, 319–20. AOM, INF, c. 122, d. 1106, "Activités anti-françaises dans le 2ᵉ territoire militaire d'octobre 1943 à mai 1945" (1 June 1945), discussed below, also makes the link between Nguyen Ai Quoc and Ho Chi Minh, perhaps independently of the Sûreté analysis. Stein Tønnesson has discovered another French intelligence report, undated but based on information from Nguyen Hai Than in about September 1944, which connects the two names as well. It does not seem to have made any impact. Tønnesson, *Vietnamese Revolution*, 138.

193. Devillers, *Paris-Saigon-Hanoi*, 61–62. Sainteny, *Histoire*, 45.

194. AOM, INF, c. 123, d. 1108, subdossier 3, DGER report, 20 July 1945.

for an Indochinese parliament elected by universal suffrage, a French governor-general until independence was granted in five to ten years, mutual economic development programs, freedoms as specified by the U.N. charter, and prohibition of the sale of opium. Thomas also informed the French of Ho's readiness to talk with a ranking French official, either in Kunming or Kim Lung.[195] The French prepared a conciliatory, if noncommittal, response but chose not to transmit it via OSS channels, apparently intending for Sainteny to present it personally to Ho.[196] Sainteny and Ho Chi Minh would not meet until 15 October, by which time conditions had changed dramatically.[197]

French commanders of troop units withdrawn into China continued to hope that their units would be reequipped in preparation for reentering Indochina. They were furious when told by an American officer in late April to route their requests for food and clothing to the United Nations Relief and Rehabilitation Administration (UNRRA), as this implied mere refugee status.[198] To make matters worse, French officers sent from Paris failed to back up their colonial colleagues. According to a blunt report of 16 May, European personnel appeared unfit to go into action again, while indigenous troops, although in better physical condition, seemed ready to desert because they had not received pay or allowances since before the Japanese takeover.[199] From June on, the government in Paris managed to forward some subsidies by a circuitous route, involving conversion of French francs into pounds sterling, which were then changed into Indian rupees, which could finally be converted to Chinese dollars.[200] In early July, Jean de Raymond, head of the French Colonial Mission in Calcutta,

195. Patti, *Why Viet Nam?* 128–29. *Viet-Nam Crisis*, ed. Cameron, 43–44. "Deer Report #1," 17 July 1945, and "Report on Deer Mission," 17 Sept. 1945, both in U.S. Congress, Senate Committee on Foreign Relations, *Causes, Origins and Lessons of the Vietnam War* (Washington, D.C., 1973), 246, 257.

196. Devillers, *Paris-Saigon-Hanoi*, 65–67. Sainteny, *Histoire*, 57–59. Sainteny made plans with Laurence Gordon of the GBT network to invite Ho Chi Minh for talks in Kunming, or, failing that, to seek out the Viet Minh leader inside Tonkin.

197. Jean Sainteny, *Ho Chi Minh and His Vietnam: A Personal Memoir* (Chicago, 1972), 43–46.

198. AOM, INF, c. 123, d. 1108, subdossier 3, DGER report, 28 Apr. 1945.

199. AOM, INF, c. 123, d. 1108, subdossier 4, report of Commandant Leporz, 16 May 1945. Only the 800-strong Rhadé battalion deserved to be integrated into DGER operations, according to Leporz. Tønnesson, *Vietnamese Revolution*, 246–47, quotes from an even more critical report by Léon Pignon dated 16 May 1945.

200. Charbonneau and Maigre, *Les Parias*, 307–8.

roundly criticized General Sabattier's proposals for early utilization of colonial units. According to de Raymond, the prestige of the French Army was already at lowest ebb in Indochina; "bad elements" would have to be weeded out, especially those who had participated in "ferocious repression" of the natives in the hills north of Hanoi.[201] Like most Gaullists, de Raymond knew very little about specific conditions in Tonkin, but he was anxious that people perceive a new France at work. Later the same month, General Alessandri was informed by China Theater that it would take six months for American Lend-Lease matériel to reach his units in Yunnan and Kwangsi.[202]

As head of M.5, the DGER operation in South China, Jean Sainteny was less interested in rejuvenating existing colonial units than in recruiting fit French and native volunteers for retraining and redeployment in small-scale intelligence and sabotage operations. After overcoming resistance from Sabattier, Alessandri, and the French Military Mission, Sainteny found the Americans at China Theater headquarters unwilling to provide equipment, training, or logistical support without French acceptance of OSS operational control. Numerous meetings failed to resolve this dispute.[203] Nonetheless, several of Sainteny's teams did manage to accumulate enough resources to go into action. Most significant was "Martinique group" in the South China Sea, composed of two customs patrol boats (supplied with fuel by American AGAS Catalina flights from Kunming) and six or seven junks. Besides providing routine radio reports on Japanese movements, these boats aimed to demonstrate in a vital strategic zone—the Bay of Ha Long and approaches to Haiphong—that France was determined to persist and eventually prevail.[204] It was a message not lost on Vietnamese nationalists and communists alike.

The French discourse on Indochina between April and early August 1945 possesses an air of unreality, owing above all to inadequate information about what was happening inside the colony, but also to petty personal recriminations, bureaucratic infighting, wishful thinking, and refusal to acknowledge material limitations. Many Gaullists remained openly con-

201. AOM, INF, c. 123, d. 1108, subdossier 3, DGER report, 7 July 1945. De Raymond became *résident* in Cambodia in 1950, only to be murdered by his Vietnamese houseboy in 1951.

202. Patti, *Why Viet Nam?* 114–15.

203. Ibid., 107–14. In his memoirs (*Histoire*), Sainteny generally maintains diplomatic silence on his April–July problems with the French colonial generals on the one hand and China Theater / OSS on the other.

204. Sainteny, *Histoire*, 15, 27, 37–43, 229–33. Mordal, *Marine Indochine*, 75–80.

temptuous of former Vichyites fleeing Indochina. Even resistance participants like General Sabattier were considered prisoners of the "old colonial mentality." On the other hand, Sabattier and other colonial personnel worried about the naive enthusiasm of self-proclaimed representatives of the "new France" coming from Paris. As the DGER labored to gain a monopoly over all continuing operations involving "occupied" Indochina, other French government organizations defended their prerogatives fiercely. Quite deliberately, General Wedemeyer and most of his China Theater subordinates dealt with the French military at the expense of the DGER.[205] No French official wished to depend heavily on the Americans or the Chinese, yet those closest to events realized they had no alternative.[206] No Frenchman wanted to admit that the natives opposed their return, yet many sensed that the longer they remained absent, the less their chances of reasserting authority.

With the exception of reports still coming from teams in Laos, DGER intelligence was derivative, no longer referring to "our agents" but dependent on American, Chinese, and British sources. Facile assumptions abounded, which undoubtedly helped to provoke policy misjudgments. For example, one analysis proclaimed that "the great majority of Indochinese people yearn for return of the French in order to live in peace," and added that the rural population of Tonkin was "not interested in political questions"; only a tiny minority opposed the French, egged on by alien interests. More specifically, according to this line of reasoning, because current native political ferment was being masterminded by the Japanese, it would collapse upon their surrender. Members of the Tran Trong Kim regime were considered ungrateful turncoats or willing enemy collaborators. Lists began to be compiled of natives who had acted in a "treasonous" manner toward France as opposed to those who had helped the French in their time of need following the coup. The latter would receive medals, while the fate of the former remained ominously unmentioned.[207] Heart-

---

205. Sabattier, *Le Destin de l'Indochine*, 258–68, 458–62. AOM, INF, c. 123, d. 1108, subdossiers 4 and 5. Tønnesson, *Vietnamese Revolution*, 317–19, provides a fine sketch of French bureaucratic confusion in April–July 1945.

206. In May 1945, the French still hoped they might be included in American landings in South China or northern Indochina in support of Chinese divisions approaching the coast. AOM, INF, c. 123, d. 1108, subdossier 3, DGER reports of 5 and 17 May 1945.

207. AOM, INF, c. 121, d. 1102, "Indochine sous l'occupation du Japon 1944–5." This dossier, like most others, chose to ignore the large number of French colonial personnel who continued to work under Japanese control after the coup.

warming stories circulated of Annamite colonial soldiers staying faithful to France in adversity, but reports of large-scale defections, especially among the Garde indochinoise, evidently dealt a blow to French plans to promote native NCOs to officer status.[208]

Some French observers also speculated that the Viet Minh, even though overtly pro-Allied, were receiving assistance from the Japanese, the germ of an idea that in a few months would blossom into a prime French explanation for Viet Minh success. It was assumed as well that Ho Chi Minh had promised the Americans future economic privileges in Indochina in exchange for current OSS support.[209] Quite possibly the Americans intended to acquire Cam Ranh Bay as a military base.[210]

Voices in the Wilderness

Amid the rhetorical hodgepodge clogging French policy channels during this period, one report on the Viet Minh, dated 1 June 1945, stands out by way of exception. Perhaps authored by Sainteny based on information provided by Commandant Reul, who had sustained clandestine contacts with the Viet Minh both before and after the March coup, it explicitly identified Ho Chi Minh as Nguyen Ai Quoc,[211] dismissed speculation that the Viet Minh were accepting help from the Japanese, and warned that dropping French teams into the border provinces would court disaster. If team members were not turned over to the Japanese by ordinary villagers, they would probably be eliminated by the Viet Minh or see their mission sabotaged by Viet Minh seizure of subsequent supply drops. According to this report, it would require at least five or six French battalions to suppress the Viet Minh in the border region following Japanese surrender. However, the Viet Minh had to be perceived as "not merely a political

208. AOM, INF, c. 138–39, d. 1247, "Le Viet Minh—L'Action de la Chine et du Japon dans sa formation et son accession au pouvoir" (25 June 1946; prepared about December 1945, based largely on information obtained before September).

209. AOM, INF, c. 134, d. 1229, "Agissements américains contre le rétablissement de la souveraineté français en Indochine" (n.d., but probably compiled in early October 1945).

210. AOM, INF, c. 123, d. 1108, subdossier 3, DGER report, 1 May 1945.

211. Despite this unambiguous linkage, and similar references by other analysts, confusion about Ho Chi Minh's identity persisted among the French for months thereafter. In late October 1945, for example, the French ambassador in Washington continued to insist to State Department listeners that Nguyen Ai Quoc had died of tuberculosis in a Hong Kong jail. Perhaps Ho really was Buu Ai, a graduate of the Stalin School, the ambassador added. USNA, DOS special files, Record Group 59, 54-D-190, c.7, d. 1.

party but rather a general movement of the population." Accordingly, France could only succeed if she abandoned old policies, avoided use of colonial personnel who had played a prominent part in previous repressions, and considered Viet Minh proposals seriously. It appeared that ranking Viet Minh leaders honestly desired French "counsel and guidance," although many subaltern chiefs would try to prevent such an arrangement.[212]

In Paris from 13 to 27 July, Sainteny failed to obtain an audience with General de Gaulle, who was preoccupied with domestic issues and postwar problems relating to Germany and the Mediterranean. Only officials with specific duties involving Indochina gave Sainteny a hearing. Charged with the mission of repenetrating Tonkin as soon as possible, Sainteny by now realized this was impossible without linking up with both the American OSS and the Viet Minh. He was disturbed to discover, however, that most French officials continued to believe that "the Indochinese await our return with impatience and prepare to greet us with open arms."[213] Most officials also refused to trust the Americans and preferred not to make any commitments to groups like the Viet Minh prior to French return in force, thus retaining maximum room for maneuver.

The highest-ranking French official to share Sainteny's sense of urgency was Henri Laurentie, head of the Political Affairs Section at the Colonial Ministry. The previous month Laurentie had urged the Indochina Committee to demonstrate France's good intent, observing: "The Indochinese, like the others, have as little faith as Saint Thomas. This is how it is. It is up to us to yield to their decisive feelings." At that time Laurentie had nothing much to suggest beyond better dissemination of the 24 March declaration and possible appointment of a Vietnamese in France to General de Gaulle's cabinet.[214] By the end of July, Laurentie was questioning whether the principles of the declaration of 24 March could be defended and arguing for an early French proclamation of "Annamite independence." Yet, he also wanted to dispatch no fewer than four army divisions and three or four thousand civilian administrators to Indochina in the wake of any Japanese capitulation. If such a commitment were not possible, Laurentie

---

212. AOM, INF, c. 122, d. 1106, "Activités anti-françaises" (1 June 1945). Tønnesson, *Vietnamese Revolution*, 348, cites a DGER report, based on information dating from 16 May 1945, that describes growing Viet Minh strength in the Cao-Bac-Lang and Thai Nguyen regions with considerable accuracy.

213. Sainteny, *Histoire*, 46–49.

214. AOM, INF, c. 123, d. 1108, subdossier 3, DGER report, 11 June 1945.

added ominously, French public opinion should be prepared for the loss of Indochina.[215]

At the end of July, the French individual possessing the most informed impression of Vietnamese attitudes was Captain Paul Mus, who sat down in Paris to type out a passionate fourteen-page "Note" to higher authority. Mus devoted almost four pages to a description of traditional, tenacious "Annamite nationalism," adding that it might well have been heightened by the recent Japanese experience, as in the case of Ba Maw in Burma, who predicted a "permanent revolution" if the European colonialists tried to return to the Far East. Certainly the 9 March Japanese takeover in Indochina had changed native impressions of the French dramatically, such that in Mus's opinion, it was ridiculous for the Ministry of Colonies to characterize current opposition as a revolt of the same manageable type as Yen Bai in 1930 or Thai Nguyen in 1917. The Annamites had a lively sense of the "historical occasion"; when "all is temporarily possible, the world is plastic"; they would take advantage of present opportunities. Mus was almost unique among French observers in looking beyond the modernizing elite to argue that the Annamite masses already possessed political and social education, "perhaps limited in form, but substantial and healthy underneath." Above all, he asserted, people would respond to evidence of virtue, not simply military force.[216]

What could France do in these circumstances to recoup its position in Indochina? Acknowledging bluntly that France probably would play only an accessory or even symbolic role in the liberation of Indochina, and that many natives might be disposed to rely on other foreigners, Paul Mus called for a major political gesture by the government, demonstrating its willingness to meet Annamites, Cambodians, and Laotians as equals, with their own ideas about the future. He particularly criticized General de Gaulle's Tet speech in February for harping on the old themes of "our dear Indochina," "loyal Indochina." The declaration of 24 March had confirmed people's doubts, especially as it came after the Japanese coup and specified a tripartite division of the Annamite nation that lacked historical basis. Mus also pointed to a lack of imagination and political stability in the métropole, a condition rendered more dangerous by the remnant colonial lobby. Unlike Laurentie, however, Mus avoided any mention of possible inde-

---

215. Laurentie memo, 31 July 1945, as cited and discussed in Tønnesson, *Vietnamese Revolution*, 366.

216. AOM, INF, c. 184, d. 1219, "Note sur la crise morale franco-indochinoise par le Capitaine Paul Mus" (Paris, 1 Aug. 1945).

pendence for the peoples of Indochina, instead referring vaguely to establishment of a "supranational constitutional framework that would engage the French people as much as those in overseas territories, today their wards, tomorrow their partners."[217]

Both Laurentie and Mus had drafted their papers in anticipation of an important Indochina Committee meeting on 2 August. Aware that high-level appointments might be discussed, Laurentie urged creation of an independent ministry for Indochina, while Mus recommended selection of some very prominent civilian representative to balance General Jacques Philippe Leclerc's impending designation as military commander. Almost surely neither of them had Admiral Georges Thierry d'Argenlieu in mind as high commissioner for Indochina—an appointment announced by General de Gaulle two weeks later.

In any event, the time for such gestures had passed; Paris was already losing the initiative to others. The day before his departure from Paris, Jean Sainteny heard of the decision at Potsdam to allocate operational responsibility in Indochina north of the sixteenth parallel to China Theater. When his plane broke down in Athens, Sainteny was offered a seat by General Donovan, head of the OSS, who was en route to India and Ceylon.[218] It would not be the last time Sainteny was forced to hitch a ride on an OSS aircraft.

ON THE EVE

At the end of July 1945, only a handful of people in the world had any inkling that the Pacific War would be over in a fortnight; none of those informed individuals had reason to consider the implications for Indochina. Each party to events discussed in this and previous chapters operated on the basis of military and political calculations made some months prior. Thus, Japanese commanders in Indochina were not particularly concerned about Chinese Army probes along the northern frontier, since in the absence of a coordinated Allied amphibious landing, which did not appear imminent, neither Haiphong nor Hanoi seemed in any jeopardy. Cut off from Tokyo and China's coastal provinces, it appeared that Japanese forces in Indochina might have to fend and forage for themselves well into 1946. Partly for this reason, General Tsuchihashi and his subordinates found time to meet with officials of the Bao Dai government to discuss administrative

217. Ibid.
218. Sainteny, *Histoire*, 49–51.

devolution, training of the Civil Guard, food supplies, and labor recruitment, but made no attempt to coerce the Vietnamese into participating directly in defense against an Allied invasion.

Even had Emperor Bao Dai and Premier Tran Trong Kim wished to mobilize tens of thousands of their countrymen to fight alongside the Japanese, both of them lacked the political talents to accomplish the task. Indeed, so far the royal government as a whole had proven itself incapable of grappling even with domestic problems of food distribution, tax collection, and local law and order, much less assuming any defense responsibilities. While Premier Kim might point with pride to particular territorial and administrative concessions extracted from General Tsuchihashi, he failed to take proper measure of student demonstrations, antigovernment leaflets, public meetings, tax protests, and the growing incidence of assaults on officials and public installations. By late July, not only the Viet Minh but also leaders of various nationalist parties and unaffiliated intellectuals had taken to mocking the government's outpouring of edicts as an exercise in "make-believe independence" (*doc lap banh ve*).

Although the Viet Minh leadership possessed a coherent strategy for seizing power and declaring "real" independence, preparations were far from complete even in the hills north of Hanoi, where Ho Chi Minh was seriously ill. No one knew how many delegates would arrive in the next week or two for the ICP's "All-Country Conference" and the "National People's Congress" designed to legitimize the Viet Minh movement. The first contingent of Viet Minh guerrillas was about to begin the short course taught by Major Allison Thomas and his OSS team. However, circumstances in mid August proved quite different from those anticipated. The most important Viet Minh attributes were intangible: patriotic songs; hand-sewn flags; stories of endurance in jail and heroism in the mountains; rumors of Allied assistance; and news of Japanese defeats. These assets circulated to almost every corner of the country, generally without benefit of ICP orders or trained cadres. The typical Viet Minh enthusiast was an eighteen-year-old with a junior high school education, aware of key political slogans, the recipient of leaflets of unknown derivation, and an avid reader of newspapers passed from hand to hand, but not part of any apparatus.

Among the Allied powers, China had most reason in late July to pay attention to Indochina. As Chinese troops marched southeast in the general direction of Fort Bayard (on the Luichou Peninsula), Canton, and Hong Kong, it was necessary to guard against a possible flank attack from Japanese forces in Tonkin. Beyond that, General Chang Fa-kwei and Yunnan's

Governor, Lung Yün, hoped to receive military resources sufficient to penetrate Tonkin at least as far as Hanoi and Haiphong. General Wedemeyer probably supported their bids in memory of President Roosevelt and his own bitter jurisdictional disputes with Admiral Mountbatten. Meanwhile, OSS operations inside Indochina were expected to expand to the extent that local groups such as the Viet Minh could offer protection and recruits for training. Beyond China Theater, however, Indochina no longer possessed strategic significance for American planners. Admiral Chester Nimitz and General MacArthur were both preoccupied with future invasion of the Japanese home islands, while General George C. Marshall and the Joint Chiefs of Staff in Washington also had to consider ways to support the Soviet Union's impending invasion of Manchuria. In the White House, Indochina had become subordinated to the question of how to improve relations with France.

Aware that he was about to be given a large chunk of MacArthur's Southwest Pacific territories to add to his South East Asia Command, Admiral Mountbatten did not try to contest the Combined Chiefs of Staff decision at Potsdam to assign him only half of Indochina. In a sense, the decision to carve up Indochina at the sixteenth parallel offers an example of the wisdom of Solomon gone awry: the two "mothers" in this case, China Theater and SEAC, each lacking enough love for the "baby" to consider relinquishing it, reluctantly accepted its operational dismemberment. Only France believed sufficiently in the unity of Indochina to oppose this solution, but France had not been consulted. Only the Vietnamese believed fervently in the unity of Tonkin, Annam, and Cochinchina, yet it is unlikely that any of the decision makers at Potsdam had ever heard the name "Vietnam" uttered, much less sensed its potential to inspire millions of people to revolution. In all this lurked a major historical irony, going to the heart of great power politics. For much of World War II, Indochina was largely of symbolic significance to leaders in Chungking, Washington, London, and even Algiers/Paris. Having "used" Indochina symbolically in wartime, the masters of the new peacetime order were quite unprepared when, in the following months, years, and decades, this small corner of the Asian continent became the vortex of conflict and tragedy of global significance.

6 The Opportune Moment

Almost all Vietnamese were acquainted with stories from folklore, the Confucian classics, or Chinese historical romances that described in vivid, absorbing detail the sudden accession to power of hitherto unknown individuals as the result of some combination of fortuitous circumstances, sound strategy, and, perhaps, moral integrity. Many people also knew how to play Asian chess (*co tuong*), in which victory often goes to the participant who perceives a temporary gap in the opponent's defenses that makes a sudden, conclusive attack possible. For Vietnamese intellectuals, such particular cultural legacies had long been endowed with abstract significance, most notably for the emperor's alleged "mandate of heaven" (*thien menh*) and reasons why it might be "revoked" (*cach menh*). In both popular and elite perceptions, there existed, too, the potent political concept of the "opportune moment" or "favorable occasion" (*thoi co; co hoi*). Many had seen the Japanese seizure of power on 9 March 1945 as such an occasion, or at least the opening of a window of opportunity that still remained to be exploited. No one realized in the first days of August that a new window would soon swing wide open.

The Royal Government

In Hanoi on 1 August, General Tsuchihashi Yūichi and Premier Tran Trong Kim completed their discussions on future political arrangements in Tonkin, Annam, and Cochinchina. With little reason to expect a full-scale Allied invasion of Indochina in the next few months, yet increasingly mindful that his troops might have to survive indefinitely in isolation from Tokyo and southern China, General Tsuchihashi was prepared to give the Vietnamese royal government additional administrative responsibilities. Most important, he now agreed that Cochinchina should revert to Hue's authority, although details remained to be ironed out. Meanwhile, in the cities of Hanoi, Haiphong, and Tourane (Da Nang), which had been under direct foreign control for the past seventy years, Vietnamese mayors could replace Japanese ones forthwith.[1] This transfer was celebrated immediately in Hanoi by destruction of French colonial statues, beginning with that of Paul Bert, the dynamic, if short-lived, resident general of Annam and Tonkin in 1886.[2] On 2 August, removal of French statues also received priority attention at the first meeting of the Vietnamese Municipal Council of Haiphong.[3] Statues remained intact in Saigon for the moment, perhaps on local Japanese instructions. In Hue, at a public ceremony on 3 August commemorating return of the three cities, Foreign Minister Tran Van Chuong took pains to compliment the Japanese representatives present.[4]

At their meeting in Hanoi, Tsuchihashi and Kim also agreed that either the Tonkin Kham Sai (imperial delegate), Phan Ke Toai, or the new mayor of Hanoi, Tran Van Lai,[5] should meet with Viet Minh leaders, explain that Japan had no intention of appropriating Indochina, and propose cooperation in the lofty cause of Vietnamese independence. It may even have been contemplated that Phan Ke Toai would seek out the mysterious Ho Chi Minh in the hills and bring a Viet Minh delegate back to Hanoi for serious talks.[6] However, there was no particular sense of urgency, and in any event it would take time to make the requisite contacts.

---

1. Tran Trong Kim, *Mot Con Gio Bui* [A Puff of Dust] (Saigon, 1969), 78–81. As noted earlier, Tran Van Lai had already been permitted to take up the mayor's position in Hanoi on 20 July.

2. *Tan A* (Saigon), no. 72 (10 Aug. 1945).

3. Foreign Broadcast Intercept Service, 7 Aug. 1945, as cited in Kenneth E. Colton, "The Failure of the Independent Political Movement in Vietnam, 1945–46" (Ph.D. diss., American University, 1969), 144. A list of members of the Haiphong Municipal Council, approved by Premier Kim, can be found in AOM, INF, GF 22.

4. Colton, "Failure," 203.

5. Tran Van Lai possessed some credibility among the Vietnamese intelligentsia because of his avowed socialist beliefs, his participation in the prewar Front populaire, and his subsequent arrest by the French for alleged pro-Japanese tendencies, one of the provocations being acceptance of a Japanese exchange student in his household. Hoang Xuan Han, interview by Huynh Kim Khanh, Paris, 24 Feb. 1966. The late Dr. Huynh Kim Khanh was kind enough to share his interview transcript with me.

6. Bōeichō, Bōei Kenshujo Senshitsu, *Shittan Meigō sakusen: Biruma sensen no hōkai to Tai, Futsuin no bōei* [The Sittang and Meigō Operations: The Collapse of the Burma Front and the Defense of Thailand and French Indochina] (Tokyo, 1969), 684.

Tran Trong Kim returned to Hue believing he had the concessions and the time necessary to take the political initiative.[7] At a cabinet session beginning 5 August, however, the premier's plans quickly unraveled. Early in the meeting, Foreign Minister Chuong complained that Kim had taken undue credit for negotiating successes in Hanoi. Kim proceeded to reveal a letter from a senior Japanese staff officer expressing no confidence in Chuong, which had led Kim to assume a direct role. As Tran Van Chuong possessed a reputation as the most "pro-Japanese" member of the cabinet, there was more than a suggestion that he had become expendable. Furious at the rebuff, Chuong left the room, and Kim adjourned the meeting briefly.[8] After reconvening, a long, multifaceted argument ensued over who should go to Saigon to complete arrangements with the Japanese concerning Cochinchina. Kim insisted on a delegation of four ministers headed by himself. Tran Dinh Nam, minister of the interior, argued that popular upheavals in Tonkin and Annam were too serious to warrant such a shift of attention to Saigon. Ho Ta Khanh, the mercurial economics minister, raised the stakes by demanding immediate discussion of policies to deal with popular unrest, the likelihood of resumed famine in a few months, and contact with Viet Minh leaders. When this discussion did not happen, Khanh tendered his resignation. He was followed on 7 August by Tran Dinh Nam and Nguyen Huu Thi, the minister of supply. Phan Anh and Vu Van Hien, the ministers of youth and finance, respectively, then moved for resignation of the entire cabinet, a resolution apparently approved over Kim's objections.[9]

Attempting to pick up the pieces, Kim quickly obtained Emperor Bao Dai's authorization to form a new cabinet, cabled Tsuchihashi that he would not be able to travel to Saigon, designated Nguyen Van Sam as imperial delegate for Nam Ky (Cochinchina), and sought a replacement in the north for Phan Ke Toai, whom Kim now considered weak and unreliable. However, a batch of cables sent to prominent personalities urgently requesting their presence in Hue for consultations went unanswered. On 12 August, Kim

---

7. Tran Trong Kim, *Mot Con Gio Bui*, 82–84.

8. Ibid., 88–89. Pham Khac Hoe, *Tu Trieu Dinh Hue den Chien Khu Viet Bac* [From the Hue Court to the Viet Bac War Zone] (Hanoi, 1983), 42–43.

9. Ho Ta Khanh, "Re[t]our des ministres de Hànôi le 3 août 1945" (notes recorded 8 Aug. 1945). Dr. Ho Ta Khanh kindly gave me a retyped copy of these notes at an interview in Paris, 1 Nov. 1984. See also Tran Trong Kim, *Mot Con Gio Bui*, 89, and Pham Khac Hoe, *Tu Trieu Dinh Hue*, 44–47. Significant discrepancies exist between these accounts. For example, Kim makes no mention of resignation of the entire cabinet. Kim and Hoe both assert that Ho Ta Khanh wanted to turn over government to the Viet Minh, but Khanh's account says nothing about this.

had no choice but to ask the old cabinet to continue on a caretaker basis.[10] At about this time, Ho Ta Khanh agreed to go to Quang Ngai, where Viet Minh adherents had clashed with Japanese units, "to try to prevent further useless bloodshed." He did manage to arrange a meeting between Viet Minh representatives and Japanese officers, but then found himself arrested by a local Viet Minh committee as he drove north toward Hue.[11] At the cabinet meeting on 5–7 August, Tran Dinh Nam had warned his colleagues repeatedly of such "revolts," particularly in Quang Ngai and Thanh Hoa. With farmers tying up village chiefs and disarming policemen, Nam's provincial mandarins had asked him whether they should fire on these rebels or not. When Nam repeated the question to the cabinet, no one answered.[12] Presumably, some crackdown was contemplated: an imperial decree of 15 August established a special court to try and punish "gangs of traitors."[13]

Despite growing political uncertainty, the administrative wheels kept turning. Clerks continued to process resignation requests, pension petitions, and applications for leave without pay. In Tonkin, the newly established Economic Police group received its August operating fund of 6,550 piastres.[14] The Tonkin Kham Sai conveyed the thanks of Japanese military and civilian officials to provincial mandarins for assistance in recruiting local auxiliaries.[15] The Hanoi Kenpeitai requested and received from the Local Economic Service two consignments of scarce cloth, totaling 650 meters.[16] Another section of the same service issued automobile permits, monitored cloth stocks, and processed petitions from citizens complaining about black-marketeering.[17] The Hai Duong provincial mandarin forwarded a local Japanese request for a blank Vietnamese tax identification card, presumably

10. Pham Khac Hoe, *Tu Trieu Dinh Hue*, 52. Nguyen Ky Nam, *Hoi Ky, 1925–1964* [Memoirs, 1925–64], vol. 2, *1945–1954* (Saigon, 1964), 195.

11. Interview with Ho Ta Khanh, Paris, 1 Nov. 1984.

12. Ho Ta Khanh, "Re[t]our." In regard to Thanh Hoa, Tran Dinh Nam may have been thinking particularly of the confrontation with Viet Minh adherents on 24 July that resulted in capture of the Hoang Hoa district mandarin together with twelve civil guardsmen. Pham Cuc, "Khoi Nghia gianh chinh quyen Thang Tam 1945 o Thanh Hoa" [The August 1945 Insurrection to Seize Power in Thanh Hoa], *Tap Chi Lich Su Dang* (Hanoi), 4-1991, 31.

13. Imperial *du* reprinted in the 18 Aug. 1945 edition of *Viet Nam Tan Bao* (Hue), several issues of which can be found in AOM, INF, GF 56.

14. AOM, INF, GF 58, dossier on Ty Liem Phong Kinh Te.

15. Kham Sai to all provinces, 6 Aug. 1945, AOM, INF, GF 25.

16. Phong Kinh Te, messages to Nha Kinh Te Bac Bo, 1 and 17 Aug. 1945, AOM, INF, GF 42.

17. "Kinh Te Cuc" outgoing message file, in AOM, INF, GF 74. Most of the messages are signed by Nguyen Manh Ha, a naturalized French citizen and prominent Catholic lawyer soon to be appointed to Ho Chi Minh's first cabinet.

for use by an undercover agent.[18] Reflecting increased responsibilities following the departure of French personnel, the new Vietnamese head of the Haiphong Sûreté requested promotions for four of his subordinates.[19]

A remarkable amount of government activity went on without reference to the Pacific War, the Viet Minh, or growing social disorder. On 10 August, Emperor Bao Dai promulgated a Vietnamese citizenship law containing detailed definitions of who was currently a citizen, who was eligible to apply, conditions under which citizenship might be lost, and procedures for changing one's status.[20] Meanwhile, Bac Giang province asked the Tonkin Kham Sai for a response to its recommendation on 6 July of a list of street-name changes in the town of Phu Lang Thuong;[21] a team in the Kham Sai's Office busied itself with a proposal to either increase the salaries of local yamen orderlies (totaling 838 individuals) from 1 September on or close out the post entirely;[22] and a different Hanoi bureau approved a detailed 1944 inventory of government property located in Hai Duong province.[23] The bylaws of a proposed consumer cooperative in Thai Binh province were the subject of four messages between 26 July and 31 August.[24] A retired village head in Bac Ninh province, humbly styling himself a "child" (*con*) and addressing the Kham Sai as "lofty great-grandfather" (*cu lon*), requested a royal certificate acknowledging his nine years of "devoted service to King, country, and village, without any mistakes."[25] On 7 August, the Kham Sai instructed all city, provincial, and district offices in Tonkin to close on the afternoon of 22 August, Vietnamese All Souls' Day, and to distribute some state rice to the poor in the spirit of that occasion.[26]

It would be a mistake to conclude that, because such routine chores continued to occupy the attention of government employees at this time of momentous change, the governing institution itself had become func-

18. Hai Duong to Kham Sai, 2 Aug. 1945, AOM, INF, GF 51.

19. Ty Liem Phong Haiphong to Kham Sai, 6 Aug. 1945, AOM, INF, Gouvernment Revolutionnaire CR 141. The request was politely denied on 3 September, following the Viet Minh takeover.

20. "Du so 103: Ve su nhap quoc-tich Viet-Nam," AOM, INF, GF 25.

21. Bac Giang to Kham Sai, 12 Aug. 1945, AOM, INF, GF 24.

22. Internal proposal, 13 Aug. 1945, backed up by files on yamen orderlies (*linh le*) dating back to 26 Aug. 1940, in AOM, INF, GF 14.

23. Approval of file submitted from Hai Duong, among fifteen assorted property inventories for 1944, 10 Aug. 1945, AOM, INF, GF 40.

24. Exchanges between Kham Sai and Thai Binh, including text of the bylaws, AOM, INF, GF 36.

25. Petition dated 7 Aug. 1945, AOM, INF, GF 10. On 8 August, an official marked the petition: "Route to province chief for consideration."

26. Kham Sai to all provinces, 7 Aug. 1945, AOM, INF, GF 25.

tionally irrelevant. First of all, administrative and technical systems remained largely intact—to be used by whichever leaders, political or military, domestic or foreign, happened to occupy the policy-making positions. In subsequent weeks and months the Viet Minh, Chinese, British, and French would all tap into these systems to one degree or another. Secondly, not all government employees had preferred to hide behind day-to-day paperwork, eschewing the bigger issues. Excited by the new possibilities offered in the wake of the March coup, some had drafted proposals for reform during the summer of 1945, circulating them internally for comment and possible action, and occasionally publishing them in Hanoi and Saigon periodicals. At government request, citizens had submitted a wide variety of proposals for reform too, all of which had to be processed bureaucratically and a few singled out for serious consideration.

The momentum of these reform discussions carried through to early August. As late as 13 August, for example, officials in Hanoi considered a forty-page proposal for political and social restructuring submitted by Nguyen Dinh Diep, a local medical practitioner. The Information Bureau bothered to append a three-page summary and commentary, which criticized the dictatorial implications of Diep's scheme. The day after Japan's surrender, petitions took on a harsher, more urgent tone. Thus, Le Tran Duc, a chartered accountant, advocated immediate detention of all French nationals, using Vietnamese servants and mistresses of the French to uncover hidden weapons caches, allowing ordinary citizens to bear arms, encouraging minority peoples to descend from the hills to help defend Hanoi, and telling the great powers that Vietnam had no further ties with France. Even sterner proposals were advanced by Dang Minh Phung, a self-styled left-wing member of the Vietnam Nationalist Party, including forbidding citizens to have any contacts with French nationals, arresting pro-French Vietnamese and suspected traitors, asking the Japanese to turn over all confiscated French military equipment, evacuating women and children from Hanoi if necessary, and seeking to cooperate militarily with the Cambodians and the Lao.[27] Engrossed in such policy formulations, which had their own apparent momentum, neither the petitioners nor government officials seemed to take much account of changes welling up from below.

Nonetheless, anyone in the Tonkin Kham Sai's Office permitted to read incoming reports in the first two weeks of August would have perceived

27. These and many more petitions, together with official marginalia, memos, and routing slips, can be found in AOM, INF, GF 66.

a pattern of growing unrest and challenges to existing authority. Already in late July, there had been a dramatic jump in the number of messages from local officials reporting illegal meetings, demonstrations, refusals to pay taxes, detention of government employees, and armed assaults. On 1 August, Hai Ninh province reported that twenty-seven functionaries had fled their posts in recent days, eleven of them to China.[28] The district mandarin of Thuan Thanh, in Bac Ninh province, informed higher echelons that a number of "liberation councils" had been formed in villages to take control of administrative and judicial affairs.[29] In Phu Tho province on 2 August, a local Viet Minh group forced the Ha Hoa district mandarin to surrender his seal of authority and administrative records.[30] An increasing number of Hanoi policemen asked to resign, continuing a trend evident in late July and reflecting the upsurge in Viet Minh threats, not to mention several killings of plainclothes personnel.[31] The PTT reported telegraph and telephone poles being chopped down and many kilometers of copper wire stolen. Son La and Lai Chau provinces could not be reached even by road; on 13 August, the Son La radio post failed to respond. Railroad officials reported essential supplies stolen from local stations.[32] Efforts to forward either rice or money to the Ha Giang province chief to help relieve the plight of one thousand people rendered homeless by an Allied air attack were abandoned for lack of any means of delivery.[33] In Thai Nguyen on 12 August, two civil guards deserted, carrying cartridges but no firearms. Three days later, a third soldier deserted, taking his Remington rifle plus ten cartridges.[34] The next day in Thai Nguyen, a band of forty men and women with firearms, identifying themselves as Viet Minh, seized a caravan of thirty-six carts carrying more than twenty tons of rice to Hanoi. Immediate appeals for redress by the woman merchant-organizer of the caravan went unheeded.[35]

---

28. Hai Ninh to Kham Sai, 1 Aug. 1945, AOM, INF, GF 5. Someone in the viceroy's Personnel Office scribbled on the margin of this message: "What should be done?"

29. Thuan Thanh to Bac Ninh, 30 July 1945, forwarded to Kham Sai, 3 Aug. 1945, in "Courrier à l'arrivée" dossier, AOM, INF, GF 25.

30. Le Thuong and Vu Kim Bien, *Lich Su Vinh Phu* [History of Vinh Phu] (Vinh Phu, 1980), 168.

31. "Phong Vien Chuc" dossier, AOM, INF, GF 44.

32. "Courrier à l'arrivée" dossier, AOM, INF, GF 25. Dossier of late July and August messages, GF 27.

33. "Khong Quan dich" folder, in AOM, INF, GF 66.

34. "Thai Nguyen" dossier, AOM, INF, GF 27.

35. Nguyen Thi Diet to Uy Ban Nhan Dan Cach Menh Bac Bo, 24 Aug. 1945, in Thai Nguyen dossier, AOM, INF, GF 29.

Amid all these incoming messages, a few officials revealed their own judgments about what was happening. When he resubmitted his resignation as head of youth affairs in Tonkin on 9 August, Ngo Bich Son intimated that his young charges were getting completely out of hand.[36] The district mandarin of Kham Khai, in Thai Nguyen, was more explicit when he urgently requested a transfer. Admitting a reputation for punishing communists and forcing citizens to turn over castor oil, sesame, peanuts, and rice to higher authority, he feared for his own life now that "the people were all following the revolution."[37] However, other officials tried to maintain the tradition of presenting a calm, authoritative face to their superiors. On 10 August, Nguyen Van Ninh, provincial mandarin of Kien An, informed the Kham Sai that he had "no difficulties." According to Ninh, people remained thankful to the Japanese for having "liberated the country" and understood their continuing dependence on Japan for protection against foreign aggressors. People also hoped the war would end soon, enabling families to get back together and live quietly again, content with their occupations. Ninh did admit that thieves were increasingly more active in Kien An, putting the police under strain and necessitating help from local youth groups and the Civil Guard. Viet Minh obstruction was making tax collection more difficult than before, yet amounts were coming in. Ninh's most pessimistic comments had to do with inflation, which he was sure continued to demoralize the public seriously.[38] From Bac Ninh province came a measured description of expanding Viet Minh activities, an estimate that one hundred villages had "refused to obey local mandarins," and a request for instructions from the Kham Sai to be able to "throttle the revolutionary movement."[39]

Faced with such information and requests, government officials in Hanoi tried to grapple with threats as they understood them. Until the new military training program agreed upon with General Tsuchihashi bore fruit, Civil Guard units were instructed simply to hold fixed positions and accompany Japanese patrols to nearby villages. Internal Kham Sai records make it clear that Japanese officers retained de facto control of the Civil Guard and various auxiliary groups. Provincial mandarins were told to round up specific numbers of young men to present to Japanese training

36. "Hoi Nghi Tu Van Quoc Gia" dossier, in AOM, INF, GF 5.

37. "Thai Nguyen" dossier, AOM, INF, GF 27.

38. Bimonthly report on Kien An province, signed 10 Aug. 1945, in AOM, INF, GF 61. As we shall see in the next chapter, the Viet Minh performed poorly in Kien An a fortnight later, so Ninh's assessment may have been valid.

39. Transfer of provincial authority report, cosigned by Than Trong Hau (outgoing) and Ha Van Vuong (incoming), 6 Aug. 1945, in AOM, INF, GF 66.

teams. On 2 August, for example, the Quang Yen province chief informed Hanoi that he was endeavoring to provide two hundred tirailleur recruits as requested by the Japanese commander at Vat Chay.[40] Four days later, in a message to all provinces, the Kham Sai thanked those who had "helped the Japanese Army select men to form auxiliary (*bo tro quan*) units," most notably the Phu Yen provincial mandarin, who had "recruited new soldiers in a most effective manner." General Tsuchihashi and other Japanese commanders also conveyed their compliments, the Kham Sai added.[41]

For some months the government had tried without much success to locate and confiscate thousands of French firearms that had fallen into civilian hands following the Japanese takeover. On 7 August, the Tonkin Kham Sai's Office promulgated a new edict on firearms, specifying several legitimate reasons for ownership, warning everyone else, and offering rewards to those who turned in illegal weapons. This edict immediately stimulated scores of applications and queries, most seeking to confirm ad hoc permits granted after 9 March. On 11 August, for example, the mayor of Haiphong forwarded two lists of current holders of firearms for favorable consideration, mostly landlords, merchants, functionaries in sensitive locations, and employees of Japanese firms. The provincial mandarin of Lang Son requested new papers for his police assistant, Ngo Kieu, to carry Dumon pistol no.129.344, which the French had captured from "Vietnamese revolutionaries" in 1940 and subsequently entrusted to him. An officer of the Union des jonquiers transporteurs indochinois, Pham Tat Hien, explained on 14 August that he had turned in his Browning 7.65 pistol on 21 June according to government instructions and was now quite prepared to pay the necessary permit fee to get it back. The entire process of relicensing firearms seems to have ground to a halt before Viet Minh seizure of the Kham Sai's Office on 19 August, however. Public posters about firearms were not ordered to be printed until 10 August, and still had not arrived as of the 18th. Nor had the consignment of new permit cards been received back from the printers. On 24 August, cables, still purporting to come from the Kham Sai, went out to all provinces deferring implementation of the firearms edict of 7 August "pending further instructions."[42]

Government coffers required urgent replenishment. The Tonkin Finance Bureau warned that "because the anti-tax movement continues to

---

40. AOM, INF, GF 27.
41. AOM, INF, GF 25.
42. "Xin phep mang sung" dossier, AOM, INF, GF 62. Additional firearms applications can be found in GF 16. See also messages between Kham Sai First Bureau and Supply Office, GF 8.

spread and quicken, the Bac Bo budget will be in extreme danger."[43] Rice collections had fallen far below expectations. On 10 August, the Kham Sai ordered all provinces to report rice stocks as of the 15th, after which the government would take stern measures against tax delinquents and the Economic Police would proceed to "severely repress" hoarders and black-marketeers.[44] Farmers had until 16 August to declare their holdings, following which illegal quantities of paddy or rice would be confiscated and allocated to charity associations.[45] Anxious not to be seen as continuing the French policy of forcing cheap rice from the peasants to supply the Japanese Army or the civilian bureaucracy, the Kham Sai's Office stressed that persons tilling less than three *mau* (one hectare) were exempted, as were quantities of harvested paddy below two tons or rice below one ton.[46] On the other hand, citizens could be arrested for transporting more than fifty kilograms of rice without a permit. On 18 August, one of those caught petitioned the Kham Sai from jail: Mai Dinh Minh admitted he had no trading permit, but argued that much bigger offenders were avoiding punishment entirely.[47]

Meanwhile, food shortages and hyperinflation continued to undermine public confidence. Sensing tougher times ahead, Vietnamese staff in a number of bureaus under the governor-general petitioned for advance payment of August and September wages and allowances. On behalf of General Tsuchihashi, General Secretary Tsukamoto Takeshi approved these forward payments on 14 August, the day before most Gouvernement général offices were transferred to local jurisdiction.[48]

In Hanoi in early August, new organizations were forming, meetings taking place, leaflets appearing, critical articles being published—all without much heed to continuing stringent legal restrictions on freedom of speech and assembly. Although government officials appreciated that calls from prominent intellectuals for immediate, wide-ranging consultations could no longer be ignored, and indeed hoped to regain the political initiative, they insisted on moving at their own pace, following customary

43. Tai Chinh Phong to Kham Sai, budget review, n.d., AOM, INF, GF 5.

44. Service économique local dossier, in AOM, INF, GF 32.

45. Kinh Te Cuc so 13, messages of 8 Aug. 1945, AOM, INF, GF 37.

46. Service économique local messages of 8 and 15 Aug. 1945, AOM, INF, GF 37.

47. AOM, INF, GF 41.

48. Administration des douanes et régies report to the governor-general, attaching a petition signed by about 180 employees, 1 Aug. 1945, in AOM, INF, GF 51. There is similar paperwork here for the Rice Bureau, Agricultural Bureau, and other offices.

procedures. A government-established Council for Administrative, Legal, and Financial Reform, which had met for the first time in mid July, seems to have foundered completely by early August.[49] Attention shifted to preparations for convening the northern branch of a new National Consultative Conference (Hoi Nghi Tu Van Quoc Gia), scheduled to deliberate for five days from 17 August on.[50]

By 10 August, however, increasing popular ferment in Hanoi led the Kenpeitai to tack up stern warnings against illegal political activity, urging everyone to keep trusting the Japanese Army and the Vietnamese royal government.[51] Word circulated of a cache of arms and ammunition discovered in a French civilian villa, followed by detention of five French nationals and pursuit of an alleged ringleader named Marcel.[52] The next day, hearing rumors that a Gaullist representative had been able to meet General Tsuchihashi to propose a landing in Haiphong, members of the Greater Vietnam National Alliance (Dai Viet Quoc Gia Lien Minh) took to the streets of Hanoi to oppose "imperialist invasion plots."[53] On 12 August, something calling itself the National Service (Phung Su Quoc Gia) group organized a meeting in Hanoi where speakers called for unity among the people. On the 13th, Dai Viet demonstrators carried banners urging the public to "consolidate Vietnam's independence."[54] The same day, a group borrowing the designation of "National Salvation Committee" from Viet Minh parlance, yet clearly not affiliated, instructed French residents to

---

49. Only four of fifteen carefully designated members of this new council (Hoi Dong Cai Cach Cai Tri Tu Phap va Tai Chinh) attended its first and perhaps only session on 16 July 1945. They were Vu Van Hien (minister of finance), Phan Ke Toai (viceroy), Nguyen Van Huyen (doctorate in literature), and Nguyen Huu Tao (professor). AOM, INF, GF 5 and GF 25.

50. Authorization for this conference had been provided by a royal edict of 8 May 1945. Not until 30 July, however, did Premier Tran Trong Kim approve the list of fifty-nine individuals to be invited to attend the northern branch meeting. AOM, INF, GF 5 and 25. Hanoi newspapers of 14 August announced the conference would begin on the 17th. *Cach Mang Thang Tam* [The August Revolution] (henceforth cited as *CMTT*), vol. 1, ed. Tran Huy Lieu (Hanoi, 1960), 34.

51. Nguyen Ky Nam, *Hoi Ky*, 195–96. For a similar proclamation two days later, see Françoise Martin, *Heures tragiques au Tonkin (9 Mars 1945–18 Mars 1946* (Paris, 1948), 112.

52. Giam Doc Ty Canh Sat Hanoi to mayor, 10 Aug. 1945, in dossier of late July and Aug. 1945 messages, AOM, INF, GF 27.

53. Hoang Van Dao, *Viet Nam Quoc Dan Dang* [Vietnam Nationalist Party] (Saigon, 1965), 215. As Hoang Van Dao was a Nationalist Party adherent, his descriptions of Dai Viet activities must be read cautiously.

54. *CMTT*, 1:33. Nguyen Quyet, *Ha Noi Thang Tam* [August in Hanoi] (Hanoi, 1980), 128.

"think and behave like people defeated in battle" if they wished to remain in Vietnam.[55] Japanese officials could be reasonably confident that the leaders of these Hanoi organizations would not let their followers get out of hand. In the nearby countryside, however, those few French nationals who had not regrouped to the city were in grave danger. Already on the 9th, M. Servais, the former chief warden of Cho Chu prison, and his wife had disappeared after being ordered out of a vehicle by Japanese and Civil Guard soldiers and forced to walk alone toward Thai Nguyen town.[56] Two days later the René Robin Catholic orphanage at Késo, in Nam Dinh province, was pillaged and one priest killed. The head of the mission, Father Dupont, was bound, taken away, and later shot dead. The remaining priests and nuns, evacuating to Hanoi with all the orphans,[57] had their supplies of soap and cloth, as well as a bicycle, confiscated en route by the Ha Nam provincial mandarin.[58]

On 15 August, the head of Civil Guard forces in Tonkin, Captain Vu Van Thu, forwarded an urgent message to the Kham Sai warning that in the current political situation, it was essential to place improvement of troop morale above all other priorities. More and more guardsmen were deserting, taking their firearms with them, the captain reported ominously. Reflecting his training in prewar French metropolitan military academies, Thu eschewed any discussion of the political or security reasons why men were vanishing, instead simply proposing immediate pay increases, reliable rice rations, and better uniforms. Without these changes, he predicted, more guardsmen would desert and either use their weapons to rob people or join "other parties where living conditions are more abundant." Rather than take any immediate action, the Kham Sai apparently referred the matter to the upcoming Consultative Conference.[59]

It is unclear from the available sources exactly when royal government officials realized that Japanese surrender might be imminent. From PTT

---

55. "Loi hieu trieu cua Uy Ban Cuu Quoc," reprinted in *Tan A* (Saigon), no. 73 (17 Aug. 1945).

56. Thai Nguyen to Kham Sai, 14 Aug. 1945, in Thai Nguyen dossier, AOM, INF, GF 27. It is not clear from the report whether the Japanese kept Servais as head warden after 9 March, although it is hard to imagine him remaining in this exposed position for any other reason.

57. Douguet to Nishimura, 13 Aug. 1945, and Shibazaki to Douguet, 17 Aug. 1945, in Van Phong Kham Sai dossier, AOM, INF, GF 58.

58. Ha Nam to Kham Sai, 19 Aug. 1945, in Ty Liem Phong Kinh Te dossier, AOM, INF, GF 58.

59. Message from Bao An Binh to Kham Sai, 15 Aug. 1945, in Hoi Nghi Tu Van Quoc Gia files, AOM, INF, GF 5.

radio monitoring they may have heard about Allied stations announcing the atomic bombing of Hiroshima on 6 August and the Soviet Army's invasion of Manchuria on 9 August.[60] A few well-positioned intellectuals also listened to Allied stations by means of private shortwave receivers. Although such bits of war information always spread rapidly by word of mouth, very few listeners in Hanoi, Hue, or Saigon possessed sufficient background knowledge to appreciate the strategic implications. By 12 August, PTT employees were spreading the exciting, if somewhat misleading, word that Japan already had accepted Allied surrender terms.[61] By the 13th, careful listeners to Domei broadcasts could infer that Japan was giving serious consideration to the terms contained in the Potsdam Declaration of late July. On the 15th, Allied stations broadcast Japan's acceptance of surrender terms; the next day, a Domei dispatch confirming this news was affixed to the front of the Japanese Information Bureau in downtown Hanoi.[62] Nonetheless, Japanese officials made it clear in public and private that they retained responsibility for order in Indochina. When the Vietnam General Association of Government Employees (Tong Hoi Vien Chuc) applied to the mayor of Hanoi for permission to organize a public meeting in front of the Opera House, it was informed on 16 August that additional approval needed to be obtained from the Japanese Army.[63]

Even as the momentous fact of Japanese capitulation began to intrude on the consciousness of people in Indochina, administrative routine persisted. On 14 August, Tsukamoto instructed all bureaus of the Gouvernement général to remain open on Assumption Day, the 15th, although office heads would need to make provision for Catholic subordinates to attend mass.[64] The next day the Tonkin Kham Sai's Office cabled Premier Kim in Hue to correct the spelling of a Haiphong municipal councillor's name.[65] Also on the 15th, the Tonkin Civil Guard Bureau forwarded a request for a batch of letterhead stationery—which duly arrived and was signed for

60. Although the Soviet Union declared war on Japan on the evening of 8 August, Moscow time, in Manchuria and Japan the date was already the 9th.

61. Hoang Anh, "Nho lai cuoc Khoi Nghia gianh chinh quyen o Hue" [Recalling the Uprising to Gain Government in Hue], *Tap Chi Cong San* (Hanoi), 8-1985, 38.

62. Martin, *Heures tragiques*, 114. Philippe Devillers, *Histoire du Vietnam de 1940 à 1952* (Paris, 1952), 136. On 17 August, newspapers carried the imperial surrender rescript, with commentaries. Martin, *Heures tragiques*, 117–20.

63. AOM, INF, GF 58. The application was lodged on 14 August for a meeting on the 18th. As we shall see, someone brought the meeting forward to the 17th.

64. Gougal to all echelons, 14 Aug. 1945, AOM, INF, GF 51.

65. Last item (15 Aug. 1945) in dossier on Conseil municipal de Haiphong, AOM, INF, GF 22.

three days later.[66] On 17 August, the provincial mandarin of Cao Bang, now surrounded by villages controlled by the Viet Minh and threatened by Chinese troops just across the border, nevertheless found time to sign a letter accompanying the personnel file of a coolie in the provincial establishment who needed to have his wage rate reassessed in Hanoi.[67]

In Hue, Tran Trong Kim continued to try to piece together a credible central cabinet and reassert authority over the administration in Tonkin. On 16 August he drafted yet another resignation announcement, but held it in reserve.[68] Two days later, messages went out announcing fourteen members of a new provisional government, and requesting the individuals named to report quickly "to assure continuity of services." Reflecting the half-baked character of this initiative, the list contained neither a minister of foreign affairs nor a minister of the interior, much less a minister of defense.[69] Simultaneously, Kim announced plans for regional "committees of national salvation," apparently in an attempt to undercut Viet Minh groups of the same title.[70] Both Tran Trong Kim and Emperor Bao Dai's secretary, Pham Khac Hoe, informed the Tonkin Kham Sai by cable that he was to be assisted by a four-person Political Committee. Later on the 18th, by imperial edict, Phan Ke Toai was replaced as Kham Sai by Nguyen Xuan Chu, one of the members of the Political Committee.[71] As we shall see, Phan Ke Toai had already resigned the previous evening.

Aside from mounting domestic problems, officials in Hue discussed what position to take vis-à-vis the victorious Allies. At a cabinet meeting on 17 August, with Bao Dai himself presiding, it was agreed that the emperor would send urgent radiogram messages to Allied leaders stressing the intent of the Vietnamese people to oppose recolonization, by force if necessary. Bao Dai's communication to General de Gaulle is worth quoting in full, as the feelings expressed proved extraordinarily similar to those Ho Chi Minh would present publicly in Hanoi less than two weeks later, and that con-

66. Dossier on Bao An Binh and Giai Phong Quan requests for stationery, in AOM, INF, GF 22. A further request of 28 August, signed by Captain Vu Van Thu, apparently went unanswered.
67. Than Hao Bac Bo dossier, AOM, INF, GF 5.
68. AOM, INF, GF 58.
69. AOM, INF, GF 4.
70. Devillers, *Histoire*, 138. Martin, *Heures tragiques*, 217–19. Archimedes L. A. Patti, *Why Viet Nam? Prelude to America's Albatross* (Berkeley and Los Angeles, 1980), 169.
71. Tong Truong Noi Cac to Phu Kham Sai, 18 Aug. 1945, and Pham Khac Hoe to Phan Ke Toai, 18 Aug. 1945, in AOM, INF, GF 34. The other three members of the Political Committee were intended to be Tran Van Lai (mayor of Hanoi), Nguyen Tuong Long, and Dang Thai Mai. Other personnel changes are detailed in Préconseil à Kham Sai, 18 Aug. 1945, AOM, INF, GF 68.

tinued to motivate many educated Viet Minh adherents during the nine-year war with France:

> I address myself to the people of France, to the country of my youth. I address myself as well to its chief and liberator, and I wish to speak as a friend rather than as Chief of State.
>
> You have suffered too much during four deadly years not to understand that the Vietnamese people, who have a history of twenty centuries and an often glorious past, no longer desire and can no longer endure any foreign domination or government.
>
> You will understand still better if you could see what is happening here, if you could feel the will for independence which has been smoldering in the hearts of all and which no human force can hold in check any longer. Even if you were to come to re-establish French government here it would not be obeyed: each village would be a nest of resistance, each former collaborator an enemy, and your officials and your colonists themselves would ask to leave that unbreathable atmosphere.
>
> I beg you to understand that the only means of safeguarding French interests and the spiritual influence of France in Indochina is to recognize unreservedly the independence of Viet-Nam and to renounce any idea of re-establishing French sovereignty or French administration here in any form.
>
> We would be able to understand each other so easily and to become friends if you would stop hoping to become our masters again.
>
> In making this appeal to the well known idealism of the French people and to the great wisdom of their leader, we hope that the peace and the joy which has come for all the peoples of the world will be equally ensured to all the inhabitants of Indochina, native as well as foreign.[72]
>
> Bao Dai

With Japanese assistance, these appeals to Allied leaders were broadcast from Saigon, Hanoi, and Tokyo, being picked up by both French and American services,[73] yet gaining little or no media attention.

72. This translation is from *Viet-Nam Crisis: A Documentary History*, ed. Allan W. Cameron, vol. 1, *1940–1956* (Ithaca, N.Y., 1971), 48–49, based on a French text in Philippe Devillers, *Histoire*, 138, which in turn was extracted from the 20 Aug. 1945 issue of *Viet Nam Tan Bao* (Hue). See also Philippe Devillers, *Paris-Saigon-Hanoi: Les Archives de la guerre, 1944–1947* (Paris, 1988), 70, 384. Other messages went to Truman, King George VI, and Chiang Kai-shek. Stalin was excluded after a bitter argument within the cabinet, although the message to Truman included a request to inform "Russia." Nguyen Ky Nam, *Hoi Ky*, 204–5, and Hoang Van Dao, *Viet Nam Quoc Dan Dang*, 213–14, contain Vietnamese translations of Bao Dai's message to Truman, which was apparently translated from French to English by Domei before radio transmission. According to Pham Khac Hoe, *Tu Trieu Dinh Hue*, 55–56, Foreign Minister Tran Van Chuong had drafted the messages in French.

73. Stein Tønnesson, *The Vietnamese Revolution of 1945: Roosevelt, Ho Chi Minh and de Gaulle in a World at War* (London, 1991), 373, 400, is able to cite

The Viet Minh

Although Viet Minh leaders had no greater foresight than royal government officials about a sudden end to the Pacific War, they knew that
anything they did to improve their position prior to an Allied invasion of
Indochina or capitulation by Tokyo would facilitate seizure of power at the
"opportune moment." As we have seen, a Viet Minh liberated zone had
been declared in the mountains north of Hanoi in early June, and beyond
that region scores of local committees were established during the next two
months. The withdrawal of Japanese Army and Civil Guard units from a
number of posts left district mandarins feeling insecure, particularly when
the Viet Minh proceeded to convene public meetings only a kilometer or
two away. On 8 August, the Japanese withdrew from the strategic town of
Cho Chu, in Thai Nguyen province.[74] Meanwhile, along the coast just north
of Haiphong, Viet Minh groups tried to gauge the intentions of well-armed
Chinese irregulars filtering back and forth across the frontier, while reacting
violently to Free French probes by patrol boat and parachute.[75]

Since June 1945 word had gone out from the hill village of Tan Trao (Kim
Lung) for representatives of provincial and district committees of the Indochinese Communist Party to attend a strategy conference in mid August,
the first in four years. A number of noncommunist sympathizers had also
been invited to participate in a subsequent National People's Congress
(Quoc Dan Dai Hoi). From as far away as northeastern Thailand, Laos, and
southern Annam, delegates began making their way covertly toward Tan
Trao.[76] Whereas a few months prior it would have been dangerous for a
delta village to hide more than two or three illegal strangers at one time,
now the Ha Dong village of Van Phuc, in the suburbs of Hanoi, managed
to host a group of twenty-nine delegates on their way to the meetings in

---

evidence from the French and American archives of Allied reception. An unat-
tributed English text of Bao Dai's message to Truman appears in Chester L. Cooper,
The Lost Crusade: America in Vietnam (New York, 1970), 46.

74. *CMTT*, 1:76.

75. Ibid., 230–31, claims that eight French officers were captured by Viet Minh
units in the coastal zone in early August, together with firearms, ammunition,
cameras, and classified documents.

76. According to Hoang Van Hoan, *Giot Nuoc trong Bien Ca: Hoi Ky Cach
Mang* [A Drop in the Ocean: Revolutionary Memoirs] (Beijing [?], 1986), 254, the
ICP members Duong Tri Trung and Tran Duc Vinh came from northeastern
Thailand and Laos. Nguyen Chi Thanh and Tran Quy Hai were selected at an
"inter-province" meeting in Quang Ngai in June. *CMTT*, vol. 2, ed. To Lich Su Cach
Mang Thang Tam (Hanoi, 1960), 118.

the hills to the north.[77] Tran Huy Lieu, a prominent ICP writer of the 1930s, traveled from Ha Dong along a well-oiled liaison pipeline, his group picking up an engineer, a physician, a pharmacist, several journalists, and a member of the Muong ethnic minority along the way. They all used pseudonyms and were under instructions not to greet old friends warmly. Much to Lieu's amusement, two young women from Hanoi recited snatches of his poetry as they walked, without knowing the author was right beside them. As the group got closer to Tan Trao, Viet Minh guides taught members proper military procedures. Nonetheless, as the group approached one village, it was mistaken for a Japanese patrol and fired upon briefly.[78]

In Vinh Yen province, a Viet Minh team was designated to escort one of the most experienced ICP Central Committee members, Hoang Quoc Viet, to attend the meeting. The team even found Viet a horse to ride. Passing through villages in the liberated zone, this diminutive, spectacled son of working-class parents was delighted to be saluted as a "top-level representative" by armed militia squads drawn up in ranks.[79] Ironically, the call to Tan Trao meant that many local committees were minus key members at the time of the Japanese capitulation. Some delegates still en route to Tan Trao decided to turn around forthwith; others received messages to do so.

Although poorly timed in view of the sudden opportunities for action throughout the country, the Tan Trao meetings offered an important chance for seventy or so key Viet Minh cadres to renew old comradeships, participate in vivid affirmations of unity, and depart convinced that they were part of history in the making. On arrival in Tan Trao, with no further need to maintain clandestine personas, many delegates encountered people with whom they had worked closely in the 1930s but then lost contact during the colonial repression in 1939–40. Tran Huy Lieu, for example, participated in joyful reunions with comrades who had been shipped to Con Son Island or Madagascar, who had escaped the Sûreté dragnet by fleeing to China, or who had shared a jail cell with him in Son La. Together they recalled comrades who could not be part of the excitement, having been

77. Dang Bo Xa, *Lich Su Dau Tranh Cach Mang cua Dang Bo va Nhan Dan Van Phuc* [Revolutionary Struggle History of the Party Organization and People of Van Phuc], vol. 1, *1936–1945* (Hanoi, 1986), 106–7.

78. Tran Huy Lieu, "Di Du Quoc Dan Dai Hoi o Tan Trao" [Attending the National People's Congress at Tan Trao], *Nghien Cuu Lich Su* (Hanoi) (cited below as *NCLS*), no. 17 (8-1960): 35–38.

79. Kim Ngoc, in *Nhung Ngay Cach Mang Thang Tam* [Days of the August Revolution] (Vinh Phu, 1974), 37.

killed in the struggle. Lieu's first remark on meeting Vo Nguyen Giap aimed to console him over the loss of his wife, Nguyen Thi Quang Thai, in a French prison.[80] The more formal Tan Trao encounters took place in the village community hall, a modest highland-style building on low stilts with a thatched roof. Divided into three sections according to traditional practice, the building's left side was used for relaxing and eating, the right side for meetings, and the middle held the village altar plus an exhibit of captured weapons and Viet Minh publications.[81]

Delegates were also taken to witness the Liberation Army contingent of almost one hundred men and women undergoing intensive training at a camp about three kilometers from the village. For most it was also their first sight of Americans. On 9 August, the seven-man OSS Deer Team headed by Major Allison Thomas had initiated its formal course emphasizing familiarization with a range of Allied weapons, including Colt pistols, carbines, M-1 rifles, Thompson submachine guns, Bren guns, other light machine guns, bazookas, 60 mm mortars, and hand grenades. Sufficient ammunition was available to give each trainee time on a rifle range carved out of the jungle.[82] The Americans were impressed by how quickly the Vietnamese learned, not realizing that many of the trainees had previously spent long hours dry firing and disassembling and assembling captured French weapons. The Vietnamese were fascinated by these strang-

80. Tran Huy Lieu, "Di Du Quoc Dan Dai Hoi . . . ," 39.

81. Hoang Dao Thuy, "Tan Trao: Thu Do cua Cach Mang" [Tan Trao: Revolutionary Capital], in Nguyen Duy Trinh, Chu Van Tan, et al., *Nhung Ngay Thang Tam* [Days of August] (Hanoi, 1961), 79–80. *Tran Danh Ba Muoi Nam* [Thirty Years of Battles], vol. 1 (Hanoi, 1983), 33. By contrast, Tran Huy Lieu, "Di Du Quoc Dan Dai Hoi . . . ," 40, recalls meetings taking place on the left side, the exhibition on the right, and the altar area untouched.

82. Maj. Allison Thomas, report to Kunming headquarters, listing weapons needed, 17 July 1945, and "Report on Deer Mission," 17 Sept. 1945, in U.S. Congress, Senate Committee on Foreign Relations, *Causes, Origins and Lessons of the Vietnam War* (Washington, D.C., 1972), 246–47, 259. Included in the three parachute drops (16 July, 29 July, and 10 August) were small arms sufficient to equip one infantry company. As it turned out, there was no time for trainees to learn how to place demolitions, operate portable radios, or read military maps. Personal correspondence with Allison Thomas. Henry Prunier, another team member, recalls the practice firing of mortars as well as rifles, but this seems unlikely given the need to husband ammunition. See Raymond P. Girard, "City Man Helped to Train Guerrillas of Ho Chi Minh," *Evening Gazette* (Worcester, Mass.), 14 and 15 May 1968. See also Ngoc An, "Bo Doi Viet-My" [The Vietnamese-American Force], *Tap Chi Lich Su Quan Su* (Hanoi), no. 10 (Oct. 1986): 20, and Le Van Tich, "Bac Ho va nhung 'san bay da chien' thoi Cach Mang Thang Tam" [Uncle Ho and "Combat Airstrips" in the August Revolution Period], *Tap Chi Lich Su Dang* (Hanoi) 3-1991, 38–39.

ers who dropped out of the sky with tons of esoteric equipment, maintained instant contact with great sources of power in the outside world, often insisted on walking around bare-chested (completely unlike the sartorially conscious French colonials), and showed every sign of wanting to kill "Japs" the minute the training program was concluded. Any books and propaganda pamphlets brought in by the OSS team were devoured by those few Vietnamese present who could read English. Hoang Van Duc, representing the Vietnam Democratic Party at the upcoming National People's Congress, was delighted to be presented with a book titled *A Short History of American Democracy*, which extolled the United States as a model for the rest of the world.[83]

Ho Chi Minh, still recovering from serious illness, managed to find the energy in the evening to query the Americans about world events and offer them his assessment of matters in Indochina. One OSS team member, René Defourneaux, recalled Ho as insisting on speaking in slightly accented English, never raising his voice, possessing the "spindly-legs and knobby knees" of Mahatma Gandhi, and the face of "an emaciated Chinese prophet."[84] As none of the Americans had been briefed in detail about current U.S. or French policies in regard to Indochina, Ho was probably disappointed that he could obtain only general background information and personal opinions.

Above all, Ho Chi Minh wanted to know if the United States, emerging from the war as the strongest nation in the world, intended to intercede in Indochina or leave matters to the French and perhaps the Chinese. He had heard about U.S. speeches at the San Francisco Conference dealing with self-determination for colonial peoples, but nothing on the implications of General de Gaulle's impending visit to Washington at the invitation of President Truman.[85] Ho convinced Thomas that the Viet Minh possessed at least three thousand armed followers prepared to resist any French

83. Interview with Hoang Van Duc, Hanoi, 19 Feb. 1994. Mr. Duc managed to preserve this book through subsequent decades of tumult in Vietnam, bringing it out with pride for me to see.

84. René J. Defourneaux, "A Secret Encounter with Ho Chi Minh," *Look* (New York), 9 Aug. 1966, 33.

85. Defourneaux recalled talking with Ho Chi Minh "many times" about a San Francisco conference speech by John Foster Dulles. It is doubtful whether either Defourneaux or Ho was familiar with key statements at the conference by the American delegate Harold Stassen arguing for "self-government" rather than "independence" in the colonies and favorably equating European colonial empires with the American system of forty-eight federated and "interdependent" states. See William R. Louis, *Imperialism at Bay, 1941–1945* (Oxford, 1977), 532–47.

attempt at recolonization vigorously. On the other hand, Ho also expressed his willingness to go to Kunming to obtain clarification of de Gaulle's March 1945 statement on Indochina and perhaps negotiate a five to fifteen year period of French "reform" prior to full independence.[86]

Possibly as early as 11 August, the Americans at Tan Trao received a radio alert from Kunming that Japanese capitulation might be imminent.[87] On 12 August, the "Provisional Command Committee" of the Viet Minh's liberated zone issued a General Uprising Order announcing that Japan had asked to surrender and asserting (a bit prematurely) that the Allies had accepted Tokyo's formulation. All local Vietnamese forces were instructed to send ultimata to Japanese and Civil Guard units; those who did not surrender were to be annihilated.[88] On 13 August, at 2300 hours, Tan Trao headquarters issued "Military Order No. 1," stating (erroneously) that Japan had capitulated as of 1200. Nonetheless, the order continued, Vietnamese forces who received this order were to attack the enemy army, cut off its routes of retreat, and seize its weapons—actions that would lead to complete victory and national independence.[89] Tran Huy Lieu, who drafted

86. Thomas, message to Wampler, 20 July 1945, and Thomas, report on "The Viet Minh Party or League," in U.S. Senate, *Causes*, 249, 266, 267, 268. These statements by Ho Chi Minh were conveyed to Kunming via the AGAS radio network.

87. At 0400 on 10 August, the Japanese cabinet accepted the terms of the Potsdam Declaration subject to the condition that the imperial house not be deposed. From 0700, this decision was transmitted by wireless to the Swiss government for presentation to the Allies, as well as broadcast to the world. S. Woodburn Kirby, *The War against Japan*, vol. 5 (London, 1969), 210. Patti, *Why Viet Nam?* 137, indicates that he received unofficial word in Kunming on 10 August.

88. Dang Lao Dong Viet Nam, *Chat Xieng: Nhung Tai Lieu Lich Su tu Chinh Bien Thang Ba den Cach Mang Thang Tam 1945* [Breaking Our Chains: Historical Documents from the Political Changes of March to the August Revolution], 3d ed. (Hanoi, 1960), 78–79. Vo Nguyen Giap, *Nhat Lenh Dien Tu va Thu Dong Vien* [Orders of the Day: Speeches and Mobilization Letters] (Hanoi, 1963), 13–14. Translated in *Vietnam: The Definitive Documentation of Human Decisions*, ed. Gareth Porter, vol. 1 (Stanfordville, N.Y., 1979), 56–57; and *Documents of the August 1945 Revolution in Vietnam*, trans. C. Kiriloff (Canberra, 1963), 57–58, which, however, mistakenly gives the date of this document as 13 August.

89. Dang Lao Dong Viet Nam, *Chat Xieng*, 73–74. Tran Huy Lieu et al., *Tai Lieu Tham Khao Lich Su Cach Mang Can Dai Viet Nam* [Reference Materials on the History of Vietnam's Modern Revolution] (Hanoi, 1958), vol. 12 (cited below as CMCD), 12:21–22. Quan Doi Nhan Dan Viet Nam, *Van Kien Quan Su cua Dang, 1930–1945* [Military Documents of the Party, 1930–1945] (Hanoi, 1969), 301–2. A declaration of the Viet Minh General Headquarters (Tong Bo) on 14 August also called on Liberation Army units to "hurl their blood and bones against the Japanese bandits to drive them out." Dang Lao Dong Viet Nam, *Chat Xieng*, 72.

this order on instructions from Vo Nguyen Giap, refused to let the swarms of mosquitoes deter him from waxing eloquent, or from privately contrasting this unique historical opportunity with the many frustrating hours that he and Giap had spent together in the late 1930s as mere pencil-pushing intellectuals.[90]

Also on 13 August, the ICP's All-Country Conference opened at Tan Trao. Reflecting the dramatic new circumstances, it first moved to establish a five-man "Uprising Committee," consisting of Party General Secretary Truong Chinh, Tran Dang Ninh, Vo Nguyen Giap, Le Thanh Nghi, and Chu Van Tan.[91] In practice, this committee does not seem to have played much of a role in rapidly unfolding events; several days later, it issued a brief "Operation Plan" designed simply to remind Party activists of previously agreed military and political methods, not attempting to control local implementation.[92] After that, committee members departed hurriedly on different assignments.

The resolution passed at the end of the ICP Conference on 15 August had a much more sober, analytical tone than the 12 August General Uprising Order or the 13 August Military Order No. 1. Although conditions for seizing power were regarded as very favorable in many locations, it did not call for attacks on the Japanese or predict quick nationwide success. Those who received these messages in sequence must have wondered which one to obey. The resolution pointed out that "the Vietnamese revolution has not as yet succeeded in winning a position on the international arena." It was essential to "win the Soviet Union and the United States over to our cause so that we can oppose French attempts to resume their former position in Indochina and the manoeuvres of some Chinese militarists to occupy our country." Nonetheless, contradictions between Britain, the United States, and France on the one hand, and the Soviet Union on the other, "might lead the British and Americans to make concessions to the French and allow them to come back to Indochina."[93]

At 0900 on 15 August, the OSS team at Tan Trao received word by radio that arrangements for final Japanese surrender were almost complete.[94]

90. Tran Huy Lieu, "Di Du Quoc Dan Dai Hoi . . . ," 40.

91. Hoang Quang Khanh, Le Hong, and Hoang Ngoc La, *Can Cu Dia Viet Bac (Trong cuoc Cach Mang Thang 8–1945)* [The Viet Bac Base Area (in the August 1945 Revolution)] (Viet Bac, 1976) (cited below as *CCDVB*), 135.

92. Dang Lao Dong Viet Nam, *Chat Xieng*, 75–77.

93. Ibid., 63–65. *CMCD*, 12:8–17. Translation in *Vietnam*, ed. Porter, 1:57–59.

94. Personal diary of Major Allison Thomas, p. 3, a copy of which he kindly made available to me.

Early that afternoon, both Allied and Japanese radio stations announced that Emperor Hirohito had personally broadcast instructions to all his subjects to capitulate.[95] Amid the general jubilation at Tan Trao, Vo Nguyen Giap and Major Thomas agreed to terminate the training program and prepare to march southward. That night, military flares were shot into the sky, a fair quantity of liquor was consumed, the Vietnamese cheered lustily for independence, and the Americans shouted "Hip-Hip Hurray!"[96]

About this time, however, AGAS Kunming also informed the Americans at Tan Trao about the Allied decision to have Chinese forces march in to take the Japanese surrender north of the 16th parallel, and the British south of that line.[97] This news, although hardly a complete surprise, must have worried Viet Minh leaders considerably, as it meant that soon they would be forced to deal with additional foreign forces, each possessing different attitudes and objectives. The Viet Minh's long-standing public support for "Chinese armies entering Vietnam" (*Hoa Quan Nhap Viet*), designed to demonstrate willingness to cooperate in attacking the common wartime foe, might now become a distinct postwar embarrassment. Having observed in Kunming the degree of influence the Americans exercised over Chinese officials, Ho Chi Minh probably hoped for a similar situation when it became necessary to establish a working relationship with the occupying forces.

Meanwhile, Viet Minh leaders were determined to put themselves in the best possible position prior to the arrival of Allied forces. Having identified

95. At an imperial conference on the morning of 14 August, Emperor Hirohito had rejected military arguments for continuation of the war, the cabinet had endorsed his views, and drafting of the capitulation rescript had begun. From 1800, messages were sent from the Army Ministry to subordinate echelons explaining the emperor's reasons and calling on all to obey. Also that evening, Tokyo central radio repeatedly foreshadowed an important broadcast at noon the next day. Formal acceptance of Allied terms was sent by wireless to Japanese ambassadors in Switzerland and Sweden at about midnight. During the night a band of young officers tried to force its way into the Imperial Household Ministry to reverse events, without success. At noon on 15 August a recording of the emperor's speech was played to a stunned audience of millions. Kirby, *War against Japan*, 5:213–17. Patti, *Why Viet Nam?* 553 n. 14.

96. Thomas diary, p. 3. Dam Quang Trung was still able to recall the strange "Hip-Hip Hurray!" slogan when he met Allison Thomas again in Hanoi in January 1990 (personal correspondence with Thomas, 28 Nov. 1992). Le Van Tich, "Bac Ho," 39, claims that the Americans shouted, "Vietnamese-American alliance!" and "Wipe out the French and Japanese!" One can only imagine this happening over drinks, the Vietnamese getting the Americans to mimic slogans without understanding them fully, accompanied by much laughter at the mispronunciations.

97. Thomas diary, p. 3, lists this news under 15 August, and mentions the 13th parallel, not the 16th. Thomas's later "Report on Deer Mission," in U.S Senate, *Causes*, 260, lists the information under 16 August.

August 1945

Dear Lt Fenn,

The war is finished. It is good for every body. I feel only sorry that all our American friends have to leave us so soon. And their leaving this country means that relations between you and us will be more difficult.

The war is won. But we small and subject countries have no share, or very very small share, in the victory of freedom and democracy. Probably, if we want to get a sufficient share, we have still to fight. I believe that your sympaty and the sympaty of the great American people will be always with us.

I also remain sure that sooner or later, we will attain our aim, because it is just. And our country get independent, I am looking forward for the happy day of meeting you and our other American friend either in Indo-China or in the U S A!

I wish you good luck & good health.

C. M. Hoo.

Figure 23. Note sent by Ho Chi Minh to Lieutenant Charles Fenn, his former OSS/AGAS contact in Kunming, on hearing definitively of Japan's capitulation. Courtesy of Charles Fenn.

publicly with the Allied cause for four long years, and more recently touted evidence of Allied support, it would not be difficult to persuade most Vietnamese that the Viet Minh represented the victors. Convincing the Japanese was another matter. Presumably after consultations with Ho Chi Minh or Vo Nguyen Giap, Major Thomas proposed by radio to his OSS superiors in China that Viet Minh units be permitted to accept Japanese prisoners and weapons for subsequent transfer to the proper authorities. This idea was quickly and firmly rejected. Chagrined but unbowed, the OSS team and Giap stuck with the 15 August decision to march toward the town of Thai Nguyen, where a significant contingent of Japanese was known to exist.[98] On the afternoon of the 16th, under the huge banyan tree at Tan Trao, the commander of the training contingent, Dam Quang Trung, drew his company-sized unit up in front of members of the National People's Congress, many of whom were deeply impressed by its crisply barked commands, soldierly bearing, and Allied firearms. Giap made a brief, firmly voiced report to the congress. Tran Huy Lieu, representing the congress, wished the unit a victorious future. Then the company, dubbed the "Vietnamese-American Joint Force" (Viet-My Lien-Quan), set off amid cheers on the difficult trek south along steep mountain paths and streambeds.[99]

At the opening session of the National People's Congress on 16 August, some of the sixty delegates noticed a frail, wan, elderly looking man in faded indigo clothing sitting in the second row, occasionally asking questions of those at the front of the room. After announcing the program, Pham Van Dong proceeded to introduce the old man as Ho Chi Minh and invited him to take the chair.[100] Up until the Tan Trao meetings, very few Viet Minh cadres knew that Ho was in fact the fabled international revolutionary Nguyen Ai Quoc, founder of the Indochinese Communist Party. At no point during the congress was Ho referred to as Nguyen Ai Quoc, a formal conspiracy of silence, designed to downplay his Comintern and Communist Party identifications, that continued for almost a decade.[101] Perhaps to heighten the mystery, however, an "Open Letter" from Nguyen Ai Quoc to all Vietnamese citizens was released at about this time, recalling his public exhortation in 1941 and pointing to major advances, but warning that

98. Thomas diary, p. 3. "Report on Deer Mission," in U.S Senate, *Causes*, 260.

99. Tran Huy Lieu, "Di Du Quoc Dan Dai Hoi . . . ," 40. Interview with Vo Nguyen Giap, Hanoi, 17 Feb. 1992.

100. *Doan Ket* (Paris), no. 370 (May 1985): 31–32.

101. Interview with Pham Binh, director of the Institute of International Affairs, Hanoi, 18 Aug. 1984.

Japanese surrender did not mean immediate success, and that only unity and struggle under the Viet Minh banner would bring independence.[102] Tran Huy Lieu recognized Ho as Nguyen Ai Quoc the moment he walked into the room, based on the carefully preserved memory of a photograph that a sailor from Marseille had given Lieu in 1929.[103] The fact that these two exalted figures were one and the same man spread quickly among congress participants and Viet Minh leaders elsewhere, becoming privileged inner knowledge that helped to define elite membership; it would be several years before the public at large became aware of it.

The main formal business of the congress was to elect a National Liberation Committee to serve as the nucleus of a provisional government. The revolutionary credentials of each nominee were outlined by another delegate, with the exception of Ho Chi Minh, about whom, paradoxically, least was known publicly. Ho was elected chairman and Tran Huy Lieu deputy chairman. Pham Van Dong, Nguyen Luong Bang, and Duong Duc Hien joined them as members of the Standing Committee. The congress also declared the banner of the Viet Minh to be the national flag. Van Cao's march "Tien Quan Ca" ("Advancing Army") became the national anthem. Some discussion ensued about the Japanese surrender and relations with the Allies. A few delegates insisted that peaceful dealings with the imperialists remained impossible: when Chinese Kuomintang troops poured in, when the French returned, it would be necessary to fight. To the disappointment of some who did not know him yet, Ho Chi Minh deliberately eschewed such emotional, heroic stances. Instead, he spoke briefly, slowly, and directly about the many difficulties that lay ahead.[104] In particular, it might be necessary to offer economic and cultural concessions to the French government in exchange for recognition of Vietnamese independence; if Paris refused such a formula and hostilities ensued, Vietnam would at least

---

102. Printed in the first Hanoi edition of *Cuu Quoc*, 24 Aug. 1945. Reprinted in Dang Lao Dong Viet Nam, *Chat Xieng*, 69–70, and Quan Doi Nhan Dan Viet Nam, *Van Kien Quan Su cua Dang*, 312–13. Translated in *Vietnam*, ed. Porter, 1:60–61, and *Documents*, trans. Kiriloff, 51.

103. Tran Huy Lieu, "Di Du Quoc Dan Dai Hoi . . . ," 41. According to Lieu, the high forehead and bright eyes provided the link between the elegant young man in the photo and the elderly gentleman with sunken cheeks at the congress. Lieu's wife had burned the photo following her husband's imprisonment, fearing police discovery. In Hue, some people figured out Ho Chi Minh's identity as soon as they saw his photograph in September 1945, because he so resembled Nguyen Ai Quoc's elder brother, Nguyen Tat Dat, who had lived in the vicinity for years. Hoang Anh, Le Tu Dong, et al., *Binh Tri Thien Thang Tam Bon Lam: Hoi Ky* [August 1945 in Binh Tri Thien Province: Memoirs] (Hue, 1985), 30.

104. Tran Huy Lieu, "Di Du Quoc Dan Dai Hoi . . . ," 32. *CCDVB*, 136.

have garnered considerable sympathy from the French people and world public opinion.[105]

Sometime during the congress, Ho dispatched a message in English to the United Nations via Lieutenant Dan Phelan, the AGAS contact now in Kunming, also intimating to Phelan that his headquarters might be shifted soon and warning that Dai Viet activists planned to terrorize French residents in Indochina in order to embarrass the Viet Minh.[106] Ho may also have tried to communicate to Paris another basic negotiating position, including acceptance of French sovereignty for five to ten years, French recognition of Vietnamese internal autonomy under a Viet Minh government, but French involvement in administration, foreign affairs, industry, and commerce.[107] On 17 or 18 August, Ho Chi Minh sent another letter to Phelan, requesting 20,000 piastres to ransom a U.S. pilot from "oversea [*sic*] Chinese bandits" at Dong Trieu (Hai Duong), apologizing that "the going of our armed boys with Major Thomas (and the staying too long of the French) drained rather heavily on our local purse."[108]

Given the need for delegates to return quickly to their localities to take part in seizure of power, the National People's Congress agenda was cut short compared to what Ho Chi Minh had originally intended. All delegates could readily agree with the final lines of the published congress resolution: "In the present post-war international situation, a people that is united and determined to demand its independence will certainly win it. We will be victorious."[109] At the solemn closing ceremony, soldiers fired a salute, the new anthem was sung, and minority villagers brought the delegates a few symbolic gifts. Ho Chi Minh pointed to a sickly, poorly clad village child

---

105. Hoang Van Hoan, *Giot Nuoc*, 255–57.

106. Ho Chi Minh letter in the possession of the late Robert Shaplen, who kindly provided me a photocopy. Although the letter is undated, the text suggests it was penned on either 16 or 17 August.

107. King C. Chen, *Vietnam and China 1938–1954* (Princeton, 1969), 107, citing a Chinese report of 10 Oct. 1945. It is uncertain whether this particular formulation ever made it to the French authorities, unlike the proposal sent via the OSS in late July (see chapter 5).

108. Ho Chi Minh letter in possession of the late Robert Shaplen. Presumably these letters were being picked up by OSS L-5 courier aircraft. "The French" Ho refers to are probably the group of civilians escorted from Tam Dao in July. See chapter 3.

109. Dang Lao Dong Viet Nam, *Chat Xieng*, 66–68.*CMCD*, 12:28–30. Quan Doi Nhan Dan Viet Nam, *Van Kien Quan Su cua Dang*, 359–61. Translated in *Vietnam*, ed. Porter, 1:59–60; *Documents*, trans. Kiriloff, 49–50; and *Viet-Nam Crisis*, ed. Cameron, 46–48. A shorter version of this resolution, designed for newspaper publication, can be found in AOM, INF, GF 48.

who had accompanied the local Tay minority representatives to bid farewell to the congress. After providing the delegates some background details about the boy, Ho stressed that the ultimate objective of everyone present, and of the Revolution as a whole, ought to be to ensure that such children throughout the country had enough to eat, to wear, to be healthy, and to be able to study.[110] Many delegates now believed fervently that Ho was the one to bring them through. As one recalled:

> Looking at Ho Chi Minh, we no longer saw a tired, elderly gentleman wearing faded indigo, but rather, through our tears of emotion, our general happiness, a leader, a symbol of the collective, representing the entire Vietnamese people in armed struggle, advancing. The nation had a government! The country had a chairman![111]

At the parting dinner that evening, Ho showed everyone his lighthearted side, cajoling Hoang Dao Thuy, a prominent Boy Scout leader, into teaching everyone a game about hopping rabbits.[112]

Hanoi and Vicinity

Although Hue was the royal capital and Saigon the commercial center of Vietnam, few doubted that Hanoi remained the most important city from the strategic, political, and cultural points of view. Taking power in Hanoi might not ensure power elsewhere, but it was impossible to govern Vietnam (or, from the French perspective, Indochina) without controlling that city.

Members of the Dai Viet Quoc Gia Lien Minh (Greater Vietnam National Alliance), on hearing news of possible Japanese surrender, convened an emergency meeting in Hanoi to determine how to react. One group favored seizing power immediately from the Kham Sai, thus preempting a likely Viet Minh takeover in the wake of Japan's capitulation. Another group opposed such action, arguing that it would be seen by the incoming Allies as collaboration with the Japanese. If Viet Minh activists did mount a coup, according to this line of reasoning, it would still be possible to join with Vietnam Nationalist Party units accompanying the Chinese Army to throw them out. At one point in the meeting, a Viet Minh representative

---

110. Tran Huy Lieu, "Di Du Quoc Dan Dai Hoi . . . ," 42. *Doan Ket* (Paris), no. 370 (May 1985): 32.

111. Hoang Dao Thuy, "Tan Trao," 80.

112. Tran Van Suy, "Ket qua buoc dau suu tam nghien cuu ve luc luong Huong Dao Sinh tham gia cuoc Cach Mang Thang Tam—1945" [Early Results of Research into Boy Scout Participation in the August Revolution—1945] (unpublished manuscript, Hanoi, 1989), 3.

was actually let in to state his case. He warned not only that any Dai Viet regime would be regarded by the Allies as collaborationist, but that such a takeover could only succeed in the city, as the rural provinces surrounding Hanoi would definitely be taken by the Viet Minh. The meeting adjourned without decision.[113]

For several weeks the Kham Sai had been putting out feelers to the Viet Minh via various intellectuals belonging to the National Salvation Cultural Association and through his son, Phan Ke Bao, a clandestine Viet Minh participant. Le Trong Nghia of the Vietnam Democratic Party appears to have gained the Kham Sai's confidence and introduced him to Tran Dinh Long, a key ICP member in the city.[114] On 13 August, Phan Ke Toai received a delegation headed by Nguyen Khang, the member of the ICP Northern Regional Committee specifically responsible for Hanoi operations. Apparently, Toai offered the Viet Minh several portfolios in the royal government and mentioned that the Japanese were prepared to turn over additional weapons to help Vietnam protect its independence. Khang flatly rejected the idea of Viet Minh participation in the existing regime, but not in such a way as to rupture communications with the Kham Sai's Office.[115] To show his good faith, Toai may have persuaded the Japanese to release some more political prisoners.[116]

That evening, just outside Hanoi, the ICP's Regional Committee, having just heard Allied radio reports of imminent Japanese capitulation, issued an urgent communiqué to subordinate echelons, ordering them to make final preparations for an uprising.[117] The next day the ICP's Hanoi City

---

113. Hoang Van Dao, *Viet Nam Quoc Dan Dang*, 216–17, does not give the date of this meeting, but from the context it seems likely to have been the evening of 12 August or the next day. Those Dai Viet members favoring a coup presumably believed they would receive Japanese assistance, although no source deals explicitly with this question. Unfortunately, we have no other source on these Dai Viet activities.

114. Hoang Van Dao, *Viet Nam Quoc Dan Dang*, 219.

115. Nguyen Khang, "Ha Noi Khoi Nghia" [Hanoi Uprising], in Nguyen Duy Trinh et al., *Nhung Ngay Thang Tam*, 133. Dang Lao Dong Viet Nam, Ban Nghien Cuu Lich Su Dang Thanh Uy Ha-Noi, *Cuoc Van Dong Cach Mang Thang Tam o Hanoi (cuoi 1939–1946)* [Activating the August Revolution in Hanoi (end of 1939–1946)] (Hanoi, 1970) (cited below as *CMTT-H*), 114–15. Nguyen Quyet, *Ha Noi Thang Tam*, 131–33, indicates that Phan Ke Toai's assistant, Pham Huu Chuong, did most of the talking on the government side. *CMTT*, 1:34, is unique in saying that this meeting took place on the 12th rather than the 13th.

116. Colton, "Failure," 176.

117. *CMTT*, 1:34–35. According to "Lich Su Nganh Thong Tin Buu Dien Viet Nam (Du Thao)" [History of Vietnam's Communications and Postal Branch (Draft)], vol. 1 (Hanoi, 1989), 66, following the 9 March coup the Regional Com-

Committee convened a special meeting of "military cadres" at a pagoda in the suburbs, where it was determined that between seven and eight hundred "self-defense" (*tu ve*) personnel were armed and ready to act.[118]

At about 2:00 P.M. on 14 August, an armed crowd of three hundred Dai Viet and Patriotic Youth Group (Thanh Nien Ai Quoc Doan) adherents marched on the Kham Sai's Palace, accompanied by four Japanese soldiers disguised as Vietnamese and carrying submachine guns. The Kham Sai met them outside the building, accompanied by two hundred rifle-toting civil guardsmen, then invited a delegation in to discuss possible turnover of government authority or at least a supply of firearms. During this meeting, a Dai Viet member rushed in with word that French soldiers detained by the Japanese inside the Citadel had dug up some hidden weapons and planned to seize the city that night. This news sent the three hundred youths rushing off toward the Citadel, where several hours later a Vietnamese working for the Kenpeitai apparently deceived them into stacking their weapons, after which they were marched to the main Civil Guard barracks and placed under detention for four days.[119] Whether intentionally or not, the Japanese had effectively neutralized those Vietnamese in Hanoi who had been closest to them during the war.

From the evening of 14 August to the morning of the 16th, the ICP's Northern Regional Committee remained in continuous session. Although some members might have preferred to wait for orders from Tan Trao, it was agreed that the Standing Bureau instructions of 12 March provided sufficient authorization for an uprising in the event of Japanese surrender, which was confirmed on 15 August. Nevertheless, the Regional Committee was not yet committed to trying to seize power in Hanoi. Instead, it decided on the 15th to mount insurrections first in ten Red River Delta provinces, taking control of government bureaus, cutting off enemy communications, and forming revolutionary people's councils in all villages that did not already have them. Messengers carried this word to the relevant provincial

---

mittee had obtained a high-quality radio receiver from To Huu Hanh, a covert ICP member employed by the colonial broadcasting service. Nguyen Khang, "Ha Noi Khoi Nghia," 132, indicates the Regional Committee also knew of the 11–12 August collapse of the Japanese Army in Manchuria. Following communist historiographical convention, no mention is made of the two atomic bombs as factors in Japan's decision to surrender. Key members of the Regional Committee at this point included Tran Tu Binh, Van Tien Dung, Nguyen Khang, and Nguyen Loc. Nguyen Quyet, *Ha Noi Thang Tam*, 129.

118. Nguyen Quyet, *Ha Noi Thang Tam*, 130–31.

119. Hoang Van Dao, *Viet Nam Quoc Dan Dang*, 220–21.

ICP leaders. Simultaneously, the Regional Committee agreed to form a Hanoi Revolutionary Military Committee (Uy Ban Quan Su Cach Mang Ha Noi), headed by Nguyen Khang, to continue preparations for conclusive action in the city.[120]

On the morning of the 16th, Nguyen Khang led a Viet Minh delegation to meet the Tonkin Kham Sai a second time. According to ICP sources, Phan Ke Toai reiterated the offer to include Viet Minh members in the existing government, thus being able to present a united front to the incoming Allies. In response, Khang bluntly urged the Kham Sai to resign and the Hue government to disband, since the Allies would consider them all Japanese collaborators. Still at an impasse, Toai warned Khang against any violent actions directed at the Japanese, who remained quite capable of defending themselves.[121]

The "Japanese question" now assumed critical importance for Viet Minh activists. At Tan Trao, as we have seen, a hard line had been taken: force Japanese units to surrender to the Viet Minh, representing the Allies, then spirit their weapons away before Allied forces arrived. An ultimatum letter was printed up hastily for Liberation Army units to use, calling on Japanese soldiers to turn over their weapons, "not only to guarantee your own survival but also to assist somewhat in the Vietnamese people's liberation efforts." At the bottom of the sheet was a blank space for units to write in the hour at which a particular ultimatum expired.[122]

For many ICP leaders it was an article of faith that revolutions required violent destruction of the existing system. It was also widely assumed that the vaunted military discipline of the Japanese would fall apart at the shock of national defeat, causing subordinate units to throw down their arms in despair, or turn them over to angry Vietnamese in exchange for safe conduct. Physically cowing the Japanese would demonstrate the strength of the Viet Minh and be greatly enjoyed by the millions of Vietnamese who

---

120. Many sources refer to this body incorrectly as the "Hanoi Uprising Committee." Besides Khang, the Hanoi Revolutionary Military Committee included Nguyen Huy Khoi (aka Tran Quang Huy), Nguyen Duy Than, Nguyen Quyet, and Le Trong Nghia (Vietnam Democratic Party), with Tran Dinh Long as "adviser." Nguyen Quyet, *Ha Noi Thang Tam*, 128–29, 134. *CMTT*, 1:36.

121. *CMTT*, 1:37. Nguyen Quyet, *Ha Noi Thang Tam*, 133. At this second meeting, Phan Ke Toai included on his side Nguyen Xuan Chu, a member of the newly formed "Political Direction Committee," as well as Pham Huu Chuong.

122. Dang Lao Dong Viet Nam, *Chat Xieng*, 80. Translated in *Documents*, trans. Kiriloff, 58–59. On 16 August, the Viet Minh's Northern Region Committee reiterated the call to overthrow the "militaristic Japanese." *NCLS*, no. 101 (8-1967): 13.

blamed the "Jap dwarfs" for wartime death and deprivation. Finally, at the higher diplomatic level, Ho Chi Minh undoubtedly appreciated the importance of demonstrating to the Americans, Chinese, British, and even the French the legitimate Allied credentials of the Viet Minh in the immediate postsurrender period, which ruled out any cozy arrangements with the Japanese.

As Viet Minh adherents encountered Japanese in the days following the Tokyo surrender announcement, they found a few individuals willing to desert, some commanders prepared to turn over captured stocks of French weapons, but no readiness to accede to ultimatums, especially regarding Japanese weapons and equipment.[123] In these circumstances, blind adherence to higher-level Viet Minh instructions to attack the Japanese would have been disastrous, resulting in thousands of casualties and widespread popular demoralization. On the other hand, many activists now sensed that it might be possible to take power at district, provincial, and even national levels without provoking major confrontations with the Japanese.

The Japanese Position

As of 16 August, it was unclear whether the Japanese authorities would make any serious effort to defend the Hue government and its local representatives, or instead withdraw from the political arena and await orders from Tokyo or from Allied commanders designated to take their surrender in Indochina. Two days earlier in Hue, Yokoyama Masayuki had finally allowed Emperor Bao Dai to proclaim abrogation of the treaties signed with France in 1862 and 1874, an act that had the effect of making Cochinchina formally a part of Imperial Vietnam (Viet Nam De Quoc).[124] That same day, Nguyen Van Sam received his credentials as Southern Region Imperial Delegate (Kham Sai Nam Ky), managed to locate sufficient fuel for his automobile, and began the potentially perilous drive toward

123. Hoang Van Hoan is the only Viet Minh leader of the period who has admitted this in his memoirs. See Hoang Van Hoan, *Giot Nuoc trong Bien Ca*, 262. All others talk ritualistically of extreme Japanese confusion, demoralization, and physical fear of the newly empowered Vietnamese.

124. Shiraishi Masaya, "La Présence Japonaise en Indochine (1940–1945)," in *Indochine française, 1940–1945*, ed. Paul Isoart (Paris, 1982), 237. Ralph B. Smith, "The Japanese Period in Indochina and the Coup of 9 March 1945," *Journal of Southeast Asian Studies* (cited below as *JSEAS*), no. 2 (Sept. 1978): 295. André Teulieres, *L'Indochine, guerre et paix* (Paris, 1985), 101, 104. It will be recalled that only the 1884 treaty making Annam a protectorate had been abrogated on 11 March 1945.

Saigon.[125] Perhaps partly to encourage Japanese officials to protect the status quo, both Tran Trong Kim and Phan Ke Toai issued public statements that reiterated their gratitude to Japan for liberating Vietnam, promised continuing close cooperation, affirmed the government's determination not to return to colonial slavery, and urged citizens to unite to safeguard national independence.[126]

On 15 August, as per previous agreement, the Japanese authorities in Hanoi formally transferred control of the Civil Guard, the police, and all educational institutions to the royal government.[127] That same day the Japanese sent letters to the last group of French guards at the Hanoi Central Prison, instructing them to cease working immediately as a consequence of the Kham Sai assuming full authority.[128] The royal government cabled the Kham Sai to fire the remaining French employees of the PTT forthwith, without pay. If they refused to "retire," they would be put before a special criminal court on security charges.[129] However, the Japanese still insisted on retaining French railway technicians and some French employees at the port of Haiphong. On the 16th, with Tokyo's capitulation confirmed formally by Yokoyama, Tran Trong Kim tried to blunt the domestic impact of this news by emphasizing that Vietnam remained independent, and that the Vietnamese people would never again subjugate themselves to France. By way of implied Japanese support, Domei broadcast this statement to the world in English on the 17th, soon doing the same with Bao Dai's messages to Allied heads of state.[130]

Although the Japanese Southern Area Command in Saigon presumably received word no later that 11 August of Tokyo's intention to sur-

125. Nguyen Ky Nam, *Hoi Ky*, 185–86, 187. Tran Trong Kim, *Mot Con Gio Bui*, 90. Sam appeared to have a Japanese escort as far as Quang Ngai, but not beyond. Pending his arrival in Saigon, Ho Van Nga was named acting viceroy.

126. Ban Nghien Cuu Lich Su Dang tinh Thua Thien, *So Thao Lich Su Cach Mang Thang Tam Thua Thien Hue* [Draft History of the August Revolution in Thua Thien Hue] (Hanoi, 1970), 58. Nguyen Quyet, *Ha Noi Thang Tam*, 127. Colton, "Failure," 211–13.

127. *CMTT*, 1:34. Nguyen Quyet, *Ha Noi Thang Tam*, 133–34. Devillers, *Histoire*, 136, asserts that these transfers occurred on 16 August. Teulieres, *L'Indochine*, 104, refers to a further order from General Tsuchihashi to subordinates in Hue, Phnom Penh, and Vientiane on 17 August for all powers to be returned to local sovereigns.

128. Japanese consul, Hanoi, dossier, in AOM, INF, GF 2. Other French guards had received similar letters in the previous three weeks.

129. Nguyen Van Huong to Kham Sai, 18 Aug. 1945, and list of twelve French PTT employees, 19 Aug. 1945, in first Kham Sai folder, AOM, INF, GF 4.

130. *New York Times*, 18 Aug. 1945, 5. Colton, "Failure," 213–14. Patti, *Why Viet Nam?* 169, 185, 554 n. 9.

render, Marshal Terauchi may have avoided notifying lower echelons. In Hanoi, however, General Tsuchihashi quickly summoned officers and diplomats to confirm what previously had been considered only enemy propaganda.[131] For a few days there was staff talk of carrying on the struggle, if necessary by retreating into previously prepared defense zones in Cambodia and Laos. However, those who listened to the Shōwa emperor's broadcast on 15 August, or who heard subsequent Domei reports, could be under no illusions: His Majesty wanted them to accept the unbearable and stop fighting. The news caused confusion, emotional trauma, and a few suicides. Not until 18 August did General Tsuchihashi order all units of the Thirty-eighth Army to cease hostilities by the morning of the 21st. Any further thoughts among high-ranking officers of continued resistance must have been scotched on 19 August, when Prince Kanin delivered the imperial surrender decree personally to Marshal Terauchi.[132] The next day, All-India Radio having established direct communication with Southern Area Command, Lord Mountbatten ordered Marshal Terauchi to send a delegation by air to Rangoon to sign a preliminary convention prior to formal surrender ceremonies planned for Singapore.[133] Similar contact by Chinese commanders was not made until 26 August.[134]

Not content to accept passively whatever British and Chinese commanders meted out, some Japanese continued to try to influence immediate developments inside Indochina. In one of the more curious episodes, an officer drove from Saigon to Loc Ninh, Admiral Decoux's place of internment, to inform the former governor-general of the war's end, and even offered him two bottles of champagne. Decoux declined the champagne, but gave the captain a letter addressed to General Tsuchihashi, proposing his immediate return to authority at Norodom Palace and the release of all other French personnel to assist him in maintaining order pending arrival of Allied forces. He also enclosed a message for transmission to the French

131. Tønnesson, *Vietnamese Revolution*, 371, based on American radio intercepts.

132. Peter M. Dunn, "An Interpretation of Documentation and Oral Primary Source Materials for the Period September 1945 until May 1946 in the Region of Cochinchina and Southern Annam" (Ph.D. diss., [University of London] School of Oriental and African Studies, 1980), ch. 5, 13. Patti, *Why Viet Nam?* 159, 553 n. 14. Devillers, *Histoire du Vietnam*, 136. Kirby, *War against Japan*, 5:218.

133. *Official History of the Indian Armed Forces in the Second World War, 1939–1945. Post-War Occupation Forces: Japan and South East Asia*, ed. B. Prasad (n.p., 1958), 172.

134. *War in Asia and the Pacific, 1937–1949*, ed. Donald S. Detwiler and Charles B. Burdick (New York, 1980), 6:34.

日本降伏す。聯合國提示條件を承認。天皇は各地軍隊に對し抵抗中止の勅令を發せられる。（正式發表に依る）	Japan has surrendered. The Allied peace terms have been accepted. The Emperor is issuing orders ending resistance everywhere— OFFICIAL.
	Japan ne hathiar dal die hain. Ittihadion ki sulah ki sharten man li gai hain. Japan ke shahinshah ne har ilaqe ki Japani faujon ko muqabla band kar dene ka hukm de dia hai.— SARKARI ELAN.
	ဂျပန် လက်နက် ချ၍ အရှုံးပြို၊ မဟာမိတ် တို့၏ ငြိမ်းချမ်းရေး စည်းကမ်းချက်များကို ဂျပန်က လက်ခံပြီးဖြစ်၏။ ဂျပန် စစ်တပ်များ နေ ရာတိုင်းတွင် ခု ခံ တိုက် ခိုက် ခြင်းကို ရပ်စဲေစရန် ဂျပန် ဘုရင်က အမိန့် ထုတ် နေ သည်။ အစိုး ရ က အ တိ အ လင်း ကျေ ညာ ကြောင်း။
	Le Japon s'est rendu. Les conditions de paix alliées ont été acceptées. L'Empereur donne des ordres pour mettre fin partout à la resistance. (OFFICIEL)

Figure 24. Leaflet dropped over Saigon in late August 1945. In five languages—Japanese, English, Hindi, Burmese, and French—the Allies spread the word of Japan's capitulation. Courtesy of Archives d'Outre-Mer, Aix-en-Provence.

government, informing Paris of these planned actions.[135] According to some sources, the Japanese did indeed radio the substance of Decoux's proposal to France, receiving a reply on 23 August to await the arrival of new chiefs.[136] It seems unlikely that Tsuchihashi would have agreed voluntarily to release and rearm French military personnel, as some might have chosen to vent their spleen on the Japanese who had attacked them in March. In any event, once Lord Mountbatten had told Marshal Terauchi to maintain the status quo pending the Rangoon meeting, it followed that Admiral Decoux should remain at Loc Ninh.

All things considered, many Japanese in authority would have liked the Vietnamese government established following the 9 March coup to remain in power. Aside from honest feelings of sympathy for people who rejected Western colonialism and for individual Vietnamese who had become personal friends, Japanese officials needed to keep dealing with someone in authority if mob violence were to be avoided, food obtained, epidemics

135. Jean Decoux, *A la barre de l'Indochine* (Paris, 1952), 339–41, 349. Claude de Boisanger, *On pouvait éviter la guerre d'Indochine* (Paris, 1977), 108–9.

136. Martin, *Heures tragiques*, 131 n. 1. Jean-J. Bernardini, *Sous la botte nippone* (Paris, 1971), 149. Arnaud Barthouet, *Indochine (au-dessus des drames, des bourrages et des comédies)*, vol. 4 (Paris, 1949), 51–52.

contained, units regrouped peacefully, and military equipment preserved for disposition according to Allied orders. If the Chinese or British occupiers then chose to overturn the existing Vietnamese government, the onus would be on them to avoid chaos.

Besides the transfer of administrative authority in Hanoi, mentioned previously, Japanese officers were present in Saigon on 14 August at the founding meeting of the United National Front (Mat Tran Quoc Gia Thong Nhut), designed to bring together all groups opposed to return of the French colonial rulers.[137] Japanese representatives also attended an impressive ceremony in Saigon of the Vanguard Youth, where up to fifty thousand young men knelt down to swear loyalty to the nation, sing patriotic songs, and march around the field. On 16 August, the Japanese began to transfer bureaus and official responsibilities to an executive body of the United National Front.[138] The next night, however, members of the Vanguard Youth, probably with Japanese connivance, "liberated" a truck convoy containing two thousand rifles and ten million cartridges, which had the effect of suddenly shifting the operational center of gravity toward one specific component of the United National Front.[139] When the newly appointed Kham Sai, Nguyen Van Sam, arrived in Saigon on 19 August, he went immediately to Japanese headquarters to talk about acquiring firearms for other groups not as heavily influenced by the ICP.[140]

During this period the Japanese withdrew large quantities of cash, about 60 million piastres, from the Bank of Indochina.[141] They did not know how they would be treated by the Allies, but assumed that all weapons would have to be relinquished, and such money could be used to secure food and services during the indefinite period of time between surrender and repatriation. Although Japanese units had stockpiled large amounts of rice, much of it was far from the ports where troops might well be ordered to concentrate.[142]

137. Members of this short-lived front included Ho Van Nga's Vietnam National Independence Party, the Vanguard Youth, Cao Dai, Hoa Hao, Phuc Quoc, Trotskyists, and several unions of workers and public servants. Devillers, *Histoire*, 140–41. Colton, "Failure," 208–9, 242–57.

138. *Dia Chi Van Hoa Thanh Pho Ho Chi Minh*, ed. Tran Van Giau, vol. 1 (Ho Chi Minh City, 1987), 345–46. Colton, "Failure," 210, 243–64 passim.

139. This feat was masterminded by Dr. Pham Ngoc Thach and Ngo Tan Nhon. *Dia Chi*, ed. Tran Van Giau, 344.

140. Devillers, *Histoire*, 141.

141. Patti, *Why Viet Nam?* 214, 556n.

142. Kyoko Kurusu Nitz, "Independence without Nationalists? Japanese and Vietnamese Nationalism during the Japanese Period, 1940–45," *JSEAS* 15, no. 1 (Mar. 1984): 129.

Takeover in Hanoi

At a meeting of the Viet Minh's Hanoi Revolutionary Military Committee on the evening of 16 August, everyone agreed that the moment for resolute action had come, but the exact forms and sequence remained open to intense discussion. By this time copies of the Viet Minh Military Order No. 1 of 13 August and the call to "drive out the Japanese bandits" of 14 August may have reached Hanoi from Tan Trao,[143] yet it was obvious that any direct attack on the well-armed Japanese in the city would be suicidal. On the other hand, it might be possible to seize power without confronting the Japanese. The meeting may have heard a report from one Viet Minh adherent who had just had a discussion with Resident Superior Nishimura in which the latter suggested that firearms might be available "informally" from outlying Japanese units, even though officially all weapons had to be surrendered to Allied representatives.[144] Eventually the meeting decided to drop the slogan about driving out the Japanese in favor of "Oppose all imperialist interference in the Vietnamese people's independence efforts."[145] Nguyen Huy Khoi was delegated to prepare a leaflet, for urgent translation into Japanese by a Viet Minh sympathizer, calling on Imperial Army members to focus on returning to their loved ones, staying clear of the efforts of the Vietnamese to liberate their country. When word arrived that the Vietnamese General Association of Government Employees had been given Japanese permission to convene a public meeting at the Opera House the afternoon of the next day, the Revolutionary Military Committee determined to employ armed self-defense teams to take control of the proceedings and, if possible, convert them into a mass Viet Minh

143. Nguyen Quyet, *Ha Noi Thang Tam*, 138–39, 140. For a recent secondary description of events in Hanoi during 16–19 August 1945, see Thanh Van, Tran Hoai Long, et al., *Thu Do Ha Noi: Lich Su Khang Chien Chong Thuc Dan Phap (1945–1954)* [Hanoi Capital: History of Resistance to the French Colonialists (1945–54)] (Hanoi, 1986), 56–78.

144. Interview with Nishimura Kumao, Tokyo, 17 Nov. 1967. More than once Nishimura volunteered his favorable impression of the Viet Minh leaders he encountered after 15 August, particularly their vigor, courage, and ability to make decisions quickly, "quite different from ordinary Vietnamese intellectuals."

145. Nguyen Khang, "Ha Noi Khoi Nghia," 140. Differing ICP behavior toward the Japanese after 15 August has never been analyzed by historians in Hanoi. Brief explanations of both "attack" and "negotiate" responses can be found in Tran Van Ty, "Tim hieu nhung kinh nghiem cua hinh thai dau tranh Cach Mang Thang Tam" [Understanding Experiences of Forms of Struggle in the August Revolution], *NCLS*, no. 20 (9-1961): 10–11, and Hoang Trung Thuc, "Tim hieu phuong cham 'Them ban bat thu' trong thoi ky Cach Mang Thang Tam" [Understand the Formula "Adding Friends and Subtracting Enemies" in the August Revolution Period], *NCLS*, no. 101 (8-1967): 12–13.

demonstration around the city. That same evening, armed "youth assault" teams belonging to the Democratic Party entered three Hanoi theaters to call on people to participate in the impending insurrection. At the To Nhu theater, a Japanese officer was shot and killed as he fled the building. Unlike in the case of previous such incidents, there was no harsh retaliation.[146]

On the morning of 17 August, the royal government's long-planned National Consultative Congress, Northern Branch, convened in the lecture hall of the Association pour la formation intellectuelle et morale des Annamites (AFIMA), about 600 meters from the Opera House, across the Returned Sword Lake.[147] The membership included many teachers, journalists, creative writers, physicians, and specialists employed by the government, but neither any avowedly pro-French individuals nor anyone publicly identified with the Viet Minh. A large contingent of police was present to keep nondelegates at a distance, but popular interest seems to have been minimal. After the Civil Guard band played the royal national anthem and the eldest delegate present declared the congress in session, Kham Sai Phan Ke Toai proceeded to read a very general keynote address, then exited the building to the tune of the most popular marching song of the day, "Call to Youth" ("Tieng Goi Thanh Nien"). Having ascertained that thirty-six of the fifty-nine delegates were present, thus constituting a quorum, his assistant, Dr. Pham Huu Chuong, declared the session legal according to the May imperial edicts, and called for nominees to positions on the "management board." Nguyen Xien proposed a slate headed by Dr. Nguyen Van Luyen, which was promptly approved, following which Dr. Chuong turned over the rostrum and excused himself to return to urgent business at the Kham Sai's Office.[148]

Almost immediately a dispute arose over whether to follow the agenda prepared in advance by the Kham Sai[149] or instead establish an emergency

146. Nguyen Quyet, *Ha Noi Thang Tam*, 135–40. *CMTT*, 1:38. Nguyen Van Tri, "Thanh Nien Xung Phong . . . ," in Nguyen Khang et al., *Ha Noi Khoi Nghia* [Hanoi Uprising] (Hanoi, 1970), 154–55. Vo Van Cam, a leader of the pro-Japanese Patriotic Youth Group, was wounded, but managed to escape, also at the To Nhu theater.

147. The following description of the meeting is taken from minutes of the Hoi Nghi Tu Van Quoc Gia, Bac Chi Bo, 17 Aug. 1945, contained in AOM, INF, GF 5.

148. Nguyen Van Luyen, a physician and respected nationalist unconnected to any political party, had published the daily newspaper *Tin Moi* (New News) from 1940 to 1943. Pham Huu Chuong was active in the Democratic Front and French Socialist Party during the late 1930s, but had moved to a conservative position by 1941.

149. Issued on 15 August, this agenda provided for seven days of deliberations, with a rest on Sunday the 19th. AOM, INF, GF 34. Another copy can be found in AOM, INF, GF 58.

"national salvation committee" (*uy ban cuu quoc*) to take action on crucial questions such as unifying diverse political groups, mobilizing troops, acquiring weapons, collecting money, obtaining a radio station, and formulating a strategy to deal with the incoming Allies. At 12:30 P.M., word arrived that the Hue government had given the new four-person Northern Region Political Direction Committee "full powers to resolve matters in the current extraordinary circumstances."[150] This news appeared to silence talk of a national salvation committee. A reply cable approved by the congress reaffirmed confidence in the emperor and his government, urged national unity in defense of independence, and pledged to sacrifice everything to the struggle "if the French are still scheming to return to rule us once again." Simultaneously, some local officials cabled Hanoi renewing their pledge of loyalty. The provincial mandarin of Son Tay went further, assuring the Kham Sai that people of all classes were solidly behind him and stating: "Have taken necessary steps to meet any eventuality. No worries on dikes situation."[151] The next day, in fact, the dikes broke in Son Tay. When the National Consultative Congress adjourned for lunch, some key members went to the Kham Sai's Palace to discuss matters with Phan Ke Toai and Nguyen Xuan Chu, head of the new Political Committee. It seems likely that Toai decided at this point that his position was untenable, but withheld announcement of his resignation until the evening. Toai did bother to inform the Japanese of the new committee and to request that it receive a quantity of firearms to facilitate resistance to return of the French.[152] When the congress reconvened at 5:00 P.M., discussion focused mainly on foreign affairs, a resolution being passed requesting the government "to protest violently" French statements, especially the Brazzaville Declaration of early February 1944. One subcommittee was selected to prepare a booklet refuting French propaganda, another to participate in the work of Nguyen Xuan Chu's committee. Well before the 7:00 P.M. adjournment of the congress, however, the attention of many members had been diverted to the loud noise of demonstrators marching along the other side of the lake.[153]

150. As mentioned earlier, the royal edict establishing the Political Direction Committee is dated 18 August; presumably informal word was telegraphed to Hanoi one day prior.

151. Son Tay, cable to viceroy (in French), 17 Aug. 1945, in dossier of late July and August messages, AOM, INF, GF 27.

152. Tønnesson, *Vietnamese Revolution*, 375, based on American radio intercepts.

153. Nguyen Quyet, *Ha Noi Thang Tam*, 147.

From sunrise on the 17th, newsboys had moved through the streets of Hanoi, yelling, "Papers! Fresh papers! Two o'clock this afternoon, a special meeting at the Opera House, organized by the General Association of Government Employees. . . . Buy the newspaper to get details!"[154] By early afternoon, in oppressively hot, humid, and overcast conditions, a crowd of at least twenty thousand had gathered in the square facing the Opera House.[155] Some came because they were ordered to by their bosses. An eleven-year-old boy watched his two brothers-in-law, staid law clerks in the colonial administration, reluctantly obey instructions, gather up their umbrellas, and walk to the square, much to the amusement of their wives, who had never seen them venture out this way before.[156] Others came because they had heard that the hitherto clandestine Viet Minh would present itself at the meeting. Several government employees who also happened to be Boy Scout leaders brought their uniformed scout troops— some carrying concealed Viet Minh flags. The owner of a local radio store, a longtime scoutmaster, contributed a microphone and loudspeakers for the occasion.[157]

At 2:00 P.M., a leader of the General Association approached the microphone to read out the program and to supervise raising of the royal flag, accompanied by trumpets playing the royal anthem. As a second leader of the association began to speak, several young men nearby spread out a Viet Minh flag in their arms, which was the signal for self-defense teams in the audience to wave small flags and yell "Hooray for the Viet Minh flag!" Pandemonium ensued, as some in the crowd clustered around the flag bearers and surged back and forth across the square. Several hundred civil guardsmen with rifles held their positions but did not intervene. Nor did the police. After perhaps five minutes, during which association leaders fruitlessly called on people to resume order, a Viet Minh armed team seized

154. Ibid., 142.
155. The following description is derived mainly from ibid., 143–47; CMTT, 1:39–41; CMCD, 12:43–51; Nguyen Khang, "Ha Noi Khoi Nghia," 135–36; Tran Van Suy, "Ket qua buoc dau," 15, 18; Tran Lam, "Doi Tuyen Truyen Xung Phong Dang Dan Chu nhung ngay tien Khoi Nghia" [The Democratic Party's Propaganda Assault Unit in the Opening Days of the Insurrection], Doc Lap (Hanoi), 28 Sept. 1988, 1–2; and Truong Ban Chinh Tri, Bac Ky Trinh Tham Cuc report to Giam Doc Ty Liem Phong Bac Bo, 18 Aug. 1945, in AOM, INF, GF 58. Thanks to this last confidential police report of the meeting and subsequent demonstrations, it is possible to cross-check some assertions made in the later memoirs of ICP leaders.
156. Memoir of Van Ngoc, "Ha Noi Mua Thu 1945" [Autumn 1945 in Hanoi], Doan Ket (Paris), no. 373 (Sept. 1985): 8.
157. Tran Van Suy, "Ket qua buoc dau," 15, 18.

the podium and cut down the government flag. Immediately thereafter, another team high on the balustrade of the Opera House unrolled a large Viet Minh flag down the front of the building, much to the amazement of the crowd, which broke into sustained applause.

The brief prepared speech that followed, by Ngo Quang Chau of the Vietnam Democratic Party, urged the crowd to participate in the "general insurrection," but carefully avoided any call to violence against either the Japanese or the "completely powerless Tran Trong Kim government." Chau warned that General de Gaulle was at that very moment pressing the Allies to bring Admiral d'Argenlieu into Indochina as governor-general and emphasized that only a "revolution by all citizens" would possess enough strength to "request the Japanese Army to withdraw from Vietnam, to concentrate French nationals in one location, and to deal with the various crazy ambitions of those eager to return to this country." Vietnam's independence and freedom could only be built on the "bones and blood" of the Vietnamese people.[158] At one point Chau became so excited that he knocked over the microphone. A young woman named Nguyen Khoa Dieu Hong then took the rostrum, wearing a demure white tunic (*ao dai*), speaking calmly in a distinct Hue accent of the need for unity and sacrifice. She concluded by leading the audience in rousing cheers for the nation and the Viet Minh.[159]

Another Viet Minh group then led the crowd in singing a series of patriotic and revolutionary tunes. This was the first time that Van Cao's "Tien Quan Ca" ("Advancing Army")—soon to become the national anthem of the Democratic Republic of Vietnam—was heard by such a large audience.[160] The same was true of Nguyen Dinh Thi's "Diet Phat-Xit" ("Wipe

158. Dang Lao Dong Viet Nam, *Chat Xieng*, 82–83. Ngo Quang Chau's mention of d'Argenlieu demonstrates careful local monitoring of the radio, as the admiral's appointment had only been announced in Paris a few hours before. Several days later in Thanh Hoa province, this information from Allied shortwave broadcasts about d'Argenlieu's appointment spurred ICP members to immediate action and gave them another slogan to disseminate to demonstrators: "Oppose All Foreign Invasion." Le Tat Dac, "Ve cuoc Tong Khoi Nghia o Thanh Hoa" [On the General Insurrection in Thanh Hoa], *Tap Chi Lich Su Dang* (Hanoi), 4-1991, 12.

159. Tran Lam, "Ngay 17 Thang 8 Nam 1945 o Ha Noi" [17 August 1945 in Hanoi], *Thong Tin Lich Su Quan Su* (Hanoi), 2-Feb. 1990, 48–50. A second woman, identified in other sources as Tu Trang, also spoke briefly after Chau and Dieu Hong.

160. Van Cao, "Ky niem ve bai hat 'Tien Quan Ca'" [Recollections of the "Advancing Army" Song], *Van Hoa Nghe Thuat* (Hanoi), no. 171–72 (Aug. 1985): 9, 19. Le Quang Dao et al., *Mot Chang Duong Van Hoa* [A Segment of the Cultural Road] (Hanoi, 1985), 109–13. Van Cao was in the crowd on 17 August.

Out the Fascists"), with its fierce charges of food confiscation, imprisonment, torture, and murder by the Japanese and their "running dogs."[161]

In this emotional climate, Nguyen Khang decided to take the next step. Mounting the rostrum, he gave a quick, impromptu speech, then urged the crowd to join in a peaceful march through the streets of Hanoi. Self-defense unit members led off down Trang Tien Street carrying a Viet Minh flag, apparently firing a few pistol shots in the air for dramatic effect. At each intersection the demonstration picked up participants. The atmosphere was festive, not confrontational, with no attempt to enter key government buildings, and no threats directed at the Japanese and French nationals encountered at several points along the way. A Civil Guard unit that had been cautiously using the sidewalks to keep abreast of the main Viet Minh contingent eventually merged with the crowd. When passing in front of the main police station, Viet Minh activists led a loud call for release of Nguyen Van Tuc, a twenty-two-year-old caught several days earlier with three pistols; but there was no move against the gate. At a five-way intersection, with thunder sounding and rain beginning to fall, the crowd split up and several large groups wandered the streets for another hour or so, yelling slogans such as "Support the Viet Minh!" "Down with Puppets!" and "Complete Independence for Vietnam!"

A senior Vietnamese police official who submitted a report the next day on the events of 17 August was particularly impressed by the public's readiness to support the actions of the Viet Minh. Following the demonstration, he said, rumors swept the city that the Viet Minh was engaged in discussions with General Tsuchihashi, that the incoming Allied mission would include Viet Minh representatives, and that General de Gaulle had welcomed an independent Vietnam. Partly on the basis of those rumors, the official concluded, people were very optimistic about the future, "believing that there will not be any incidents of bloodshed occurring in our country."[162] General Tsuchihashi's civilian deputy, Tsukamoto Takeshi, in a message to Tokyo, noted the "truly strange sight" of Viet Minh flags appearing in the midst of the General Association's meeting, adding that the French were "panic stricken."[163]

---

161. Huy Du, "An Anti-Fascist Song," *Vietnam* (Pictorial), no. 317 (May 1985): 25. Le Quang Dao et al., *Mot Chang Duong Van Hoa*, 105–8. Long after Japanese departure, the lyrics continued to be sung at mass rallies. The tune is still used each morning to open the Voice of Vietnam radio schedule.

162. "Truong Ban Chinh Tri . . . ," AOM, INF, GF 58.

163. Tønnesson, *Vietnamese Revolution*, 375, who quotes from the American decryption of Tsukamoto's radiogram.

On the night of 17 August, members of the ICP's Northern Regional Committee, meeting at the outskirts of the town of Ha Dong, ten kilometers from Hanoi, were able to assess the extraordinary changes of that day. On the "enemy" side, the government's National Consultative Congress had failed to reconstitute itself for executive action, the Kham Sai had resigned or been removed, the Civil Guard seemed confused, and the Japanese had chosen not to suppress a large Viet Minh march around the city. On the "revolutionary" side, people had responded with alacrity when Viet Minh teams took over the Opera House meeting, followed the Viet Minh flag eagerly from one neighborhood to another, and avoided violent behavior likely to provoke Japanese counteraction. Given this dramatic shift in fortunes, the committee reversed its priorities of only two days before, now giving its primary attention to seizing power in Hanoi and the adjacent province of Ha Dong, rather than the surrounding rural areas.[164]

That same night, an "enlarged" meeting of the Hanoi Revolutionary Military Committee drew up detailed plans for the takeover. Participants agreed that to devote many days to careful organizing would risk loss of popular enthusiasm and a possible preemptive coup by opponents of the Viet Minh. The 18th being too soon to spread the word effectively, Sunday the 19th was selected as the target date. The events of the 17th were now seen as a dress rehearsal for the 19th, except that the aims on Sunday would be to bring at least a hundred thousand people into the same Opera House square and to gain control of key government buildings during subsequent mass demonstrations. Places occupied by the Japanese would be avoided, notably the Governor-General's Palace, the Imperial Army Staff Headquarters, the naval base on the river, and the old Citadel, where French Army personnel remained under detention. If the Japanese moved to disarm Viet Minh teams, or otherwise provoked a confrontation, it would be necessary to withdraw to the suburbs, regroup, initiate guerrilla tactics, and wait for Liberation Army units from the hills before attempting to take the city. The Military Committee adjourned just as roosters began to crow and red streaks could be seen on the eastern horizon.[165]

Eager to disseminate word of the Viet Minh success of 17 August to the surrounding provinces, Democratic Party members marched into the offices of *Tin Moi* daily and ordered the publisher, Mai Van Ham, to

164. *CMTT-H*, 125–26.
165. Ibid., 126–27. *CMTT*, 1:41–42. Nguyen Quyet, *Ha Noi Thang Tam*, 148–53, notes the roosters and red streaks.

include their article on events in his morning edition. Shortly thereafter, another group, representing the National Salvation Cultural Association, entered the premises to make an identical demand, necessitating hasty, embarrassed consultations and the decision to feature both articles on the front page. While the printing presses were running, two individuals dressed in Japanese uniforms, wearing swords, and claiming to be Kenpeitai officers also arrived on the scene. Deciding they were Dai Viet members in disguise, workers sympathetic to the Viet Minh overpowered the two men, tied them up, and tossed them into a back room. The press run complete, Viet Minh adherents took consignments of papers for distribution, Ham and his employees were locked up in the building, and the key was dropped off at the local police station, together with a note to corroborate Ham's subsequent story that he had printed the articles under duress.[166]

On the morning of the 18th, an automobile festooned with Viet Minh flags, with youths standing on the running boards yelling through megaphones, moved slowly through the city streets, followed by a pack of cyclists passing out leaflets announcing the Sunday morning meeting. Other flag-carrying teams spread the word on foot, pasting up leaflets, shouting slogans, and drawing noisy, excited crowds at each intersection. Tailor shops busily turned out flags, while families sought scarce pieces of red and yellow cloth to sew their own. At some factories and shops, workers took control of the premises on the 18th, prepared banners, and guarded machinery and supply inventories against looting or sabotage.[167]

Increasingly confident, the Revolutionary Military Committee moved its headquarters from the suburbs into the middle of the city, to an empty villa belonging to the daughter of Hoang Trong Phu, a notorious collaborator mandarin. The committee now possessed a good radio, a typewriter, and a commandeered automobile.[168] As one key participant recalled the scene:

> The work of revolution kept pouring in. Comrades from suburban villages who had already seized power came to us asking for advice on organizing authority and wanting the names of members of the uprising committee. Those who had not yet risen up asked for directions, for some of our self-defense members to assist. Workers belonging to national salvation groups in factories or enterprises asked about how to deal with own-

166. Le Quang Dao et al., *Mot Chang Duong Van Hoa*, 163–66. Tran Lam, "Ngay 17 Thang 8," 50–51. Tran Lam, "Doi Tuyen Truyen Xung Phong," 2.
167. Nguyen Quyet, *Ha Noi Thang Tam*, 156–57.
168. Nguyen Khang, "Ha Noi Khoi Nghia," 137–38.

ers and supervisors. People came in to ask for struggle slogans, or wanted a cadre to come and give a speech. Every request was urgent, pressing.[169]

The committee sent a letter to the main Civil Guard base with an ultimatum ordering it to "surrender to the revolution," but received no reply.[170]

During 18 August, Nguyen Xuan Chu, head of the government's new Political Direction Committee, and de facto Kham Sai of Tonkin, tried frantically to assert his authority. However, communication with a number of provinces was restricted by cuts in the telegraph and telephone lines, as well as blockages on railroad tracks.[171] Inside Hanoi, armed Viet Minh groups made official movement increasingly hazardous. Many policemen put themselves out of contact on the pretext that it was a weekend.[172] The city health department reported to the mayor that three armed men had seized two ambulances and 160 liters of fuel alcohol, saying they needed to go to Haiphong and Bac Giang.[173] Meeting for its second day, the National Consultative Congress summoned the Civil Guard commander, Captain Vu Van Thu, for urgent consultations, only to be told that he was "too busy."[174]

In an extraordinary last-minute initiative on 18 August, three senior royal government officials went to the Viet Minh Military Committee's new headquarters in downtown Hanoi to try to head off a confrontation. Headed by Professor Hoang Xuan Han, the minister of education, and including Dr. Nguyen Xuan Chu and Pham Huu Chuong, they obviously risked detention unless some intermediary had gained Viet Minh assurances in advance. According to Communist Party sources, Hoang Xuan Han proposed that the Viet Minh take control outside Hanoi, while the royal government secured additional firearms from the Japanese and retained control inside the city; together they would meet incoming Allied representatives. According to Hoang Xuan Han, he mainly wished to show good faith by conveying a Japanese offer to dump weapons and inform him of the location subsequently.[175] Whatever the substance of Dr. Han's proposal,

169. Nguyen Quyet, *Ha Noi Thang Tam,* 157.
170. Ibid., 166.
171. Hoa Xa Viet Dien report to Chinh Phu Lam Thoi, 24 Aug. 1945, in AOM, INF, GF 48. On the night of 18 August, someone removed tracks at a point on the Hanoi-Haiphong line, causing an accident in which five were killed.
172. Vu Ngu Chieu, "Political and Social Change in Viet-Nam between 1940 and 1946" (Ph.D. diss.,University of Wisconsin, 1984), 420–21.
173. Dr. Nguyen Viem Hai to Tran Van Lai, 18 Aug. 1945, in AOM, INF, GF 27.
174. AOM, INF, GF 5. Second Lieutenant La apparently went in Captain Thu's stead.
175. Interview with Hoang Xuan Han, Paris, 3 Nov. 1984. The previous day, Dr. Han had requested of Tsukamoto Takeshi that all Viet Minh adherents still in

it met with flat rejection from Viet Minh representatives present, although he and the other two officials were not impeded from returning to the Kham Sai's Palace.[176] Several hours later some three thousand workers from the Stai factory, Aviat auto repair facility, and other enterprises arrived to demonstrate in front of the Kham Sai's Palace, loudly denouncing the "puppet regime," but making no attempt to enter the premises.[177]

While there is no direct evidence, it seems likely that during 18 August, the Revolutionary Military Committee was able to convey to Japanese officials the essential proposition that Viet Minh organizations be allowed to seize certain installations in Hanoi in exchange for leaving Japanese and French nationals alone pending arrival of the Allied mission. Phan Ke Toai, the former Kham Sai, may have served as the key intermediary; according to one source, he was under Viet Minh "escort" from the afternoon of the 18th on.[178] Hoang Minh Giam, appointed head of a "Japanese-Vietnamese Liaison Office" by Tran Trong Kim only three weeks earlier, probably maintained even more reliable contacts with Viet Minh leaders.[179] On the other hand, prominent intellectuals associated with the Vietnam Democratic Party could also have played this role.[180] The Japanese would particularly have wanted to assess the capacity of Viet Minh leaders to keep the mob in check following their initial successes. Meanwhile, as its own way of clearing the decks, the Kenpeitai on 18 August released all remaining political prisoners, both declared Viet Minh adherents and individuals who had worked for the French prior to the 9 March coup.[181] A Japanese under-

---

Japanese custody be released forthwith. Tønnesson, *Vietnamese Revolution*, 375, citing Allied radio intercepts.

176. Nguyen Quyet, *Ha Noi Thang Tam*, 159–60. *CMTT-H*, 129. An interpretation more antagonistic to Hoang Xuan Han can be found in Bui Huu Khanh, *Ha Noi trong thoi ky Cach Mang Thang 8* [Hanoi in the August Revolution period] (Hanoi, 1960), 43.

177. *CMTT*, 1:43.

178. Hoang Van Dao, *Viet Nam Quoc Dan Dang*, 225. The fact that Phan Ke Toai subsequently received various ministerial positions under the DRV suggests some collusion in the Viet Minh takeover. However, no source has surfaced yet to clarify this intriguing question.

179. Nghi Dinh, 28 July 1945, in AOM, INF, GF 66. I base my supposition about Giam's Viet Minh connections on his assignment shortly thereafter to positions of considerable responsibility in the DRV.

180. One obvious possibility was Dang Thai Mai, a teacher and writer with contacts across the political spectrum. However, an official telegram to Sam Son beach resort on 15 August inviting Mai to join the four-man Political Direction Council does not appear to have been answered. AOM, INF, GF 34.

181. *CMTT*, 1:43–44.

cover agent named Tachibana turned over five or six automatic rifles to a Viet Minh contact, receiving in return a travel pass signed by "V.T.V."[182]

As it happened, an incident on the afternoon of 18 August served to test both sides. Two workers from the Aviat repair shop had been sent across the river with a commandeered automobile to receive some twenty clandestine firearms. As they recrossed the Paul Doumer (Long Bien) Bridge, rashly planting a Viet Minh flag on the roof of the car, Japanese guards stopped the vehicle, uncovered the weapons, and insisted on detaining the offenders. A crowd gathered, word spread like wildfire through the city, and thousands more people converged on the street in front of the Japanese General Staff headquarters where the two men and the car had been taken. Some workers wanted to attack the Japanese, and shouts of "Who's afraid of the defeated dwarfs!" and "Down with the Japanese fascists!" were met with warm rounds of applause. The Japanese sent in reinforcements, including four light tanks, yet the demonstrations spread, with the shopkeepers on Trang Tien Street, for example, hauling furniture out on the road to impede Japanese movement. Several young men stood in front of the tanks, while a young woman comrade called out to the crowd, "Countrymen, don't retreat, they won't dare to kill us!"[183] Eventually a meeting was arranged between a Japanese officer and Tran Dinh Long, member of the Viet Minh Revolutionary Military Committee, the latter assuring the former that the weapons were for gaining independence, and saying, "If members of the Japanese Army do not interfere in our work, we will guarantee their physical security." After nightfall, with crowds still surging around, a Japanese officer, as a token of good faith, presented Long with the Viet Minh flag from the truck and two pistols, allegedly promising to turn over the other weapons the next day. Declaring a victory, Viet Minh leaders managed to persuade people to disperse.[184]

182. Yoshizawa Minami, "Watashitachi no naka no Ajia no sensō—Nihon to Betonamu no aida" [The War among Us in Asia—Between Japan and Vietnam], *University Press* (Tokyo), no. 143 (Sept. 1984): 29. "V.T.V." may have been Vuong Thua Vu, although other sources indicate he did not arrive in Hanoi until some days later.

183. Tran Trung Thanh, "Nho Mai Ha-Noi" [Always Remembering Hanoi], in *Ha-Noi Chien Dau* [Hanoi Fights] (Hanoi, 1964), 5.

184. Nguyen Quyet, *Ha Noi Thang Tam*, 160–64. *CMTT*, 1:44. A similar tense encounter occurred on the 18th at the nearby provincial seat of Ha Dong, in front of the Civil Guard post, violence being avoided by a meeting between a Japanese lieutenant colonel and a member of the ICP Northern Region Committee. *CMTT-H*, 131. As we shall see, however, this same post was the scene of considerable bloodshed three days later.

As Viet Minh leaders in Hanoi made final preparations on the night of 18–19 August, they could count almost eight hundred self-defense unit members under their direct control, formed into ten "companies" equipped with about ninety firearms, as well as machetes, swords, spears, and knives. At least half of the firearms were in the hands of one company, however, the "Hoang Dieu Youth Assault Group" (Doan Thanh Nien Xung Phong Hoang Dieu) organized by the Democratic Party.[185] During the night, several more self-defense units arrived from the nearby countryside, carrying an additional thirty to thirty-five guns.[186] Ammunition was extremely scarce, perhaps ten or fifteen rounds to a rifle or pistol, and not necessarily reliable or interchangeable. Against these organized Viet Minh units might be ranged fifteen hundred civil guardsmen, all carrying rifles, plus an assortment of armed Dai Viet, Patriotic Youth, and Vietnam Nationalist Party groups. Nonetheless, the mood at Viet Minh headquarters was exuberant. Thousands more young men and women had not been structured into self-defense units yet, but they knew the Viet Minh line and appeared ready to follow instructions. As one 24-year-old leader watched a unit clean its weapons and sing Viet Minh marching tunes, he recalled a phrase drilled into him by an ICP military instructor in late 1944: "Defense is the road to death in an armed insurrection."[187]

During the afternoon of 18 August, word arrived in Hanoi of a serious breach in the Red River dike system upstream. It had rained heavily since June, and the Kham Sai's Office had been aware by 13 August that a grave situation was developing, indeed using it as a pretext to warn Viet Minh representatives against disruptive actions.[188] The first break in Vinh Yen province did not alleviate danger downstream, although the dikes in Hanoi itself remained firm; within days, 150 breaks were reported around the delta, about one-third of Tonkin's summer rice crop being flooded as a result.[189]

185. Nguyen Quyet, *Ha Noi Thang Tam*, 93, 130–31, 141. *CMTT*, 1:41. Hoang Dieu was commander of Hanoi when the French attacked in 1882 and committed suicide rather than escape or surrender. Published sources are not consistent on the number of firearms held by the Viet Minh in Hanoi, but no one claims more than 120.
186. Bui Huu Khanh, *Ha Noi trong thoi ky Cach Mang Thang 8*, 41.
187. Nguyen Quyet, *Ha Noi Thang Tam*, 165–67.
188. Ibid., 133.
189. Bo Cong Chinh report, October 1946, in AOM, INF, GF 19. Pham Quang Trung, "Nan Lut Nam At Dau voi cuoc Tong Khoi Nghia gianh chinh quyen o Dong Bang Bac Bo Nam 1945" [The 1945 Flood and the General Insurrection to Seize Power in the Northern Delta], *NCLS*, no. 251 (4-1990): 56–60. Although some local

While some Viet Minh leaders fretted that the flooding might divert their countrymen from immediate insurrection,[190] others must have realized that it had the temporary merit of inhibiting vehicle movement by both Japanese and Chinese troops, as well as dissipating any remaining credibility the royal government might have, since by neglecting the dikes, it had just failed one of the most ancient tests of political legitimacy in Vietnam. How many of their countrymen might die in the flood or its aftermath was not an immediate preoccupation of the Viet Minh leaders, although some groups did help subsequently to organize local relief and repair efforts.

Specific members of the Revolutionary Military Committee assumed responsibility for different aspects of the final planning. Nguyen Huy Khoi took charge of the program of the Opera House rally, including drafting the main speech. Nguyen Khang made sure that banners bore acceptable slogans, and that each group knew where to stand in the square, as well as which mass march to take part in following the rally. Khang was also designated to lead the takeover of the Kham Sai's Palace and Mayor's Office, while Nguyen Quyet was responsible for seizure of the main Civil Guard barracks, estimated to contain one thousand men. Other committee members made the rounds of the city, checking the preparations of each self-defense group and receiving reports on the enemy.

In the early hours of 19 August, tens of thousands of villagers began marching toward the city to the sound of drums, cymbals, and horns. The marchers had a few firearms but mostly brandished spears, machetes, knives, reaping hooks, and sickles. Some also carried picks, shovels, and adzes, having already dug up roads and rail tracks to try to isolate the city. In Ha Dong province, Truong Thi My had earlier allocated groups the tasks of making flags and banners, preparing food, and requisitioning weapons from village chiefs. At 3:00 A.M., she led several hundred people onto the road, picking up more demonstrators during the thirteen-kilometer march to Hanoi. Japanese troop trucks passed the crowd without incident.[191] Although these eager bands of peasants provided valuable additional numbers, the Revolutionary Military Committee must have worried about

---

mandarins abandoned dike preservation efforts in frustration, others seem to have thrown themselves into last-minute efforts along the river banks, probably leaving their offices more vulnerable to seizure by Viet Minh adherents.

190. Nguyen Quyet, *Ha Noi Thang Tam*, 155.

191. Truong Thi My, in *Niem Tin Khong Bao Gio Tat* [Belief Is Never Extinguished] (Hanoi, 1967), 40–48. Dang Cong San Viet Nam, *So Thao Lich Su Cach Mang Huyen Hoai Duc (1926–1945)* [Preliminary History of Revolution in Hoai Duc District (1926–45)] (Hanoi, 1982), 76–78.

whether or not they would accept predetermined insurrection plans and follow orders from students and young workers during the crucial phase of capturing government buildings. One large group of villagers decided en route to seize a district office in the suburbs, causing the mandarin to flee and a Civil Guard squad to surrender its weapons.[192]

The morning of 19 August was auspiciously sunny and breezy, unlike the heavy clouds and torpid humidity of the preceding few days. A team from the Hoang Dieu Youth Assault group moved into the Opera House square early to disarm or disperse the few police in the vicinity.[193] At this point the Japanese could easily have preempted Viet Minh plans by cordoning off the streets around the Opera House, but presumably they chose not to because it might have provoked the repelled crowds to rampage through the rest of the city. A number of self-defense units formed up at their work sites or schools, then marched behind banners and flags toward the square, singing and yelling slogans such as "Down with the puppet Tran Trong Kim regime!" and "Long live Viet Nam!" A couple of units tried to outfit themselves in similar clothing—for example, light brown shirts, dark shorts, and white rubber sandals for young men, and head scarves, brown blouses, and black trousers for young women. Workers favored their standard dark blue garb. Intellectuals, students, and shopkeepers dressed in their neatest white shirts. Peasants mostly wore indigo or black. The mood en route to the square was festive, with everyone laughing and swapping rumors. It was claimed, for example, that five self-defense unit members had stood in front of the four Japanese tanks and forced them to withdraw, that the Japanese had just delivered a truckload of guns, that power had already been seized in most rural districts surrounding the city. Slowly the square and adjacent streets filled up with as many as two hundred thousand people, at which point the Hoang Dieu Assault Youth group arrived in ranks of three, marching behind a large Viet Minh flag newly embroidered with its name, accompanied by waves of applause from the crowd.[194] Formal

192. Nguyen Quyet, *Ha Noi Thang Tam*, 157–58, 167–69. *CMTT*, 1:45–46. *CMTT-H*, 132. A poem by Le Minh titled "Trang Dem" [Night Moon], apparently written the night of 18–19 August, captures the collective excitement of an armed Viet Minh unit moving into a suburban village preparatory to marching into Hanoi. Reprinted in *Doan Ket* (Paris), no. 373 (Sept. 1985): 9.

193. *CMTT*, 1:46.

194. Nguyen Van Tri, "Thanh Nien Xung Phong Thanh Hoang Dieu" [The Hoang Dieu Assault Youth], in Nguyen Khang et al., *Ha Noi Khoi Nghia*, 156–57. Nguyen Quyet, *Ha Noi Thang Tam*, 169–70. *CMTT*, 1:46. *CMCD*, 12:51–59. In this case, Vietnamese sources on crowd size are not likely to be inflated. One photograph in Bui Huu Khanh, *Ha Noi trong thoi ky Cach Mang Thang 8*, end of

proceedings began at 11:00 A.M. with a minute of silence for those who had sacrificed themselves in the struggle for independence, a three-round rifle salute, and flag-raising to the tune of "Advancing Army." Already much of the crowd had learned to employ the Viet Minh military salute, drawn from prewar labor union practice—the right arm thrust back, bent sharply at the elbow, the fist clenched close to the temple.[195] On top of the Opera House, self-defense unit members released thousands of leaflets into the breeze.[196] At some point during the meeting, an Allied plane flying over Hanoi captured the attention of the crowd and encountered Japanese anti-aircraft fire.[197]

The main speech by Nguyen Huy Khoi was brief, undramatic, and devoid of standard Viet Minh hyperbole. "Following orders from their emperor, the Japanese have ceased fighting on all fronts," he announced. The plan, Khoi explained, was to "very moderately avoid all senseless fighting or brawling, of no use to either side, while simultaneously employing diplomacy to get Japan to understand clearly the situation, agree with the Vietnamese revolution, and deliver weapons to us." Khoi ignored the royal government almost entirely, obviously considering it a spent force. On the other hand, in regard to those French elements who "nurtured the crazy ambition to reestablish sovereignty in Indochina," it was absolutely essential to stand up to them, if necessary by war, "opposing their aggression and that of any other imperialists." To this end, it was necessary immediately to establish a Vietnamese revolutionary people's government that would "promulgate free rights for all citizens, improve the material and spiritual conditions of the people, and at the same time mobilize the forces of the entire country to protect and strengthen the legitimate independence of our nation."[198]

---

text, shows the crowd extending from the Opera House square down Trang Tien Street all the way to Hoan Kiem Lake. Martin, *Heures tragiques*, 130, who resided in Hanoi at the time, also says that "about 200,000 persons" attended.

195. See the 19 Aug. 1945 Opera House photo in Devillers, *Paris-Saigon-Hanoi*, facing p. 196. See also the photo of Vo Nguyen Giap and comrades with Archimedes Patti on 2 Sept. 1945, in R. Harris Smith, *OSS: The Secret History of America's First Central Intelligence Agency* (Berkeley and Los Angeles, 1972), 355.

196. Nguyen Quyet, *Ha Noi Thang Tam*, 171.

197. Patti, *Why Viet Nam?* 146. Jean Sainteny, *Histoire d'une paix manqueé: Indochine, 1945–1947* (Paris, 1953), 69.

198. Dang Lao Dong Viet Nam, *Chat Xieng*, 85–86. CMCD, 12:60–62. Translations of excerpts are my own. Full translations can be found in *Breaking Our Chains: Documents of the Vietnamese Revolution of August 1945* (Hanoi, 1960), 85–87; *Vietnam*, ed. Porter, 1:61–62; and *Documents*, trans. Kiriloff, 61–63.

Figure 25. The climactic 19 August 1945 meeting of Viet Minh adherents in front of the Opera House in Hanoi. Courtesy of the Centre militaire d'information et de documentation sur l'Outre-Mer.

Following rousing slogans and mass repetition, members of the Revolutionary Military Committee gave final instructions over the microphone for the armed, but, it was hoped, bloodless, moves to occupy preselected installations. The group marching on the Kham Sai's Palace had only about two blocks to go. When the crowd's exhortations to the two hundred civil guardsmen behind the palace gates had no effect, some particularly audacious youths scaled the iron picket fence and confronted the soldiers directly. Apparently lacking clear orders from their officers and convinced by Viet Minh sympathizers in their ranks that they would not be ill treated, the guardsmen dumped their rifles in a big pile and walked away. While the firearms were being distributed and people moved to take over the adjacent, much larger Kham Sai's Office building, a worker climbed on the roof, pulled down the royal standard, and ran up the Viet Minh flag. Tran Tu Binh, the most senior ICP leader present in Hanoi, proceeded to arrest Nguyen Xuan Chu and several associates, sending them in fetters to Phu Dong village in Bac Ninh province.[199] Binh then took

199. According to *CMTT*, 1:49, they were released following establishment of the DRV provisional government.

Figure 26. Viet Minh followers occupying the Kham Sai's Palace on the afternoon of 19 August. This building is now the State Guest House, across from the renovated Métropole Hotel. Courtesy of the Centre militaire d'information et de documentation sur l'Outre-Mer.

control of the Kham Sai's switchboard, using it to call mandarins in a number of provinces, informing them of the Viet Minh takeover in Hanoi, and ordering them to surrender. Resistance would be "punished severely," he warned.[200]

Having accomplished its mission at the Kham Sai's Palace, the main body of this crowd marched on the Hanoi City Hall, where Mayor Tran Van Lai was waiting to receive Nguyen Huy Khoi and readily agreed to transfer authority "to the people." At the adjacent police headquarters, the director was able to convene sixty of his men to participate in formal turnover ceremonies, although control of the Hanoi Central Prison was not transferred until four days later.[201] At Phu Doan Hospital, three shots from a Viet Minh team sent the Japanese director and French vice director

200. Nguyen Quyet, *Ha Noi Thang Tam*, 173–74.
201. *CMTT*, 1:51. Quan Khu Thu Do, *Thu do Ha Noi: Lich su khang chien chong thuc dan phap (1945–1954)* [The Capital of Hanoi: History of Resistance to French Colonialism (1945–54)] (Hanoi, 1986), 78. Viet Minh leaders were not quick or resourceful enough to prevent the police from destroying a lot of confidential records.

running, the former trailing his long sword, the latter clutching a brief-case full of hospital records.[202] Occupation of the PTT building and the Treasury proceeded without incident. However, when a crowd approached the Bank of Indochina building they were met by carefully positioned Japanese machine guns. Attempts to persuade the Japanese to withdraw fell on deaf ears, although the unit commander did allow the Viet Minh to leave several self-defense group members to "share" guard duties.[203] A similar outcome awaited demonstrators who tried to seize the radio station at Bach Mai.[204]

The most serious confrontation of the day occurred at the Civil Guard barracks, the prime target of the second crowd leaving the Opera House square.[205] When guards refused to open the main gate, Nguyen Quyet instructed a self-defense team to force it, which apparently caused the commander, Captain Vu Van Thu, to reverse his orders and invite Viet Minh representatives into the compound. An extended parley ensued in Thu's office, with Quyet insisting that all civil guardsmen surrender their weapons, after which they could either be "assisted by the revolution" to return to their home villages or volunteer to join the Viet Minh forces. Thu expressed a willingness to "follow the revolution" and turned over the keys to the armory, but insisted that his unit be kept intact and questioned the ability of the poorly trained Viet Minh irregulars to take on the French if they returned. Quyet shot back, "Not only can we defend, but if they dare to come to bother Vietnam once again we will grab them by the neck and throw them into the ocean." When Quyet decided that Thu was merely stalling for time, he gestured for several comrades to leave the room, take up key positions in the encampment, and begin persuading guardsmen to give up their weapons. Already a couple of impeccably dressed Viet Minh women had entered the Civil Guard living quarters to talk politely and gently with members of the marching band.

While this was happening inside the base, an angry roar went up from the crowd that remained outside the gate. Japanese tanks and troops had

202. Ton That Tung, *Duong vao Khoa Hoc cua toi* [My Path to Science] (Hanoi, 1978), 42.

203. Bui Huu Khanh, *Ha Noi trong thoi ky Cach Mang Thang 8*, 50. Nguyen Quyet, *Ha Noi Thang Tam*, 174. CMTT, 1:50. These Viet Minh guards withdrew several days later.

204. Nguyen Quyet, *Ha Noi Thang Tam*, 180.

205. Nguyen Quyet, "Chiem Trai Bao An Binh" [Seizing the Civil Guard Barracks], in Nguyen Khang et al., *Ha Noi Khoi Nghia*, 33–41. Dinh Ngoc Lien and Dinh Cong Thuan, "Ra Doi cung Cach Mang Thang Tam" [Coming of Age in the August Revolution], *Thong Tin Lich Su Quan Doi* (Hanoi), 2 Apr. 1990, 52.

arrived on the scene and taken up firing positions. Nguyen Quyet managed to telephone Nguyen Khang, while associates approached the Japanese officer in charge, who initially demanded that Viet Minh forces be disarmed and the Civil Guard barracks returned. Some Viet Minh followers wanted to fight, but it was agreed to try to persuade the Japanese to withdraw. Tension mounted when a portion of the crowd that had previously taken the Kham Sai's Palace and Mayor's Office arrived on the other side of the tanks. The Revolutionary Military Committee urgently dispatched Tran Dinh Long and Le Trong Nghia to the Japanese General Staff headquarters, where they concentrated on trying to persuade the officers present that their newly acquired weapons would not be used against Japanese personnel. Either this delegation or other Viet Minh representatives in Hanoi invited Tsukamoto Takeshi to lunch; surprisingly, he accepted. Concerned at the unyielding attitude of some Viet Minh adherents, and mindful that some Japanese Army officers wanted to teach the Viet Minh a lesson, Tsukamoto worked for a compromise.[206] At 4:00 P.M., Japanese forces withdrew from in front of the Civil Guard barracks, much to the delight of the crowd.[207] Unlike Nguyen Xuan Chu, Captain Thu was not arrested. Indeed, some Civil Guard units retained their identity into the first months of the DRV provisional government, with Thu as "director."[208]

On the evening of the 19th, members of the Dai Viet Party and the Vietnam Nationalist Party met in Hanoi to assess their position. Most Dai Viet adherents reluctantly accepted the Viet Minh takeover and were prepared either to cooperate or to withdraw from action to await developments. One Nationalist Party leader, Le Khang, argued passionately against this position. To allow the communists to gain the upper hand was to commit suicide, he warned. Claiming that the Japanese still offered thousands of firearms, Khang favored an immediate countercoup, followed by imprisonment of all Communist Party members. When even his own Nationalist Party comrades failed to support him, Khang stalked out of the meeting, gathered some followers, and departed Hanoi for Vinh Yen with

---

206. Tønnesson, *Vietnamese Revolution*, 382, citing American intercepts of Tsukamoto's reports to Tokyo.

207. Nguyen Quyet, *Ha Noi Thang Tam*, 175–80. Nguyen Quyet, "Chiem trai," 39–41. Tran Trung Thanh, "Nho Mai Ha-Noi," 7–8. Interview with Nguyen Van Tran, Hanoi, 17 Feb. 1992. Nguyen Khang, in "Ha Noi Khoi Nghia," 142, indicates that he too was in the delegation to Japanese headquarters, but chose to remain incognito.

208. As late as November 1945, Captain Thu retained his title of "director" and was corresponding with the DRV authorities about appropriate official housing for himself. AOM, INF, GF 58.

the intention of turning that province into a base from which to oppose the Viet Minh.[209]

While this secluded meeting took place in a mood of somber reassessment, the atmosphere on the streets of Hanoi was euphoric. Revolutionary change was symbolized that evening by people removing the black air-raid blinkers on all street lamps, giving a bright glow to the city for the first time in years. Viet Minh flags hung from hundreds of buildings. Thousands of citizens promenaded the sidewalks downtown, enjoying the new sense of freedom. People stopped to admire the new armed guards in front of public buildings, especially one proud sentinel in front of the Kham Sai's Palace who sported a belt of ammunition strung across his chest. They also marveled at the huge flag fluttering from the tall lightning rod on the Palace.[210] According to French sources, this makeshift flagpole collapsed at some point, provoking much superstitious comment.[211] If so, it was only a shadow amid general cheerfulness. As one young participant ruminated, not in his wildest imagination could he have expected such a transformation in one day.[212]

209. Hoang Van Dao, *Viet Nam Quoc Dan Dang*, 222–24.
210. *CMTT*, 1:52. Nguyen Quyet, *Ha Noi Thang Tam*, 180–81.
211. George Gautier, *9 Mars 1945, Hanoi au soleil de sang: La Fin de l'Indochine française* (Paris, 1978), 290.
212. Tran Trung Thanh, "Nho Mai Ha-Noi," 6.

7 Beyond Hanoi

The August insurrection was much more than a series of demonstrations followed by occupation of government buildings in Hanoi. If Hanoi had been the sole focus of attention, the Chinese or the French would have encountered little difficulty in isolating the insurrectionaries, engineering a countercoup, and coming up with more amenable Vietnamese with whom to construct a postwar administration. As it was, uprisings in other cities, and especially in the countryside, made a foreign coup quite impractical, something the Chinese probably came to understand by late September, but that continued to elude French comprehension for much longer.

Events in many rural districts of Vietnam in late August went well beyond political transfer of power, involving social revolutionary behavior the consequences of which no one could predict at the time. The administration established by the Viet Minh in Hanoi became as much a prisoner of the thousands of revolutionary committees emerging around the country as the directing authority. Although members also identified enthusiastically with the new central government, and particularly with its preparations to meet foreign threats, each committee had its own agenda. This tension between center and locality, already apparent in late August and destined to influence the course of events in Vietnam for decades, could not be acknowledged as legitimate by Viet Minh activists—steeped as they were in various mixtures of adulation for ancient Vietnamese centralizing monarchs, dominant interpretations of the French Revolution, Sun Yat-sen's three stages of political development, and belief in Leninist "democratic centralism." Even if such influences could somehow have been set aside, the immediate fear that foreigners would once again "divide in order to rule" (*chia de tri*) drove many activists to equate localism with crass selfishness, even treason. Yet they themselves often represented particular interests, however uncomfortably.

Haiphong and Vicinity

Whoever controlled Hanoi needed to look eastward to the important port city of Haiphong and the nearby coastal provinces of Quang Yen and Hai Ninh, where large coal reserves, rich fishing banks, and intricate ethnic relations made for unsettled conditions even in peacetime. For Viet Minh leaders, there were added concerns that incoming Chinese forces would take a proprietary interest in both Haiphong and the coal mines, while the French might well intend to use Haiphong as springboard to recapture Hanoi and the entire Red River Delta. In the short term, everything depended on the actions of the local citizenry, who were not particularly inclined to take orders from Hanoi.

The approach on 16 August of two French patrol boats, the *Frézouls* and the *Crayssac*, slowly threading their way through Allied-planted mines, proudly flying the tricolor, had thrown Haiphong into turmoil. French civilians rushed to the docks to give the crews a frantic welcome. Interned colonial troops sought immediate release from their Japanese captors. Just as the French looked to the sea for salvation, the Vietnamese perceived a grave threat from it. The Dai Viet Party organized an anti-French demonstration, while the Viet Minh prepared for an insurrection. Sensing a volatile situation, the Japanese ordered Lieutenant Commander Blanchard to move his patrol boats to a secluded anchorage. On the 19th, however, the *Crayssac* suddenly hoisted anchor and tried to steam up the Bamboo Canal in the direction of Hanoi. Encountering Viet Minh gunfire at Ninh Giang, Blanchard retreated to Haiphong, where the Japanese put the crews of both boats under arrest.[1] Two days later, Blanchard and five subordinates were taken under Japanese armed guard to Hanoi, traveling much of the way by foot and sampan because of the recent flooding of roads and railway lines.[2] Even movement of these six white men through the countryside was enough to spark rumors in Hanoi of a French unit

1. Jacques Mordal, *Marine Indochine* (Paris, 1953), 115–16. Jean Sainteny, *Histoire d'une paix manquée: Indochine, 1945–1947* (Paris, 1953), 69, 82. *Cach Mang Thang Tam* [The August Revolution] (cited below as *CMTT*), vol. 1, ed. Tran Huy Lieu (Hanoi, 1960), 274.
2. Sainteny, *Histoire*, 83. The date is mistakenly printed as 12 August, probably a typographical transposition.

killing rural demonstrators, which led to more Vietnamese threats against French civilians.[3]

From 21 August on, Viet Minh cadres worked openly in Haiphong, setting up an office, arranging production of flags, and contacting the Civil Guard, the police, and youth groups established by the Japanese. On the 22d, the mandarin of Haiphong province, which encircled but did not include the city itself, agreed to relinquish authority. That night, armed Viet Minh units from the "Fourth War Zone" north of Haiphong arrived to participate in the takeover, now planned for the 23d. In a deliberate, if smaller-scale, replay of events in Hanoi four days earlier, the Haiphong Opera House provided the venue for a public meeting, followed by a march and occupation of key buildings not guarded by the Japanese. Among the eight members of the new Haiphong Revolutionary People's Committee introduced at a second mass meeting on the 27th, at least three had participated in the former administration, although they would be pushed out a few weeks later. The highest priority was assigned to disciplining or disarming a number of armed groups operating autonomously in the city and nearby countryside.

The new Haiphong authorities even ordered citizens to stop wearing Viet Minh insignia without written permission and stated that only vehicles (including bicycles) belonging to the People's Committee could display the Viet Minh flag. On the 29th, a workers' committee was established to nationalize French-owned companies and begin to direct production toward state-defined targets, especially in the area of defense.[4] The two hundred French soldiers and approximately fifteen hundred French civilians were ordered not to show themselves on the streets.[5] Only in September, however, were the remaining French employees of the Haiphong port authority ordered to stop work.[6] Meanwhile, Haiphong residents of Chinese origin ignored the Viet Minh, resuscitated the local branch of the Kuomintang, and prepared to welcome Chinese troops when they arrived in the city.[7]

3. Françoise Martin, *Heures tragiques au Tonkin (9 Mars 1945–18 Mars 1946)* (Paris, 1948), 137–38.

4. *CMTT*, 1:232, 274–78. "Bao cao hang thang Hai Phong" dossier, in AOM, INF, GF 53. *Dan Chu* (Haiphong), no. 4 (28 Aug. 1945). The names of Revolutionary People's Committee participants are different in these sources, suggesting that either the membership remained in flux or some individuals possessed multiple identities.

5. Minutes of meeting of provincial committee representatives at Bac Bo Phu, 1–2 Sept. 1945, in AOM, INF, GF 68.

6. Northern Region People's Committee decision, 10 Sept. 1945, in first folder, AOM, INF, GF 4.

7. Esta S. Ungar, "Chinese Policy in Vietnam, 1945–1946: Its Impact on the Chinese Community of Haiphong and Hanoi" (unpublished seminar paper, Canberra, 1989), 6–7.

Along the coast north of Haiphong, in Quang Yen and Hai Ninh provinces, a variety of armed groups contested for power, profit, or simple survival. Besides the Viet Minh committees established in June, Chinese and Nung ethnic minority bands, Chinese Nationalist irregulars, adherents of the Vietnam Revolutionary League (Viet Nam Cach Menh Dong Minh Hoi), and French-led mercenaries roamed the rugged limestone hills, coal mining towns, fishing villages, and nearby islands. Sizeable Japanese garrisons remained at three locations. On 18 August, a Viet Minh group managed to clean out the small Civil Guard armory in Quang Yen, then moved to confiscate 167,944.91 piastres and an unspecified number of lottery tickets from the provincial treasury.[8] Six days later, the Viet Minh announced a provisional Revolutionary People's Committee for Quang Yen. However, with well-armed Viet Minh units commanded by Nguyen Binh and Hai Thanh away in Haiphong city, the committee still could count on only twenty rifles. It thus had no choice but to make concessions to other forces, in particular the Vietnam Revolutionary League, which demanded that its blue-and-white flag be flown side by side with the Viet Minh banner. Two regular Chinese Army battalions also arrived and demanded support. Rather than turn over French weapons to the incoming Chinese, a Japanese colonel donated them to the Viet Minh. Forms of indirect resistance had already become the stock-in-trade of small Viet Minh groups in this coastal region, including destroying bridges and roads, concealing ferryboats, hiding food and equipment from enemy patrols, and providing false intelligence.[9] In early September, Viet Minh adherents at Hon Gai managed to capture the *Crayssac* when it put in to unload wounded, and snared another boat, the *Audacieuse*, when it came looking for its partner.[10]

8. Kho Bac Quang Yen to So Kho Bac Bac Bo, 20 Aug. 1945, in AOM, INF, GF 68. The provincial treasurer complained furiously to superiors, then was rash enough to renew his complaint nine days later; the Hanoi provisional government tried twice to obtain an explanation from the new Quang Yen Revolutionary People's Committee, apparently without success.

9. *CMTT*, 1:231–34. Ban Nghien Cuu Lich Su Dang Quang Ninh, *So Thao Lich Su Cach Mang Thang Tam tinh Quang Ninh* [Preliminary History of the August Revolution in Quang Ninh Province] (Quang Ninh, 1970), 40–45. Ban Nghien Cuu Lich Su Dang, *Lich Su Dang Bo Tinh Quang Ninh* [History of the Quang Ninh Province Party Apparatus], vol. 1, *1928–1945* (Hanoi, 1985), 194–205.

10. Mordal, *Marine Indochine*, 117–18. An unnamed American OSS lieutenant was aboard the *Crayssac*. See also René Charbonneau and José Maigre, *Les Parias de la victoire: Indochine–Chine, 1945* (Paris, 1980), 369, which adds that the captain of the *Crayssac*, Lieutenant Vilar, was killed by the Viet Minh a few days later.

Upheavals in the Red River Delta

As the ancient heartland of Vietnamese culture, and one of the most densely populated rural areas in the world, the Red River Delta posed both major opportunities and substantial problems for any ruling group in Hanoi in 1945. Proud of their heritage, skilled at grappling with the elements, and quick to mobilize themselves, the people of the delta could determine whether a regime survived on local sources of food and manpower or was forced to depend on more distant and tenuous supplies. However, demographic growth during the colonial period, wartime economic disruptions, and the terrible famine of early 1945 had altered delta society irretrievably, calling every assumption into question. When they took action in late August, the inhabitants of the delta were trying to reconstruct their own lives and ward off another impending famine, not just support or attack a particular organization or political tendency.

From 17 August on, news of Japan's capitulation and the dramatic events in Hanoi precipitated action in every province of the Red River Delta. In Thai Binh province, southeast of Hanoi, word arrived on the morning of the 18th that the city was "in the midst of an uprising." Some local ICP members urged immediate action, while others wanted to wait for orders. Already on the 13th in Tien Hai, scene of the worst starvation only four months earlier, a crowd had marched on government offices, causing the district mandarin to flee and six civil guardsmen to surrender after firing token volleys into the air. Three days later the captured district mandarin, Ha Ngoc Hien, was brought before a crowd of about five thousand people, accused of helping the "Japanese pirates" during the famine, sentenced to death, and shot on the spot. Other "henchmen of the Japanese" were dragged out of their homes, forced to lower their heads, beaten, and imprisoned.[11] At the Thai Binh province seat on the 18th, a youth group with no ICP links moved to hang up Viet Minh flags, distribute leaflets, and lead a march on the local Civil Guard post, where they secured forty-nine firearms and one hundred grenades. The next morning, in heavy rain, a crowd of four thousand people swooped into town, frightening a Japanese soldier into fatally shooting one demonstrator. Further bloodshed was averted by talks between Japanese officers, the provincial mandarin, Nguyen Huu Tri, and Viet Minh activists. Attention then shifted to arrangements for a public meeting on the 20th, with each of the three parties

11. *CMTT*, 1:436. David W. P. Elliott, "Vietnam's August Revolution: The Origins of Legitimacy" (unpublished seminar paper, Cornell University, 1972 [?]), 28–31.

insisting that its flag be displayed prominently. The Japanese rejected a Viet Minh proposal to haul down the Rising Sun ceremoniously at the meeting, arguing quite logically, "We have been defeated by the Allies, not by you."[12]

Fifteen kilometers from Thai Binh town, also on the 20th, a mob stopped a Japanese automobile on the road, hauled out the two occupants, an Imperial Army officer and his enlisted driver, then killed them and dumped their bodies into the nearby river. When a Japanese company moved into the area and prepared to retaliate, a Viet Minh activist named Thanh managed to defuse the situation by offering himself as culprit, also making sure the officer's sword was returned with formal apologies.[13] Two days later, Nguyen Huu Tri cabled his resignation to Hanoi, adding that Viet Minh adherents had arrested two of his district mandarins and forced others to flee their posts. Only a Viet Minh cadre could bring order to the province, Tri concluded.[14] In fact, a revolutionary people's committee had already been formed, but was experiencing considerable difficulty in gaining control. Four villages in Thai Binh proceeded to execute accused traitors without waiting for higher-level authorization; other villages reluctantly deferred similar action, meanwhile protesting outside interference in their right to eliminate traitors expeditiously.[15] Failing to gain recognition from the provincial committee, several groups fired off urgent telegrams or letters to Hanoi.[16]

In adjacent Hai Duong province, after hearing on 16 August of Japan's capitulation, Viet Minh adherents called a demonstration for the next morning. No attempt was made to seize power, the demonstrators limiting themselves to the symbolic act of removing the royal banner from in front of the provincial office and substituting the red flag with yellow star. The afternoon of the 17th, a joint leadership committee was established, which

12. Ngo Huy Dong, in *Thai Binh Khoi Nghia* [The Thai Binh Uprising] (Thai Binh, 1965), 150–55. Dong asserts that only the Viet Minh flag was evident during the speechmaking portion of the meeting on 20 August.

13. Ibid., 156–57. Two weeks later, the new Thai Binh People's Committee cabled Hanoi an explanation of the 20 August incident and requested help in obtaining Thanh's release. Thai Binh to Bac Bo, 5 Sept. 1945, in Thai Binh dossier, AOM, INF, GF 16. Dong indicates that Thanh later regained his freedom.

14. Thai Binh to Bac Bo, 22 Aug. 1945, in Thai Binh dossier, AOM, INF, GF 16.

15. Uy Ban Thai Binh, handwritten report to Bac Bo, 10 Sept. 1945, in Thai Binh dossier, AOM, INF, GF 16.

16. See, e.g., UBNDCM Khu Tien Phong to Bac Bo Phu, 28 Aug. 1945, requesting authorization papers, firearms, and armed reinforcements to be able to guard the bridge across the Duong River, in AOM, INF, GF 44.

included Tran Van Tuyen, deputy provincial mandarin and a successful youth organizer, along with the adjutant of the local Civil Guard post, the province veterinarian, and three Viet Minh representatives. That evening the Civil Guard post declared its allegiance to the Viet Minh, bringing two hundred firearms. The local Japanese garrison still refused to acknowledge Viet Minh predominance, however. On the 20th, a public ceremony introduced the new administration to the public, followed by a cheerful march around the provincial seat. Two days later, members of district- and village-level Viet Minh groups attended an ICP-dominated planning session, paving the way for announcement on the 25th of a Hai Duong Revolutionary People's Committee, which effectively demoted the original committee to town significance only.[17] Viet Minh leaders must have been pleasantly surprised when the provincial mandarin turned over a treasury containing 3,263,499.98 piastres in cash. Most of this money had been accumulated to buy paddy for the Japanese Army, but it was now taken to a Viet Minh hiding place.[18] A Japanese-controlled distillery continued to consume five tons of paddy per day, leading the Hai Duong committee to request intercession by the provisional government in Hanoi.[19]

Although most Viet Minh takeovers in the Red River Delta occurred without major armed confrontations, the province of Ha Dong was an exception. Between 18 and 20 August, Viet Minh groups gained control with little difficulty in six out of eight districts of the province. Truong Thi My was even able to march her group, which had taken part in the insurrection in Hanoi on 19 August, back to Hoai Duc district to seize power that same day. She spent two hours deflecting crowd demands to kill the district mandarin, in the end gaining their agreement to hang a "Vietnamese traitor" (*Viet gian*) sign around his neck and send him to the ICP Regional Committee for a decision.[20] At the provincial seat, however, a Viet

17. *CMTT*, 1:258–60.

18. Hai Duong financial report to Bac Bo, 22 Nov. 1945, in Hai Duong folder, AOM, INF, GF 53. Tran Van Tuyen resigned as province committee treasurer on 30 Aug. 1945, subsequently becoming an implacable enemy of the ICP.

19. Minutes of 1–2 Sept. 1945 meeting of provincial committee representatives at Bac Bo Phu, in AOM, INF, GF 68.

20. Truong Thi My, *Niem Tin Khong Bao Gio Tat* [My Belief Was Never Extinguished] (Hanoi, 1967), 45–54. According to Dang Cong San Viet Nam, *So Thai Lich Su Cach Mang Huyen Hoai Duc (1926–1945)* [Preliminary History of the Revolution in Hoai Duc District (1926–45)] (Hanoi, 1982), 78, Truong Thi My did order the execution of a different "pro-Japanese traitor," but the case was subsequently transferred to the provincial level for determination. Nearby, in the village of Van Phuc, two individuals were also sentenced to death but then held for subsequent dispensation by higher authority. Dang Bo Xa Van Phuc, *Lich Su Dau*

Minh mob attempt on the 21st to force surrender of the Civil Guard post went horribly wrong, the frightened guardsmen first shooting at youths trying to scale the fence, then at the crowd beyond. Within minutes, forty-seven people were dead, thirty wounded. Guardsmen then pursued demonstrators through the streets, capturing forty. A PTT employee in Hanoi, hearing by telephone of the bloodshed, ran to inform the Northern Region Revolutionary People's Committee, which resulted in another crowd marching on Ha Dong. The next day, a representative of the committee arrived to try to break the impasse.[21] In the midst of all this, four Frenchmen parachuted into Ha Dong, were detained, then escaped. One was recaptured and delivered much later to police headquarters in Hanoi.[22]

On 24 August, the provincial mandarin of Ha Dong, Ho Dac Diem, agreed to relinquish his position at a public ceremony the next day, leaving the Civil Guard commander, Quan Duong, a member of the Vietnam Nationalist Party, isolated and soon forced to flee for his life.[23] The Civil Guard post was quickly stripped of all food, equipment, and clothing. When seizing control in the two remaining districts of Ha Dong, Viet Minh activists targeted Dai Viet Party adherents.[24] More than other provinces in the north, Ha Dong in late August witnessed a host of arrests or kidnappings of alleged traitors, as well as several violent disputes between competing Viet Minh local organizations. On the 25th, for example, about forty armed Viet Minh adherents swept into two villages and told citizens to march on the Thuong

Tranh Cach Mang cua Dang Bo va Nhan Dan Van Phuc, 1936–1945 [Revolutionary Struggle History of the Van Phuc Party Apparatus and People, 1936–45] (Hanoi, 1986), 115.

21. *CMTT,* 1:342–45. *Cach Mang Can Dai Viet Nam* (cited below as *CMCD),* 12:85–88. "Lich Su Nganh Thong Tin Buu Dien Viet Nam (Du Thao)" [History of Vietnam's Post and Communications Branch (Draft)], vol. 1 (Hanoi, 1989), 68. Other Communist Party sources prefer to evade discussion of this Ha Dong altercation, the bloodiest to occur in the north in August.

22. Ha Dong to Bac Bo, 25 Oct. 1946, in outgoing message file, AOM, INF, GF 31. The four officers were identified as Captain Dupre, Lieutenant Mook, Second Lieutenant Ferrace, and Second Lieutenant Marc Julien (recaptured).

23. Hoang Van Dao, *Viet Nam Quoc Dan Dang* [The Vietnam Nationalist Party] (Saigon, 1965), 227, asserts that Quan Duong was executed in early September, after attempting to escape with Japanese assistance. *CMCD,* 12:88, says Duong fled the area, was captured two months later, and then sentenced to death by a people's court. A petition from Duong's family to Chairman Ho Chi Minh on 21 Jan. 1946 requesting leniency indicates that Duong was condemned to execution by a Ha Dong court, but then reprieved while his case was considered by a military tribunal. "Viec xay ra tai tinh" [Ha Dong] dossier, in AOM, INF, GF 28.

24. *CMTT,* 1:345–46.

Tin district seat to help capture a group of traitors. Out on the road, an altercation developed between village Viet Minh representatives and the other group, with shots being exchanged. When a delegation of villagers went to higher echelons to complain, they were assaulted, tied up, stripped of their shoes, money, and watches, and imprisoned.[25]

Across the river from Hanoi, in Bac Ninh province, a peasant group identifying itself with the Viet Minh cut telegraph wires, dug up poles, destroyed a railroad station, and allegedly provoked a train accident in which a number of Vietnamese were killed. A local petitioner angrily asked why these "rural revolutionaries" were smashing things, when "all this property now belongs to Vietnam and the Vietnamese?"[26] Meanwhile, Tran Dinh Nam, head of the Bac Ninh "uprising leadership committee," succeeded on 20 August in winning over the Civil Guard post and organizing a mass march toward the sports field. However, when the front of the march had already reached the field, the tail decided to break off and harass Japanese soldiers at the Bac Ninh citadel. Adventurous youths who tried to climb the flagpole and pull down the Rising Sun were driven away by gunfire. Viet Minh self-defense members then tossed grenades on the roof of the building, only to have them roll back and explode amid the crowd, killing and wounding several people. Eventually Tran Dinh Nam entered the citadel and persuaded the Japanese officer in charge to hoist a Viet Minh flag alongside his own, then join him in addressing the crowd. The sports-field meeting was abandoned in favor of an immediate march on the Bac Ninh provincial offices, which were taken without further incident.[27]

In Bac Giang province, just to the northeast of Bac Ninh, Viet Minh committees were already functioning openly in all districts before news of Japan's capitulation arrived, enabling ICP leaders to focus solely on taking control of the provincial seat, Phu Lang Thuong. In the early morning of the 18th, armed teams infiltrated the town, seized the provincial offices, and persuaded the provincial mandarin to call the Civil Guard commander over for discussions. Apparently caught by surprise, the commander reluctantly

25. Petitions and cover letter of 10 Sept. 1945 (signed by the general secretary of the Vietnam Democratic Party) to Bac Bo, in Ha Dong dossier, AOM, INF, GF 52. Other incidents of late August are detailed in petition from Son Lang Thuong villagers to Bac Bo, 29 Aug. 1946; Phuong Vien village committee message to Bac Bo, 15 Sept. 1945; and Ha Dong province report to Bac Bo, 27 Aug. 1945, in AOM, INF, GF 18, GF 28, and GF 53, respectively.

26. Anonymous petition addressed to Ong Thanh Tra Can Bo Viet Minh [Mr. Viet Minh Cadres Inspector], 20 Aug. 1945, in AOM, INF, GF 69.

27. *CMTT*, 1:223–26. This Tran Dinh Nam should not be confused with the royal government minister of the same name.

agreed to accompany a Viet Minh team back to the post, housing three hundred guardsmen, to hoist the red flag with yellow star. The provincial mandarin then telephoned the Japanese garrison to arrange a meeting, with himself as intermediary. By 8:30 A.M., an understanding had been reached for a Viet Minh administration, the Japanese rejecting only the demand that they surrender their weapons. Subsequently, they chose to donate four machine guns and thirty rifles to the Viet Minh. A Dai Viet group in Phu Lang Thuong offered no resistance to Viet Minh takeover. In town, the Viet Minh discovered the former Chinese Nationalist consuls for Hanoi and Haiphong, who had been incarcerated there by the Japanese. This provided the opportunity to convene a meeting of overseas Chinese in Bac Giang province to explain Viet Minh policies, and eventually to deliver the two consuls safely to incoming Chinese troops.[28] Nonetheless, Chinese irregular bands roaming the uplands of Bac Giang, often claiming to be adherents of the Vietnam Revolutionary League, continued to bedevil local Viet Minh committees for months thereafter.[29]

In Phuc Yen, with its provincial seat only twenty-eight kilometers northwest of Hanoi, Viet Minh activists did not hear of Japan's capitulation until 18 August, which was the day the dikes broke. By the next morning, however, some ten thousand villagers, stiffened by five hundred Viet Minh self-defense unit members, were already marching eagerly on the provincial seat. Participants especially recalled the festive sounds of the demonstration, from round drums, wooden slit drums (*mo*), work chants (*ho*), loud cheers, and the yelling of Viet Minh slogans. Entering Phuc Yen town, they bumped into a Dai Viet youth group carrying its blue flag with three yellow stripes. Allegedly sending the Dai Viet scurrying with great roars of *Da dao!* (Overthrow!), the crowd then moved to the Civil Guard camp, hoping to persuade the two hundred soldiers there to surrender. When this failed, attention shifted to the provincial mandarin, including threats to harm his family if he did not transfer power immediately. No sooner had he agreed, spoken deferentially to the crowd, and turned over thirty-nine firearms than word arrived of a Japanese platoon approaching from nearby Vinh Yen. People scrambled to erect barricades and prepare for a siege. A messenger from the Japanese ordered surrender of all firearms in half an hour or they would attack. Two Viet Minh messengers were dispatched to explain, and the night passed without incident. On the morning of the 20th, a Japanese officer who approached the barricades was invited to parley;

---

28. *CMTT*, 1:208–11.
29. Bac Giang to Bac Bo, 30 Oct. 1945, in AOM, INF, GF 45.

eventually he agreed to withdraw in exchange for food for his troops. The Civil Guard unit remained in place, neither opposing nor obeying the Viet Minh.[30] When a combined Dai Viet–Vietnam Nationalist Party armed contingent from Vinh Yen attempted subsequently to force the Phuc Yen Civil Guard unit to submit, it was repulsed with heavy casualties.[31] In all likelihood the guardsmen subsequently joined the Viet Minh or dispersed quietly to their home villages.

On the northwestern edge of the Red River Delta, in the strategic triangle formed by Son Tay, Phu Tho, and Vinh Yen provinces, the Viet Minh scored some early victories but also suffered significant setbacks. From 16 August on, following minor skirmishes with Civil Guard squads, small armed Viet Minh groups took control of three district seats in Son Tay province.[32] On the 21st, demonstrators marched on the provincial seat from several directions, listened to Viet Minh speeches for an hour, then took part in peaceful liberation of the Son Tay mandarin's office, the Civil Guard post, power station, and water plant.[33] That same day the Northern Region Revolutionary People's Committee in Hanoi sent an urgent cable to the ICP committee of Son Tay, urging "extreme moderation" in establishing the provincial people's committee, as well as assiduous avoidance of any confrontations with the Japanese. The benefits of this posture became evident the next day, when the Japanese commander of the Son Tay fortress agreed not to destroy a substantial quantity of French military booty when his unit departed—including mortars, machine guns, two hundred rifles, ammunition, medicines, gasoline, an equipment repair facility, and even six light aircraft, plus bombs, at the nearby airstrip.[34] Also,

30. Vu Ngoc Linh, in Ban Nghien Cuu Lich Su Dang Vinh Phu, *Nhung Ngay Cach Mang Thang Tam* [Days of the August Revolution] (Vinh Phu, 1974), 113–27. Le Tuong and Vu Kim Bien, *Lich Su Vinh Phu* [History of Vinh Phu] (Vinh Phu, 1980), 169. *CMTT*, 1:191–93. Pham Cuong and Nguyen Van Ba, *Revolution in the Village: Nam Hong, 1945–1975* (Hanoi, 1976), 13–14.

31. Hoang Van Dao, *Viet Nam Quoc Dan Dang*, 336–38.

32. Nguyen Quoc Hong, in *Hoi Ky Cach Mang Ha Tay* [Ha Tay Revolutionary Memoirs], vol. 2 (Ha Tay, 1970), 48–53.

33. *CMTT*, 1:357–61.

34. Nguyen Quoc Hong, in *Hoi Ky Cach Mang Ha Tay*, 55–65, 75–76. *CMTT*, 1:361–62. A message from Son Tay to Bac Bo on 29 Aug. 1945 reported imminent Japanese withdrawal and urgently requested assistance in shifting a large cache of military supplies. Son Tay dossier, in AOM, INF, GF 16. A partial list of this booty is in AOM, INF, GF 71. From 1 September on, officials in Hanoi were trying especially to round up sufficient containers to transport 2,000 liters of gasoline from Son Tay. As late as April 1946, Chinese officers were trying by various means, including the jailing of Vietnamese government representatives, to obtain these military stores. *CMTT*, 1:363–64.

rather than transport twenty-seven tons of stored grain to Hanoi, the Japanese sold it cheaply to local government representatives.[35]

Simultaneously, however, Viet Minh units in Son Tay were hunting down several armed, "pro-Japanese" Dai Viet groups without pity. On the 20th, a Dai Viet contingent of about one hundred men retreated to the Mo Chen plantation in Tung Thien district. Allegedly refusing Viet Minh written ultimata, this group endured a series of firefights and retreats until its remnants were surrounded and wiped out thirty kilometers south of the provincial seat. Among the bodies were those of three Japanese.[36] The harshness of early Viet Minh rule in Son Tay was revealed, too, by a chilling cable to Hanoi on 28 August requesting immediate dispatch of an electrical generator and a police specialist to torture "Vietnamese traitors."[37] Several days later, the Thach That district people's committee jailed two representatives of the Hanoi provisional government, stole their belongings, and damaged their automobile, despite presentation of authentic travel permits.[38] On the other hand, the former provincial mandarin of Son Tay was still taking part in routine administrative affairs as of early September, and he agreed to serve as adviser to the provincial people's committee when it was finally established a month later.[39] Some of the tensions in Son Tay were undoubtedly ethnic in origin, particularly between upland Thai and lowland Kinh (Vietnamese). With the arrival of Chinese troops and Vietnam Nationalist Party adherents in late September, the situation in Son Tay became all the more volatile.

Just upriver from Son Tay, in Phu Tho province, a Viet Minh group swept into the Lam Thao district offices on 17 August, seizing seven rifles, one shotgun, one pistol, and two typewriters, then burning government documents. At the specific request of the district mandarin they fired shots into the air before withdrawing so that he could report to higher authority that he had not surrendered voluntarily.[40] Two days later, a participant in the Tan Trao meetings returned to Phu Tho with specific insurrection orders, and on the 20th copies of *Tin Moi* newspaper arrived with news of Viet Minh accomplishments in Hanoi. Even so, the lack of a single com-

35. Son Tay, report to Hanoi, 6 Sept. 1945, in AOM, INF, GF 71.

36. *CMTT*, 1:359, 362–63.

37. Son Tay dossier, in AOM, INF, GF 16.

38. Noi Vu to UBND Thach That, 9 Sept. 1945, in Son Tay dossier, AOM, INF, GF 16.

39. Son Tay to So Y-te Bac Bo, 1 Sept. 1945, in Le Thi Van file, AOM, INF, GF 8.

40. "Phong trao Viet Minh xa Kinh Ke" [The Viet Minh Movement in Kinh Ke Village], in *Nhung Ngay Cach Mang*, 171–72.

mand structure or coherent policy continued to bedevil Viet Minh efforts in Phu Tho. On the 21st, the Japanese reacted to the killing of a Vietnamese employee of theirs by positioning machine guns to cover major intersections in the provincial seat, arresting suspects, and confiscating all weapons from the wavering Civil Guard garrison. During discussions the next day, the Japanese promised to turn over administrative authority to the Viet Minh and to donate five hundred French and Civil Guard firearms, but this agreement was jeopardized on the 23d when a different Viet Minh unit ambushed a Japanese truck convoy arriving from Tuyen Quang province. Following acrimonious and extended talks, the Japanese allowed a Viet Minh public meeting and march through Phu Tho town on the 25th. The next day the provincial mandarin formally ceded authority and a Viet Minh delegation presented itself at Japanese headquarters to announce the transfer.[41] By the end of the month, 125 prisoners dating from the French administration had been released, but an unspecified number of new detainees were soon being subjected to "very light torture," and the Phu Tho People's Committee requested Hanoi to dispatch a "judicial specialist" to speed proceedings.[42]

In Vinh Yen province, following breaks in the dikes, Viet Minh cadres managed to locate about 150 youths with twenty-seven firearms and thirty boats to paddle through the floodwaters toward the Civil Guard post at Vinh Tuong, where the district mandarin agreed on 21 August to order his men to surrender their weapons. Both guardsmen and mandarin were then made to stand at attention and salute at a Viet Minh flag-raising ceremony, after which a bonfire consumed the district records. Khuat Thi Vinh, a young female ICP leader present, was disconcerted to find two old men about to prostrate themselves in front of her in gratitude for having their "lives saved." She attempted to convince these gentlemen that it was the Communist Party and the Revolution that had already saved her, and would surely save them.[43] Only eleven kilometers away, however, at the Vinh Yen provincial seat, Vietnam Nationalist Party members under the leadership of Le Khang joined with civil guardsmen and a Dai Viet youth

41. *CMTT*, 1:158–62. Le Tuong and Vu Kim Bien, *Lich Su Vinh Phu*, 170–71. "Thi xa Phu Tho vuon minh trong Cao Trao Cach Mang . . . " [Phu Tho Town Stretches Itself in the Revolutionary High Tide . . .], in *Nhung Ngay Cach Mang*, 95–96, 111–12. A petition from Nguyen Bach's wife, Nguyen Thi Hue, dated 19 Oct. 1945 indicates that he was jailed subsequently. Phu Tho dossier, in AOM, INF, GF 59.

42. Phu Tho periodic report to Bac Bo Phu dated 29 Oct. 1945, in AOM, INF, GF 68.

43. Khuat Thi Vinh, in *Nhung Ngay Cach Mang*, 92–94.

group headed by Do Dinh Dao to neutralize all Viet Minh attempts to seize power. A five-person Viet Minh negotiating team was incarcerated. On the 31st, Viet Minh demonstrators approaching the town of Vinh Yen from the east, then from the west, were fired upon repeatedly, several being killed and the rest eventually falling back in confusion. This local bloodshed undoubtedly hardened ICP attitudes toward the Nationalist Party elsewhere. After arrival of Chinese troops a few days later, it proved impossible to dislodge Nationalist Party adherents from Vinh Yen; until mid 1946, they were able to control and tax movement up and down the Red River corridor to Yunnan.[44] In the Vinh Yen countryside, however, citizens identifying themselves with the Viet Minh had proceeded in late August 1945 to seize plantation property and distribute it to the poor. Only a few days later, the absentee owner of these plantations, Ung Ngan Nhie, filed a protest with the provisional government; because he was an overseas Chinese, Ung's case received quick, favorable attention from the fledgling Department of Foreign Affairs.[45]

In Hung Yen, on the opposite side of Hanoi, the provincial mandarin was still attempting on 19 August to uphold royal government authority. He reported establishment of a special team of young cyclists to keep in touch and begged the Kham Sai's Office for "essential orders" to obey in the current difficult circumstances.[46] That same day, a crowd of Viet Minh followers brandishing only two rifles took control of the Van Lam district seat. About the same time, Viet Minh adherents overpowered guards in front of the My Hao district office, marched the district mandarin out the gate for public execution, burned official documents, and then withdrew temporarily from town. Another group stormed a French-owned plantation at Cau Lac, confiscating everything that could be moved and distributing parcels of land to local peasants.[47] Elsewhere in Hung Yen, landlords "donated" large tracts of land to the Revolution, leaving Viet Minh adherents temporarily nonplussed about what to do with them.[48] On the 21st, the An Thi district mandarin, Nguyen Van Giao, was seized by demonstrators, jailed, and four weeks later hauled before a "people's court,"

44. *CMTT*, 1:195–96. Le Tuong and Vu Kim Bien, *Lich Su Vinh Phu*, 170. Hoang Van Dao, *Viet Nam Quoc Dan Dang*, 332–36, 338–43.

45. File titled "Bao ve quyen loi cua Hoa Kieu," in AOM, INF, GF 68.

46. Tong Doc Hung Yen to Kham Sai, 19 Aug. 1945, in AOM, INF, GF 51.

47. *CMTT*, 1:307–9.

48. Minutes of meeting of provincial committee representatives at Bac Bo Phu, 1–2 Sept. 1945, in AOM, INF, GF 68.

which sentenced him to indefinite detention.[49] On the 22d, having reached an understanding with the local Japanese unit, ICP and Democratic Party activists led a crowd into the Hung Yen province compound, from which the mandarin had fled the previous day.[50]

Not all Viet Minh adherents had their minds fixed primarily on seizing power. In Kien An province, adjacent to Haiphong, a group in one district allowed the royal administration to continue functioning while it concentrated on capturing two boats containing ninety barrels of gasoline. In a nearby district, Viet Minh activists devoted their time to liberating several boats filled with alleged Japanese rice and coal. On 22 August, bands from two different districts of Kien An opened fire on each other, three people being killed. A senior ICP leader, Le Thanh Nghi, rushed to the scene to convince each side that the other was legitimate. The province revolutionary people's committee established a few days later reflected Kien An's immediate political complexities: the chairman was from the Democratic Party, his deputy was an ICP member, and the others were a former colonial clerk, a former education mandarin, a former district mandarin, a member of the Vietnam Nationalist Party, and a representative of the Viet Minh Women's National Salvation Association.[51]

South of Hanoi, in Ha Nam, Nam Dinh, and Ninh Binh provinces, Viet Minh organizing at village and district levels appears to have lagged behind other parts of the Red River Delta, perhaps reflecting the relative strength of the Catholic Church here. In two districts of Ha Nam, for example, rather than mobilize crowds to march on government offices, small Viet Minh teams used ruses to capture the mandarins and force them to order subordinates to surrender. Viet Minh cadres met with the Ha Nam provincial mandarin, Dam Duy Huyen, to arrange a mass march and peaceful transfer of authority on 24 August, yet subsequently decided to arrest Huyen and execute him in secret.[52] The police chief of Phu Ly town was also detained in late August and apparently killed soon after.[53]

---

49. Petitions from Giao's family to Bac Bo, 12 Nov. and 1 Dec. 1945, in AOM, INF, GF 32. As of mid February 1946, Giao's dossier was still going back and forth between Hanoi and Hung Yen, with no decision in sight.

50. *CMTT*, 1:309–10. *Dan Chu* (Haiphong), no. 4 (28 Aug. 1945).

51. *CMTT*, 1:289–92. *Dan Chu* (Haiphong), no. 4 (28 Aug. 1945).

52. *CMTT*, 1:413–17. Petitions from the family of Dam Duy Huyen to Ho Chi Minh, 2 Nov. and 14 Dec. 1945, in Phu Ly dossier, AOM, INF, GF 1. As late as March 1946, Huyen's relatives had not been notified officially of his execution, been provided with any explanation for his disappearance, or assisted in locating his body.

53. Petitions from Pham Van Dan's family, Nov.–Dec. 1945, in Phu Ly dossier, AOM, INF, GF 1. In March 1946, the Ha Nam People's Committee still had not

In Nam Dinh, the provincial mandarin apparently felt no pressure to resign until a carload of Viet Minh representatives arrived from Hanoi on 20 August to convince him that all of northern Vietnam possessed a new government.[54] The next day he was still sending official telegrams, including a request for information on seven Nam Dinh activists jailed for political offenses in 1944 and early 1945; it was soon learned from file clerks in Hanoi that these prisoners had been amnestied following Bao Dai's edict of 17 May.[55] In Ninh Binh province, after taking power in Kim Son district on its own initiative, a Catholic group managed to bypass local ICP members when linking up with the Northern Region People's Committee in Hanoi. The new bishop of Phat Diem, Le Huu Tu, did likewise. In Yen Khanh district, a Viet Minh crowd persuaded civil guardsmen to relinquish their guns and ammunition.[56] By the 25th, Van Tien Dung, senior ICP member in the area, was able to introduce to the public a Ninh Binh Provincial Revolutionary People's Committee, with himself as chairman.[57] Four days later, Dung forwarded a specimen of his signature to the Ninh Binh treasury and requested a batch of check forms to begin to draw funds from existing accounts.[58] Soon he was approaching Hanoi about the need of local families with relatives in France to receive remittances, which would require re-opening of the overseas postal money order (*mandat*) system.[59]

The Northern Hills

The hills north of Hanoi have always possessed vital strategic significance because of their proximity to China, the complex ethnic mix of the population, and the proven difficulty of rooting out any dedicated band of

---

responded to repeated queries from Hanoi about Dan, although someone in the Bac Bo Phu had marked the file in bold letters: "? Committee has killed him already."

54. *CMTT*, 1:427. *Ha Nam Ninh Chong Thuc Dan Phap Xam Luoc* [Ha Nam Ninh Opposes French Colonial Invasion] (Ha Nam Ninh, 1979), 26–27. A report from the Nam Dinh People's Committee on 30 Sept. 1945 acknowledges that as of mid August, the province possessed few Viet Minh adherents, and most of those were new. Nam Dinh dossier, in AOM, INF, GF 45.

55. Messages in Phong Vien Chuc dossier, 21 and 29 Aug. 1945, AOM, INF, Gouvernement Revolutionnaire/GF 141.

56. Ninh Binh province mandarin to UBNDCM Hanoi, 21 Aug. 1945, in AOM, INF, GF 62.

57. *Ha Nam Ninh*, 383. *CMTT*, 1:370–73.

58. UBNDCM Ninh Binh to Chu Su Kho Bac Ninh Binh, 29 Aug. 1945, in AOM, INF, GF 62.

59. Minutes of meeting of provincial committee representatives at Bac Bo Phu, 1–2 Sept. 1945, in AOM, INF, GF 68.

dissidents. As we have seen, Ho Chi Minh and his lieutenants devoted considerable effort to crafting bases in this region, which, although of little immediate utility when power was assumed in the lowlands by the Viet Minh, did remain important as a "rear area," particularly in the event of foreign troops forcing the fledgling government out of Hanoi. In late August 1945, however, Viet Minh activists in the northern hills were intent on dealing with remnants of the royal government, Japanese military units, and incoming Chinese forces.

In this region, royal government representatives had mostly lost the initiative to Viet Minh committees in the two or three months before Tokyo's capitulation. Where Japanese military posts existed, provincial- and district-level functionaries still clustered for protection, hoping for a reversal of fortunes. Immediately following the Shōwa emperor's rescript on 15 August, however, Japanese units began to abandon their remaining small posts in favor of the provincial towns, then withdrew hastily toward the delta. This left Vietnamese functionaries and remaining Civil Guard units the option of either attempting to flee southward on their own or submitting to the triumphant Viet Minh units entering each town.

Meeting local Viet Minh representatives in the town of Cao Bang on 21 August, Japanese officers firmly rejected demands to surrender their own weapons, but agreed to leave a cache of French weapons conveniently unguarded at a designated time. A few hours later, Chinese Nationalist troops began to arrive near the town, causing the Japanese to withdraw toward the delta that same night. Skirmishes between Viet Minh and Chinese units led to impromptu parleys, the Viet Minh trying to obtain recognition as the new administrative authority, the Chinese criticizing the Viet Minh for "opposing the Allied army" and refusing to provide food. Late on the 22d, Viet Minh units withdrew hastily to the nearby hills; not until November would it be possible to negotiate a return to Cao Bang town with the Chinese.[60] Meanwhile, the provincial mandarin and a few functionaries from the former government continued to conduct affairs under Chinese supervision.[61]

In Lang Son on 25 August, both the Japanese and the provincial mandarin, Linh Quang Vong, agreed to Viet Minh units entering the provincial seat and occupying government facilities. That same day, however, Chinese

60. Hoang Quang Khanh, Le Hong, and Hoang Ngoc La, *Can Cu Dia Viet Bac (trong cuoc Cach Mang Thang 8–1945)* [The Viet Bac Base Area (in the August 1945 Revolution)] (Viet Bac, 1976), 144–46. Cited below as *CCDVB. CMTT,* 1:101–84.

61. Cong Chinh Cao Bang to So Cong Chinh Bac Bo, 18 Sept. 1945, in AOM, INF, GF 16.

forces crossed the border at Nam Quan in strength, arriving at Lang Son town the next day. With them were units of the Vietnam Revolutionary League and Vietnam Restoration League (Viet Nam Phuc Quoc Dong Minh Hoi), also intent on asserting local authority. When the main Viet Minh group was surrounded and ordered to surrender, most members wanted to try to shoot their way out, but this was overruled by ICP leaders. One squad leader blew himself up with a grenade in protest after being forced to relinquish firearms. Some 170 guns were turned over, the Chinese soldiers then adding insult to injury by taking all watches and fountain pens before imprisoning the entire Viet Minh unit. Several days later, two Viet Minh representatives from outside succeeded in negotiating departure of the unit from Lang Son town, minus its weapons. On the 30th, the Viet Minh began an economic blockade of the town, which was not lifted until an understanding was reached between higher-echelon Chinese and DRV representatives in Hanoi.[62]

In Bac Can province, Viet Minh units had already forced government personnel to abandon all posts except the provincial seat by early August. On 19 August, and again on the 23d, Nong Van Lac, the Viet Minh provincial chairman, met with Japanese officers to offer food supplies in exchange for weapons. Under orders to remain in Bac Can town until units evacuating Cao Bang arrived safely, the Japanese commander eventually assented and allegedly turned over 1,800 French firearms, 500 boxes of ammunition, one case of mines, and 210,000 piastres. On the 25th, with the provincial mandarin and other officials having fled the scene, Viet Minh leaders organized a public meeting and march around town. On the 28th, Bac Can citizens enjoyed their first provincewide market day in some months.[63]

Immediately to the west of Bac Can, at the provincial seat of Tuyen Quang, Viet Minh adherents led by Song Hao, an experienced young organizer, managed on 17 August to persuade the provincial mandarin and a Civil Guard unit to surrender. They then captured a Japanese liaison officer and seven Vietnamese assistants, releasing the former after giving him a propaganda lecture. However, several violent attempts to induce a Japanese platoon stationed in a nearby hilltop fort to surrender its weapons proved futile. In subsequent discussions, the platoon leader explained that since his su-

62. *CCDVB*, 146–47. *CMTT*, 1:109–13. Archimedes L. A. Patti, *Why Viet Nam? Prelude to America's Albatross* (Berkeley and Los Angeles, 1980), 233–34. Harold E. Meinheit, "The Chinese Intervention in Vietnam: 1945–1946" (unpublished paper, Dec. 1976), 59–60.

63. *CCDVB*, 143–44. *CMTT*, 1:125–26.

periors already possessed a radio report of his weapons, he could not arrive in Hanoi with anything less. To complicate matters, on the 20th a member of the Vietnam Revolutionary League by the name of Vu Tien Duc presented himself to Viet Minh leaders at Tuyen Quang, claiming to command one thousand men with two hundred firearms, and wanting urgently to meet Ho Chi Minh. Judging Duc a potential ally, particularly since he vehemently rejected cooperation with the Vietnam Nationalist Party and was willing to donate six guns as a token of good faith, Viet Minh representatives wrote out two travel permits to Hanoi and loaned him five hundred piastres for expenses.[64] On the morning of the 22d, two Japanese automobiles approached town from the direction of Hanoi, bringing news of peaceful arrangements there. Two days later, seventy Imperial Army soldiers arrived from Ha Giang to the north, joining the Tuyen Quang platoon to evacuate downstream without further incident. On the 25th, Viet Minh units marched ceremoniously into the hilltop fort, where they established the Tuyen Quang People's Committee, headed by Nguyen Van Chi.[65] Several weeks later, however, this fledgling committee was pleading for help from Hanoi to deal with the influx of Chinese troops demanding food and the Vietnam Nationalist Party cadres urging joint administration.[66]

West of Tuyen Quang, at Yen Bai, the provincial mandarin, Dao Van Binh, arranged a meeting on 16 August between the commander of a Japanese unit positioned in the former French fort and local Viet Minh representatives. Failing to reach any understanding on a transfer of weapons, both sides agreed to a forty-eight-hour truce, which was broken by the arrival of a separate Viet Minh group descending from the hills and seizing the Civil Guard post in Yen Bai town, including an armory containing three hundred firearms and ten cases of ammunition. After four days of desultory shooting, another meeting was arranged, the Japanese now agreeing to leave behind a further quantity of French weapons, equipment, and stockpiled food when they withdrew a few days later. Just prior to arrival of Chinese troops from Yunnan, a Yen Bai Revolutionary People's Committee was formed, headed by Ngo Minh Loan. Office workers were invited to remain in government employ, while railroad employees received three months' back pay owed them by the Japanese.[67]

64. UBND Tuyen Quang to UBND Bac Bo, 21 Aug. 1945, in Tuyen Quang dossier, AOM, INF, GF 16.

65. *CCDVB*, 138–41. *CMTT*, 1:139–42.

66. UBND Tuyen Quang report to Bac Bo, 10-8 lunar calendar (15 Sept. 1945), in Tuyen Quang dossier, AOM, INF, GF 16.

67. *CMTT*, 1:179–81. *CMCD*, 12:62–66.

Further upstream, in Ha Giang and Lao Cai provinces, no groups identifying themselves as Viet Minh seem to have surfaced in August. The only
excitement in Lao Cai involved Kenpeitai capture on the 13th of two French
captains, Singenes and Delalande, as they attempted to infiltrate from
China and make contact with a Vietnamese public works official. Nine days
later, the Lao Cai provincial mandarin reported Japanese detention of the
official. Remarkably, this mandarin was still sending messages in September to the long-defunct Tonkin Kham Sai.[68]

Lai Chau province, on the Black River west of Lao Cai, remained quiet
throughout August. However, downstream in Son La province, word arrived on 21 August of the successful Viet Minh insurrection in Hanoi,
spurring a group of Thai minority youths to take control in four districts
in the name of the Viet Minh on the night of the 22d. On the 26th, the
Japanese stood aside while a small Civil Guard unit in Son La town opened
its gates to the Viet Minh. A provincial revolutionary committee was
announced the following day. Nonetheless, very few people had any idea
of who the Viet Minh might be. Traditional clan leaders among the Thai
remained aloof from these young upstarts, with the exception of one
former district mandarin, Cam Van Dung, who had been arrested by the
French and had befriended some ICP members in Hanoi Central Prison.
The first Chinese troops arrived in Son La town on the 31st, not only
disarming the Japanese but doing likewise to a fledgling Viet Minh unit,
as well as jailing a number of youths. Only in late October was it possible
for a representative from the provisional government in Hanoi to begin
pulling together a Son La provincial administration, mainly from among
clan elders and former officials.[69]

Further down the Black River, in Hoa Binh province, several Viet Minh
groups had been operating clandestinely since late 1944. Immediately on
hearing of the Uprising Order of 12 August, a guerrilla team marched into
Lac Son and, after persuading the district mandarin to turn over seal and
files, proceeded to invite him to become chairman of the new revolutionary
people's committee. Some one hundred youths carrying an assortment of
bird guns, old muskets, and rifles taken from civil guardsmen were organized into five squads for the 57-kilometer walk to the provincial seat,
picking up another three thousand people en route. Hearing of the crowd's

68. Lao Cai to Kham Sai, 22 Aug. and 6 Sep 1945, in Lao Cai personnel dossier,
AOM, INF, GF 51.

69. Cam Trong, *Nguoi Thai o Tay Bac Viet Nam* [The Thai People of Northwest
Vietnam] (Hanoi, 1978), 513–20. *CMTT*, 1:448–49.

approach, the provincial mandarin crossed the Black River by boat to meet it and donate some firearms. On the 23d, the Hoa Binh Revolutionary People's Committee was established, with a hereditary Muong minority leader as chairman.[70] A Viet Minh team sent out to Luong Son district to take power apparently stole the property of one or more functionaries there.[71] By contrast, the new committee at Hoa Binh town meticulously itemized acquisitions from the former administration, including 114 French rifles of 1902 and 1916 vintages, one machine gun, three swords, 155,274 piastres, 23.73 kilograms of opium, 220 tons of salt, and assorted quantities of rice, soap, cloth, matches, and sugar. The committee also reported to Hanoi that 14 civil guardsmen had deserted or were absent without leave, leaving 114 men.[72] On the 26th, a Vietnam Nationalist Party unit of company size arrived in Hoa Binh demanding to share power; the resulting firefight allegedly ended with the Nationalists fleeing, leaving behind fifty guns.[73]

The provincial seat of Thai Nguyen, on the northern edge of the delta, with key roads running south and west, became the scene of the only substantial clash of arms between Viet Minh and Japanese forces after Tokyo's submission. Presumably ICP leaders wanted to test the combat capabilities of the "Vietnamese-American Joint Force" that had been put together and trained briefly at Tan Trao, hoping to gain a clear-cut victory for psychological and political purposes, then push through quickly to liberate Hanoi, only sixty-five kilometers away—unaware that the city had been in Viet Minh hands since 19 August. Meanwhile the Japanese commander at Thai Nguyen, with some 120 soldiers at his disposal, apparently had orders to retain the town as the obvious collecting point for units withdrawing from provinces further north and northwest.

On 19 August, local Viet Minh representatives in Thai Nguyen were willing to discuss a peaceful transfer of authority with the Japanese. They

---

70. Ngo Tien Chat, "Ve nhung cuoc Dau Tranh Vu Trang cua Nhan Dan cac Dan Toc tinh Hoa Binh trong cuoc Khang Chien Chong Phap (1945–1954)" [Armed Struggles of the People of Various Nationalities in Hoa Binh Province during the Anti-French Resistance], *Nghien Cuu Lich Su* (Hanoi) (cited below as *NCLS*), no. 109 (4-1968): 44–45. *CMTT*, 1:402–4.

71. Petition of Vu Thi, listing about a hundred items stolen, including a pistol, clothing, furniture, and 740 piastres, 15 Nov. 1945, in Hoa Binh dossier, AOM, INF, GF 11.

72. Hoa Binh to Bac Bo, 30 Aug. 1945, in "Hoa Binh 1945" dossier, AOM, INF, GF 53.

73. *CMTT*, 1:405. A second Nationalist Party group was allegedly ambushed and captured the next day.

also met with the provincial mandarin, visited the jail to assure inmates of early release, exhorted Civil Guard members not to resist the Liberation Army when it arrived, and convened a public meeting at the sports field. Early on the morning of the 20th, however, the mood changed abruptly, with a Liberation Army unit under the command of Vo Nguyen Giap and Dam Quang Trung moving into attack positions and sending surrender ultimata to both the Civil Guard and the Japanese. By 5:30 A.M., 160 guardsmen and the provincial mandarin had given up, bringing six hundred firearms, some of which were quickly distributed to another Viet Minh unit arriving from Bac Giang in the east. The provincial mandarin and a Japanese civilian were then used to make the rounds under white flag to the four Japanese defense positions, urging surrender. Written ultimata were presented, one signed by "Van" (Vo Nguyen Giap), the other by Major Allison Thomas, head of the OSS team accompanying the Liberation Army unit.[74] When these actions had no effect, Viet Minh units commenced intermittent fire, continuing through the night and following morning. A further parley extracted only a Japanese promise not to interfere in Vietnamese affairs, but no surrender or willingness to turn over weapons.[75]

At 3:00 P.M. on the 21st, Viet Minh units opened up for about ten minutes with most of the firepower they possessed, including bazookas, antitank rifle grenades, and light machine guns as well as rifles.[76] The effect on the Japanese was negligible. According to Major Thomas: "The Japs were well installed in their concrete fortifications and it is doubtful if any were even wounded at this time. But the townspeople were duly impressed by the 'attack.'"[77] Several more attempts at negotiation were made by the Viet Minh, interspersed with shooting. The persistence of Viet Minh hostility in Thai Nguyen must have puzzled General Tsuchihashi in Hanoi. If the Japanese garrison had been seriously threatened and Tsuchihashi had

74. Ngoc An, "Bo Doi Viet My" [The Vietnamese-American Force], *Tap Chi Lich Su Quan Su*, no. 10 (10-1986): 20.

75. *CCDVB*, 141–42. *CMTT*, 1:77–79. *CMCD*, 12:40–43. A more detailed, if highly exaggerated, account of the Thai Nguyen confrontation can be found in *Lich Su thoi ky van dong Cach Mang Thang 8 cua Dang Bo va Nhan Dan Thanh Pho Thai Nguyen (1939–1945)* [History of the August Revolution Campaign of the Thai Nguyen City Party Branch and People (1939–45)], vol. 1 (Thai Nguyen, 1971), 36–46.

76. Although several mortars had been provided by the OSS team, they do not seem to have been employed at Thai Nguyen, perhaps because of lack of training in pinpoint targeting and a desire to conserve limited stocks of ammunition.

77. Allison Thomas, "Report on Deer Mission," 17 Sept. 1945, reproduced in U.S. Congress, Senate Committee on Foreign Relations, *Causes, Origins and Lessons of the Vietnam War* (Washington, D.C., 1973), 261.

Figure 27.   A Liberation Army unit at the outskirts of Thai Nguyen, 20 August, preparing to attack Japanese positions. The American is Major Allison Thomas, and the person on his right is Phan Dinh Huy. Courtesy of U.S. National Archives.

decided to commit to combat the units approaching Thai Nguyen from the north and west, thus expanding the battle, the cautious modus vivendi developing in Hanoi and other locations might have evaporated. Two out of four Japanese positions at Thai Nguyen were eventually occupied by the Viet Minh, producing little immediate military advantage, but yielding up a booty of TNT (French), gasoline, guns, eight horses, and considerable quantities of rice, salt, and sugar.[78]

On the 22d, a student arrived at Thai Nguyen by bicycle carrying a recent Hanoi newspaper, the first knowledge Vo Nguyen Giap had of the dramatic events in the city. When Truong Chinh reached Thai Nguyen from Tan Trao on the 23d, it was decided to detach a portion of the Liberation Army and march it to Hanoi posthaste, although the recent flooding meant that part of the distance had to be covered in small boats.[79] Two days later, with assistance from a Japanese civilian intermediary, the Imperial Army and Viet Minh forces in Thai Nguyen arranged a cease-fire. The next day representatives of both the Japanese General Staff and the Vietnamese provisional government arrived from Hanoi to terminate the

78. Ibid., 262. *CMTT*, 1:79.
79. Interview with Vo Nguyen Giap, Hanoi, 17 Feb. 1992.

confrontation completely.[80] Japanese soldiers could keep their arms and await Chinese orders; Viet Minh forces would control the town and provide some food to the Japanese. Townspeople quickly came into the open again, Viet Minh flags appeared on most buildings, parades were organized, and unarmed Japanese soldiers circulated through the town, "where they were surprised to find seven equally surprised Americans out strolling the streets on a shopping and picture taking tour."[81]

Central Vietnam

Like few other countries in the world (only Norway and Chile come to mind), Vietnam's long north-south geographical configuration has deeply influenced its modern history. Central Vietnam, the 1,300 kilometers of territory positioned between the Red River Delta and the Mekong Delta, with its diverse climates, topography, cultural underpinnings, and ethnic composition, has long been difficult to govern. Breaking with precedent, Emperor Gia Long, founder of the Nguyen dynasty in 1802, chose to establish his capital in Hue rather than far to the north. Although the subsequent French decision to focus on Hanoi and Saigon rendered the royal capital increasingly anachronistic, Hue still held the imagination of millions of Vietnamese in 1945, and the administrative unit of Annam (Trung Ky; Trung Bo), a colonial creation, retained sufficient meaning to be acknowledged by all political actors, including the Viet Minh leaders taking power in Hanoi.

News of Tokyo's impending capitulation came rapidly to a number of provinces in central Vietnam usually via employees of the PTT with access to radio receivers. By 22 August, even people in distant districts of the central highlands had heard not only of Japan's surrender but also about Viet Minh takeovers in Hanoi and several coastal provinces. ICP committees were quick to take advantage of the new circumstances, yet with the notable exception of Quang Ngai province, they lacked an established network of village- and district-level Viet Minh groups upon which to rely for sustained action, not to mention any experience at coordinating operations in a multi-district "liberated zone." As a result, ICP members in central Vietnam relied more on contacting royal government officials directly, demanding immediate transfer of power "to the Revolution"—generally a cluster of eager youths, former political prisoners, and acknowledged intellectuals. Except for those in Quang Tri, Quang Ngai, and Hue, the crowds that fol-

---

80. *CCDVB*, 143. *CMTT*, 1:80.
81. Thomas, "Report on Deer Mission," 262.

lowed these leaders tended to be small, on the order of two hundred to two thousand people. "Colonial Route 1," the main north-south road, became the focus of much Viet Minh political activity, in effect denying all other groups except the Japanese regular movement between Hanoi and Saigon until Chinese, British, and French units moved into the area months later.

Hoang Quoc Viet has left us a vivid impression of the first days of revolution along Route 1 in central Vietnam.[82] Dispatched from the Tan Trao meetings to establish contact with ICP members in the south, Viet arrived in Hanoi on the first leg of his journey only hours after the Viet Minh had seized power on the 19th. Avoiding the temptation to get involved, Viet and his companion, Cao Hong Linh, managed to secure the automobile and driver that had carried Nguyen Thi Thap and an unnamed Hoa Hao leader from Saigon a few days prior, and by 7:00 P.M. that same evening they were on the road southward.[83] Entering Nam Dinh town, the vehicle was stopped by a self-defense woman, sword in hand, who demanded a travel pass. At the office of the former French colonial *résident*, Comrade Van Tien Dung assured them all was under control. Back on the road, it proved impossible to drive fast because of the clusters of people and numerous security checkpoints. At Thanh Hoa, in the middle of the night, Viet Minh youths were hoisting several banners across the main street.[84] At Ngang Pass, on the border between Ha Tinh and Quang Binh provinces, Viet obtained his first good view of the ocean after years of furtive existence in the northwestern forests and hills. Near Hue, Nguyen Chi Thanh and To Huu reported to Viet that Emperor Bao Dai was ready to abdicate.

At Hai Van pass, just north of Da Nang, Japanese guards stopped the car, observed several firearms, and notified their commander; after taking

82. Hoang Quoc Viet, "Nhan Dan ta rat Anh Hung," in Ho Chi Minh et al., *Nhan Dan ta rat Anh Hung* [Our People Are Very Heroic] (Hanoi, 1969), 203–8. Translated in Ho Chi Minh et al., *A Heroic People* (Hanoi, 1965), 251–58. See also Hoang Quoc Viet, "Like Wildfire . . . ," *Vietnam Courier*, 8-1985, 13–14.

83. We do not know if Viet and Linh talked with Thap prior to departing Hanoi. If so, it may well have influenced the way they dealt with factional disputations after their arrival in Saigon. See chapter 8. AOM, INF, GF 64, contains a driver's report on Citroën TG-997, which also left Hanoi for Hue and Saigon on the 19th, with three passengers, but this may be a different group. The identity, role, and subsequent fate of the Hoa Hao member who accompanied Nguyen Thi Thap has never been explained.

84. There are puzzling discrepancies between Hoang Quoc Viet's chronology and other sources. For example, he claims to have met an ICP member, Le Tat Dac, in the offices of the former French resident of Thanh Hoa early on the 20th, whereas according to *CMTT*, 1:396, the Viet Minh did not take power in the provincial seat until the 23d.

a look at their Viet Minh flag and travel papers, he waved them on. In Quang Ngai, Viet noted an "atmosphere of tense struggle." While his papers were scrutinized skeptically, local self-defense women, their hair cut short as a revolutionary statement, aimed spears at the car's tires to obstruct it. Eventually they introduced Viet to their superiors, including Comrade Tran Quy Hai, who somehow had come even more quickly from the Tan Trao congress. In Phu Yen, a full morning had to be devoted to resolving a quarrel between an "old" Viet Minh group and a "new" one; according to Viet, on hearing that the unknown Ho Chi Minh was in fact Nguyen Ai Quoc, everyone was jubilant and agreed to work together.

Because no village in Annam is very far from the forest, a higher proportion of bird rifles and old hunting muskets appeared among the demonstrators than in Red River Delta. Obviously these were no match for the repeating rifles possessed by the Civil Guard, yet in almost every case guard commanders decided to "make their units available" to the new revolutionary committees, rather than try to get their men to shoot. Except in Quang Ngai, where demonstrations had previously given way to guerrilla ambushes, none of the insurrectionaries tried seriously to persuade the Japanese to surrender to them. As in the north, however, Japanese units proved willing to donate captured French weapons. By 25 August, mandarins had been replaced by revolutionary committees in all but one province of central Vietnam.

In Thanh Hoa, adjacent to Tonkin, the ICP provincial committee happened to be meeting when word arrived of Japan's surrender. Plans were immediately drawn up to take power in ten of the thirteen lowland districts on the night of 19 August. Only in Thieu Hoa district did the insurrectionaries meet armed resistance from about fifty civil guardsmen and a group of Dai Viet adherents, spurred on by the district mandarin. In two engagements, twelve poorly equipped Viet Minh followers and three guardsmen were killed, yet the Civil Guard unit nonetheless felt constrained to withdraw to the provincial seat. Apparently, most guardsmen deserted soon after, as a small band of youths entering the main post on the 20th found only the post commander and thirty rifles. Three days later, several thousand armed demonstrators came from nearby villages to witness establishment of the Thanh Hoa Revolutionary People's Committee. On the 24th, the committee seized 1.7 million piastres in the provincial bank, released all prisoners, abolished existing taxes, and instructed half of the armed youths who had converged on the town to return home. No attempt was made to alter administration in the six upland districts where Muong hereditary chieftains held sway, except that the Viet Minh flag went up over government buildings and people were encouraged to join national salvation associations.[85]

South of Thanh Hoa, in Nghe An province, a crowd surged into the Quynh Luu district compound on 16 August, fired several shots in the air, arrested the clerks, and compelled the mandarin to turn over his seal. A number of alleged agents for the French and the Japanese were tracked down and shot. ICP cells in other districts, probably hoping for precise orders from the Central Committee, chose to wait four or five days before taking similar action. In Nghi Loc district, a crowd marched into the Catholic bishop's office and demanded that French missionaries cede authority to Vietnamese priests. On the 19th, some two hundred youths and workers on bicycles, waving Viet Minh flags, rode around the streets of Vinh, the provincial seat, urging people to take part in a mass demonstration the following day. By that time, Le Viet Luong, a key ICP member in Nghe An, had returned from Tan Trao with top-level confirmation of the uprising strategy delineated in March. A meeting with local Japanese officers produced a promise of five hundred rifles, ten thousand cartridges, and almost a thousand grenades from the Civil Guard post—which was honored a few weeks later. Not until the 23d did Viet Minh organizers feel sufficiently confident to take power in Vinh, where they immediately convened a "people's court" to try and execute four alleged counterrevolutionaries. Teams were then dispatched to three upland districts to persuade minority hereditary leaders to form revolutionary people's committees. From the 18th, rumors circulated of French units in Laos preparing to move east into Nghe An. Crash military instruction was begun for young Viet Minh adherents, who were then combined with most Civil Guard members to establish the first local Liberation Army unit.[86] A courier was dispatched to Hanoi to request one thousand firearms, with unknown results.[87]

85. *CMTT,* 1:388–97. Le Tat Dac, "Ve cuoc Tong Khoi Nghia o Thanh Hoa" [On the General Insurrection in Thanh Hoa], *Tap Chi Lich Su Dang* (Hanoi), 4 Apr. 1991, 11–12. Pham Cuc, "Khoi Nghia gianh chinh quyen Thang Tam 1945 o Thanh Hoa" [The August 1945 Insurrection to Seize Power in Thanh Hoa], *Tap Chi Lich Su Dang* (Hanoi), 4 Apr. 1991, 30–33.
86. *CMTT,* vol. 2, ed. To Lich Su Cach Mang Thang Tam (Hanoi, 1960), 11–19. Ban Nghien Cuu Lich Su Dang, *So Thao Lich Su Tinh Dang Bo Nghe An* [Preliminary History of the Party in Nghe An Province] (Nghe An, 1967), 83–90. Tinh Uy Nghe Tinh, *Lich Su Dang Bo Dang Cong San Viet Nam Tinh Nghe Tinh* [History of the Vietnam Communist Party Apparatus in Nghe Tinh Province], vol. 1, *1925–1954,* 186–94.
87. UBND Nghe An Ha Tinh to UBND Hanoi, 30 (?) Aug. 1945, in dossier on firearm permits, AOM, INF, GF 16.

Instructed by the interim cabinet in Hue to drive to Hanoi with his assistant, Ta Quang Buu, to make contact with all parties, the royal government's minister of youth, Phan Anh, found himself unintentionally caught up in revolutionary events in Nghe An. Phan Anh's automobile was allowed past several Viet Minh checkpoints, and he even managed to address a youth assembly at Vinh on 18 August. Continuing north the next morning, however, his car was stopped by a crowd of suspicious demonstrators in the village of Thanh Son. When crowd members asked if they had any weapons, Phan Anh's orderly foolishly pulled out a pair of scissors, causing all of them to be arrested and detained in the house of an old Confucian scholar, with whom Anh swapped lines of poetry to pass the time, including fatalistic snatches from Nguyen Du's immortal *Truyen Kieu* (The Tale of Kieu). Observing two airplanes flying from north to south, villagers eagerly persuaded themselves that a delegation from the new Vietnamese government in Hanoi was traveling to meet an Allied mission and secure international recognition. Released by Le Viet Luong, Phan Anh was permitted on the 24th to continue to Hanoi. He was particularly impressed that his captors returned every bit of his baggage, money, and documents.[88]

In Ha Tinh province, where ICP promotion of national salvation groups had proceeded somewhat further than most locations in Annam, it was relatively easy to organize marches on most district offices between 17 and 19 August. No resistance was encountered, although in Can Loc one Viet Minh group arrested another, which had captured the district mandarin and Civil Guard post, requiring urgent conciliation by provincial-level cadres. In the town of Ha Tinh, Viet Minh adherents delivered a letter in classical Chinese to the local Japanese garrison on the 17th, requesting noninterference. Early the next day, they appropriated all seven provincial motor vehicles, using one to drive up to the residence of the provincial mandarin, Ha Van Dai, from whom a letter was extracted ceding authority to the "uprising committee." Another auto full of activists entered the Civil Guard post and managed to take custody of a hundred rifles, shifting them

---

88. Phan Anh, "Con duong di toi Cach Mang Thang Tam cua toi" [My Path toward the August Revolution], *Nhan Dan* (Hanoi), 21 Aug. 1960. Phan Anh, "Toi da tham gia Chinh Phu Lien Hiep Khang Chien (3-3-1946) nhu the nao?" [How I Took Part in the Resistance Union Government (3 March 1946)], *Tap Chi Lich Su Quan Doi* (Hanoi), no. 36 (12 Dec. 1988): 8. When it became known in Hue that Phan Anh had not made it to Hanoi, Bao Dai may have sent Prince Ung Uy, a former minister of rites, on the 21st. See Kenneth E. Colton, "The Failure of the Independent Political Movement in Vietnam, 1945–46" (Ph.D. diss., American University, 1969), 223, 227.

to a more secure location in the countryside. The first act of the "provisional people's authority" established on the 18th was to inform Hanoi, Hue, and adjacent provinces that "the Ha Tinh Viet Minh has seized power."[89]

In Quang Binh province, after hearing the 15 August radio announcements concerning Japan's surrender, a member of the three-month-old clandestine Viet Minh committee quickly notified the ICP province committee, then printed a batch of leaflets for transport to other locations and pasted up messages in classical Chinese addressed to Japanese soldiers, four of whom decided to desert to the ranks of the insurrectionaries. However, it took several days to put together an uprising committee, and Viet Minh groups did not march on provincial and district offices until the 23d, perhaps reflecting delicate relations with the large Catholic minority in Quang Binh. Some days later, a people's court was convened to try and punish the judicial mandarin, Dang Hieu An, plus a number of secret policemen and other "colonial lackeys."[90]

ICP activists in Quang Tri province did little but debate their options until two comrades returned from adjacent Thua Thien on 21 August, carrying copies of the Tan Trao uprising order and confirmation of the success of the Viet Minh in Hanoi. Deciding to seize power on the night of the 22d, they remained worried about reaction from the many Japanese troops withdrawing from Thailand along Route 9 to staging areas in Quang Tri. After several discussions, Japanese officers made it clear they had no intention of interfering, and indeed subsequently donated a substantial quantity of weapons to the Viet Minh.[91] Just to be sure, ICP leaders deliberately avoided any attempt to take power in the district containing the largest Japanese camp. At midnight on the 22d, several rifle shots announced marches on the Quang Tri provincial office and Civil Guard post, both of which were occupied without incident. More impressive were the demonstrations on 23 August in Vinh Linh, where an estimated ten thousand villagers converged on the district seat from different directions. At one point, when three alleged enemy agents were exposed at the mass meeting, Tran Giac, one of the ICP organizers, was barely able to persuade

89. *CMTT*, 2:26–32.
90. Ibid., 36–38.
91. Ibid., 52–54. This may be the "10,000 rifles . . . in the Hue area" referred to in Kiyoko Kurusu Nitz, "Independence without Nationalists? The Japanese and Vietnamese Nationalism during the Japanese Period, 1940–45," *Journal of Southeast Asian Studies* 15, no. 1 (Mar. 1984): 122. However, no Vietnamese source mentions obtaining a quantity of firearms of that magnitude anywhere in central Vietnam.

people to jail rather than kill them. After the district mandarin was delivered to him in fetters, Giac removed the bonds and ordered the official to hand over all documents and money, which turned out to be a paltry sum.[92]

In Quang Nam province, just south of the royal capital, word arrived on the 13th of probable Japanese surrender, causing the ICP provincial committee to plan district-level takeovers for the night of 17–18 August. On the afternoon of the 17th, however, hearing of plans by the Frontline Youth (Tien Tuyen Thanh Nien) group to grab power in the provincial seat of Hoi An ahead of the Viet Minh, the provincial committee decided to take that town as well the same night. At 3:00 A.M. on the 18th, fewer than a thousand farmers and artisans from three nearby villages began to advance on the Civil Guard post, yelling slogans, beating round drums, clacking wooden slit drums, and lighting firecrackers to imitate guns. No resistance was offered by the sixty guardsmen, who delivered up 125 firearms. Next the demonstrators released all prisoners at the provincial jail and took the Hoi An treasury, where they discovered that the Japanese had already carried away all large-denomination currency, leaving only twenty-eight stacks of small bills. The provincial mandarin, Ton That Gian, met the crowd deferentially and attempted to make a speech, but he was cut off by youths eager to pull down the royal flag and run up the Viet Minh banner. Automobiles were then appropriated to alert nearby districts and hide documents, money, and some firearms for fear of a Japanese counterattack. One group of cars filled with flag-waving, armed Viet Minh adherents played a key role in liberating four districts to the south of Hoi An that same day.[93]

Probably influenced by events in adjacent Quang Ngai province, where Viet Minh adherents had been trying to kill Japanese for months, ICP leaders in Quang Nam made their uprising preparations on the assumption that violent clashes with the "dwarf bandits" (*giac lun*) were inevitable, indeed desirable, despite news of Tokyo's capitulation. Plans for district

92. Ban Nghien Cuu Lich Su Dang Tinh Binh Tri Thien, *Mot Long vi Dang vi Dan* [Of One Heart Because of the Party and People], vol. 1 (Hue, 1984), 194–97. *CMTT*, 2:55–59. Hoang Anh, Le Tu Dong, et al., *Binh Tri Thien Thang Tam Bon Lam: Hoi Ky* [August 1945 in Binh Tri Thien: Memoirs] (Hue, 1985), 127–31, 163–65.

93. Ban Nghien Cuu Lich Su Dang Tinh Quang Nam, *Cuoc Van Dong Cach Mang Thang Tam tinh Quang Nam* [The August Revolution Campaign in Quang Nam Province] (Thanh Hoa, 1973), 76–94. *CMTT*, 2:97–98. Dang Bo Huyen Hoa Vang, *Lich Su Dau Tranh Cach Mang Huyen Hoa Vang, 1928–1954* [History of Revolutionary Struggle in Hoa Vang District] (Da Nang, 1985), 60–71.

takeovers included destruction of several bridges, sinking of river ferries, and felling of hundreds of trees on selected roads—all designed to inhibit Imperial Army counteraction. The effect, however, was to provoke a higher level of Japanese military activity than otherwise would have been the case. On 18 August, Japanese troops fired on crowds surrounding roadblocks in Dien Ban district, killing twenty-three. Frustrated at having wasted twenty-four hours evading obstacles, two truckloads of Japanese soldiers dispatched to relieve the small fort in Dai Loc district killed at least twelve demonstrators and burned down forty houses. Two other encounters, in Tam Ky and Duy Xuyen districts, left an additional six demonstrators dead. Because so many Japanese troops were stationed in Da Nang, no attempt was made to take power in that important city until the 26th, by which time it was obvious that no confrontation was necessary. Le Van Hien, nationally known for his 1938 memoir about the abysmal conditions at Kontum Prison, and now a key member of the Quang Nam uprising committee, not only reached an understanding with the Japanese about Da Nang and vicinity, but agreed to go south to Quang Ngai to help arrange a cease-fire there. En route back to Da Nang, he was forcibly detained for two days by local Viet Minh activists who insisted on continuing to shoot at Japanese convoys and sentry posts.[94]

As elsewhere, newly formed revolutionary people's committees at various levels in Quang Nam had no time to study their responsibilities or contemplate long-term programs. Problems had to be tackled on a day-to-day basis. On 21 August, five French and associated Vietnamese commandos who had parachuted down near the ancient My Son temple complex, thirty-two kilometers south of Da Nang, were captured complete with weapons and radio transmitter. On the 24th, Mai Trong Tanh, a supporter of Prince Cuong De, the royal pretender residing in Tokyo, was apprehended.[95] Four days later, the Quang Nam provincial committee cabled Hanoi that it had intercepted Dinh Khac Thiec and thirteen other members of the pro-Japanese "Vietnam Patriotic Youth Group," traveling in three

94. Ban Nghien Cuu Lich Su Dang Tinh Quang Nam, *Cuoc Van Dong Cach Mang*, 79, 82, 86, 89, 92–93, 95–96. *CMTT*, 2:99–100. According to Nitz, "Independence without Nationalists?" 130, based on a 1962 interview, Ishida Masao, assistant consul in Hue, was called to Da Nang to negotiate with the Viet Minh after demonstrators had killed three Japanese nationals. Since no available Vietnamese source mentions such killings, a meritorious achievement in those days, we may speculate that they occurred in Quang Ngai, and that Ishida was brought in primarily to resolve continuing hostilities in that province.

95. Ban Nghien Cuu Lich Su Dang Tinh Quang Nam, *Cuoc Van Dong Cach Mang*, 95, 106.

automobiles.[96] The Japanese do not seem to have tried to protect their former associates. By the end of the month, they were turning over French military equipment, but not weapons, to the Da Nang committee. An angry dispute in the first days of September over stocks of Japanese gasoline being stolen from Da Nang airfield was resolved peacefully. Meanwhile, new committees in rural areas concentrated more on confiscating the property of absent French nationals and "Vietnamese traitors," pressuring landlords to reduce rents, reallocating communal land, and convening the occasional court to execute a hated policeman or former colonial employee. To show their sentiments, people in Quang Nam greeted each other with a military salute and the salutation "Fight!" (*Chien Dau!*).[97]

Ho Ta Khanh, the economics minister in the Hue government, was being driven north from Quang Ngai on 19 or 20 August when his auto was brought to a halt in Tam Ky district, Quang Nam, by a series of slit trenches dug across the road. Soon it was surrounded by curious peasants, and eventually a Viet Minh team came with orders to escort Khanh to the Tam Ky People's Committee office, where he was detained for several days, then transferred to Hoi An. Although he was fed regularly and allowed to wash, more than once Khanh feared that he was about to be taken away to be killed. He was thus not unhappy to be put on display, minus all clothes except his shorts, for passersby to goggle at. Some days later, Khanh was taken in his own car back to Hue, and in September he was permitted to return to his family home in Phan Thiet.[98]

In Quang Ngai province, news of the imminent Japanese capitulation served simply to heighten the enthusiasm of Viet Minh activists for attacking enemy posts and vehicles. On 13 August, Quan Tran, commander of the Civil Guard post at Di Lang, was lured to the home of a guardsman sympathetic to the Viet Minh, given dinner, abducted, and forced to order his subordinates to surrender. Thirty-seven rifles were collected, with ammunition. As a hated opponent of the ICP, dating back to the 1930–31 "White Terror," Tran was later put before a people's court and executed.[99] Also on the 13th, two Viet Minh guerrillas were killed when Japanese

---

96. UBND Faifo to Bac Bo, 28 Aug. 1945, in AOM, INF, GF 45. The same day Hanoi replied: "Detain them carefully." One can surmise that Thiec and his group were fleeing Hanoi and hoped to reach Saigon.

97. Ban Nghien Cuu Lich Su Dang Tinh Quang Nam, *Cuoc Van Dong Cach Mang*, 101, 105, 106. *CMTT*, 2:101–2.

98. Interview with Ho Ta Khanh in Paris, 1 Nov. 1984.

99. Pham Kiet, *Tu Nui Rung Ba To* [From the Hills and Forests of Ba To] (Hanoi, 1977), 107–12. *CMTT*, 2:119–21.

guards on the Route 1 bridge over the Tra Bong River foiled a surprise attack. The next day a Japanese officer, Kenpeitai soldier, and Vietnamese interpreter were ambushed and killed at the village of Xuan Pho. Toward evening, when a Japanese platoon arrived in search of the missing men, it too was ambushed in a field of sugarcane, both sides losing one combatant before the platoon withdrew in the dark. On the 17th, another Viet Minh group tore up a section of railroad track south of the town of Quang Ngai and sprang two ambushes on Japanese truck convoys, managing to burn several vehicles. Imperial Army units reacted to these harassments by launching sweeps through nearby villages, setting fire to houses. At the same time, however, both sides sent representatives to meet and try to arrange a cease-fire, with the provincial mandarin serving as reluctant intermediary. At district level, except where protected by Japanese troops, the vestiges of royal government were being swept away by crowds of armed demonstrators.

On 28 August, an agreement was signed that committed the Viet Minh in Quang Ngai to ending attacks and no longer withholding food and services, in exchange for the Japanese withdrawing from outlying posts and not interfering in popular meetings or demonstrations. Two days later, two well-armed companies from the Ba To guerrilla zone marched into Quang Ngai town accompanied by more than ten thousand Vietnamese peasants and highland minority peoples, to be greeted by shopkeepers, clerks, and workers waving Viet Minh flags. A revolutionary people's committee was announced, composed mostly of tough ICP survivors of jail and several months' guerrilla struggle. Junks sailing from Saigon to Tonkin were stopped as before, alleged to be serving Japanese interests, and stripped of their cargoes of rice. People's courts were established to try and punish "a large number of reactionaries"; many of those sentenced to death also had their family property confiscated or sealed up pending future disposal. Subsequent intervention by the ICP Central Committee in Hanoi apparently persuaded Quang Ngai militants to reduce some of these sentences.[100]

Sometime in the week or two following Tokyo's capitulation, Viet Minh adherents at the Ve River train station in Quang Ngai arrested Ta Thu Thau, Vietnam's most gifted Trotskyist writer and orator, as he was returning from Hanoi to Saigon. Thau vehemently rejected charges that

100. Pham Kiet, *Tu Nui Rung Ba To*, 112–17. *CMTT*, 2:121–30. *Vietnamese Studies* (Hanoi), no. 81 (1985): 172. Dang Bo Huyen Son Tinh, *So Thao Lich Su Dang Bo Huyen Son Tinh* [Preliminary History of the Party Apparatus in Son Tinh District], vol. 1, 1929–1945 (Ho Chi Minh City, 1986), 129–340.

he was a reactionary, had misled revolutionary public opinion, and even somehow sabotaged the local railway bridge. It is possible that he had been followed from Hanoi, and that ICP agents chose blood-spattered, chaotic Quang Ngai as the best place to eliminate him. In any case, after a perfunctory trial, he was taken to a nearby beach and shot.[101] Thau's death shocked intellectuals of all political complexions and led some to suspect that the ICP had a nationwide hit list that included prominent anticolonialists as well as collaborators.

Binh Dinh, the equally populous province just south of Quang Ngai, was beset by dissension between two Viet Minh groups that had grown up since the Japanese coup, one based at the Delignon textile mill in the town of Qui Nhon, the other among farmers in three rural districts, with each also boasting adherents among railway employees at train stations along the main north-south line. On 23 August, the Delignon group convened a mass meeting at the Qui Nhon sports field, then led two crowds to seize the provincial mandarin's office and Civil Guard compound without incident. Japanese soldiers barred entry to the local Bank of Indochina branch, but subsequently donated a quantity of arms and ammunition. Vo Xan, head of the Delignon group and now chairman of the new Binh Dinh provisional revolutionary people's committee, decided to travel to the countryside to meet leaders of the second Viet Minh organization. His additional status as an ICP member and veteran of Son La prison did not, however, prevent him from being summarily executed on the 27th. Further internecine bloodshed was averted when the two sides met four days later and agreed on the membership of town and province people's committees, although mutual distrust continued to impede Viet Minh activities in Binh Dinh for years thereafter.[102]

In adjacent Phu Yen province, local ICP members needed to be prodded by a Party representative from Quang Ngai to organize a march on the provincial seat of Song Cau on 23 August, where the provincial mandarin and the Civil Guard commander both proved willing to concede authority.

---

101. Phuong Lan, *Nha Cach Mang Ta Thu Thau* [Ta Thu Thau the Revolutionary] (Saigon, 1973), 431–37. Ho Huu Tuong, a fellow Trotskyist who earlier had accompanied Thau north from Saigon, decided to remain a bit longer in Hanoi, and indeed is listed as one of the "prominent personalities" invited to meet the new minister of interior, Vo Nguyen Giap, on 27 August. *Cuu Quoc* (Hanoi), no. 34 (31 Aug. 45): 1.

102. Do Quyen, *Lich Su Dang Bo Tinh Binh Dinh* [History of the Party Apparatus in Binh Dinh Province], vol. 1, *1930–1945* (Qui Nhon, 1990), 124–59. *CMT T*, 2:142–45. In 1949, the ICP criticized unnamed individuals for executing Vo Xan, and in 1985 he was officially extolled as a true revolutionary.

In the town of Tuy Hoa, two groups asserted their Viet Minh credentials against each other. Despite Hoang Quoc Viet's invocation of the name of Nguyen Ai Quoc / Ho Chi Minh, mentioned above, several bloody confrontations occurred before a higher-level team intervened to force peaceful resolution. Meanwhile, when the Japanese refused to relinquish a large sugar refinery and storehouse in the vicinity, one of these Viet Minh groups established a cordon and carried out sniping attacks until Japanese troops withdrew three months later.[103]

In Khanh Hoa province, several ICP activists returned from Quang Ngai on 13 or 14 August eager to organize armed attacks. At about the same time, covert ICP activists in several royal government bureaus in the town of Nha Trang heard radio reports of imminent Japanese surrender. It was decided to take control of a royal government-sponsored Frontline Youth meeting already scheduled for Sunday the 19th. Nguyen Van Sam, newly appointed Kham Sai for Cochinchina, was detained in Khanh Hoa for several days by Viet Minh adherents, then mysteriously released and allowed to continue south.[104] The meeting of the 19th was duly co-opted by the Viet Minh, then transformed into a march on the provincial offices, police station, and treasury. At one point in the march, a Japanese officer chose to engage the crowd in the following lively colloquy:

> "Can Vietnam be independent?"
> "Yes! Yes!"
> "If another country comes to seize Vietnam, what will the Vietnamese people do?"
> "We'll fight back!"
> "Without Japan to help, can Vietnam possibly fight effectively?"
> "Why not?!"[105]

By the 27th, it was possible to convene a meeting of representatives of all people's committees in Khanh Hoa to begin to unify provincial administration. Four "enemy agents" of the Japanese were executed, yet this did not prevent the Japanese from transferring French civilians detained in Nha Trang to Viet Minh custody.[106]

---

103. *CMTT*, 2:151–54.

104. Nguyen Ky Nam, *Hoi Ky, 1925–1964* [Memoirs, 1925–64], vol. 2, *1945–54* (Saigon, 1964), 34–37, 41–45. The author was traveling in the same car as the viceroy. After release, they still feared being stopped on some obscure stretch of Route 1 and eliminated.

105. Minh Vy, in Nguyen Duy Trinh, Chu Van Tan, et al., *Nhung Ngay Thang Tam* [Days of August] (Hanoi, 1961), 206.

106. *CMTT*, 2:160–64.

In Ninh Thuan province, a meeting of the Frontline Youth at the Thap Cham primary school on 21 August was forcibly taken over by Viet Minh adherents, who then urged crowd members to march on the town of Phan Rang, five kilometers distant. There the provincial mandarin, Phan Van Phuc, readily turned over his pistol, dossiers, and treasury key, before accompanying demonstrators to the Civil Guard barracks to arrange delivery of one hundred rifles. The provincial people's committee established the next day took care to recruit individuals from the old administration, including Phuc, but also felt the need to execute seven "enemy agents." All French-owned plantations were confiscated, a large consignment of salt transported to the hills for use in any future fighting, and seven youths dispatched to Hanoi for training. Professional divers were located to go down and secure weapons on several Japanese ships that had been sunk by American aircraft.[107]

In Binh Thuan, Viet Minh adherents disguised as lumber merchants gained entry to the office of the provincial mandarin, Huynh Du, persuading him to release an ICP member in police custody and agree to transfer authority the following day. However, a subsequent demonstration in the town of Phan Thiet to celebrate the Viet Minh takeover was forcibly dispersed by Japanese soldiers. When Du went to Kenpeitai headquarters to ask that the troops be withdrawn, he was subjected to a humiliating dressing-down and allegedly threatened with sword and pistol. Eventually the demonstration was allowed to proceed and Du for his troubles was elected a member of the provincial people's committee. After a French parachute team was captured in Ham Tan district, all local committees organized regular armed patrols of both upland and coastal sections of the province. On 2 September, up to forty thousand citizens converged on the Phan Thiet sports field to celebrate national independence.[108]

In the highland provinces of central Vietnam, changes were usually triggered by telegrams from the lowlands reporting Japanese surrender, Viet Minh takeover in Hanoi, and Bao Dai's decision to abdicate. Ethnic Vietnamese took the local initiative, but because they were very much a minority among the Rhadé, Sedang, Ede, Jarai, and other tribal groups, some sort of consultation and cooperation was generally deemed desirable.

107. Ibid., 167–72. Truong Sinh, in Nguyen Duy Trinh, Chu Van Tan, et al., *Nhung Ngay Thang Tam*, 208–17, contains an hour-by-hour eyewitness account of events in Ninh Thuan on 21–22 August.

108. *CMTT*, 2:176–85. Ho Chi Minh's Independence Proclamation was allegedly read to the Phan Thiet crowd, but it seems highly unlikely that Hanoi could have transmitted the text in time.

In Pleiku province, Vietnamese youths organized a demonstration on 25 August, then established a people's committee, with the deputy chair reserved for a tribal representative. Hereditary tribal leaders previously confirmed by the French were not displaced unless they showed signs of opposition. French-owned plantations came under control of the workers, who sold stocks of coffee beans and tea leaves accumulated during the war to obtain revenue for local committees.[109] In adjacent Kontum province, members of the Sedang tribe took part in the formation of the new administration. Nay De became chairman of the provincial committee, and hundreds of Sedang youths opted to join nascent army units.[110] In Darlac province on the 20th, a small Viet Minh group persuaded Y Bih and Y Blok, two Ede commanders of tribal Civil Guard units, to withdraw from a royal government flag-raising ceremony, then participate in seizure of power four days later. The resulting provincial people's committee contained six tribal members out of a total of thirteen. An Italian plantation owner named Delfante, who had avoided Japanese detention because of his nationality, was executed for rejecting committee edicts. In Dalat, following Viet Minh takeover on the 23d, a dispute arose with the Japanese over the six hundred resident French civilians: Viet Minh leaders wanted to keep them all in military barracks, but the Japanese successfully insisted that most be allowed to reside and circulate elsewhere in the town. To the southwest of Dalat, in Dong Nai Thuong province, the new committee administration remained mostly in the hands of existing officials and clerks.[111]

Hue and Vicinity

With cable reports coming in by the hour, particularly of the Viet Minh takeover in Hanoi, but also concerning disturbing events closer to the royal capital, in Thanh Hoa and Ha Tinh, for example, Premier Tran Trong Kim finally abandoned his attempts to reconstitute a cabinet. On 20 August he issued a statement, actually drafted four days prior, claiming to have accomplished his two overriding objectives of unifying the territory of Vietnam and sustaining its administrative capabilities. "Before history, the mission of our cabinet is now complete," he wrote. With international

---

109. Ibid., 189–92. Do Quyen, *Lich Su Dang Bo Tinh Binh Dinh,* 179–80.

110. Tran Van Than, "Tim hieu Phong Trao Chong Thuc Dan Phap cua nguoi Sedang o vung dong bac Kontum" [Understanding the Anti–French Imperialist Movement of the Sedang People in Northeastern Kontum], *NCLS* 150 (5/6-1973): 26–27.

111. *CMTT,* 2:197–203, 211–13, 217–19.

circumstances changing, Kim acknowledged that others needed to carry on. In his last official breath, Kim pleaded for political unity, pointing out that the enemy was "looking for divisions."[112]

Also on 20 August, Emperor Bao Dai issued an order, drafted three days earlier, in which he acknowledged Japan's help to Vietnam in regaining its independence, indicated his desire for a new cabinet, and, most important, stated a personal willingness to sacrifice his position if necessary. In words that moved many of his subjects, Bao Dai said he would "prefer to be a citizen of an independent country rather than king of an enslaved one."[113] This language had been debated vigorously at the cabinet meeting on 17 August (see chapter 6), in the context of Bao Dai's expressed readiness to attract Viet Minh ministers and place national defense above all. Tran Dinh Nam, minister of the interior, had provoked the argument by suggesting that even the emperor should be prepared to withdraw, causing Tran Trong Kim to accuse Nam of lèse-majesté. Vu Van Hien, the finance minister, favored offering power to the Viet Minh in the framework of a constitutional monarchy, and the cabinet eventually decided to send Phan Anh to Hanoi with that proposal. However, the text as subsequently drafted clearly raised the possibility of Bao Dai's abdication, perhaps termination of the monarchy entirely, ideas that continued to bother Kim profoundly, yet received strong endorsement from Ho Ta Khanh and Phan Anh, since they demonstrated the emperor's commitment to the national interest. Finally, in a rare display of personal initiative, Bao Dai rejected any change in the wording.[114] The Japanese-controlled radio station in Hue broadcast Bao Dai's statement on the afternoon of the 21st, giving a decided boost to Viet Minh confidence.[115] The next day the statement was rebroadcast as well as

112. "Tuyen cao cua Chinh Phu Thuan Hoa" [Declaration of the Thuan Hoa Government] to Kham Sai Hanoi, Saigon, and all ministries, 16 Aug. 1945, actually dispatched 20 Aug.; contained in dossier "Phuong sach doi voi thoi cuc 1945," AOM, INF, GF 58.

113. "Viet Nam Hoang De Ban Chieu" [Vietnam Imperial Proclamation], 17 Aug. 1945, released 20 Aug.; contained in dossier "Phuong sach doi voi thoi cuoc 1945," AOM, INF, GF 58.

114. Pham Khac Hoe, *Tu Trieu Dinh Hue den Chien Khu Viet Bac* [From the Hue Royal Court to the Viet Bac War Zone] (Hanoi, 1983), 56–59. By the 17th, Phan Anh had his own understanding with the local Viet Minh about avoiding youth group confrontations. See *CMTT*, 2:81.

115. Hoang Anh, "Nho lai cuoc Khoi Nghia gianh Chinh Quyen o Hue" [Recalling the Insurrection to Take Power in Hue], *Tap Chi Cong San* (Hanoi), 8 Aug. 1985, 40. Hoang Anh mistakenly recalls the statement including a specific offer to abdicate.

telegraphed to subordinate government echelons, but this time adding a specific invitation to the Viet Minh to form a new cabinet.[116]

Since Viet Minh declarations had been utterly consistent in foreshadowing a republican government, any last-minute proposal from Hue to accept a constitutional monarchy was doomed to failure. Among intellectuals unaffiliated with the Viet Minh, the eminent literatus Huynh Thuc Khang was probably the first to suggest Bao Dai's abdication, in a conversation with Pham Khac Hoe, the emperor's private secretary, in March 1945.[117] In early August, Ton Quang Phiet, a respected writer, high school principal, and covert Viet Minh adherent, persuaded Hoe to try to convince the emperor to abdicate. To strengthen his case, Hoe returned to the palace library to look up regicide precedents. On 12 August, after telling Bao Dai that he doubted any leftist candidates for the new cabinet would accept office, Hoe mentioned the sad fate of Louis XVI in the French Revolution, then added, "Perhaps Your Highness ought not wait until the water reaches your feet before jumping."[118] That same day, a Japanese general from Saigon offered Imperial Army assistance in suppressing the Viet Minh, but Bao Dai demurred.[119] On the morning of the 19th, Hoe briefed Bao Dai on reports of Viet Minh seizures of power in districts of Ha Tinh and Quang Ngai, as well as the increasingly serious unrest in and around Hue itself. Repeatedly Bao Dai asked to be able to meet any available Viet Minh leaders, but Hoe's main contact, Ton Quang Phiet, proved unresponsive.[120] Probably Phiet would have liked to comply, but there were no senior ICP or Viet Minh representatives available, only eager young members of provincial- and city-level committees.[121]

That same morning of 19 August, Viet Minh adherents seized the district offices in Phu Loc, thirty-eight kilometers southeast of Hue. The mandarin having fled beforehand, his staff readily turned over the official seal and district records. After a revolutionary people's committee was announced, individual activists set off to organize self-defense groups and

116. Philippe Devillers, *Histoire du Vietnam de 1940 à 1952* (Paris, 1952), 138. *Hung Viet* (Saigon), no. 21 (24 Aug. 1945): 1, reprints the 22 Aug. text.

117. Nguyen Quoc Thang, *Huynh Thuc Khang: Con Nguoi va Tho, Van (1876–1947)* [Huynh Thuc Khang: His Life and Letters] (Saigon, 1972), 219.

118. Pham Khac Hoe, *Tu Trieu Dinh Hue*, 51–53.

119. Nguyen Ky Nam, *Hoi Ky*, 188–89. Nam's source for this information was Trinh Dinh Thao, minister of justice at the time.

120. Pham Khac Hoe, *Tu Trieu Dinh Hue*, 60.

121. Phiet had arranged one month earlier for Phan Anh to meet the ICP provincial secretary, Hoang Anh. Hoang Anh, Le Tu Dong, et al., *Binh Tri Thien*, 26–28.

Figure 28. Pham Khac Hoe, private secretary to Emperor Bao Dai in the summer of 1945. Courtesy of Archives d'Outre-Mer, Aix-en-Provence.

track down "traitors and reactionaries" from a list prepared in advance. Six days earlier, members of the ICP committee for Thua Thien province and Hue had argued vehemently about whether to wait for Standing Bureau orders or proceed to mount uprisings in the countryside immediately upon confirmation of Japan's surrender—finally opting for the latter course by a 3–2 vote. Two comrades were dispatched north to locate the Party center, another sent to Quang Ngai to coordinate with ICP leaders there. On the 15th, a provincial uprising committee was established, the texts of five different leaflets were drafted, and individual letters were dispatched to ranking members of the royal government. A letter was sent as well to Ambassador Yokoyama, urging him to instruct Japanese troops not to interfere in Viet Minh endeavors to secure independence, in return for which, "we shall make every effort to avoid bumping against the Japanese Army."[122] The uprising leaflets were held up for four days owing to a difference of opinion between the two Viet Minh groups active in Hue— one of them taking exception to wording that delineated French colonialists and French progressives. Once that problem was cleared up, a consignment of ten thousand leaflets was produced overnight by a covert team in a local

---

122. Ban Nghien Cuu Lich Su Dang Tinh Thua Thien, *So thao Lich Su Cach Mang Thang Tam Thua Thien-Hue* [Preliminary History of the August Revolution in Thua Thien-Hue] (Hanoi, 1970), 55–63. Hoang Anh, "Nho lai cuoc Khoi Nghia," 38–39. Hong Thuy, in Nguyen Duy Trinh, Chu Van Tan, et al., *Nhung Ngay Thang Tam,* 191–94. CMTT, 2:82–84.

printing house, many copies being dispatched to rural areas the next morning.[123]

As the moment of possible confrontation approached, attention focused on Lieutenant Phan Tu Lang, commander of Civil Guard units in Thua Thien–Hue, and by all accounts a resourceful, respected officer. Earlier Ton Quang Phiet had introduced Lieutenant Lang to Le Tu Dong, a key ICP committee member, who tried to answer Lang's wide-ranging questions about Viet Minh policies, international as well as domestic. On 17 August, the ICP provincial secretary, Hoang Anh, paid a surprise visit to Lang's home, catching him stripped to the waist, chopping firewood. Lang agreed to let Viet Minh representatives speak to his Civil Guard units, and subsequently provided advice on which subordinates might be regarded as sympathetic, indifferent, or antagonistic. Nonetheless, Lieutenant Lang does not appear to have committed himself to disobeying direct imperial or government orders.[124]

On the morning of 20 August, word reached the ICP's Thua Thien–Hue committee of Viet Minh success in Hanoi the previous day. That afternoon, three ICP representatives, Ho Tung Mau, Nguyen Duy Trinh, and To Huu, arrived in Thua Thien from the north with Central Committee orders to guide the takeover of Hue. A few hours later, To Huu was made chairman of the Hue uprising committee, with Hoang Anh as deputy.[125] That night, two district headquarters in the countryside near Hue were taken by the Viet Minh, while mandarins at two others indicated their readiness to step aside. On the 21st, a small group of armed Viet Minh adherents marched around the streets of Hue without encountering opposition; the group even tried to persuade Japanese soldiers at the Mang Ca garrison, where French troops were interned, to share guard duties. Hearing of royal government plans to convene a public meeting on the 23d to celebrate the reincorporation of Cochinchina, the Hue uprising committee determined to seize power on that day. Meanwhile, during the 22d, groups of demonstrators, some

123. Hoang Anh, Le Tu Dong, et al., *Binh Tri Thien*, 21, 150.

124. Ibid., 23–24, 65–69. Thirty years later, Le Tu Dong met Phan Tu Lang again in Saigon, where the latter was chief inspector in the office of metal engineering.

125. There is considerable confusion in the sources about when To Huu in particular arrived in Thua Thien–Hue. Some claim he was present as early as 14 August, but assertions by Hoang Anh and Le Tu Dong of the 20th appear more credible. Nguyen Chi Thanh also arrived back in Thua Thien from Tan Trao at about this time, with responsibility for rebuilding the ICP's Trung Bo (Central Region) Committee, as well as developing contacts in Laos. See Ban Nghien Cuu Lich Su Dang Tinh Binh Tri Thien, *Mot Long vi Dang vi Dan*, 91.

armed, took control of several government installations, raised a big Viet Minh flag over the Information Office, and attempted to share guard responsibilities with Japanese soldiers at a bridge over the Perfume River.[126]

Hue, normally a quiet town of about fifty thousand inhabitants, was now awash with extraordinary rumors, excited clusters of high school students, and increasing numbers of peasants filtering in from the countryside. Members of the government-sponsored Frontline Youth group were ordered to stand guard at the Citadel, but their rifles contained no firing pins, and many were less interested in defending the government or royal family than in reading Viet Minh leaflets and discussing the dramatic changes elsewhere. One Hue youth, feeling like a piece on a chessboard, ruminated how only a few months earlier he had dropped the French language so as not to be considered procolonial, switching to the study of Japanese; soon he would be face to face with some mysterious Vietnamese revolutionary front.[127] Other Hue youths were already more directly involved in Viet Minh activities. As one participant recalled:

> Whatever was needed, from going out to buy cloth for making flags, to painting slogans, hammering weapons together, giving a propaganda speech at a theater or marketplace, [we] did it immediately, happily. For us, time no longer divided into days and nights, there was no longer one place versus another or individual versus group preoccupations.[128]

As the uprising committee made its final preparations, a merchant came to donate a typewriter and paper, a printshop owner offered his press and workers to crank out leaflets, and groups of women at the Dong Ba marketplace provided food for demonstrators.[129]

By 22 August, the gravity of their position was finally becoming evident to royal government officials and Emperor Bao Dai alike. When Tran Trong Kim called in Lieutenant Lang to ask if the Civil Guard and Frontline Youth could be depended upon, he received an equivocal answer. On checking, Kim realized that even the several-hundred strong Palace Guard had been infiltrated by the Viet Minh and was generally demoralized. Recalling for Bao Dai the dire examples of Louis XVI and Czar Nicholas II, Kim advised him to abdicate quickly rather than struggle further. "We lack strength, the Viet Minh possess popular support, let them take responsibility for

126. Ban Nghien Cuu Lich Su Dang Tinh Thua Thien, *So thao Lich Su Cach Mang*, 63–67. *CMTT*, 2:84–85.

127. Thach Ha, *Mat Troi Chieu* [Afternoon Sun] (Saigon, 1963), 30–32.

128. Trinh Xuan An, in Nguyen Duy Trinh, Chu Van Tan, et al., *Nhung Ngay Thang Tam*, 197.

129. Ibid., 198–99.

protecting national independence," Kim concluded.[130] Whatever Bao Dai's fate, Kim was about to become Vietnam's Kerensky, although it is unlikely he appreciated the historical parallel.

Two days earlier, Pham Khac Hoe had made the same points to Bao Dai as Tran Trong Kim, adding some complimentary remarks about the revolutionary Nguyen Ai Quoc, whose "Open Letter" issued in the north was now being pasted up in the streets of the royal capital. Hoe described to Bao Dai a cryptic Nghe An prophecy that could point to Nguyen Ai Quoc becoming savior of his country. Warming to the theme of omens, Bao Dai described to Hoe how several months prior, on the anniversary of the Nguyen dynasty's foundation in 1802, a heavy wooden beam had fallen on the path where Bao Dai had passed in his sedan chair only a few seconds before.[131]

Also on the 22d, Bao Dai was visited by the Japanese colonel in charge of the Hue garrison, who explained that he had taken measures to ensure the security of the Imperial Palace and its occupants, in line with orders from the Allied commander. Bao Dai rejected this protection, saying, "I do not wish a foreign army to spill the blood of my people."[132] That evening, a young man engaged recently as tutor for the crown prince came to the emperor with a proposal to flee to the valley of the imperial tombs, just outside Hue. Remembering Louis XVI's deadly mistake of trying to escape Paris, Bao Dai politely rejected the idea. A bit later, the PTT director in Hue was ushered in with a telegram from a "Committee of Patriots" in Hanoi, respectfully urging the emperor to remit his powers as a historic act in support of national independence.[133] That telegram grew out of a public meeting called by the General Association of Students the previous day, which had demanded Bao Dai's abdication, installation of a republican system, and immediate Viet Minh negotiations with other parties to form a provisional national government.[134]

130. Tran Trong Kim, *Mot Con Gio Bui* [A Puff of Dust] (Saigon, 1969), 92–93.

131. Pham Khac Hoe, *Tu Trieu Dinh Hue*, 60–63. Bao Dai, *Le Dragon d'Annam* (Paris, 1980), 111, confirms the episode of the dropping beam, adding that his mother took it to signify that he was at a turning point in his life.

132. Bao Dai, *Le Dragon*, 117. A Japanese officer who visited Tran Trong Kim with a proposal to defend the palace received a similar answer. Tran Trong Kim, *Mot Con Gio Bui*, 93.

133. Bao Dai, *Le Dragon*, 117–18. According to Devillers, *Histoire*, 139, Viet Minh adherents in Hue were also informed of this telegram. AOM, INF, GF 69, contains several petitions from northern citizens urging Bao Dai's abdication, one as early as 15 August addressed to the "Viet Minh Delegate."

134. Devillers, *Histoire*, 137. By contrast, someone in the Northern Region Revolutionary People's Committee told Nishimura Kumao on the 21st that they

On the morning of the 23d, Bao Dai, feeling very isolated, recalling the fallen beam omen, unable to locate any ministers in the palace, and particularly upset that some youths had replaced the royal banner on the main flagpole with the Viet Minh flag unopposed by palace guards nearby, decided to cable the "Committee of Patriots" his willingness to transfer power to someone in authority if they came to Hue.[135] His telegram crossed one from the Northern Region Revolutionary People's Committee that amounted to an ultimatum:

> A Provisional revolutionary people's government has been established with Ho Chi Minh as chairman. Request Your Majesty abdicate immediately in order to consolidate and unify the independence of Vietnam.[136]

Given raucous events in the streets of Hue during 23 August, it was by no means certain that Bao Dai and his family would be permitted a dignified exit from the palace and from history. Early that morning Ambassador Yokoyama had observed Viet Minh irregulars coming in from surrounding rural districts, barefoot, carrying flags and bamboo spears, singing the "Internationale." Mindful of Allied instructions to maintain order, the Japanese commander particularly stationed guards around the French quarters.[137] Reversing the sequence in Hanoi four days earlier, Viet Minh leaders in Hue sent groups first to occupy public buildings and Civil Guard barracks, to be followed by a mass meeting in the late afternoon at the sports stadium. The atmosphere was festive, with much laughter and cheering, children beating small drums, citizens trying to march in formation to the call of "one, two, one, two." People noticed that many lesser members of the royal family were participating. There was no resistance: functionaries in each government bureau made a small ceremony of turning over records "to the Revolution." Hoang Anh was delighted to discover that the royal treasury contained 3,600 kilograms of silver ingots. However, ICP squads did hunt down and arrest specific "traitors," includ-

---

awaited "recognition" from Hue, which led the puzzled Japanese to attempt last-minute mediation, abandoned on the 23d. Stein Tønnesson, *The Vietnamese Revolution of 1945: Roosevelt, Ho Chi Minh and de Gaulle in a World at War* (London, 1991), 389, based on Allied radio intercepts. The exact positions of individual ICP and Democratic Party leaders on the question of Bao Dai's abdication remain murky.

135. Bao Dai, *Le Dragon*, 118–19. Pham Khac Hoe, *Tu Trieu Dinh Hue*, 63–64.
136. "Uy Ban Nhan Dan Cach Mang Bac Bo gui Duc Kim Thuong" [Northern Region Revolutionary People's Committee to His Majesty], 23 Aug. 1945, in dossier "Phuong sach doi pho voi thoi cuoc 1945," AOM, INF, GF 58.
137. Interview with Yokoyama Masayuki in Tokyo, 16 Nov. 1967.

ing the former premier Pham Quynh, the former minister Ngo Dinh Khoi, and the latter's son, Ngo Dinh Huan, who had worked for Ambassador Yokoyama. No attempt was made to enter the royal palace itself, although a Viet Minh ultimatum was delivered that required an answer by 1:30 P.M.[138]

At 12:25 P.M. on 23 August, Bao Dai presided over his last cabinet meeting, convened hastily to respond to the Viet Minh ultimatum and discuss the abdication edict.[139] Participants agreed to accept the Viet Minh terms, which included relinquishment of all weapons and ammunition in the palace, notification to the Japanese that all powers had been transferred to the revolutionary government, and orders to all provincial mandarins to turn over their responsibilities to the local representatives of the Viet Minh. In return, the Viet Minh promised to guarantee the lives and property of the royal family. The abdication edict was endorsed with one minor amendment and the meeting adjourned.[140] Pham Khac Hoe was then dispatched to report to Viet Minh leaders before the 1:30 P.M. deadline, encountering a sea of people on the streets and in the sports stadium, but no one who knew where the uprising committee could be located. Peasants in brown, black, or indigo mixed easily with elders in traditional tunics, townsfolk in shirt and tie, khaki shorts, or school uniforms. Suddenly Hoe realized he was the only one among tens of thousands who was wearing the ivory badge of a royal mandarin. With some relief he eventually located Ton Quang Phiet, who took him to meet To Huu. After conveying his message, Hoe was told that the safety of the royal family was assured. Returning to the palace, Hoe went directly to the emperor's private lounge, where he recalls:

> Bao Dai hastened in and appeared almost ready to embrace me. The sound of Buddhist chants, the prayers to Jesus Christ coming from the inner chambers, suddenly ceased. Both the queen mother [a Buddhist] and the empress Nam Phuong [a Catholic] came out to see me.[141]

138. Hoang Anh, "Nho lai cuoc Khoi Nghia," 40–41. Ban Nghien Cuu Lich Su Dang Tinh Thua Thien, *So thao Lich Su Cach Mang*, 67–69. Hoang Anh, Le Tu Dong, et al., *Binh Tri Thien*, 32–34, 72–73, 113, 115–16, 151.

139. According to Pham Khac Hoe, *Tu Trieu Dinh Hue*, 65, the ministers present were Tran Trong Kim, Tran Van Chuong, Tran Dinh Nam, Trinh Dinh Thao, Vu Van Hien, and Nguyen Huu Thi. The fact that the cabinet had resigned on the 20th seems to have been ignored.

140. Pham Khac Hoe asserts that he drafted the abdication edict on the evening of 20 August and kept it in his pocket for the opportune moment. Bao Dai says that he prepared the edict with the help of his cousin and faithful adviser Vinh Can.

141. Pham Khac Hoe, *Tu Trieu Dinh Hue*, 65–67. Hoe admits, however, that the royal family's attitude quickly cooled toward him, as he was now considered

The worst fears of the royal family, that a crowd would sweep into the palace, killing, looting, and burning, now subsided.

Formal proceedings began at the sports stadium at about 4:00 P.M., with thousands of people having to stand outside because the inside was packed. To Huu declared the end of both imperialist and feudalist systems and the establishment of a revolutionary people's regime. Many were surprised at To Huu's youth, but delighted by his Hue accent. He then introduced Ton Quang Phiet as chairman of the Thua Thien provisional revolutionary people's committee. Phiet read a short prepared statement and the meeting concluded. Late into the night, groups continued to march around the town in quasi-military formation, singing and chanting slogans.[142] A poem subsequently sought to capture the passionate mood of Hue on the 23d:

> Four thousand years our chests were crushed.
> Today at noon a mighty wind swells them again.
> Suddenly the heart turns sun,
> There is a bird in our hair which hops and dances.
> How joyful, delightful the song it sings!
> Wind, O wind, become a tempest, a typhoon.
> Unroll and raise the flag,
> So much blood, so much youth!
> Star so golden and beautiful, fly through the air!
> I fall into the stream of men,
> A whirlpool sweeps me along.
> O heavens! My greedy ears can no longer bear so much music
> From ten thousand directions the sound of tramping feet.
> Vietnam! Vietnam, ten thousand years![143]

Bao Dai had second thoughts on the 24th. After he informed the royal family council of his intention to abdicate, some members expressed dis-

---

perhaps to be a long-standing agent of the Viet Minh. Meanwhile, Tran Trong Kim had apparently taken refuge in Ambassador Yokoyama's office, but he agreed to leave the next day and was not arrested. *CMCD*, 12:76. Pham Khac Hoe may have brokered an understanding with the Viet Minh whereby no ministers of the Kim cabinet would be jailed.

142. Ban Nghien Cuu Lich Su Dang Tinh Thua Thien, *So thao Lich Su Cach Mang*, 69–71. Trinh Xuan An, 199–200. Hoang Anh, "Nho lai cuoc Khoi Nghia," 40–41. *CMTT*, 2:86. Hoang Anh, Le Tu Dong, et al., *Binh Tri Thien*, 155–57. The provincial committee of seven included at least two men not previously associated with the Viet Minh: Buu Tiep, a teacher; and Nguyen Tai Duc, former mandarin of Phu Vang district, a heavily Catholic area.

143. Portion of "Hue Thang Tam" [Hue in August], an anonymous poem apparently composed soon after the events, translated in Nguyen Khac Vien and Huu Ngoc, *Vietnamese Literature* (Hanoi, 1983[?]), 704–5.

may and urged him to reconsider.[144] No one seriously considered putting the young crown prince, Bao Long, on the throne in Bao Dai's place. Nor did anyone else volunteer. The emperor sought practical options, to no avail. Bao Dai was also unhappy that the stated leader of the provisional government was someone called Ho Chi Minh, not Nguyen Ai Quoc. Pham Khac Hoe sought out the eminent scholar Dao Duy Anh, who unearthed a number of pseudonyms for Quoc in the documentary sources, but Ho Chi Minh was not among them. Remembering that one of the royal cabinet members, Vu Van Hien, had only recently returned from Hanoi, Hoe was able to ascertain from him that the two men were almost surely one. Based on this information, Bao Dai cabled Hanoi an invitation to the chairman of the provisional government to come to Hue to accept authority.[145] The next day the abdication edict was posted outside the palace, as well as cabled to Hanoi, Saigon, and every province of central Vietnam.

Bao Dai's abdication edict stands very much in the Confucian literary tradition, yet most of its content is modern, a product of nationalist discourse dating back to Phan Boi Chau and Phan Chu Trinh in the first decades of the twentieth century.[146] On the one hand, we find the classical rhetoric of a thwarted ruler chastising himself for not living up to the lofty accomplishments of his dynastic forebears, not unlike that of Emperor Tu Duc in the 1870s, who had anguished in edicts about his individual incapacity to prevent further French incursions. On the other hand, Bao Dai placed himself proudly in the immediate patriotic context, claiming to be stepping aside to avoid further domestic conflict, inviting all parties and social classes to join him in support of the Democratic Republic, and asking the new government to treat all the parties that had struggled for Vietnam's independence fraternally, "even though these did not always follow the popular movement." On the personal level, he asked only that the new

144. Pham Khac Hoe, *Tu Trieu Dinh Hue*, 70. Bao Dai signed a separate statement to the royal family, which is reprinted in Nguyen Ky Nam, *Hoi Ky*, 215–16.

145. Pham Khac Hoe, *Tu Trieu Dinh Hue*, 68–69. *Cuu Quoc* [National Salvation] (Hanoi), no. 32 (27 Aug. 1945).

146. The abdication edict seems to have been composed in Vietnamese, although following standard court procedure a classical Chinese text may exist as well. The Vietnamese text is reproduced in *Cuu Quoc*, no. 33 (29 Aug. 1945), as well as in Nguyen Ky Nam, *Hoi Ky*, 214–15. A French translation appears in *La République* (Hanoi), no. 1 (1 Oct. 1945), and much later in Bao Dai, *Le Dragon*, 120–21. English translations can be found in *Vietnam: The Definitive Documentation of Human Decisions*, ed. Daniel Gareth Porter, vol. 1 (New York, 1979), 62–63; *Viet-Nam Crisis: A Documentary History*, ed. Allan W. Cameron, vol. 1 (Ithaca, N.Y., 1971), 49–50; and *New Cycle in Asia*, ed. Harold Isaacs (New York, 1947), 161–62.

authorities care for the dynastic temples and royal tombs, and promised to allow no one to "utilize our name, or the name of the royal family, to sow dissension among our compatriots" (an affirmation Bao Dai himself was to violate less than a year later). At the national level, Bao Dai explicitly conceded authority to the government of the Democratic Republic without any negotiation of terms, and asserted that he would be happy to "be a free citizen in an independent country."

Citizens in Hue who read posted copies of the abdication edict were deeply moved, causing ICP uprising leaders to warn Pham Khac Hoe against any further provocation of the "backward emotions of the masses."[147] From the point of view of these ICP militants, Bao Dai should have denounced the evils of his feudalist ancestors and openly admitted his puppet status under the French. In their eyes, it was not the prerogative of Bao Dai to concede an authority that he had never possessed, but to acknowledge that the people had seized power away from the Japanese imperialists and their Vietnamese lackies. However, ICP leaders in Hanoi, presumably appreciating the awe in which many Vietnamese still regarded their king, were clearly quite pleased by Bao Dai's statement, above all the repeated affirmations of support for the Democratic Republic.

It had already been decided to send Tran Huy Lieu, deputy chairman of the National Liberation Committee, to Hue to accept Bao Dai's abdication in a public ceremony.[148] Together with Nguyen Luong Bang, representing the Viet Minh General Headquarters, and Cu Huy Can, included perhaps because of his literary status and membership in the Vietnam Democratic Party, Lieu needed first to borrow Western suits from functionaries in the former Tonkin Kham Sai's Office, then find gasoline for two cars commandeered from the French-owned Stai garage. Departing Hanoi early on the 27th, the drivers found progress slowed repeatedly by crowds on the road waving Viet Minh flags, each group wanting the government delegates to stop, meet the local committee, and give a speech. The crowds were not accidental, cables having been sent in advance to each province along the route, yet people were willing to wait patiently for many hours, even at

147. Pham Khac Hoe, *Tu Trieu Dinh Hue*, 71. The ICP message was delivered via Ton Quang Phiet.

148. As of the morning of 27 August, presumably owing to cable transmission difficulties, Tran Huy Lieu in Hanoi was still not aware that the abdication edict had been issued on the 25th, although he knew the basic contents. In the name of the provisional government, Lieu sent a message urging Bao Dai to "officially promulgate [your] abdication to set the minds of the people at rest" and informing him that the government delegation was about to come to Hue. See dossier "Phuong sach doi pho voi thoi cuoc 1945," in AOM, INF, GF 58.

night or in heavy rain, in anticipation of the delegation's arrival. Lieu—slight, bespectacled, and a skilled orator—frequently climbed on a table or the top of one of the autos to address an assembly, recalling for the audience the bitter days of colonial enslavement, describing the general insurrection sweeping the country, and urging everyone to unite to defend Vietnamese independence and build a happy, prosperous nation. People in some places were not yet familiar with the "modern" customs of applauding and responsive yelling of slogans and preferred instead to beat drums and blow horns, or simply offered a deferential "yes" when queried rhetorically. In one village an elderly scholar presented Lieu with a poem in classical Chinese celebrating the "new dynasty," shrinking back from shaking hands, but adding, allegedly with tears in his eyes, that he had never expected to live long enough to witness such a transformation.[149]

Arriving in Hue at noon on 29 August, the government delegation was taken directly to the sports stadium, where some people had been camped since the 27th. Group after group filed past the rostrum, saluting and chanting slogans. That afternoon, Lieu, Bang, and Can received Pham Khac Hoe at the headquarters of the revolutionary people's committee, formerly the offices of the French résident. Hoe requested that the new government care for the royal tombs and dynastic temples, treat the royal family without discrimination, and permit former mandarins to contribute to the country's future according to their "attitudes and abilities." Accepting those requests, Lieu then instructed Hoe that following the abdication ceremony, Bao Dai would be expected to vacate the palace, all property except the personal effects of the emperor, empress, and queen mother would revert to the revolutionary state,[150] and any future rituals at the tombs or temples would require government permission. Hoe promised to persuade Bao Dai to accept these conditions, then conveyed the emperor's personal wish that the royal banner be allowed to fly one last time when he read the abdication edict publicly the next day. Hoe also suggested that the delegation's automobiles drive directly through the middle entrance of the Zenith (*Ngo Mon*) gate, a privilege previously reserved for the

149. Tran Huy Lieu, "Tuoc An Kiem cua Hoang De Bao Dai" [Taking the Seal from Emperor Bao Dai], in *NCLS*, no. 18 (9-1960): 46–48. Huy Can, "Vao Hue: Nhan su thoai vi cua Bao-dai" [Entering Hue: Accepting Bao Dai's Abdication], *Nhan Dan* (Hanoi), 30 Aug. 1970, 3. Cu Huy Can, "The Last Moments of a Dynasty," *Vietnam Courier* (Hanoi), 7 Sept. 1970, 8. Hoang Anh, "Nho lai cuoc Khoi Nghia," 41.

150. Anticipating this issue, Hoe already had spent a day conducting an inventory of palace property. Pham Khac Hoe, *Tu Trieu Dinh Hue*, 72, 74.

monarch and the French governor-general. Lieu agreed to both proposals. At 4:30 P.M., Bao Dai greeted the delegation on the front steps of the Kien Trung Palace, using the polite third-person "grandfather" (*ong*) to refer to each member, and styling himself in the impersonal "I" (*toi*). Prior to this meeting, delegates had debated how to address the retiring monarch, agreeing that "Your Imperial Highness" (*Hoang Thuong*) and "Sire" (*Be Ha*) were no longer appropriate, yet also rejecting anything insulting. Eventually they had settled on "Excellency" (*Ngai*). Conversation remained stilted, except for Bao Dai's expression of delight at being able to transfer authority to the "famous revolutionary Nguyen Ai Quoc."[151]

On the afternoon of 30 August, a crowd gathered in front of the Zenith gate to witness the last act in a thousand-year drama of Vietnamese monarchy.[152] Once again the cars went through the middle entrance, this time stopping at the foot of the gate, where Pham Khac Hoe and Prince Vinh Can greeted the government delegation. At the head of the steps, Bao Dai received them solemnly, wearing embroidered imperial robes, a golden turban, and glass-bead shoes. With the aid of loudspeakers, Tran Huy Lieu introduced himself and read a cable just received, announcing that Chairman Ho Chi Minh would read the Declaration of Independence three days hence in Hanoi. Then Bao Dai read his abdication edict with considerable emotion, getting a big ovation when he expressed his happiness to be a free citizen in an independent country.[153] For some in the audience, it seemed sad to hear the emperor speak for the first time ever when it was also his final act as monarch.[154] The royal standard was pulled down slowly, to be replaced (again) by the yellow star on a red background, amid applause and a 21-gun salute. Members of the Frontline Youth, who only ten days earlier had saluted with the face of the hand outward, now employed the Viet Minh clenched-fist salute. Bao Dai formally presented the royal regalia to Tran Huy Lieu, who almost dropped the seven-kilogram gold seal as he

151. Ibid., 74–76. Huy Can, "Vao Hue," 3. Tran Huy Lieu, "Tuoc An Kiem," 49–50. Huy Can and Tran Huy Lieu recall the pronoun issue a bit differently from each other; I have leaned toward the former. See also Alexander B. Woodside, *Community and Revolution in Modern Vietnam* (Boston, 1976), 231–32.

152. Estimates on the size of this crowd vary dramatically. Cu Huy Can, "Last Moments," 7, claims 50,000–60,000. Pham Khac Hoe, *Tu Trieu Dinh Hue*, 77, says "tens of thousands." Bao Dai, *Le Dragon*, 120, recalls only "some thousands." Given the unprecedented nature of the ceremony, one imagines at least ten thousand people coming out of curiosity alone.

153. Buu Tien, "Recollections of a Dramatist," *Vietnam Courier* (Hanoi), 9-1988, 29.

154. Thach Ha, *Mat Troi Chieu*, 33.

lifted it up for the crowd to see, which would have been bad luck indeed. Cu Huy Can noticed that the royal sword, although sheathed in magnificent jade inlay, had specks of rust on the blade. Following a prepared speech by Lieu, Bao Dai caught the delegation off guard by asking for a souvenir of the occasion; after brief consultation, Nguyen Luong Bang took one of their own Viet Minh lapel badges and pinned it on Bao Dai, while Can led the crowd in a number of rousing cheers for "Citizen Vinh Thuy." When the former emperor had taken his leave, a mass march was organized through the streets on the left bank of the Perfume River and across the Trang Tien Bridge.[155]

On the morning of 31 August, Ton Quang Phiet brought Pham Khac Hoe an urgent cable from the provisional government inviting "Mr. Vinh Thuy" to come to Hanoi as "Supreme Adviser" as soon as possible. Although Phiet put a good face on it, saying that only the great revolutionary Nguyen Ai Quoc would do something so original, Hoe could not help but think again of the tragic fates of Louis XVI and Czar Nicholas II. Breaking the news to a dismayed Bao Dai, Hoe argued that it was an offer he could not refuse. During the next two days, as Bao Dai prepared to leave, there were anguished scenes in the lesser buildings of the palace complex, with relatives who remained behind wondering what would happen to them and employees asking about back pay and future prospects. The most poignant dilemmas involved several surviving wives of the emperor Khai Dinh (r. 1916–25), and even one spouse of the emperor Dong Khanh (r. 1885–89).[156]

There can be little doubt that the ICP and the provisional government mainly wanted control over the person of the former monarch, although the gesture of making Bao Dai "Supreme Adviser" had obvious political and diplomatic rewards. In Hue, Viet Minh leaders worried about possible Japanese or French attempts to "rescue" Bao Dai. On 24 August, Japanese troops had tried halfheartedly to liberate the former premier Pham Quynh, Ngo Dinh Khoi, Ngo Dinh Huan, and others from the Hue jail. On the 28th, a six-man French commando team parachuted in twenty kilometers north of the royal capital, with orders to make contact with Emperor Bao Dai. Local Viet Minh adherents, impressed by documents identifying the team as official Allied representatives, invited the Frenchmen to take up resi-

155. Pham Khac Hoe, *Tu Trieu Dinh Hue*, 77–79. Cu Huy Can, "Last Moments," 7. Tran Huy Lieu, "Tuoc An Kiem," 50–51. Thach Ha, *Mat Troi Chieu*, 33. David Alexander, "Reviving Hue—Vietnam's Broken Heart on the River of Perfumes," *Smithsonian* (Washington, D.C.), June 1986, 53–54. Bao Dai, *Le Dragon*, 120–21, mistakenly recalls this public ceremony as occurring on the 25th.
156. Pham Khac Hoe, *Tu Trieu Dinh Hue*, 80–88.

dence in a local church pending higher authorization to proceed to Hue. After several days investigation, however, ICP members in Hue decided that the mission aimed to link up with French personnel detained by the Japanese, as well as with procolonial Vietnamese mandarins at court. In a subsequent violent altercation, four commandoes were killed, and the two others imprisoned until June 1946.[157]

These incidents not only influenced the ICP decision to move Bao Dai but probably sealed the fate of Pham Quynh and his fellow inmates—all of whom were apparently executed in the first week of September.[158] The killing of Pham Quynh in particular stunned Vietnamese intellectuals, many of whom admired his tireless cultural endeavors, although often disapproving of his enthusiastic collaboration with the French colonial administration. The violent death of Ngo Dinh Khoi and his son made any future Viet Minh rapprochement with this influential Catholic clan most unlikely, although Ho Chi Minh would try later to win over his younger brother, Ngo Dinh Diem.[159]

Southern Vietnam

With its heritage of frontier settlement, millenarianism, and entrepreneurial hustle, Cochinchina (Nam Ky; Nam Bo) was bound to react to external events differently from Tonkin and Annam. As we have seen, wartime security controls and Allied bombing raids had largely isolated southern intellectuals from political developments further north. General

157. Philippe Devillers, *Paris-Saigon-Hanoi: Les Archives de la guerre, 1944–1947* (Paris, 1988), 73. Hoang Anh, "Nho lai cuoc Khoi Nghia," 41–42. An additional four French commandoes were captured on 8 September when they disembarked from a motorized junk at the Thuan An estuary near Hue. René Charbonneau and José Maigre, *Les Parias de la victoire: Indochine–Chine 1945* (Paris, 1980), 368. According to ICP sources, the men on the junk kept calling out "Où est Pham Quynh, où est Bao Dai?" Local Viet Minh adherents offered to serve as guides, then captured three commandoes once out of sight of the junk. Hoang Anh, Le Tu Dong, et al., *Binh Tri Thien*, 74. While the story may be apocryphal, there is no denying that the French were sufficiently out of touch with recent developments to be capable of making such an error.

158. Ban Nghien Cuu Lich Su Dang Tinh Thua Thien, *So thao Lich Su Cach Mang*, 74–75. Although anticommunist Vietnamese subsequently accused the ICP of killing prominent individuals in August–September 1945 according to a predetermined hit list, I have found no evidence to substantiate this charge.

159. Days before the killing of Ngo Dinh Khoi, a third brother, Ngo Dinh Thuc, was listed in Hanoi as one of the "prominent personalities" invited to meet the new minister of the interior, Vo Nguyen Giap. *Cuu Quoc* (Hanoi), no. 34 (31 Aug. 1945): 1. No mention was made of the influential status Thuc had already attained within the Catholic clerical hierarchy, even though that presumably accounted for the invitation.

Tsuchihashi had responded only slowly to Hue government proposals to incorporate Cochinchina into Imperial Vietnam, and the process, once it commenced, was quickly swamped by news of the Japanese surrender and then the abdication of Emperor Bao Dai. Suddenly, southern nationalists not affiliated with the Viet Minh were deprived of key planks in their platform. Even had incorporation begun earlier, it is likely that southern Vietnamese functionaries, entirely unaccustomed to administrative procedures further north, would have found ways to sabotage the effort.

On 15 August, hearing confirmation of Tokyo's capitulation, the small standing group of the ICP Regional Committee headed by Tran Van Giau picked a four-man Uprising Committee, then proceeded to discuss the crucial questions of the timing, location, and tactics of the insurrection, and contacts with the Japanese.[160] Although some members wanted to make decisions immediately, others had strong reservations, leading to a stopgap agreement to convene an "enlarged" meeting of the Regional Committee on the evening of the 17th at Cho Dem, in the Saigon suburbs. At that meeting, which extended through the afternoon of the 18th, with the participants fueling themselves repeatedly with bowls of chicken soup (*chao ga*), there was bitter argument between those who insisted on quick action and those anxious either to receive instructions first from ICP center in Tonkin or to be assured at least that any southern initiative would not occur in isolation. Those attending could not even agree whether the objective was to seize power or simply to organize mass demonstrations celebrating Allied victory and future cooperation with a progressive French government. By way of temporary compromise, it was decided to continue mobilizing adherents locally for future action while awaiting developments in the north.[161] Behind these policy differences lurked the unresolved southern ICP leadership dispute between the "Vanguard" (Tien Phong) group, led by Tran Van Giau, and the "Liberation" (Giai Phong) group, led

160. According to Huynh Van Tieng, "'Len Dang' lam Cach Mang" ["Setting Out" to Make Revolution], *Dac San* (Ho Chi Minh City), 8-1987, 24, the Uprising Committee included Tran Van Giau, Huynh Van Tieng, Nguyen Van Tran, and "a military comrade."

161. Interview with Tran Van Giau, Ho Chi Minh City, 19 Mar. 1988. *Dia Chi Van Hoa Thanh Pho Ho Chi Minh* [Geography, History, and Culture of Ho Chi Minh City], ed. Tran Van Giau, vol. 1 (Ho Chi Minh City, 1987), 346–50. In a 1989 interview with Stein Tønnesson, Tran Van Giau revealed that two prominent southern communists, Bui Cong Trung and Nguyen Van Nguyen, argued against the insurrection, while a third, Nguyen Van Tao, remained skeptical. Tønnesson, *Vietnamese Revolution*, 383. Since all three of these men were respected veterans of 1930s struggles, it was impossible for Giau to ignore them entirely.

by Nguyen Van Tay from his headquarters in Can Tho. Separately each group tried to make its case with ICP center, Ha Huy Giap of "Vanguard" already having been dispatched to attend the Tan Trao meetings, and Nguyen Thi Thap of "Liberation" apparently arriving in Hanoi on the 18th or 19th, as mentioned above. Exactly what discussions took place with Truong Chinh and others has never been revealed, but Ha Huy Giap's claim to be second-in-charge of the Cochinchina Regional Committee was refused, and it proved impossible for him to return to Saigon until after 2 September,[162] suggesting that he was deliberately delayed.

News of the Viet Minh takeover in Hanoi on 19 August reached Saigon quickly by cable and was spread by word of mouth throughout the Mekong Delta in the next few days. On the evening of the 20th, the ICP's Saigon City Committee organized a general meeting to introduce the Viet Minh publicly, as well as to encourage members of the Vanguard Youth (Thanh Nien Tien Phong) to identify openly with the Viet Minh.[163] The next day, tracts signed by the Viet Minh appeared around Saigon, asserting its legitimacy as a powerful resistance organization that had fought alongside the USSR, China, and America against the Vichy French and the Japanese.[164] The Viet Minh flag was raised over a large working-class restaurant, where ICP cadres proceeded to recruit young men into "assault" units. The "enlarged" ICP Regional Committee reconvened at Cho Dem, yet failed once again to reach a consensus. A number of participants now voiced their fear that Japanese units in the south, unlike those in Hanoi, would suppress any Viet Minh attempt to take power. With no guerrilla bases to withdraw to, the outcome might be a bloodbath, worse than the terrible losses that had followed the uprising of 1940. However, these participants at the meeting eventually did agree to a plan whereby Tan An province, forty kilometers southwest of Saigon, and with two key bridges on the main road to My Tho, would be used to test Japanese intentions.

On the evening of the 22d, Viet Minh adherents in Tan An took control of the provincial and district offices there with no opposition from either the Japanese or the Vietnamese Civil Guard. They followed this up the next day with an armed demonstration of eleven thousand people marching behind both ICP and Viet Minh flags. On receiving this news, ICP representatives at Cho Dem quickly approved plans to seize power in Saigon on the night of 24–25 August. Following the Bolshevik precedent of Oc-

162. Interview with Tran Van Giau, Ho Chi Minh City, 25 Mar. 1980.
163. *CMTT*, 2:226–27. Huynh Van Tieng, "'Len Dang,'" 24–25.
164. Devillers, *Histoire*, 141.

Figure 29. Tran Van Giau, key ICP leader in Cochinchina. Courtesy of Archives d'Outre-Mer, Aix-en-Provence.

tober 1917, Tran Van Giau and his comrades felt no need to camouflage the key role of the Communist Party.[165]

Other political groups in southern Vietnam were far from quiescent. Members of the United National Front, a freshly formed coalition of religious groups and secular nationalists, although stunned to hear of Tokyo's surrender, and worried about being accused by the Allies of collaboration, nonetheless managed to blitz Saigon with manifestos opposing French imperialism and foreign invasion, calling for the elimination of reactionaries, yet also urging preservation of public order.[166] On 19 August, three well-known nationalists identified with the Front left in a Japanese convoy for consultations in Hue, only to be stopped by a barricade in Nha Trang and compelled to turn back.[167] On 21 August, the Front sparked a march through the streets of Saigon of up to one hundred

165. *Dia Chi Van Hoa*, ed. Tran Van Giau, 350–51. Interview with Tran Van Giau, Ho Chi Minh City, 25 Mar. 1980. *CMTT*, 2:227, 326.

166. Document reprinted in *Tan A* [New Asia] (Saigon), no. 73 (17 Aug. 45).

167. Tønnesson, *Vietnamese Revolution*, 383, 404. The three nationalists were Ngo Dinh Diem, Tran Van An, and Vu Dinh Dy.

thousand citizens.[168] Behind the scenes, however, leaders of organizations affiliated with the Front found it impossible to work together. The Trotskyist "Struggle" (Tranh Dau) group called publicly for resignation of the new southern Kham Sai, Nguyen Van Sam, as well as for establishment of people's committees and implementation of radical land reform in the countryside.[169] This contrasted with a large march on the 23d by Cao Dai, Civil Guard, and Red Cross groups designed specifically to uphold the royal government and the new Kham Sai.[170] More seriously, on the 22d, banners and leaflets had announced incorporation of the Vanguard Youth into the Viet Minh, information that, if confirmed, left other United National Front affiliates with very few firearms in the event of an armed confrontation.[171]

Also on the 22d, Front leaders argued bitterly with one another over whether or not to cooperate with the ICP under the Viet Minh banner. Surprisingly, they chose to invite Tran Van Giau, chairman of the ICP Regional Committee, to address their meeting. Giau was large for a Vietnamese, with a deep voice and vehement manner; if he was angered, his face would darken and his gestures become menacing. Like many intellectuals, he punctuated his arguments with French expressions. Giau's main point on this occasion, that the Front would be seen by the incoming Allies as a creation of the Japanese, hence reducing the chances of international recognition of Vietnam's independence, was difficult for anyone present to refute.[172] Phan Van Hum, a Trotskyist, was delegated to continue confidential discussions with Giau; he came back on the 23d opposed to any Front amalgamation with the Viet Minh.[173] Then came rumors of the impending abdication of Emperor Bao Dai, which for some Front participants raised serious doubts about the political legitimacy of their endeavor. One newspaper associated with the Front complained that any acceptance by the emperor of Viet Minh demands for a democratic republic would violate his earlier promise to convene a nationwide assembly to

---

168. Nguyen Ky Nam, *Hoi Ky*, 50.

169. Colton, "Failure of the Independent Political Movement," 261, 263–64.

170. Tran Quang Vinh, "Lich Su Dao Cao Dai trong thoi ky 'Phuc Quoc,' 1941–1946" [History of the Cao Dai Religion in the "National Restoration" Period, 1941–46] (Saigon, 10 Sept. 1946), 44–45. A copy of this report was kindly provided me by the author in 1967.

171. Nguyen Ky Nam, *Hoi Ky*, 51. See chapter 2 for details of the Vanguard Youth's establishment and earlier activities.

172. Devillers, *Histoire*, 141. John T. McAlister, Jr., *Vietnam: The Origins of Revolution* (New York, 1969), 203. Colton, "Failure of the Independent Political Movement," 266.

173. Colton, "Failure of the Independent Political Movement," 267.

determine Vietnam's future form of government. On the same page, however, the paper published a Front announcement that endorsed the democratic republican system and a Viet Minh government.[174] Front members also agreed to march in the Viet Minh demonstration planned for the 25th, which meant accepting the rule that a Viet Minh flag accompany the flag of each of the participating organizations. The chief of the Cao Dai paramilitary units, Tran Quang Vinh, mindful of his public image as a close friend of the Japanese, agreed to step aside in favor of a colleague who was expected to work constructively within the Viet Minh framework.[175]

On the morning of 24 August in downtown Saigon, a large Communist Party hammer-and-sickle flag fluttered in the breeze over the clinic and residence of Dr. Pham Ngoc Thach, chairman of the Vanguard Youth, attracting a crowd of curious spectators. Japanese officers also stopped to take a look, then drove away. It may have been on this day that Pham Ngoc Thach and Tran Van Giau met with Field Marshal Terauchi, hoping to obtain weapons. Giau recalls telling Terauchi, "You are defeated, now it's our turn to fight the white imperialists," deliberately tossing in "white" to exclude the Japanese. Terauchi replied that orders from the Shōwa emperor forbade him to surrender Imperial Army weapons to anyone except the Allies, but added that confiscated French equipment might be another matter. Then, in a remarkable gesture of support, Terauchi presented Thach with his short sword and gave Giau a stunning silver revolver, an act the two Vietnamese also took to mean that the marshal did not intend to commit suicide.[176]

At 6:00 P.M. on the 24th, deliberately imitating the behavior of Lenin in Petrograd in 1917, Tran Van Giau appeared before a public meeting to declare the insurrection under way. When a young associate, Tran Bach

174. *Hung Viet* (Saigon), no. 21 (24 Aug. 1945): 1. This was probably the last issue of *Hung Viet*.

175. Tran Quang Vinh, "Lich Su Dao Cao Dai," 45–48, 51–52. Interview with Tran Quang Vinh, Saigon, 12 Apr. 1967.

176. Interview with Tran Van Giau, Ho Chi Minh City, 12 Feb. 1990. The way in which Tran Van Giau told this story, complete with vivid gestures and facial expressions, suggested that he had been deeply impressed by Japanese attitudes and behavior in general, although he might well reject that interpretation. He also indicated that the 15 August surrender was a big surprise, as he fully expected the Japanese to await Allied landings on the main islands and try to take as many of the enemy as possible to a common death. Stein Tønnesson also interviewed Tran Van Giau in Ho Chi Minh City, November 1989, and this meeting with Terauchi came up toward the end. Pham Ngoc Thach allegedly told Terauchi, "You've been defeated by the whites. It's up to us to keep going." No mention was made by Tran Van Giau of the silver revolver. My thanks to Tønnesson for sharing his notes.

Dang, unfurled a banner proclaiming "All Power to the Viet Minh, Long Live the Indochinese Communist Party!" a great roar went up and people threw anything that came to hand into the air, even their shoes.[177] The Viet Minh Uprising Committee issued operational orders to activists from the ICP, Vanguard Youth, Vietnam Democratic Party, General Labor Group, Public Servants Union, and "several religious organizations," probably a contingent of young Catholics and devotees from a number of Buddhist temples identified with the Vanguard Youth.[178] It was the armed and reasonably disciplined Vanguard Youth units, however, that received the most important occupation assignments, including the treasury, power plant, water-pumping station, main PTT building, Cochinchina Governor's Palace, main fire station, local police stations, and key bridges. Units were also sent to positions close to several Imperial Army garrisons, as well as to the main French civilian quarter and the camp of the Eleventh Colonial Infantry Regiment, where French soldiers were interned. No attempt was made to enter facilities guarded by Japanese troops, which included the Governor-General's Palace, the Bank of Indochina, the military docks along the Saigon River, and Tan Son Nhut Airport. Also avoided for the moment was the main police station on Catinat Street, which was commanded by Huynh Van Phuong, a Trotskyist.[179]

By 10:00 P.M., Vanguard Youth messengers reported all objectives secured. The only drama occurred at the Governor's Palace, where a team of seven young government clerks, armed with one pistol, walked past the two guards at the entrance, replaced the royal standard on the balustrade with the Viet Minh flag, nonchalantly locked the Kham Sai in his bedroom, and waited for sunrise. At 6:00 A.M., a squad of working-class Viet Minh adherents approached the building and almost shot their predecessors in error. When the Kham Sai's staff showed up for work, they were lined up to listen to a reading of the uprising order and a Viet Minh proclamation.[180]

---

177. Interview with Tran Bach Dang, Ho Chi Minh City, 17 Mar. 1988.

178. For brief descriptions of Catholic and Buddhist involvement in the events of August 1945 in southern Vietnam, see the articles by Vo Van Khai and Ky Phuong in *Dac San* (Ho Chi Minh City), 8-1987, 26–30.

179. Huynh Van Tieng, "'Len Dang,'" 25. *Dia Chi Van Hoa*, ed. Tran Van Giau, 352. Interview with Tran Van Giau, Ho Chi Minh City, 25 Mar. 1980. *CMTT*, 2:227–28.

180. Ung Ngoc Ky, "Chiem Dinh 'Kham Sai'" [Seizing the Palace of the "Imperial Delegate"], *Dac San* (Ho Chi Minh City), 8-1987, 33–35. Mai Van Bo, "Phong Trao Thanh Nien, Sinh Vien va Tri Thuc trong nhung Nam 40" [The Youth, Student, and Intellectual Movement in the 1940s], *Tap Chi Khoa Hoc Xa Hoi* (Ho Chi Minh City), no. 18 (4-1993): 28.

Huynh Tan Phat, a young architect, was assigned the task of constructing a fifteen-meter-high tower overnight at the intersection of Bonard
(now Le Loi) and Charner (Nguyen Hue) boulevards to display the names
of the new administrative committee. A speakers' platform and parade
review stand was also thrown together behind the Cathedral, at the intersection of Norodom (Le Duan) and Blancshubé (Pham Ngoc Thach)
boulevards. During the early morning hours of the 25th, several hundred
thousand peasants entered Saigon from the adjoining provinces, together
with smaller but more organized contingents coming from points as far
south and west as Long Xuyen province. By 9:00 A.M., when formal
proceedings began, there may have been half a million rural and urban
citizens swamping the downtown streets of Saigon, perhaps one-third of
them armed with bamboo spears, pitchforks, machetes, and shotguns.[181]
The Vanguard Youth's flag with its red star on a yellow field had largely
been replaced by its inversion, the Viet Minh's yellow star on a red field,
together with a sprinkling of ICP banners. Red and white banderoles
proclaimed "Long Live Independent Vietnam!" and "All Power to the Viet
Minh!"

Tran Van Giau led off with a rousing speech to those within earshot of
the few loudspeakers, a band played the "Internationale" and "Len Dang"
(Setting Out), a recently composed patriotic song by Luu Huu Phuoc, then
the crowd formed itself into a huge procession through the main streets of
the city, guided by parade wardens in uniform sporting white gloves.
According to one source, "progressive" French civilians and some British
and American POWs joined the parade, carrying Viet Minh flags and
singing the "Internationale" with everyone else.[182] At noon, Dr. Pham
Ngoc Thach read the names of the newly established Southern Provisional
Administrative Committee (Uy Ban Hanh Chanh Lam Thoi Nam Bo) from
the balcony of the Mayor's Office, asking for and receiving a loud roar of
confidence from the crowd below. Following speeches by representatives of
the Viet Minh and the ICP Regional Committee, the procession continued
in a festive mood until 6:00 P.M., concluding with another rendition of "Len

---

181. Most Vietnamese communist sources put the crowd on 25 August at a
million or more, half of them armed. Given the total population of Saigon and
nearby provinces in 1945, I think this must be an exaggeration. On the other hand,
based on eyewitness accounts, particularly references to specific streets all packed
with people, half that number does not seem unreasonable.

182. Huynh Van Tieng, "'Len Dang,'" 25. One of these individuals was a
French citizen named Sauterey, who joined the ICP either before or after the events
of 25 August and was killed two months later. *Co Giai Phong* (Hanoi), no. 51 (5
Nov. 1945): 2.

Dang" plus the "Thanh Nien Hanh Khuc" (Youth March).[183] Even according to French eyewitnesses, some of whom feared for their lives, the entire demonstration of the 25th in Saigon passed off in orderly fashion, without incident, although demonstrators did enjoy toppling colonial statues, with the notable exception of that of the Swiss bacteriologist Dr. Alexandre Yersin, founder of the Indochinese branch of the Pasteur Institute, who discovered the plague bacillus in Hong Kong in 1894 and developed a vaccine against it.[184] The next day, Nguyen Van Sam, imperial delegate for the south, cabled Hue his resignation, news of which greatly pleased Ho Chi Minh in distant Hanoi, as it meant that the last legal representative of the monarchy was gone.[185]

Behind the scenes, however, all was far from settled in southern Vietnam. If the Viet Minh was designed to encompass all patriotic, anti-imperialist elements, as claimed, many in Saigon found it unacceptable that the new nine-member Southern Provisional Administrative Committee contained five avowed ICP members and four individuals who had already demonstrated their willingness to obey ICP orders.[186] No attempt had been made to incorporate Hoa Hao, Cao Dai, or Catholic representatives. As for the Trotskyists, ICP leaders tipped their hand on 25 August by forcibly evicting Huynh Van Phuong and his comrades from the Catinat Street police station.[187] To complicate matters, on the 25th, the Japanese publicly released 101 political prisoners of various tendencies who had been serving time in Con Son Island (Poulo Condore).[188] Several days later, the spiritual

---

183. *Dia Chi Van Hoa*, ed. Tran Van Giau, 352–54. Tran Van Giau, "May dac diem cua cuoc Khoi Nghia Thang 8 o Sai Gon" [Special Characteristics of the August Insurrection in Saigon], *Dac San* (Ho Chi Minh City), 8-1987, 18. *CMTT*, 2:228–29. The music and lyrics for "Len Dang" and "Thanh Nien Hanh Khuc," also composed by Luu Huu Phuoc, can be found in *Dac San*, 8-1987, 20, 42.

184. Devillers, *Histoire*, 141–42. *Les Lendemains qui ne chantaient pas (1944–1947)*, ed. Gilbert Guilleminault (Paris, 1962), 247.

185. Patti, *Why Viet Nam?* 203.

186. The five ICP members were Tran Van Giau, Nguyen Van Tao, Nguyen Van Tay, Duong Bach Mai, and Nguyen Phi Oanh. Among the other four, Pham Ngoc Thach was a clandestine ICP member. Hoang Don Van represented the General Labor Group, Ngo Tan Nhon the Independent Nationalist Party, and Huynh Van Tieng the Democratic Party.

187. Duong Bach Mai was made police chief of Nam Bo. Nguyen Van Tran was placed in charge of the Saigon police force. T. N., "Nhung ngay dau . . . " [The First Days . . .], *Dac San* (Ho Chi Minh City), 8-1987, 40.

188. Thanh Giang and Thanh Nguyen, "Vung Len" [Rise Up], *Dac San* (Ho Chi Minh City), 8-1987, 15. Nguyen Van Sam, the imperial delegate, had insisted on his arrival in Saigon that all political prisoners be released. One of the first beneficiaries was the ICP member Tran Van Tra, who was trucked from Saigon

leader of the Hoa Hao, Huynh Phu So, allegedly drawing on Sûreté dossiers obtained by Huynh Van Phuong, accused Tran Van Giau of having been a secret agent for the French. In the eyes of some, Giau appeared to confirm such suspicions by choosing to meet with Jean Cédile, France's "commissioner of the Republic for Cochinchina," who had just arrived by parachute (see chapter 8).[189]

The Mekong Delta

Tran Van Giau and his Uprising Committee had concentrated on Saigon, arguing that success there would make takeovers in other locations relatively easy. ICP and Vanguard Youth groups in nearby provinces were instructed to encourage as many people as possible to converge on the city, participate in seizure of power, and then return home to complete the process. That is the way it happened in large part. From adjacent Cho Lon, for example, a large contingent of overseas Chinese workers took part in the demonstration in Saigon on 25 August, chanting slogans in various Chinese dialects as well as Vietnamese; the next day, local officials in Cho Lon readily conceded authority to the Viet Minh.[190] In Bien Hoa, railway workers made available a locomotive and train cars sufficient to carry six hundred delegates of diverse organizations in style to Saigon. Others walked behind a huge ICP banner that had been hastily sewn the previous afternoon. Returning to Bien Hoa town, these demonstrators had no difficulty taking power on the 26th and were surprised only at the bonus of three hundred firearms in the local armory.[191] In Gia Dinh province, by way of contrast, ICP members in several districts felt no obligation to wait for orders from higher echelons to rise, convening rallies as early as the 20th,

---

prison to Cao Dai headquarters on the 22d, offered a position, and allowed to refuse politely and depart. Tran Van Tra, "Cach Mang Thang Tam: Mo dau doi linh cua toi" [The August Revolution: The Beginning of My Life as a Soldier], *Dac San*, 8-1987, 13.

189. Nguyen Ky Nam, *Hoi Ky*, 29–30, 88. According to Tran Van Giau at our interview in Ho Chi Minh City on 19 March 1988, members of the Giai Phong ICP group also said they suspected him of being a "lackey" (*tay sai*) of the French and Japanese. If so, this demonstrates how deep the southern ICP cleavage had become in late August 1945, and helps to explain why, even forty-three years later, the surviving leaders of the two groups have not sat down together to discuss the events in question.

190. Han Truong Vu contribution in "Hao Khi Nhung Ngay Cach Mang Thang 8 tai Saigon" [Days of Courage in the August Revolution in Saigon], *Dac San* (Ho Chi Minh City), 8-1987, 42–43. *CMTT*, 2:235–36.

191. *CMTT*, 2:310–11.

then during the next few days forcing local officials to turn over keys, weapons, dossiers, and public monies. After walking to Saigon early on the 25th, some Gia Dinh demonstrators reversed tracks that same afternoon and marched straight into the compound of the provincial chief, whose surrender was secured without bloodshed.[192]

In a number of provinces more distant from Saigon, ICP members either received early private encouragement from Tran Van Giau's group to mount their own insurrections, despite refusal of the "expanded" Regional Committee to authorize such action until the 23 August meeting, or they took matters into their own hands without reference to ongoing deliberations elsewhere.[193] Because other groups were also moving into the political vacuum created by sudden Japanese passivity and the apparent collapse of the Vietnamese royal government in Hue, a delay of more than a few days was seen as potentially disastrous by many local ICP militants. In Chau Thanh district of My Tho province, where the ICP's "Liberation" faction predominated, teams acted from the evening of the 20th to persuade former colonial soldiers in seventeen small posts to relinquish their weapons. Brandishing those fifty-two firearms, insurgents took the nearby district seat of Cai Lay on the 23d, leaving the provincial town for the 26th.[194] Vanguard Youth leaders, who only a few days prior had provided a useful screen and some legitimacy among urbanites, now were bypassed entirely at the big My Tho rally.[195] In Bac Lieu province, deep in the delta, ICP members turned a government celebration on 23 August of Nguyen Van Sam's appointment as Kham Sai into an opportunity to debut the Viet Minh, not to mention relieving twenty soldiers of their weapons. That same day, they received orders from the ICP Regional Committee to take power on the 25th, which proved surprisingly easy.[196] In Thu Dau Mot, rubber

192. T. B., "Vanh Dai Do" [Red Turban], *Dac San* (Ho Chi Minh City), 8-1987, 17–18. *CMTT*, 2:317–18, 322–23.

193. There is ample evidence in vol. 2 of *CMTT* that a number of ICP provincial-level representatives to the Cho Dem meeting on 21 August returned home determined to take power as soon as possible despite the lack of formal authorization. Whether they made up their minds individually or were quietly encouraged remains unclear. Do Thuc Vinh, *Mua Ao Anh* [Season of Mirages] (Saigon, 1962), a quasi-fictional narrative, refers specifically (139–40) to a poster signed by Tran Van Giau that appeared in My Tho on 21 August calling for general demonstrations on the 25th.

194. *CMTT*, 2:332–33.

195. Do Thuc Vinh, *Mua Ao Anh*, 141–46.

196. *CMTT*, 2:293–94. The speed with which the Regional Committee's decision of 23 August reached distant Bac Lieu suggests some coded use of the telegraph system.

plantation workers gravitated toward the Loc Ninh–Saigon railway line, then walked south to Ben Cat and the provincial seat, where they joined with Vanguard Youth groups, townspeople, farmers, and a sprinkling of Stieng minority members to sing revolutionary songs, salute the Viet Minh flag, listen to speeches, yell "Long Live the ICP!" and eventually occupy government facilities.[197]

In most provinces of southern Vietnam, however, it was leaders of the Vanguard Youth, not the ICP, who took the insurrectionary initiative, moving with remarkable consistency to seize control on 25–26 August. For example, in Ba Ria, sixty kilometers southeast of Saigon, members of the Vanguard Youth persuaded more than ten thousand unarmed peasants to converge on the provincial seat early on the morning of the 25th, prudently carrying both red- and yellow-starred flags. After extended discussions with a Japanese officer and the Ba Ria provincial chief, it was agreed that the latter could continue working for a few days under the Viet Minh banner, after which he would give way to a provisional people's committee.[198] In Go Cong, Vinh Long, Tra Vinh, Sa Dec, and Rach Gia, meetings between Vanguard Youth leaders and provincial chiefs paved the way for reasonably smooth transfers of authority, followed invariably by popular demonstrations and rousing speeches. In Ha Tien, the provincial chief became a member of the new people's committee. In Thu Dau Mot, the Uprising Committee agreed to appoint the deputy provincial chief as chairman of the people's committee.

Most demonstrations sported a mixture of Vanguard Youth yellow flags with red stars and Viet Minh red flags with yellow stars. In Ben Tre province, cloth merchants quickly sold out both colors; sewing shops worked day and night to meet the sudden demand for Viet Minh flags. ICP cells in some provinces still insisted on giving equal status to their hammer-and-sickle banners. Perhaps the most complex "battle of flags" occurred in Long Xuyen, where a mass meeting at noon on the 25th began with a mix of Vanguard Youth, Viet Minh, ICP, and even royal government flags. Angry cries of "Take down the trigram!" soon disposed of the Hue standard. ICP members then began to pressure for elimination of the Vanguard Youth flag, but were opposed by about a thousand town dwellers, "children of upper-class families" according to communist sources.[199] A similar con-

197. *Lich Su Dang Cong San Viet Nam Tinh Song Be* [History of the Vietnam Communist Party in Song Be Province], ed. Nguyen Minh Duc and Huynh Lua, vol. 1, *1930–1945* (Ho Chi Minh City [?], 1989), 192–210.

198. *CMTT*, 2:241–42.

199. Ibid., 246–49, 260–65, 269–73, 278–81, 302–5, 340–42, 387–94, 400–402, 407. Ban Nghien Cuu Lich Su Dang Tinh Uy An Giang, *Lich Su Dang Bo Tinh An*

frontation occurred in neighboring Chau Doc province, with ICP members pushing Vanguard Youth leaders off the platform and ordering all yellow banners with red stars to be put away.[200] At a rally in My Tho on 26 August, the trigram was hauled down the flagpole with propriety and a single Viet Minh banner, already styled the "national flag" (*quoc ky*), raised in its place. When instructions passed through the crowd to fold up hundreds of Vanguard Youth flags, some people complied, others did not.[201]

Within a few weeks, Vanguard Youth flags had disappeared, and ICP banners could be seen in only a few locations. The red flag with yellow star flew triumphant. However, behind all those Viet Minh standards in the Mekong Delta marched a wide variety of groups, often possessing only the barest knowledge of the movement they now fervently upheld and claimed to represent. Much policy confusion was evident. In some provinces, government employees were invited to stay on, in others they faced permanent dismissal and harassment. While Viet Minh adherents in many locations quickly confiscated property belonging to absent French colonials or to Vietnamese families regarded as lackeys of the French or the Japanese, there was no consistency as to what to do next—whether, for example, to nationalize acquired property or simply distribute it to worthy followers. Some of the most substantial confiscations took place around Can Tho, including tens of thousands of hectares of French-owned plantation land, hundreds of thousands of tons of paddy or rice stored in warehouses, several thousand head of cattle, and all the boats and ferries belonging to the Société d'exploitation forestiére de l'ouest. In Tra Vinh province, and probably elsewhere, peasants seized the land of Vietnamese landlords, as well as rice stores and agricultural equipment, without particular reference to the political history of the victims. ICP members urged peasants to keep calm and "wait for directions from higher echelons," with mixed results.[202]

Some of the groups taking over provincial or district administration rapidly turned their attention to executing individuals who allegedly "owed many blood debts to the people." In Ben Tre town, for example, the public was urged to go to the sports field on 27 August, where people listened to an ICP member read the multifold charges against a Sergeant Hien of the Civil Guard, endorsed the death penalty by acclamation, and watched Hien

Giang (1927–1945) [History of the Party Apparatus in An Giang Province (1927–45)] (An Giang, 1986), 172–80.

200. Ban Nghien Cuu Lich Su Dang Tinh Uy An Giang, *Lich Su Dang Bo Tinh An Giang*, 187–88.

201. Do Thuc Vinh, *Mua Ao Anh*, 42–44.

202. *CMTT*, 2:279, 358.

shot. Four canton chiefs, an education official, a noncommissioned officer, and an accused enemy agent met similar fates in the Ben Tre countryside. In Tra Vinh province, Le Quang Liem, a prominent landlord and member of the Constitutionalist Party, was executed along with a Sergeant Cang, alleged to have hidden French firearms and attempted to sabotage the new revolutionary administration. In Tan An, two colonial army adjutants who had taken part in violent suppression of the 1940 Nam Ky uprising were tracked down and killed, while in Vinh Long a former province chief, three canton chiefs, three former Sûreté agents, and the head of the local public works department met similar fates.[203] In My Tho, several members of the professions who were considered too pro-French were tied up and drowned, their bodies being left to float downriver.[204]

As in northern and central Vietnam following word of Tokyo's capitulation, Japanese commanders in the south quickly began to shift small units toward the main towns, brushing aside Vietnamese attempts to induce them to relinquish Imperial Army weaponry, but sometimes donating captured French weapons or leaving stocks unattended. The biggest arms success was in Thu Dau Mot province, twenty-five kilometers north of Saigon, where deserting Japanese soldiers led the Viet Minh to hidden stores containing several thousand guns and tons of ammunition and explosives. On the opposite side of Saigon, in Cho Lon province, Viet Minh members uncovered another store of explosives, as well as some firearms. In Ben Tre, by contrast, a Japanese platoon created a furor when it moved to eject the new provincial revolutionary committee from its offices in order to install a radio transmitter; eventually, the Japanese agreed to shift to an alternate site. The only reported shoot-out between Viet Minh and Imperial Army forces came on 28 August in Tay Ninh, when the Japanese surrounded the provincial people's committee building to try to gain release of some Vietnamese prisoners. A market strike the next day seems to have persuaded the Japanese to withdraw.[205]

Tay Ninh also saw leaders of the Cao Dai religious sect divide into pro–Viet Minh and anti–Viet Minh camps, the beginnings of a schism that would assume serious proportions later on. On 26 August, Viet Minh adherents allocated only one seat for a Cao Dai representative on the new people's committee of Tay Ninh province, the Cao Dai's spiritual heartland.

203. Ibid., 263, 272, 279–80, 326.
204. Do Thuc Vinh, *Mua Ao Anh*, 149.
205. *CMTT*, 2:236, 263–64, 304–5, 371–72. *Lich Su Dang Cong San Viet Nam Tinh Song Be*, ed. Nguyen Minh Duc and Huynh Lua, 197.

In Ben Tre, a Cao Dai leader sent to collect donations from the faithful was arrested by the new provincial people's committee. ICP cadres in Sa Dec province deliberately included Cao Dai, Hoa Hao, and Independent Nationalist Party representatives on the people's committee, while making sure the ICP controlled the chairmanship, police force, and self-defense organization.[206] The lack of any consistent stance toward the Cao Dai—an important regional force by anyone's reckoning—reflected the southern ICP's more general incapacity in the year or two preceding the August 1945 upheavals to plan or to communicate effectively. Meanwhile, Cao Dai adherents tried hard to persuade Japanese commanders at several different locations to give them stocks of captured French weapons. Tran Quang Vinh secured a promise from Imperial Army Staff Headquarters in Saigon of supplies of firearms, which never materialized, although he did receive ten truckloads of cloth, sandals, soap, matches, medicine, and gasoline, together with twenty truckloads of rice and at least a million piastres in cash.[207]

The most serious domestic altercations anywhere in Vietnam quickly occurred between Viet Minh and Hoa Hao adherents in at least five provinces of the lower Mekong Delta, despite efforts by Nguyen Van Tay and the Giai Phong ICP group to achieve a working alliance. Furious that Tran Van Giau had excluded his people from the Southern Provisional Administrative Committee, Huynh Phu So, the fiery, unpredictable founder of the Hoa Hao, dispatched Chung Ba Khanh, a wealthy landowner and recent convert, to the delta with instructions to protect and advance Hoa Hao political interests, if necessary by throwing ICP members and other opponents off the newly formed provincial and district people's committees. Anticipating a confrontation, ICP and Vanguard Youth activists in Chau Doc province had already disarmed and jailed three hundred Hoa Hao believers, provoking a series of demonstrations aimed at gaining release of these people.[208] The first real test came in Long Xuyen province, where eager Vanguard Youth members had taken control of the town of Cho Moi, only seven kilometers from the village of Hoa Hao itself, with barely a passing nod to adherents of that religion.[209] In response, Chung Ba Khanh

206. *CMTT*, 2:263, 341.
207. Tran Quang Vinh, "Lich Su Dao Cao Dai," 49–50. Presumably to avoid charges of corruption, Vinh carefully describes how he distributed most of this bounty to Cao Dai subordinates.
208. *CMTT*, 2:380. A Hoa Hao offer to divide responsibility for seizing key points in Chau Doc was angrily rejected by local ICP leaders. Ban Nghien Cuu Lich Su Dang Tinh Uy An Giang, *Lich Su Dang Bo Tinh An Giang*, 180.
209. Ngu Giang, "Nho ve nhung ngay Khoi Nghia Nam Xua" [Recalling Those Insurrectionary Days of Long Ago], *An Giang*, no. 381 (14 Aug. 1983): 2. According

urged local Hoa Hao members to arm themselves and march into Cho Moi to demand reorganization of the administrative committee. On 29 August, more than thirty thousand Hoa Hao adherents converged on Cho Moi, but they were forcibly dispersed by better-armed units brought in from Long Xuyen town and adjacent Chau Doc province by ICP and Vanguard Youth leaders. The next day a number of local Hoa Hao leaders were tracked down and arrested. As a sop, one member of the Hoa Hao was made commissioner of social affairs on the provincial revolutionary committee.[210]

Attention now focused on the town of Can Tho, nicknamed the "Western Capital" (Tay Do), and considered the key to the lower Mekong Delta by all political elements. Already the Hoa Hao felt tricked at having their local leader, Tran Van Soai (Nam Lua), take part in the Viet Minh delegation to Saigon for the demonstrations on 25 August, only to see the ICP seize power in Can Tho the following day. Backed up by Nguyen Xuan Thiep, a Trotskyist adviser to Huynh Phu So, Chung Ba Khanh urged the Hoa Hao faithful to reverse the ICP success. Rather than repeat mistakes made in Long Xuyen, however, Hoa Hao members concentrated first on appropriating firearms from local landlords and taking control of several district administrations before moving on Can Tho. In Saigon, meanwhile, Huynh Phu So urged Tran Van Giau to accept some form of power-sharing arrangement under the Viet Minh mantle. Rather than parley, ICP and Vanguard Youth leaders in Can Tho called for and received loyal armed reinforcements from five nearby provinces.

On 7 September, Nguyen Xuan Thiep, together with Huynh Phu So's younger brother and Tran Van Soai's son, led about twenty thousand Hoa Hao demonstrators to converge on the town of Can Tho from three directions, yelling such slogans as "Arm the population to oppose the French imperialists!" and "Cleanse the Southern Administrative Committee of corrupt elements!" Halting the crowds at the outskirts, Hoa Hao leaders entered town to try to persuade the chairman of the Can Tho Administrative Committee, Tran Van Kheo, to approve peaceful demonstrations in support of "independence." Cables exchanged with Saigon failed to resolve the impasse. At daybreak on the 8th, shooting broke out at several locations, hundreds of Hoa Hao demonstrators being killed or wounded. All three

---

to a close associate of Tran Van Giau's, Hoa Hao leaders demanded explicitly that ten Mekong Delta provinces be turned over to them. Interview with Duong Quang Dong (Nam Dong), Ho Chi Minh City, 19 Mar. 1988.

210. *CMTT*, 2:391–93. Hue-Tam Ho Tai, *Millenarianism and Peasant Politics in Vietnam* (Cambridge, 1983), 138.

demonstration leaders were captured on the 8th and executed a month later. Hoa Hao adherents were quick to exact revenge for the Can Tho shootings, however, killing hundreds of ICP and Vanguard Youth cadres at other locations, dumping their bodies in tied-up clusters to float down rivers and canals or exhibiting them at public sites.[211]

To further complicate matters, members of the substantial Khmer minority in the Mekong Delta, excited by rumors of national independence for Cambodia, decided to take matters into their own hands too, mounting public demonstrations and forming armed youth groups. In Vinh Long province, Vietnamese villagers feared a violent Khmer uprising directed against them. In Chau Doc, bands of Khmer moved back and forth across the border, sometimes pillaging whole villages and causing the new Vietnamese provincial administrative committee to organize their suppression. When news arrived of a French military unit returning to Phnom Penh, Viet Minh adherents began to worry about the Khmer being used to sabotage the Vietnamese Revolution. Nonetheless, Khmer residing in southern Vietnam were encouraged to join the Viet Minh and participate in local government committees in the name of anti-imperialist solidarity. In Soc Trang, a Khmer liberation youth group that agreed to change its name to "National Salvation Youth" in accordance with Viet Minh nomenclature became an important force in the province. In Ha Tien, Vietnamese cadres made sure to include Khmer as well as Chinese representatives on district and canton administrative committees. With characteristic patriotic zeal, Kinh activists in several provinces took to calling ethnic minority participants "New Vietnamese" (which must have grated on some minority ears).[212]

One hundred kilometers off the coast of southern Vietnam, the three thousand inmates on the prison island of Con Son sensed that something dramatic was happening when the Japanese garrison suddenly departed on 25 August, taking with them all French personnel and smashing the radio facility. Le Van Tra, the prison administrator recently appointed by the royal government, was left with a few score Vietnamese wardens, a Civil Guard unit of questionable reliability, dwindling food supplies, and no idea

---

211. A rare Hoa Hao account of these events can be found in Nguyen Long Thanh Nam, "Cuoc bieu tinh 9-1945 tai Can Tho cua PGHH de lam gi?" [What Was the Purpose of the Hoa Hao Buddhist Demonstration in September 1945 in Can Tho?], *Duoc Tu Bi* (Santa Fe Springs, Calif.), 15 Nov. 1987, 8–14. See also Hue-Tam Ho Tai, *Millenarianism*, 138–39, and *CMTT*, 2:356–61.

212. *CMTT*, 2:272, 281, 287, 381, 407. *Lich Su Dang Cong San Viet Nam Tinh Song Be*, ed. Nguyen Minh Duc and Huynh Lua, 183–84.

when assistance would arrive from the mainland. Tra responded by opening the gates during daytime and agreeing to a proposal from the inmates that they form a "citizens' council" composed of representatives from both the prison staff and the almost two thousand political prisoners, but excluding the common criminals. By the first days of September, one radio receiver had been repaired, enabling the inmates to pick up news of the outside world. Upon hearing of events in Hanoi, the exhilarated ICP committee, chaired by Pham Hung, organized a flag-raising ceremony and begin to print a news sheet titled *Doc Lap* (Independence). Some three hundred members of a hastily formed "island defense unit" commenced to train daily with about forty rifles and pistols obtained from the Civil Guard and Le Van Tra. Meanwhile, the Viet Minh on the mainland managed to bring together a small ship and thirty-two sampans to go to Con Son on 16 September. Seven of the sampans were scattered by a storm, but the remaining vessels carried most of the political prisoners back to a rousing welcome on the 23d.[213] Any later and the British and French might well have sealed off the island.

Given the lack of organizational hegemony in the Mekong Delta, as well as the preexisting political, religious, and ethnic animosities, it is unlikely that anyone could have prevented serious outbreaks of domestic violence following the Japanese surrender. Although Vanguard Youth units and ICP cells possessed weapons and a quasi-military structure, in many locations around the delta this grouping was a mere marriage of convenience, without ideological consensus, or any awareness of what the Viet Minh was supposed to represent beyond defense of Vietnam's independence.

The ICP itself was bedeviled by internal differences. In Bien Hoa, for example, two provincial party committees competed for authority. In Chau Doc, while two different provincial party committees did agree to merge, separate Viet Minh organizations continued to operate at cross-purposes until early 1946. In Cho Lon and Long Xuyen provinces, the split was between "old" Viet Minh groups formed before the Japanese takeover on 9 March and new ones that cropped up in subsequent months. Perhaps most seriously, the ICP's "Liberation" group headquartered at Can Tho continued to question the authority of the Nam Bo Regional Committee dominated by Tran Van Giau's "Vanguard" group.[214] There can be little doubt that such intramural confusion contributed to the ICP's erratic, poorly

213. Ban Nghien Cuu Lich Su Dang Dac Khu Vung Tau—Con Dao, *Nha Tu Con Dao, 1862–1945* [Con Son Island Prison, 1862–1945] (Hanoi, 1987), 168–78. Many of these Con Son veterans immediately became involved in fighting the French.

214. *CMTT,* 2:237, 309, 354, 379, 387.

coordinated reaction to domestic challenges in the south after 25 August, and left it ill prepared to deal with the arrival of Allied forces.

Conclusion

Viewed from Hanoi, the upheavals around Vietnam that followed the news of Japan's surrender seemed cut out of the same cloth: people marched on administrative bureaus, Japanese troops watched in stunned silence, mandarins fled, the red flag with yellow star fluttered everywhere, citizens committed themselves joyfully to defense of Vietnam's independence, and there was practically no violence. This was what the new central leadership wanted to see, and in large part what the public wanted to be told had happened. Very soon this characterization of "the August Revolution" had circulated nationwide and become engraved in the popular imagination, even among those who had experienced a rather different set of events.[215]

From the somewhat laborious province-by-province descriptions offered in this chapter, it should be evident that events in late August did not fit any single pattern. In some places, power was seized, not by a mass of demonstrators, but by a tiny coterie. While the Japanese were undoubtedly stunned by the Shōwa emperor's announcement, this did not prevent them from playing significant roles in numerous local dramas. Many mandarins did flee, yet others turned over their seals of office with dignity, and not a few accepted invitations to join the new administration. It was the demoralization or breaking away of key elements of the existing regime—combined with popular discontent and disaffection among the intelligentsia—that caused events to move so rapidly in mid August. The Viet Minh banner did quickly become the preeminent national symbol, but many who carried it proudly had almost no idea what the Viet Minh organization represented. Almost all Vietnamese were ecstatic at the idea of independence, even among those who had benefited from the French colonial presence, but this did not prevent individuals or groups from taking a variety of actions that had nothing to do with independence. Finally, as we have seen, there was, in fact, a fair amount of bloodshed, although not by prior design of the leaders of the insurrection and less than in many such affairs elsewhere.

---

215. By early September, based on confidential reports from provincial committees and a profusion of citizens' petitions, leaders in Hanoi must have known that the characterization was woefully inadequate, yet it served a valuable political purpose, and has continued to dominate the history books to this day.

For all the diversity in the way people acted, however, there was a psychological aspect to the August insurrection(s) in which millions shared. It included a desire for moral purification, the readiness of young people to take the initiative (and of older people to follow), a willingness to behave unorthodoxly, to speak directly, to ignore taboos, to refuse to worry about one's personal future or safety. Alongside the iconoclasm and the bravado, there was a longing to identify with something certain, to find new order in one's soul and throughout the universe. In this context, Viet Minh slogans, songs, and flags both prompted individuals to take unprecedented action and provided a new sense of belonging, which ICP leaders were quick to build upon in subsequent months. Youthful heroics and the wish for order came together in the rush to join self-defense (*tu ve*) units, where demonstrated initiative and discipline counted for more than social origin, schooling, or wealth, and where men and women could associate openly without necessary reference to marriage or compromising the woman. The quest for guns, and knowledge of how to use them, became more important than careers, money, or sex.

The complete collapse of royal government authority and quick formation of revolutionary committees throughout Tonkin, Annam, and Cochinchina helped shape the course of the Vietnamese Revolution quite as much as events in Hanoi. The proliferating revolutionary committees gave the Revolution a depth and resilience that no amount of top-level planning or maneuvering could have provided. This vitality at the local level would also impose certain restrictions on higher-echelon leaders, whether in the ICP Central Committee, the Viet Minh General Headquarters, or the nascent provisional government of the Democratic Republic of Vietnam. On the other hand, without firm guidance from Hanoi, provincial, district, and village committees might well have marched off in many different directions, canceled each other out, or even disintegrated—to the benefit of the perceived enemies of the republic. It was this dialectic between center and locality, only dimly visible at the end of August, that lay at the institutional and social core of the Vietnamese Revolution for years thereafter.

8   A State Is Born

On the morning of 20 August, the young leaders of the insurrection in Hanoi could congratulate themselves on a job well done. Key government installations had been secured with practically no loss of life. Electricity and water-pumping systems continued to operate. Trains and buses came and went, albeit erratically because of Red River flooding. Most telegraph and telephone lines were either functional or being repaired rapidly.[1] The Japanese showed no signs of reversing the Viet Minh takeover. Perhaps most important, tens of thousands of ordinary people, rural as well as urban, had taken part enthusiastically in the seizure of power in Hanoi. Desperately eager to cast off seventy years of subjugation by foreigners, prepared to identify with the still somewhat mysterious Viet Minh, wishing to believe that it was possible to sustain independence and freedom amid the new perils of Chinese and British troop occupation, these people would reject any return to old patterns of behavior. They could either become a disciplined force to protect the gains of 19 August or quickly dissipate their political potential in looting and mob violence.

That morning, a Northern Region Revolutionary People's Committee was announced, with Nguyen Khang as chairman, Le Trong Nghia responsible for liaison with the Japanese, Nguyen Duy Than in charge of government bureaus, and Tran Dinh Long as "adviser."[2] A spate of official

---

1. Nguyen Khang et al., "Ha Noi Khoi Nghia" [Insurrection in Hanoi] (Hanoi, 1970), 143.
2. On the evening of 20 August, "Provisional" was appended to the committee's title, and two individuals added for administration (Nguyen Van Tran) and for propaganda (Ngo Xuan Dan). A Hanoi committee also was appointed, with Nguyen Huy Khoi as chairman. Nguyen Quyet was placed in charge of "military forces" until arrival a few days later of Vuong Thua Vu. *Cach Mang Thang Tam* [The Au-

instructions went out the same day. Formalizing the telephone calls of the previous afternoon (see chapter 6), the committee directed all northern province chiefs by telegraph to fly the Viet Minh flag, tell citizens to do likewise, and "continue administrative activity until further orders."[3] The committee also issued a plan to mobilize large numbers of citizens to shore up the city's threatened dike system.[4] The PTT was ordered to retain all its Vietnamese employees but to sack any remaining French personnel.[5] Any private person still possessing a radio transmitter was told to deposit it for "temporary use" by the committee. In the existing "special situation," the committee decided to reiterate royal government press censorship regulations, editors being instructed to bring their copy to Viet Minh headquarters at 101 Gambetta Street for screening.[6] When journalists who attended a press conference on the 20th asked when censorship restrictions would be lifted, an unnamed cadre in charge of propaganda replied, "very soon."[7] All political groups, including those who had disagreed previously with the Viet Minh, were encouraged to present themselves to the former Kham Sai's Office to discuss how to deal with French preparations to "trample down the people of Vietnam once again."[8]

In the afternoon of the 20th, rumors swept the city of a plot between Vietnamese members of the former colonial Sûreté and the French to seize control. The new Viet Minh authorities claimed to have uncovered a cache of enemy firearms, ammunition, and even poison gas. Other rumors had it that the Japanese had released and rearmed French soldiers, or that French prisoners had broken out and were attacking Vietnamese in nearby Ha

---

gust Revolution] (cited below as *CMTT*), vol. 1, ed. Tran Huy Lieu (Hanoi, 1960), 54–55. Nguyen Quyet, *Ha Noi Thang Tam* [Hanoi in August] (Hanoi, 1980), 185. Bui Huu Khanh, *Ha Noi trong thoi ky Cach Mang Thang 8* [Hanoi in the Period of the August Revolution] (Hanoi, 1960), 54. Tran Dinh Long was killed by Vietnam Nationalist Party adherents several months later.

3. Uy Ban Nhan Dan Cach Menh Bac Ky to all provinces, 20 Aug. 1945, in AOM, INF, GF 66. The handwritten draft of this message, apparently penned by Nguyen Khang, is on *Mairie de Hanoi* stationery.

4. Tung Hiep, in *Trung Bac Chu Nhat* (Hanoi), no. 259 (26 Aug. 1945): 24. *CMTT*, 1:56–57.

5. UBNDCM Bac Bo to Nha Buu Dien, 20 Aug. 1945, in AOM, INF, GF 45.

6. Dossier 96, "Kiem duyet 1945," in AOM, INF, GF 38.

7. *Cuu Quoc* (Hanoi), no. 31 (24 Aug. 1945): 2. Five days later, the new chief of information and propaganda, Tran Huy Lieu, told a press conference that censorship must continue, because "many covert, dark types of opposition" continued to threaten the Revolution. *Cuu Quoc*, no. 34 (31 Aug. 1945): 2. My thanks to Allison Thomas and Christopher Goscha for making August editions of this newspaper available to me.

8. Dossier 95, "Thong Cao 1945," in AOM, INF, GF 48.

Dong.[9] Thousands of Hanoi residents poured onto the streets, armed mostly with machetes, knives, and spears, prepared, as one periodical said, to "drink the blood of the invader."[10] Citizens in some neighborhoods threw up barricades of furniture, bullock carts, and rickshaws.[11] A further spate of petitions, now addressed to the revolutionary government and not the Kham Sai, called for detention of French nationals and acquisition of firearms from the Japanese or the Americans.[12] The Regional Committee issued a statement urging people to ignore stories about French prisoners attacking Hanoi, insisting that Japanese commanders intended to keep the "French bandits" in jail.[13] On the 23d, it ordered any individuals searching French houses to cooperate with the Kenpeitai, to be cautious about detaining French nationals, and to forward information on abduction cases in previous days.[14]

Amid this popular outcry, French civilians not under forced detention found themselves molested, their homes pillaged under the placid gaze of Japanese soldiers. As many as two hundred French nationals were incarcerated briefly, then released.[15] The fear of being massacred gripped French residents of Hanoi.[16] Even the arrival of a single Allied airplane over the city in the early evening of the 20th caused excited speculation among the French about their imminent deliverance.[17] Two days later, after careful preparations against possible Viet Minh ambush, the Japanese shifted a contingent of French prisoners from Hoa Binh province back to the Citadel in Hanoi.[18] Those prisoners were more fortunate than the former resident

9. Bui Huu Khanh, *Ha Noi*, 56.
10. Tung Hiep, in *Trung Bac Chu Nhat* (Hanoi), no. 260 (2 Sept. 1945): 5–6.
11. *CMTT*, 1:55–56.
12. Files of petitions in AOM, INF, GF 66 and GF 69.
13. Dossier 95, "Thong Cao 1945," in AOM, INF, GF 48. Privately, the Hanoi police bureau reported that Japanese guards were no longer vigilant in guarding the Pasquier and Carnot camps. Three French prisoners had escaped, two of them being captured by the police. Undated message from Ty Canh Sat, in dossier 83, "Quan Su (linh tinh) 1945," AOM, INF, GF 38.
14. "Huan Lenh" file in AOM, INF, GF 68.
15. "Le Viet Minh," Service de Documentation Extérieure et de Contre-Espionnage report, 25 June 1946, 37, in AOM, INF, c. 138–39, d. 1247. This report appears to have been drafted in December 1945, but not circulated until six months later.
16. Philippe Devillers, *Histoire du Vietnam de 1940 à 1952* (Paris, 1952), 137.
17. Françoise Martin, *Heures tragiques au Tonkin (9 Mars 1945–18 Mars 1946)* (Paris, 1948), 137.
18. Georges Gautier, *9 Mars 1945, Hanoi au soleil de sang: La Fin de l'Indochine française* (Paris, 1978), 223–26. This group, which included General Mordant as well as Gautier, had been moved from Hanoi to Hoa Binh on 4 August.

superior of Annam, Jean Haelewyn, and two associates, who, after being shifted from one place to another by their Japanese guards, were suddenly beheaded in distant Kratié, Cambodia.[19]

Allied Representatives Arrive

The Potsdam agreement demarcating China Theater and South East Asia Command at the 16th parallel had been designed to meet wartime operational requirements, not to govern the transition from war to peace in Indochina. Only a few weeks later, however, Allied leaders suddenly needed to designate specific commanders to receive the Japanese surrender in dozens of different locations, all the way from the Kurile Islands in the north to Burma in the west. The Americans held the initiative: drafting of "General Order No. 1" on surrender dispositions began in Washington on 10 August. Although both the State Department and the Joint Chiefs of Staff now favored restoration of French rule in Indochina, no attempt was made to reposition all of Indochina inside South East Asia Command, or even to insert a clause specifying that French troops would accompany Chinese forces to northern Indochina. Washington planners had too many other issues to deal with worldwide, and neither the British nor the French were quick enough in making their wishes felt. On the 14th, a new paragraph was inserted to warn Japanese forces against surrendering to any commander not listed in the order. While designed to encourage the Japanese to resist Communist Chinese efforts to disarm them, this wording also made it improbable that Imperial Army units in Indochina would accede to Viet Minh surrender demands. Once General Order No. 1 was sent by President Harry Truman to other Allied heads of state on the afternoon of the 15th, the likelihood of any country or political group securing substantial modifications was minimal.[20]

The French official most immediately concerned about China Theater jurisdiction was Jean Sainteny, who, from a villa in Kunming, tried desperately with the paltry resources available to him to project French sovereignty over Indochina. On 12 August, Sainteny cabled Paris an urgent warning that the Chinese were inhibiting operations of his commandos and

19. Haut commissariat de France pour l'Indochine, *Neuf Mars 1945–Neuf Mars 1948* (Saigon, 1948), 34. Gautier, *9 Mars 1945*, 225–26.

20. The exception was Hong Kong: complaints from London led President Truman on 21 August to pressure Chiang Kai-shek to accept a change in the order enabling the British to take the Japanese surrender in that colony. Marc S. Gallicchio, *The Cold War Begins in Asia: American East Asian Policy and the Fall of the Japanese Empire* (New York, 1988), 77–85.

raising obstacles to participation by General Alessandri's troops in the liberation of northern Indochina.[21] The next day, Sainteny went further, complaining to Paris that occupation of northern Indochina by the Chinese must be considered "the worst of all possible solutions," and that it would profoundly undermine the prestige of the "white race in the Far East."[22] When French representatives in Chungking tried to recruit American Ambassador Patrick Hurley to their cause, he dutifully reported the conversation to Secretary of State James Byrnes.[23] On the 14th, Byrnes instructed the American ambassador in Paris to inform Foreign Minister Georges Bidault that the operational demarcation at the 16th parallel possessed "no political significance whatsoever," and that the United States was suggesting to both China and Great Britain that they invite French representatives to be present at Japanese surrender ceremonies in Indochina.[24]

This was far less than the French desired. Frustrated through official channels, Paris government sources began from 14 August on to reveal to the press their efforts to obtain American, British, and Soviet agreement to immediate assumption by France of postwar responsibilities in Indochina, which also would require Allied assistance in reequipping military forces and transporting them to the colony.[25] On the 17th, Foreign Minister Bidault insisted publicly that France take part in the capitulation of Japanese forces in Indochina, specifically mentioning the availability of General Alessandri's units in southern China, General Blaizot's 750 men in Ceylon, and two French divisions commanded by General Jacques-Philippe Leclerc de Hautecloque.[26] Such open badgering may well have proven counter-

21. Jean Sainteny, *Histoire d'une paix manquée: Indochine, 1945–1947* (Paris, 1953), 50. Already on 11 August the Chinese government had announced that its troops would be disarming the Japanese in northern Indochina. Philippe Devillers, *Paris-Saigon-Hanoi: Les Archives de la guerre, 1944–1947* (Paris, 1988), 67.

22. Sainteny, *Histoire*, 51. By contrast, Jean de Raymond, head of the Colonial Ministry's office in India, simply requested "firm instruction" from Paris regarding Chinese entry to Indochina. De Raymond to MinCol, 14 Aug. 1945, in AOM, INF, c. 133, d. 1211.

23. Archimedes L. A. Patti, *Why Viet Nam? Prelude to America's Albatross* (Berkeley, 1980), 138–39. W. Macy Marvel, "Drift and Intrigue: United States Relations with the Viet Minh, 1945," *Millennium* (London) 4, no. 1 (1975): 16, 18.

24. Byrnes to Caffery, 14 Aug. 1945, in *Viet-Nam Crisis: A Documentary History*, ed. Allan W. Cameron, vol. 1, *1940–1956* (Ithaca, N.Y., 1971), 45–46.

25. Kenneth E. Colton, "The Failure of the Independent Political Movement in Vietnam, 1945–46" (Ph.D. diss., American University, 1969), 293–94. A very defensive draft accord dealing with administrative and juridical issues raised by the presence of non-French Allied forces in Indochina can be found in "Négociations franco-chinoises, 1945–46," AOM, INF, c. 209, d. 1572.

26. *New York Times*, 18 Aug 1945, 5. As early as June 1945, de Gaulle had ordered General Leclerc to prepare to reoccupy Indochina.

productive in Chungking: on the 11th, General Ho Ying-chin, chief of staff of the Chinese Army, had given General Alessandri assurances about French participation; however, by the 20th, Alessandri was convinced that the Chinese government intended to block return of his troops to Indochina.[27] Alessandri also approached General Wedemeyer about releasing a fleet of air transports to return French units to Indochina in style, but was offered the use of only one French plane. Aside from real shortages of China Theater aircraft and fuel, Wedemeyer knew that Chiang Kai-shek had no intention of allowing French troops to arrive ahead of his own units, most of whom would be required to walk overland to Hanoi or Haiphong.[28] American officers also continued to turn a blind eye to French requests to reequip General Alessandri's units; eventually, French staff officers found money to purchase arms, munitions, vehicles, and clothing that had been pilfered from the Americans by the Chinese.[29]

If regular French troops could not be inserted quickly, another option was to dispatch a small commando contingent directly to Hanoi to try to take control of events. On 12 August, Jean Sainteny called on Archimedes Patti, the OSS member in Kunming responsible for Indochina activities, to seek cooperation in flying to Hanoi as soon as possible. Patti offered only to seek permission for Sainteny and a few assistants to be included in the first "Mercy" flight, designed primarily to seek out and safeguard Allied prisoners of war. After initial rejection, General Wedemeyer's headquarters in Chungking agreed on the 15th that Sainteny plus four staff members could be listed on the flight manifest.[30] When the Americans then delayed takeoff, citing heavy rainfalls, Sainteny managed to locate an Air France Dakota, just arrived from India, whose pilot was willing to take the risk. Arriving at the airport in the early hours of the 17th, they found armed Chinese soldiers preventing any departure. Apparently, the orders had come from General Ho Ying-chin, to ensure that the French did not finesse China's occupation prerogatives. Sainteny angrily accused the Americans of participating in this sabotage of French initiatives.[31] Meanwhile, General Alessandri was also being stymied in separate attempts to

27. Devillers, *Histoire*, 151, 152. René Charbonneau and José Maigre, *Les Parias de la victoire: Indochine–Chine, 1945* (Paris, 1980), 361. Alessandri to Paris, 20 Aug. 1945 (relayed by DGER, 24 Aug.), in AOM, INF, c. 133, d. 1211.

28. Patti, *Why Viet Nam?* 138–40.

29. Charbonneau and Maigre, *Les Parias*, 297.

30. Patti, *Why Viet Nam?* 142–45.

31. Sainteny, *Histoire*, 67–69. François Missoffe, *Duel Rouge* (Paris, 1977), 21–22. French military attaché, Chungking, to Paris, 25 Aug. 1945, in AOM, INF, c. 133, d. 1211. Patti, *Why Viet Nam?* 145–46.

fly to Hanoi.[32] To complete French frustration, word arrived that Lieu-tenant Commander Blanchard, under orders from Sainteny to reach Hanoi by any means possible, had been detained by the Japanese in Haiphong on the 19th.

It is likely that American delays in flying to Hanoi were owing neither to the weather nor to any particular desire to thwart the French, but mainly to the requirement by General Douglas MacArthur, who was in charge of implementing the terms of surrender with the central Japanese authorities, that all Allied theater commanders defer further operations in enemy-occupied territories until it was clear that local Japanese commanders had received their surrender orders from Tokyo.[33] Certainly, a message from General Wedemeyer to Fourteenth Air Force headquarters in Kunming on 17 August ruled out dispatching aircraft of any nationality to Hanoi until the Japanese commander's reaction to Tokyo's capitulation had been as-certained.[34] By the 20th, however, Wedemeyer's deputy, General Mervin Gross, had decided that a "Mercy" flight could proceed as soon as weather permitted; formal clearance was provided in Kunming the next day.[35]

While Sainteny and Alessandri were still fretting in China, DGER Calcutta received permission from Admiral Mountbatten's command to proceed with audacious plans to employ Royal Air Force Special Duty B-24s to parachute French government officials directly into Tonkin, Annam, Cochinchina, and Cambodia.[36] Months earlier, a French commando group fleeing Annam to Laos had reported the practical value of including at least one American as insurance against native attack,[37] and Sainteny's units

32. Colton, "Failure of the Independent Political Movement," 298. *New York Times*, 18 Aug. 1945, 5.

33. Peter Dennis, *Troubled Days of Peace: Mountbatten and South East Asia Command, 1945–46* (Manchester, 1987), 13. Peter M. Dunn, *The First Vietnam War* (London, 1985), 122–23.

34. Sainteny, *Histoire*, 68. Patti, *Why Viet Nam?* 145. R. Harris Smith, *OSS: The Secret History of America's First Central Intelligence Agency* (Berkeley, 1972), 348.

35. Patti, *Why Viet Nam?* 147. Patti used the delay to meet on the 19th with members of the Kunming branch of the Viet Minh, who had just received infor-mation (by shortwave radio?) of the demonstrations in Hanoi on 17 August.

36. Cedille to MinCol, 15 Aug. 1945, relayed by DGER, 16 Aug., in AOM, INF, c. 133, d. 1211. Devillers, *Histoire*, 150. The original plan had been for civilian advisers from the French Ministry of Colonies to accompany any Allied force entering Indochina.

37. L. H. Ayrolles, *L'Indochine ne répond pas* (Saint-Brieuc, 1948), 77, 107–8, 156. An American officer named Hughett, who earlier had managed to flee the Saigon area to northern Annam, joined Ayrolles's team in walking across Laos to China.

operating along the Chinese frontier generally followed this advice, but DGER Calcutta chose to go it alone. Possessing only a tiny smattering of information about events since the Japanese takeover on 9 March, these Gaullist cadres hoped that they would be hailed as antifascist liberators, or at least respected as representatives of the sovereign power in Indochina. Léon Pignon, the Colonial Ministry's specialist on Indochina, stressed that these vanguard officials must know exactly what to say, since "for the Annamites, the letter is more important than the spirit," apparently meaning that form was more important than content. General Alessandri used the identical formula that same day, adding his opinion that the word *indépendance* could be accepted as a way for the Annamites to save face without jeopardizing essential French interests.[38] Neither Pignon nor Alessandri seemed to appreciate that "form" or "face" was no less meaningful to French citizens at this critical moment.

On the evening of 22 August, Pierre Messmer, carrying credentials as "commissioner of the Republic for Tonkin," prepared to parachute in near the Tam Dao mountain spur, some thirty kilometers northwest of Hanoi, together with a radio operator, Warrant Officer Marmont (who had jumped with Major de Langlade the previous year), and Medical Captain André Brancourt, a prewar resident of Indochina. At the last moment, noting the peaceful appearance of Hanoi below, Messmer urged his Australian pilot to drop the three of them directly over the city's Gia Lam airport, but the pilot insisted on sticking to prior orders. After hitting the ground, Marmont was able to make radio contact twice with Rangoon before the team was placed under detention by armed Viet Minh adherents led by a woman, then marched into the hills. All three Frenchmen subsequently became seriously ill and were convinced they had been poisoned.[39] Brancourt died under the curious stares of Vietnamese villagers. Messmer and Marmont were subsequently rescued by a Chinese troop unit and made it to Hanoi in late October.[40]

38. Pignon (Kunming) to Calcutta, 20 Aug. 1945, and Alessandri (Kunming) to Paris, 20 Aug. 1945, both quoted in Devillers, *Paris-Saigon-Hanoi*, 72–73.

39. This is the story according to Paul Mus, "L'Indochine en 1945," *Politique étrangère* (Paris) 11 (1946): 359. See also Dunn, *First Vietnam War*, 38–40. On the other hand, Jean-Michel Hertrich, *Doc-Lap! (L'Indépendence ou la mort!): Choses vues en Indochine* (Paris, 1946), 12, recounts that Captain Brancourt suffered a heart attack and was given the wrong medicine by a local Vietnamese practitioner.

40. Hertrich, *Doc-Lap!* 10–16. Georges Gautier, in *Histoire de l'Indochine: Le Destin, 1885–1954*, ed. Philippe Héduy (Paris, 1983), 249–50. Paul Mus, "L'Indochine en 1945," 359–60, makes a point of contrasting his polite reception in early 1945 with the Messmer team's harsh treatment in late August, when the "mandate

Also on the night of 22 August, Jean Cédile, "commissioner of the Republic for Cochinchina," parachuted with three comrades into the rice paddies of Tay Ninh province, some eighty-five kilometers northwest of Saigon. Like Messmer, Cédile had instructions to reestablish French authority as quickly as possible. His team was surrounded by a crowd of Vietnamese farmers, apparently Cao Dai adherents, who gave way only when a Japanese platoon arrived on the scene. Stripped naked, their hands tightly bound, the French found themselves being interrogated harshly, then forced to march through the night to brigade headquarters. At one point a Japanese officer tested Cédile's mettle by drawing his sword and preparing to decapitate his prisoner, smiling when Cédile refused to be intimidated. Piled aboard a truck still naked, the portly Cédile and his subordinates presented quite a spectacle as they were driven through Vietnamese villages. In Saigon, a French-speaking Japanese colonel, after listening sympathetically to Cédile's story that he was on a fact-finding mission, restored the team's clothing and put them in a schoolroom under loose detention.[41]

As mentioned earlier, the six-man commando team that dropped into Annam just north of Hue suffered a fate worse than any of the others, with four members killed and two incarcerated well into 1946. In Cambodia, by contrast, the eight-member team that parachuted in near Phnom Penh on 29 August found itself not only transported to the city without incident but able to plot the overthrow of the nationalist regime established two weeks earlier.[42] In Laos, additional Force 136 personnel, code-named "Buckmaster," had already been parachuted into several key

---

of heaven" had shifted. Messmer, who later became prime minister of France, remained convinced as late as 1977 that a single planeload of French operatives, if dropped together on 22 August, could have penetrated Hanoi and reversed the Viet Minh's preponderance. See Dunn, *First Vietnam War*, 40–41. It seems more likely that there would have been a spontaneous bloodletting, with French civilians the prime targets and the Japanese forced to restore order pending arrival of Chinese troops.

41. René Pléven, "Reception du Gouverneur Jean Cédile," *Comptes rendus trimestriels des séances de l'Académie des Sciences d'Outre-Mer* (Paris) 37, no. 4 (21 Oct. 1977): 657–58. Mus, "L'Indochine en 1945," 360. Hertrich, *Doc-Lap!* 7–10. Gautier, in *Histoire*, ed. Héduy, 249–50. Devillers, *Histoire*, 153. Dunn, *First Vietnam War*, 45–46. Patti, *Why Viet Nam?* 260, 275. *Dia Chi Van Hoa Thanh Pho Ho Chi Minh* [Geography, History and Culture of Ho Chi Minh City], ed. Tran Van Giau, vol. 1 (Ho Chi Minh City, 1987), 354.

42. David P. Chandler, "The Kingdom of Kampuchea, March–October 1945: Japanese-sponsored Independence in Cambodia in World War II," *Journal of Southeast Asian Studies* 17, no. 1 (Mar. 1986): 89.

locations with instructions to reestablish French administration.[43] On the 29th, Colonel Imfeld, commander of a French unit that had retreated to China in May, returned to Luang Prabang, was welcomed by King Sisavong Vong, and assumed the position of commissioner of the Republic in Laos.[44] Further south, however, Vietnamese residents in Vientiane had mounted demonstrations in favor of independence, and on the 23d they established a provisional administrative committee. A week later, Vietnamese in Savannakhet organized a meeting of some fifteen thousand people, including many Lao, while Vietnamese functionaries who had continued to work following the 9 March coup turned over their offices ceremoniously to local Lao representatives. An envoy of the Viet Minh General Headquarters, Tran Duc Vinh, arrived to provide guidance and up-to-date information on the dramatic developments in Vietnam to the east.[45] Hanoi newspapers printed upbeat bulletins about anti-French activities in Laos. Soon ICP cells in Laos and northeast Thailand were linked in with the Central Committee in Hanoi, initially via Nguyen Chi Thanh in Hue. Whatever the aspirations of the Lao and other ethnic groups, the fear that France would use Laos as a springboard to return in force to northern and central Vietnam prompted ICP leaders to encourage anti-French activities of any kind in that territory.

It was left to Jean Sainteny to establish the first French presence in a part of Indochina occupied predominantly by the "Annamites." On 22 August, Sainteny's grudging readiness to hold onto OSS coattails again bore fruit when the first C-47 Dakota "Mercy" flight carrying a thirteen-man OSS contingent, headed by Archimedes Patti, managed to find room for Sainteny's five-man team as well. Flying over the city of Hanoi, the French observed hundreds of "strange red flowers" dotting the streets, which on closer inspection turned out to be red flags. Finding Bach Mai airstrip blocked, the pilot circled Gia Lam Airport on the opposite side of the Red River. Noting the presence of small tanks and anti-aircraft guns, but encountering no hostile fire, Patti decided to parachute in a four-man re-

43. *Histoire*, ed. Héduy, 273.

44. Geoffrey C. Gunn, "Road through the Mountains: Vietnamese Communist Power in the Lao Struggle for National Independence, 1901–1954" (Ph.D. diss., Monash University, Sept. 1983), 506.

45. Le Manh Trinh, *Cuoc van dong Cuu Quoc cua Viet Kieu o Thai Lan* [National Salvation Activities of Overseas Vietnamese in Thailand] (Hanoi, 1961). Tran Xuan Cau, "Cach Mang Thang Tam Lao Nam 1945" [Laos's August Revolution in 1945], *Nghien Cuu Lich Su* (Hanoi) (cited below as *NCLS*), no. 163 (7/8-1975): 33–34. Ky Son, "The Special Vietnam-Laos Relationship," *Vietnam Courier* (Hanoi), July 1980, 12.

connaissance party, which soon radioed all clear for the plane to land.[46] As the aircraft taxied to a stop, however, it was surrounded by fully armed Japanese, while another Japanese detachment moved to block several hundred Indian Army POWs who had broken out of the nearby internment camp hoping to greet the Allied team. A possible bloodletting was averted when the senior POW, British Lieutenant Commander Simpson-Jones, was permitted by the Japanese to approach and make a report to Patti, who was then invited to meet a Japanese major at a nearby building and offered iced towels and cold beer. The major particularly suggested that the French contingent return with the C-47 to China, a proposal that began to look more sensible when one of Sainteny's men was caught by the Japanese trying to slip into the city on his own. After Patti vouched for the French, however, everyone was invited to pile into vehicles for the short trip across the Long Bien (Doumer) Bridge to Hanoi.[47]

Both the Americans and the French were surprised to see the city streets not only bedecked in Viet Minh flags but draped with banners proclaiming in English, Vietnamese, French, Chinese, and Russian: "Independence or death"; "Long live Vietnamese independence"; "Vietnam for the Vietnamese"; "Death to French imperialism"; "Welcome to the Allies"; "Allow countries to determine their own fate"; and even "Hurrah for the Allied countries arriving to liberate us," which would not have been a preferred ICP slogan.[48] After a short stop at the Japanese-occupied Governor-General's Palace, where Sainteny unsuccessfully demanded access to Bach Mai radio station, everyone continued to the Hotel Métropole in downtown Hanoi. There they encountered a large group of French civilians, who boisterously greeted Sainteny as their liberator and recounted the maltreatment and killing of Frenchmen by Japanese and Annamites. Meanwhile, a crowd of angry Vietnamese gathered outside the hotel, chanting anti-imperialist slogans, held back only by a line of bayonet-wielding Japanese. Fearing that their presence might jeopardize the lives of French civilian residents of the Métropole, and eager to project an aura of incipient

46. According to Sainteny, *Histoire*, 72, if the American reconnaissance party had signaled in the negative, the French intended to jump out of the plane anyway.

47. Patti, *Why Viet Nam?* 151–55. Sainteny, *Histoire*, 70–73. Missoffe, *Duel Rouge*, 23.

48. For these slogans I rely mainly on reports in *Trung Bac Chu Nhat* (Hanoi), no. 260 (2 Sept. 1945): 6, 23. See also Patti, *Why Viet Nam?* 155, and Sainteny, *Histoire*, 79. When the four parachutists first appeared over Gia Lam airfield, a rumor swept Hanoi that they were Viet Minh representatives, causing the Revolutionary People's Committee to dispatch its own reception team, apparently missing the Patti group. "Huan Lenh" file in AOM, INF, GF 68.

government authority, Sainteny got the Japanese to allow his team to move into the Governor-General's Palace.[49] Although he considered this something of a coup, it turned out to be his greatest blunder, since it enabled the Japanese to isolate Sainteny's team in a "golden cage" and gave the Vietnamese public at large the distinct impression that France intended to turn back the clock completely, beginning with occupation of the prime physical symbol of colonial rule.

Both French and American teams were quick to establish radio contact with their superiors. "Political situation in Hanoi worse than we could have foreseen," Sainteny notified the DGER. "Have found Hanoi decked out solely with Masque [French code-name for the Viet Minh] flags."[50] Meanwhile, Patti signaled OSS Kunming: "Viet Minh strong and belligerent and definitely anti-French. Suggest no more French be permitted to enter French Indo-China and especially not armed."[51] Since Patti's recommendation was in flat opposition to Sainteny's desire to bring in M.5 reinforcements, relations between the two men deteriorated rapidly in subsequent days.

While Sainteny was being snubbed by both the Japanese and the Viet Minh Committee, not least because he lacked any official accreditation from his own government, not to mention the China Theater commander,[52] Major Patti found both parties ready to acknowledge him as Allied plenipotentiary pending arrival of higher-ranking representatives. Ushered in to meet General Tsuchihashi early on the 23d, Patti stated his mission as determining the whereabouts and condition of Allied POWs, as well as serving as "initial intermediary" for implementation of the surrender of Japanese forces in northern Indochina. Going further, he said the Japanese authorities remained responsible for public order in the region until relieved by the Allied powers. This statement caused considerable disquiet among the Japanese staff officers present, according to Patti,[53] which was not surprising in view of the fact that they had permitted the Viet Minh to take over in Hanoi four days earlier and undoubtedly knew of the ferment sweeping the provinces.

49. Sainteny, *Histoire*, 74–79, 80–81. Patti, *Why Viet Nam?* 156–58.
50. Sainteny, *Histoire*, 80.
51. Hanoi to Kunming, 23 Aug. 1945, as quoted in Ronald H. Spector, *United States Army in Vietnam. Advice and Support: The Early Years, 1941–1960* (Washington, D.C., 1983), 57.
52. Even though Sainteny soon established that Pierre Messmer was in captivity, Paris did not choose to empower him as replacement commissioner for Tonkin and northern Annam until 1 October.
53. Patti, *Why Viet Nam?* 158–60.

Determined to make his own evaluation of Viet Minh capabilities, Patti had already begun to receive a string of Vietnamese visitors to his hotel suite, beginning with Le Trong Nghia, representing the Hanoi Provisional Revolutionary Committee. In a considerable simplification of reality, Patti assured Nghia that Sainteny's team was only on a "humanitarian mission to look after the [French] POWs at the Citadel," that no French troops were anticipated, and that the United States did not support colonialism.[54] On 25 August, Patti met with a delegation of Vietnamese journalists headed by Vu Van Minh, a Catholic youth leader formerly employed by the governor-general's bureau of information, now fulfilling a similar role for the Hanoi Committee and the provisional government.[55] In his memoirs, Patti recalled emphasizing to the journalists that he was not chief of an "Allied Commission," and that America pursued a policy of noninterference, although it was sympathetic to their aspirations.[56] In a Vietnamese press account following the meeting, however, Patti was said to have stressed that: (a) the French had no role in discussions between the Allies and the Japanese in Indochina; (b) the Allies were not assisting or authorizing French military return; (c) the United States was well aware that Vietnam was a civilized country, "not barbaric as still thought by some"; and (d) when the official Allied mission arrived to take the Japanese surrender, Vietnamese citizens ought to mount peaceful demonstrations demanding independence.[57] Readers of this news report could be forgiven for believing that the United States opposed French return to Indochina and favored Vietnamese independence, neither of which was true at the time.

Patti clearly suggested more sympathy and support for Vietnamese aspirations than his American superiors were prepared to deliver. He was probably acting as he thought President Roosevelt would have wanted,

54. Ibid., 156–57. Patti identifies his first Vietnamese visitor as Le *Trung* Nghia, but this was almost certainly Le Trong Nghia. The second element of Patti's team arrived on 24 August, bringing its total strength to twenty-two and necessitating a shift to the elegant villa near the Returned Sword Lake formerly occupied by Georges Gautier, secretary-general to the governor-general. Ibid., 173.

55. *Tong Tuyen Cu 6–1–46* [The 6 January 1946 General Election] (Hanoi, Dec. 1945), 14–15.

56. Patti, *Why Viet Nam?* 182–83.

57. *Trung Bac Chu Nhat* (Hanoi) no. 260 (2 Sept. 1945): 23–24. Patti indicates that Vu Van Minh served as interpreter, which would be rather surprising, since most of those present would have spoken French. Another account of this meeting on 25 August in *Dan Chu* (Haiphong), no. 4 (28 Aug. 1945), places more emphasis on Patti's reluctance to comment on political issues. The Vietnamese journalists present expressed frank disbelief when Patti made his claim about Sainteny's "humanitarian mission."

even though broadly aware that Washington's policy had changed since April. The OSS had been Roosevelt's creation, its members in the field had often managed to interpret central instructions creatively, and Patti, deeply impressed by what he saw in Hanoi, probably wanted to make his mark before the general officers arrived. Enjoying his role as amateur plenipotentiary, Patti said too much. On the other hand, his Vietnamese listeners, desperately eager for American recognition, heard even more than Patti uttered. It was, moreover, in the interests of the Viet Minh to exaggerate its connections with the United States and the benevolent intentions of the U.S. government. Already in late August of 1945, then, a gap was opening up between Vietnamese and American perceptions that would influence the behavior of the two nations for decades thereafter.

Determined to show Patti how popular and well-organized their movement was, the Viet Minh leaders in Hanoi arranged a quasi-military parade on the morning of Sunday the 26th. The former Civil Guard band positioned itself outside the building occupied by the OSS team (still referred to in the press and on banners as the "Allied Peace Commission"), Vo Nguyen Giap and three colleagues arrived for a brief discussion, and Giap then invited Patti out to the front gate to be "welcomed." With careful attention to international protocol, the American, Soviet, British, Chinese, and Vietnamese flags each received precedence in turn while the band played their respective national anthems. The subsequent march in review included civil guardsmen reconstituted as a Liberation Army unit, self-defense teams, and a variety of unarmed civilian affiliates of the Viet Minh, walking ten abreast, carrying placards in English, Russian, and Chinese (but not French), and chanting patriotic slogans. Saying goodbye to Patti, Giap added that he would long remember this occasion as "the first time in the history of Viet Nam that our flag has been displayed in an international ceremony, and our national anthem played in honor of a foreign guest."[58] Interviewed by Vietnamese reporters, Giap conveyed Patti's alleged remark that "the independence of Vietnam is quite clear already; it simply needs to be consolidated."[59]

The more frustrated Sainteny became at his own inability to influence events, the more furious he was at Patti's reported statements and behavior. On 23 August, Sainteny was joined at the Governor-General's Palace by

58. Quoted in Patti, *Why Viet Nam?* 198–99. See also, *Cuu Quoc* (Hanoi), no. 33 (29 Aug. 1945). Vo Nguyen Giap and Tran Huy Lieu had addressed the civilian participants at a rally preceding the review.

59. *Trung Bac Chu Nhat*, no. 260 (2 Sept. 1945): 25. Six photographs of the march on 26 August are also reproduced in this issue.

Figure 30. Archimedes Patti and Vo Nguyen Giap saluting the flags of the
United States, Great Britain, the Soviet Union, and Vietnam at a review in
Hanoi, 26 August 1945. Note the civilian salute used by Giap and his compa-
triots. Courtesy of Archimedes Patti.

Blanchard's naval group, as a result learning something about setbacks in
Haiphong.[60] The next day Sainteny complained to Patti about the lead story
in a local Hanoi paper, which carried the headline "Viet Minh Fighting
[together] with U.S. Troops in Tonkin Will Soon Be Here to Oust the
French Oppressors Who Last Year Starved 2 Million People" and listed
Major Allison Thomas by name.[61] On the 25th, the Japanese permitted
General Chamagne, former director of the Supply Service, to visit Sainteny
in his "golden cage" for the purpose of arranging shipments from China
of medicines and other essentials for the interned French troops. In sub-

60. Sainteny, *Histoire*, 81. Patti agreed to Sainteny's request that Blanchard be
flown to Kunming on 25 August. Patti, *Why Viet Nam?* 190.
61. Patti, *Why Viet Nam?* 171, 173. Patti subsequently radioed Kunming a
recommendation that OSS teams be withdrawn from both the Viet Minh unit at
Thai Nguyen and several French-led units along the Sino-Indochina frontier.

sequent meetings, Chamagne was able to slip Sainteny notes about the situation in Hanoi, including an estimate that only 5 percent of the native population actively supported the Viet Minh.[62] Through Chamagne, ranking officials detained in the Citadel appealed urgently to Sainteny for armed intervention by outside French forces, or at least weapons to rearm colonial units.[63] Sainteny tried without luck to persuade Patti to join him in instructing General Tsuchihashi to rearm one thousand colonial troops to patrol the neighborhoods in which French civilians were concentrated.[64] Perhaps in desperation, Sainteny told Patti that the French government was prepared to extend five billion francs in credit to selected Americans to invest in Indochina, coyly asking Patti for recommendations.[65]

Matters became byzantine on the 28th, when Patti's Japanese liaison officer showed him an alleged radio message from Sainteny to Calcutta, intercepted in Saigon, that complained about "a concerted Allied maneuver aimed at eliminating the French from Indochina." Although the radiogram was genuine, Patti understandably wondered if it was, rather, a Japanese attempt to sow dissension.[66] The next day Sainteny went further, warning DGER Calcutta of a "total loss of face" for France, of being forced to "go through Patti for everything," of the Allied attitude being "more harmful to us than that of the Viet Minh."[67] Such messages would eventually undercut Patti completely, the first sign being a "blistering" 30 August radiogram from Patti's superior in Kunming, upbraiding him for failing to provide assistance to Sainteny's team.[68]

Nonetheless, Sainteny and Patti treated each other cordially on the surface, often sharing information over lunch or dinner. On 28 August, they had just finished lunch at the Governor-General's Palace when someone noticed three young French women walking slowly along the adjacent street, one dressed in blue, the middle woman in white, the third in red. Tears came to the eyes of the Frenchmen at this inventive act of patriotism,

---

62. Sainteny, *Histoire*, 85. DGER report, 29 Aug. 1945, in AOM, INF, c. 133, d. 1211.

63. Gautier, *9 Mars 1945*, 291–92. Along with General Mordant, Gautier himself took the initiative in these appeals.

64. Patti, *Why Viet Nam?* 205.

65. Ibid., 210. There is no evidence that Sainteny had authorization from Paris to make such an offer.

66. Ibid., 215. Sainteny, *Histoire*, 91. It remains unclear whether Sainteny was foolish enough to send such messages in the clear or the Japanese had cracked his codes.

67. Sainteny, *Histoire*, 91.

68. Patti, *Why Viet Nam?* 228–29.

so similar in spirit to what they recalled from the period of German occupation in France. When Patti commented ironically that this was probably
the first French flag they had seen since arriving, Sainteny shot back, "Yes,
but I give you my word that it is not the last."[69]

Viet Minh leaders in Hanoi were understandably puzzled by the conflicting information they garnered in regard to Franco-American relations.
From the 26th on, Ho Chi Minh was available to help his younger associates
sift the evidence, having traveled from Tan Trao on foot and by boat to the
outskirts of Hanoi and then been escorted by Party Secretary Truong Chinh
in a commandeered automobile to a secret residence on Hang Ngang
Street.[70] Remarkably, this was the first time that Ho had ever seen Hanoi,
yet there was no time to reflect on how he, a Nghe An provincial, had
traveled across the world for more than three decades, as far as New York
City, to reach the cultural and political center of his country as head of
government. On Sunday the 26th, Ho invited Patti to lunch.[71] Patti was
shocked by Ho's emaciated appearance in comparison with their meeting
in China four months prior, yet thoroughly charmed by his informality,
seeming frankness, political sophistication, and knowledge of current
events. Picking up questions raised by Giap with Patti earlier that day, Ho
particularly wanted to know why Sainteny, the head of French intelligence
operations in China, was now in Hanoi through the good offices of the
Americans. When Patti answered that Sainteny's team had come to minister
to the needs of the French POWs, Ho was skeptical, remarking "that may
be your purpose but certainly it is not theirs." Ho revealed his overriding
concern that the French, British, and Chinese in tandem would jeopardize
the independence of Vietnam. Probing for some sign of U.S. help in these

69. Sainteny, *Histoire*, 89. Sainteny even lists the names of the three women
in his memoirs.

70. "Chu Tich Ho Chi Minh: Bien Nien Tom Tat (tu 14-8-1945 den 20-12-
1946)" [Chairman Ho Chi Minh: Abbreviated Itinerary (from 14 Aug. 1945 to 20
Dec. 1946)], *Tap Chi Cong San* (Hanoi), 8-1985, 18. Le Dinh, "Khu di tich lich su
cua Trung Uong Dang o noi Ngoai Thanh Ha Noi" [Historical Site of Party Center
in the Hanoi Suburbs], *Van Hoa Nghe Thuat* (Hanoi), no. 171–72 (Aug. 1985): 15.
Nguyen Quyet, *Ha Noi Thang Tam*, 186. "Nguoi Ve" [He Returns], *Doan Ket*
(Paris), no. 370 (May 1985): 34–35. Truong Chinh, "August 1945: Welcoming
President Ho Chi Minh to Hanoi," *Vietnam Courier* (Hanoi), Nov. 1988, 6. Ho Chi
Minh reached the Hanoi suburbs on the 25th, rested overnight, then drove into the
city on the 26th.

71. Also at the table were Vo Nguyen Giap, Truong Chinh, Le Xuan (a Viet
Minh intellectual serving as liaison with Patti), and a sixth person, perhaps Nguyen
Khang. After lunch, these four excused themselves to allow Ho and Patti to talk
privately for another hour or more. Patti, *Why Viet Nam?* 197, 199–200.

potentially desperate circumstances, especially since it was Patti, an American, who had led the first Allied contingent to Hanoi, not a Chinese officer, Ho seemingly received from Patti only a promise to convey messages expeditiously to higher echelons. At the personal level, Patti also pledged not to reveal Ho's whereabouts to either the French or the Chinese.[72]

Although at lunch Ho Chi Minh politely rejected Patti's suggestion that he establish direct contact with the French team, by evening he was willing for Giap to meet Sainteny if Patti were present as well. This encounter was arranged the next morning, with Sainteny choosing one of the largest, most elegant salons in the Governor-General's Palace to receive his guests formally.[73] Sainteny already considered Giap "one of the most brilliant products of our culture," yet still felt the need to lecture him about recent expressions of "Annamite" animosity toward the French, which he claimed had led the Allies to call on China and Great Britain to disarm the Japanese, rather than relying on France. Giap made it clear that he too did not relish the arrival of Chinese troops, but his attempts to get Sainteny to spell out proposals for "French-Annamite cooperation" in these urgent, difficult times produced only vague generalities. In truth, Sainteny was uncomfortably aware that he possessed no authority from Paris to negotiate anything. Knowing that the Viet Minh leaders were about to announce a provisional government for the whole country, Sainteny simply warned Giap that he would be keeping a "watchful eye," judging for himself whether its members were worthy of positions of authority in the future Indochina. Following this meeting, Sainteny radioed Léon Pignon an optimistic interpretation of Giap's attitude.[74] However, for the next week or more, Sainteny's main hope seems to have been that the French government, taking advantage of General Jacques-Philippe Leclerc's attendance at the surrender ceremonies in Tokyo Bay, would instruct the Japanese to recognize Sainteny as "forerunner of the French delegation," thus enabling him to seize the initiative in Hanoi before the arrival of Chinese troops.[75] This was not to be.

---

72. Ibid., 201–3. Ho's lieutenants worried often about his physical security. While the Kenpeitai clearly knew where he was, Viet Minh leaders by this time felt the Japanese had no reason to intervene forcibly.

73. Sainteny, *Histoire*, 86–87. Patti, *Why Viet Nam?* 207–10. Giap was accompanied by Duong Duc Hien, a Democratic Party leader about to be named minister of youth in the provisional government.

74. Sainteny to Pignon, 27 Aug. 1945, as quoted in Devillers, *Paris-Saigon-Hanoi*, 78–79.

75. Sainteny to Roos (Calcutta), 31 Aug. 1945, quoted in Devillers, *Paris-Saigon-Hanoi*, 79–80.

High-Level Deliberations and Actions

One of the reasons why officials in Paris failed to respond to Sainteny's urgings through the month of August was their preoccupation with overall Allied affairs, notably attempts to place Franco-American relations on a better footing. With top-level French policy makers sizing up President Truman in comparison with the late President Roosevelt, with the postwar shape of Europe still in the balance, the pleas of a junior operative in faraway Kunming and then Hanoi tended to be routed to middle-level officials who relied on months-old government statements for guidance. This is not to say that Indochina was ignored. The most important decisions for the future involved the appointments of Admiral Thierry d'Argenlieu as high commissioner for Indochina and General Leclerc as commander of French Armed Forces in the Far East, both announced on 17 August.[76] Also on the 17th, a meeting of the National Defense General Staff, chaired by General de Gaulle, discussed the legal problem of sending soldiers to Indochina who had signed up only for the duration of the war against Japan, as well as the logistical difficulties of reequipping units for tropical conditions and finding sufficient sea transport.[77] A mere 979 men and seventeen vehicles were immediately available in Ceylon for inclusion with Lord Mountbatten's British and Indian contingents. Another 2,300 in Madagascar would be ready in two weeks to board ships, while the 17,000-strong Ninth Colonial Division in France could embark by mid September.[78] One of Admiral d'Argenlieu's first official acts before leaving France was to request from the General Staff an increase in the number of C-47 Dakota aircraft allocated for Indochina.[79] This request may have been stimulated by receipt of an assessment from General Leclerc, just arrived in Ceylon, that the only ways to get French troops into Indochina north of the 16th parallel were by parachute or shallow-draft landing craft.[80]

When General de Gaulle arrived in Washington on 22 August to meet President Truman, he planned to include Indochina in the discussions, above

76. Institut Charles-de-Gaulle, *Le Général de Gaulle et l'Indochine, 1940–1946* (Paris, 1982), 30, 67 (cited below as *DGI*). Devillers, *Paris-Saigon-Hanoi*, 68. Joseph Buttinger, *Vietnam: A Dragon Embattled*, vol. 1 (New York, 1967), 307–8, 612.

77. General staff minutes, 17 Aug. 1945, in AOM, INF, c. 134, d. 1221.

78. Dennis, *Troubled Days of Peace*, 33–34.

79. D'Argenlieu to Juin, 22 Aug. 1945, AOM, INF, c. 134, d. 1221. This request was forwarded to the Ministry for Air on the 26th, together with a suggestion that civilian flights on other routes be reduced to accommodate the requirements of Indochina if necessary.

80. Leclerc to d'Argenlieu, 22 Aug. 1945, AOM, INF, c. 133, d. 1211.

all to obtain an American reaffirmation of French sovereignty that would help France seize the political initiative, and, it was hoped, result in Allied allocation of more ships and aircraft. He may also have wanted Truman to reconsider China's occupation rights in northern Indochina.[81] However, with Chiang Kai-shek angry over suddenly losing the right to take the Japanese surrender in Hong Kong, Truman was not about to offend the Generalissimo further with another alteration of General Order No. 1 that downgraded Chinese responsibilities. The most that de Gaulle could secure from Truman, amid all the other pressing items of business, was a promise not to do anything that hindered return of the French to Indochina.[82] In subsequent messages to the relevant American diplomats, the State Department added the proviso, "It is not the policy of this [government] to assist the French to re-establish their control over Indochina by force and the willingness of the U.S. to see French control re-established assumes that French claim to have the support of the population of Indochina is borne out by future events."[83] Nonetheless, the United States did permit France to use Lend-Lease supplies, originally provided for operations against Germany and Japan, to reequip General Leclerc's forces earmarked for postwar Indochina; and some weeks later American ships would be employed to transport at least thirteen thousand French troops to Saigon.[84]

General de Gaulle also used Washington as a platform to make several unilateral statements on Indochina, most notably a message from "the Mother Country addressed to her children," which managed to infuriate Vietnamese who heard it via Allied radio broadcasts or by word of mouth.[85] At a press conference on the 24th, de Gaulle insisted: "The position of

81. As late as 28 August, the French Embassy in Washington was proposing to the State Department that Indochina be considered a single surrender area, with the British in charge. U.S. Department of State, *The Foreign Relations of the United States, 1945*, vol. 7 (Washington, D.C.), 513. Harold E. Meinheit, "The Chinese Intervention in Vietnam, 1945–1946" (unpublished seminar paper, Cornell University, Dec. 1976), 8–9.

82. George C. Herring, "The Truman Administration and the Restoration of French Sovereignty in Indochina," *Diplomatic History* (Wilmington, Del.) 1, no. 2 (Spring 1977): 111–12. Christopher Thorne, *Allies of a Kind: The United States, Britain and the War against Japan, 1941–1945* (London, 1978), 633. Clarke W. Garrett, "In Search of Grandeur: France and Vietnam, 1940–1946," *Review of Politics* 29, no. 3 (July 1967): 314. Gautier, *9 Mars 1945*, 303.

83. Dept. of State to secretary of American Commission at New Delhi, 30 Aug. 1945, as quoted in *Viet-Nam Crisis*, ed. Cameron, 1:51.

84. George McT. Kahin, *Intervention: How America Became Involved in Vietnam* (New York, 1986), 7–8, 435.

85. Devillers, *Paris-Saigon-Hanoi*, 75, corrects those sources that place this message on 19 August in Paris, rather than the 25th in Washington.

France in Indochina is very simple. France means to recover its sovereignty over Indochina."[86] On the other hand, de Gaulle was not averse to talking privately about eventual independence for the peoples of Indochina. The word *independence* must have been used in his discussions with Truman, although Mme Chiang Kai-shek undoubtedly overstated matters when she reported that the president had told her on the 29th that de Gaulle had given assurances that immediate steps would be taken by France to give Indochina its independence.[87] While in Washington, de Gaulle received a message from the Quai d'Orsay advising him to speak only of the "Annamite nation" and to avoid any public mention of independence. This advice was meant to rebut a radiogram on 22 August from General Alessandri and Léon Pignon in Kunming, who used the term *Vietnam* in the context of Bao Dai's message to de Gaulle, and suggested that independence not be ruled out in future negotiations.[88] As Stein Tønnesson has pointed out, it was the Colonial Ministry that favored concessions to Vietnamese nationalism, even acceptance if necessary of the principle of unity of the three parts of Vietnam, in order to be able quickly to secure a French official presence there, no matter how small. By contrast, according to Tønnesson, it was de Gaulle's principle "never to offer promises from a position of weakness, but to show generosity once in a position of force."[89] Within weeks of de Gaulle's return to Paris, the Colonial Ministry's position would be rejected by the government's Committee for Indochina.[90]

In Calcutta, French intelligence personnel and journalists had been hearing Radio Saigon broadcasts since 22 August asserting the independence of Vietnam and vehemently denouncing French colonial rule. Their first reaction was indignation, but then some listeners began to wonder if French government statements bore any relationship to current realities in the colony. On the 25th, when Radio Saigon announced the abdication of Bao Dai and formation of an independent republic, Calcutta listeners speculated about Japanese intentions behind the scenes and whether or not leaders in Paris had any idea of how to deal with the quickly developing

---

86. *DGI*, 68. Allied radio stations broadcast this assertion on the 25th and it was reprinted by *Cuu Quoc* (Hanoi), no. 32 (27 Aug. 1945), which appended three exclamation marks in parentheses by way of angry editorial comment.

87. Herring, "Truman Administration," 111. *DGI*, 68. Gautier, *9 Mars 1945*, 273–74. Patti, *Why Viet Nam?* 265, 560. Meinheit, "Chinese Intervention," 32.

88. Devillers, *Paris-Saigon-Hanoi*, 74–76.

89. Stein Tønnesson, *The Vietnamese Revolution of 1945: Roosevelt, Ho Chi Minh and de Gaulle in a World at War* (London, 1991), 366–67.

90. *DGI*, 15.

situation.[91] Seemingly unruffled, a government spokesman in Paris categorically denied a Reuters news report that material difficulties made it impossible for France to administer Indochina, asserting, "We definitely are taking over."[92] However, General Wedemeyer was still not inclined to reequip and supply the Indochina Army elements that had earlier fled to China, and even the few DGER personnel operating out of Kunming could not be sure from day to day whether the Americans and Chinese, not to mention the Vietnamese, would tolerate their activities. If de Gaulle was to seize the high ground, he would have to rely on General Leclerc's forces, which were still scattered from Ceylon to the métropole.

On 24 August, following discussions with Lord Mountbatten in Kandy, General Leclerc formulated a plan for resumption of French control throughout Indochina. The entire region south of the 16th parallel would be secured in the wake of British landings. Meanwhile, a maximum number of political agents, as well as military equipment for the interned French colonial troops, would be parachuted to northern locations. As reinforcements arrived from France, they would be assigned to take over the Chinese-occupied zone.[93] To make things more difficult for the Chinese troops, not to mention the Vietnamese population in the starvation-torn north, Admiral d'Argenlieu appears to have obtained a British promise not to transport Cochinchinese rice surpluses to Tonkin unless all Indochina was placed in Lord Mountbatten's zone.[94] On the 28th, Leclerc cabled to Paris a list of the types of ships he would need from either the British in India or the Americans in the Philippines to enable the Ninth Colonial Division to reenter Tonkin. Mountbatten warned him that French flags would have to be used, not British.[95] From this and other signals, Leclerc came to understand that Britain's desire to help the French regain control was conditioned by its concern not to disturb relations with the United States, particularly in regard to Chinese prerogatives north of the 16th parallel.[96]

91. Hertrich, Doc-Lap! 20–21, 26. The Japanese released an official report on the abdication through the Domei English-language service, 28 Aug. Patti, Why Viet Nam? 554.

92. Press reports, 23 and 24 Aug., as quoted in Patti, Why Viet Nam? 191–92, 556.

93. Claude Paillat, Dossier secret de l'Indochine (Paris, 1964), 47.

94. D'Argenlieu (Kandy) to Paris, 25 Aug. 1945, AOM, INF, c. 133, d. 1211.

95. Leclerc to Paris, 28 Aug. 1945, AOM, INF, c. 133, d. 1211. At about this time, the former director of the Haiphong port estimated that it would take five years to rebuild facilities there. The only points currently available for debarking in Tonkin were Hon Gai and Cam Pha—provided a fleet of minesweepers cleared the approaches in advance.

96. Dennis, Troubled Days of Peace, 34. According to Adrien Dansette, Leclerc (Paris, 1952), 184, Mountbatten urged Leclerc on the 22d to obtain a more favorable

Arriving in Yokohama to act as French representative on the USS *Missouri* at the formal surrender of Japan, Leclerc must have been delighted to hear General MacArthur advise him to "bring in troops, more troops, and still more troops" to Indochina.[97] There is no evidence that MacArthur offered any of his own troop transports or landing craft, however.

For the moment the French remained heavily dependent on the good graces of the British. Fortunately for them, the chiefs of staff in London assigned occupation of Saigon a priority second only to that of Singapore, the purpose being to take control of Marshal Terauchi's Southern Area Army headquarters.[98] Existing plans were thrown into confusion by General MacArthur's insistence that his Tokyo surrender arrangements precede all others; Lord Mountbatten protested vehemently for about a week, then proceeded to evade the restriction by instructing Marshal Terauchi to send a delegation to Rangoon to sign a preliminary agreement on 27 August.[99] From the 28th on, Royal Air Force planes dropped leaflets, food, and medicine over known POW camps in Indochina. No one could be sure how Japanese troops, mostly undefeated in combat, would react on seeing Allied personnel landing in their midst and proceeding to give orders. The directive issued to General Douglas Gracey, commander of the Allied units preparing to enter southern Indochina, instructed him to secure the Saigon area, disarm the Japanese, rescue POWs and internees, maintain law and order, and "liberate Allied territory in so far as your resources permit."[100] However, Gracey's superiors were anxious that British obligations be of an essentially military character, leaving all civil matters to French representatives on the Allied Control Commission.[101] To further complicate mat-

---

demarcation of SEAC and China Theater zones. Perhaps Mountbatten was thinking of a last-minute approach by de Gaulle to President Truman in Washington. However, Mountbatten knew enough about the acrimonious background to the existing demarcation not to be optimistic.

97. Dansette, *Leclerc*, 185–86. Devillers, *Histoire*, 150. According to Patti, *Why Viet Nam?* 253–54, Leclerc repeated MacArthur's words over Radio Delhi on 2 Sept., giving French listeners misplaced hopes and leaving Vietnamese listeners stunned.

98. F. S. V. Donnison, *British Military Administration in the Far East, 1943–1946* (London, 1956), 407.

99. Dennis, *Troubled Days of Peace*, 13–14, 35. Dunn, *First Vietnam War*, 119–30. *Official History of the Indian Armed Forces in the Second World War, 1939–1945. Post-War Occupation Forces: Japan and South East Asia*, ed. B. Prasad (n.p, 1958), 172–73.

100. Dunn, *First Vietnam War*, 125. Dennis, *Troubled Days of Peace*, 39–40.

101. *Official History*, ed. Prasad, 195. Mountbatten suggested to the War Office on 8 August that a formal civil affairs agreement needed to be negotiated with the

ters, even before the first small British unit landed at Tan Son Nhut airport on 6 September, it was accepted that some Japanese troops would be required to remain under arms to help ensure internal security.[102] Although some sort of confrontation was probably inevitable in Saigon, poorly defined orders and British evasion of political responsibilities made matters much worse.

In Chungking, meanwhile, plans went ahead to move substantial numbers of Chinese troops into northern Indochina. Chiang Kai-shek had at least three motives when he accepted responsibility for taking the Japanese surrender there. First, the assignment reaffirmed China's status as a victorious Allied power, capable of sharing international leadership with the United States, the Soviet Union, and Great Britain. In a speech on 24 August taking the diplomatic high ground, Chiang disclaimed any territorial ambitions in Indochina and expressed the hope that the territory would "emerge to independence."[103] Only later did it become clear that Chiang was prepared to let France return to northern Indochina if she paid an appropriate price to the Nationalist government, starting with former French concessions and property holdings in China.

Secondly and more immediately, Haiphong or smaller ports nearby offered the most convenient venues to load military units from Kwangsi and Yunnan aboard American vessels for transport to northern and central China so as to get there ahead of Chinese Communist units marching east and northeast from bases around Yenan. Chiang must have been particularly mindful of this race for territory, as preparations had been completed to receive Mao Tse-tung, who arrived in Chungking aboard a U.S. plane on 28 August.[104]

Finally, Chiang Kai-shek wanted to rid himself of a long-standing irritant in the form of Lung Yün, governor of Yunnan province. By giving occupation prerogatives in Indochina to Lung Yün rather than to General Chang Fa-kwei, commander of the Fourth Army Area in Kwangsi-Kwangtung, as might have been expected, Chiang ensured that many of Lung Yün's troop units would be away at the time when units loyal to himself

---

French in regard to Indochina, but by the end of the month, little had been accomplished. Negotiations would continue until early October. Donnison, *British Military Administration*, 405–6.

102. Dunn, *First Vietnam War*, 135–36.
103. *New York Times*, 25 Aug. 1945, 3.
104. Robert Payne, *Chiang Kai-shek* (New York, 1969), 271–74.

engineered a coup in Kunming, which had been planned even before the Japanese capitulation.[105]

Because the Yunnanese forces, commanded by General Lu Han, had little knowledge of Indochinese conditions, the General Staff in Chungking arranged for a unit headed by General Hsiao Wen to be detached from Fourth Army Area and placed under General Lu's orders. Officers in these two groups possessed different outlooks and objectives, the Yunnanese often treating northern Indochina as alien territory to be exploited for as long as circumstances permitted, the Kwangsi contingent more eager to immerse themselves in local politics, perhaps with an eye to longer-term hegemony. General Lu had a reputation for disliking the French, perhaps because of some abortive commercial discussions in Hanoi in 1940,[106] yet General Alessandri's officers in China found his subordinates cordial, businesslike, and willing to appropriate arms, munitions, and equipment from American Lend-Lease stocks to sell to the French.[107]

Nonetheless, at some level, probably in Chungking, it was decided to exclude French units from participation in occupation duties. On 24 August, a small French commando unit, accompanied by several American OSS personnel, tried on its own to enter Indochina east of Cao Bang, but was fired upon by Chinese troops and forced to turn back.[108] Three days later, it became clear to the French that none of their reequipped commando units in China would be allowed to enter Tonkin.[109] Also on the 27th, Major Patti in Hanoi received a message from OSS sources in Yunnan to the effect that "temporarily at least the Chinese want no, repeat no, French to move to Indochina."[110] This was a major blow to Sainteny's plans to seize the initiative in Hanoi, especially since he probably sensed by this time that Leclerc's idea of parachuting in political agents and military equipment was likely to be foiled by the Viet Minh. Not until January 1946 were several

105. Lloyd E. Eastman, *Seeds of Destruction: Nationalist China in War and Revolution, 1937–1949* (Stanford, 1984), 35. Patti, *Why Viet Nam?* 217. It is unclear whether Lung Yün readily accepted the occupation mission because of the economic benefits that would follow or was pressured into this risky dispersal of forces by Chiang Kai-shek. The successful coup took place on 4 October 1945.

106. Patti, *Why Viet Nam?* 213.

107. Charbonneau and Maigre, *Les Parias*, 297, 358. Governor Lung Yün's sons had graduated from the prestigious Saint-Cyr military academy.

108. Ibid., 371. One commando was killed and several wounded, including an American.

109. DGER (Calcutta?) to Paris, AOM, INF, 30 Aug. 1945, c. 133, d. 1211.

110. Patti, *Why Viet Nam?* 213.

French units in China permitted to return to Indochina, and then only to Laos, not Tonkin.[111]

Ignoring General MacArthur's instructions to defer local surrender initiatives until formalities were completed in Tokyo, one of General Hsiao Wen's groups, accompanied by members of the Vietnam Revolutionary League, crossed the Tonkin frontier near Lang Son on 20 August.[112] On the evening of the 21st, as mentioned previously, Japanese troops at Cao Bang chose to withdraw south rather than treat with arriving Chinese units. Two days later, when one of General Tsuchihashi's subordinates delivered a note to Patti expressing concern at Chinese border crossings, Patti refused to accept it, suggesting that a message to Tokyo would confirm the validity of Chinese actions.[113] On the 26th, General Tsuchihashi's headquarters in Hanoi received a radio message from General Lu Han to dispatch representatives to K'ai-yuan, 160 kilometers south of Kunming.[114] The following day, Patti received instructions via OSS channels to facilitate Sino-Japanese contacts. Accompanied by Captain Imai Ichio, Patti met with General Tsuchihashi to discuss air transport to and from K'ai-yuan, as well as local issues, including urgent medical care for the POWs and the inflammatory behavior of agents working for Sainteny.[115]

On the 28th, without waiting for parleys in K'ai-yuan, Yunnanese and Chinese central government divisions began to pour across the border at Lao Cai. Clearly worried about how Chinese troops might treat disarmed Japanese soldiers after eight years of bitter warfare, General Tsuchihashi probably hoped that Major Patti's leadership of the advance Allied team was a sign that Americans would be playing an important restraining role. Six days earlier, however, General Wedemeyer in Chungking had received orders from Washington to suspend all training of Chinese troops, which soon led as well to disbanding of the elaborate American network of advisory

111. Charbonneau and Maigre, *Les Parias*, 361. Raoul Salan, *Mémoires: Fin d'un empire*, vol. 1 (Paris, 1970), 271.

112. King Chen, "The Chinese Occupation of Vietnam, 1945–46," *France-Asie/Asia* (Paris), no. 196 (1969): 10.

113. Patti, *Why Viet Nam?* 167–68.

114. *War in Asia and the Pacific, 1937–1949*, ed. Donald S. Detwiler and Charles B. Burdick (New York/London, 1980), vol. 6, *The Southern Area* (Part I), 34.

115. Patti, *Why Viet Nam?* 212–15. Captain Imai was designated interpreter in the four-man Japanese delegation to K'ai-yuan, which eventually flew out of Hanoi on 2 September, but Patti suspected he was the ranking member in disguise. An advance party of the Chinese occupational staff landed at Gia Lam airport the next day.

and liaison units.[116] Although some U.S. officers did accompany Chinese forces to Indochina, their influence was already on the wane. The Japanese would have to rely on their own wits when dealing with General Lu Han.

The Vietnamese were about to learn the same thing. Hearing quickly of the Lao Cai border crossings, Vo Nguyen Giap came to see Patti, complaining that to his personal knowledge Yunnanese troops were the "most rapacious and undisciplined of the entire Chinese army." As in previous conversations, Giap also worried that the Chinese planned to overthrow the provisional government and replace it with Vietnamese "renegades" and "reactionaries." Giap wanted to know from Patti if the Americans knew what they were doing. When Patti tried to explain that Chiang Kai-shek was in charge, the following significant exchange occurred:

> Looking straight at me, Giap asked if I was not arranging for the surrender. He wanted to understand how it was possible for me, an American representative, to be arranging matters and not be responsible for what was happening. Again, I pointed out that I was not participating in the decision-making process, negotiation of terms, or surrender procedures but was only acting in a liaison capacity. Giap shook his head, unconvinced and worried, and said he hoped things would turn out all right.[117]

Two days later, worried about the Chinese, Ho Chi Minh asked Patti to send a provisional government message to President Truman requesting that both the United States and the "Viet Nam Republic" be represented on any Allied Commission for the territory. Patti advised Ho that such a proposal had almost no chance of acceptance, and that in any event he was unable to communicate with the president. He did, however, agree to forward the message to Ambassador Hurley in Chungking.[118] Ironically, OSS Director William Donovan sent President Truman a very different report on the 31st conveying the opinion of the OSS representative in

---

116. S. Woodburn Kirby, *The War against Japan*, vol. 5, *The Surrender of Japan* (London, 1969), 146.

117. Patti, *Why Viet Nam?* 218. In Giap's memoirs of this period, he claims to have observed the first scraggy Chinese units walking into Hanoi on 25 or 26 August. Vo Nguyen Giap, *Nhung Nam Thang khong the nao quen* [Unforgettable Months and Years] (Hanoi, 1970), 21. He must be in error by several weeks, unless a few Chinese soldiers were brought in by plane.

118. Patti, *Why Viet Nam?* 230–34. Patti could instead have sent Ho's message via OSS channels to General Donovan, but perhaps he chose not to because his OSS superiors in Kunming and Chungking were already questioning his objectivity. On 21 and 22 August, Donovan had given President Truman messages from Vietnamese in China insisting that the French must not return. See Herring, "Truman Administration," 109–10.

Hanoi that the provisional government was politically immature, misled by "Japanese agents-provocateurs and Communist elements," and inclined to use terms like *liberalism, democracy,* and *nationalization* without understanding what they meant.[119] This assessment almost surely owed much less to Patti than to one of his superiors in Kunming.

Ho Chi Minh was more mindful than most of his associates that the formation of a new state required not only commitment from prospective citizens but recognition of its right to exist by other states. He could assert Vietnam's independence eloquently, and millions of people could believe in it fervently, yet this particular infant might be strangled in its crib unless one of the major powers acknowledged its position in postwar Asia. While it was impossible for Ho to know in detail about deliberations in distant Allied capitals on the future of "his" country, he appreciated that one of his most important functions was to assess Allied intentions and try to influence foreign attitudes in Vietnam's favor. Ho would not have approached this task naively: ever since his bitter experience at the Versailles Conference in 1919, when he had been shown the door after attempting to present a petition applying the principles of Wilsonian self-determination to his own country, Ho had pondered the predicament of weak, oppressed peoples in a world dominated by the great powers.

On 1 September, Ho Chi Minh invited Patti to a formal dinner at the Northern Region Office. For three hours, Ho, Vo Nguyen Giap, and Hoang Minh Giam probed Patti for insights into American policy and sought to educate him on the perfidy of the French and the Chinese. As before, they were particularly irritated that the Allies at Yalta, San Francisco, and Potsdam had made decisions involving Vietnam without bothering to consult the Vietnamese. Patti's regular answer to such charges was to reiterate President Roosevelt's commitment to Vietnamese self-determination, which grossly overstated Roosevelt's interest in the question, ignored changes under Truman, and unwittingly led the Vietnamese astray. Ho asked Patti to convey to the American government his immediate concern that the Chinese occupation forces would requisition so much food as to bring mass starvation back to northern Vietnam. Giap offered indirect assurances that the Viet Minh, although dominated by communists, had no intention of substituting Soviet domination for French. Giam painted a picture of future American and French investment capital assisting the

119. Memorandum for the president, 31 Aug. 1945, in the Conway Files (OSS), Harry S. Truman Library. My thanks to Stein Tønnesson for making a copy of this document available to me.

Vietnamese to develop a modern economy.[120] By this time, however, all three men may well have been losing faith in the good offices of the United States. Further attempts would be made in the coming months, but meanwhile it was understood that the Viet Minh and the provisional government would have to face the Chinese in the north, as well as the French and British in the south, essentially alone.

The Provisional Government Begins to Function

While the young activists who took power in Hanoi on 19 August had little, if any, practical experience in governing, they were not caught entirely unawares. From Chinese and Vietnamese precedents, from study of the French and Russian revolutions, ICP training sessions, and observation of colonial administration, they appreciated the need to take matters firmly in hand and demonstrate competence before assorted enemies had a chance to regroup or the mob ran amok and undermined the existing sense of common purpose. Although faith in the Viet Minh was currently very high, it could dissipate rapidly. Already on the 20th, for example, the Northern Region Revolutionary People's Committee, on hearing of "a lot of characters carrying weapons and collecting money in our name," ordered the Police Department to arrest and punish any such impostors.[121] In the following days, it tried to gain control over the various paramilitary groups in Hanoi that claimed allegiance to the Viet Minh by the device of issuing Civil Guard uniforms (the old insignia replaced by a red armband with yellow star) and forbidding anyone in civilian clothes to carry firearms unless in possession of a newly issued permit. After accusing one particular youth group of being "divisive and disputatious" to the point of provoking fights, the Northern Viet Minh Committee warned it ominously that in current circumstances such behavior amounted to a "major crime before the Fatherland."[122] The committee also instructed newspapers to print announcements, aimed specifically at guerrilla units in the provinces, to cease all previously ordered sabotage operations and to cooperate with employees of the Public Works and PTT departments in repairing existing damage.[123]

120. Patti, *Why Viet Nam?* 233, 243–47.
121. UBNDCM Bac Ky to Giam Doc So Canh Sat, 20 Aug. 1945, in AOM, INF, GF 16. An announcement was also drafted informing the public that the new government had not sent out anyone to collect money on its behalf.
122. Messages in "Huan Lenh" file, 21 Aug. 1945, AOM, INF, GF 68.
123. Ky Bo Viet Minh to *Dong Phat*, *Tin Moi*, and *Binh Minh* papers, 21 Aug. 1945, in AOM, INF, GF 48.

Communications were among the fledgling government's top priorities. Since people continued to cut down and remove telegraph wires in a number of places, telegrams could for the moment only be certain to reach six or seven northern provinces. Other locations often had to rely on messages carried by horse cart.[124] ICP members in Tuyen Quang province, having somehow secured a small radio transmitter, urgently requested Hanoi to send ciphers, countersigns, and contact times; this became an important link after Vietnam Nationalist Party adherents consolidated control of Vinh Yen between the capital and the northwestern region.[125] The vital telegraph line between Hanoi, Hue, and Saigon appears to have stood up well, and by the end of August the majority of provincial connections in the north had been restored. However, railway tracks continued to be blocked and railroad property stolen, causing the new leadership to order all local authorities to regard the railroad system as state property and to protect it accordingly.[126] Japanese personnel continued to help operate the train system; the kidnapping on 25 August of two Japanese railway workers does not appear to have provoked Imperial Army retaliation.[127]

The Northern Revolutionary People's Committee made it clear that it wanted Vietnamese employees of the former Gouvernement général and the royal government to remain on the job, with the exception of some civil guardsmen, police, and judicial personnel. Most employees complied, until the provisional government ran out of funds to pay them in late 1945. Account ledgers, receipt books, duty officer rosters, and message logs continued to be filled in faithfully according to long-established procedures, although often a new numbering sequence was utilized after either 19 August or 2 September.[128] The *mandat* system of transmitting money via the PTT functioned without pause, as did confidential government analysis of who was using the service and for what purposes. It took functionaries

124. Buu Dien to Kham Sai, 22 Aug. 1945, in dossier of late July and Aug. 1945 messages, AOM, INF, GF 27. Nha Giam Doc Buu Dien Mien Bac to Toa An Hanoi, regarding telegraph wire losses of 21–22 Aug., 27 Sept. 1945, in AOM, INF, GF 25. Son La and Lai Chau were the only provinces in the north entirely out of PTT communication.

125. UBND Tuyen Quang to Dong Chi Xien, Chanh Chu Tich Bac Bo, 27 Aug. 1945, in Tuyen Quang dossier, AOM, INF, GF 16.

126. Thong Cao cua UB Giai Phong Dan Toc Viet Nam, 27 Aug. 1945, in d. 95, AOM, INF, GF 48.

127. Report of Nguyen Nhu Quy, railroad director, 29 Aug. 1945, in AOM, INF, GF 68; and Bac Bo to Phuc Yen and Vinh Yen, 26 Sept. 1945, in AOM, INF, GF 71.

128. See, e.g., the official receipt book in AOM, INF, GF 9, which was opened on 13 June 1945 and has its last entry dated 18 Dec. 1946.

in Hanoi some days to accustom themselves to new terminology. For example, as late as 23 August, the Economic Office dispatched a message headed "Imperial Vietnam." That same day, however, a letter went out addressed to M. Pierre Fourquet, butcher, containing the first "proper" designation of "Northern Region Revolutionary People's Committee" at the top. Previously stencilled royal government message forms and gun permits continued to be used until the 31st.[129] On the other hand, by the 21st some clerks were taking the old Résident Supérieur file folders, which only a few months earlier had been turned inside out and marked "Imperial Vietnam," and recycling them yet again with the aid of hastily cut rubber stamps specifying the Revolutionary People's Committee. To heighten the sense of change, folders were often turned upside down before being stamped.[130] Simultaneously imitating and negating the style of French Indochina, official correspondence after the first few days of September bore the words "Democratic Republic of Vietnam" in the upper left-hand corner, followed by the motto "Independence, Freedom, and Happiness."[131] Private citizens quickly began writing the same formula at the top of letters as a patriotic gesture. In dating letters, some offices dropped mention of 1945 in favor of "Year One of the Revolution."

From 20 August on, the Northern Region Revolutionary People's Committee used the existing administrative system to blitz the region with edicts. The earliest ones provided information on the Allied victory, urged people not to listen to unfounded rumors, and invited all political parties to join with the new government in preparing to resist any return of the French. On the 23d, the market tax and the slaughter tax were abolished. The next day, restrictions on transporting rice were lifted, but merchants were threatened with unspecified punishments if they hoarded supplies rather than selling them immediately on the market. On the 25th, all armed groups were ordered to disband and enroll in the Vietnam Liberation Army. About the same time, a statement was drafted to inform everyone that the Japanese Kenpeitai no longer possessed the right to demand identification

129. Kinh Te Cuc, Cong Van Gui Di, in AOM, INF, GF 37. Dossier of gun permits, in AOM, INF, GF 16.

130. Phong Vien Chuc dossier, in AOM, INF, Gouvernement Revolutionnaire/GF 41. Much the same recycling occurred with official mailing envelopes.

131. There was some early confusion of sequence and syntax. For example, a message from the Northern Region People's Committee to all offices on 3 Sept. 1945 ordered that the motto be placed on top, and that the institutional designation below be Chinh Phu Dan Chu Cong Hoa Viet Nam (Government-Democratic-Republic-Vietnam), rather than the soon-dominant Viet Nam Dan Chu Cong Hoa (Vietnam-Democratic-Republic). AOM, INF, GF 13.

papers or inspect people for weapons; however, this announcement does not seem to have been promulgated. On the 28th, citizens were told that henceforth all outdoor meetings, demonstrations, or armed training exercises would require government authorization. The following day, sale or purchase of gold and silver was prohibited until further notice, with offenders being warned of "very serious punishments."[132] While many of these edicts had little immediate effect, at least beyond Hanoi, they did give citizens who cared to read them an idea of what could be expected from the new government as it consolidated its authority.

The first capital issue of the Viet Minh's main newspaper, *Cuu Quoc* (National Salvation), appeared in Hanoi on the 24th, with bright red and yellow ink splashed in a big flag across the front page. Because events had moved so fast, *Cuu Quoc* staff members had been forced to jettison two previous editions entirely on the 10th and the 19th at their clandestine base in Dan Phuong district, twenty kilometers west of Hanoi. On the 20th, the team had been located by a comrade from Hanoi and driven into the city in style to take control of the most modern publishing plant available.[133] Feature articles on the 24th recalled past struggles against foreign aggressors, listed places where revolutionary forces had already seized power, urged all (male) "youths" between 18 and 40 to sign up for the army, and chastised students who "continued to clutch books instead of weapons."

On the 24th, *Cuu Quoc* announced formation of a national "Provisional People's Government," listing ten individuals, headed by Ho Chi Minh, but indicating that this was not a complete roster.[134] Four days later, an official circular released five additional names.[135] However, five ICP and National Salvation Cultural Association members were dropped in favor of a Catholic intellectual, two Democratic Party members, and two nonparty educators in the cabinet of the "Provisional Democratic Republic of Vietnam"

132. "Thong Cao 1945," d. 95, AOM, INF, GF 48.

133. Pham Van Hao, "Lam Bao Bi Mat" [Producing Newspapers in Secret], in Chanh Thi et al., *Len Duong Thang Loi* [On the Road to Victory] (Hanoi, 1960), 131–34. At this time, Xuan Thuy was in charge of *Cuu Quoc*, with Pham Van Hao apparently functioning as editor after Tran Huy Lieu's departure for Tan Trao. They were joined in Hanoi by Nhu Phong, Nguyen Hong, Xuan Dieu, and other prominent members of the National Salvation Cultural Association.

134. The ten were Ho Chi Minh, Tran Huy Lieu, Vo Nguyen Giap, Nguyen Luong Bang, Chu Van Tan, Duong Duc Hien, Cu Huy Can, Nguyen Dinh Thi, Pham Van Thach (probably Pham *Ngoc* Thach), and Nguyen Huu Dang.

135. These were Le Quoc Hien (probably Le *Van* Hien), Pham Van Dong, Nguyen Chi Thanh, Nguyen Van Xuan, and Bui Van Hach. Pham Ngoc Thach was jumbled in yet another way as "Tran Thach Ngoc." "Thong Cao 1945," d. 95, AOM, INF, GF 48.

announced to the press on the 27th or 28th.[136] Almost certainly this change of personnel was the work of Ho Chi Minh, who had just arrived and wanted to emphasize the broad, united-front character of his government.[137] On the other hand, among the six ICP members still included in the cabinet, none came from the group that had engineered the insurrection in Hanoi on its own initiative on 19 August. Perhaps this was meant as a disciplinary slap from the Party secretary, Truong Chinh, although the Northern Regional Committee had certainly been consulted on the take-over.[138] In a reshuffle of the Hanoi People's Committee in late August, individuals who had played leadership roles were also dropped in favor of a left-wing physician and an ICP journalist who had been prominent in the 1930s.[139] While some of those ignored or replaced lacked sufficient "Party age" (*tuoi Dang*) to be taken seriously by the Central Committee, that was not the case with all members of the Hanoi group. It seems likely that Truong Chinh was unhappy with the way they had relied extensively on the Vietnam Democratic Party when seizing power and distrustful of their

136. Those dropped were Nguyen Luong Bang, Nguyen Chi Thanh, Bui Van Hach, Nguyen Dinh Thi, and Nguyen Huu Dang. The additions were Nguyen Manh Ha, Nguyen Van To, Vu Trong Khanh, Dao Trong Kim, and Vu Dinh Hoe. Thong Cao cua Chinh Phu Lam Thoi, 28 (?) Aug. 1945, in d. 95, AOM, INF, GF 48. *Cuu Quoc* (Hanoi), no. 34 (31 Aug. 1945): 1. *Trung Bac Chu Nhat* (Hanoi), no. 260 (2 Sept. 1945): 6. See also *Doc Lap* (Hanoi), no. 1 (4 Sept. 1945), as cited in Vu Ngu Chieu, "Political and Social Change in Viet-Nam between 1940 and 1946" (Ph.D. diss., University of Wisconsin, 1984), 425–26; and Patti, *Why Viet Nam?* 557. In an interview in Hanoi on 17 February 1992, Vo Nguyen Giap indicated that he was responsible for sounding out additional "intellectual luminaries," having known many of them from the 1930s. At least three members of the cabinet were not yet physically present: Pham Van Dong was en route from Tan Trao, Pham Ngoc Thach was in Saigon, and Le Van Hien was in Hue. Tran Huy Lieu and Cu Huy Can had departed Hanoi for Hue on the 27th to receive Bao Dai's abdication. Nguyen Van Xuan, a former Vietnam Nationalist Party adherent and current ICP member, should not be confused with Colonel Nguyen Van Xuan of the French Army.

137. Truong Chinh, "August 1945," 7, admits that on arrival in Hanoi, Ho criticized him and other Party members present for "narrow-mindedness" in their prior selection of cabinet members. Ho's changes gave more weight to the Democratic Party and the *Thanh Nghi* publishing circle.

138. It is perhaps worth pointing out as well that none of that "19 August" group ever made it very high in either the Party or the DRV administration in subsequent decades.

139. Thong Cao, 28 Aug. 1945, d. 95, AOM, INF, GF 48. The new chairman was Tran Duy Hung, a 33-year-old doctor, and his journalist deputy was Khuat Duy Tien, neither of whom are mentioned in published accounts of the Hanoi takeover. Others on the new Hanoi People's Committee were Vu Nhu Hung, Nghiem Tu Trinh, and Trinh Van Bo.

contacts with members of the royal administration, the Civil Guard, and even Japanese officials.

Ho Chi Minh convened his first cabinet meeting on the 27th, at which time it was decided to fix Sunday, 2 September, as National Independence Day, with formal observances to be organized in as many locations as possible. While some thought six days too short a time to prepare properly, the overriding consideration was to hold the meetings before arrival of Allied troops.[140] Also on the 2d, all clocks would be moved back one hour, reversing a change imposed by the Japanese in March.[141] Ho was careful to notify Major Patti of cabinet proceedings, while Vo Nguyen Giap forwarded a letter to Japanese Consul General Tsukamoto, bringing to his attention the abdication of "S. E. le Mikado à Huê" on 25 August and announcing establishment of the provisional government of the Republic of Vietnam, "in response to the legitimate aspirations of our people."[142] Also following the cabinet meeting of the 27th, a concise public statement was issued over the name of the provisional government, linking its formation to the 16–17 August National People's Congress at Tan Trao, the 19 August seizure of power in Hanoi, and the "willing abdication of the king," but stressing that the new government was for everyone, not just the Viet Minh or a coalition of political parties. For this reason, the statement continued, the cabinet had been reorganized in accordance with instructions from Chairman Ho Chi Minh to incorporate some eminent personalities (*nhan si*); it would continue to function until the day when a National Assembly designated an authoritative government. With the people "ready to rise up to oppose foreign invaders and smash French plots to reestablish colonial rule," the prime governmental slogan was declared to be: "All citizens unite! Fight for complete independence!"[143] This message was not

140. Interview with Vo Nguyen Giap, 17 Feb. 1992. Nguyen Huu Dang accepted responsibility for organizing the main Hanoi ceremony. *Dat Nuoc* (Canberra) 9-1994, 4; 7–8.

141. Nghi Dinh of Interior Ministry, 1 Sept. 1945, in AOM, INF, GF 71, and Trung Uong Buu Dien to Chinh Phu Lam Thoi Dan Chu Cong Hoa Viet Nam, 1 Sept. 1945, in AOM, INF, GF 27. On about 22 August, the Hanoi public had also been informed that, in addition to the regular 10:00 A.M. single blast of the siren, henceforth three blasts would signify a breach in the dikes and five a foreign attack. Dossier 95, AOM, INF, GF 48.

142. Giap to Tsukamoto, 29 Aug. 1945, amid loose papers in AOM, INF, GF 16. Giap also requested that Tsukamoto transmit this message to Ambassador Yokoyama in Hue. Giap omitted "Democratic" from the title of the provisional government, a common practice for some months thereafter when communicating with foreign powers.

143. "Loi Hieu-Trieu cua Chinh-Phu Lam-Thoi Nuoc Dan-Chu Cong-Hoa Viet-Nam" [Appeal of Provisional Government of the Democratic Republic of

only communicated via Viet Minh channels but taken up with alacrity by groups of very different origins and persuasions. Thus, *Duoc Tue* (Torch of Knowledge), the weekly journal of the Vietnam Buddhist Association, which previously had focused almost entirely on religious matters, now suddenly called for readers to support the "people's government," to enroll in the Liberation Army, and to resist all aggression. At the end of August, *Duoc Tue* announced formation of a National Salvation Association of Buddhist Monks and Nuns, dedicated to "eliminating superstitious and outmoded customs" and to establishing both "suicide units" (*doi quan Cam tu*) and Red Cross groups for the purpose of defending Vietnam's independence.[144]

In late August, government-authorized articles about Vietnam's position in the world exhibited decidedly schizophrenic tendencies, on the one hand asserting that there was a favorable international environment, on the other warning that enemies were everywhere and that great sacrifices would be required before independence was assured. China continued to be pictured as a vital friend, using much the same rhetoric employed in Viet Minh publications the previous year. A radio report that thirty thousand Chinese *Communist* troops were coming to help Vietnam to resist foreign invaders was printed, then denied.[145] The United States allegedly remained sympathetic to national liberation movements in general and to Vietnamese aspirations in particular. The British could hardly be characterized as sympathetic, according to these Vietnamese writers, yet the old imperialist Churchill had been replaced by a presumably less hostile Labour prime minister, and in any event London was increasingly preoccupied with problems in Egypt and India. That left the French, but Hanoi thought de Gaulle was encountering ever more domestic opposition to his plans to reconquer Indochina. Side by side with these optimistic assessments, how-

---

Vietnam], 27 Aug. 1945, published in *Cuu Quoc* (Hanoi), no. 34 (31 Aug. 1945): 1–2. Reprinted in Dang Lao Dong Viet Nam, *Chat Xieng: Nhung Tai Lieu Lich Su tu Chinh Bien Thang Ba den Cach Mang Thang Tam 1945* [Breaking Our Chains: Historical Documents from the Political Changes of March to the August Revolution], 3d ed. (Hanoi, 1960), 89–91, and Tran Huy Lieu et al., *Tai Lieu Tham Khan Lich Su Cach Mang Can Dai Viet Nam* [Reference Materials on the History of Vietnam's Modern Revolution], vol. 12 (Hanoi, 1958) (cited below as *CMCD*), 12:124–25. Translation in *Documents of the August 1945 Revolution in Vietnam*, trans. C. Kiriloff (Canberra, 1963), 64–65.

144. *Duoc Tue* (Hanoi), nos. 255–56 (1–15 Aug. 1945) and 257–58 (15–30 Aug. 1945). Thanks to Do Thien for bringing this journal to my attention.

145. *Cuu Quoc* (Hanoi), no. 31 (27 Aug. 1945): 1; and *Co Giai Phong* (Hanoi), no. 16 (12 Sept. 1945): 1.

ever, were printed somber admonitions that mass preparedness to fight overshadowed any ability of Vietnamese leaders to negotiate, and that much more blood would have to be shed before anyone could enjoy happiness and freedom. Although to some degree these different interpretations reflected temporary information gaps and rapidly changing international conditions, at a more fundamental level they represented divergent attitudes within the ICP and the provisional government about geopolitics, revolution, and human nature. Formulas would be found to subsume these variations, but at a heavy price.

Despite constant exhortations about resisting foreigners, several of the government's more immediate problems were economic in character. Most seriously, the multiple breaks in the Red River dikes had left at least 300,000 hectares of rice fields flooded. Although new people's committees in the eight provinces most affected moved with alacrity to mobilize citizens to seal breaches and drain off excess water, about one-third of the total crop normally harvested in November was lost—leaving the north once again facing a desperate shortfall.[146] On 28 August, Thai Binh province reported all twelve of its districts still inundated, evidence of considerable crop destruction, and rapidly rising food prices. Eleven days later, Thai Binh requested 100,000 tons of relief rice from the central government, an impossible amount.[147] Aware that some provinces possessed modest surpluses, the Economy Ministry repeated orders removing all restrictions on the movement and sale of rice; however, local revolutionary committees were often very reluctant to see any stored rice shifted out of their jurisdictions. A government campaign to grow corn, yams, and beans as short-term replacements for rice achieved much more success.[148]

One obvious solution to the threat of renewed famine in the north was to secure some portion of the rice surplus remaining in the south. As early as 21 August, the Northern Region Revolutionary People's Committee alerted three coastal provinces to protect boats owned by the Tien Loi Transport Company that were carrying rice northward on behalf of the

---

146. Hoa Binh to Kham Sai, 21 Aug. 1945, in AOM, INF, GF 25. Bo Cong Chinh report, Oct. 1946, in AOM, INF, GF 19. Phan Quang Trung, "Nan Lut Nam At Dau voi cuoc Tong Khoi Nghia gianh chinh quyen o Dong Bang Bac Bo Nam 1945" [The 1945 Flood and the General Insurrection to Seize Power in the Northern Delta], *NCLS*, 251 (4-1990): 56–60.

147. Thai Binh dossier, in AOM, INF, GF 16. One month later, many fields in Thai Binh remained inundated.

148. Service économique local dossier, in AOM, INF, GF 34. The work of rehabilitating the northern dike system before the 1946 danger season served as a basic test of DRV capacity to govern, although as it happened the peak water flows of 1945 would not be repeated until 1970.

previous government.[149] Hanoi periodicals described the fleets of pirate junks, some equipped with black-powder cannon, that preyed on defenseless commercial vessels.[150] On the 29th, the Kim Son district revolutionary committee in Ninh Binh province requested one 37 mm cannon and two machine guns to deal with heavily armed pirates in fifty boats who were seizing junks laden with grain from the south.[151]

At a more ambitious level, someone conceived the idea of using French vessels sequestered by the Japanese following the 9 March coup. Apparently responding to queries, a Vietnamese employee of the former Gouvernement général submitted a faintly whimsical report on the status of these ships, stating that eleven had been destroyed or damaged by Allied air attacks, leaving five cargo vessels anchored in the Mekong River and theoretically capable of hauling rice north. Vietnamese crews would need to be found to replace French personnel, however, and the author knew of only two Vietnamese qualified to serve as captains. Beyond that, he wondered if the harbor pilots, who were all French, would agree to place themselves under a Vietnamese captain. Finally, before anyone could move downstream, someone would need to clear the mines that had been laid by Allied aircraft in the Mekong River.[152] Undeterred by these obstacles, the new minister of the economy, Nguyen Manh Ha, telegraphed an urgent request to the new minister of health, Dr. Pham Ngoc Thach, in Saigon, to ascertain the current status of these ships. Simultaneously, Thach was instructed to investigate the possibility of shipping grain north by train, and to consider seeking assistance from the International Red Cross in relieving the "alarming situation" in a number of Tonkin provinces.[153]

When British forces moved into Saigon several weeks later, they apparently began to restrict further shipments of rice to the north. Some grain continued to be smuggled out of the south by various means. In the end, however, according to confidential DRV records, at least 11,458 people died of starvation as a consequence of the August 1945 floods.[154]

149. UBND Bac Bo to Nghe An, Ninh Binh, and Nam Dinh, 21 Aug. 1945, in "Riz de Cochinchine 1945" dossier, AOM, INF, GF 58.
150. Phan Huu Hai, a junk captain, offers suggestions for defeating the pirates in *Trung Bac Chu Nhat* (Hanoi), no. 259 (26 Aug. 1945): 17–18.
151. Dossier 83, "Quan Su (linh tinh) 1945," in AOM, INF, GF 38.
152. Report titled "Ham Doi Hang Hai Dong Duong," 29 Aug. 1945, in AOM, INF, GF 36.
153. Bo Truong Bo Kinh Te to Bo Y Te (two telegrams), 3 Sept. 1945, in Kinh Te Cuc, Cong Van gui di, AOM, INF, GF 37. Nguyen Manh Ha had already had experience dealing with the rice problem as head of the Tonkin Economic Service under the royal government.
154. Uy Ban Hanh Chinh Bac Bo to Bo Noi Vu, 7 Nov. 1946, in "Cuu te va y te" dossier, AOM, INF, GF 12. Uy Ban Hanh Chinh Bac Bo to Nha Cuu Te Trung

Vietnamese employees of the former Gouvernement général and the royal administration proved useful to the provisional government in a variety of ways—for example, helping to locate and itemize any stocks of scarce commodities that remained. Messages went out early to every northern province to ascertain how much rice committed to the Japanese by the former regime had not yet been turned over, presumably with an eye to spiriting these supplies away. In the same vein, the "Office du credit populaire" reported 458 tons of castor-oil seeds sitting in warehouses for delivery to the Japanese.[155] Several warehouses filled with cloth probably represented the most valuable discovery. Thus, "Grousfate," the French-established textile control board in Hanoi, reported 18,267.5 meters of cloth in stock—at a time when much of the population was walking around in rags.[156] Other uses for the cloth received priority, however. On 24 August, the Milk Supply Office requested 100 meters of white muslin to filter milk, receiving a government ration slip for this purpose five days later. On 1 September, the minister of youth, Duong Duc Hien, asked for 1,000 meters of white cloth and 25 meters of yellow to decorate the Opera House for his upcoming speaking engagement.[157] However, first preference often went to Liberation Army units for uniforms. The government unwisely allowed some stocks of cloth to remain in Hanoi until Chinese troop units began to arrive; within days there was nothing.

The provisional government had very little money to buy essentials. The new minister of finance, Pham Van Dong, found only 1,230,720 piastres, including 586,000 in old notes waiting to be burned, in the treasury of the former royal government.[158] As mentioned earlier, some provincial treasuries proved rather better endowed when secured by Viet Minh adherents. On 24 August, Nguyen The Khang, representing the Northern People's

---

Uong, 10 Sept. 1946, in AOM, INF, GF 12. It should be added that many of these people might not have died if Chinese commanders had not demanded Vietnamese rice to feed their troops.

155. Service économique local dossier, in AOM, INF, GF 34. The location of stored commodities was a priority topic at the meeting of provincial committee representatives at the Bac Bo Phu in Hanoi on 1–2 Sept. 1945 (discussed further below).

156. "Cong Van de ky" dossier, in AOM, INF, GF 31. Denis Frères d'Indochine was another source of textiles.

157. "So Xin Vai" dossier, in AOM, INF, Gouvernement Revolutionnaire/GF 141.

158. *Kinh te Viet Nam, 1945–1960* [Vietnam's Economy, 1945–60], ed. Bui Cong Trung (Hanoi, 1960), 6. However, a report from the Central Treasury to the Bac Bo Phu on 5 Sept. 1945, contained in AOM, INF, GF 68, also lists 5.9 million piastres in ten-xu coins, probably withdrawn from circulation during the war.

Committee, took custody of the "secret fund" of the Kham Sai's Office, containing 150,000 piastres, from Nguyen Van Huong, the former chief secretary.[159] Five days later, the provisional government invited Jean Laurent, French director of the Bank of Indochina, to its headquarters for discussions.[160] The encounter must have been fruitless, since on 12 September, Laurent gleefully passed out notices that the provisional government was bankrupt.[161] While this was not entirely accurate, the government certainly faced an uphill struggle to acquire liquid assets, particularly since it felt obliged to honor prior Viet Minh pledges to abolish many types of colonial taxes. Indeed, some farmers soon petitioned the government for return of past taxes unfairly collected by village administrators.[162] Many people were owed money by the former colonial and royal administrations, a daunting total of 263,594,312 piastres according to treasury books,[163] but few if any citizens tried to persuade the new government to honor these debts. No consideration appears to have been given by the government at this point to printing new currency to replace the existing system of Bank of Indochina piastres.

On 1–2 September, a remarkable meeting of Northern Region officials and representatives of thirteen provincial revolutionary committees took place in Hanoi.[164] Arranging this gathering on such short notice demonstrated more than the reliability of the PTT: the new central administration was eager to assert its leadership, and local activists showed by their presence and behavior that they wanted to be part of the larger state system in the making. Hanoi participants in this meeting especially wanted each province, district, and village to designate a single legitimate political body, which would bear the standardized name of "people's committee," consist of from five to seven members (appointed or elected, "depending on conditions"), and be more broadly representative than appeared to be the

159. "Nguyen The Khang" is presumably Nguyen Khang. The receipt for this transaction is found in AOM, INF, GF 52.

160. Invitation to "Monsieur le directeur français," 29 Aug. 1945, in AOM, INF, GF 16. Two days later the government notified the bank that it had appointed Nguyen Van Khoat as treasurer-general to replace Consul General Okunuri. AOM, INF, GF 68.

161. Patti, *Why Viet Nam?* 287.

162. See, e.g., the Duc Tho village petitions in the My Duc district dossier, AOM, INF, GF 18.

163. *Kinh te Viet Nam,* ed. Bui Cong Trung, 6. Treasury records also carried old debts to the Bank of Indochina totaling 300,773,210 piastres.

164. This account is drawn from fourteen pages of handwritten notes of the meeting taken by an unidentified Northern Region Office participant, now filed in AOM, INF, GF 68. The ranking administrator present was Nguyen Xien, newly designated chair of the Northern Region People's Committee.

case with many of the committees that had hitherto emerged. They also warned that the provisional government would not be in a position to disburse funds to cover local expenses, so that each province would need to mount patriotic fund-raising campaigns and use whatever money there was extremely conservatively. Provincial participants in the meeting were encouraged to state their own priorities, and most did so with alacrity, ranging from concern about losing income from likely termination of the salt monopoly in Nam Dinh to Son Tay's urgent need for additional youths to guard military equipment obtained from the Japanese. The discussion repeatedly came back soberly to which taxes would be abandoned and which retained, how victims of the recent floods and earlier disasters could be fed, what sort of criteria should be applied when confiscating or requisitioning property, and how to keep former French enterprises functioning to Vietnamese benefit.

In the country at large, however, state symbolism took precedence over economic substance. Speeches, songs, flags, and parades captured the imagination of millions of Vietnamese savoring their release from colonial bondage. The new Ministry of Information and Propaganda realized this, not only establishing contact with journalists and local revolutionary committees but seeking custody of a quantity of musical instruments belonging to the Civil Guard.[165] Overseas Chinese in Vietnam were criticized sharply for hoisting the flag of China all around their neighborhoods while ignoring the red flag with yellow star entirely. "You have wittingly or unwittingly made a big mistake: not to respect the sovereignty of the country in which you reside," *Cuu Quoc* intoned somberly. Giving at least equal precedence to the flag of Vietnam would help to "stamp out suspicions of the Vietnamese populace toward you," the article concluded.[166]

State power also was evoked by physical custody of public buildings, the most important for the provisional government being the former Kham Sai's Palace (and adjacent offices) just across from the Métropole Hotel, now designated the Northern Region Office (Bac Bo Phu), but in fact housing national cabinet offices as well. French and Vietnamese agents in

165. The new minister, Tran Huy Lieu, held his first press conference on 25 August. *Cuu Quoc* (Hanoi), no. 33 (29 Aug. 1945): 1–2; and no. 34 (31 Aug. 1945): 2. The request for musical instruments of 1 Sept. 1945 is in "Kiem duyet 1945," d. 96, AOM, INF, GF 38. Permission was granted three days later.

166. *Cuu Quoc* (Hanoi), no. 34 (31 Aug. 1945): 2. Such concerns were not restricted to Viet Minh followers. Only a week earlier the Southern Region Police Bureau in Saigon had published a warning to overseas Chinese that flying the Chinese flag without the flag of Imperial Vietnam was unacceptable. *Hung Viet* (Saigon), no. 21 (24 Aug. 1945): 2.

those two edifices literally tried to stare each other down, the road between them becoming a dividing line between two worlds. On 28 August, the day after Ho Chi Minh's first cabinet meeting, a request was forwarded to the director of the Hanoi power plant for a technician to check all the lamps outside the Northern Region Office and replace burned-out light bulbs.[167] In 1945, light bulbs were worth their weight in gold in Vietnam, with no early prospect of imported replacements.

The story of Le Tuc Chuyen, a member of the Vietnam Democratic Party in the Hanoi suburbs, offers some insight into the mood of late August. On the 20th, returning from an armed demonstration in the nearby town of Ha Dong, Chuyen was arrested by a Viet Minh self-defense team newly attached to the central Sûreté (Liem Phong) station. Although released the next day and given back his bicycle, no one seemed to know what had happened to his treasured Browning pistol. Chuyen had requested a receipt when the pistol was taken, only to have a self-defense unit member put a rifle in his face and order him to keep quiet. Over the next few weeks, Chuyen tried to obtain satisfaction, but even a letter from Le Trong Nghia, ranking member of the Democratic Party, got him nowhere. Eventually, Chuyen went to the Northern Region People's Committee, which instructed the director of the Sûreté to investigate with an eye to returning Chuyen's pistol. We do not know from the archives if Chuyen ever got his pistol back, but even if he did, the whole disconcerting experience must have led him to question the legitimacy of the new system, or at least the behavior of individual officials.[168] Hung Chan Ho, an overseas Chinese resident of Hanoi, was more fortunate in his petition, apparently receiving his Browning pistol back in September, just before the arrival of Chinese divisions.[169] Most people who lost firearms to Viet Minh groups probably never even dared to petition for their return.

By the end of August, the Northern Region People's Committee had issued new gun permits to some eighty-five individuals, the first being a hastily scribbled note signed by Nguyen Khang for Anh Tam, a guard at the Bac Bo Phu, to carry. From 1 September on, a two-part printed card was available, the right-hand section to be torn off and given to the firearm

167. UBNDCM Bac Bo to Ong Chanh Giam Doc So May Den Hanoi, dossier of late July and Aug. 1945 messages, 28 Aug. 1945, in AOM, INF, GF 27.

168. Correspondence, 20 Aug.–31 Oct. 1945, in dossier on firearm permits, AOM, INF, GF 16. See also the unsuccessful requests from individuals in Quang Yen and Thai Nguyen. Another rejection can be found in the Thanh Tri district (Ha Dong) dossier, AOM, INF, GF 28.

169. Dossier on firearm permits, AOM, INF, GF 16.

holder, the left-hand portion retained for the files. In some cases these cards served as permits to go out and purchase firearms, with the type of weapon and serial number being inserted later. Early cardholders included Viet Minh leaders as well as security personnel, miners, workers at sensitive locations like the power plant, public servants required to travel extensively, and even a private accountant named Le Tran Duc, who ten days earlier had petitioned the Kham Sai for immediate detention of all French nationals. Gone were the permits to landlords, merchants, and employees of the Japanese. A request by the Hanoi police bureau for fifty rifles with ammunition was rejected apologetically, citing the higher-priority needs of the Liberation Army.[170] Meanwhile, in distant Lao Cai province, a former civil guardsman reported his efforts to get back for the "new Vietnamese government" some 250 firearms taken by the Japanese and distributed to their followers. He was instructed to link up with the Lao Cai People's Committee and formally ask the Japanese to return the weapons.[171]

Dealing with Enemies Past and Present

Although some French observers now claimed to see a deliberate plot between the Viet Minh and the Japanese to thwart French return,[172] the reality was more complicated. Early on 28 August, for example, the provisional government formally notified Imperial Army headquarters in Hanoi that one hundred of its soldiers would be arriving in the city that day, and asked that appropriate orders be issued to Japanese units so as to avoid any "regrettable incidents."[173] A self-defense (*tu ve*) unit and the former Civil Guard music band were sent across the Doumer Bridge to greet this Liberation Army company, which had marched from Thai Nguyen, as well as to provide its members with Civil Guard uniforms to wear. As both units prepared to march into the city, it appeared the Japanese intended to block entry and even confiscate weapons. Slogans were yelled at the Japanese soldiers and tempers rose, but neither side resorted to force. Eventually the self-defense unit formed ranks and took the lead in approaching the bridge. Two remaining Japanese guards gave way at the last moment.

170. Ty Canh Sat to UBND Bac Bo, 24 Aug. 1945, in dossier on firearm permits, AOM, INF, GF 16.
171. Bui Van Nanh to UBND Bac Bo, 31 Aug. 1945, in dossier 83, "Quan Su (linh tinh) 1945," AOM, INF, GF 38.
172. For example, a message from military attaché, Chungking, to Paris of 25 Aug. 1945 speaks of "extensive Japanese-revolutionary collaboration," presumably basing this conclusion on reports from Sainteny. AOM, INF, c. 133, d. 1211.
173. Loose document in AOM, INF, Gouvernement Revolutionnaire/GF 141.

Figure 31.   Minority women in the Liberation Army. The inclusion of this contingent caused a minor sensation in Hanoi. Courtesy of Archimedes Patti.

Accompanied by the band, all the marchers sang triumphantly as they entered the city, followed by a crowd chanting slogans. Tens of thousands of citizens lined the march route to the Civil Guard barracks.[174]

At the provincial level, as noted previously, the Viet Minh managed to reach ad hoc understandings with Japanese commanders, often involving supplying the Japanese with fresh food in exchange for political and administrative noninterference. Undoubtedly, some of the new local leaders remained uncertain about how to deal with the Japanese in the areas under their jurisdiction, as suggested by a request from the Thai Binh provincial

174. Tran Trung Thanh, "Nho mai Ha-Noi" [Forever Remembering Hanoi], in *Ha-Noi Chien Dau* [Hanoi Fights] (Hanoi, 1964), 13–16. Dinh Ngoc Lien and Dinh Cong Thuan, "Ra doi cung Cach Mang Thang Tam" [Coming of Age in the August Revolution], *Thong Tin Lich Su Quan Su* (Hanoi), 2 Apr. 1990, 54. At the Bac Bo Phu, a Civil Guard unit, now headed by Nguyen Quyet, a key Viet Minh actor in the events of 19 August, as we have seen, had apparently waited in vain since 11:00 A.M. to formally welcome the Liberation Army contingent. UBNDCM Bac Bo to Anh Quyet, 27 Aug. 1945, in d. 83, "Quan Su (linh tinh) 1945," AOM, INF, GF 38.

committee on 28 August for specific top-level guidance on this question.[175] In the current volatile public mood, Japanese civilians sometimes found themselves subjected to harassment or robbery, and Japanese soldiers were instructed not to walk the streets alone. On the 23d, the Dainan Koosi office in Hanoi reported to the Northern Region Revolutionary People's Committee that three of its Japanese employees had been arrested by Viet Minh followers at the Hung Hoa mica mine in Thai Nguyen province while attempting to pack up company property for transport to the city. The office requested travel permits so as to allow the task to be completed.[176] Although the archives provide no clue as to the outcome, it seems likely that the employees were released eventually, minus the company property. By the end of the month, Japanese companies in Hanoi were routinely requesting and receiving permission to visit employees as far away as Da Nang and Thanh Hoa.[177] Meanwhile, a Mr. K. Hayashi, identifying himself as agricultural manager for a Japanese firm, submitted a formal complaint in Vietnamese alleging that on the 25th, some twenty armed Vietnamese, claiming to represent the Cam Giang people's committee (Hai Duong province), had seized eight buffaloes, a bicycle, a clock, blankets, and assorted papers from a property he had leased privately since 1942. Two months later, the Hai Duong provincial committee defended the confiscations, saying that a villager had illegally leased a parcel of public land (*cong dien*) to Hayashi.[178]

On 29 August, Consul General Tsukamoto responded quickly to Vo Nguyen Giap's letter announcing establishment of the provisional government. We lack the text of Tsukamoto's letter, but it was sufficiently promising for Giap to reply immediately with a polite request that the Japanese hand over the Indochina General Services and the Bank of Indochina (including subordinate bureaus and branches), as well as the "palace of the old governor-general."[179] The next day, General Tsuchihashi relinquished all police powers to the provisional government, except for protection of the Bank of Indochina and Kenpeitai operations.[180] Two days later, at the Governor-General's Palace, where Sainteny's team remained,

175. Thai Binh dossier, in AOM, INF, GF 16.

176. In dossier "Giay thong hanh o Bac Bo 1945," AOM, INF, GF 48.

177. See, e.g., the request from Taiwan Takushoku Kabusiki Kaisha of 29 Aug. 1945, with travel papers issued the same day, in AOM, INF, GF 66. The Japanese sometimes corresponded in Vietnamese, a sharp departure from colonial practice.

178. In Hai Duong dossier, AOM, INF, GF 63.

179. Président du Gouv. Prov. de la République du Viet Nam [signed by Giap] à S.E. le Consul Gen. Tsukamoto, 29 Aug. 1945, in AOM, INF, GF 67.

180. Patti, *Why Viet Nam?* 231.

Japanese guards were replaced by Vietnamese ones, who limited their patrols to the outer walls of the garden.[181] About the same time, the Japanese handed over remaining public facilities to Viet Minh representatives, including the important Bach Mai radio transmitter. French railway personnel still employed by the Japanese were particularly dismayed at this turn of events, since they had hoped to make a direct and smooth transition back to French administration. It must have rankled them particularly when, on specific orders from the provisional government, trains began to fly the Viet Minh flag and carry the slogans "Aid the government" and "Liberty or death." After Japanese guards departed, the De Lanessan Hospital was stripped of equipment by Viet Minh adherents. The French director of the Société indochinoise d'électricité, M. Drouin, managed to retain some influence on the pretext that it was necessary for him to prepare a complete diagram of the power grid before departing.[182] General Tsuchihashi's motives in effecting these transfers to the provisional government probably had little to do with embarrassing the French or sabotaging their eventual return. Rather, he was concerned to make dealings with the incoming Chinese generals as uncomplicated as possible, an objective he hoped would be served by referring them to Ho Chi Minh on all matters not directly influencing the fate or welfare of his own troops.[183]

In these new circumstances, it was unclear who accepted responsibility for the tens of thousands of unarmed French men, women, and children in Indochina. General Tsuchihashi kept guards around camps where French military personnel were detained, but the vigilance of his soldiers appeared to decline with every passing day. French civilians often found themselves dependent on the good graces or otherwise of local Vietnamese people's committees. At the 1–2 September meeting of Northern Region officials and local representatives, described above, each participant tried to report on how many French nationals remained in his province. In several locations where killings had occurred, they were blamed on "fake Viet Minh." The Vietnamese wives or mistresses of Frenchmen were also vulnerable to attack. More often, the movable property of French nationals and their spouses was confiscated by local revolutionaries, leaving them with little

181. Sainteny, *Histoire*, 92. Already on 29 August, the Vietnamese domestic staff attached to the Governor-General's Palace had departed their posts abruptly, leaving Sainteny and his team to prepare their own food and wash the dishes.

182. Gautier, *9 Mars 1945*, 295–96. DGER report, 4 Oct. 1945, in AOM, INF, c. 121, d. 1102.

183. An advance party of General Lu Han's staff accompanied the Japanese delegation from K'ai-yuan by plane back to Hanoi on 3 September. Patti, *Why Viet Nam?* 260.

or nothing with which to purchase food and firewood. The provisional government forbade Vietnamese citizens from selling food to, working for, or otherwise interacting with French military personnel.[184] From here it was only a small step to isolating all French nationals as a threat to Vietnamese security, just at the time when Ho Chi Minh was trying to signal the French government his readiness to work out a cooperative relationship in the future.

The fate of Vietnamese who had worked for the French or the Japanese became fraught with uncertainty. In principle, the provisional government, as part of its patriotic united-front platform, and in accordance with traditional ethics, wished to amnesty citizens who had served the foreigner, provided they openly admitted their misdeeds and demonstrated a firm commitment to the new order. As one Viet Minh newspaper article explained, "Except for a few persons whose crimes cannot possibly be forgiven, the people's government is generous with those who have made mistakes and know enough to correct themselves." However, the article itself was headlined "Traitors should still watch out!" and went on to accuse "a lot of vile individuals" of ignoring the government's generosity, instead spreading disruptive rumors, slandering members of the government who had sacrificed many years struggling on behalf of the country, or making excessive demands that had the effect of undermining the united front at a crucial moment. Those who did these things were traitors and had to be punished. The author urged citizens to form "traitor elimination committees" (*uy ban tru gian*) in every neighborhood and village, tied in with the local authorities.[185]

One man who could never be forgiven was Cung Dinh Van, the former provincial mandarin of Thai Nguyen, who over the years had pursued ICP members with particular ruthlessness. At his subsequent public trial, Van claimed to have urged villagers in August to support the Viet Minh and personally to have turned over weapons and property to the provisional government, but the highly emotional testimony of citizens concerning Van's prior torture and killing of revolutionaries sealed his fate. A crowd of ten thousand witnessed his execution by firing squad.[186] Such mass episodes were comparatively rare. It was more common for small groups of Viet Minh to arrest individuals and spirit them away. Nationwide, on

---

184. Sac Lenh no. 6 (4 Sept. 1945), in AOM, INF, GF 64.

185. K.V., "Bon Phan Quoc hay coi chung!" [Traitors Should Still Watch Out!], *Cuu Quoc* (Hanoi), no. 33 (29 Aug. 1945).

186. "Bien Ban Chung Nhan viec hanh hinh Cung Dinh Van," in Thai Nguyen dossier, 16 Dec. 1945, AOM, INF, GF 29.

the basis of subsequent petitions by family members to the government (still preserved in the archives in Aix-en-Provence), we can estimate that several thousand alleged enemies of the Revolution failed to survive abductions of this kind in late August and September. Tens of thousands remained under detention for periods of a few weeks to many months, during which time local committees often confiscated or requisitioned their property.

Having only recently been emptied of political prisoners, the Hanoi Central Prison was soon filling up with alleged "enemies of the people," "traitors," and "antirevolutionary elements." Already on 26 August, Liberation Army headquarters labeled certain Hanoi detainees as wicked traitors, others as deserving of early release.[187] Just prior to the Independence Day celebrations, a number of Dai Viet Party and other "pro-Japanese" nationalists were arrested.[188] Nguyen The Nghiep and Nguyen Ngoc Son, two Vietnam Nationalist Party leaders in Hanoi, were grabbed and apparently killed a week or two later.[189] While these political arrests appear to have been carried out on high-level ICP instructions, we do not know from available sources why certain individuals were killed, others detained indefinitely, and still others released after a short while. In later years, ICP leaders would criticize themselves publicly for not eliminating more enemies of the Revolution in August 1945.

On 1 September, the provisional government placed Hanoi under martial law, including a midnight-to-six curfew, no carrying of weapons without a permit, and punishment according to military law for those who "violated the lives or property of the people."[190] In the first days of September, someone in the Northern Region People's Committee office drafted a message to all subordinate committees, instructing them to

187. Truong Ban Giai Phong Quan to UBNDCM Bac Bo, 26 Aug. 1945, loose paper in AOM, INF, GF 45. A note penciled on the message indicates that "a large proportion have been released."

188. Devillers, *Histoire*, 178. A subsequent government edict dissolved the Dai Viet Quoc Gia Xa Hoi Dang and the Dai Viet Quoc Dan Dang, but did not bother to mention the arrest of selected members. Sac Lenh no. 8 (5 Sept. 1945) of the provisional government, in AOM, INF, GF 64.

189. Hoang Van Dao, *Viet Nam Quoc Dan Dang, 1927–1954* [Vietnam Nationalist Party, 1927–1954] (Saigon, 1965), 226. Nguyen Ngoc Son had also written for the Dai Viet newspaper *Hai Phong Nhat Bao*. His wife was arrested too but not killed.

190. Sac Lenh, signed by the minister of the interior, Vo Nguyen Giap, 1 Sept. 1945, reprinted in *Viet-Nam Dan-Quoc Cong-Bao* [Vietnam Official Journal], 29 Sept. 1945. My thanks to Ralph B. Smith for providing me with a copy of this publication.

examine the cases of all those jailed following the insurrection carefully with an eye to releasing those who were the victims of private vendettas, while compiling proper dossiers on the others for forwarding to provincial judicial commissions.[191] However, due process would not prove to be a high priority of the Revolution, and neither were the events of August as nonviolent and devoid of retribution as subsequent Communist Party historiography would have everyone believe.

Independence Day

With the provisional government in Hanoi having set Sunday, 2 September, as the day to celebrate Vietnam's national independence, Viet Minh groups around the country tried frantically in the few days available to them to organize suitably impressive commemorations. In Saigon, Norodom Square, just behind the central cathedral, was selected as venue for a mass meeting at which people would be able to listen to a direct broadcast from Hanoi of Ho Chi Minh's Independence Declaration, piped to the crowd by means of loudspeakers. Organizers must have been aware, however, that the mood of the city was distinctly less festive and more surly than had been the case at the demonstrations on 25 August, largely owing to persistent rumors of the imminent return of the French and the angry accusations being traded between the leaders of various Vietnamese political groups.

The most concrete manifestation of French intent at the end of August in Saigon was the robust figure of Jean Cédile. Although humiliated by the Japanese during his first day or two in Cochinchina, as we have seen, Cédile soon found his captors quite willing to let him talk with anyone he pleased, beginning with Mario Bocquet, a rubber planter who had secretly passed information to the Allies until he was tossed in jail following the Japanese takeover in March 1945. Bocquet introduced Cédile to several local members of the French Socialist and Communist parties, who easily put him in touch with Viet Minh leaders. On 27 August, Cédile met with Tran Van Giau, Pham Ngoc Thach, and Nguyen Van Tao.[192] According to Giau, Cédile merely recited the terms of General de Gaulle's outmoded declaration of 24 March and refused to negotiate, leading the Vietnamese to

191. "Viec xu cac nguoi bi can day bi giam tu khi Khoi Nghia," 4 Sept. 1945, in outgoing message file, AOM, INF, GF 13. It is not clear whether this message was actually dispatched.

192. *DGI*, 87. Devillers, *Histoire*, 115, 153. Patti, *Why Viet Nam?* 275, 310, 561, 564.

conclude that he was stalling for time until the arrival of British and French troops.[193] Giau was not aware of Cédile's status as "commissioner of the Republic for Cochinchina"; if Cédile had revealed this, Giau stated in a later interview, "I would have chased him out."[194]

Four days later, under Japanese escort, Cédile drove to Loc Ninh to meet former Governor-General Decoux, who was shocked to hear that Chinese and British forces, not French, would be responsible for taking the Japanese surrender and maintaining order. From his sickbed, Decoux apparently berated Cédile for the way in which his proposal to return to Saigon to rearm French troops had been ignored by Paris. Cédile reacted angrily. Although Decoux's loyal assistant, Claude de Boisanger, subsequently apologized to Cédile for the rude tone of Decoux's remarks, he too was stunned to discover that Cédile intended to leave them both under Japanese guard in Loc Ninh, with no access to outside information.[195] Back in Saigon, Cédile made an equally poor impression among less senior French colonial personnel, who felt he was treating them like pariahs, or "Vichy virus," of no use to incoming Gaullist officials. They also took offense at his willingness to talk with Viet Minh leaders, whom they considered responsible for the growing climate of hostility, and a definite threat to French interests.[196]

Having accomplished nothing with Cédile, the Southern Provisional Administrative Committee tried to go over his head, securing Japanese permission for Pham Ngoc Thach to broadcast an appeal in French to the Allies over Radio Saigon to recognize the "young Vietnam Democratic Republic." Dr. Thach professed astonishment that the French government, having only recently fought against German domination, should now seek to reimpose "a colonization going against the progress of humanity" on Vietnam. By contrast, he pointed out, the United States had promised that the entire administration of the Philippines would be in Filipino hands by 1 September 1946, leading Thach to suggest plaintively that "President Truman and all the people [of the United States] will no

193. *Dia Chi*, ed. Tran Van Giau, 355.

194. Interview with Tran Van Giau, Ho Chi Minh City, 12 Feb. 1990.

195. Jean Cédile, " 'Discordances'alliées en 1945: Les Relations franco-anglaises en 1945 au Proche-Orient et en Extrême-Orient," *Comptes rendus trimestriels des séances de l'Académie des Sciences d'Outre-Mer* (Paris) 36 (1976): 408–9. Claude de Boisanger, *On pouvait éviter la guerre d'Indochine: Souvenirs, 1941–1945* (Paris, 1977), 109–10. Decoux and de Boisanger remained in Loc Ninh for another month, then were driven directly to Tan Son Nhut airport and packed aboard a flight to Bangkok, with no French official present to bid them farewell.

196. Maurice Ducoroy, *Ma trahison en Indochine* (Paris, 1949), 211–12. Jacques Le Bourgeois, *Ici Radio Saigon, 1939–1945* (Paris, 1985), 307–9.

doubt defend our cause in the arena of world politics and recognize all the effort, all the courage, we have shown these last 80 years to make heard the voice of a people who want to be free and sovereign."[197] In a leaflet addressed to the French population of Saigon, Tran Van Giau warned that any attempt to dominate even "the smallest part of our Vietnam" would result in "annihilation to the last enemy."[198] To its own people, the Southern Committee issued a statement on the 29th acknowledging that an Allied delegation was about to arrive to take the Japanese surrender, instructing citizens to treat them respectfully, to eschew disorder, and to fly the new Vietnam national flag alongside the four flags of Great Britain, the United States, the Soviet Union, and China—deliberately excluding France.[199]

Behind such brief public statements lay many doubts and differences of opinion, however. Would the British accept anything short of disarming the Viet Minh and reinstalling French administrators? Would the Americans play a separate role, as in Hanoi? Would Paris see the merits of avoiding a bloody confrontation before it was too late? On the Vietnamese side, could people be persuaded to demonstrate their patriotic, revolutionary convictions in a disciplined, nonviolent manner, thus offering fewer pretexts for Allied suppression? Could sufficient trust be generated in the Southern Provisional Administrative Committee to enable it to make day-to-day decisions without harsh public criticism? If armed conflict became inevitable, would it be possible to play for time in order to mobilize forces and place the onus of aggression squarely on the shoulders of the foreigners? Negative answers to most of these questions would be forced upon Vietnamese leaders in Saigon during the next four weeks. As September began, however, Tran Van Giau and his circle had no option but to make educated guesses and act accordingly.[200]

197. Saigon Radio, 28 Aug. 1945, reported in the British *Fortnightly Intelligence Report* (New Delhi), 16–31 Aug. 1945, and reprinted in *Vietnam: The Definitive Documentation of Human Decisions*, ed. Gareth Porter, vol. 1 (Stanfordville, N.Y., 1979), 63–64. Other passages in this appeal were addressed to "the people of France," China, Great Britain, and "the great Soviet Republic."

198. Undated leaflet reproduced in *Saigon, 1925–1945: De la "belle colonie" à l'éclosion révolutionnaire ou la fin des dieux blancs*, ed. Philippe Franchini (Paris, 1992), 211. Internal evidence suggests this flyer was composed and circulated in the last days of August 1945.

199. Nguyen Ky Nam, *Hoi Ky, 1925–1964* [Memoirs, 1925–64], vol. 2, *1945–1951* (Saigon, 1964), 217.

200. A thoughtful discussion of the dilemmas facing Vietnamese activists in Saigon at this moment in time can be found in Buttinger, *Vietnam*, 313–20.

Even among members of the ICP in Saigon, there was serious dissension. The arrival from Hanoi of Hoang Quoc Viet, representing the ICP Central Committee and the Viet Minh General Headquarters, might have been expected to facilitate quick resolution of differences between "Vanguard" and "Liberation" factions, but Viet seems to have been a poor choice for the task, having little or no understanding of southern conditions, and perhaps quietly disparaged by some because of his lack of formal education. As to the substance of discussions, Viet remarks vaguely in his memoirs that "some asked about one policy, others inquired about another," and all wanted to know the true identity of Ho Chi Minh, which he readily provided, to their general acclamation.[201] However, Viet's demand that Pham Ngoc Thach dissolve the Vanguard Youth met with vehement opposition from Tran Van Giau, who still regarded that organization as the "main force of the Revolution" in the south. Even when Viet insisted that the dissolution order came "from above," presumably meaning the ICP Central Committee, Thach refused to make the required public statement,[202] although in practice local Vanguard Youth units did begin to relabel themselves national salvation groups. Not until 9 September was it possible to convene a broader meeting under Viet's aegis, which agreed to expand the Southern Provisional Administrative Committee to include several representatives of groups other than the ICP and Vanguard Youth.[203] Meanwhile, the Hoa Hao, Cao Dai, and Trotskyists not only remained

201. Hoang Quoc Viet, "Nhan Dan ta rat Anh Hung," in Ho Chi Minh et al., *Nhan Dan ta rat Anh Hung* [Our People Are Very Heroic] (Hanoi, 1969), 207–8. Translated in *A Heroic People* (Hanoi, 1965), 257–58. I have not been able to find any memoir by Cao Hong Linh, who accompanied Viet to Saigon.

202. Interview with Tran Van Giau, Ho Chi Minh City, 12 Feb. 1990. Giau insists that Hoang Quoc Viet lied in his memoir, particularly about the date of his arrival in Saigon, which was no earlier than 2 September. Viet does not give a date explicitly, but within the context of the narrative, he wants readers to believe that it was no later than 27 August. The whole question of ICP Central Committee–Southern Regional Committee differences in late 1945 and beyond remains politically sensitive in Vietnam today. With most of the key actors now deceased, we can only hope that they left unpublished memoirs, or that relevant archival documents will emerge in due course.

203. To Thanh, "Cuoc dau tranh nham cung co va giu vung Chinh Quyen Cach Mang o Nam Bo: Thoi Ky 1945–46" [The Struggle to Consolidate and Defend the Revolutionary Regime in the South: 1945–46 Period], *NCLS*, no. 229 (4-1986): 18, 24. Luu Phuong Thanh, "Nam Bo trong buoi dau Khang Chien Chong Thuc Dan Phap xam luoc (9-1945–3-1946)" [The South in the Early Days of Resistance to French Colonial Aggression (Sept. 1945–Mar. 1946)], *Tap Chi Lich Su Quan Su* (Hanoi), no. 16 (4-1987): 11.

unrepresented, but found some of their leaders arrested or eliminated by ICP and Vanguard Youth "police" squads.[204]

For the commemorations in Saigon on 2 September, it was agreed that participating organizations would form up at different places in the city, march to Norodom Square carrying weapons, as in the demonstration on 25 August, listen to Ho Chi Minh's speech from Hanoi, then march in disciplined fashion through the downtown streets.[205] Hearing that the Allied mission might arrive that same day, additional banners were prepared in English and hung across the streets, proclaiming "Down with fascism and colonialism!" "Vietnam has suffered and bled under the French yoke!" "Long live the USSR and the USA!" and "Long live Vietnamese independence!"[206] On the morning of the 2d, before any official activities were scheduled, more than five hundred Vietnamese youths armed with hunting rifles, swords, and bamboo spears demonstrated in front of one of the military camps where French troops remained interned by the Japanese. Reacting to this "provocation," the French soldiers inside hoisted several tricolors, sang the "Marseillaise" lustily, and traded insults across the fence. Although the Japanese sent reinforcements to ensure that this confrontation did not get out of hand, French participants still were convinced that Japanese agents had instigated and perhaps led the entire demonstration.[207] It was an additional source of irritation for French internees that the Japanese now permitted English, Australian, Dutch, and American POWs to walk around freely, while they remained imprisoned. On occasion, Allied POWs loaned their distinctive clothing to Frenchmen to enable them to move about without being insulted or menaced.[208]

By noon, in extremely hot and humid weather, several hundred thousand people had gathered in Norodom Square, with many more packing the

204. Nguyen Ky Nam, *Hoi Ky*, 30, 79, asserts that Hoang Quoc Viet at one point anointed the Hoa Hao leader Huynh Phu So as chairman of the Viet Minh in the south, yet a few days later "the communists" (presumably Tran Van Giau's group) tried without success to capture and punish So on charges of plotting to overthrow the government.

205. *Dac San* (Ho Chi Minh City), 25 Aug. 1987, 16, 29, 32, 39, 40, 44.

206. Nguyen Ky Nam, *Hoi Ky*, 219. Le Bourgeois, *Ici Radio Saigon*, 310. The account in the latter book of the events of 2 September is a slightly amended version of the original description in Jacques Le Bourgeois, *Saigon sans la France (Des Japonais au Viet-Minh)* (Paris, 1949), 199–209.

207. Lucien Félixine, *L'Indochine livrée aux bourreaux* (Paris, 1959), 64–66. The author was an internee at this camp.

208. Ducoroy, *Ma trahison*, 210–11. Report on POW experiences of U.S. Marine Corps Private James McCorne, 1 Oct. 1945, in USNA, DOS special file Record Group 59, 54-D-190, c. 10, d. 7.

adjacent streets. Urbanites stared at the units of bare-footed farmers from the countryside, while rural folk gawked at the stylishly dressed young Saigon women. On nearby Catinat Street, renamed Paris Commune Street, an eight-man drill team in white shirts and trousers, with black shoes, armed with pistols, went through its paces smartly under the admiring eyes of thousands of bystanders.[209] At the square, with the aid of a microphone and loudspeakers, Pham Ngoc Thach, in his role as DRV minister of health, promised that the central government would remain faithful to the program of the Viet Minh front and resolutely defend the independence and unity of the country. Nguyen Van Nguyen, representing the southern branches of the ICP and the Viet Minh, led the crowd in a solemn pledge not to work for the French, not to serve as soldiers for them, not to sell them food, and not act as guides if they came back as invaders.[210]

At 2:00 P.M., people pressed in closer to the loudspeakers to catch the words of President Ho Chi Minh reading the Independence Declaration in Hanoi. However, the radio connection failed to perform as planned.[211] After twenty minutes of waiting, people began to mutter impatiently, "They've sabotaged us." Realizing that a change of program was necessary, Tran Van Giau, wearing a borrowed suit and red tie, took the microphone to exhort the audience, among other things warning that some traitors were becoming brazen, causing trouble for the new Democratic Republic, creating incidents to justify foreign invasion. They would be "punished severely by people's courts," he threatened.[212] Meanwhile, many in the crowd were annoyed to see scores of French faces gazing down at them from the upper balconies of the central post office, the Jean Compte automobile firm, and the Catholic presbytery adjacent to the cathedral. When people vigorously applauded calls for Vietnamese independence, the French refused to join in.[213]

Speeches completed, the parade began. Just as the lead group swung around the cathedral and started to march down Paris Commune Street, a series of shots rang out. According to a French eyewitness, there was a moment of stunned silence, then loud tumult as people stampeded in all

209. Nguyen Ky Nam, *Hoi Ky*, 219.

210. *Dia Chi*, ed. Tran Van Giau, 355. This "Four No's" pledge had been employed by the Viet Minh in the north for several years.

211. Nguyen Ky Nam, *Hoi Ky*, 219. As if this technical lapse were irrelevant, almost all DRV-published accounts of events in Saigon on 2 September have asserted that Ho Chi Minh's speech was heard. *Dia Chi*, ed. Tran Van Giau, 355, finally (in 1987) acknowledged that Ho Chi Minh's voice did not reach Saigon.

212. Interview with Tran Van Giau, Ho Chi Minh City, 12 Feb. 1990. Nguyen Ky Nam, *Hoi Ky*, 219–20.

213. Le Bourgeois, *Ici Radio Saigon*, 309–11.

directions.[214] According to a Vietnamese witness, word quickly spread among the agitated crowd: "The French are sabotaging us, the French have shot into the marchers!"[215] Tran Van Giau, who had remained on the speaker's platform, asserts that the garage doors of the Jean Compte building opened up and someone began to fire at him specifically; after lying flat for a few moments, he stood up to order people in that direction.[216] Some parade members, certain they saw snipers on the second floor of the Jean Compte building, quickly scaled the intervening wall and seized the alleged perpetrators.[217] However, others were convinced that the firing had come from the upper floor of the presbytery, causing hundreds of angry youths to surge onto the grounds to gain revenge. Father Tricoire, a bearded prison chaplain and quietly respected by many Vietnamese former political prisoners, was shot as he stood at the main door of the building, then left to bleed to death in the garden. Monsieur Trinquecoste, former *contrôleur principal* of the Saigon-Cholon Region, who had come to the square with his ten-year-old son on a Sunday stroll, was grazed by a bullet and stabbed several times by bamboo spears, but remained sufficiently mobile to be marched to the nearby Sûreté compound.[218] Additional French nationals were taken away with him, although one group managed to hide in the attic of the presbytery until early the next morning, when they were escorted home by Viet Minh police.[219]

Meanwhile, other bands of Vietnamese had roamed the streets during the late afternoon of the 2d, looking for anyone French to beat up and

214. Ibid., 311.

215. Tran Khac Minh, "Nho lai Mua Thu 1945" [Recalling Autumn 1945], Dac San (Ho Chi Minh City), 25 Aug. 1987, 39.

216. Interview with Tran Van Giau, Ho Chi Minh City, 12 Feb. 1990.

217. Long Dien, "Hao Khi Nam Bo Khang Chien" [Courage in the Southern Resistance], Giac Ngo (Ho Chi Minh City), no. 59 (1 Oct. 1978): 5. It is also possible that some anti-ICP Vietnamese group fired the first shots, or that it began with undisciplined demonstrators simply shooting into the air, but this would require discarding the assertions of Tran Van Giau and other ICP witnesses. One is reminded here of the two shots fired in Berlin in March 1848 that provoked street fighting and revolutionary upheaval. Much historiographical ink has been spilled over the question of who fired those shots and whether the March 1848 Revolution would have occurred without them. See, e.g., Max Weber, *The Methodology of the Social Sciences*, trans. E. A. Shils and H. A. Finch (New York, 1964), 165–66, 181–87.

218. Undated statutory declaration by Trinquecoste, in AOM, INF, CP 108. Trinquecoste's fellow Sunday stroller M. Vegini was killed at the main door of the presbytery.

219. Le Bourgeois, *Ici Radio Saigon*, 311–13. The author was one of those hiding in the attic.

perhaps deliver to the local police station. According to one source, the French wife of Dr. Pham Ngoc Thach had her teeth punched in.[220] A handful of Allied POWs rushed from one place to another, trying with occasional success to rescue terror-stricken Frenchmen, women, and children.[221] Hoodlums took advantage of the confusion to loot French and Chinese stores and houses. Sporadic gunfire echoed through the city until about 6:00 P.M., when heavy rain caused people to retreat indoors.[222] It was claimed that Viet Minh adherents had uncovered weapons hidden in the attic of the Jean Compte building.[223]

At 3:00 P.M. on the 2d, a four-man OSS team from Burma landed at an airstrip close to the main Saigon airport, with orders to locate American POWs and civilian internees. The Japanese greeted the team respectfully and took them to the downtown Continental Hotel, where POWs briefed them on events and spoke highly of French assistance during the difficult months and years of their imprisonment. "[POW] sympathies are entirely with [the] French and many stated they wished to remain to help them," the OSS team subsequently reported to headquarters.[224] "Black Sunday," as the French immediately began to style 2 September in Saigon, sounded the death knell to any compromise solution in the south. Viet Minh leaders stated vehemently, and probably believed, that French agents had fired down on the marchers in order to discredit the Democratic Republic on the eve of the arrival of Allied forces. French nationals quickly convinced themselves that either the Viet Minh "police" or prisoners recently released from Con Son Island by the Japanese were responsible for the entire incident.[225] A French version of events reached the British in Rangoon within hours, perhaps via the radio of the OSS team, including a claim that at least a hundred French civilians had been massacred. SEAC transmitted stern orders to Marshal Terauchi to restore order immediately.[226] General Gracey and his staff undoubtedly became more inclined than ever to reject any proposal to cooperate with the Provisional Administrative Committee on arrival.

220. Hertrich, *Doc-Lap!* 46.
221. Somehow these efforts by POWs were inflated subsequently by one official history into suppression of "a serious riot . . . against the French authority." See *Official History*, ed. Prasad, 197.
222. Nguyen Ky Nam, *Hoi Ky*, 220–21. Patti, *Why Viet Nam?* 253, 256–58.
223. T.N., "Nhung ngay dau . . . " [First Days], *Dac San* (Ho Chi Minh City), 25 Aug. 1987, 40.
224. Dunn, *First Vietnam War*, 134–35.
225. Le Bourgeois, *Ici Radio Saigon*, 311. Hertrich, *Doc-Lap!* 45–46.
226. Dunn, *First Vietnam War*, 135. Patti, *Why Viet Nam?* 253–54, 256.

The Japanese stepped up patrols of French neighborhoods, permitted some dependents to join soldiers in the internment camps for their own protection, and pressed the Provisional Administrative Committee's police chief, Duong Bach Mai, to free the two hundred or so French nationals detained on the 2d. Tran Van Giau issued a statement the next day indicating that French "provocateurs" were indeed being released, in order to "demonstrate to the Allies our peaceful intentions, in contrast to the savagery of the French colonialists."[227] With these releases, local journalists asserted that only five French nationals had been killed, plus as many as fourteen Vietnamese. About thirty Frenchmen, women, and children required hospitalization.[228] While Giau's statement remained truculent—for example, taking credit for cowing the French on the 2d, Ho Chi Minh in Hanoi took pains to ask Major Patti to inform the Allies that, regardless of who had initiated the trouble in Saigon, the Viet Minh would accept responsibility for ensuring that there would be no recurrence.[229] Exactly how remained unclear. No formal investigation was launched into the events of 2 September. After the much greater bloodshed on both sides that occurred three weeks later, the truth became politically irrelevant.[230]

A number of provincial centers also organized Independence Day celebrations. At Tan An in the Mekong Delta, for example, a band of youths borrowed a radio receiver from the local veterinarian to try to pick up Ho Chi Minh's speech from Hanoi. At the appointed moment, however, they couldn't start the electric generator, the disappointed crowd having to be content with patriotic music, a flag-raising ceremony, and cheering the new people's committee. Only much later did citizens in Tan An realize that Ho Chi Minh was Nguyen Ai Quoc.[231]

227. Nguyen Ky Nam, *Hoi Ky*, 221–22.
228. These figures are from ibid., 223. I have not been able to locate a French source for comparison.
229. Patti, *Why Viet Nam?* 259.
230. Subsequent published Vietnamese accounts of 2 September in Saigon continued to assert that French "reactionaries" opened fire on the crowd and made no mention of unarmed French civilians being killed. Meanwhile, most French accounts continued to assume top-level Vietnamese culpability for the killings. Father Tricoire's martyrdom became a particularly potent symbol for the French. Even Philippe Devillers, normally a careful historian, wrote (without attribution) in 1952 of Father Tricoire being "dragged outside, stabbed and finished off by a gun on the threshold of the cathedral, where his body remained for more than an hour, with arms forming a cross." Devillers, *Histoire*, 154. How Father Tricoire's body got from the presbytery to the cathedral, a distance of about one hundred meters, is not explained.
231. H.S., "Ngay 2 Thang 9 Nam 1945 o Thi Xa Tan An" [2 September 1945 in Tan An Town], *Long An* (Long An), no. 336 (30 Aug. 1982): 4–5.

In Hue, early on 2 September, two chauffeured automobiles set out on the road northward to Hanoi, carrying former Emperor Bao Dai, his cousin Vinh Can, his personal secretary Pham Khac Hoe, two retainers, the new DRV minister of labor (recently arrived from Da Nang), and two armed Viet Minh guards from the former "Frontline Youth" group. At several stops along the way, Bao Dai particularly noticed how leaders of the local people's committees had difficulty reconciling their new egalitarian ideals and traditional deferential attitudes toward the monarch.[232] At the Gianh River ferry, however, Bao Dai, an avid and knowledgeable collector of hunting rifles, made the mistake of showing too much interest in the weapon held by a local Viet Minh militiaman, causing the latter to berate him loudly.[233] At Thanh Hoa, Bao Dai encountered Prince Souphanouvong, cousin of the king of Luang Prabang, who was also en route to Hanoi.[234] Arriving in Hanoi on the 4th, Bao Dai was driven to his new official quarters as "supreme adviser" to the DRV, located at 51 Boulevard Gambetta, then taken the next day for his first meeting with Ho Chi Minh.[235]

The fledgling republic's prevailing tone was to be set by 2 September in Hanoi, with the outburst in Saigon providing an ominous minor chord. The weather was clear and hot, with a light breeze from the west. Many people treated the morning as they would the Lunar New Year festival (Tet), making sure the house was clean, burning incense at the family altar, lighting a string of firecrackers. Shops reduced prices or promised to donate half the proceeds to help the Liberation Army.[236] Because this Sunday was coincidentally the Catholic "Feast of Vietnamese Martyrs," commemorating those who had died for their faith, particularly in the nineteenth century, Hanoi's churches were crowded that morning with people at-

232. Bao Dai, *Le Dragon d'Annam* (Paris, 1980), 127–28. Unlike other sources, Bao Dai recalls departing Hue on the 4th, not the 2d. His memoir contains numerous small errors of chronology.

233. Pham Khac Hoe, *Tu Trieu Dinh Hue den Chien Khu Viet Bac* [From the Hue Court to the Viet Bac War Zone] (Hanoi, 1983), 93.

234. Bao Dai, *Dragon*, 128. Souphanouvong was soon back in Laos, having allied his Lao group with the DRV in resisting French recolonization.

235. Pham Khac Hoe, *Tu trieu dinh Hue*, 88–101. At this meeting, according to Bao Dai, *Dragon*, 129, Ho Chi Minh claimed to have sent a message on 22 August proposing that Bao Dai remain as head of state, with himself a leader of the new government. Since Ho Chi Minh did not reach the outskirts of Hanoi until the 23d, it would have been almost impossible for him to initiate a message to Hue before that. On the other hand, in his conversation with Bao Dai on 5 September, Ho probably did wish to distance himself from the pressure tactics employed to secure Bao Dai's abdication.

236. Tung Hiep, "Hom nay la Ngay Doc Lap!" [Today Is Independence Day!], *Trung Bac Chu Nhat* (Hanoi), no. 261 (9 Sept. 1945): 5–6.

tending Mass. In a move deliberately designed to identify the Vietnamese church with the new government, priests subsequently led their flocks through the streets toward the spacious square, not far from the former Governor-General's Palace, where the main Independence Day ceremonies were to take place.[237] The head monks of several Buddhist temples did likewise. Schoolteachers armed with whistles or megaphones walked at the head of bands of children singing revolutionary songs. Young men particularly noticed how the bright red national flags held by groups of young women contrasted with their chaste white tunics.

As on 19 August, two Sundays prior, large numbers of rural folk trooped to Hanoi to take part, but this time many of them came as village communities, led by elders and Viet Minh organizers, wearing traditional tunics and turbans, sometimes proudly bearing ceremonial scimitars and bronze clubs from local shrines and pagodas. Ethnic minority contingents from the hills were present as well, wearing their distinctively colored headgear, skirts, and sashes.[238] Vietnamese organizers guessed the crowd at close to a million; American aerial photographs taken that day produced an estimate of between five and six hundred thousand. More than four hundred thousand people seems improbable, yet this would still have been the largest gathering ever seen in Hanoi.[239] One group that could not participate in the meeting was able to take part vicariously: common criminals at the

237. Nguyen Manh Ha, in *Doan Ket* (Paris), no. 373 (Sept. 1985): 20. Patti, *Why Viet Nam?* 248. French observers were clearly surprised by overt Catholic participation in Independence Day proceedings. See, e.g., Sainteny, *Histoire*, 92, and André Falk, "Le Coup d'Hanoi (19 décembre 1946)," in *Les Lendemains qui ne chantaient pas (1944–1947)*, ed. Gilbert Guilleminault (Paris, 1962), 252.

238. *Doan Ket* (Paris), no. 370 (May 1985): 35. Vo Nguyen Giap, *Nhung Nam Thang*, 25–26. Sainteny, *Histoire*, 92. Patti, *Why Viet Nam?* 248–49.

239. Patti, *Why Viet Nam?* 559. A closer-range photograph of one portion of the crowd can be found in Sainteny, *Histoire*, facing p. 96. Considering that Hanoi's total population in 1945 was no more than 200,000, and assuming an equivalent number of people arrived from nearby provinces, the crowd in Hanoi on 2 September is unlikely to have exceeded 400,000. When a senior Vietnamese historian recently suggested that the figure of 1,000,000 was unrealistic, he was sharply reprimanded by the Communist Party history journal. Duong Trung Quoc, "Nghien Cuu Cach Mang Thang Tam 1945" [Researching the August 1945 Revolution], *NCLS*, no. 251 (4-1990): 14, 73. Kim Van, "Bao Nhieu Nguoi Tham Du cuoc Mit Tinh ngay 2-9-1945?" [How Many People Attended the 2 Sept. 1945 Meeting?], *Tap Chi Lich Su Dang* (Hanoi), 3-1991, 40. On the other hand, no one complained in 1986 when army historians stated that 500,000 attended the meeting. Thanh Van, Tran Hoai Long, et al., *Thu Do Ha Noi: Lich Su Khang Chien Chong Thuc Dan Phap (1945–54)* [Hanoi Capital: History of Resistance to the French Colonialists (1945–54)] (Hanoi, 1986), 81–82.

Central Prison received three pigs to slaughter, cook, and consume "in celebration of Vietnam's Independence Day."[240]

The venue for the ceremony had been named Puginier Square under the French in honor of a famous Catholic missionary. During the summer of 1945, the mayor of Hanoi, Tran Van Lai, had redesignated it Ba Dinh Square to commemorate a particularly stubborn defense against French colonial forces in 1886–87. A tall flagpole gave the place its colloquial Vietnamese name (Cot Co). Nearby, a high platform, decked out with white and red cloth, had just been constructed to accommodate dignitaries. Below the platform were positioned a traditional bronze gong and big drum. The former Civil Guard band, now dressed in spiffy Boy Scout shorts, forage caps, and new leather shoes, warmed up the audience with a medley of march tunes.[241] Although a loudspeaker system was functioning, the provisional government's plan to broadcast Ho Chi Minh's address to the nation was defeated by Japanese roadblocks that prevented the motor vehicle containing the transmitter equipment from reaching the square.[242] Considerable thought had been given to security matters. A Liberation Army honor guard encircled the platform facing outward, trusted organizations stood in formation about fifty meters from the podium, and the general public took positions behind. Armed workers and students were positioned at all corners of the square, and a self-defense unit was on alert against any harassment from the direction of the Citadel, where French troops remained under detention. Prior to the meeting, Japanese soldiers on the grounds of the Governor-General's Palace had set up machine guns pointed at the square, causing organizers to interpose a human screen of self-defense unit members with orders to die rather than retreat.[243]

240. Nguyen Van Hinh, food contractor, to the director of Hanoi Central Prison, 2 Sept. 1945, in AOM, INF, GF 56.

241. Discussion with Tran Quoc Vuong, Ithaca, N.Y., 20 July 1991. Dinh Ngoc Lien and Dinh Cong Thuan, "Ra doi cung Cach Mang Thang Tam," 54.

242. Discussion with Duong Trung Quoc, senior researcher at the History Institute, Hanoi, 12 Mar. 1990. The transmitter, which had previously linked up French mines in Tonkin, had been requisitioned with the assistance of the son of Nguyen Van Vinh (1882–1936), a prominent journalist, translator, and apologist for French colonial policy. It was not possible to hook up the microphone at Ba Dinh Square to the bigger radio transmitter at Bach Mai, although after the meeting, the text of Ho Chi Minh's Independence Declaration was read over the air by a member of the station's staff. The provisional government's "Voice of Vietnam" went on the air officially from 7 September. Interview with Tran Lam, Hanoi, 5 Mar. 1988.

243. Tran Trung Thanh, "Nho mai Ha-Noi," 17–19. Nguyen Quyet, *Ha Noi Thang Tam*, 185. Photograph in Bo Quoc Phong, *Lich Su cuoc Khang Chien Thuc Dan Phap, 1945–1954* [History of Resistance to French Colonialism, 1945–54], vol.

Although the program was supposed to begin promptly at 2:00 P.M., prewar American automobiles carrying members of the DRV cabinet were twenty-five minutes late making their way through the crowd. Ho Chi Minh led the others up to the top of the platform at a brisk pace, which surprised many observers because they expected rulers to walk in a measured, stately manner. While almost all his colleagues on the platform wore Western suits and ties, Ho had deliberately chosen a faded khaki jacket with a high collar and white rubber sandals[244] —his trademarks as head of state for the next twenty-four years. After the national anthem was played, two young women, Dam Thi Loan of the Liberation Army, and Le Thi from a Hanoi middle school, were given the honor of raising the flag.[245]

Vo Nguyen Giap then stepped to the microphone to introduce Ho, who was greeted with loud, prearranged chants of "Independence! Independence!" For several minutes, Ho waved to the audience, then he raised both hands to obtain silence. In his distinctive Nghe An province accent, Ho then proceeded to read the Independence Declaration.[246] After several sentences he stopped short and asked his listeners, "Countrymen, can you hear me clearly?" A roar came back, "Clearly!" From that moment forward, a special bond had been struck.[247] Giap was not distorting when he wrote much later that "Uncle [Ho] and the sea of people became one."[248] Tran Trung Thanh, a young self-defense cadre who was supposed to be watching the Japanese machine gunners, recalled that, although not yet knowing who Ho Chi Minh was exactly, this simple exchange of words moved him to tears, and caused him to take one particular motto on a banner as a personal commitment: "Independence or Death!"[249] Emerging from the void, Ho was already evoking admiration and awe, fulfilling the need of people for a just, invincible leader, projecting the collective dream, weaving the new

---

1 (Hanoi, 1985), facing p. 40. Interview with Nguyen Van Tran, Hanoi, 17 Feb. 1992.

244. Tung Hiep, "Hom nay la Ngay Doc Lap!" 23. Photographs reveal that Ho also wore a pith helmet, but unlike the jacket and sandals, this did not remain his standard attire.

245. Si Tam, "Nguoi keo co trong le Tuyen Ngon Doc Lap 2–9–1945" [Flag Raisers at the 2 September 1945 Independence Declaration Ceremony], *Thong Tin Lich Su Quan Su* (Hanoi), 2-1990, 56.

246. Several available photographs show that someone held a parasol over Ho while he was reading the declaration, perhaps an unconscious continuation of royal tradition.

247. Nguyen Quyet, *Ha Noi Thang Tam*, 187. Patti, *Why Viet Nam?* 250.

248. Vo Nguyen Giap, *Nhung Nam Thang*, 28.

249. Tran Trung Thanh, "Nho mai Ha-Noi," 20.

myth. A recording of this speech, admittedly made by Ho a decade later, and without benefit of audience, reveals a firm, resonant voice with obvious rhetorical talents, for example, in the emphasis given to particular words and the use of pauses for dramatic effect.[250]

The declaration itself, not long, was designed to set the overall tone for both domestic and foreign consumption.[251] Anxious to link Vietnam's present with past world revolutionary traditions, and to bow diplomatically in several directions, Ho Chi Minh opened with quotations from the 1776 American Declaration of Independence[252] and the 1791 French Declaration of the Rights of Man and the Citizen. These ideals of life, liberty, happiness, and equality were then contrasted sharply with more than eighty years of French colonial practice—Ho particularly mentioning the division of Vietnam into three administrative systems, the killing or imprisonment of patriots, the sale of opium and liquor to "weaken our race," expropriation of land and raw materials, and the levying of "hundreds of unfair taxes." Although France asserted responsibilities as "protector" of Vietnam, in reality she had sold the territory twice to Japan in the past five years. The populace had become ever poorer and more miserable, leading to the terrible famine early in the year, when "more than two million of our countrymen" had died of starvation. When Japan capitulated to the Allies, "our entire people rose up to gain power and founded the Democratic Republic of

250. This recording is included on a tape cassette that accompanies the *Tu Dien Ho Chi Minh: So Gian* [Ho Chi Minh Dictionary: Basic Version] (Ho Chi Minh City, 1990).

251. The text of the declaration was printed in several contemporary periodicals, including *Co Giai Phong* (Hanoi), no. 16 (12 Sept. 1945). More accessible reprints can be found in Dang Lao Dong Viet Nam, *Chat Xieng*, 92–95; *Ho Chi Minh Toan Tap* [The Complete Works of Ho Chi Minh], vol. 3 (Hanoi, 1983), 383–86; and *Tong Tap Van Hoc Viet Nam* [Vietnam Literature Compendium], ed. Nguyen Khanh Toan, vol. 36 (Hanoi, 1980), 812–23. Some texts append the names of all fifteen cabinet members, signifying formal government assent, but there is no doubt that Ho Chi Minh wrote the declaration. The first English translation was included in a DRV booklet from late 1945 entitled *Documents*, with a cover of bright red plus the yellow star; a copy can be found in AOM, INF, GF 46. For foreign eyes, the country was styled "Republic of Vietnam," minus "Democratic." Other translations are available in *New Cycle in Asia*, ed. Harold R. Isaacs (New York, 1947), 163–65; *Documents of the August 1945 Revolution*, trans. Kiriloff, 66–70; *Vietnam*, ed. Porter, 64–66; and *Viet Nam Social Sciences* (Hanoi), no. 3 (1985): 145–47.

252. Ho Chi Minh had tried out this speech opening on Patti four days earlier. Patti initially was incredulous, then strained his memory to correct a transposition of "life" and "liberty," and finally became "uncomfortably aware that I was participating—however slightly—in the formulation of a political entity." Patti, *Why Viet Nam?* 223–24.

Figure 32. Ho Chi Minh reading the Independence Declaration, 2 September 1945. To his left a photographer is employing a studio-style camera to capture the proceedings. The guards apparently kept their pistols drawn throughout the ceremony. Note the "fat" yellow star on the platform bunting, common in Hanoi at this time but soon to be replaced by the more pointed version that originated in the south in 1940. Courtesy of Allison K. Thomas.

Vietnam."[253] With the abdication of Bao Dai, the people had also put an end to several millennia of monarchism.

Having devoted more than two-thirds of the declaration to a concise, if colored, lesson in history, Ho Chi Minh turned in his final passages to the immediate diplomatic circumstances. He announced that the provisional government was canceling all treaties signed by France dealing with Vietnam and abolishing all French special privileges. He warned that the Vietnamese people were "determined to oppose every plot of the French colonialists." Somewhat plaintively, Ho called on the Allied powers to recognize the right of the Vietnamese people to independence, in the spirit of the Teheran and San Francisco conferences. If they did not, Ho's last words announced to the world that in any case:

> Vietnam has the right to enjoy freedom and independence, and in fact has become a free and independent country. The entire Vietnamese people are determined to mobilize all their physical and mental strength, to sacrifice their lives and property, in order to safeguard their freedom and independence.

Once the clapping and cheering had died down, Ho Chi Minh introduced each of his ministers, and all took an oath of office promising to lead the people in defense of the Fatherland and implementation of the Viet Minh program, no matter what the personal sacrifice.[254] Vo Nguyen Giap then stepped forward to provide a sober gloss to the president's declaration. In an impromptu speech,[255] more than twice as long as Ho's, Giap rambled through praise of Vietnam's heroic ancestors, the Liberation Army, the "worldwide democratic movement," Buddhist and Christian clergy, even Emperor Bao Dai. He foreshadowed democratic elections to a national assembly, which would then devise a constitution and provide a legal government. The army would be reorganized and broadened, the economy rebuilt, and education given high priority. Giap admitted that the provisional government, lacking finances to accomplish these tasks, would need to resort to "loans, subscriptions and income taxes." The government was confident that citizens would help out, since "if the country is lost, the individual's home must also be lost, if independence and the Democratic

---

253. It is not certain that Ho Chi Minh used the word "Democratic" in his speech, although subsequent reprints contain the term. In the late 1945 English translation cited above, he refers in this passage to "the present Republican Government."

254. *CMCD*, 12:101.

255. Ibid., 107–19. *Vietnam*, ed. Porter, 66–71. *Documents* booklet, in AOM, INF, GF 46.

Republic[256] are shaky, personal rights will also not be perfect." Censorship would remain until the political situation had "cleared up."

Even more openly than Ho Chi Minh, Giap appealed for support from the Allied powers, particularly the United States and China (neither speaker mentioned the Soviet Union or Great Britain), claiming that the "Vietnamese masses had eagerly risen to fight Japan," whereas the French colonialists had collaborated with the Japanese fascists throughout the war. He paraphrased President Roosevelt on how oppression and cruelty made people appreciate what freedom meant, and quoted Generalissimo Chiang Kai-shek on the likelihood of a Third World War if the oppressed peoples of Asia were not given freedom and equality. Giap also provided his audience with a chilling, yet essentially accurate, appraisal of current French government statements and actions, mentioning the appointment of a new "governor-general," preparations to bring troops back to Indochina, and local schemes to reclaim public offices. If no one outside chose to help Vietnam to ward off the French diplomatically, the nation, united, would have to go it alone. In such circumstances, Giap warned ominously, "division, doubt, and apathy are all a betrayal of the country." In a concluding apocalyptic vision, Giap intoned: "Following in the steps of our forefathers, the present generation will fight a final battle, so that generations to follow will forever be able to live in independence, freedom, and happiness."

Following Giap's speech, Tran Huy Lieu reported to the audience on Bao Dai's abdication ceremony in Hue three days earlier, then presented the royal sword and seal to Ho Chi Minh. A gifted public performer, Lieu apparently had the crowd laughing and clapping at his description of the demise of the monarchy. Entering into the spirit of things, Ho declared that the sword, previously used to oppress the people, would now be employed to "cut off traitors' heads."[257] Representing the Viet Minh General Headquarters, Nguyen Luong Bang then spoke briefly on the need for unity and struggle. Paraphrasing Lenin (without attribution), he stressed that while gaining political power was difficult, keeping it was more so. Taking a more intractable position than either Ho or Giap, Bang flatly

256. Giap definitely used "Democratic," since the translation of his speech in *Documents* repeats the term several times, unlike the translation of Ho's Independence Declaration.

257. *CMCD*, 12:119–22. Tran Trung Thanh, "Nho mai Ha-Noi," 20–21. *Doc Lap* (Hanoi), no. 1 (4 Sept. 1945), as quoted in Vu Ngu Chieu, "Political and Social Change," 380–81.

asserted that it would be necessary to fight the French, and that Vietnam "should not rely on [*y lai*] anyone else."[258] At some point in the afternoon's proceedings, however, two American P-38 Lightnings swooped down low over the crowd, an event immediately declared and believed by the people to represent a coordinated U.S. salute to the fledgling Vietnamese government.[259]

The final item on the program involved the audience reciting a solemn oath of allegiance to the provisional government and to President Ho Chi Minh, a vow to preserve the independence of the Fatherland, "even to the sacrifice of our lives," and a promise not to help the French if they invaded again.[260] On a last cautionary note, Ho took the microphone again to predict: "We shall have to pass through much more adversity and suffering. [You] countrymen must support the government, so that later on there will be many more celebrations and victories!"[261] Organized groups in the square then marched downtown, disbanded at Returned Sword Lake, and joined in the general merriment until the hour of curfew.[262]

Prismatic Colors

There can be no doubt that the meeting in Hanoi on 2 September deeply impressed many people who had not previously taken part in Viet Minh activities. As one avowedly anticommunist writer has commented, "The majority clearly welcomed Ho and his men—the mysterious and awesome figures emerging from prisons, jungles, mountains, and foreign countries."[263] At the time, trying to capture the essence of events, Tran Xuan Sinh wrote:

> The souls of the earth and water [also signifying the nation] have returned to the former capital on this imperishable day, and all social strata of the Ascending Dragon Citadel [Hanoi's traditional name]

258. Dang Lao Dong Viet Nam, *Chat Xieng*, 96–98. *CMCD*, 12:122–23.

259. Sainteny, *Histoire*, 93. Patti does not mention this incident in his book but recalled it vividly in a radio interview, emphasizing that the flyby was entirely accidental. See Michael Charlton and Anthony Moncrieff, *Many Reasons Why: The American Involvement in Vietnam* (Harmondsworth, 1979), 13–14.

260. *CMCD*, 12:102. Vo Nguyen Giap, *Nhung Nam Thang*, 28–29. Tran Trung Thanh, "Nho mai Ha-Noi," 21. Vu Ngu Chieu, "Political and Social Change," 381.

261. Tung Hiep, "Hom nay la Ngay Doc Lap!" 23.

262. Patti, *Why Viet Nam?* 253. Tung Hiep, "Hom nay la Ngay Doc Lap!" 23–24.

263. Vu Ngu Chieu, "Political and Social Change," 382.

have just demononstrated the brave spirit of a people who have decided
to retake their free life.[264]

Phan Anh, former minister of youth, arriving in Hanoi from his brief
detention in Nghe An in time to witness the Independence Day ceremonies,
noted especially the firm commitment of Hanoi's citizenry to the Revolution, a factor he expected would impress the Allied powers decisively.[265]
In the evening, a young dragon dance group pranced the streets, pledging
loudly to drink the blood of invading bandits and chanting, "Today is
Independence Day!" At a nearby hotel, an elderly gentleman recalled the
first bitter days of French occupation of Hanoi sixty years prior, explained
how for so many decades he had not dared to speak his inner thoughts, but
now was able to yell "Long Live Independence!" to his heart's content.
Claiming never to have imbibed before, the old man insisted on joining his
friends in a drink so that his face could be as red as the flag draped on the
wall.[266]

Ho Chi Minh had invited Major Patti to be present on the official
Independence Day platform, but Patti decided it would be preferable to
come with three of his OSS teammates as observers, positioning themselves among some local dignitaries in front of the stand. While listening
to his Viet Minh liaison-interpreter, Le Xuan, provide a running rendition
of Ho's speech, Patti watched the responses of the crowd. Ho "was reaching
them," he easily concluded. Provided later in the afternoon with the
Vietnamese text of the declaration, Patti made sure it was translated and
transmitted by radio to Kunming. By air courier, Patti added his own vivid
interpretations, describing Ho's appearance, for example: "Head high,
wisps of hair and beard agitated by the slight breeze, and exerting a
powerful emotional delivery."[267] While by this time some of his superiors
must have thought that Patti had "gone native," they faithfully transmitted his reports to OSS Director William Donovan in Washington, who
arranged for them to be summarized as memos for the attention of Secretary of State James Byrnes, who, having many more urgent things to
read, probably ignored them completely.[268]

264. *Dan Moi* (Hanoi), no. 10 (5 Sept. 1945), as quoted in Vu Ngu Chieu,
"Political and Social Change," 382.
265. Phan Anh, "Toi da tham gia Chinh Phu Lien Hiep Khang Chien (3-3-1946)
nhu the nao?" [How I Took Part in the Resistance Union Government (3 Mar.
1946)], *Tap Chi Lich Su Quan Su* (Hanoi), no. 36 (12-1988): 8–9.
266. Tung Hiep, "Hom nay la Ngay Doc Lap!" 24.
267. Patti, *Why Viet Nam?* 249–52.
268. *Vietnam*, ed. Porter, 71–72.

Jean Sainteny watched from the Governor-General's Palace on 2 September as tens of thousands of Vietnamese filed past on adjacent Brière-de-l'Isle Avenue to enter the botanical gardens. He was struck by the orderliness of the crowd, the absence of any disruptive behavior. No one even made hostile gestures in his direction. Sainteny was mainly irritated by the presence of the "American delegation" at the ceremony and the low-level flyover by U.S. aircraft. When he obtained detailed reports on speeches at the meeting, Sainteny noted that Ho Chi Minh had taken a more moderate line than his younger comrades.[269] The next day, one of his assistants, Lieutenant François Missoffe, walked brashly into the Northern Region Office and talked productively with Ho Chi Minh and Hoang Minh Giam, Ho's aide for foreign relations. Missoffe emerged deeply impressed by Ho and convinced that negotiations were possible.[270] Sainteny desperately wanted to open discussions with Ho, but still could get no instructions from Paris.

When texts of the Independence Day speeches reached Paris, they appear to have been ignored. Some months later, an intelligence analyst described the content sarcastically as "a bastard combination of bookish internationalism and chauvinistic patriotism, a melange of intellectual Marxism and primitive social demands, corresponding exactly to the aspirations of a section of the backward masses of these Asiatic deltas."[271] In reality, Paris was neither interested in the ideas of Ho Chi Minh or Vo Nguyen Giap nor eager for Sainteny to develop his tentative contacts. The emphasis was on moving as many troops as quickly as possible to Saigon, from whence selected units might penetrate Tonkin. Once a preponderance of power was achieved, deliberations with various native elements claiming to represent one thing or another could begin. Such hubris would cling to the French government and army for years. Then it was the turn of the Americans.

269. Sainteny, *Histoire*, 92–93.
270. Missoffe, *Duel Rouge*, 24–27. Sainteny, *Histoire*, 96–97.
271. "Le Viet Minh," report dated 25 June 1946, p. 37, in AOM, INF, c. 138–39, d. 1247.

Epilogue

The organizers of the celebrations in Hanoi and Saigon on 2 September 1945 made a point of displaying the flags of the Allied powers, minus the French tricolor, alongside the banners of the Viet Minh–Democratic Republic of Vietnam. The American OSS team in Hanoi already boasted a villa in front of which the Stars and Stripes was hoisted proudly; soon other villas were flying British and Chinese standards, and the first small French military unit to enter Saigon along with the British naturally risked a fight by flaunting the tricolor. The Japanese had put away the Rising Sun, yet their influence on events was not quite finished. The story of Vietnam during the next fifteen months is symbolized by the removal of one after another of these flags, until only the banners of the French and the DRV remained, held by citizens about to lock together in mortal combat.

On 6 September, a *British* advance party landed at Tan Son Nhut airport to prepare for arrival in Saigon of the Twentieth Indian Division, whose commander, General Douglas Gracey, also had responsibility for all other Allied units, civilian as well as military, about to enter Indochina south of the 16th parallel. When Gracey himself arrived a week later, he immediately ordered his Gurkha escort to accompany a Japanese unit to evict the Vietnamese Southern Provisional Executive Committee from the former Governor-General's Palace. On the 22d, Gracey accepted Jean Cédile's urgings that he rearm fourteen hundred French soldiers and civilians, who then, in the name of restoring law and order, proceeded to rampage through the city, cursing, beating up, detaining, and otherwise offending any native encountered. Although Gracey angrily disarmed the former internees as punishment, Vietnamese bands of different political tendencies struck back ruthlessly, killing more than a hundred and fifty French civilians, many of them women and children. As the hatred and bloodshed escalated, no leader, British, French, or Vietnamese, was in a position to reverse the cycle. One-sided news accounts quickly reached Paris and Hanoi, provoking public outrage and strengthening the hands of those who argued that no negotiated solution was possible.

In London, as well as at SEAC headquarters in Kandy, word of these violent outbursts in Saigon led Great Britain to place a ceiling on the number of its own forces entering southern Indochina, while simultaneously attempting without success to speed up the arrival of French troops. On 3 October, the French cruiser *Triomphant* debarked the first thousand-man contingent of the Fifth Colonial Infantry Regiment. Three weeks later, sufficient strength existed for Gracey to launch a combined British-French-Japanese attack on the town of My Tho in the Mekong Delta. During November, a French armored column swept northwest to Tay Ninh, while Japanese and British units cleared armed Viet Minh adherents from the region immediately north and northwest of Saigon. A French infantry battalion landed at Nha Trang on the central coast, backed up by the big guns of the *Triomphant*. British/Indian ground forces increasingly avoided participation in offensive operations, although Spitfire aircraft continued to roam the skies, swooping down occasionally to strafe Vietnamese hamlets and river craft. With Lord Mountbatten facing difficulties elsewhere in Southeast Asia, one Indian infantry brigade departed Indochina for Borneo in late December, and another headed for Malaya in mid January 1946. Amid much ceremony, the French made Gracey a *citoyen d'honneur* of the city of Saigon before he departed on 28 January. General Jacques Philippe Leclerc took the salute of the last British forces to leave two months later, which concluded Britain's direct involvement in Indochina except for repatriation of Japanese personnel still awaiting sea transport.

Once the shock of national defeat had been absorbed, most of the eighty thousand or so *Japanese* nationals positioned in Indochina in September 1945 turned their thoughts to home and to avoiding local dangers until such time as Allied commanders found spare ships to send them there. General Gracey often ordered Japanese forces positioned south of the 16th parallel to take part in offensive operations, however, and he gave them a variety of patrol, police, guard, and logistical duties as well. Because Japanese officers refused to take orders from French personnel, an elaborate network of British liaison officers had to be constructed. In the north, meanwhile, the Chinese general Lu Han ordered most Japanese personnel to concentrate in the vicinity of Haiphong, while temporarily retaining the services of a few technicians. General Tsuchihashi's fears about ill-treatment of his men at the hands of incoming Chinese forces proved unfounded; Yunnanese recruits in particular seemed awed by Japanese combat units, who maintained their discipline and composure even in defeat. It helped that Japanese commanders were well supplied with piastre banknotes, reducing the likelihood of confrontations over food, fuel, and other scarce resources.

By August 1946, the big holding camps for Japanese at Cap Saint-Jacques in the south and Haiphong in the north had been emptied, but the French continued to detain at least nine hundred Japanese officials, Kenpeitai members, prison guards, and alleged secret agents. The exact fate of many of these individuals is uncertain, although we know that a few were executed, while others eventually managed to make their way back to Japan. Marshal Terauchi had been transferred to Singapore earlier by the British for possible trial as a war criminal, but died of natural causes before the issue could be resolved. General Tsuchihashi made his way home unobtrusively, despite the desire of the French to punish him for the events of March 1945, above all for the summary execution of Indochina Army officers at Lang Son.

Meanwhile, perhaps five hundred Japanese officers and enlisted men had chosen to join the Viet Minh and other armed groups, especially in the south. Each was given a Vietnamese name and otherwise encouraged to blend in. They were particularly useful as weapons instructors and in the establishment of small equipment repair and ordnance facilities. Casualty rates were high, but a few survivors arrived back in Japan quietly in the late 1950s. At about this time, other Japanese with experience in Indochina returned to Saigon at the encouragement of Ngo Dinh Diem, now president of the fledgling Republic of Vietnam; some of these became quite wealthy in the wartime economic boom of the 1960s. Former Ambassador Matsumoto visited Saigon several times as Tokyo's special representative. Although the 1975 communist victory meant financial setbacks for Japanese businessmen, a decade later they were in the vanguard of renewed trading contacts with Vietnam. In January 1993, as if to tie up a loose end, Hanoi announced that it intended to return the remains of eighteen Japanese servicemen killed during or immediately after World War II.

In fulfillment of Allied General Order No. 1, the first *Chinese* troop units reached Hanoi on 9 September 1945, unceremoniously evicting Jean Sainteny from that city's former Governor-General's Palace the next day. Sainteny's requests that colonial troops be released and rearmed were rejected. A week later General Lu Han met with Ho Chi Minh, implicitly accepting the DRV provisional government as a suitable partner, providing it delivered sufficient provisions to Chinese troops, did not protest massive Chinese financial manipulations, and kept popular discontent about the occupation under control. General Hsiao Wen was not happy that his plans to install the Vietnam Revolutionary League, headed by Nguyen Hai Than, had been finessed; later he pressured Ho Chi Minh to accept Revolutionary League and Nationalist Party members into the government, a tactical arrangement that satisfied no one.

At the ceremony organized by Lu Han to take General Tsuchihashi's surrender on 28 September, neither France nor the DRV was represented officially. Not long afterward, however, Generalissimo Chiang Kai-shek received the new French high commissioner for Indochina, Admiral d'Argenlieu, in Chungking, and by the end of October, French Ambassador Zinovi Pechkoff was able to inform Paris that China might well return northern Indochina to France in exchange for substantial economic concessions. As the diplomatic bargaining continued into 1946, thousands of Chinese carpetbaggers took advantage of the military occupation to reap quick rewards at the expense of the long-suffering inhabitants, while division after division of troops from Yunnan and Kwangsi transited Haiphong en route to northern China and eventual battle with Mao Tsetung's forces. On 28 February, Chungking agreed with Paris to withdraw the remaining Chinese forces in exchange for France relinquishing territorial and concessional rights extracted from China in the nineteenth century, providing a free port and customs transit for Chinese goods moving through Tonkin, and granting special status to Chinese nationals residing in Indochina. Although Chinese generals in Hanoi wanted more than this, and managed to delay final withdrawal for six months, French troops began landing at Haiphong on 8 March.

As Chiang Kai-shek's confrontation with the Chinese Communist Party and Red Army intensified in 1947, Indochinese affairs slid toward inconsequentiality. Many Kwangsi and Yunnan generals had deserted the Nationalist cause by early 1949, making the southern provinces a less promising venue for Chiang's forces to retreat to than the island of Taiwan. In January 1950, the new People's Republic of China became the first government to recognize the DRV. Stocks of American weapons and ammunition captured in Korea and transported to the Sino-Vietnamese border enabled General Vo Nguyen Giap to outfit entire new divisions. Chinese anti-aircraft units played a key role in Giap's 1954 victory over the French at Dien Bien Phu. The CCP exerted considerable influence over Vietnamese communists until the Great Proletarian Cultural Revolution of the late 1960s. Relations cooled markedly following President Richard Nixon's 1972 visit to China, and eventually degenerated into armed hostilities in 1979. At least four hundred thousand overseas Chinese fled Vietnam. A decade later, as the "socialist world" disintegrated, elderly communist rulers in Beijing and Hanoi saw cause to resolve their differences, yet Vietnamese suspicions about the long-term motivations of the Chinese persisted. Meanwhile, the Republic of China (Taiwan), taking advantage of Hanoi's sweeping economic reforms, could boast in 1993 that it was the largest single foreign investor in Vietnam.

Following the Japanese capitulation in mid August 1945, the government of the *United States* saw no reason to become extensively involved in Indochina, having already agreed that Chinese and British forces would assume occupation responsibilities, and having formally reendorsed French sovereignty over the territory. Even so, American theater-level momentum persisted a bit longer, and Washington was embarrassed by a series of articles by journalists who arrived with Allied units that expressed outrage at the general disregard for native aspirations to independence. American largess, personal contacts, and political favor became the object of intense local competition and complaints. Given general perceptions of its massive power and its prestige, decisions by the United States *not* to act took on causative significance in themselves.

During late 1945, the most important question was the degree to which the United States would assist France to regain sovereign authority over Indochina, above all by facilitating the arrival of French troops, equipment, and supplies. The Allied Shipping Pool decided to assign a far higher priority to repatriation of U.S. and British troops, as well as to transporting Indian soldiers home from the Mediterranean, although eight troopships were provided by the United States to move the French Ninth Colonial Infantry Division to Saigon. Most French soldiers were outfitted with U.S. weapons and uniforms, and they roared around in U.S. jeeps, trucks, and armored cars—a startling, depressing sight for Vietnamese who had hoped for American neutrality, if not outright support.

For a while, contradictory signals from the Americans abounded. In Saigon, much to the ire of General Gracey, OSS Lieutenant Colonel Peter Dewey publicly protested French behavior and met repeatedly with Viet Minh representatives, until he was killed by unknown Vietnamese assailants on 26 September. In Chungking, General Wedemeyer still chose not to reequip French troops in southern China, and neither did he try to persuade Chiang Kai-shek to reverse General Lu Han's decision to exclude French forces entirely from northern Indochina. Brigadier General Philip Gallagher, the senior American adviser to General Lu Han, was taken by Major Patti to meet President Ho Chi Minh, and it was not long before Hanoi newspapers proclaimed Gallagher co-founder of a Vietnamese-

American Association. Patti was ordered by his OSS superiors to depart Indochina forthwith and appears to have been placed in career purgatory by the U.S. Army. He was probably fortunate not to be dragged out for condemnation by Senator Joseph McCarthy during the witch-hunts for communists in the 1950s.

The Truman administration gave more consistent support to French efforts in Indochina as the Cold War intensified in 1948, and especially following communist victory in China, when Indochina came to be seen as a vital segment of the global anticommunist front line. Even before the outbreak of the Korean War in June 1950, Washington increased its military aid to the French substantially, and by fiscal 1953–54, the United States was paying 78 percent of France's total costs in Indochina. As Paris withdrew troops in stages following the 1954 Geneva Conference, the Eisenhower administration took up full sponsorship of the fledgling Vietnamese Army created by the French and supported the resolutely anticommunist Ngo Dinh Diem in his efforts to build a new Republic of Vietnam with its capital in Saigon.

In 1963, dissatisfied at Diem's lack of progress in quelling the communist-led insurgency in South Vietnam, President John F. Kennedy backed a military coup that resulted in the killing of Diem and his younger brother; a third brother was executed a few months later. From that time on, it was probably inevitable that Washington would commit American combat forces to South Vietnam, although President Lyndon Johnson held back until March 1965. Four years later, when it was clear that even 550,000 U.S. troops could not provide the desired results, President Nixon began gradual reductions in the name of "Vietnamization" of the conflict. The agreement finally signed in Paris in January 1973 traded complete withdrawal of U.S. troops for the return of American POWs and the continued functioning of two separate administrations in the south pending further negotiations. These negotiations never got off the ground, however, and when Hanoi launched its massive military offensive in early 1975, President Gerald Ford decided not to send U.S. aircraft back over Vietnam to counter it. The Republic of Vietnam collapsed quickly, and America accepted hundreds of thousands of Vietnamese refugees. Subsequently, the United States maintained an economic embargo on Hanoi, which was not lifted until 1994. Begun so well-meaningly in the middle of World War II, America's Vietnam involvement produced domestic wounds second only to those of the 1861–65 U.S. Civil War.

French determination to return to Indochina in late 1945 was matched by neither the physical resources necessary to accomplish the task forcibly nor the political flexibility to negotiate power-sharing arrangements with Ho Chi Minh and other DRV leaders. French gunboats coursed up and down the tributaries of the Mekong, and armored columns dashed as far as Ban Me Thuot in the central highlands, but General Leclerc lacked sufficient troops to control the southern countryside. It would take years to reconstitute a native militia, and even longer to create a Vietnamese officer corps. As for Tonkin, Leclerc possessed no minesweepers or landing craft to mount an early amphibious operation around Haiphong, and lacked sufficient transport aircraft to drop even one battalion over Hanoi—assuming Chinese agreement to French reentry there, which was not forthcoming until six months later. Given those limitations, regaining control over Cambodia and Laos became all the more important. By January 1946, King Norodom Sihanouk had accepted French terms for Cambodia. Laos took a bit longer, because of Chinese objections to French forces operating north of the 16th parallel and armed resistance from bands of young Vietnamese and Lao, but by late April it was possible to install a commissioner of the French Republic in Vientiane. French forces from Laos had already penetrated central Vietnam to seize the former royal capital of Hue. Although these developments enabled Admiral d'Argenlieu to talk with more authority of an "Indochina Federation," they simultaneously reinforced the fears of the Vietnamese about what lay in store for them if effective national resistance could not be organized.

While working to achieve military supremacy, the French did not abjure political discussions with prominent Vietnamese entirely. In Hanoi on 12 October 1945, Jean Sainteny and Léon Pignon met with Nguyen Hai Than, head of the Vietnam Revolutionary League, without result. Three days later, Sainteny had his first meeting with Ho Chi Minh. In Paris, de Gaulle met secretly with Prince Vinh San, who had been deposed as boy emperor (Duy Tan) by the French in 1916, exiled to Réunion for twenty-five years, and then enrolled in the Free French forces. Apparently, Vinh San was to be touted as the monarch who had never abdicated, a symbol of both Vietnamese patriotism and Franco-Vietnamese cooperation. That the prince was completely out of touch with events in his homeland must have been considered an asset by de Gaulle. The idea of de Gaulle and Vinh San going to Saigon together was, however, aborted when the prince died in an airplane crash in Africa in December.

De Gaulle's sudden resignation of the provisional presidency of France in January 1946, and France's return to party government, gave Saigon greater weight in decision making with respect to Indochina. D'Argenlieu quickly lined up several wealthy, malleable Vietnamese to participate in a

Cochinchina Consultative Council. By contrast, Leclerc and Sainteny, increasingly mindful of France's military limitations overall, showed more interest in reaching an understanding with Ho Chi Minh that enabled French forces to return unchallenged to the north following the anticipated Paris-Chungking agreement, and that began to set the parameters for future Franco-DRV cooperation. This led to the Preliminary Accord of 6 March 1946, in which the DRV agreed to receive fifteen thousand French troops amicably in exchange for formal recognition as a "free state having its own government, parliament, army and finances, and forming a part of the Indochina Federation and French Union." Cochinchina's unification with the rest of the country was to be the object of a popular referendum. For a brief moment, it appeared that both governments had overcome history, surmounted opposition in their own ranks, and made the concessions that could produce a long-term peaceful relationship.

Six days later, however, Jean Cédile publicly characterized the accord as a "local convention," not committing France to a unified Vietnam; and on 12 March the minister for overseas territories, Marius Moutet, declared that Cochinchina would be treated as a separate "free state" within the federation, an interpretation totally unacceptable to the DRV. Moreover, some French leaders seemed to interpret "free state" to mean French rule with native support, whereas for Ho Chi Minh it signified cultivation of a special relationship by mutual consent. Subsequent diplomatic encounters at Dalat and Fontainebleau failed to resolve these fundamental differences.

During the rest of 1946, a shift to the left in France's political climate appeared to suggest that diplomatic settlement with Ho Chi Minh was feasible. Precisely for that reason, Admiral d'Argenlieu in Saigon was determined to increase military pressure on the DRV. In late November, a dispute over customs controls in Haiphong harbor escalated quickly into French naval bombardment of the city, killing as many as six thousand people. Four weeks later, the DRV ordered a nationwide counterattack. Within months, French forces had seized almost all of Vietnam's cities and towns, yet were experiencing difficulty pacifying the villages or penetrating the forests. In October 1947, French units almost captured Ho Chi Minh in a surprise assault in the hills of Bac Can province; Nguyen Van To, then chairman of the National Assembly, was caught in this raid and died shortly thereafter.

With each passing year, French casualties mounted and the Indochina war became a more divisive issue at home. Protracted discussions with the former emperor Bao Dai and an assortment of noncommunist associates eventually produced a "state of Vietnam" alternative to the DRV, but all important decisions continued to be made by the French. In early 1954, hoping to lure General Vo Nguyen Giap into a set-piece battle, French commanders committed sixteen thousand troops to the distant valley of Dien Bien Phu, near the frontier with Laos. In an unprecedented logistical maneuver, Giap shifted sufficient soldiers, artillery, anti-aircraft guns, ammunition, and food 220 kilometers across the mountains of northern Vietnam to be able to isolate, bombard, assault, and finally force the surrender of the entire French garrison.

In July 1954, a new French government took the occasion of an international conference at Geneva to negotiate a cease-fire and regroupment formula with a DRV delegation headed by Pham Van Dong. French troops withdrew south of the 17th parallel, and were then sent home, the last unit departing Saigon in 1956. Paris henceforth had no choice but to accept predominant American influence in South Vietnam. Sainteny was dispatched to Hanoi as France's "general delegate" to the DRV in the hope of building a new economic and cultural relationship, but this came to naught; he returned for the last time in 1969 to represent France at the funeral of Ho Chi Minh. In early 1993, President François Mitterrand became the first Western head of state to visit Vietnam since the end of the Vietnam War in 1975. "I am here to close a chapter, and even more so, to open another," Mitterrand declared.

Between its Declaration of Independence on 2 September 1945 and the outbreak of full-scale hostilities with the French in December 1946, the *Democratic Republic of Vietnam* was transformed from a handful of men issuing edicts in Hanoi into a revolutionary state commanding the loyalty of the vast majority of the people living in the former Tonkin, Annam, and Cochinchina. The DRV's flag, anthem, and motto ("Independence, Freedom, Happiness") stood above all other political symbols. Ho Chi Minh's frail image was revered widely as that of the national savior; his voice was conveyed by radio even to guerrilla fighters in the distant jungles of southern Vietnam. In the north and in large parts of central Vietnam, the DRV possessed an administrative apparatus, an army, a zealous militia, a police force (both public and secret), and tens of thousands of dedicated, if unpaid, literacy teachers, hygiene instructors, youth organizers, and cultural cadres. Citizens throughout the country joined Viet Minh groups according to occupation, age, gender, religion, or ethnic origin. Although officially dissolved in November 1945, the ICP continued quietly to restructure, recruit new members, attempt to control vital state sectors, and monitor society at large.

People did not identify with all these changes in equal measure. Pride in the new symbols of the Vietnamese state and faith in President Ho Chi Minh went deeper and extended further than confidence in government ministries, local administrative committees, or Viet Minh cadres. The army also won considerable admiration from the public, partly because of its crisp, no-nonsense style, but especially because of its early dispatch of troops to the south (most of whom never returned), and its stated readiness to fight elsewhere whenever ordered. Amid the general exuberance, some elements of society remained cautious about ICP / Viet Minh intentions. Thus, the substantial Catholic minority (about 10 percent of the population) worried about being punished for its historical links with the foreigner. Ho Chi Minh proved adept at alleviating those concerns, to the extent that Vietnamese bishops willingly lobbied the Vatican and Paris for recognition of the DRV, and thousands of young Catholics joined the army and militia. Several years later, many Catholics became alienated from "the Revolution," yet very few returned to full-fledged cooperation with the French.

Local committees sometimes ignored national directives by seizing the property of landlords, harassing merchants, jailing individuals arbitrarily, extorting heavy financial "contributions" from anyone perceived as having benefited from the colonial system, and prohibiting a range of traditional customs. Anyone who complained risked being labeled a "traitor," "reactionary," or "counterrevolutionary." Particularly flagrant violations of government instructions came to the attention of higher echelons, with special investigators being sent with powers to search and arrest. However, compliance was achieved more often by patiently explaining to obstreperous local revolutionaries the importance of engaging the vast majority of citizens in united-front activity, while isolating and neutralizing those few who refused to go along.

Different tactics were employed against any group considered a potential challenger to the monopoly of political power held by the ICP / Viet Minh. In the north, local struggles quickly broke out with members of the Revolutionary League and the Nationalist Party, even while Ho Chi Minh met cordially with their leaders and accepted several into his government. By April 1946, ICP / Viet Minh activists had forced the adherents of the Revolutionary League and the Nationalist Party out of the political arena entirely except in the capital of Hanoi and a few towns along the communication routes to China. Nguyen Hai Than, for a short while vice president of the DRV, had already fled the country. Nguyen Tuong Tam attended the Dalat conference as DRV foreign minister, but disappeared to

China in June. DRV police soon made it impossible for independent political activity to continue even in Hanoi, yet in the name of an ever-expanding united front, some Revolutionary League and Nationalist Party members were permitted to keep their seats in the National Assembly. Others rotted in detention camps in the northern hills or made abject confessions to the police in order to avoid incarceration.

In the south, bitter disputes continued to erupt between the ICP / Viet Minh and other groups committed to fighting the French, notably the Hoa Hao and Cao Dai religious groups. Following arrival of Nguyen Binh from the north at the end of 1945, a degree of basic communication and tactical coordination across competing groups was achieved. During 1946, small-scale attacks on French personnel and Vietnamese identified with the "Republic of Cochinchina" increased in urban as well as rural locations. Ironically, this momentum became apparent to the outside world in a nonviolent manner on 30 October, when almost all resistance units in the south observed a cease-fire agreement reached earlier by Ho Chi Minh and Marius Moutet in Paris. This surprisingly disciplined response helped to convince Admiral d'Argenlieu that pacification could not be achieved in Cochinchina until the DRV government was toppled in Hanoi. Meanwhile, throughout north, center, and south, the objectives of fighting separatism and achieving territorial integrity had become the touchstone of Vietnamese patriotism—around which the DRV and the Communist Party could consolidate political hegemony for the next three decades.

From the beginning, the DRV's main weakness was its economy. Another terrible famine in the north was barely averted in late 1945 by a variety of short-term measures, although at least ten thousand people nonetheless died of starvation. The May 1946 rice harvest was reasonably bountiful, and the government subsequently mobilized hundreds of thousands of people to repair the Red River dikes, thus preventing a possible repetition of the August 1945 floods. The revenues of the central government remained very precarious, however, several taxes having been abolished in conformity with Viet Minh promises, and others being difficult to collect in the revolutionary conditions prevailing. "Voluntary" contributions to support the army and other defense-related initiatives did flow in, but that still left other government ministries with minuscule budgets. Although the central authorities assigned high priority to resuming plantation agriculture, to reopening colonial-period mines and industries, and to stimulating commerce, the early results were disappointing. Paris repeatedly held out the lures of economic aid, technical assistance, and capital investment as part of a larger diplomatic settlement, but even if Vietnamese and French negotiators had announced an agreement in late 1946 and begun to implement its provisions, it is not at all certain that Ho Chi Minh could have persuaded local committees to relinquish French property in the interests of joint reconstruction and development. French analysts often predicted the collapse of the DRV as a result of internal economic contradictions, not appreciating the degree to which people were willing to tighten their belts for a patriotic cause, or the capacity of Vietnamese society to keep afloat on village-level rice cultivation and cottage industries.

Withdrawal under fire from Hanoi and other cities and towns at the end of 1946 heightened the trends in the DRV toward economic decentralization, barter, and local taxation in kind, although leaders set ambitious production and collection quotas, which were often achieved. So long as foreigners denied Vietnamese unity and threatened the existence of the DRV, people seemed prepared, with varying degrees of enthusiasm, to work longer hours and live on a bare minimum. This "war economy" system persisted beyond the DRV's 1954 return to Hanoi, now bolstered by Stalinist/Maoist ideology and injections of aid from the Soviet Union and China that masked its inefficiencies. Not until 1979 did Communist Party leaders begin to lose confidence in the existing system, and it was another ten years before the economy underwent fundamental transformations.

The generation of ICP members who had survived repression and jail in the 1930s, and who disseminated the Viet Minh message before August 1945, went on to govern the DRV and command its armed forces for the next forty years. The generation of youths who joined patriotic groups in the summer of 1945, practiced marching, demonstrated, took control of offices, and formed local revolutionary committees became the vital middle echelon of Party, state, and military hierarchies for those same four decades, although not a few died in battle or were purged during the bitter 1950s campaigns against "class enemies." Each subsequent generation has grown up in an atmosphere imbued with the mystique of 1945, whether conveyed by parents and grandparents or by Party cadres, schoolteachers, and writers.

As prior generations disappear from the scene and the circumstances of life change, heroic stories inevitably lose their glow. Because the legitimacy of the Communist Party in Vietnam is so closely linked to the events of 1945, efforts to revitalize the memory of that year are common, but no new interpretations have yet made their way past the censors. It seems only a matter of time, however, before novelists, filmmakers, and historians (perhaps in that order) find ways of looking afresh at this watershed in Vietnam's modern history.

Glossary

Complete Vietnamese diacritics are provided here for all names and terms introduced in the main text and for those mentioned in the footnotes, apart from source listings. The arrangement is alphabetical, but not in standard Vietnamese fashion (i.e., broken down by diacritical markings, multiple-letter initial consonants, etc.), since this might confuse some readers. Only one non-English initial consonant demands differentiation in the alphabet here: Đ (in lower case, đ), which follows D.

An Châu
An Nam
An Nhơn
Ân Thi
An Toàn Khu
Anh Tâm
áo dài
Ba Đình
Bà Rá
Bà Rịa
Ba Tơ
Bắc Bộ
Bắc Bộ Phủ
Bắc Cạn
Bắc Giang
Bắc Kỳ
Bắc Kỳ Khâm Sai Đại Thần
Bạc Liêu
Bắc Mã

Bắc Ninh
Bắc Sơn
Bạch Mai
Ban Mê Thuột
Bần-yên-nhân
Bảo An Binh
Bảo Đại
Bảo Đại cũng bại đảo
Bảo Long
Bệ Hạ
Bến Cát
Bến Tre
Biên Hòa
Bình Định
Bình Gia
Bình Giang
Bình Sơn
Bình Thuận
binh vận

Bộ Đội Việt Mỹ
bộ trợ quân
bọn cướp
Bùi Bằng Đoàn
Bùi Công Trừng
Bùi Quang Chiêu
Bùi Văn Hách
Bùi Văn Thụ
Bửu Tiếp
cách mạng
cách mạng giải phóng dân tộc
Cách Mạng Tháng Tám
Cai Lậy
Cẩm Giàng
Cẩm Phả
Cam Ranh
Cầm Văn Dung
Can Lộc
Cần Thơ
Cang
Cao-Bắc-Lạng
Cao Bằng
Cao Đài
Cao Duệ
Cao Hồng Lĩnh
Cao Ngọc Liên
Cầu Lác
Chấn Tốn
cháo gà
Châu Đốc
Châu Thành
chia để trị
chiến đấu
chiến khu
Chợ Chu
Chợ Đệm
Chợ Lớn
Chợ Mới
Chợ Rã
chó săn
chủ lực
Chu Văn Tấn
Chung Bá Khánh

Chương Mỹ
Cờ Giải Phóng
cơ hội
cờ tướng
con
Côn Sơn
công điền
Cột Cờ
Cù Huy Cận
cụ lớn
Cung Đình Vận
Cường Để
Cứu Quốc
Cứu Quốc Quân
Dân Sinh
dân tộc
Di Lăng
Diên Khánh
Diệt Phát-Xít
Dương Bá Trạc
Dương Bạch Mai
Dương Công Hoạt
Dương Đức Hiền
Dương Trung Quốc
Duy Tân
Duy Xuyên
đả đảo
Đà Lạt
Đà Nẵng
Đại Lộc
Đại Việt
Đại Việt Quốc Dân Đảng
Đại Việt Quốc Gia Liên
    Minh
Đại Việt Quốc Gia Xã Hội
    Đảng
Đàm Duy Huyến
Đàm Quang Trung
Đàm Thị Loan
Đan Phượng
Đảng Dân Chủ Việt Nam
Đăng Đàn
Đảng Hiếu An

Đặng Ming Phụng
Đặng Thái Mai
Đào Duy Anh
Đào Trọng Kim
Đáp Cầu
Đề Thám
Đệ Tứ Chiến Khu
Đèo Khế
đi bí mật
Điện Bàn
Điện Biên Phủ
đình
Đình Bảng
Đinh Hòa
Đinh Khắc Thiếc
Đinh Xuân Lâm
Đỗ Đình Đạo
Đỗ Đức Dục
Đỗ Huy Liêm
Đồ Sơn
Đỗ Văn Bình
đoàn
đoàn thể cứu quốc
Độc Lập
độc lập bánh vẽ
đội danh dự
đội quân cảm tử
đội xung phong
Đông Á
Đông Ba
Đồng Đăng
Đông Dương Cộng Sản Đảng
Đồng Khánh
Đồng Kỵ
Đồng Mu
Đồng Nai
Đồng Nai Thượng
Đồng Phúc Quận
Đồng Triều
Đuốc Tuệ
Đuống
Gia Định
Gia Hòa

Gia Lai
Gia Lâm
Gia Lộc
Gia Long
giặc
giặc lùn
Giải Phóng
Giải Phóng Dân Tộc
Gianh
Giao Thủy
Gò Công
Hà Đông
Hà Giang
Hạ Hòa
Hà Huy Giáp
Hà Huy Tập
Hạ Long
Hà Nam
Hà Ngọc Niên
Hà Nội
Hà Tiên
Hà Tĩnh
Hà Văn Đại
Hà Văn Vượng
Hà Vị
Hải Ấn
Hải Dương
Hải Hậu
Hải Ninh
Hải Phòng
Hải Thanh
Hải Vân
Hàm Tân
Hàn Thuyên
Hàng Ngang
Hậu Giang
Hiền
Hiệp Hòa
hò
Hồ Chí Minh
Hồ Đắc An
Hồ Đắc Điểm
Hồ Diệc Lan

Hồ Học Lãm
Hồ Hữu Tường
Hồ Ngọc Lãm
Hồ Tá Khanh
Hồ Tùng Mậu
Hồ Văn Ngà
Hoa
Hòa Bình
Hòa Hảo
Hoa Kiều
Hỏa Lò
Hoa Quân Nhập Việt
Hoài Đức
Hoàn Kiếm
Hoàng Anh
Hoàng Đạo Thúy
Hoàng Diệu
Hoàng Đình Ròng
Hoàng Đôn Văn
Hoẳng Hóa
Hoàng Hữu Nam
Hoàng Minh Chính
Hoàng Minh Giám
Hoàng Quốc Việt
Hoàng Qúy
Hoàng Sâm
Hoàng Thượng
Hoàng Trọng Phu
Hoàng Văn Đức
Hoàng Văn Hán
Hoàng Văn Hoan
Hoàng Văn Thái
Hoàng Văn Thụ
Hoàng Xuân Hãn
Hội An
Hội Đồng Cải Cách Cai Trị Tư Pháp
 và Tài Chính
Hội Khai Trí Tiến Đức
hồi ký cách mạng
Hội Nghị Tư Vấn Quốc Gia
Hội Phụ Nữ Việt Nam
hội tương tế
Hội Việt Nam Thanh Niên Ái Quốc

Hòn Gai
hợp pháp
Huế
Hưng Yên
Hương Tích
Huỳnh Dư
Huỳnh Kim Khánh
Huỳnh Ngọc Thu
Huỳnh Phú Sổ
Huỳnh Sanh Thông
Huỳnh Tấn Phát
Huỳnh Thúc Kháng
Huỳnh Văn Phương
Huỳnh Văn Tiếng
Kẻ Sở
Khải Định
Khâm Khai
Khâm Sai
Khâm Sai Nam Kỳ
Khánh Hòa
khởi nghĩa
Khu Giải Phóng
Khuất Duy Tiến
Khuất Thị Vĩnh
khủng bố đỏ
Kiến An
Kiến Trung
Kiến Xương
Kim Lũng
Kim Sơn
Kinh
Kinh Thầy
Lạc Hồng
Lạc Sơn
Lạc Song
Lai Châu
Lâm Thao
Lạng Sơn
Lao Bảo
Lào Cai
Lê Duẩn
Lê Đức Thọ
Lê Giản

Lê Hồng Phong

Lê Hữu Từ

Lê Khang

Lê Lợi

Lê Mậu Hãn

Lê Minh

Lê Quảng Ba

Lê Quang Liêm

Lê Quang Tảo

Lê Quốc Hiến

Lê Tất Đắc

Lê Thanh Nghị

Lê Thi

Lê Thiết Hùng

Lê Trần Đức

Lê Trọng Nghĩa

Lê Tự Đồng

Lê Tức Chuyên

Lê Tung Sơn

Lê Văn Hiến

Lê Văn Huến

Lê Văn Trà

Lê Viết Lượng

Lê Xuân

Lên Đàng

Liêm Phóng

Liên Đoàn

lính cơ

lính dõng

lính lệ

Linh Quang Vọng

Lộc Ninh

Long An

Long Biên

Long Xuyên

Lũ Phong

Lục Văn Lợi

Lục Vân Tiên

Lục Yên

Lụng

Luộc

Lương Đại Bân

Lương Sơn

Lương Văn Chi

Lưu Hữu Phước

Lưu Văn Lang

Ly

Lý Chiến Thắng

Lý Thường Kiệt

Mai Đình Minh

Mai Trọng Tánh

Mai Văn Bộ

Mai Văn Hàm

Mán Tiền

Mang Cá

Mặt Trận Quốc Gia Thống Nhứt

mẫu

mấy ông Trung Ương

Mèo

Minh Vương

mõ

Mỏ Chén

Mỏ Nhài

Móng Cái

Mường

Mỹ Độ

Mỹ Hào

Mỹ Sơn

Mỹ Tho

Nà Ngần

Nam Bộ

Nam Cao

Nam Định

Nam Hải

Nam Kỳ

Nam Long

Năm Lửa

Nam Phương

Nam Quan

Nga Thiên Hương

Ngài

Ngân Sơn

Ngang

Nghệ An

Nghĩa Lộ

Nghiêm Kế Tổ
nghiêm trị
Nghiêm Tử Trinh
Ngô Bích Sơn
Ngô Đình Diệm
Ngô Đình Huân
Ngô Đình Khôi
Ngô Hoàng Oanh
Ngô Kiều
Ngô Minh Loan
Ngọ Môn
Ngô Quang Châu
Ngô Quyền
Ngô Tấn Nhơn
Ngô Văn Hòa
Ngô Xuân Đan
Nguyễn
Nguyễn Ái Quốc
Nguyên Bình
Nguyễn Bình
Nguyễn Chí Thanh
Nguyễn Công Hòa
Nguyễn Công Hoan
Nguyễn Điền
Nguyễn Đình Chiểu
Nguyễn Đình Diệp
Nguyễn Đình Phách
Nguyễn Đình Thi
Nguyễn Duy Thân
Nguyễn Duy Thông
Nguyễn Duy Trinh
Nguyễn Hải Thần
Nguyễn Hòa Hiệp
Nguyễn Hồng
Nguyễn Huệ
Nguyễn Hữu Đang
Nguyễn Hữu Tạo
Nguyễn Hữu Thân
Nguyễn Hữu Thi
Nguyễn Hữu Trí
Nguyễn Huy Khôi
Nguyễn Huy Tưởng
Nguyễn Khang

Nguyễn Khoa Diệu Hồng
Nguyễn Khoa Phong
Nguyễn Lộc
Nguyễn Lương Bằng
Nguyễn Mạnh Hà
Nguyễn Ngọc Sơn
Nguyễn Phi Oanh
Nguyễn Quyết
Nguyễn Tài Đức
Nguyễn Tất Đạt
Nguyễn Thái Học
Nguyễn Thể Đức
Nguyễn Thế Khang
Nguyễn Thế Nghiệp
Nguyễn Thị Bích Thuận
Nguyễn Thị Lào
Nguyễn Thị Minh Khai
Nguyễn Thị Quang Thái
Nguyễn Thị Thập
Nguyễn Trực Hiến
Nguyễn Tường Long
Nguyễn Tường Tam
Nguyễn Văn Chì
Nguyễn Văn Chính
Nguyễn Văn Cừ
Nguyễn Văn Cung
Nguyễn Văn Giao
Nguyễn Văn Hương
Nguyễn Văn Huyện
Nguyễn Văn Khoát
Nguyễn Văn Luyện
Nguyễn Văn Nguyễn
Nguyễn Văn Ninh
Nguyễn Văn Rạng
Nguyễn Văn Sâm
Nguyễn Văn Sỹ
Nguyễn Văn Tạo
Nguyễn Văn Tây
Nguyễn Văn Thủ
Nguyễn Văn Tố
Nguyễn Văn Trân
Nguyễn Văn Trấn
Nguyễn Văn Túc

Nguyễn Văn Vĩnh
Nguyễn Văn Xuân
Nguyễn Xiển
Nguyễn Xuân Chữ
Nguyễn Xuân Thiệp
Nha Trang
nhân sĩ
Nho Giáo
Như Phong
Ninh Bình
Ninh Giang
Ninh Thuận
Nội Bài
Nông Văn Lạc
Nùng
ông
Ông Ké
Pác Bó
Phác
Phai Khắt
Phạm Công Tắc
Phạm Hùng
Phạm Hữu Chương
Phạm Khắc Hoè
Phạm Ngọc Thạch
Phạm Quỳnh
Phạm Tất Hiểm
Phạm Văn Bạch
Phạm Văn Đồng
Phạm Văn Thạch
Phạm Việt Tử
Phạm Vũ Phiệt
Phan Anh
Phan Bội Châu
Phan Chu Trinh
Phan Đăng Lưu
phản đế cứu quốc hội
Phan Đình Phùng
Phan Hữu Hải
Phan Huy Quát
Phan Kế Bảo
Phan Kế Toại
Phan Mỹ

Phan Rang
Phan Thiết
Phan Tử Lăng
Phan Văn Hùm
Phan Văn Phúc
Phát Diệm
Phổ Yên
Phù Cát
Phủ Doãn
Phù Đổng
Phủ Lạng Thương
Phú Lộc
Phủ Lý
Phù Mỹ
Phú Ninh
Phù Thọ
Phú Yên
Phục Quốc Quân
Phúc Yên
Phùng Chí Kiên
Phụng Sự Quốc Gia
phương
Quản Dưỡng
Quản Trân
Quảng Bình
Quảng Nam
Quảng Ngãi
Quảng Trị
Quảng Yên
Qui Nhơn
Quốc Dân Đại Hội
Quốc Gia Đồng Minh
quốc kỳ
quốc ngữ
Quỳnh Côi
Quỳnh Lưu
Rạch Giá
Sa Đéc
Sài Gòn
Sầm Sơn
Sóc Trăng
Sơn La
Sơn Tây

Sông Cầu

Song Hào

Tà Lài

Tạ Quang Bửu

Tạ Thu Thâu

Tạ Uyên

Tam Đảo

Tam Kỳ

Tân Á

Tân An

tân dân chủ

Tân Sơn Nhứt

Tân Trào

Tân Việt Nam Hội

Tày

Tây Đô

Tây Ninh

tay sai

Tết

Thạch Thất

Thái

Thái Bình

Thái Nguyên

Thân Trọng Hậu

Thanh

Thanh Hóa

Thanh Miện

Thanh Nghị

Thanh Niên Ái Quốc Đoàn

Thanh Niên Hành Khúc

Thanh Niên Tiền Phong

Thanh Niên Xung Phong Hoàng Diệu

Thanh Phong

Thanh Sơn

Thanh Thủy

Tháp Chàm

thiên mệnh

Thiệu Hoa

Thổ

thổ phỉ

thời cơ

Thủ Dầu Một

Thừa Thiên

Thuận An

Thuận Thành

Thường Tín

Tiên Giang

Tiên Hải

Tiến Lợi

Tiền Phong

Tiến Quân Ca

Tiền Tuyến Thanh Niên

Tiếng Dân

Tiếng Gọi Thanh Niên

Tin Mới

Tơ

Tô Hoài

Tố Hữu

Tô Hữu Hạnh

Tố Như

Tổ Quốc

tôi

Tôi là Tây mà!

Tôn Quang Phiệt

Tôn Thất Gián

Tôn Thất Tùng

Tổng Bộ

Tổng Hội Cứu Tế

Tống Văn Kim

Trà Bồng

Trà Ngọc Anh

Trà Vinh

Trầm

Trần Bửu Kiếm

Trần Cung

Trần Dân Tiên

Trần Đăng Ninh

Trần Đình Long

Trần Đình Nam

Trần Độ

Trần Đức Tảo

Trần Đức Vĩnh

Trần Duy Hưng

Trần Giác

Trần Hưng Đạo

Trần Huy Liệu

Trần Quang Bình
Trần Quang Huy
Trần Quang Vinh
Trần Quí Hai
Trần Trọng Kim
Trần Trung Thành
Trần Tử Bình
Trần Văn Ân
Trần Văn Chương
Trần Văn Giàu
Trần Văn Khéo
Trần Văn Lai
Trần Văn Soái
Trần Văn Trà
Trần Văn Tuyên
Trần Xuân Sinh
Tràng Tiền
Tranh Đấu
Tri Tân
Trịnh Đình Thảo
Trịnh Văn Bộ
Trưng
Trung Bộ
Trung Kỳ
Trung Việt Du Kích Quân
Trương Bội Công
Trường Chinh
Trường Quân Chính Kháng Nhật
Trường Sơn
Trương Thị Mỹ
Truyện
Tự Đức
Tư Kỳ
Từ Sơn
Từ Trang
Tự Vệ
Tùng Thiện
tuổi Đảng
Tương Trực
Tuy Hà
Tuyên Quang
Ứng Úy
Ung Văn Khiêm

Uông Bí
Ủy Ban Chỉ Huy Lâm Thời
Ủy Ban Cứu Quốc
Ủy Ban Dân Tộc Giải Phóng
Ủy Ban Hành Chánh Lâm
　Thời Nam Bộ
Ủy Ban Nhân Dân Cách
　Mạng
Ủy Ban Quân Sự Cách Mạng
　Bắc Kỳ
Ủy Ban Quân Sự Cách Mạng
　Hà Nội
ủy ban trừ gian
Ủy Ban Việt Nam Thanh
　Niên Thể Thao Tổng Hội
Văn Cao
vấn đề dân tộc
Văn Lâm
Vạn Phúc
Văn Tạo
Văn Tiến Dũng
Vạt Chay
Vệ
Việt gian
Việt Minh
Việt-Mỹ Liên Quân
Việt Nam Ái Quốc Đảng
Việt Nam Cách Mệnh Đồng
　Minh Hội
Việt Nam Dân Chủ Cộng
　Hòa
Việt Nam Dân Tộc Giải
　Phóng Đồng Minh
Việt Nam Đế Quốc
Việt Nam Độc Lập
Việt Nam Độc Lập Đoàn
Việt Nam Độc Lập Đồng
　Minh
Việt Nam Độc Lập Đồng
　Minh Hội
Việt Nam Giải Phóng Quân
Việt Nam Phản Xâm Lược
　Đồng Minh

Việt Nam Phục Quốc Đồng Minh Hội
Việt Nam Quốc Dân Đảng
Việt Nam Quốc Gia Độc Lập Đảng
Việt Nam Sử Lược
Việt Nam Tuyên Truyền Giải Phóng
 Quân
Việt Trì
Vinh
Vĩnh Cẩn
Vĩnh Linh
Vĩnh Long
Vĩnh San
Vĩnh Thụy
Vĩnh Tường
Vĩnh Yên
Võ Nguyên Giáp
Võ Văn Cầm
Võ Xán
Voi Phục
Vũ Anh
Vũ Đình Dy
Vũ Đình Hoè
Vũ Hồng Khanh
Vũ Huy Phúc
Vũ Lăng

Vũ Ngọc Anh
Vũ Ngọc Cừ
Vũ Nhai
Vũ Như Hùng
Vũ Quốc Uy
Vũ Tiến Đức
Vũ Trọng Khánh
Vũ Văn An
Vũ Văn Hiền
Vũ Văn Minh
Vũ Văn Thụ
Vũng Tàu
vườn không nhà trống
Vương Thừa Vũ
xã hoàn toàn
Xích Thắng
Xuân Diệu
Xuân Phổ
Xuân Thủy
ỷ lại
Yên Bái
Yên Khánh
Yên Phú
Yên Thế

Selected Bibliography

ARCHIVES

Centre des Archives d'Outre-Mer, Aix-en-Provence (AOM)
    Fonds conseiller politique (CP)
    Fonds du gouvernement de fait (GF)
    Indochine nouveau fonds (INF)
Trung Tam Luu Tru Quoc Gia-1 [National Archives Center No. 1], Hanoi
    DRV Government Files, 1945–46
Cuc Luu Tru-2 [Archives Bureau No.2], Ho Chi Minh City
    Fonds du Goucoch (Cochinchina Government Files)
    Nghi Dinh Thong Doc Nam Ky [Edicts of the
        Governor of Cochinchina / Southern Vietnam]
National Archives, Washington, D.C. (USNA)
    Record Group 59: Department of State Decimal Files
    Record Group 226: OSS Records

INTERVIEWS

Duong Quang Dong (Nam Dong), Ho Chi Minh City, 19 March 1988
Ho Huu Tuong, Saigon, 3 March 1967
Ho Ta Khanh, Paris, 1 November 1984
Hoang Van Duc, Hanoi, 19 February 1994
Hoang Van Hoan, Beijing, 13 September 1980
Hoang Xuan Han, Paris, 3 November 1984
Huynh Van Tieng, Ho Chi Minh City, 19 March 1988
Kubota Kanichiro, Tokyo, 19 January 1967
Matsushita Mitsuhiro, Saigon, 2 June 1967
Minoda Fujio, Tokyo, 20 January 1967
Nguyen Van Tran, Hanoi, 17 February 1992
Nishimura Kumao, Tokyo, 27 November 1967
Pham Binh, Hanoi, 18 August 1984

Phan Anh, Hanoi, 7 March 1988
Tan, Frank, by telephone, 29 June 1994
Tran Bach Dang, Ho Chi Minh City, 17 March 1988
Tran Lam, Hanoi, 5 March 1988
Tran Quang Vinh, Saigon, 12 April 1967
Tran Van Giau, Ho Chi Minh City, 25 March 1980, 19 March 1988, 12 February
    1990
Urabe Kiyoji, Tokyo, 15 November 1967
Vo Nguyen Giap, Hanoi, 17 February 1992
Yokoyama Masayuki, Tokyo, 16 November 1967

SERIAL RUNS CONSULTED

Co Giai Phong (Red River Delta; Hanoi)
Cuu Quoc (Red River Delta; Hanoi)
Dan Bao (Saigon)
Doan Ket (Paris)
Journal of Asian Studies (Ann Arbor)
Journal of Southeast Asian Studies (Singapore)
L'Armée française (Paris)
Lich Su Dang (Hanoi)
Lich Su Quan Su (Hanoi)
New York Times (New York)
Nghien Cuu Lich Su (Hanoi)
Tan A (Saigon)
Thong Tin Lich Su Quan Su (Hanoi)
Trung Bac Chu Nhat (Hanoi)
Van Su Dia (Hanoi)

SELECTED BOOKS AND ARTICLES

Aldrich, Richard. "Imperial Rivalry: British and American Intelligence in Asia,
    1942–46." *Intelligence and National Security* 3, no. 1 (Jan. 1988): 5–55.
Alzon, Claude Hesse d'. See Hesse d'Alzon.
Ayrolles, L. H. *L'Indochine ne répond plus.* Saint-Brieux: Les Presses bretonnes,
    1948.
Bang Ba Lan. "Doi, doi . . . " [Hunger, Hunger . . .]. *Vietnam Forum*, no. 5 (Winter–
    Spring 1985): 101–7. Translated by Huynh Sanh Thong.
Bao Dai. *Le Dragon d'Annam.* Paris: Plon, 1980.
Bauchar, René. *Rafales sur l'Indochine.* Paris: Fournier, 1946. The author's real
    name: René Charbonneau.
Bernardini, Jean-J. *Sous la botte nippone.* Paris: Editions de la pensée universelle,
    1971.
Bigot, A., and R. F. Auriol. "Le Problème des mèdicaments en Indochine de 1940
    à 1945." *Produits Pharmaceutiques* 2, no. 3 (Mar. 1947): 109–19. Also pub-
    lished in *Bulletin de la Société des Études Indochinoises* 21, no. 3–4 (1946): 81–
    107.

Bōeichō [Japan Defense Agency]. Bōei Kenshujo Senshitsu [War History Office]. *Shittan Meigō sakusen: Biruma sensen no hōkai to Tai, Futsuin no Bōei* [The Sittang and Meigō Operations: The Collapse of the Burma Front and the Defense of Thailand and French Indochina]. Tokyo: Chōun Shinbunsha, 1969.

Boisanger, Claude de. *On pouvait éviter la guerre d'Indochine: Souvenirs, 1942–1945.* Paris: A. Maisonneuve, 1977.

Boulé, Etienne. *Ici Tananarive: L'Empire libre parle à l'Indochine.* Tananarive: Mission indochinoise d'information, 1945.

Bourgeois, Jacques Le. *Ici Radio Saigon, 1939–45.* Paris: Editions France-Empire, 1985.

Brocheux, Pierre. "La Revue *Thanh Nghi* et les questions littéraires (1941–1945)." *Revue française d'histoire d'Outre-Mer* 75, no. 280 (1988): 347–56.

————. "La Revue *Thanh Nghi*: Un Groupe d'intellectuels Vietnamiens confrontés aux problèmes de leur nation (1941–1945)." *Revue d'histoire moderne et contemporaine*, no. 3 (1987): 317–31.

Bui Huu Khanh. *Ha Noi trong thoi ky Cach Mang Thang 8* [Hanoi in the August Revolution Period]. Hanoi: Su Hoc, 1960.

Bui Phung. *Tu Dien Viet-Anh* [Vietnamese-English Dictionary]. Hanoi: Truong Dai Hoc Tong Hop Ha Noi, 1986.

Buttinger, Joseph. *Vietnam: A Dragon Embattled.* 2 vols. New York: Frederick A. Praeger, 1967.

Cameron, Allan W., ed. *Viet-Nam Crisis: A Documentary History.* Vol. 1, *1940–1956.* Ithaca, N.Y.: Cornell University Press, 1971.

Cao Van Bien. "Ve Nan Doi Nam At Dau (1945)" [On the Famine of 1945]. *NCLS* 251 (4-1990): 50–55, 60.

Chanh Thi et al. *Len Duong Thang Loi* [On the Road to Victory]. Hanoi: Van Hoc, 1960.

Charbonneau, René, and José Maigre. *Les Parias de la victoire: Indochine-Chine, 1945.* Paris: Editions France-Empire, 1980.

Chen, King C. *Vietnam and China, 1938–1954.* Princeton: Princeton University Press, 1969.

Chiang Yung-ching. *Hu Chih-ming tsai Chung Kuo: I ko yüeh nan min tsu chu i wei chuang che* [Ho Chi Minh in China: A Person Who Disguised Himself as a Nationalist]. Taipei: Chuan Chi Wen Hsüeh Ch'u Pan She, 1972.

Chu Van Tan. *Reminiscences on the Army for National Salvation.* Translated and annotated by Mai Elliott. Ithaca, N.Y.: Cornell Southeast Asia Program, 1974. Originally published as *Ky Niem Cuu Quoc Quan.* Hanoi: Quan Doi Nhan Dan, 1971.

Colton, Kenneth E. "The Failure of the Independent Political Movement in Vietnam, 1945–46." 2 vols. Ph.D. diss., American University, 1969.

Cong Hoa Xa Hoi Chu Nghia Viet Nam. See Vietnam.

Cotter, Michael. *Vietnam: A Guide to Reference Sources.* Boston: G. K. Hall, 1977.

Cruikshank, Charles. *SOE in the Far East.* Oxford: Oxford University Press, 1983.

Dang Cong San Viet Nam. See Vietnam.

Dang Lao Dong Viet Nam. See Vietnam.

Dang Ngoc Tot, Duong Duc Hien, and Nguyen Dinh Thi. *Suc Song cua Dan Viet Nam* [The Living Strength of the Vietnamese People]. Hanoi: Lua Hong, 1944.

David, Gilbert. *Chroniques secrètes d'Indochine (1928–1946).* 2 vols. Paris: L'Harmattan, 1994.

Decoux, Jean. *A le barre de l'Indochine: Histoire de mon gouvernement général, 1940–1945.* Paris: Plon, 1952.

Dennis, Peter. *Troubled Days of Peace: Mountbatten and South East Asia Command, 1945–46.* Manchester: Manchester University Press, 1987.

Detwiler, Donald S., and Charles B. Burdick, eds. *War in Asia and the Pacific, 1937–1949.* 15 vols. New York/London: Garland Publishing, 1980. Vol. 6, *The Southern Area* (Part I).

Descours-Gatin, Chantal, and Hugues Villiers. *Guide de recherches sur le Vietnam: Bibliographies, archives et bibliothèques de France.* Paris: L'Harmattan, 1983.

Desiré, Michel. *La Campagne d'Indochine, 1945–1954: Bibliographie.* 4 vols. Vincennes: Service historique de l'Armée de terre, 1971.

Devillers, Philippe. *Histoire du Vietnam de 1940 à 1952.* Paris: Editions du seuil, 1952.

———. *Paris-Saigon-Hanoi: Les Archives de la guerre, 1944–1947.* Paris: Editions Gallimard/Julliard, 1988.

Dinh Trong Hy and Nguyen Quang Truc. "Cuu Quoc Quan, mot Chang Duong Lich Su" [The National Salvation Army: A Historical Phase]. *Thong Tin Lich Su Quan Su,* 4-1991, 31–39.

Do Thuc Vinh. *Di Mo* [Auntie Mo]. Saigon: Tu Do, 1957.

———. *Mua Ao Anh* [The Season of Mirages]. Saigon: 1962.

Doan Quoc Sy. *Ba Sinh Huong Lua* [Three Generations in the Flames]. Saigon: 1962.

Drachman, Edward R. *United States Policy toward Vietnam, 1940–1945.* Cranbury, N.J.: Associated University Press, 1970.

Dreifort, John E. "Japan's Advance into Indochina, 1940: The French Response." *JSEAS* 13, no. 2 (Sept. 1982): 279–95.

Ducoroy, Maurice. *Ma Trahison en Indochine.* Paris: Editions internationales, 1949.

Duiker, William J. *The Communist Road to Power in Vietnam.* Boulder, Colo.: Westview Press, 1981.

Dunn, Peter M. *The First Vietnam War.* London: C. Hurst, 1985.

Duong Kinh Quoc. *Chinh Quyen Thuoc Dia o Viet Nam truoc Cach Mang Thang Tam nam 1945* [Colonial Government in Vietnam before the August 1945 Revolution]. Hanoi: Khoa Hoc Xa Hoi, 1988.

Duong Trung Quoc. "Nghien Cuu Cach Mang Thang Tam 1945: Tu Hien Thuc den Nhan Thuc" [Researching the August 1945 Revolution: From Reality to Cognition]. *NCLS* 251 (4-1990): 8–14, 73.

———, compiler. *Viet Nam: Nhung Su Kien Lich Su, 1858–1945,* [Historical Events in Vietnam, 1858–1945]. Vol. 4, 1936–1945. Hanoi: Khoa Hoc Xa Hoi, 1989.

Eastman, Lloyd E. *Seeds of Destruction: Nationalist China in War and Revolution, 1937–1949.* Stanford: Stanford University Press, 1984.

Elsbree, Willard H. *Japan's Role in Southeast Asian Nationalist Movements, 1940 to 1945.* New York: Russell & Russell, 1970.

Fenn, Charles. *Ho Chi Minh: A Biographical Introduction.* New York: Charles Scribner's Sons, 1973.

Fonde, Jean Julien. "Giap et le maquis de Cho-ra (mars 1945–mars 1946)." *Revue historique des armées* 2 (1976): 112–27.

France. Gouvernement général de l'Indochine. *Souveraines et notabilités d'Indochine.* Hanoi: Imprimerie d'Extrême-Orient, 1943.

———. Haut commissariat de France pour l'Indochine. *Les Crimes japonais après le 9 Mars 1945: Conditions d'internement des Français en Indochine.* Saigon: Imp. France d'Outre-Mer, 1948.

———. Statistique générale de l'Indochine. *Annuaire statistique de l'Indochine.* Vol. 11, *1943–1946.* Saigon: 1948.

Franchini, Phillippe, ed. *Saigon, 1925–1945: De la "belle colonie" à l'éclosion révolutionnaire ou la fin des dieux blancs.* Paris: Editions autrement, 1992.

Gaudel, André. *L'Indochine française en face du Japon.* Paris: J. Susse, 1947.

Gautier, Georges. *9 Mars 1945, Hanoi au soleil de sang: La Fin de l'Indochine française.* Paris: Societé de production littéraire, 1978.

Girard, Raymond P. "City Man Helped to Train Guerrillas of Ho Chi Minh." *Evening Gazette* (Worcester, Mass.), 14 and 15 May 1968. Interview with Henry Prunier, member of OSS "Deer Team" in July–Sept. 1945.

Gouvernement general de l'Indochine. See France.

Ha Thi Que. "Rung Yen The" [The Yen The Forest]. In Le Thiet Hung et al., *Rung Yen The.* Hanoi: Quan Doi Nhan Dan, 1962.

Hammer, Ellen J. *The Struggle for Indochina, 1940–1955.* Stanford: Stanford University Press, 1966.

Hardy, Andrew. "La politique économique française en Indochine, 1944–1948." Maîtrise d'histoire, University of Paris, 1991.

Haut commissariat de France pour l'Indochine. See France.

Héduy, Philippe, ed. *Histoire de l'Indochine: Le Destin, 1885–1954.* Paris: Société de Production Littéraire / Henri Veyrier, 1983.

Hémery, Daniel. *Ho Chi Minh: De l'Indochine au Vietnam.* Paris: Gallimard, 1990.

Herring, George C. "The Truman Administration and the Restoration of French Sovereignty in Indochina." *Diplomatic History* (Wilmington, Del.) 1, no. 2 (Spring 1977): 97–117.

Hertrich, Jean-Michel. *Doc-Lap! (L'Indépendence ou la mort!): Choses vues en Indochine.* Paris: Jean Vigneau, 1946.

Hess, Gary R. "Franklin D. Roosevelt and Indochina." *Journal of American History* 59 (Sept. 1972): 353–68.

Hesse d'Alzon, Claude. "L'Armée française d'Indochine pendant la seconde guerre mondiale, 1939–1945." In *L'Indochine française, 1940–1945,* ed. Paul Isoart, 86–89. Paris: Presses universitaires de France, 1982.

———. *La Présence militaire française en Indochine (1940–1945).* Paris: Service historique de l'Armée de terre, 1985.

Ho Chi Minh. *Ho Chi Minh Toan Tap* [Complete Works of Ho Chi Minh]. Vol. 3, *1930–1945.* Hanoi: Su That, 1983.

———. *Nhat Ky Trong Tu* [Prison Diary]. Hanoi: Van Hoa, 1960. Translation into Vietnamese of *Nguc Trung Nhat Ky,* a poetry collection in Chinese. The best

English-language translation is by Huynh Sanh Thong, in *Reflections from Captivity*, ed. David G. Marr. Athens, Ohio: Ohio University Press, 1978.

Ho Chi Minh, Nguyen Luong Bang, et al. *Nhan Dan Ta Rat Anh Hung* [Our People Are Very Heroic]. 2d ed. Hanoi: Van Hoc, 1969. Most of the first edition was translated into English as *A Heroic People: Memoirs from the Revolution*. Hanoi: Foreign Languages Publishing House, 1965.

Hoai Thanh et al. *Bac Ho, Hoi Ky* [Recollections about Uncle Ho]. Hanoi: Van Hoc, 1960.

Hoang Anh. "Nho lai cuoc khoi nghia gianh chinh quyen o Hue" [Recalling the Uprising to Take Power in Hue]. *Tap Chi Cong San*, 8-1985, 34–42, 86.

Hoang Anh, Le Tu Dong, et al. *Binh Tri Thien, Thang Tam Bon Lam: Hoi Ky* [August 1945 in Binh Tri Thien Province: Memoirs]. Hue: Thuan Hoa, 1985.

Hoang Quang Khanh, Le Hong, and Hoang Ngoc La. *Can Cu Dia Viet Bac (Trong cuoc Cach Mang Thang 8-1945)* [The Viet Bac Base Area (in the August 1945 Revolution)]. Viet Bac: Viet Bac, 1976.

Hoang Van Dao. *Viet Nam Quoc Dan Dang, 1927–1954* [Vietnam Nationalist Party, 1927–54]. Saigon: Nguyen Hoa Hiep, 1965.

Hoang Van Hoan. *Giot Nuoc trong Bien Ca: Hoi Ky Cach Mang* [A Drop in the Ocean: Revolutionary Memoirs]. Beijing [?]: Tin Viet Nam, 1986.

Hodgkin, Thomas. *Vietnam: The Revolutionary Path*. London: Macmillan, 1981.

Huang Cheng. *Hu Chih-ming yü Chung Kuo* [Ho Chi Minh and China]. Beijing: Chien Fang Chün Ch'u Pan She, 1987.

Huynh Kim Khanh. "The Vietnamese August Revolution Reinterpreted." *Journal of Asian Studies* 30, no. 4 (Aug. 1971): 761–82.

———. *Vietnamese Communism, 1925–1945*. Ithaca, N.Y.: Cornell University Press, 1982.

Huynh Van Tieng. "'Len Dang' lam cach mang" [Setting Out to Make Revolution]. *Dac San*, 8-1987, 21–25.

Institut Charles-de-Gaulle. *Le Général de Gaulle et l'Indochine, 1940–1946*. Paris: Plon, 1982.

Isaacs, Harold R. *No Peace for Asia*. New York: Macmillan, 1947. 2d ed.: New York: MIT Press, 1967.

Isoart, Paul. *Le phénomène national vietnamien: De l'indépendance unitaire à l'indépendance fractionée*. Paris: Librairie Général de Droit et de Jurisprudence, 1961.

———, ed. *L'Indochine française, 1940–1945*. Paris: Presses universitaires de France, 1982. Essays by Paul Isoart, Claude Hesse d'Alzon, Pierre Brocheux, William Duiker, and Shiraishi Masaya.

Kaneko Noboru. "Annan himitsu butai" [Annam Secret Unit]. *Shūkan yomiuri*, special ed., 8 Dec. 1956, 161–63.

Kashima Heiwa Kenkyūjohen. *Nihon Gaikōshi* [A History of Diplomacy in Japan]. Vol. 24. Tokyo: Kashima Kenkyūjo Shuppankai, 1971.

Katz, Mark N. "The Origins of the Vietnam War, 1945–1948." *Review of Politics* 42 (1980): 131–51.

Kirby, S. Woodburn. *The War against Japan*. Vol. 5, *The Surrender of Japan*. London: Her Majesty's Stationary Office, 1969.

Kiriloff, C., trans. *Documents of the August 1945 Revolution in Vietnam.* Canberra: Department of International Relations, Australian National University, 1963. Translation from Vietnamese via Russian of most of Vietnam, Dang Lao Dong Viet Nam, *Chat Xieng* (see below).

La Feber, Walter. "Roosevelt, Churchill and Indochina, 1942–45." *American Historical Review* 80, no. 5 (Dec. 1975): 1277–95.

La Roche, Jean de. "Indo-China in the New French Colonial Framework." *Pacific Affairs* 18, no. 1 (Mar. 1945): 62–75.

Lattimore, Eleanor. "Indo-China: French Union or Japanese 'Independence.'" *Far Eastern Survey*, no. 14 (23 May 1945): 132–34.

Le Hien Mai. "Lua Sang Trong Rung Sau" [Bright Fire in the Deep Forest]. In Chanh Thi et al., *Len Duong Thang Loi.* Hanoi: Van Hoc, 1960.

Le Quang Dao. "Vai Mau Chuyen Hoi Bi Mat" [Some Stories from the Clandestine Period]. In Chanh Thi et al., *Len Duong Thang Loi.* Hanoi: Van Hoc, 1960.

Le Quang Dao et al. *Mot Chang Duong Van Hoa* [A Segment of the Cultural Road]. Hanoi: Tac Pham Moi, 1985.

Le Tat Dac. "Ve cuoc Tong Khoi Nghia o Thanh Hoa" [Concerning the General Uprising in Thanh Hoa]. *Tap Chi Lich Su Dang*, 4-1991, 11–14.

Le Thiet Hung. "Lay Sung" [Getting Firearms]. In Le Thiet Hung et al., *Rung Yen The.* Hanoi: Quan Doi Nhan Dan, 1962.

Loane, Shannon Smith. "Franklin D. Roosevelt and Indochina: United States Policy during World War II." Master's thesis, Cornell University, May 1991.

Lockhart, Greg. *Nation in Arms: The Origins of the People's Army of Vietnam.* Sydney: Allen & Unwin, 1989.

Louis, William Roger. *Imperialism at Bay, 1941–1945: The U.S. and the Decolonization of the British Empire.* Oxford: Oxford University Press, 1977.

Luu Phuong Thanh. "Nam Bo trong buoi dau Khang Chien Chong Thuc Dan Phap Xam Luoc (9-1945–3-1946)" [Southern Vietnam in the Early Resistance to French Colonial Invasion (Sept. 1945–Mar. 1946)]. *Tap Chi Lich Su Quan Su*, no. 16 (4-1987): 11–18, 78.

McAlister, John T., Jr. *Vietnam: The Origins of Revolution.* New York: Knopf, 1969.

McAlister, John T., Jr., and Paul Mus. *The Vietnamese and their Revolution.* New York: Harper, 1970.

Mai Van Bo. "Phong Trao Thanh Nien, Sinh Vien va Tri Thuc trong nhung Nam 40" [The Youth, Student, and Intellectual Movement in the 1940s]. *Tap Chi Khoa Hoc Xa Hoi*, no. 18 (4-1993): 22–28.

Marr, David G. "Vietnam Biographical Database" (VNBIOG). Canberra: Research School of Pacific and Asian Studies, 1994. Computerized records on 1,550 individual Vietnamese, particularly those active during the 1920–55 period.

———. "Vietnam: Harnessing the Whirlwind." In *Asia, the Winning of Independence*, ed. Robin Jeffrey. London: Macmillan, 1981.

———. *Vietnamese Anticolonialism, 1885–1925.* Berkeley and Los Angeles: University of California Press, 1971.

———. "Vietnam 1945: Some Questions." *The Vietnam Forum*, no. 6 (Summer–Fall 1985): 155–93.

————. *Vietnamese Tradition on Trial, 1920–1945*. Berkeley and Los Angeles: University of California Press, 1981.

————. "World War II and the Vietnamese Revolution." In *Southeast Asia under Japanese Occupation*, ed. Alfred W. McCoy. New Haven: Yale University, Southeast Asia Studies Monograph Series No. 22 (1980): 125–58.

Martin, Françoise. *Heures tragiques au Tonkin (9 mars 1945–18 mars 1946)*. Paris: Berger-Levrant, 1948.

Marvel, W. Macy. "Drift and Intrigue: United States Relations with the Viet Minh, 1945." *Millennium* 4, no. 1 (1975): 10–27.

Mehlert, Calvin E. "Miscellaneous Comments on the Vietnamese Nationalist Movement, 1925–1946." Unpublished paper, University of California, Berkeley, 1969.

Meinheit, Harold E. "The Chinese Intervention in Vietnam: 1945–1946." Unpublished Cornell University Seminar paper, Dec. 1976.

Mordant, Eugène. *Au service de la France en Indochine, 1941–1945*. Saigon: Imp. française d'Outre-Mer, 1950.

Morley, James W., ed. *The Fateful Choice: Japan's Advance into Southeast Asia, 1939–1941*. New York: Columbia University Press, 1980. Japanese studies in translation.

Murakami, Sachiko. "Japan's Thrust into French Indochina 1940–1945." Ph.D. diss., New York University, 1981.

Mus, Paul. *Le Vietnam chez lui*. Paris: Centre d'études politiques étrangères, 1946.

————. "L'Indochine en 1945." *Politique étrangère* 11 (1946): 329–74, 433–64.

————. *Viet-Nam: Sociologie d'une guerre*. Paris: Editions du seuil, 1950.

Ngo Huy Dong. *Thai Binh Khoi Nghia* [The Thai Binh Uprising]. Thai Binh: Ty Van Hoa Thong Tin, 1965.

Ngo Minh Loan. "Doi Du Kich Au-Co" [The Au Co Guerrilla Unit]. In Le Thiet Hung et al., *Rung Yen The*. Hanoi: Quan Doi Nhan Dan, 1962.

Ngo Vinh Long. *Before the Revolution: The Vietnamese Peasants under the French*. Cambridge, Mass.: MIT Press, 1973.

Ngoc An. "Bo Doi Viet-My" [The Vietnamese-American Unit]. *Tap Chi Lich Su Quan Su*, no. 10 (10-1986): 18–20, 31.

Nguyen Anh Dung. *Dau Tranh Vu Trang trong Cach Mang Thang Tam* [Armed Struggle in the August Revolution]. Hanoi: Khoa Hoc Xa Hoi, 1985.

Nguyen Cong Binh. "Ve Moc Khoi Dau va Ket Thuc cua cuoc Cach Mang Thang Tam" [Concerning the Beginning and Conclusion of the August Revolution]. *NCLS*, no. 51 (6-1963): 17–22.

Nguyen Dinh Hoa. *Hoa's Vietnamese-English Dictionary*. Saigon: Binh Minh, 1959.

Nguyen Dong Chu, comp. *Tong Muc Luc va Sach Dan Tap San "Van Su Dia" va Tap Chi "Nghien Cuu Lich Su," 1954–1973* [A General Catalog and Guide to the Journal of "Literature, History and Geography" and the Journal of "Historical Research," 1954–1973]. Hanoi: Vien Su Hoc, 1976.

Nguyen Duy Trinh, Chu Van Tan, et al. *Nhung Ngay Thang Tam* [Days of August]. Hanoi: Van Hoc, 1961.

Nguyen Khac Vien and Huu Ngoc, eds. *Anthologie de la littérature vietnamienne.* Vol. 3, *Deuxième moitié du XIXe siècle–1945* . Hanoi: Foreign Languages Publishing House, 1975.

Nguyen Khang. "Ha Noi Khoi Nghia" [Hanoi Insurrection]. In Nguyen Duy Trinh, Chu Van Tan, et al., *Nhung Ngay Thang Tam.* Hanoi: Van Hoc, 1961.

Nguyen Khang, Nguyen Quyet, et al. *Ha Noi Khoi Nghia* [Hanoi Insurrection]. Vol. 2. Hanoi: Ban Nghien Cuu Lich Su Dang Thanh Uy Ha Noi, 1970.

Nguyen Khanh Toan et al. *Cach Mang Thang Muoi va Cach Mang Viet Nam* [The October Revolution and the Vietnamese Revolution]. Hanoi: Khoa Hoc Xa Hoi, 1977.

Nguyen Khanh Toan, general editor. *Tong Tap Van Hoc Viet Nam* [General Collection of Vietnamese Literature]. Volume 36 is devoted entirely to Ho Chi Minh's writings up to 2 Sept. 1945. Hanoi: Khoa Hoc Xa Hoi, 1980.

Nguyen Ky Nam. *Hoi Ky, 1925–1964* [Memoirs, 1925–1964]. Vol. 2, *1945–1954.* Saigon: Dan Chu Moi, 1964.

Nguyen Long Thanh Nam. "Cuoc bieu tinh 9–1945 tai Can Tho cua PGHH de lam gi?" [What Was the Purpose of the Hoa Hao Buddhist Demonstration of September 1945 in Can Tho?]. *Duoc Tu Bi,* 15 Nov. 1987, 3–14.

Nguyen Luong Bang, Vu Anh, et al. *Uncle Ho.* Hanoi: Foreign Languages Publishing House, 1980.

Nguyen Quoc Dinh and Nguyen Dac Khe. *Le Futur statut de l'Indochine: Commentaire de la declaration gouvernementale du 24 Mars 1945.* Paris: Dalloz, 1945.

Nguyen Quyet. *Ha Noi Thang Tam: Hoi Ky* [Hanoi in August: Memoirs]. Hanoi: Quan Doi Nhan Dan, 1980.

Nguyen The Anh. "La Campagne nord-vietnamienne de la dépression économique de 1930 à la famine de 1945." *Review française d'histoire d'Outre-Mer* 74, no. 274 (1987): 43–53.

———. "La Famine de 1945 au Nord-Vietnam." *Vietnam Forum,* no. 5 (Winter–Spring 1985): 81–100.

Nguyen Van Rang. "Nam Thang o Giai Phong Quan Khang Nhat" [Five Months in the Liberation Army Resisting the Japanese]. In Le Thiet Hung et al., *Rung Yen The.* Hanoi: Quan Doi Nhan Dan, 1962.

———. *Toi Len Chien Khu* [I Go Up to the War Zone]. Hanoi: Pho Thong, 1961.

Nitz, Kyoko Kurusu. "Independence without Nationalists? The Japanese and Vietnamese Nationalism during the Japanese Period, 1940–45." *JSEAS* 15, no. 1 (Mar. 1984): 108–33.

———. "Japanese Military Policy towards French Indochina during the Second World War: The Road to the *Meigō Sakusen* (9 Mar. 1945)." *JSEAS* 14, no. 2 (Sept. 1983): 328–53.

Oey Giok Po et al., compilers. *Southeast Asia Catalog.* 7 vols. Boston: G. K.Hall, 1976. Includes publications relating to Vietnam housed at the Cornell University Library.

Patti, Archimedes L. A. *Why Viet Nam? Prelude to America's Albatross.* Berkeley and Los Angeles: University of California Press, 1980.

Pedrazzani, J. M. *La France en Indochine de Catroux à Sainteny.* Paris: Arthaud, 1972.

Pham Cuc. "Khoi Nghia gianh Chinh Quyen Thang Tam o Thanh Hoa" [The August 1945 Uprising to Take Power in Thanh Hoa]. *Tap Chi Lich Su Dang*, 4-1991, 30–33.

Pham Khac Hoe. *Tu Trieu Dinh Hue den Chien Khu Viet Bac* [From the Hue Court to the Viet Bac War Zone]. Hanoi: Ha Noi, 1983.

Pham Kiet. "Nhung Nguoi Tu An Tri Cang Ba To" [Prisoners at the Ba To Displacement Center]. In Le Thiet Hung et al., *Rung Yen The*. Hanoi: Quan Doi Nhan Dan, 1962.

———. *Tu Nui Rung Ba To* [From the Hills and Forests of Ba To]. Hanoi: Quan Doi Nhan Dan, 1977.

Pham Quang Trung. "Nan Lut nam At Dau voi cuoc Tong Khoi Nghia gianh Chinh Quyen o Dong Bang Bac Bo nam 1945" [The 1945 Flood and the General Insurrection to Seize Power in the Northern Delta]. *NCLS* 251 (4-1990): 56–60.

Pham Van Hao. "Lam Bao Bi Mat" [Producing Clandestine Newspapers]. In Chanh Thi et al., *Len Duong Thang Loi*. Hanoi: Van Hoc, 1960.

Phan Anh. "Con Duong di toi Cach Mang Thang Tam cua Toi" [My Path to the August Revolution]. *Nhan Dan* (Hanoi), 21 Aug. 1960, 4, 6.

———. "Toi da tham gia Chinh Phu Lien Hiep Khang Chien (3-3-46) nhu the nao?" [How I Took Part in the Resistance Union Government (3 March 1946)?]. *Tap Chi Lich Su Quan Su*, no. 36 (12-1988): 8–11, 16.

Phan Ngoc Lien. "Tim Hieu ve Cong tac Van Dong, Giao Duc Quan Chung cua Ho Chu Tich trong thoi gian Nguoi o Pac-Bo" [Understanding Chairman Ho's Mobilization and Mass Education Activities When He Was at Pac Bo]. *NCLS* 149 (2-1973): 13–21, 30.

Porter, Daniel Gareth. "Imperialism and Social Structure in Twentieth-Century Vietnam." Ph.D. diss., Cornell University, 1976.

Porter, Gareth, ed. *Vietnam: The Definitive Documentation of Human Decisions.* 2 vols. Stanfordville, N.Y.: Coleman Enterprises, 1979.

Quan Doi Nhan Dan Viet Nam. See Vietnam.

Rageau, Christiane, compiler. *Catalogue du Fonds indochinois de la Bibliothèque nationale.* Vol.1, *Livres vietnamiens imprimés en quoc ngu, 1922–1954.* Paris: Bibliothèque nationale, 1980.

Rosenfeld, F. *Indices économiques indochinois* 3d ser. Saigon: Statistique générale de l'Indochine, July 1947.

Rueff, Gaston. "The Future of French Indo-China." *Foreign Affairs* 23, no. 1 (Oct. 1944): 140–46.

———. "Postwar Problems of French Indochina: Economic Aspects." *Pacific Affairs* 18, no. 2 (June 1945): 137–55.

———. "Postwar Problems of French Indo-China: Social and Political Aspects." *Pacific Affairs* 18, no. 3 (Sept. 1945): 229–45.

Ruscio, Alain. *Les Communistes français et la guerre d'Indochine, 1944–1954.* Paris: L'Harmattan, 1985.

———. *La Décolonisation tragique, 1945–1962.* Paris: Editions Messidor, 1987.

———. "Tran Van Giau et la révolution d'août 1945 au Nam Bo (Sud du Viet-Nam)." *Approaches Asie*, no. 10 (1989–90): 182–96.

Sabattier, Gabriel. *Le Destin de l'Indochine: Souvenirs et documents, 1941–1951*. Paris: Plon, 1952.

Sainteny, Jean. *Histoire d'une paix manquée: Indochine, 1945–1947*. Paris: Fayard, 1953.

———. *Ho Chi Minh and His Vietnam: A Personal Memoir*. Chicago: Cowles Book Co., 1972.

Sbrega, John J. " 'First catch your hare': Anglo-American Perspectives on Indochina during the Second World War." *JSEAS* 14, no. 1 (Mar. 1983): 63–78.

Shiraishi Masaya. "La Présence japonaise en Indochine (1940–1945)." In *Indochine française 1940–1945*, ed. Paul Isoart. Paris: Presses universitaires de France, 1982.

———. "Vietnam under the Japanese Presence and the August Revolution." In *1945 in South-East Asia*, Part 2. London: Suntory Toyota International Centre for Economics and Related Disciplines, London School of Economics and Political Science, 1985.

Shiraishi Masaya and Furuta Motoo. "Taiheiyō sensō ki no Nihon no tai-Indoshina seisaku: Sono futatsu no tokuisei o megutte" [Japan's Policy toward Indochina during the Pacific War: Concerning Two Peculiarities]. *Ajia kenkyū* 23, no. 3 (1976): 1–37. This article is translated in *Indochina in the 1940s and 1950s*, ed. Shiraishi Takashi and Furuta Motoo.

Shiraishi Takashi and Furuta Motoo, eds. *Indochina in the 1940s and 1950s*. Ithaca, N.Y.: Cornell University Southeast Asia Program, 1992.

Smith, R. Harris. *OSS: The Secret History of America's First Central Intelligence Agency*. Berkeley and Los Angeles: University of California Press, 1972.

Smith, Ralph B. "The Japanese Period in Indochina and the Coup of 9 March 1945." *JSEAS* 9, no. 2 (Sept. 1978): 268–301.

———. "The Vietnamese Elite of French Cochinchina, 1943." *Modern Asian Studies* 6, no. 4 (1972): 459–82.

Spector, Ronald H. "Allied Intelligence and Indochina, 1943–1945." *Pacific Historical Review* 51, no. 1 (Feb. 1982): 23–50.

———. *United States Army in Vietnam. Advice and Support: The Early Years, 1941–1960*. Washington, D.C.: Center of Military History, U.S. Army, 1983.

———. "What the Local Annamites Are Thinking: American Views of Vietnamese in China, 1942–1945." *Southeast Asia* 3, no. 2 (1974): 741–51.

Statistique générale de l'Indochine. See France.

Tabuchi Yukichika. "Dai Tōa kyōeiken to Indoshina: Shokuryō kakutoku no tame no tame no senryaku" [The Greater East Asia Co-Prosperity Sphere and Indochina: A Strategy for Securing Food Supplies]. *Tōnan Ajia: Rekishi to bunka*, no. 10 (June 1981): 39–68. Translated in *Indochina in the 1940s and 1950s*, ed. Shiraishi Takashi and Furuta Motoo (see above).

Tang Xuan An. "Nan Doi Nam At Dau (1945)" [The 1945 Famine]. Mimeographed compilation. New Haven: Yale University, 1981, pp. 37–41.

Tarling, Nicholas. "The British and the First Japanese Move into Indo-China." *JSEAS* 21, no. 1 (Mar. 1990): 35–65.

Thanh Van, Tran Hoai Long, et al. *Thu Do Ha Noi: Lich Su Khang Chien Thuc Dan Phap (1945–1954)* [Hanoi Capital: History of Resistance to the French Colonialists (1945–1954)]. Hanoi: Ha Noi, 1986.

The Tap, compiler. "Chu Tich Ho Chu Minh: Bien Nien Tom Tat (Tu 14-8-1945 den 20-12-1946)" [Chairman Ho Chi Minh: Summary Chronology (from 14 August 1945 to 20 December 1946)]. *Tap Chi Cong San*, 8-1985, 18–25.

Thorne, Christopher. *Allies of a Kind: The United States, Britain and the War Against Japan, 1941–1945*. London: Hamish Hamilton, 1978.

———. "Indochina and Anglo-American Relations, 1942–1945." *Pacific Historical Review* 45 (1976): 73–96.

To Huu. "Nho lai mot thoi ky Cach Mang Ve Vang" [Recalling a Glorious Revolutionary Period]. *Tap Chi Lich Su Dang*, 4-1991, 15–17.

Tønnesson, Stein. *The Vietnamese Revolution of 1945: Roosevelt, Ho Chi Minh and de Gaulle in a World at War*. London: SAGE, 1991.

Tran Cung. "Khoi nghia o De Tu Chien Khu"[Uprising in the Fourth Battle Zone]. *NCLS*, no. 126 (9-1969): 44–57.

Tran Dan Tien. *Nhung Mau Chuyen ve Doi Hoat Dong cua Ho Chu Tich* [Stories about the Working Life of Chairman Ho]. Hanoi: Van Hoc, 1960.

Tran Do. "Nhung Mau Truyen . . . Sung" [Some Anecdotes on . . . Guns]. In Chanh Thi et al., *Len Duong Thang Loi*. Hanoi: Van Hoc, 1960.

Tran Huu Ta. "Doc Hoi Ky Cach Mang, Nghi ve Ve Dep cua Nguoi Chien Si Cong San Viet-Nam" [Reading Revolutionary Memoirs, Thinking of the Attractiveness of Vietnamese Communist Combatants]. *Tap Chi Van Hoc*, 2-1977, 17–28.

Tran Huy Lieu. "Di Du Quoc Dan Dai Hoi o Tan-Trao" [Attending the National People's Congress at Tan Trao]. *NCLS*, no. 17 (8-1960): 35–43.

———. *Nghia Lo Khoi Nghia* [Uprising at Nghia Lo]. Hanoi: Hoi Van Hoa Cuu Quoc, 1946.

———. "Tien Tren Duong Nghia" [Advancing on the Righteous Path]. In Bui Cong Trung et al., *Nguoi Truoc Nga, Nguoi Sau Tien*. Hanoi: Van Hoc, 1960.

———. "Tuoc An Kien cua Hoang De Bao Dai" [Taking the Seal from Emperor Bao Dai]. *NCLS*, no. 18 (Sept. 1960): 46–51.

——— et al., eds. *Cach Mang Thang Tam: Tong Khoi Nghia o Ha Noi va cac Dia Phuong* [The August Revolution: General Insurrection in Hanoi and Various Localities]. 2 vols. Hanoi: Su Hoc, 1960.

Tran Huy Lieu et al. *Tai Lieu Tham Khao Lich Su Cach Mang Can Dai Viet Nam* [Reference Materials on the History of Vietnam's Modern Revolution]. 12 vols. Hanoi: Van Su Dia, 1955–58.

Tran Lam. "Doi Tuyen Truyen Xung Phong Dang Dan Chu nhung ngay tien khoi Nghia" [The Democratic Party's Propaganda Assault Unit in the Opening Days of the Insurrection]. *Doc Lap*, 28 Sept. 1988, 1–2.

———. "Ngay 17 Thang 8 Nam 1945 o Ha Noi" [17 August 1945 in Hanoi]. *Thong Tin Lich Su Quan Su*, 2-1990, 47–51.

Tran Trong Kim. *Mot Con Gio Bui* [A Puff of Dust]. Saigon: Vinh Son, 1969.

Tran Trung Thanh et al. *Ha-Noi Chien Dau* [Hanoi Fights]. Hanoi: Quan Doi Nhan Dan, 1964.

Tran Van Giap et al. *Luoc Truyen cac Tac Gia Viet Nam* [Biographical Outlines of Vietnamese Authors]. Vol. 2. Hanoi: Khoa Hoc Xa Hoi, 1972.

Tran Van Giau. "Khoi Nghia Thang Tam 1945 o Saigon" [The August 1945 Insurrection in Saigon]. *To Quoc*, 8-1985, 7–10.

———. "May dac diem cua cuoc Khoi Nghia Thang 8 o Sai Gon" [Special Characteristics of the August Insurrection in Saigon]. *Dac San*, 8-1987, 3–5, 18.

Tran Van Giau, ed. *Dia Chi Van Hoa Thanh Pho Ho Chi Minh* [Geography, History and Culture of Ho Chi Minh City]. Vol. 1, *History*. Ho Chi Minh City: Thanh Pho Ho Chi Minh, 1987.

Truong Buu Lam. "Japan and the Disruption of the Vietnamese Nationalist Movement." In *Aspects of Vietnamese History*, ed. Walter Vella. Honolulu: University Press of Hawaii, 1973.

Truong Chinh. *The August Revolution*. Hanoi: Foreign Languages Publishing House, 1962.

———. *Cach Mang Dan Toc Dan Chu Nhan Dan Viet-Nam* [The Vietnamese People's Democratic National Revolution]. 2 vols. Hanoi: Su That, 1975.

———. "Mot So Van De ve Cach Mang Thang Tam Viet Nam" [Some Issues Regarding the Vietnamese August Revolution]. *Hoc Tap*, 9-1963, 1–10.

Truong Sinh. "Len duong Thang Loi" [On the Road to Victory]. In Chanh Thi et al., *Len Duong Thang Loi*. Hanoi: Van Hoc, 1960.

———. "Nguoi Truoc Nga, Nguoi Sau Tien" [The Front Rank Falls, the Rear Advances] and "Toi di tim Ly Tuong" [I Look for an Ideal]. In Bui Cong Trung et al., *Nguoi Truoc Nga, Nguoi Sau Tien*. Hanoi: Van Hoc, 1960.

Truong Thi My and Nguyen Thi Hung. *Niem Tin Khong Bao Gio Tat* [Feelings of Trust Never Extinguished]. Hanoi: Phu Nu, 1967.

Tsuchihashi Yūichi. "Furansu-gun o busō kaijo" [Disarming the French Army]. Special ed. of *Shūkan Yomiuri*, 8 Dec. 1956.

Tung Hiep. "Hom Nay la Ngay Doc Lap!" [Today Is Independence Day!]. *Trung Bac Chu Nhat*, no. 261 (9 Sept. 1945): 5–6, 23–24.

United States. Department of Defense. *United States–Vietnam Relations, 1945–1967*. 12 vols. Washington, D.C.: Government Printing Office, 1971. Better known as "The Pentagon Papers."

———. Department of State. *The Foreign Relations of the United States*. Washington, D.C.: Government Printing Office, various years.

———. Department of State. *Political Alignments of Vietnamese Nationalists*. Washington, D.C.: State Department Office of Intelligence Research, Oct. 1949. Compiled by Milton Sachs.

———. Office of Strategic Services. *Programs of Japan in Indochina*. Honolulu: OSS, Aug. 1945. Compilation and translation of wartime radio intercepts.

———. Senate Committee on Foreign Relations. *Causes, Origins and Lessons of the Vietnam War*. 92d Congress, 2d sess. Hearings, 9, 10, and 11 May 1972. Washington, D.C.: Government Printing Office, 1973. Contains both transcripts of the hearings and one hundred pages of OSS documents from 1945–46.

Valentine, Daniel B. "The British Facilitation of the French Re-entry into Vietnam." Ph.D. diss., University of California, Los Angeles, 1974.

Van Tao, Thanh The Vy, and Nguyen Cong Binh. *Lich Su Cach Mang Thang Tam* [History of the August Revolution]. Hanoi: Su Hoc, 1960.

Van Tien Dung. "Di Tim Lien Lac" [Trying to Establish Contact]. In Chanh Thi et al., *Len Duong Thang Loi*. Hanoi: Van Hoc, 1960.

———. "Nuoc Song Hong len rat cao nhung De Van Vung" [The Red River Waters Rise High but the Dikes Hold]. In Le Thiet Hung et al., *Rung Yen The*. Hanoi: Quan Doi Nhan Dan, 1962.

Viet Minh. Tong Bo. *Bac Son Khoi Nghia* [The Bac Son Uprising]. Hanoi: Tu Sach Cuu Quoc, 1946.

Viet nam. Cong Hoa Xa Hoi Chu Nghia Viet Nam. Thu Vien Khoa Hoc Xa Hoi. "Thu Muc ve Cach Mang Thang Tam tai Nam Bo va Nam Trung Bo qua nguon Sach Bao Chi Dia Phuong cac tinh phia Nam sau Giai Phong" [Bibliography on the August Revolution in Southern and South Central Vietnam as Found in Publications Appearing in Southern Provinces after Liberation]. Typescript. Ho Chi Minh City: Vien Khoa Hoc Xa Hoi, Sept. 1984.

———. Dang Cong San Viet Nam. Ban Nghien Cuu Lich Su Dang Quang Ninh. *Lich Su Dang Bo Tinh Quang Ninh* [History of the Quang Ninh Province Party Apparatus]. Vol. 1, *1928–1945*. Hanoi: Tien Bo, 1985.

———. Dang Cong San Viet Nam. Ban Nghien Cuu Lich Su Dang Trung Uong. *Cach Mang Thang Tam (1945)* [The August Revolution (1945)]. Hanoi: Su That, 1980.

———. Dang Cong San Viet Nam. Ban Tuyen Huan Trung Uong. *Lich Su Dang Cong San Viet Nam: Trich Van Kien Dang* [History of the Vietnam Communist Party: Extracts from Party Documents]. Vol. 1, *1927–1945*. Hanoi: Sach Giao Khoa Mac Len-Nin, 1979.

———. Dang Cong San Viet Nam. Vien Lich Su Dang. *Tong Khoi Nghia Thang Tam 1945* [The August 1945 General Insurrection]. Hanoi: Su That, 1985.

———. Dang Lao Dong Viet Nam. *Chat Xieng: Nhung Tai Lieu Lich Su tu Chinh Bien Thang Ba den Cach Mang Thang Tam 1945* [Breaking Our Chains: Historical Documents from the Political Changes of March to the August Revolution, 1945]. 1946. 3d ed., Hanoi: Su That, 1960. Preface by Nguyen Van To. See, too, in English, *Breaking Our Chains: Documents of the Vietnamese Revolution of August 1945*. Hanoi, 1960. Also see C. Kiriloff, trans. *Documents of the August 1945 Revolution in Vietnam*.

———. Dang Lao Dong Viet Nam. *Cuoc Van Dong Cach Mang Thang Tam o Ha Noi (cuoi 1939–1946)* [Mobilizing the August Revolution in Hanoi (end of 1939–1946)]. Hanoi: Ban Nghien Cuu Lich Su Dang Thanh Uy Ha-noi, 1970.

———. Dang Lao Dong Viet Nam. *Ngon Co Giai Phong* [Liberation Flag]. Hanoi: Su That, 1955.

———. Dang Lao Dong Viet Nam. *So Thao Lich Su Cach Mang Thang Tam Thua Thien-Hue* [Preliminary History of the August Revolution in Thua Thien-Hue]. Hanoi: Le Van Tan, 1970.

———. Dang Lao Dong Viet Nam. *Ve Su Lanh Dao cua Dang tren Mat Tran Tu Tuong va Van Hoa, 1930–1945* [Concerning the Party's Leadership on the Ideological and Cultural Front, 1930–1945]. Hanoi: Su That, 1960.

———. Dang Lao Dong Viet Nam. Ban Nghien Cuu Lich Su Dang Ha Tay. *Hoi Ky Cach Mang Ha Tay* [Ha Tay Revolutionary Memoirs]. 2 vols. Ha Tay: Ban Nghien Cuu Lich Su, 1970.

———. Dang Lao Dong Viet Nam. Ban Nghien Cuu Lich Su Dang Tinh Quang Nam. *Cuoc Van Dong Cach Mang Thang Tam Tinh Quang Nam* [Mobilizing the August Revolution in Quang Nam Province]. Thanh Hoa: Ban Nghien Cuu Lich Su, 1973.

———. Dang Lao Dong Viet Nam. Ban Nghien Cuu Lich Su Dang Tinh Uy Lang Son. *Lich Su Dau Tranh Cach Mang Huyen Bac Son (1935–1945)* [History of Revolutionary Struggle in Bac Son District (1935–1945)]. Lang Son: Ty Van Hoa, 1974.

———. Dang Lao Dong Viet Nam. Ban Nghien Cuu Lich Su Dang Trung Uong. *Nhung Su Kien Lich Su Dang* [Party Historical Events]. Vol. 1, *1920–1945*. Hanoi: Su That, 1976.

———. Dang Lao Dong Viet Nam. Ban Nghien Cuu Lich Su Dang Trung Uong. *Tim Hieu Cach Mang Thang Tam* [Understanding the August Revolution]. Hanoi: Su That, 1967.

———. Dang Lao Dong Viet Nam. Ban Nghien Cuu Lich Su Dang Vinh Phu. *Nhung Ngay Cach Mang Thang Tam* [Days of the August Revolution]. Vol. 1. Vinh Phu: Ban Nghien Cuu Lich Su, 1974.

———. Viet Nam Giai Phong Quan. *Chien Thuat Co Ban* [Basic Military Tactics]. Hanoi: 1945.

———. Quan Doi Nhan Dan Viet Nam. Ban Nghien Cuu Lich Su Quan Doi. *Lich Su Quan Doi Nhan Dan Viet Nam* [History of the People's Army of Vietnam]. Vol. 1. Hanoi: Quan Doi Nhan Dan, 1974.

———. Quan Doi Nhan Dan Viet Nam. *Van Kien Quan Su cua Dang, 1930–1945* [Military Documents of the Party, 1930–1945]. Hanoi: Quan Doi Nhan Dan, 1969.

Viet Nam, Democratic Republic of. *History of the August Revolution*. Hanoi: Foreign Languages Publishing House, 1972.

Vo Nguyen Giap. *Tu Nhan Dan ma ra* [From the People]. Hanoi: Quan Doi Nhan Dan, 1964.

———. *Unforgettable Months and Years*. Ithaca, N.Y.: Cornell Southeast Asia Program Data Paper No. 99, May 1975. Translated and with an introduction by Mai Elliott. Originally published as *Nhung Nam Thang khong the nao quen*. Hanoi: Quan Doi Nhan Dan, 1970.

Vu Ngu Chieu. "Political and Social Change in Viet-Nam between 1940 and 1946." Ph.D. diss., University of Wisconsin–Madison, 1984.

———. "The Other Side of the 1945 Vietnamese Revolution: The Empire of Viet-Nam (Mar.–Aug. 1945)." *Journal of Asian Studies* 45, no. 2 (Feb. 1986): 293–328.

Vuong Thua Vu. *Truong Thanh trong Chien Dau: Hoi Ky* [Growing Up in Battle: Memoir]. Hanoi: Quan Doi Nhan Dan, 1979.

White, David Henry, Jr. "The United States and Indochina, 1942–1945." Ph.D. diss., Tulane University, 1974.

Wise, Edward Tayloe. "Vietnam in Turmoil: The Japanese Coup, the OSS and the August Revolution in 1945." Master's thesis, University of Richmond, 1991.

Woodside, Alexander B. *Community and Revolution in Modern Vietnam.* Boston: Houghton Mifflin, 1976.

Yoshizawa Minami. "The Nishihara Mission in Hanoi, July 1940." In *Indochina in the 1940s and 1950s,* ed. Shiraishi Takeshi and Furuta Motoo, 9–54. Ithaca, N.Y.: Cornell University Southeast Asia Program, 1992.

———. "Watashitachi no naka no Ajia no sensō—Nihon to Betonamu no aida" [The War among Us in Asia: Between Japan and Vietnam]. *University Press* (Tokyo), no. 141 (July 1984): 1–10; no. 142 (Aug. 1984): 10–15; and no. 143 (Sept. 1984): 23–31.

Index

Designer: Nola Burger
Compositor: Braun-Brumfield, Inc.
Text: Aldus
Display: Aldus
Printer: Braun-Brumfield, Inc.
Binder: Braun-Brumfield, Inc.

DATE DUE
